The Mythographic Chaucer

The Mythographic Chaucer

THE FABULATION OF SEXUAL POLITICS

Jane Chance

University of Minnesota Press

Minneapolis

London

Published by the University of Minnesota Press
111 Third Avenue South, Suite 290, Minneapolis, MN 55401-2520
Printed in the United States of America on acid-free paper

Library of Congress Cataloging-in-Publication Data

Chance, Jane, 1945–
    The mythographic Chaucer : the fabulation of sexual politics /
Jane Chance.
        p.   cm.
    Includes bibliographical references and index.
    ISBN 0-8166-2276-0 (alk. paper). — ISBN 0-8166-2277-9 (pbk. :
alk. paper)
        1. Chaucer, Geoffrey, d. 1400—Political and social views.   2. Sex
role in literature.   3. Chaucer, Geoffrey, d. 1400—Knowledge—
Mythology.   4. Man-woman relationships in literature.   5. Sex
(Psychology) in literature.   6. Sex—Political aspects—England—
History.   7. Mythology, Classical, in literature.   I. Title.
PR1933.S35C43   1994
821'.1—dc20   94-10265

For my beloved Paolo, Antony, Joe

"Silence itself—the things one declines to say, or is forbidden to name, the discretion required between different speakers—is less the absolute limit of discourse ... than an element that functions alongside the things said, with them and in relation to them within over-all strategies."
　　　　　—Michel Foucault, *The History of Sexuality*

Contents

ix

Contents

Abbreviations

Abbreviations for Chaucerian works and contemporary journals are those found in the annual bibliography published in *Studies in the Age of Chaucer.*

AHDLMA   *Archives d'histoire doctrinale et littéraire du Moyen Âge*

AM   *Annuale Mediaevale*

Allen, "Mythology"   Judson Boyce Allen. "Mythology in the Bible Commentaries and *Moralitates* of Robert Holkot." Diss., Johns Hopkins University, 1963.

Arnulf   Arnulf of Orleans. *Allegoriae super Ovidii Metamorphoses.* In "Arnolfo d'Orléans, Un Cultore di Ovidio nel Seculo XII." Ed. Fausto Ghisalberti. *Memorie del Reale Istituto Lombardo di Scienze e Lettere* 24 (1932): 157–234.

[Bern. Sil.] *Aen.*   [Bernardus Silvestris.] *The Commentary on the First Six Books of the Aeneid Commonly Attributed to Bernardus Silvestris.* Ed. Julian Ward Jones and Elizabeth Frances Jones. Lincoln and London: University of Nebraska Press, 1977.

[Bern. Sil.] *Aen.*, trans.   *Commentary on the First Six Books of Virgil's Aeneid.* Trans. Earl G. Schreiber and Thomas E. Maresca. Lincoln and London: University of Nebraska Press, 1979.

[Bern. Sil.] *Mart.*   *The Commentary on Martianus Capella's De nuptiis Philologiae et Mercurii Attributed to Bernardus Silvestris.* Ed. Haijo Jan Westra. Studies and Texts, 80. Toronto: Pontifical Institute of Mediaeval Studies, 1986.

Bersuire, "De formis"   Pierre Bersuire. "De formis figurisque deorum." Chap. 1 of *Reductorium morale, liber XV: Ovidius moralizatus.* Ed. J. Engels. Utrecht: Instituut voor Laat Latijn der Rijksuniversiteit, 1966.

Bersuire, *Ovidius* ———. *Reductorium morale, liber XV, cap. ii-xv: Ovidius moralizatus.* Ed. J. Engels. Utrecht: Instituut voor Laat Latijn der Rijksuniversiteit, 1962.

Bersuire, *Ovidius,* trans. ———. "The *Ovidius Moralizatus* of Petrus Berchorius: An Introduction and Translation." Trans. William Reynolds. Diss., University of Illinois-Urbana, 1971.

Boccaccio Giovanni Boccaccio. *Genealogia deorum gentilium.* Ed. Vincenzo Romano. 2 vols. *Opere,* vols. 10–11. Scrittori d'Italia, no. 200–201. Bari: Giuseppe Laterza and Sons, 1951.

Bode Mythographi Vaticani. *Scriptores rerum mythicarum latini tres Romae nuper reperti.* Ed. Georgius Henricus Bode. 2 vols. 1834. Repr. 1 vol., Hildesheim: Georg Olms, 1968.

Boethius *De consolatione Philosophiae.* Ed. L. Biehler. CC, vol. 164. Turnhout: Brepols, 1957. References are to book and either poem (m) or prose (p) numbers.

Boethius, trans. ———. *The Consolation of Philosophy.* Trans. Richard H. Green. Indianapolis and New York: Bobbs-Merrill, 1962.

Bryan and Dempster W. F. Bryan and Germaine Dempster, eds. *Sources and Analogues of Chaucer's Canterbury Tales.* 1941. Repr. Atlantic Highlands, N.J.: Humanities Press, 1958.

CC Corpus Christianorum, series latina

ChauR *Chaucer Review*

CN *Chaucer Newsletter*

CSEL Corpus scriptorum ecclesiasticorum latinorum

Chance, *Mythographic Art* Jane Chance, ed. *The Mythographic Art: Classical Fable and the Rise of the Vernacular in Early France and England.* Gainesville: University of Florida Press, 1990.

DAI *Dissertation Abstracts International*

Dante Dante. *The Divine Comedy.* Trans. John Sinclair. 3 vols. 1939. Repr., New York: Oxford University Press, 1981.

EETS Early English Text Society

ELH *English Literary History*

ELN *English Language Notes*

ES *English Studies*

FVM First Vatican Mythographer. *See* Bode.

Fulg. *Expos.* Fabius Planciades Fulgentius. *Expositio continentiae Virgilianae secundum philosophos moralis.* In *Opera.* Ed. Rudolf Helm. 1898. Repr., Stuttgart: B. G. Teubner, 1970.

Fulg. *Expos.,* trans. (or *Mit.,* trans.). *Fulgentius the Mythographer.* Trans. Leslie George Whitbread. Columbus: Ohio State University Press, 1971.

Fulg. *Mit.* ———. *Mitologiae. See* Fulg. *Expos.*

Guillaume, *Roman* Guillaume de Lorris and Jean de Meun. *Le Roman de la Rose par Guillaume de Lorris et Jean de Meun.* Ed. Ernest Langlois. 5 vols. Société des Anciens Textes Français, vols. 117–21. Paris: Librairie ancienne Honoré Champion, 1914–24.

Guillaume, *Roman,* trans. ———. *The Romance of the Rose by Guillaume de Lorris and Jean de Meun.* Trans. Charles Dahlberg. Princeton: Princeton University Press, 1971.

Hoffman, *Ovid* Richard L. Hoffman. *Ovid and the Canterbury Tales.* Philadelphia: University of Pennsylvania Press, 1967.

Holkot, *In librum duodecim* Robert Holkot [Holcot]. *In librum duodecim prophetas.* Oxford. MS. Bodleian 722.

Holkot, *In librum Sapientiae* M. *Roberti Holkoth … In librum Sapientiae Regis Salomonis praelectiones CCXIII.* Basel, 1586.

Holkot, *Moral.* ———. *Moralitates.* Venice, 1514 and Basel, 1586.

Holkot, *Super librum* ———. *Super librum Ecclesiastici.* Venice, 1509.

Holkot, *Super librum Sapientiae* ———. *Super librum Sapientiae.* Venice, 1509.

Hyginus Hyginus. *Fabulae.* Ed. H. J. Rose. Leiden: A. W. Sijthoff, 1934.

Hyginus, trans. ———. *The Myths.* Trans. and ed. Mary Grant. University of Kansas Publications: Humanistic Studies, no. 34. Lawrence: University of Kansas Publications, 1960.

JEGP *Journal of English and Germanic Philology*

Jean, *Roman* *See* Guillaume, *Roman.*

John of Garland John of Garland. *Integumenta Ovidii: Poemetto inedito del secolo XIII.* Ed. Fausto Ghisalberti. Testi e documenti inediti o rari, 2. Messina and Milan: Giuseppe Principato, 1933.

John of Garland, trans. ————. *Integumenta Ovidii*. Trans. Lester
Kruger Born. In "The Integumenta on the Metamorphoses of Ovid by
John of Garland—first cited with Introduction and Translation." Diss.,
University of Chicago, 1929.

John Scot   John Scot [Joannes Scottus]. *Annotationes in Marcianum.*
Ed. Cora Lutz. 1939. Repr., New York: Kraus Reprint Co., 1970.

MAE   *Medium Ævum*

MGH   *Monumenta Germaniae historica*

M & H   *Mediaevalia et Humanistica*

MLN   *Modern Language Notes*

MLQ   *Modern Language Quarterly*

MLR   *Modern Language Review*

MLS   *Modern Language Studies*

MP   *Modern Philology*

MS   *Mediaeval Studies*

Macrobius   Ambrosius Theodosius Macrobius. *Macrobius.* 2 vols. Ed.
James Willis. Leipzig: B. G. Teubner, 1963.

Macrobius, trans. ————. *Commentary on the Dream of Scipio.* Trans.
William Harris Stahl. Records of Civilization: Sources and Studies, no.
48. 1952. Repr., New York and London: Columbia University, 1966.

Martianus   Martianus Capella. *Martianus Capella.* Ed. Adolf Dick.
Rev. Jean Préaux. Bibliotheca Scriptorum Graecorum et Romanorum
Teubneriana. Stuttgart: B. G. Teubner, 1969.

Martianus, trans.   ————. *Martianus Capella and the Seven Liberal
Arts,* vol. 2: *The Marriage of Philology and Mercury.* Trans. William
Harris Stahl and Richard Johnson with E. L. Burge. New York:
Columbia University Press, 1977.

McCall   John P. McCall. *Chaucer Among the Gods: The Poetics of
Classical Myth.* University Park: Pennsylvania State University Press, 1979.

NM   *Neuphilologische Mitteilungen*

N & Q   *Notes and Queries*

Ovid   Ovid. *Metamorphoses.* Ed. and trans. Frank Justus Miller. 2 vols.
Loeb Classical Library. 3d ed. Cambridge, Mass.: Harvard University
Press; London: W. Heinemann, 1977.

Ovide moralisé.   *Ovide moralisé: Poème du commencement du quatorzième siècle.* Ed. C. de Boer et al. *Verhandelingen der Koninklijke Akademie van Wetenschappen te Amsterdam. Afdeeling Letterkunde. Nieuwe Reeks* 15 (1915): 1–374; 21 (1920): 1–394; 30 (1931): 1–303; 37 (1936): 1–478; 43 (1938): 1–429. Repr., 5 vols. Wiesbaden: Martin Sändig, 1966–68.

PL   *Patrologiae cursus completus, series latina,* ed. J.-P. Migne (cited by volume and column)

PMLA   *Publications of the Modern Language Association*

PQ   *Philological Quarterly*

Pietro   Pietro Alighieri. *Petri Allegherii super Dantis ipsius genitoris Comoediam commentarium nunc primum in lucem editum.* Ed. Vincentio Nannucci. Florence, 1845.

RES   *Review of English Studies*

Remigius, *Boeth.*   Remigius of Auxerre. Mythological Glosses from the Commentary on Boethius. In "The Study of the Consolation of Philosophy in Anglo-Saxon England." Ed. Diane K. Bolton. *AHDLMA* 44 (1977): 61–78.

Remigius, *Mart.*   ———. *Commentum in Martianum Capellam libri I-II,* and *III-IX.* Ed. Cora E. Lutz. 2 vols. Leiden: E. J. Brill, 1962 and 1965.

Robertson, *Preface*   Robertson, D. W., Jr. *A Preface to Chaucer: Studies in Medieval Perspectives.* Princeton: Princeton University Press, 1962; repr. 1969.

SAC   *Studies in the Age of Chaucer*

SP   *Studies in Philology*

SVM   Second Vatican Mythographer. *See* Bode.

Schoeck and Taylor   Richard J. Schoeck and Jerome Taylor, eds. *Chaucer Criticism.* 2 vols. Notre Dame: University of Notre Dame Press, 1960–61.

TAPA   *Transactions and Proceedings of the American Philological Association*

TVM   Third Vatican Mythographer. *See* Bode.

Theodulf   Theodulf of Orleans. "The Books I Used to Read." In Peter Godman, ed. *Poetry of the Carolingian Renaissance.* Norman: University of Oklahoma Press, 1985.

Virgil   *Virgil.* Trans. H. Rushton Fairclough. 2 vols. Rev. ed. Cambridge, Mass.: Harvard University Press; London: W. Heinemann, 1978.

Walsingham   Thomas Walsingham. *Archana deorum.* Ed. Robert A. van Kluyve. Durham, N.C.: Duke University Press, 1968.

William, *Boeth.*   William of Conches. Glosses on Boethius. Excerpts in Édouard Jeauneau, "L'Usage de la notion d'*integumentum* à travers les gloses de Guillaume de Conches." *AHDLMA* 32 (1957): 35–100.

William, *Macrob.*   ———. Glosses on Macrobius. In Peter Dronke, *Fabula: Explorations into the Uses of Myth in Medieval Platonism.* Mittellateinische Studien und Texte, vol. 9. Leiden and Cologne: E. J. Brill, 1974, pp. 114–18, 167–83.

William, *Mart.*   In Dronke.

A Chronology of Major
Medieval Mythographers

4th–7th centuries

Servius (ca. 389), Commentaries on Virgil's *Eclogues, Georgics,* and *Aeneid*
Macrobius (ca. 433), *Saturnalia;* Commentary on the *Somnium Scipionis*
Fulgentius (fl. 468–533), *Mitologiae; Expositio continentiae Virgilii; Super Thebaiden*
Isidore (fl. 602–36), *Origines* (8.11.1–104, "De diis gentium")

8th–11th centuries

First Vatican Mythographer (8th–9th c.?), Mythography
Second Vatican Mythographer (8th–9th c.?), Mythography
Theodulf of Orleans (ca. 786), "De libris quos legere solebam et qualiter fabulae poetarum a philosophus mystice pertractentur"
Rabanus Maurus (776?-856), "De diis gentium" of Isidore copied in *De universo*
Remigius of Auxerre (ca. 841–908), Commentaries on Martianus Capella and Boethius
Ecloga Theoduli (9th c.)
Notker Labeo (d. 1022), Commentaries on Martianus and Boethius
Bernard of Utrecht (11th c.), Commentary on *Ecloga Theoduli*
Baudri of Bourgueil (1046–1130), Poem CCXVI: Fragment of a Moralized Mythology

12th–13th centuries

William of Conches (1090–1145), Glosses on Boethius, Macrobius, the *Timaeus,* Martianus Capella
Bernardus Silvestris (1085–1178), Commentaries on the *Aeneid* and Martianus Capella
Third Vatican Mythographer (12th c.), *De diis gentium et illorum allegoriis*
Arnulf of Orleans (fl. 1175), Glosses on Lucan, Ovid's *Metamorphoses,* and Ovid's *Fasti*
John of Garland (1180–1252), *Integumenta Ovidii*

14th–15th centuries

Nicholas Trevet (ca. 1314), Commentaries on Boethius, St. Augustine's *City of God*, Seneca's *Tragedies*

John Ridevall (fl. 1331), *Fulgentius metaforalis*, Commentary on *City of God*, 1–3, 6–7

Robert Holkot (fl. 1332–34, d. 1349?), Commentaries on the Book of Wisdom, the Twelve Prophets, Ecclesiastes

Pierre Bersuire (ca. 1342), *Ovidius moralizatus*

Ovide moralisé (14th c.)

Giovanni del Virgilio (fl. 1332–33), *Allegorie librorum Ovidii Metamorphoseos*

Pietro Alighieri (ca. 1340–41), Commentary on Dante

Giovanni Boccaccio (fl. 1313–75), *Genealogia gentilium deorum*, Commentary on the *Inferno*

Coluccio Salutati (1331–1406), *De laboribus Herculis*

Christine de Pizan (ca. 1399), *Epistre d'Othéa*

Cristoforo Landino (fl. 1481), Commentaries on Virgil and Dante

Preface

The concealment of embarrassing secrets, often sexual in nature, and the burden of political alliances and strategies — what together might be termed sexual politics — motivated Chaucer in much of his work (an idea long evident but for the most part ignored by Chaucer critics). Because Chaucer had treated Criseyde (and therefore all women) so shamefully in the *Troilus* through his misogynistic depiction of her as fickle, he was accused of having abrogated courtly norms of decorum. Having well documented his offense in the *Prologue* to the *Legend of Good Women,* Chaucer proscribed as poetic penance for himself (through the authority of the God of Love) the writing of the legends of good women, a task that he never completed and that was exchanged for the more inviting task of constructing the drama of class subversion in the *Canterbury Tales.*

Although he never finished either project, Chaucer learned well from his offense. Even in his mostly classical legendary and mythological tales, women are not merely manipulated *as tales* (something that critics have only recently begun to observe); that is, if as a consequence of the Fall woman is linked by the cleric with desire and the body, and if reading a text literally rather than figuratively implies a prohibited carnal reading, then allegorical reading leaves women out of the text. Therefore Chaucer avoids allegory in most of his later writing. But he also returns the female, and the "female" — the essentialized idea of the female as different, other, alien — to the text.[1] What remains the same in all the phases of Chaucer's developing poetic, despite the social and political demands placed upon him, is his abiding interest in the use of mythological imagery as a means of protection for the helpless from charges such as misogyny, immorality, or treason.

Mythography, focused as it is upon moral theology in the tradition of medieval poetic, is indeed a political technique. Chaucer's own valorization of the vernacular in place of Latin has been recently perceived as a means of empowerment of the marginalized in relation to language, country, class, a "premature Reformation," to borrow Anne Hudson's phrase.[2] This valorization may also have carried with it — by means of a similar adaptation of the essentially Latin tradition of fabulous narrative and clerical tradition of allegorical reading—a concomitant valorization in relation to gender. Termed the most feminist writer since Richardson by Derek Brewer,[3] Chaucer appropriates these conflicted sets of images for politically subversive reasons to undermine "allegory" as a traditional and patriarchal form of discourse. Of the political possibility of allegory, David Aers (drawing upon his previous work and that of Herbert Marcuse), declares that "Allegory is inextricably bound up with the *power* of a particular social institution. It is not surprising that resistance to allegory is seen as 'infidelity', for 'infidelity', like heresy, was defined as obstinate opposition to the authority of the institution, the Catholic Church and its officials."[4]

Most problematic is Chaucer's participation in the religious literary debates of the fourteenth century. The Wycliffites, with whom some of Chaucer's aristocratic friends shared sympathies, opposed the use of images— they were antimendicant, anti-Franciscan, and antiglossation (that is, opposed to the practice of glossing, in Latin, biblical texts) in their insistence on the vernacular.[5] If Chaucer were similarly sympathetic, as scholars recently have surmised, then how could he have rationalized his borrowing from the commentators? Yet for some reason his "fables," as they were termed, were specifically exempted from the 1542–43 Parliamentary Act "for the advancement of the Religion" that sought to ban early English books, which suggests that Chaucer was never in his own day, much less thereafter, suspected of explicitly heretical or subversive inclinations.[6] But, then, was his poetic so concealing a veil, so conservatively managed, that his use of mythological imagery was by 1542 acceptable practice?

The Mythographic Chaucer analyzes mythological references, images, and characters throughout Chaucer's poetry in the light of the medieval mythographic tradition, with the goal of clarifying those truths hidden within the text, whether for literary, social, or political reasons. Medieval mythographers are generally well known for their moralizing and allegorizing penchants; Chaucer, in contrast, often inverts typically allegorical signification for psychological or political and ironic purposes in developing characterization. In so doing, he rewrites—vernacularizes—the Latin and patristic tradition from an English and medieval perspective: his is an antimythography. The result of this mythographic reading is, I hope, new answers to both old and new questions about the shape and significance of Chaucer's writings. The mythographic "method"—if I may call it that— focuses closely on the text, retains an abiding interest in the structure of the work, and invokes only what it needs from the large and sometimes seemingly amorphous mythographic tradition. This method should, by its very nature, suggest the medieval scholastic approach to literature that a poet like Chaucer or Dante would have acquired during his education, and consequently its readings ideally reconstruct what a medieval reader would have seen in Chaucer's poems if they, rather than those of Virgil and Ovid, had appeared in the school curriculum. This method does not, however, substitute a mechanical process of allegorization for poetic responses that are more selective, more sensitive, and more responsive to nuance. Chaucer is rarely mechanical or narrow in his usage of myth: he will often deliberately conjure up an ambiguous range of readings, some *in bono*, some *in malo*, to enrich his poetry.

Surprisingly little, given the wealth of mythographic materials in the Middle Ages, has been written about Chaucer's subversive and gendered use of pagan mythology, with attention to the mythographic tradition. Although scholars have begun to investigate Chaucer's use of mythological figures, most of the work has focused on individual lines in poems, or has ignored the existence of the medieval mythographic tradition, despite a scholarly interest in allegoresis that has surfaced at various periods during the past century. From the beginning, scholarly essays have either related the mythological references to topical allegory and the political situation in fourteenth-century England, or uncovered Chaucer's use of mythographic sources, or established the astrological background of some planetary figures.[7] In the second half of this century, especially in the sixties and early seventies, patristic exegesis as a critical method (the "Robertsonian school") was ushered in by D. W. Robertson, Jr., and his monumental *Preface to Chaucer: Studies in Medieval Perspectives*. His patristic exegetical approach, while not necessarily focused on the mythological, nevertheless resulted in new attention to the gods in Chaucer, mostly linked to Ovid and Virgil references, by Robertson and others over a period of thirty years.[8] More recently, the complexity of Chaucer's mythographic and polysemous imagery has been revealed in studies that acknowledge his dependence on various mythographic traditions and their appearance in intermediary vernacular sources.[9] Other books on Chaucer's women characters and the issue of female textuality have generally bypassed the question of myth and mythography, and therefore Chaucer's feminizing poetic, in their attention to Chaucerian sexuality or misogyny.[10]

To understand Chaucer's recuperation of myth depends upon acceptance of that tradition as part of his literary heritage. One humanist misunderstanding has been that he generally drew upon original classical sources and ignored medieval commentators on those sources. Based on Chaucer's direct and indirect references to authors, one study argues that the poet intimately knew the works of Boethius and Ovid and was familiar with the works of Cicero, Seneca, Statius, and Virgil: "It is possible to say only that Chaucer *knew* very few classical authors but that he *used* approximately twenty-seven with some degree of regularity."[11] Although support for such dependence is encouraged by Chaucer's own Man of Law, who portrays Chaucer as an English Ovid ("For he hath toold of loveris up and doun / Mo than Ovide made of mencioun / In his Episteles, that been ful olde" [53–55]), scholars have nevertheless maintained an appropriately skeptical attitude toward this attribution as they have learned more about the glossing of classical authors in the Middle Ages and the difficulty in isolating Chaucer's exact mythographic sources. True, the last four fabulous tales of the *Canterbury Tales* derive mythological images or characters or fables either from Ovid or from Ovidian works like the *Roman de la Rose,* as this study will examine. But Chaucer's extensive knowledge of Ovid may in fact reflect his familiarity with the much-read mythographic schoolbook of the *Ecloga Theoduli,* which has been established to be part of his library and the source for many of his references.[12] The nature of the mythographic, scholastic process differs in figurative complexity from that of the poetic mythological process,[13] but Chaucer would have been well aware of both by education, travel, the coterie of courtly poets with whom he associated, and geographical proximity.

Although Chaucer did not travel extensively or frequently, he probably had access to a surprising collection of important commentaries and handbooks, whether in or out of school (and he may have attended St. Paul's School, with its own significant book holdings).[14] Important mythographic manuscripts were also housed at Cambridge and Oxford (for example, Bernardus's commentary on Martianus, or manuscript Digby 221); he might have seen others on trips to Avignon, Florence, and Milan (for example, works by the Vatican Mythographers, Dante, and the Dante commentators). The commentaries and handbooks he most often read, judging from the evidence in his poetry, were mostly written in the twelfth to the fourteenth centuries and glossed a variety of classical texts, by Virgil, Ovid, Statius, Boethius, and Martianus Capella. In his earliest dream visions (*Parlement, Hous of Fame*), Chaucer was most conscious of the *Aeneid* commentaries (or at least the commentary attributed to Bernardus Silvestris). As he started on the *Troilus,* he became fascinated by the Boethius commentaries (especially by Remigius and Nicholas Trevet), as well as the Ovid commentaries and mythographic handbooks (Arnulf of Orleans, Pierre Bersuire, John of Garland, the Vatican Mythographers). Certainly his interest in Dante as a poetic "glossator" similar to other medieval commentators (and Dante's son Pietro Alighieri) is evidenced in *Hous of Fame,* the *Troilus,* and the *General Prologue.* Chaucer also owes a substantial debt in the *Knight's Tale* to the classicizing friars Robert Holkot and Thomas Walsingham (from whom he draws so much of his material). In the Marriage Group, he plays with Martianus on Marriage (and the commentators John Scot and Remigius of Auxerre). In the last tales, his interest in metamorphosis conjoins with an interest in Ovidian commentary in particular as filtered through the *Roman de la Rose,* which takes on the hue of a commentary in itself.

Given Chaucer's complex commentary reading, the provenance of some of these handbooks and mythographies deserves closer attention, especially the Oxford and Cambridge manuscripts containing later commentaries and mythographic tracts (and in them *florilegia,* or collections of excerpts, or "flowers," from earlier glosses). By the mid-fourteenth century, the library holdings at Oxford's Merton College numbered 340 volumes[15] and included Isidore's encyclopedia and Seneca; by 1374, according to a preserved indenture, also available were Macrobius's commentary on Cicero's *Somnium Scipionis,* Martianus Capella, Alan of Lille's *Anticlaudianus,* and Boethius's *Consolatio.* Before 1410, Merton also held a copy of Bersuire's *Ovidius moralizatus.*

Oxford's Bodleian Library manuscript Digby 221 is a famous example of a single manuscript containing four influential commentaries, mostly twelfth-century: a mythographic handbook, the *Scintillarii* of Albericus; Alexander Neckham's commentary on Martianus Capella; a work attributed to Hermes Trismegistus; and the Digby mythography. (Alexander Neckham's commentary on Martianus also appears in Cambridge, Trinity College manuscript R.14.1429, fols. 38–63.) Nicholas Trevet's important fourteenth-century expansion of earlier Boethius commentaries (especially Remigius's) is contained in Bodleian Library manuscript Rawlinson 167. Twelfth-century Hugutio of Pisa's dictionary containing much mythographic material identical in many cases to the glosses of Arnulf of Orleans and entitled *Derivationes* appears in Bodleian Library manuscript 376. And, of course, not least in importance for the issue of accessibility are Robert Holkot's manuscripts:[16] at Balliol College, manuscript 26 includes *In librum duodecim prophetas* (his commentary on the Twelve Prophets, full of mythographic glosses), as does Bodleian Library manuscript 722. Holkot's important and much-copied *Moralitates,* exempla intended for preachers and appended to his commentary on the Book of Wisdom in the Bale printed edition of 1586, can be found in Magdalen College manuscript 68, as well as in many manuscripts now housed in the British Library (Additional 21429, Arundel 386, Egerton 2258, Royal VI.E.3), Gray's Inn Library in London (Gray's Inn 2, fols. 1r-72r), and on the continent in the Marziana in Venice (Marcianus lat. 2771 [III:75]) and the Vatican Library in Rome (Palatinus lat. 1726). Thomas of Walsingham, who died in 1422, wrote his *Archana deorum* in England, copies of which appear in St. John's College manuscript 124, and in London, British Library manuscript Lansdowne 728.

At Cambridge, the *Ecloga Theoduli* is contained in Peterhouse 207, along with other schoolbook texts.[17] The important eleventh-century K-Reviser of Remigius's Boethius glosses (full of Fulgentian additions to Remigius) appears in full in University Library manuscript KK.III.21, 104ff. Bernardus Silvestris's supposed twelfth-century commentary on Martianus Capella (a very important synthesis of earlier *florilegia* and commentaries and full of the same glosses found in his astonishing *Aeneid* commentary) can be found in University Library manuscript Mm.1.18. (An earlier version of the alleged commentary by Bernardus on the *Aeneid* has been ascertained to be English in provenance—in fact, contained in Peterhouse manuscript 158.)[18] John de Foxton (1369–1450) continued Ridevall's *Fulgentius metaforalis* in a treatise contained in Trinity College manuscript R.15.21, and dated 1408.

These varied mythographic and commentary influences were expressed and emphasized at different times during Chaucer's career, but consistently account for the nature of the classics and classical mythological imagery as simultaneously authoritative and marginalized, because pagan and "other," "female," and therefore accessible to medieval scholars and poets only through the mediating if politicized role of patristic exegesis and allegorical reading. The classical gods and heroes in Chaucer's poems—images, exempla, and characters—reveal feminizing and subversive attitudes not readily apparent on the surface because he appropriates the essentially patriarchal discourse of medieval exegesis for ironic (or even antiphrastic) use. For this reason, so many of the myths involve, center on, elaborate female figures and characters.

The three parts of *The Mythographic Chaucer* treat different, evolving aspects of feminized Chaucerian subjectivity through the major phases of his career. In the first, on the dream visions, Chaucer's interest in female authority, subjectivity, and women's experience is reflected in the female heroes Alcyone and Alceste, both drawn from the Latin mythographic and epic tradition. His valorization of their lives makes them paradigmatic in a tradition that is often perceived as patristic and masculinized. More self-consciously, Chaucer constructs his own subjectivity as feminized poet through the figures of Dido, Ganymede, and "Marcia" in his dense scholastic parody of mythographic conventions and traditions, the *Hous of Fame,* which finds her/him abandoned by the mythographic (male) heroes of that Latin tradition, specifically Aeneas, as interpreted by Virgil, Ovid, Dante. The embodiment of female experience is authorized by the goddess Venus, whose multiple significations (influenced by the Neo-Stoic mythography of Bernardus Silvestris and Alan of Lille) recast specific aspects of women's sexuality in the *Parlement of Foules* as a function of natural law.

The second part, a long chapter on the *Troilus,* examines mythographic cross-dressing—both the blending of usually discrete traditions of commentary and the disgendering of specific myths by characters' sexual crossover within the narrative. Troilus may function as a type of Paris in his affair with Criseyde, but he also is cast as Cupid to the Venus of maternal Criseyde in the third book, and ends as Eurydice to her Orpheus, Meleager to Atalanta and Meleager's vengeful mother. The tale-teller fuses poetic narrative inexorably with gloss—embeds it, exploits it, challenges it. Where Ovidian mythography may work best in one instance—as a contextualization for Criseyde's "metamorphoses" in the fourth book—Statian versions of Theban myth historicize the epic clash between nations and the difference in their cultures at the end.

In the third part, as Chaucer responds to the Peasants' Revolt and the social and political confusion engendered by its consequence in the 1380s, his use of mythography as a political tool depends upon subversion of the sources he exploits in the *Tales*. He radically transforms—anglicizes, or feminizes, or both—the myths of Zephirus, Theseus, Ceres, Mercury and Philology, Echo, Pygmalion, and Proteus by contextualizing them within a narrator's own subjectivity. The tale spoken by his character is allowed to shape the "objective" tradition of commentary on the mythological figure; the subjectivity of speaker is both filter and gloss. The Roman figure for the West Wind is allied with a historical figure, Thomas à Becket, whose martyrdom becomes important politically within England as a sign of ecclesiastical subversion by the state. Theseus's masculine martiality—his allegiance to Mars—must be feminized by means of the wisdom of Pallas Athena: chivalry and war must make room for women, for Hippolyta, for Emelye. Alisoun's appropriation of clerical exegesis on Ceres and Bacchus and her bold alteration of Ovidian myth and mythography in her invention of Midas's wife stud her prologue and tale with myths that reveal—comment upon, define—her own life, the narrative of her autobiography. The Merchant pragmatically invokes Martianus Capella as a mythographic context for an ideal marriage in the earthly underworld that weds May's eloquence to the very unphilological ignorance—blindness—of Januarie. The upwardly mobile Franklin criticizes the self-absorbed and homosocial chivalry of the knight and squire and explains the lack of self of the aristocratic lady by glossing Arveragus as Narcissus, Aurelius as Echo, and Dorigen as Narcissus's reflected image. Toward the end of the *Tales*, Chaucer becomes increasingly interested in speakers who absorb his own roles as king's man, public official, and poet. In their tales, the Physician uses Pygmalion and the Pardoner, Proteus, at least implicitly, whose power in transformation of other or self seduces them into the illusion of a kind of omnipotence—similar to that of the artist who populates his fictional world with his own creations, variations on his self.

One inference of this study is that greater continuity exists between Chaucer's early works and his later, major ones than scholars have posited—his work is much more of a single piece, a seamless web. This makes sense, for Chaucer worked on the *Tales* off and on all his life. This continuity is best seen in his favorite myths to dramatize flawed love and betrayal, of Venus, Bacchus, Ceres, or Venus and Hymen, Venus and Adonis, Venus and Mars, Venus and Cupid, or the blinding of Argus by Mercury, the deception of Medea by Jason and her revenge, the treachery of Sinon or Agenor, the doomed love of Narcissus and Echo, the fall of Phaethon and Icarus, the blindness of Orpheus or Oedipus, the seduction of Europa by Jove, or of Pasiphaë by Neptune. Here the familiar themes of narcissism, selfishness, lechery, deceit, incest, scandalous secrets that Macrobius would have avoided in writing *narratio fabulosa,* converge. But for the court poet, telling secrets—about Alisoun's husbands as poor lovers, or as murderers, about Criseyde and Pandarus, and a possibly incestuous relationship, about the weaknesses of the Black Knight as a thinly disguised John of Gaunt— is a business he must approach with the greatest of care. The school short-hand of mythography, which many of his contemporaries would have known, provides a means of dissemination without ignobility. In the delicious ambiguity that Chaucer traces, of *in bono, in malo,* rests all his art.

Acknowledgments

All of Chaucer's poems containing some mythological reference or allusion are discussed in this study. The individual legends of the *Legend of Good Women* constitute the one exception: they are much more complex than most Chaucer scholars have realized and deserve an entire book of their own. My discussion invokes them only insofar as they pertain to the overall frame of the *Legend* as defined by the *Prologue*. As legends, these stories of good classical women depend more on the tradition of Ovidian tale than Ovidian mythography, and Chaucer's direction in the unfinished work is not yet clear to me.

This study depends upon the research and conclusions of other scholars interested in the interrelationship between classical fable and vernacular poetics, most especially the work of the late Richard Hamilton Green, Judson Boyce Allen, and D. W. Robertson, Jr., but including the monumental studies of Don Cameron Allen, Ernst Curtius, Erwin Panofsky, Fritz Saxl, Jean Seznec, and Beryl Smalley. Much of what I propound is indebted to the more recent work on this subject or on its relationship to gender and sexuality by R. Howard Bloch, Emerson Brown, Rita Copeland, Sheila Delany, Marilynn Desmond, Carolyn Dinshaw, George Economou, Margaret Ehrhart, Joan Ferrante, John Block Friedman, John Fyler, Robert Hanning, Susan Schibanoff, Winthrop Wetherbee, James Wimsatt, and Chauncey Wood.

To acknowledge fully the help I have received in writing this book, I must begin with an explanation. I came to write this book to help in completing another. At the 1984 New Chaucer Society meeting in York, where I delivered a report on my research-in-progress on another, longer, book on the history of the mythographic tradition, Julia Bolton Holloway advised me first to study the mythographic tradition as it intersects the work of a specific poet, perhaps Chaucer, and then write the study that would describe its parameters. Although she suggested this approach to help define audience and organize material, the result has strengthened my understanding of both Chaucer and the mythographic tradition; I am deeply grateful to her as the presiding genius of this book as it has evolved over the past ten years.

Thanks are also due to the National Endowment for the Humanities for granting me the Summer Seminar for College Teachers on "Chaucer and Mythography" in 1985 during which I formulated the early lectures on Chaucer that provided the core for this book. I am indebted to the seminar participants, whose presence, contributions in class and out, and encouragement in a variety of ways inspired the shape of this book—especially Deborah D. Rubin, Charles B. Moore, Sister Rose Marie Julie Gavin, Judith Kellogg, and Jeanne Nightingale.

Much of the background information on the mythographic tradition was gleaned from research pursued during a National Endowment for the Humanities Fellowship leave in London in 1977–78 and a Guggenheim leave in Rome and Venice in 1980–81; I am grateful to both of these foundations for permitting me the released time to work up this tradition and thereby apply my insights to Chaucer in this study.

Acknowledgments are also due Rice University for the research grant in 1984–86 that subsidized travel and student help required to complete this book, particularly in transcribing oral lectures on cassette, and for the sabbatical semester in the fall of 1987, during which I pulled together much earlier writing. The English Department and the Dean of Humanities supplied funds for research assistance in rechecking documentation, transcriptions, and abbreviations, as well as funds for the index.

Many friends, colleagues, and scholars have read portions of this study as it progressed and offered invaluable responses (whatever errors the book contains are, of course, my own). I am especially grateful to the late Judson Allen, David Anderson, Chris Baswell, Rita Copeland, Helen Eaker, Peggy Ehrhart, John Hurt Fisher, John Block Friedman, Britton Harwood, Laura Hodges, the late Bernard F. Huppé, Roy Laird, Seth Lerer, D. W. Robertson, Jr., Lois Roney, R. A. Shoaf, Lorraine Stock, and Winthrop Wetherbee. As readers for the Press, Julia Bolton Holloway and Chauncey Wood also offered helpful suggestions for revision.

Many others, including graduate and undergraduate students and secretaries, have helped in the completion of this book. Faye Walker rechecked bibliographic documentation against notes for consistency, and Kathye Bergen added abbreviations in the notes. Caroline Levander rechecked transcriptions and documentation; Larry Kraemer helped with problems here. Dejan Kuzmanovic read proofs. Cindy Pfeiffer, my secretary for the 1985 National Endowment for the Humanities Summer Seminar for College Teachers, valiantly collected texts and compiled an initial bibliography. Undergraduates who doggedly transcribed my cassettes included the uncomplaining Kristine Hain, Robert Barber, and Jennie Hyan. I am grateful to the following individuals for their contributions to the production of *The Mythographic Chaucer*: David Thorstad, Deborah Ausman, and (at the

University of Minesota Press) Mary Byers, Laura Westlund, Elizabeth Knoll Stomberg, Kathy Wolter, Becky Manfredini, and Biodun Iginla.

Acknowledgments for permission to reprint are as follows. A portion of the Introduction and small portions of the chapters on the *Merchant's Tale* and the *Parlement of Foules* derive from "Chaucer and Mythology," *The Chaucer Newsletter* 6 (Winter 1984): 1, 2. Portions of two articles on Chaucer's short poems have been used in the chapter on the *Parlement* and the short poems; thanks to *Mediaevalia* for allowing me to reprint relevant sections in revised form, and to *Papers on Language and Literature* for permission to reprint in revised form from "Chaucerian Irony in the Verse Epistles 'Wordes unto Adam,' 'Lenvoy a Scogan,' and 'Lenvoy a Bukton'" (vol. 21 [1985]; copyright 1985 by the Board of Trustees, Southern Illinois University, reprinted by permission). The chapter on Zephirus in the *General Prologue* is reprinted in revised form from *The Mythographic Art: Classical Fable and the Rise of the Vernacular in Early France and England*, ed. Jane Chance (Gainesville: University of Florida Press, 1990). *Philological Quarterly* has allowed me to reprint a portion of my chapter on the Pardoner from the special issue published in 1988 (vol. 67), which included papers and responses from the 1987 Midwest Modern Language Association session on medieval studies and literary theory.

Some of the material in this book has been delivered as conference papers or lectures; acknowledgment will be provided within the notes to individual chapters.

All references to Chaucer derive from the *Riverside Chaucer*, ed. Larry D. Benson, rev. from the 2d ed. (Boston: Houghton Mifflin, 1987), and will be quoted by poem or tale and line number(s) and parentheses within the text.

Introduction
"Fables and Swich Wrecchednesse"

Chaucer rarely comments on his own life or poetic career, aside from the prefatory pseudoautobiographical narrative frames in the dream visions, the two tales of the pilgrim Chaucer (*Sir Thopas* and the *Melibee*), and the Retraction at the end of the *Canterbury Tales*. The lone passage of what might be defined as literary biography is voiced by one of his own characters (and alter ego), the Canterbury pilgrim Man of Law, in the introduction to his tale (45–89). Apart from the fascinating Borges-like situation of a character commenting on the authority of his own creator, the most important aspect of this literary biography is the Man of Law's singular isolation of classical mythological figures used by Chaucer, particularly pairs of lovers. Mentioned are Ceys and Alcyone (57), from *The Book of the Duchess*, written "In youthe," and Dido and Aeneas, Lucretia and Thisbe, Phyllis and Demophon, Deianira and Hermione, Hero and Leander, Helen, Briseyde, Laodamia, Medea and Jason, Hypermnestra, Penelope, and Alceste, all from the "saint's legend of Cupid" (in actuality, *The Legend of Good Women* [61]).[1] In later lines within the tale, the Man of Law also refers to myths about heroes used elsewhere by Chaucer, including "the deeth of Ector, Achilles" and "whan Pirrus brak the wal" (198, 288, from the *Troilus*), "The strif of Thebes" (200, from the *Knight's Tale*), and even the *de casibus* version of the story of Hercules, Samson, Turnus, and Socrates (201, from the *Monk's Tale*).

In relation to use of these pagan figures, the Man of Law most commends his creator for noticeably avoiding "unnatural abominations" ("unkynde abhomynacions") in his writings, which the Man of Law terms "sermons." In the most legal fashion, the Man of Law appears to be defending Chaucer from potential accusations of immorality, perhaps not entirely understanding the poet's means of using mythological fable as a cloak for immoral "secrets," or truths. He cites as examples of such "abhomynacions" the classical fables detailing the incest of Canacee with her own brother and of Antiochus with his own virgin daughter (77–85). Of course Chaucer does begin the story of Canacee in the *Squire's Tale*—a story that would have ended in incest with her brother[2]—and he suggests in the

1

most elliptical manner the possibility of incest in the *Troilus*, between Pandarus and Criseyde, as well as between Helen and Paris's brother, Deiphebus. In addition, the Man of Law himself has inadvertently touched on those immoral fables in this little *occupatio*, although he claims, "Ne I wol noon reherce, if that I may" (89).

Yet the Man of Law tells a tale about incest between Constance and her father. His point is that the tale is not figuratively about incest; his point is exactly what Carolyn Dinshaw has claimed that it is—an ideological and patriarchal desire for the reconciliation of opposites (male and female, father and daughter), and perhaps also the suppression of female power and desire by means of the manipulation of the "principle of similarity and difference" (p. 112). Chaucer *the poet*, by drawing attention to the discrepancy between the narrator's desire for concealment of the ugliness of incest and the actual secret, clarifies an important feature of his own poetic in his *character's* own preface to an exemplary tale.

In the *Tales*, Chaucer employs mythological imagery to gloss the characters populating tales that are told by speakers who are themselves fictional and driven by their own needs and desires—layer upon layer of sexual truth interwoven into a fabric poetical and political. It may come as no surprise, then, that in the penultimate tale Chaucer provides the reader with the "naked text"—a tale relayed by a character not so different from himself, the Manciple, that is actually a classical fable, the ancient Ovidian story of Apollo and the crow. But Chaucer's "naked text," ironically, exemplifies what this study will analyze in detail—the usefulness of fabulation to cover up the body for political and social reasons. Understanding Chaucer's purpose in this tale will change how the Retraction is read. It will also help to sum up the mythographic direction of his artistry throughout his work. One leads inexorably to the other.

At the end of his tale, placed by modern editors in the penultimate position of the *Tales*, the Manciple warns against telling the truth, for the sake of life and friendship. The Parson, in contrast, insists on the need of the eternal soul to understand the truth. The necessary lies of the former, unfortunately, seem to have no place in the stripped-down clarity of the latter. In many ways, the Manciple's view of truth as cloaked by fiction is a most conventional literary theory, so that Chaucer's juxtaposition of the *Manciple's Tale* with the *Parson's Tale* suggests a tension between classical fable and homiletic Gospel sermon that is, for Chaucer, art itself.

The Parson, a man of great authority who enters the *Canterbury Tales* at its end, very like the unknown figure who ends the *Hous of Fame* at the moment Chaucer muses over the problem of tidings and rumor, desires to praise God through sounding moral truths. But at the opening of the *Parson's Prologue*, when the Host asks the Parson to " 'Telle us a fable anon' " (29), the Parson replies, " 'Thou getest fable noon ytoold for me' " (31). The reason derives from the counsel of Paul in the letter to Timothy (32), " 'Repreveth hem that weyven soothfastnesse / And tellen fables and swich wrecchednesse' " (33–34). In the context of such Gospel authority, the Parson questions why he should flout Christian tradition: " 'Why sholde I sowen draf out of my fest, / Whan I may sowen whete, if that me lest?' " (35–36). In contrast to the immoral lies of the poets, he posits the "wheat" of "Moralitee and vertuous mateere" (38), which he is glad to share with an audience in reverence of Christ. This *occupatio* nevertheless keeps before the reader the concept of fable, all the while the Parson continues with a confession of his ignorance of poetry and the "rum, ram, ruf" of the Northern poets. And of course he then proceeds in the best Lollard fashion to deliver his sermon in the vernacular, his dislike of figuration also typical of the Wycliffites.[3]

At the other—political and worldly—end of the spectrum, the homilist or poet can tell too much "truth" about the wrong person, as the life of the politically insensitive Saint Thomas à Becket signifies. In a sense, actual gossip, tattling, tale-telling, according to the gloss on the tale provided by the Manciple at its end, is dangerous and should be shunned altogether. He counsels the pilgrims to " 'be war, and be noon auctour newe / Of *tidynges*, wheither they been false or trewe' " (357–58). Whatever the source of this news, " 'amonges hye or lowe' " (361), he admonishes them to " 'Kepe wel thy tonge and thenk upon the crowe' " (362).

This curious injunction against tidings-bearing should remind us of the whirling house of Rumor at the end of the unfinished *Hous of Fame*, wherein there is no porter through whom tidings can enter, "No maner *tydynges* in to pace" (1955; my emphasis). A secular "other world," its eternal flux also marks the repository of all extant tidings, which cannot be disseminated or stopped: "Ne never rest is in that place / That hit nys fild ful of tydynges, / Other loude or of whisprynges" (1956–58). The house of Rumor in the *Hous of Fame*, like the tavern full of pilgrims along the way to Canterbury, is chock full of pilgrims and shipmen about whose gossip Chaucer fantasizes: "Were the tydynge soth or fals" (2072), it passes from one to the other, north and south, until, like a fire burning up a city, it flies out the window to Fame. Given the nature of the *Hous of Fame* as an allegorization of the poetic process, particularly in relation to "love-tydinges" (2143), what role do *tidynges* play in fabulous narrative and homily? How does a courtier like Chaucer tell tales, or how should he?

Although Chaucer never says directly, the whirling house of Rumor, filled so with tidings, represents exactly the kind of situation the poet as well as the courtier and the homilist should avoid. The political and social dangers inherent in poetry writing and public position had been well documented in the Middle Ages through the examples of the exile of Ovid and the imprisonment of Boethius. When the Manciple advises us to "thenk on

3

the crowe"—one dare not, like the crow, report to a husband that his wife has been "dighted" (335), if one desires freedom from bodily harm—the gossiping of the crow also illustrates a peculiar problem for the court poet.

Ovid's story of Coronis's adultery and Apollo's homicide reveals a divine baseness normally excluded from fabulous narrative, at least according to Macrobius, or, if included, then covered up with integument, according to his commentator William of Conches. The medieval model for the poetic concealment of immoral or scandalous secrets had been propounded by this fifth-century North African scholar whose concept of literary aesthetic was generally known to and used by poets throughout the Middle Ages. His theory of fiction appeared in his commentary on Cicero's *Somnium Scipionis*, or the *Dream of Scipio*, a "commentary" itself on the tenth book of Plato's *Republic* (on the superiority of philosophy to the fables of the poets). Among his literary definitions that were treated as canonical in the Middle Ages were a categorization of dreams (in 1.3) influential in the development of the dream vision and a theory of "fabulous narrative" (in 1.2) useful as a vehicle for mythographic imagery.[4] Macrobius describes *narratio fabulosa* as a means of veiling nature's secrets from the eyes of base men, presumably secrets of the gods or of the soul. For fabulous narrative to be appropriate, it must present "a decent and dignified conception of holy truths [*sacrarum rerum*], with respectable events and characters, ... beneath a modest veil of allegory [*sub pio figmentorum velamine*]" (1.2.11). When a philosopher is not prudent and openly reveals these *arcana*, or "secrets of Nature," as did Numenius when he interpreted the Eleusinian mysteries, not only does he debase and offend the gods (1.2.19) but he also allows base men to see Nature "apertam nudam [openly naked]" (1.2.17). Specifically excluded from fiction as immoral, and hence as inappropriate, is a second type of fabulous narrative, "which philosophers [*philosophi*] prefer to disregard altogether"—bawdy stories of the gods involving adultery, castration, and overthrowing of father by son. This type of fabulous narrative is inappropriate because "the presentation of the plot [*contextio narrationis*] involves matters that are base and unworthy of divinities [*per turpia et indigna numinibus*] and are monstrosities of some sort [*monstro similia*]" (1.2.11).

The concealment of divine immorality was humanized by the twelfth-century William of Conches, who himself glossed Macrobius's commentary and these very sections on fabulous narrative (1.1–16 in *Macrobius*, pp. 68–78). For this Neoplatonist philosopher and commentator, the *satura* becomes a means of safely cloaking dangerous political truths or unfortunate traits of eminent or worthy persons (rather than the gods). The conventional twelfth-century literary term to describe this "cloak," *integumentum*, literally means "cover" and is found in definitions of *fabula* going back to Macrobius's commentary, where Nature's nakedness is cloaked by the *velamen figmentorum,* "veil of images." According to William, Juvenal used *satura* to reveal the gluttony of the emperor while disguising his purpose because such an activity was dangerous.[5] Thus, as a literary mode, *satura* means satire, literally a mixture, a stew, as in the *prosimetrum* of Martianus Capella, and relates to *narratio fabulosa* in that both provide discreet ways of covering up unworthy, sinful, often sexual activities of worthy individuals, particularly emperors and gods from the pagan period.

By means of this moral strategy of concealment, whether in fabulous narrative or satire, the medieval poet could protect such immoral secrets from "base men" (but not women?), presumably the vulgar and literalistic auditors or readers who may have commanded sufficient power and authority to object. Such a strategy might also have protected the medieval poet from the hardship of exile, as experienced by Ovid in the classical period, and the related political and social dangers of truth telling in a medieval court, as the fable of Apollo's truth-telling crow testifies at the end of the *Canterbury Tales,* in the *Manciple's Tale.*

In the *Manciple's Tale,* however, the Manciple's story of the god exemplifies the consequence of jangling, tale-telling, offering hard truths to others. It illustrates his dame's early counsel to him, which functions as a *moralitas* for the tale structured by a litany of ten apostrophes to "My sone" (318–62). Again and again she warns him: first, of the literal fable of the crow, " 'My sone, thenk on the crowe, a Goddes name' " (318); second, of its moral sense, " 'My sone, keep wel thy tongue, and keepe thy freend' " (319); third, of its allegorical sense, " 'A wikked tonge is worse than a feend' " (320); fourth, of its anagogical sense, " 'My sone, from a feend men may hem blesse' " (321).

Here is a social, moral, and religious injunction against tale-telling of which Chaucer, as a courtier and public official with intimate connections to the royal household, must have been acutely aware. If Chaucer's tongue did not wag loosely, nevertheless it did wag, as in "Envoy a Scogan" and the *Book of the Duchess,* among others, both poems about a friend or relative. Chaucer's fabulous practice throughout his poetry is justified through the *moralitas* provided by the Manciple's Mother, a justification reaffirmed by the Manciple who recollects her advice and by the pilgrim and poet Chaucer who writes all this down.

Elsewhere Chaucer has remarked on the contrast between foolish garrulity and decorous and measured art that conceals, using a bird image to suggest the means by which information is conveyed. The Man of Law, another alter ego for the public official Chaucer, in his *Prologue* compares himself as a tale-teller with Chaucer by means of a humbling classical fable that, if we understand it literally, portrays him as garrulous in contrast to the eloquent, inspired true poet; that is, the Man of Law associates himself as tale-teller with those false but talkative daughters of Pierides who attempted to compete with the Muses and were therefore transformed into magpies. If we read the comparison allegorically to understand what the clever poet Chaucer is saying (after all, he deliberately created the garrulity and literalism of the Man of Law, too), we learn, at least according to Bersuire, commenting on *Metamorphoses* 5.297ff., that the Pierides are those with frivolous opinions who compete with the wise. Those frivolous ones are thereafter transformed into magpies, or borne into the air, because of their presumption and strengthened with the wings of birds, that is, adorned with types of duplicity. The reader may recall the garrulous Eagle bearing the poet Geffrey through the air in the *Hous of Fame,* an echo of this bird image that invites questioning of the difference between frivolous and serious tale-telling. That the Sergeant of Law may deceive others (in the *General Prologue,* for example, "And yet he semed bisier than he was" [322]) couples him with Chaucer, the court poet who uses the lying fictions of the classical poets to conceal the immodest and indiscreet. Literature truly is gossip, or tidings. But it is controlled, balanced, decorous, and, for Chaucer, written down. Chaucer demonstrates its nature by having the Manciple recite a classical tale as paradigm for the purpose of *narratio fabulosa*— a perfect inversion of his usage of mythographic image to gloss his characters throughout his work.

The *Manciple's Tale* emphasizes the need both for decorous, concealing speech and for silencing at the appropriate moment: it repeats the Ovidian fable of Apollo and the tale-telling crow (*Metamorphoses* 2.533ff.) whose tidings about Coronis's adultery resulted in the bird's change of color from white to black and, at least in Chaucer, the loss of his voice. This tale has been undeservedly ignored by critics in the past, studied only for its relationship with its sources,[6] or debated as comic or serious in tone,[7] and not usually granted the structural and thematic importance of the *Parson's Tale.*[8] More recently, however, it has received attention it should have, given its penultimate position in sequence of the *Tales.*[9] This fable has been analyzed for its emphasis on speech or its silencing, and on more structured forms of discourse such as penitential sermons, in the ecclesiastical realm, and court poetry, in the social realm.[10] The tale should be read with an eye to how it modifies the final shape of the *Canterbury Tales* and also of Chaucer's aesthetic, particularly his use of classical fable and *integumentum.* Losing one's voice is a terror a courtly poet—and a woman like Philomela or Alisoun of Bath—would not recommend to anyone.

Through changes in his sources, omissions and additions, and reshaping in the *Tale* itself, Chaucer provides an *ars poetica* voiced by a character similar to the Man of Law, described as Chaucer's alter ego. The Manciple, buyer of provisions at an Inn of Court (where Chaucer was believed to have studied),[11] in his practicality and vocation seems to parallel Chaucer in his role as Controller of Customs and is also a member of the "Rogues' Group" (among whose members Chaucer also numbers himself) at the end of the *General Prologue*. In these changes we can detect clues about the harmonizing if deceptive and lying nature of poetry, despite the omnipresent warnings about tale-telling in the *moralitas* for the tale (which Chaucer will adapt for his own purposes in constructing the end of the *Canterbury Tales*). First, Chaucer will redesign the tale itself to make coherent the underlying mythographic pattern of meaning in its focus on poetry and the problem of tale-telling. Second, through the Host's interchanges with the Manciple and then with the Parson, he will provide a "frame" for the most conventional (in medieval terms) literary solution to the problem of tale-telling voiced at the end of the tale. Third, by reworking the personae of his sources, he will radically transform the nature (and gender) of the Ovid commentator who provides conventional *moralitas* for this fable about *tidynges*. Fourth, he will designate the Manciple as an alter ego for Chaucer the poet, whose fable making is guided by the voice of his mother in the incongruous role of mythographer.

Chaucer's changes in Ovid's tale narrow the focus to the relationship between Apollo and the crow: he does not name Apollo's "wife" (lover Coronis in Ovid) and he omits her death at the hands of the angry, jealous god and his delivery of her unborn son Aesculapius on her funeral pyre. Chaucer also transforms Apollo into a neophyte romance hero and the crow into his faithful, pathetically unrewarded, squirelike servant, and apparently, but only apparently, erases Coronis and Aesculapius altogether. Their seeming disappearance from the poem masks their more important resurrection, as the abstract idea of mother and son, which will color Chaucer's introduction of other mothers and sons in the *Manciple's Prologue and Tale*, as we shall see, particularly and most importantly, motherless Bacchus, god of wine, known as "the twice-born son," whose presence informs most crucially Chaucer's definition of poetic.

Medieval mythographers generally glossed Phoebus Apollo, the god of truth and prophecy, also as the god of poetry, a tenth Muse, an interpretation echoed by Chaucer in the figure of the God of Love in the *Legend of Good Women* and the *Hous of Fame*, as we shall see.[12] Chaucer accordingly portrays him as a minstrel, for "Pleyen he koude on every mynstralcie, / And syngen that it was a melodie / To heeren of his cleere voys the soun" (113–15). He casts Apollo more positively than is usual in adaptations of this tale from "olde bookes" (106)—the god appears as a "lusty bachiler" (107), or knight bachelor—perhaps to suggest in its opening lines the heroic role of the poet within society (he is also "the beste archer" in the world [108]). Chaucer perhaps had used one of his sources in which the tale is summarized, the *Ovide moralisé*, to gloss this as "une aventure galante réelle" (2.2130–2548, p. 168). Specifically, Phoebus inculcates the aristocratic chivalric ideal, for he is "flour of bachilrie, / As wel in fredom as in chivalrie" (125–26). Of the many exploits of the classical god Chaucer highlights only one reference in explanation of his aristocratic heroism — his battle with the "Phitoun, the serpent," and then only his facile victory over this beast depicted sleeping in the sun (109–10). The ease of the battle perhaps characterizes what Fulgentius and Arnulf of Orleans view as the struggle between true and false belief.[13]

Chaucer's changes in his sources, further, enhance the typing of the crow as the poet, faithful but unrewarded servant of Apollo in the *Ovide moralisé*. A raven in Ovid, Chaucer's crow not only changes color from white to black as a consequence of his tattling, but he also loses his voice. Perhaps Chaucer takes his allegorization from Ovid's moral: "But his tongue was his undoing [*lingua fuit damno*]. Through his tongue's fault the talking bird, which once was white, was now the opposite of white" (*Metamorphoses* 2.540–41). Certainly the crow represents *vox* in the gloss on the tale in an expanded version of John of Garland's *Integumenta Ovidii*: "ad Phebum pertinet vocum interpretacio."[14] For these reasons Chaucer describes him as able to "countrefete the speche of every man/ ... whan he sholde telle a tale" (134–35) like any poet — like the poet Chaucer in the *General Prologue*, for that matter. In relation to the second change, from the raven, *corvus*, traditionally associated with Apollo because of its prophetic ability, to the crow, *cornix*, protected by Apollo, Chaucer may have had in mind the Fulgentian exposition on the latter bird's unnatural practice of laying eggs in the middle of summer as an example of the unnatural (artificial, lying) methods of the poet.[15] The equivocation of its name, *corvus/cornix*, may also bear on the Manciple's (Platonic) discussion of the meaning of words (207ff.).

Significantly, the only mythological poet (and the only other classical reference) mentioned by the Manciple is Amphion (116), represented as an ideal poet in the *Merchant's Tale*, Dante's *Commedia*, and Gower's *Confessio Amantis*. Amphion's musical skill in the *Merchant's Tale* illustrates by antithesis old January's sexual impotence and fantasy in marrying and creating the enclosed garden for his bride; that is, Amphion, King of Thebes, with the aid of the Muses, charmed the mountain rocks with his lyre so that they leapt into place of their own accord and built protective walls for Thebes. Chaucer refers to this miracle in comparing the musical ability of Amphion, the "king of Thebes" who "with his syngyng walled that citee" (116–17), with the superior talents of Apollo (118). Amphion's ability to construct protective city walls leads to his interpretation as a type of *amor civium*, according to Guido da Pisa in his comments on Dante's *Inferno*, canto 32,[16] the opposite of those in Antenora who destroy cities and countries and an ironic foil for January as builder of garden walls.

This gloss on Amphion also pertains to the social and political role of the poet that Chaucer seeks to construct in the *Manciple's Tale*. As a type of restorer of harmony, Amphion becomes a model of fidelity to truth necessary for Dante (or Chaucer) to emulate. In this process, specifically in describing the bottom of the universe, Dante invokes the help of the Muses, "who aided Amphion to wall in Thebes, *so that the telling may not be diverse from the fact* [*sì che dal fatto il dir non sia diverso*]" (1:395). The harmony instilled by Amphion in Martianus's *De nuptiis,* 2.352 (par. 908) and its commentaries, results from his bringing to life bodies stiff with cold, animating mountains, and granting sensibility to rocks, amazing skills that link him by association with other masters of the underworld, the poets Orpheus and Arion. For Chaucer, that harmony may be more social and political in nature.

This rather positive allegorization of the tale of Apollo and the crow drawn from medieval mythographers makes coherent many of Chaucer's changes in his sources, to demonstrate our poet's interest in the nature of poetry and the role of the poet within society. But within the tale, the Manciple's warning in fact derives from the advice of his mother. Her long (forty-four-line) address (318–62) to her son in Chaucer's major sources—Jean de Meun, the poet of the *Ovide moralisé,* John Gower—represents the *moralitas* for the tale of Apollo and the crow. Although many of these sources include a similar warning against tale-telling, others also include what might be termed an "apology for poetry" that encourages safe poetry making by prudent and philosophic men. With what must have been subversive delight, Chaucer transforms the speaker of these counsels from the rational, even avuncular, voice in his sources to the Manciple's Mother.

The most likely direct inspiration for Chaucer's imaginative use of the homily itself was Jean de Meun's thirteenth-century continuation of the *Roman de la Rose,* in lines 6901–7230. This passage became crucial to the "Querelle de la Rose" that later pitted Christine de Pizan against university officials in a debate over reading texts. Although Chaucer retains the concept of mythographic *moralitas* found in the *Ovide moralisé* and the role of the priest as instructor in the Genius of the *Confessio,* he nevertheless invokes the lecture of Raison as context for the admonitions of the Manciple's Mother. Plato, says Jean de Meun's Raison, indicated that " 'speech was given to make us understand / And willingly to teach as well as learn,' " suggesting that the university should be the place where such learning and teaching occurs—" 'Si dist l'en bien en noz escoles / Maintes choses par paraboles / Qui mout sont beles a entendre / Si ne deit l'en mie tout prendre / A la letre quanque l'en ot [In our schools indeed they say many things in parables that are very beautiful to hear; however, one should not take whatever one hears according to the letter]' " (*Roman de la Rose* 7153–57, 3:32–33; trans. p. 136).

This argument of figurative reading (Augustine's well-known levels of allegory from *De doctrina Christiana*) would be used by Christine's opponent, the Provost of Lille, Jean de Montreuil, to justify the pornographic ending of the *Roman de la Rose* when Amant violates the Rose. In this passage, Raison bolsters her lecture on the need to bridle the tongue with a similarly figurative justification of her use of the lewd word "cullions."

> En ma parole autre sen ot,
> Au meins quant de coilles palaie,
> Don si briement paler voulaie,
> Que celui que tu i veauz metre;
> E qui bien entendrait la letre,
> Le sen verrait en l'escriture
> Qui esclarcist la fable ocure;
> La verité dedenz reposte
> Serait clere s'ele iert esposte;
> Bien l'entendras se bien repetes
> Les integumenz aus poetes.

[In my speech there is another sense, at least when I was speaking of testicles, which I wanted to speak of briefly here, than that which you want to give to the word. He who understood the letter would see in the writing the sense which clarifies the obscure fable. The truth hidden within would be clear if it were explained. You will understand it well if you review the integuments of the poets.] (*Roman de la Rose* 7158–68, 3:32–33; trans. p. 136)

Such truthful meaning hidden within the "obscure fable" requires exegesis to be extricated and, as philosophical explanation, justifies the letter— a concept clear to Macrobius and William of Conches. In her justification, Raison refers explicitly to the "integuments of the poets" and to Plato's *Timaeus*—and thus implicitly to Macrobius's commentary on the *Somnium Scipionis* and (as we shall see) William of Conches's supposed glosses on Juvenal. Such fables, she continues, are used especially by philosophers whom we might identify as commentators, mythographers, or early literary critics:

> La verras une grant partie
> Des secrez de philosophie,
> Ou mout te voudras deliter,
> E si pourras mout profiter;
> En delitant profiteras,
> En profitant deliteras,
> Car en leur jeus e en leur fables
> Gisent deliz mout profitables,
> Souz cui leur pensees couvrirent
> Quant le veir des fables vestirent;

Si te couvendrait a ce tendre,
Se bien vequz la parole entendre.

[There you will see a large part of the secrets of philosophy. There you will want to take your great delight, and you will thus be able to profit a great deal. You will profit in delight and delight in profit, for in the playful fables of the poets lie very profitable delights beneath which they cover their thoughts when they clothe the truth in fables. If you want to understand my saying well, you would have to stretch your mind in this direction] (*Roman de la Rose* 7169–82, 3:33; trans. p. 136).

Amant's problem is that he has understood the word "testicles" literally to denote the male sex organ rather than any figurative meaning and therefore responds literally, or naturally, to the lady with desire for her in herself, not as the Rose: " 'Mais puis t'ai teus deus moz renduz, / E tu les as bien entenduz / Qui pris deivent estre a la letre / Tout proprement, senz glose metre [But afterward I pronounced these two words—and you understood them well—which should be taken quite strictly according to the letter, without gloss]' " (7181–84, trans. p. 136). He responds as a man with testicles rather than as Amant, the Lover—but because in fact he is a *figura* in a *narratio fabulosa*, he therefore responds inappropriately.

The spiritual and intellectual profit and delight that Raison detects in the "speculations of philosophy" strikingly anticipate the Host's injunction to the Manciple to turn earnest into game in the prologue to the *Manciple's Tale*. "O Bacus, yblessed be thy name, / That so kanst turnen ernest into game!" (99–100), cries the Host, when he sees the Manciple melt the rancor of the drunken Cook by passing him his "gourde." But the Manciple's ability to calm wrath transcends mere apt use of the grape—or of the figure Bacchus, in Chaucer's hands. A skill inspired by the Manciple's Mother's homely warning to hold one's tongue—and also the point of the tale of the wrathful Apollo and the tattling Crow—it extends as well to the articulation of a poetic credo in the Manciple's own tale. How, then, does the poet also respect the Parson's counsel, to avoid fabulizing untrue chaff (*draf*) while preserving moral truths? The Parson views earnest without game—earnest that depends upon praise of God—as key to spiritual harmony; the Host in contrast views the transformation—transubstantiation—of earnest into game as key to social harmony.

Only the Manciple's Mother worries about tale-telling, whether true or false, but tale-telling especially for a wicked purpose: "a wikked tonge is worse than a feend" (320); she cites as her authorities against jangling, "as clerkes teche," the Old Testament—the Song of Solomon, David's Psalms—and the Roman Seneca (344–45), who frequently used classical fables (especially concerning Hercules) in his plays. Her son demonstrates his skill at

11

following her advice when he pacifies the Cook with his wine and the Host with his moral fable to suggest a way of bridging both the social and the spiritual problem. Indeed, in the Middle Ages schoolmasters would have expounded in particular the Old Testament in the light of the New Testament and classical fable as trope and allegory. Neither kind of text would have been interpreted literally, at least according to Jean's Raison. Such exegesis and mythography constituted the tools of the commentator that allowed him to articulate a theory of poetic. It is no accident that this learned woman's words end this tale—and introduce the *Parson's Prologue.*

Given the derivation of this *moralitas* from sources either associated with the patriarchal mythographic tradition or with moralistic literature (the "My son" rhetorical formula can also be found in wisdom literature),[17] Chaucer alters the male voice of the moralizing mythographer often asserted at the end of the tale (in the best tradition of mythographic commentary)—the personification of the faculty of Reason, the moralizer of the *Ovide moralisé,* or the allegorical priest Genius—to that of the Manciple's Mother. Female like Raison, the *dame* seems to represent a more practical authority than the intellectual and clerical voice of the philosopher-exegete.

Perhaps she represents the Wife of Bath's *experience,* unlettered and proverbial knowledge transmitted from (in this case) mother to son orally and naturally, within the context of domestic social life. In this respect it may be important to recall the antecedent of the *Wife of Bath's Prologue and Tale* in that of the Man of Law, who also discourses, as we have seen, on artistry versus garrulity, but on form rather than substance. Or perhaps she characterizes as maternal the protection of mythography for the poet, as we can see from Chaucer's primary source for the voice of the Manciple's Mother: the moralizing voice of the commentator is *like* that of a mother worried about her son. Or perhaps Chaucer is somehow caught up in combining both of these: the Manciple should hear the concern of his mother, expressive of her experience and prudence, and adapt the strategies of protective concealment in the philosopher's fables to the contemporary poet's need to incarnate truth in the carnal text.

In addition to the fact that Gower was one of the first poets to use the word and concept of genius as inventive ability,[18] Chaucer's use of the Genius as a prototype for the Manciple's Mother makes clear the problem of truth telling for the poet—and the necessity for artistry to be informed by *moralitas,* given the role of the figure Genius as didactic moralizer as well as tale-teller. This priest of human nature and confessor to the lover Amans in the contemporary *Confessio Amantis* frames the entire abbreviated tale of the crow as an exemplum (the third book uses classical tales to illustrate the sin of wrath) with the formulaic "Mi Sone" address. Genius tells Amans to hold his tongue "stille clos" (769), to hold counsel (778) and keep other men's affairs secret (777), and he concludes with the advice that he should not jangle, or tell tales (831–35).[19] The advice echoes that of the Manciple's Mother.

Chaucer's change of gender of Genius to the *dame* suggests that we should not essentialize gender, as we should not interpret as literal the appearance of divine baseness in a classical fable. Note that the Manciple deliberately interchanges genders in the exempla used to gloss the restricting of a wife's liberty as unnecessary or futile activity (148–54). In these examples, the Manciple underscores his lack of misogyny, for his main purpose is indeed to communicate the moral character of false (untrue, adulterous) husbands and to illustrate as vain the labor of guarding any wife, whether a shrew or a good wife: " 'Alle this ensamples speke I by thise men / That been untrewe, and nothyng by wommen' " (187–88). Drawn from the counsel of the "olde clerkes" Theophrastus and Jerome, no doubt in response to Alisoun's marriage question, his first two examples involve male animals and the third involves a female. First is the caged bird that desires liberty (loosely based on *Le Roman de la Rose* of Jean de Meun [13941–58]); second is the well-fed cat that allows his appetite to overcome his discretion when he sees a mouse (Jean de Meun [14039–52]); and third is the she-wolf who picks any available wolf when she lusts for a mate (Chaucer here adds a new source, Gaston Phebus's *Le Livre de Chasse*, ca. 1387).[20]

A realist (a philosopher) who refuses to essentialize, or a nominalist (a grammarian) who understands the importance of using classical fable politically in ways the philosopher has often countenanced (a poet), this Manciple (who, we know from the *General Prologue*, fancies himself as smarter than the law students for whom he works) seems to epitomize the philosopher-poet. He understands the difference between the name and the thing and realizes that the underlying meaning determines the truth, not the fictional "name," the lying surface — an idea in accord with the theory of integument, *satura,* and fabulous narrative, especially as articulated in Raison's lecture on integument in the *Roman.* For example, in lines 212–22 the Manciple admits that no moral difference exists between an aristocratic woman who is "dishonest" with her body and a poor wench, except that the woman is called "his lady, as in love," and the poor woman "his wenche or his lemman." Using a concept of words like that explained in the Neoplatonic passage from the *Roman* cited earlier, one that involves both surface and real levels of reality, the Manciple explicitly refers to Plato (207), who indicated that the word must accord with deed, "cosyn be to the werking" (210). At the same time, he understands there are differences among women, aristocratic or common, and seeks to particularize experience and to heed what he has learned outside the schools — has learned, in fact, from female authority, from his mother. Despite this array of examples of seemingly arbitrary gender change, Chaucer has not changed Genius's gender without good reason.

Maternal figures actually predominate in this tale (or its sources), both implicitly and explicitly, despite Chaucer's depersonalization of the Ovidian Coronis to Apollo's unnamed *wyf* and his omission of her pathetic and dying appeal to Apollo about their unborn son, which in Ovid leads to the god's impromptu delivery of Aesculapius on her funeral pyre and his sending the son to be reared by the centaur Chiron.[21] Chaucer may retain Ovid's interest in the aborted, abortive, mother-son relationship and the father's maternal concern for his son through the maternalization of the Moralizer. Further, the son of Mary (*sone*) is introduced by Chaucer through a well-known pun on the setting sun (*sonne*) at the beginning of the *Parson's Prologue*, "By that the Maunciple hadde his tale al ended" (1), in one of the significant links between fragments: "The *sonne* fro the south lyne was descended / so lowe that he has nat, to my sighte, / Degreës nyne and twenty as in highte" (2-4; my emphasis).

The emphasis on the *sonne* (mentioned twelve times by the Manciple's Mother) reminds us that the archetypal relationship between mother and son — especially a son whose life ends prematurely — is that of Mary and Jesus, a "twice-born" son reborn when he ascends to heaven after his own death. Most significantly, given our earlier discussion of *satura* and integument, another motherless god — Bacchus — normally designated as "the twice-born [*bis natus*] son"[22] and glossed in William on Macrobius 1.2.11, on fabulous narrative, is invoked by the Host immediately before the *Manciple's Tale* begins. Bacchus's mother died when she longed to know Jupiter in his real form; Jupiter, assuming the role of mother, then nurtured him in his thigh. Thus, the frame for the tale itself emphasizes sons. In each case Apollo, God the Father, or Jupiter has a son he must mother, ultimately, because of the death or helplessness of the child's mother.

Chaucer may be suggesting that the relationship between tradition and the individual talent for the fourteenth-century poet resembles that between mother and son, beginning with pregnancy and followed by wise rearing. The wifeless male poet must mother his own poem, provide for its delivery and birth, and then ensure its survival (and his own), specifically through the protective techniques of *satura* and *integumentum*. Such an interpretation is not unheard of in the fourteenth century: the poet of the *Ovide moralisé* interprets the tale as an allegory of the soul's relationship with God, with Apollo as God, Coronis as the soul, the seducer as the Devil, and Aesculapius as the soul revived by God to mortal life, *en vie pardurable* (p. 168).

Yet, this essentialized reading of the female "text" does not entirely square with Chaucer's concern in empowering and quickening the female voice in his works, in the figures of Alcyone, Alceste, Dido, Venus, Natura, Emelye and Diana, Minerva, Alisoun, Dorigen, May, Virginia. Through the Manciple's Mother he may be expressing an imperative for such a voice to exist at all, in whatever form possible. She is one of the few mothers to exist in mythographized tales within the Canterbury sequence.

One solution to the philosophical problem outlined in the Mother's warning is the theory of medieval *satura* as articulated by William of Conches as a rustic or pagan means of safely disguising dangerous truths about emperors and other worthy individuals. At the end of the *Manciple's Prologue*, when the Host invokes Bacchus as a metonymy for the power of the grape (99) and praises the Manciple's transformation of earnest into game, the reference by now conveys mythographic resonances deriving from Bernardus Silvestris on Martianus used to explain passages from the *Parlement*, the *Wife of Bath's Prologue*, and the *Merchant's Tale*. His particular moralization of the god, as the potency of the vine, was used by William in his commentary on Macrobius in this same passage on fabulous narrative[23] and again in his gloss on *satura* in Juvenal (a mixture or medley of poetry and prose that for William suggests its original derivation from *satur*, full of food, and therefore meaning a food composed of various ingredients).

One of four major significations for the god, as the earth's natural potency, this allegorization stresses his role as "twice-born son" of Semele instead of his other mythological relationships and roles, with the giants, as Briseus, or with Jupiter's other son Apollo.[24] William actually uses the figure of Bacchus as well as Ceres to define how pagan enjoyment of *temporalia* may shed light on the literary enjoyment derived from such gods' appearances in *integumentum*. The products of life obtained from crops were honored by the uncultivated pagans through feasts devoted to Ceres and Bacchus; that is, "Deinde sibi indulgendo, commendo, et bibendo magnam partem diei consumebant [through indulging themselves, through eating and drinking, they consumed a great part of the day]."[25] Later, in a gloss on *Satire* 1.49–50 and the phrase "et fruitur dis [iratis]" ("and [Marius] revels in the wrath of Heaven," according to the G. G. Ramsay Loeb translation of Juvenal), William explains such enjoyment (of the exiled extortioner Marius) as depending on Ceres and Bacchus; both gods were used by classical poets (Horace especially) as metonymies for bread and wine. To explain how the pagans apotheosized such temporal things into gods, William draws from Saint Augustine's *De doctrina Christiana*, as if to say that the pagans enjoyed bread and wine (or any temporal thing) for themselves instead of for the love of God; in effect, they enjoyed them too much, making gods— Ceres and Bacchus—out of them.[26] William thus provides a gloss on how the pagans enjoyed their "text," important if we recall Raison's lecture on *integumentum* and the profit and enjoyment deriving from an understanding of its secrets of philosophy. With this explanation of Bacchus, we need to reexamine the role of the Manciple, who calms the Cook (important figure) with his own wine, and whose job entails the stocking of a buttery with provisions.

Like the poet Amphion, but happily unlike the ineffective crow-poet who provokes Apollo's wrath, the Manciple restores harmony to the community by quelling the wrath of the Cook. Following the apt advice of his mother, he also follows the advice of previous moralists and philosophers, even if in a cautious and deceptive manner (remember his mother's warning to "Dissimule as thou were deef" [line 347]). The Manciple as tale-teller is not so incongruous if we recall that the cunning used by the buyer of *vitayles* to "set the cap" of the young clerks at court mirrors the "counterfeit" of the crow—and the cloaking integuments ("fables and swich wrecchednesse") of the poet. The Manciple, then, from one perspective a cunning liar, from another, a homely fabulist, a man guided by the prudent and experiential authority of his mother, sees beneath the cover of fable and of nature. It is the both/and that seems novel—the combination of mother and son, wisdom and eloquence, rational genius voiced and fabulated. It is a perspective that dominates Chaucer's work from the earliest poem to the latest.

PART 1

Mythography and Female Authority
in the Dream Visions

CHAPTER 1

"A wonder thing"
The *Descensus ad Inferos* of the Female Heroes Alcyone and Alceste

The female mythological figures Alcyone and Alceste, from the two rarely compared poems *Book of the Duchess* and the *Prologue* to the *Legend of Good Women*, share related sources.[1] Although critics have primarily focused on their French[2] rather than Latin or learned mythographic sources,[3] in both poems the narrator Chaucer learns about its central female character from a "bok" of fables. Alcyone appears in "A romaunce" that Chaucer reads one night when he cannot sleep—apparently Ovid's *Metamorphoses* 11.410–749, but possibly the *Ovide moralisé.*

> And *in this bok were written fables*
> That clerkes had in olde tyme,
> And other poetes, put in rime
> To rede and for to be in minde,
> While men loved the lawe of kinde.
> This bok ne spak but of such thinges,
> Of quenes lives, and of kinges,
> And many other thinges smale.
> Amonge al this I fond a tale
> That me thoughte *a wonder thing.* (52–61; my emphasis)

Into the *Prologue* to the *Legend of Good Women* is also woven how to read a classical fable. Called a "wonder thing," the classical fable in the *Book of the Duchess* involves this "small" life of the pagan queen Alcyone, as the classical fable in the *Prologue* involves the pagan queen Alceste.[4] The God of Love asks Chaucer in the *Prologue* if he remembers Alceste from a book he owns (perhaps the mythological collection of Hyginus, or the fables drawn from Hyginus that reappear in later collections such as the Vatican mythographies):

> "Hastow nat *in a book*, lyth in thy cheste,
> The grete goodnesse of the quene Alceste,
> That turned was into a dayesye;
> She that for hire housbonde chees to dye,

And eke to goon to helle, rather than he,
And Ercules rescowed hire, parde,
And broght hir out of helle agayn to blys?" (F 510–16; my emphasis)

In Chaucer's individual legends, Ovid's *Metamorphoses* also has clear influence—those legends of Thisbe (4.55–166), Hypsipyle and Medea (7), Ariadne (7.456–58, 8.6ff.), and Philomela (4.424ff.)—as does Ovid's *Heroides*—Dido (7), Hypsipyle and Medea (6.12), Ariadne (10), Phyllis (2), and Hypermnestra (14).

The contextual similarity of these two female heroes, Alcyone and Alceste, invites a comparison of their fables and how those fables are read within each poem. Both women descend into the underworld—a favorite theme and narrative digression in the classical epic, but one usually performed by a male hero such as Ulysses or Aeneas, or elsewhere in classical mythology by Hercules, who rescues Alceste from hell, or Orpheus, who attempts to rescue Eurydice. Chaucer uses the idea of death—entry into the classical underworld, the place of the shades below, the *infernii*, or the *inferii*, the dead, or inferior things—as a dominating pattern to control the other mythological references in each of the two poems. Because the Black Knight's queen has died in the *Book of the Duchess*—lost in the integumental "chess game" with Fortune—he suffers the torments of hell; her own "descent" is repeated psychologically through his emotional experience, one artificially or artistically rendered by the classical fable of Alcyone and Seys. In Chaucer's version of that fable, the grieving Alcyone dies of mourning for her husband Seys after three days, a mirror image of the Black Knight, despite the vision of the resurrected body of her husband retrieved by Morpheus and Eclympasteur, almost demonic figures, and despite her invocation of Juno, goddess of weddings and childbirth. Similarly, in the *Legend of Good Women*, the noble Alceste enjoys the privileged position of accompanying the God of Love in a dream because she chose to join the shades in exchange for the life of her husband Admetus; unlike Alcyone, she was rescued from the underworld by Hercules, medieval exemplar of *sapientia et fortitudo.*

The difference between the two female heroes is that Alcyone does not have to die and is in fact instructed by her husband to "Awake," but she rebels against him, whereas Alceste does not have to die but volunteers to save her husband's life. The women about whom Chaucer reads in his "books" provide two different recourses to the problem of grief and suffering, the power of earthly attachments. Thus the meaning of the descent into the underworld in each case differs: Alcyone descends first into what the mythographers describe as a destructive emotionality, spiritual death, a "vicious descent," before her literal "descent" into the underworld to join her dead husband. In contrast, again according to a mythographic interpretation, Alceste descends virtuously—armed with the virtue of loyalty and with wisdom.

Alceste also differs from Alcyone in providing a mythographically glossed model for the women in the sketchily delineated legends that follow the *Prologue.* As we shall see, comparing the two figures will help to explain the nature of the unfinished tales in the legends and the relationship of the women they describe with both Alcyone and Alceste. It is perhaps no accident that these legends in large measure were inspired and influenced by Ovid's *Heroides.* Chaucer may have been aware of the medieval gloss on the title of the antique poet's work as a derivation from the Greek masculine word *heros,* often used to characterize the nature of the heroic spirit after death, which nevertheless denotes "noble woman."[5]

To these two women correspond the other mythological references in each poem concerning underworld descents by epic heroes. These descents, based on the sixth book of the *Aeneid* and on *Consolatio* 3m12 (specifically, Orpheus's descent into the underworld to retrieve Eurydice), unify both this poem and the *Prologue* to the *Legend of Good Women.* As we trace this pattern we shall discover the poems' indebtedness to other works of classical fable, often moralized, which provide insights into characterization and narrative pattern not previously recognized by critics.

In each case, the major mythographic pattern is based upon the descent of Aeneas into the underworld in book 6 of the *Aeneid,* and its concomitant glosses in the commentaries on the *Aeneid* and related glosses on Orpheus's descent in *Consolatio* 3 meter 12. Whereas Alcyone seems at first to descend in the manner of Eurydice, or what the commentators termed the vicious pursuit of the temporal, in actuality Alcyone, like Alceste in the *Prologue* to the *Legend,* descends (or perhaps reascends) in the manner of Orpheus, Theseus, and especially, Hercules, that is, either in pursuit of her spouse or virtuously, to arm herself with an understanding of the created world in order to protect herself against its temptations. Further, her more heroic signification is revealed to the reader (and the dreaming narrator) only in stages of literary unmasking.

Before examining each of these poems with their attendant mythological references, a brief definition of the descents into the underworld and their glosses will help provide a focus and a context for our discussion, coupled with an analysis of Chaucer's use in his poems and translations of the particular exemplary heroes associated with infernal descents in the Middle Ages—Hercules and Orpheus.

The Heroic Descent in the Commentaries and Chaucer

Whatever Chaucer's emphasis on heroic descents into the underworld, Aeneas's descent into the underworld in the sixth book of the *Aeneid,* rather than the descents of Hercules and Orpheus, initially captured the medieval imagination in schoolbook commentaries, primarily because the *Aeneid* was the first classical epic heavily glossed in the schools.[6] In this descent commentators found a metaphor for engagement with other types of vicious involvement, or involvement of soul from body — first, at birth; next, in pursuit of vice, involving the clouding of reason; third, in education, which involves understanding the ways of this (under)world in order to control its temptations; and finally, art that separates technical skill from understanding, demonic consultation. From this commentary on the sixth book of the *Aeneid* and from glosses on *Consolatio* 3 meter 12 (specifically, Orpheus's descent into the underworld to retrieve Eurydice) come the concepts of the four descents into the underworld used to unify both this poem and the *Prologue* to the *Legend of Good Women.*

According to Bernardus Silvestris in his important twelfth-century commentary on the first six books of the *Aeneid,* Paradise can be defined as the superior Aplanon, the sphere of fixed stars, and the underworld either as the inferior world below or the human body. The latter he regards as inferior (*inferius*) because it is composed of inferior things (*inferos*).[7] Four descents into an underworld are possible: natural, virtuous and vicious (or sinful), and artificial (or magical). In a misogynistic aside, Bernardus notes that although Aeneas descended into the underworld according to the second, or virtuous, descent, in the manner of Orpheus and Hercules, in contrast Eurydice descended sinfully (6.1, trans. pp. 32–33):

> *The natural descent is the birth of man:* for by it the soul naturally enters this fallen region and thus descends to the underworld and thus recedes from its divinity and gradually declines into vice and assents to pleasures of the flesh; this is common to everybody. *The second descent is through virtue, and it occurs when any wise person descends to mundane things through meditation,* not so that he may put his desire in them, but so that, having recognized their frailty, he may thoroughly turn from the rejected things to the invisible things and acknowledge more clearly in thought the Creator of creatures. In this manner, Orpheus and Hercules, who are considered wise men, descended. *The third is the descent of vice, which is common and by which one falls to temporal things,* places his whole desire in them, serves them with his whole mind, and does not turn away from them at all. We read that Eurydice descended in this way. Her descent, however, is irreversible. *The fourth descent is through artifice, when a sorcerer by necromantic operation seeks through execrable sacrifice a conference with demons and consults them about future life.*[8] (P. 30, trans. pp. 32–33; my emphasis)

Both Hercules and Orpheus were heavily glossed in the Boethius commentaries in the schools, beginning in the ninth century and continuing through the fifteenth century.[9] Certainly Boethius was read in schools, and the attendant glosses on his work might very well have been part of Chaucer's education. Although Chaucer is not believed to have completed his translation of Boethius at the time he wrote the *Book of the Duchess*, nevertheless he may have been aware of the tradition in the Middle Ages: many of his short poems can be grouped together because of their Boethian aspects, and much of the *Book of the Duchess* shares the values, themes, and images of the *Consolatio*.[10] Chaucer's glosses on the descents of Hercules and Orpheus will be used to greater ironic advantage in the *Troilus* in relation to the Trojan hero's love for Criseyde, who, in preparing them for the imminent separation, compares herself to Eurydice and Troilus to Orpheus (4.791).

In the Middle Ages, Hercules' Labors were catalogued primarily in commentaries on Boethius in 4m7, wherein he antithesizes the selfish exemplar Agamemnon (who sacrificed his own daughter for his ambition), but exemplifies the cunning Ulysses (who overcame the one-eyed and therefore morally blind monster Polyphemus). "Celebrable for his harde travailes," states Chaucer of Hercules in his translation of *Boece* (4m7, p. 456); also glorious, like Ulysses, for his triumph over "erthly lust," as glossed conventionally in the *moralitas* for this meter: "Goth now thanne, ye stronge men, ther as the heye wey of the greet ensaumple ledith yow. O nyce men! why nake ye your bakkes? (*As who seith, 'O ye slowe and delicat men! whi flee ye adversites, and ne fyghte nat ayeins hem by vertu, to wynnen the mede of the hevene?'*) For the erthe overcomen yeveth the sterres. (*This to seyn, that whan that erthly lust is overcomyn, a man is makid worthly to the hevene*)" (p. 457).

Hercules is described by Chaucer's Monk as an exemplar of *De casibus* (Boethian) tragedy, although it is not at first glance clear how his magnificent life full of difficult Labors constitutes a tragedy or fall in the medieval sense — that is, the fall from Fortune's grace, or more figuratively, the internal fall into irrationality or despair as a result of the turning of Fortune's wheel. He *does* die, but unconventionally does not apotheosize into a constellation (line 2135). Recited literally in 2095 through 2135, without mythographic glossing, the Labors of Hercules — the only Roman legend recited in the *Monk's Tale* — illustrate the pilgrim Monk's overall, eccentric thesis that Hercules' adventures (especially the ultimate problem, of Deianira's deadly cape) reflect the power of Fortune rather than the power of individual choice, or of *sapientia et fortitudo* (exemplified by Hercules, according to the mythographers).[11] "Lo, who may truste on Fortune any throwe?" the Monk asks (2136). "Ful wys is he that kan hymselven knowe!" he suggests as a weapon against Fortune (2139). Fortune is aided by Deianira, although the Monk unconventionally—that is, unlike most clerics—embellishes the episode of her cape to refocus the entire list of Labors and thereby avoid blaming her for wrongdoing (2127–29).

But Chaucer is aware of the mythographic tradition behind the hero's descent into the underworld. In the list of Labors, the Monk catalogs Hercules' descent into the underworld by means of this compressed but conventional one-line account: "He drow out Cerberus, the hound of helle" (2102)—without mention of Alceste, rescued on the same trip. Finally, however, he is described as famous for his strength and his bounty (2114), in what might be termed a variation on the *sapientia et fortitudo* topos, to emphasize merely *fortitudo*: "He was so stroong that no man myghte hym lette" (2116). Perhaps swayed by the literalism of the then-popular commentary of Nicholas Trevet on Boethius, the Monk mostly ignores this long-standing topos with which the figure is usually associated:[12] Hercules is "the sovereyn conquerour," because "in his tyme of strengthe he was the flour" (2095, 2097).

Like this human Hercules, Chaucer's more irrational Orpheus descends into the underworld, or "the houses of helle" (in *Boece* 3m12). Here our translator reveals the Thracian's "blaundysschinge songes" tempered with "resounynge strenges," the grief for his lost wife expressed in artful songs "lavyd out of the noble welles of his modir Callyope the goddesse" (p. 439). Like Alcyone and the Black Knight in the *Book of the Duchess* and Alceste in the *Prologue,* Orpheus has lost a spouse or beloved; unlike them, he attempts to retrieve her, but makes the mistake of looking back to see if she follows once "the juge of soules" has released Eurydice to him. The inhabitants of hell are also moved by his songs—Cerberus, the "porter of helle," the Furies, Ixion, Tantalus, Tityus, all are "overcomen," in the words of that Judge. Unfortunately, "Whanne Orpheus and his wif weren almost at the termes of the nyght (*that is to seyn, at the laste boundes of helle*), Orpheus lokede abakward on Erudyce his wif, and lost hire, and was deed" (p. 440). The moral is glossed conventionally (and significantly, in terms of the similar mistake of Alcyone and near mistake of the Black Knight), as a tropological example of lamentable ties to the underworld of temporal good—earthly things valued excessively:

This fable apertenith to yow alle, whosoevere desireth or seketh to lede his thought into the sovereyn day, that is to seyn, to cleernesse of sovereyn good. For whoso that evere be so overcomen that he ficche his eien into the put of helle, that is to seyn, whoso sette his thoughtes in erthly thinges, al that evere he hath drawen of the noble good celestial he lesith it, whanne he looketh the helles, that is to seyn, into lowe thinges of the erthe. (P. 440)

The descents of Orpheus and Eurydice, Hercules, and Aeneas all deploy a model Chaucer will use for his own psychologizing purposes in the *Book of the Duchess* and the *Legend of Good Women.*

The "Descents" of Seys, Alcyone, and the Black Knight

Chaucer's artistry consists in showing the resolution of the Black Knight's grief through his coming to understand by means of therapeutic dialogue the meaning of the story of Alcyone as mediated by the commentary tradition. In the scene at the moment of the narrator's "awakening" in his own dream vision, the classical narratives "are painted on the glass with sun streaming through them to comment on their typical medieval use as filters for truth and morality, and ... the love poem is represented on the wall to suggest its subjective opacity," as if the poet proposed to epitomize here "the two central and related literary traditions he had so handily bypassed in his prologue,"[13] that is, the vernacular and Latin traditions, the courtly and learned. More important, the light streaming through the stained-glass windows and onto the painted mural on the wall locks the narrator—Chaucer the poet—between the two traditions. What the windows tell him about how to write contemporary poetry, how to use classical fable, is expressed through his Wonderland-meeting with one of his own characters—the complex, integumental Black Knight, an image or icon summoned from Chaucer's poetic Cave of Dreams in much the same way the body of Seys is summoned for Alcyone from the Cave of Sleep. The way the Black Knight is identified allies him with the Trojan lovers and heroes from the *Iliad* (a work generally not directly accessible to medieval poets because of its Greek) and the *Aeneid* depicted on the wall. Understanding his relationship with Chaucer the narrator will help us understand Chaucer the poet's perplexity in dealing with classical fable—in particular, the Ovidian story of Alcyone that lulls him to sleep, which provides a feminized, if pagan, model of rebirth as a heroic recourse to loss and the problem of grief.

The key to Chaucer's changes in his Ovidian source is the medieval and Christian idea of the needs of the body mediated by the soul, as expressed by images of awakening from sleep, seeing and not seeing. In Chaucer, Alcyone dies after her husband's body appears in a dream—it *is* Seys's body borne by Morpheus, but it appears to her soul while her body slumbers as an image, or figure; she recuperates the lost husband, the lost body, through her dreams, whereas in Ovid, Alcyone kills herself after seeing her husband's body. Similarly, the dreamer Chaucer "awakens" refreshed from his sleep at the end of the poem—and from his spiritual daze and confusion experienced at the poem's beginning: he "sees" (or "hears," in the case of the bells ringing) clearly. Alcyone is read positively by Bersuire, as the "wife of Christ," or the soul who needs healing after the shock of death by means of penitence, devotion, contemplation.[14] In contrast, Ovid's pagan Alcyone cannot accept, that is, understand, this healing message. Chaucer's Alcyone heeds the message advanced by resurrected Seys, but chooses her own way of interpreting it.

Chaucer's story of Seys and Alcyone marries the text from Ovid 11.410ff. to the substory of Juno, Morpheus, and Eclympasteyr. Chaucer's classical fable of Seys and Alcyone (62–230) has been colored by Guillaume de Machaut's version of the story in *Le dit de la fonteinne amoureuse,* but the classical fable-within-a-fable, involving Juno, Morpheus, and Eclympasteyr (129–211), has been shaped by Bernardus's commentary on the *Aeneid* and Pierre Bersuire's fourteenth-century *Ovidius moralizatus.* Both the Ovidian fable of Ceyx and Alcione and also the mythographers' gloss on Somnus and his sons are conjoined in Robert Holkot's commentary on the Book of Wisdom, which was available to Chaucer in manuscript at Oxford.[15]

Chaucer feminizes the classical account by means of his changes, which underscore the infernal in the *Book of the Duchess*: instead of the omniscient narrator in Ovid, only Alcyone's point of view remains in the story. And Juno as the goddess of childbirth is associated with the concept of the underworld of this earth, the inferior place into which all souls are born, or "Awake," literally, in the fashion instructed by Seys. The emphasis falls not on death and the material world, as in Ovid, so much as on the awakening and need for rebirth: in Ovid, we hear about Ceyx's actual death; in Chaucer, we never see him die. In Ovid, Morpheus conveys an image of the dead man; in Chaucer, Morpheus brings the actual dead man to Alcyone. True, in relation to Seys, the figures Morpheus and Eclympasteur are associated with the underworld of death, the afterlife of *manes* (shades), but in relation to Alcyone, primarily with sleep. In Ovid, his message is, "mourn for me," and in Chaucer, "awake—don't mourn." Further, in Ovid, the characters metamorphose to kingfishers; however, there are no birds in Chaucer, an omission that consequently emphasizes the necessity for spiritual consolation, nor is there transformation or happy ending, a medievalization in line with Macrobian literary theory and generally consistent with Chaucer's practice in the legends themselves.

Within that specifically focused and feminized account of Alycone, Chaucer stresses the power of dreams, related to his Macrobian end point that integumental art masks truths. He transforms source Ovid, who expends much narrative description on the Cave of Sleep and Morpheus's three sons; he may have conflated Machaut's narrative of petition to Juno for help (provided by Iris's mission to the god of sleep) with the wonderful digression on dreams and fantasies that follows and the narrator's offer to Morpheus to exchange a feather bed for sleep. More likely, he borrowed from Holkot, whose story of Ceyx and Alcione is relayed in a discussion of dreams and their interpretations. Chaucer retains the description of the

Cave of Sleep and Morpheus's sons, the emphasis on dreams and fantasies, and the petition for sleep, but he imbues them with comedy, and he adds to them the more serious signification of sleep as delusion, numbness, irrationality, even moral viciousness, and the implications of awakening as rational acceptance, insight, self-control.

Chaucer's Alcyone appropriately summons Juno to aid the rebirth of the soul in the dead body of Seys because this goddess of childbirth, or *dea partus*, according to Bernardus in his commentary on the *Aeneid*, aids the natural descent, birth. At birth the soul descends into the body or *through* the air—Juno—

> because material things derive from air. She is called Jove's consort because air receives heat from fire and is subject to it. She is also called the goddess of birth because the young are conceived, formed, brought forth, and nourished by the heat and moisture of air. Thus she is called Juno, as if *novos iuvans,* "helping the young." She is called Lucina, as if *lucem natis prebens,* "giving light to the born." (*Aen.* 1, Pref., p. 4, trans. pp. 6–7)

Juno turns to Morpheus and Eclympasteur, demons of the Cave of Sleep, because the summoning of Seys will not involve a birth, a natural descent into the underworld, but an artificial one, involving consultation with demons. Their temporary, artificial renewal of his body may also suggest the knitting up of care's raveled sleeve by means of sleep, which we all enjoy; it is certainly not a permanent renewal. The Cave of Sleep is visualized as infernal, meaning both of the underworld and the body itself, in line with Bersuire's moralization that "All these are ruled and sent by King Sleep—that is sin. Romans 5:14: 'Death ruled from Adam to Moses'" (Bersuire, *Ovidius,* p. 162, trans. pp. 373–75 [11.633]). Chaucer writes, "This cave was also as derk / As helle-pit overal aboute" (170–71). It is accordingly ruled by the god of sleep Morpheus and his heir Eclympasteyr, "That slep and dide noon other werk" (169). These icons, as demons, infernal inhabitants, by means of their own nature emphasize Alcyone's ties to earthly good, to her husband—and to the body.

The emphasis on sleep—Somnus—throughout the *Book of the Duchess* is meant to be understood pejoratively and spiritually, with awakening seen as the correlative virtue. Sleep is like death (the underworld governed by Morpheus), or numbness, denial, from which it is natural and necessary to awaken. So Bersuire, in line with his moralization of hell as the underworld of earthly good, interprets Somnus as having three sons, meaning three types of care sent by the Devil into the hearts of those "worldly sleepers." These concerns reflect earthly attachments, whether to fame, honor, dignity (Morpheus), lust and other animal desires (Icelos), or gluttony for food, drink, love, and rest—the lowest appetites (Phantasos).[16]

A group of underworld images piled one atop another by the Black Knight mourning behind his oak tree type him as an Orpheus in his grief—someone overwhelmed by the ties of this world, this "hell." Many of the mythological references he cites parallel those found primarily in Boethius's *Consolatio* 3 meter 12, involving Orpheus's descent into the underworld. In the mythographic glosses on this meter the infernal inhabitants cited by the Black Knight all represent different vices, the "underworld" construed as a moral sewer. Ticius (Tityus) signifies lust; Tantalus, pride; Orpheus, rationality lost to concupiscence, because of his backward look at Eurydice, an act that sums up the general defeat of rationality at the hands of concupiscence. Generally, the Black Knight acknowledges he suffers similar hell-like torments because he lost the chess game played with false Fortune (618)—a moral theme dear to the *Consolatio* and its commentators. The Black Knight swears that he has lost his mind, an unnatural situation about which the "god of kynde" (Pan, 511) is unhappy; no one can heal or help him, including the similarly plagued Orpheus (569, cited in 3m12), who also lost his wife Eurydice, or the inventor Daedalus (570), who lost his son Icarus (and who also created the labyrinth as an underground prison for the monstrous Minotaur—cited as the "hous of Didalus" in Boethius book 3 prose 12). The sorrows of the Black Knight are so great that even Cesiphus in hell (587: either Sisyphus, condemned eternally to roll a mountain up a hill in hell, or else Tityus, condemned eternally to have his liver plucked and eaten by an eagle because of his lust for Juno; also cited in 3 meter 12) could not tell of more. The list of infernal inhabitants with whom the Black Knight compares himself in his sorrow concludes with Tantalus (709; also in 3 meter 12), who suffered the torment of having food and drink placed just outside his reach in hell because he had served his son Pelops to the gods to test their divinity.

The Black Knight inhabits the underworld of despair, into which this rational man has descended like Orpheus searching for Eurydice, but unlike his female alter ego Alcyone he is guided by a benevolent friend and therefore rescued, as if by Hercules. The grieving Black Knight's suggestion of suicide is opposed by the narrator by means of a list of classical lovers (726–35) who did not snuff out their misery along with their lives—and, of course, because they were not Christians, were not then "dampned" (725), as the Black Knight would be. Rather ironically, these models for lovers in 726–35, however, include figures who have appeared previously in the poem, in the stained-glass windows of Chaucer's bedroom, as deceived and deceiving lovers: Medea and Jason's love led to her murder of their children (726–27), no doubt a link expressive of the influence of classical source on medieval poetic. Also mentioned in the *Squire's Tale,* this couple reappears in the *Legend of Good Women*: in all these examples Medea figures forth the late medieval view of the saint for love.[17] Unfortunately, in a similarly destructive way, the love of Phyllis for deceitful Demophon, who had broken his "term-day" to come to her, led to her suicide by hanging (728–31). So also did angry, foolish Queen Dido's love for false Aeneas result in her suicide (731–34). Dido, whom Aeneas meets again in his descent to the underworld in *Aeneid* 6, may in this affair demonstrate some of the immoderation characteristic of her former marriage to Sicheus, a union that meets with Bernardus's opprobrium in his commentary because it signifies the false spiritual good of "the vices of gluttony and intoxication" ("vicium ingluviei et crapule," [Bern. Sil.] *Aen.* 6.450–76, p. 96, trans. p. 91). (Bernardus glosses the marriage of Sicheus and Dido as the union of gluttony and lechery, for "Venus grows cold without Ceres and Bacchus.") Another lady who died for love is Ecquo, who wasted away from love for Narcissus (735–37; also mentioned in a different context in the *Knight's Tale* and *Franklin's Tale*). Here the Black Knight with his own skewed emotional travails eclipses the sufferings of the mythological lovers.

These mirror images appropriately relay to the reader the Black Knight's emotional situation, one like that of Orpheus without his love, although expressed in female terms: they more precisely identify Alcyone, who does in fact die—of grief. They also forecast similar situations in the *Legend of Good Women*, the *Troilus*, and the *Squire's Tale*, as if Chaucer had written in miniature a table of contents for his future progress. But the mythological references in both the comparisons of the Black Knight and the narrator also suggest, usually by antithesis, the need for healing in love, wholeness, rather than deceit, death, destruction. Chaucer seems fond of linking this antithesis with the double levels of fable—with the "deceit" of artifice that in *fabula* can mask hidden truths. We are reminded again of the situation of the narrator awakening in his Neoplatonic Cave of Dreams to the shadows of the Idea of the Good flickering on the wall—reflecting the light that has passed *through* the stained-glass windows in the bedroom of the dreaming narrator.

Interestingly enough, it is only when the narrator ventures *outside* his bedroom and into the countryside that he meets the grieving Black Knight and overheard mythological references used to define the Knight's emotional state, his temperament, and his love for the White Queen. This horseless chevalier embodies the narrator's reading, fictionalizes in the present the idea of the Trojan and Greek warriors in the stained glass. The narrator here meets his own literary character in this dream Wonderland, a character whose literary ancestors derive from Troy (or the *Deduit* of the *Roman de la Rose*, whose garden figures grace the walls of Chaucer's dream bedroom), and whose psychology, character, and temperament match those of the bedroom's classical epic (and contemporary romance) heroes.

Unlike the politically naive Queen Alcyone, who perceived no error en-
suing from the nation's loss of Seys or of the queen herself, the epic figures
incarcerated in the stained glass (326–33), like the other mythological fig-
ures in the poem, warn, in this gendered context, of contemporary England,
and the Black Knight as John of Gaunt, of the dangerous political conse-
quences of grief and excessive love. The figures appear here because Lon-
don is the New Troy, inhabited by the descendants of Brutus, grandson of
Aeneas (as *Sir Gawain and the Green Knight* reminds us),[18] and John of
Gaunt has a powerful political role to play in managing the kingdom—the
Black Knight needs to return to ruling rather than grieving in isolation;
that is, the references to these figures—Hector, Priam, Achilles, Laome-
don, Medea, Jason, Paris, Helen, and Lavinia (328–31)—once understood in
the light of glosses by medieval commentators, can be used to "gloss" (or
develop our understanding of) Chaucer's own characters and their histori-
cized plight. These epic figures share a relationship with either the begin-
ning or the ending of Troy ("For hooly al the story of Troye / Was in the
glasynge ywroght thus" [326–27]), about which Chaucer will write in the
Troilus and to which he will allude in the first book of his *Hous of Fame.*

Paris (*Book of the Duchess* 331) and Achilles (*Book of the Duchess* 329)
also interlocked in the classical story in a way that suggests beginning and
ends: Paris killed Achilles to avenge the latter's defeat of his brother Hec-
tor. In a gloss once again centered on beginnings and endings, Bernardus
claims (in 6.56) that Paris's hand was guided by Apollo in that he hid be-
hind Apollo's statue in order to shoot Achilles and thus avenge his brother
Hector, that is, allegorically, his hand was guided by the Creator, tropologi-
cally, by sense (*sensus*) killing sadness (*tristitia*):

> If we take this allegorically, we interpret Phoebus to be the Creator
> himself, who always pitied the labors of Troy, because He makes the
> labors of the body pass away, and He nourishes the body with helpful
> things. He likewise killed Achilles with Paris's hand. Achilles, as if
> *acherelaos*, means *dura tristitia*, "harsh sadness": for *a* is *sine*,
> "without," *chere* is *leticia*, "joy," *laos* is *lapis*, "stone." Paris, in the
> proper interpretation, means sense. Indeed, Paris's arrows are the rays
> of the two eyes by which Achilles is killed, that is, sadness is
> extinguished. ([Bern. Sil.] *Aen.* 6.56, p. 45, trans. p. 46)

Thus the first several references incorporate variations on the ideal of
sapientia et fortitudo associated with Hercules in the destiny of nations
like Troy and therefore indicative of what princes like the Black Knight
need to *be* and *do* as men. The reference to "Troy" at the beginning is fol-
lowed by "Priam," king of Troy, and his son "Hector," killed by the Greek
hero Achilles at the time of Troy's fall. The glosses on Priam sustain the
images of beginning and ending, and of force: Bernardus declares:

Priam is so called as if *iperamus*, that is, *superior pressura*, "greater force." By him we understand the passion which, rising at the moment of birth, sustains the life of the body for a whole lifetime, and therefore one reads that he reigned in Troy. He is said to be an old man since (as we have said before) that age has the greatest miseries. (*Aen.* 6.494–97, pp. 99–100, trans. pp. 93–94)

The names of Achilles and Laomedon are associated respectively with the destruction and construction of Troy, as we have seen, whereas the names of Paris, Helen, and Lavinia are associated with the cause of the Trojan War that led to the fall of Troy (Paris's abduction of Helen) and the creation of a new nation after the war ended—Italy, founded by Aeneas through his marriage to Lavinia. In this catalog, however, Laomedon is not to be read negatively, as is generally the case, but rather positively—*in bono*; that is, as Priam, king of Troy at the time of its fall, suggests force, so Laomedon, founder or past king of Troy, suggests wisdom—as if Bernardus is pointing to the need for a good king to possess both *fortitudo* and *sapientia*: "Phoebus founded the city with the assistance of Neptune. Laomedon by his own wisdom founded it, and from the confluence of the seas he supplied many necessary things by trade" (*Aen.* 6.56, p. 45, trans. p. 45). Further, whereas Achilles kills Hector, Priam's son, Chaucer couples Achilles with King Laomedon—perhaps because the death of Hector marks the death of Troy's future, as its creation was marked by King Laomedon's building of Troy's walls with the help of Neptune and Hercules.

These references trace the rise and fall of Troy, a fall attributed allegorically by the commentators to Trojan self-indulgence and lechery that began, not with Paris's abduction of and adultery with Helen but with his choice of Venus in the Judgment of three goddesses, Juno, Venus, and Pallas Athena, the duplication of which, therefore, modern princes should avoid.[19] In Bernardus's commentary on the *Aeneid*, the Trojan skill with horses helps to explain the national flaw, lechery, or *luxuria*: "The Greeks made the horse, since the drunkenness and gluttony of lechery are in Troy, according to that saying: 'Venus grows cold without Ceres and Bacchus'" (6.515–16, p. 96, trans. p. 96). Because Paris is the king's son, perhaps, Bernardus declares, "Paris, in the proper interpretation, means sense [*sensus*]"[20] (6.56, p. 45, trans. p. 46). Bernardus explains Paris's initial flawed judgment in *Aeneid* 6.64, when he chose the wrong goddess, Venus, during the competition at the wedding of Peleus and Thetis and thereby caused the fall of Troy through the subsequent competition and anger of the other two goddesses, Juno and Pallas Athena; the three goddesses represent three very different ways of life—pleasure, the active life, and contemplation—which appeal to Epicureans, politicians, and philosophers.[21]

Finally, to the mythographer as well as to the Black Knight, Paris's union

31

with Helen (*Book of the Duchess* 331) spells tropological disaster because, as if *helenne*, she represents those earthly riches that rule earth, or the *dea inhabitans*, the "goddess residing," because *Hel* is *dea*, "goddess," and *enne* is *inhabitans*, "residing."

> She is said to have been the most beautiful woman because she was thought more worth seeking than other goods. Therefore, Helen was first given to Menelaus because earthly riches were first made to serve virtue, but she was seized by Paris, when she turns from the virtuous to the sensual man. For *Paris* in Greek is *sensus*, "sense," in Latin, as we have said. Therefore, after Helen forgot Menelaus, she chose Paris, because after earthly riches abandon the virtuous man, they give themselves up to the sensual man. Thus philosophers show that earthly wealth is bad because it frequently joins with evil. After Helen marries Paris, the Greeks wage war against Troy—after wealth joins with the sensual person, vices begin to attack the body. ([Bern. Sil.] *Aen.* 6.494–97, p. 99, trans. p. 93)

Because Italy is the goal of Aeneas after the fall of Troy, the last mythological reference in this passage, Lavinia (331)—also a character from the *Aeneid*—as the daughter of Italy's king (and hence associated with the third goddess, Pallas Athena, in three lives' commentaries) provides a kind of closure that matches the emphasis at the beginning of the passage, on the Judgment of Paris with which it all started. Lavinia, like Medea and Jason, is not mentioned in Bernardus's commentary, although, in commentaries on all twelve books, Lavinia represents the union of the virtuous man with wisdom, as in Fulgentius: she represents the *laborum uia*, the "road of toil," "for at this stage of life Everyman [*unusquiuis*] learns the value of toil in furthering his worldly possessions" (*Expos.*, p. 104, trans. fable 24). Italy, or Ausonia, on the other hand, in the same passage is etymologically construed as "increase of good [*boni crementa*], to which every desire of wise men hastens with eager pace."

Like the other references mirroring forth a warning to the male prince to act responsibly in love and in governance, the reference to Medea and Jason (330) nevertheless seems out of place in this stained-glass catalog, sandwiched as it is between the reference to Achilles and Laomedon (329) and the reference to Paris, Helen, and Lavinia (331). An explanatory gloss on this incongruous insertion can be found in the *Squire's Tale*, wherein Jason alone is similarly coupled with Paris. There the references communicate their mutual deception of two women, Medea and Hypsipyle, in Jason's case, and Oenone and Helen (presumably through the arguments he uses to persuade her to leave Menelaus), in Paris's; that is, Jason and Paris are described by the Squire as less skillful in feigning humility, reverence, and joy than the tercelet, so "ful of doublenesse," who deceives the falcon

("Jason? certes, ne noon oother man / Syn Lameth was, that alderfirst bigan / To loven two, as writen folk biforn" [549–51]).

This "gloss" on the *Book of the Duchess* from the *Squire's Tale* shows that deceit draws forth deceit. In the *Squire's Tale*, the cause of the fall of Troy is explained likewise by the deceit of the lover, on one hand, and on the other by the deceit of the traitor, although the tale attributes the fall to a cause different from the one in the *Book of the Duchess* catalog. In the *Squire's Tale*, the more macrocosmic deceit of Sinon the Greek (209), who pretended to be a deserter in order to allow into Troy the wooden horse concealing Ulysses and the Greeks that leads to the nation's fall, anticipates the deceit of Paris toward the shepherd girl Oenone, whom he deserts for Helen—which starts the Trojan War. In the *Squire's Tale*, like the integumental artistry and "magic" of fable and fantasy, such deceit can mask hidden emotional truths—as a further protection against pain in love, in the case of Canacee's falcon, or as a means of communicating truth to others, in the case of the *Aeneid*, the *Consolatio*, or Ovid's *Metamorphoses*, from which the story of Seys and Alcyone comes. Alcyone, if not Seys, is a bearer of truth. Deceit in the *Squire's Tale*, however, is most dramatically linked with the power of magic and artifice, as if typifying the lying fables of the poet.

The *Squire's Tale* can be used to gloss the *Book of the Duchess* and the artifice of its stained-glass windows through the knight's magical aids, which arouse both popular delight and suspicion. In the *Squire's Tale*, when the knight enters Cambyuskan's court riding on a brass steed (and carrying a mirror and wearing a thumb ring and a naked sword), the steed he offers as a gift from the King of Arabia and India has the magical ability to bear its rider anywhere in twenty-four hours, just as the mirror allows its viewer to discern the treason and subtlety of any lover, and the ring allows its bearer to understand the language of any bird and the healing properties of every grass. About these aids the folk "maden skiles after hir fantasies, / Rehersynge of thise olde poetries" (205–6).

If the deceitful horse suggests the deceits of the body to which the Trojans were known to fall prey, the way of Venus, as indicated by the folk's comparison of the brass steed with the Trojan horse led into Troy (along with some hidden Greeks) by Sinon (207–10), then their other comparison, with Pegasus the flying horse, can be understood as the antithesis, the fame gained by art, or the way of Minerva. From Medusa's blood Pegasus was born—that is (according to Fulgentius), after Perseus, with the help of Minerva, overcame the Gorgon by shining back into her eyes a mirror that turned her to stone (*Mit.* 1.21, p. 62). Fulgentius explains Perseus's victory as manliness aided by wisdom overcoming terror; renown is shaped as a horse like Pegasus and therefore said to have wings because fame is winged. Pegasus strikes out a fountain for the Muses with his hoof because the Muses either follow their own method of describing the renown of heroes or derive theirs from the ancients. Thus, as a source of poetry, in the flight of imagination, this winged horse presents a positive image to counter that of the treacherous Trojan horse; experientially, he rises out of the blood of Medusa, or from terror, to suggest that art grows out of, and transmutes, suffering and anxiety, in order to transcend human limitation.

The female perspective, the perspective of Alcyone, is privileged, identified, by Canacee's receipt of the ring and mirror (of the magical gifts, the only ones to come into her possession, for the horse vanishes and the king closes up the bridle with other jewels in the tower). When Canacee, wearing the ring, is able to hear the falcon's confession of her tercelet's perfidy, she also hears what might be called the falcon's echo of the Black Knight's similar "confession." This ironic, artful disguise of the falcon's own sorrow from the tercelet implies that her deceit provides a necessary defense against further pain and hence a lesson for all women:

> As I best myghte, I hidde fro hym my sorwe,
> And took hym by the hond, Seint John to borwe,
> And seyde hym thus: "Lo, I am youres al;
> Beth swich as I to yow have been and shal."
> What he answerde, it nedeth noght reherce;
> Who kan sey bet than he, who kan do werse? (595–600)

Here the falcon relays *her* tale, of the beginning—and end—of her own love affair, and the deceit and artfulness that went into its creation and maintenance, just as the Black Knight has relayed the tale of his affair with and marriage to the White Queen—especially concerning the beginning of his relationship, for it is the end he cannot face except through denial, subterfuge and artifice. In the background for both confessions is the tale of the rise and fall of Troy, the rise and fall of Italy, the rise (and potential) fall of England, and the double loves and deceits associated with each.

The dreaming narrator has "read" all these *Aeneid* figures in the stained glass of his bedroom, through which sunlight pours. But unlike them, the Black Knight (Chaucer's own figure as well as the figure representing John of Gaunt) has reached the point where he can blurt out "She is dead" to the deliberately dense narrator and thereby accept the loss of his Queen—or, in other words, return Orpheus-like *from* the underworld of sorrow he inhabits. In this sense, having experienced the role of Trojan Paris overwhelmed by love for Helen, skillful in the use of love-sophistry and self-delusion, he now takes on the guise of the Trojan Aeneas who weds Lavinia and discovers wisdom. Like Aeneas, the Black Knight needs to journey to Italy, and the ultimate goal of wisdom, signified by the goddess Pallas Athena (Minerva), although he says only that, had he been as wise as

Minerva, he would nevertheless have still loved his queen (1072–74), whom he compares in her goodness and loyalty to various Greek and Roman women (Penelope [1081], Lucrecia [1082]).

Even though the Black Knight compares himself, a brave lover, with various heroes from the *Aeneid*, if the Black Knight had refused to love, he would have betrayed himself, just as the Trojan Antenor captured by the Greeks and offered in exchange betrayed his country (1117–20). Indeed, Trojan Cassandra, who prophesied the destruction of Troy, never saw woe like his (1246–49). The Black Knight swears he would have loved his lost lady no matter who he was, even Alcipyades or Alcides, known for his beauty (and elsewhere, strength; 1056, 1057). In his joy over the memory of his love, he compares himself with Hector and then Achilles, the former slain by Achilles for love of Polixena; Antiolochus (Archilogus) and Achilles were then both slain, the latter by the vengeful Paris, as Achilles made ready to marry Polixena (1065–71).

Like Alcyone, suffering from a kind of spiritual death, the despairing Black Knight will, unlike Alcyone, be reborn by the end of the poem. Rebirth imaged as the awakening of the world from winter correlates with the "rebirth" of the Black Knight at the end of the poem, the "awakening" of the narrator during the dream—and contrasts with the perpetual "sleep" of Alcyone. It is not clear whether the verdant meadow scene in the *Book of the Duchess* represents the goodness of rational nature—outside of which the irrational Black Knight (and his artificial classical antecedent lovers) exists, and outside of which also our distraught narrator-dreamer therefore exists—or instead the paradise of temporal good to which Eurydice was attracted. That the Black Knight is accordingly alienated from his natural state as a husband and a man, and needs to be healed sufficiently to return whole to society, is suggested by the dreamer's venture into a flowery meadow after he is "awakened" from his state of limbo between source and influence, text and gloss. Its verdant beauty reminds the dreamer of the realm of Flora and Zephirus—"They two that make floures growe" (403)—the goddess of flowers wed to the West Wind. For the reader, the healing power of this "floury grene" mirrors its divine source: "For hit was, on to beholde, / As thogh the erthe envye wolde / To be gayer than the heven, / To have moo floures, swiche seven, / As in the welken sterres bee" (405–8). This power of rebirth, from the suffering and poverty of winter to the forgetfulness found in the green consolation of spring, hints at a Christian source, in the symbol of the incarnational dew to which it attributes its strength: "Hyt had *forgete* the povertee / That wynter, thorgh hys colde morwes, / Had mad hyt suffre, and his sorwes; / *All was forgeten*, and that was sene, / For al the woode was waxen grene; / Swetnesse of dewe had mad hyt waxe" (410–15; my emphasis). The power of recovery anticipates the green fuse that drives the flower in the *Prologue* to the *Legend of Good Women*—also Flora and Zephirus, who there mirror the ideal natural principle as the natural balance within oneself, within nature, within marriage: Alceste and the God of Love.

Alceste's Descent in the *Prologue* to the *Legend*

Chaucer, like the late medieval mythographers, stresses Alceste's role in his rendition of her myth, accordingly diminishing the role of her husband and omitting his premarital petition entirely (although one might argue that he substitutes the God of Love for Admetus). In focusing on Alceste's descent into the underworld and her rescue by Hercules, he adds the *Metamorphoses*-like daisy symbolism, perhaps by analogy with flower metamorphosis in the Ovidian fables of Clytie, Daphne, Narcissus, Crocus, and Hyacinthus,[22] to adapt her classical fable to the religion of love often associated with *fin amour*. He also dramatizes her significance as *praesumptio*, boldness, courage, succor: through her relationship with Chaucer as narrator, she does provide succor to this heretic paralyzed by fear.

The succor appears through the process of his "reading" or understanding Alceste—from his first encounter with her, as the daisy, to the idea the daisy represents, to the goddess accompanying the god, and his final recognition that this is the character he has read about in the book; the daisy (symbol) is both the literary figure (Alceste) and a real woman.

Her appearance with the God of Love suggests that her mythographic meaning is equally tied to his—in terms of love, in terms of rebirth and revivification, with which this *Prologue* teems and abounds. Scholars have long recognized the equivocal nature of the daisy as "The 'dayesye,' or elles the 'ye of day'" (F 184), which would be the sun, and also "The emperice and flour of floures alle" (F 185), the ruler or queen of flowers. As an empress she is therefore capable of materializing before the startled eyes of the narrator (which are in fact closed in sleep)—an event that indeed happens very soon after his praise of the daisy. When the God of Love appears, accompanied by a queen in green with a "fret" of gold upon her hair that bears a "whit corowne" with "flourouns smale" (F 213–17), the narrator at first does not recognize her, despite his worship and understanding of the daisy and her description in terms of daisy imagery. "For al the world, ryght as a dayesye / Ycorouned ys with white leves lyte, / So were the flowrouns of hire coroune white," the narrator marvels (F 218–20). Her white crown of flowers, which heightens her resemblance to the literal daisy, is made of pearl: "For of o perle fyn, oriental, / Hire white coroune was ymaked al" (F 221–22). "Pearl," as most Middle English scholars realize, is *margarita* in Latin, although *marguerite* in French refers to the daisy and links this poem with the French Marguerite poems often cited as sources for Chaucer here. But we should not forget her appearance in conjunction with the God of Love, to whose court Chaucer has been brought as a heretic in his dream vision. Between this god and the poet the queen Alceste acts as intermediary, an analogue to the Virgin Mary in the religion of love; because she pleads Chaucer's case to the god, this sinner is let off with a penance of writing a kind of corrective, in this case a hagiography of love's saints.

Although Alceste identifies herself as queen of Thrace in line F 432 (when she intercedes on behalf of errant Chaucer to the God of Love "That ye him never hurte in al his lyve" [F 434]), nevertheless, her "legend" and its significance is not relayed until lines F 511ff. At that point the God of Love identifies her as a literary character in a book owned by Chaucer (which book is not clear): "Hastow nat in a book, lyth in thy cheste, / The grete goodnesse of the quene Alceste" (F 510–11). Then he identifies her as a figure whose goodness is represented by the daisy ("That turned was into a dayesye" [F 512]) and as a loyal wife married to Admetus, who agrees to die and enter hell in his place ("She that for hire housbonde chees to dye, / And eke to goon to helle, rather than he" [F 513–14]). Finally, he identifies her as a shade rescued by Hercules "out of helle agayn to blys" (F 516).

In other words, the God of Love positions Alceste's meaning on four different levels—first, as a historical figure, wife of Admetus and queen of Thrace; second, as a symbolic daisy, part of the natural or physical world; third, as a moral virtue, exemplified in the heroic descent into the underworld so like that of Hercules—or Christ; and fourth, as a literary figure, whose artificial existence in a book grants her a kind of immortal life.

To an extent, these four levels echo at least three of the descents outlined by Bernardus Silvestris on the *Aeneid* and William of Conches on Boethius, namely, the natural, virtuous, and artificial descents. They are also all linked by Alceste's descent into hell and its late medieval signification, which identifies her as *praesumptio* or *animositas*—boldness, courage, confidence, audacity—and the power of the soul to withstand the terrors of death. Chaucer intensifies this signification, and Alceste's role, by means of his own changes in the tradition.

In contrast to Chaucer's compressed account, late antique and early medieval versions of the tale of Alceste place greater emphasis on the petition of Admetus for Alceste's hand in marriage than on the descent of Alceste into hell.[23] The sixth-century Fulgentius in effect divides the fable in two and thereafter focuses greater attention on Alceste's role in the second part by delaying the second gift of Apollo to Admetus—the possibility of changing places with a relative—until the actual moment of death.[24] The second part of the myth shifts to Alceste as the relative who chooses to make the exchange: "This his wife undertook; and so Hercules, when he went down to drag away the three-headed Cerberus, also freed her from the lower world" (*Mit.* 1.22, p. 34, trans. p. 63).

Nevertheless, Fulgentius stresses only the first (premarital, or Admetus) part of the fable in his very influential etymological moralization of it as an "allegory of the mind," "in modum mentis":

> He is named Admetus as one whom fear (*metus*) could seize upon (*adire*). Also he desired Alcestis in marriage, for *alce* in the Attic dialect of Greek is the word for succour, whereby Homer says: "There is no other strength [*uirtus*] of mind and no other succour [*praesumptio*]." Thus the mind hoping for succour [*praesumptio*] harnessed two opposed wild beasts to its chariot—that is, adopted two strengths [*uirtutes*], of mind and body—the lion for strength of mind and the wild boar for strength of body. (P. 34, trans. p. 63)

To the description of Alceste as a loyal wife, Fulgentius adds a brief misogynistic digression about bad and good wives that will prove persuasive to later mythographers:

> As there is nothing nobler than a well-disposed wife, so there is nothing more savage than an aggressive one. For a prudent one offers her own soul as a pledge for the safety of her husband, to the same degree that a malevolent one counts her own life as nothing compared with his death; thus the legally espoused wife is taken up either with the honeyed sweetness of pleasant ways or with the gall of malice and is either a permanent solace or an endless torture. (P. 34, trans. p. 62)

Later medieval accounts, beginning with the eighth-to-ninth century First Vatican Mythographer and culminating in the fifteenth century with Thomas Walsingham, gradually elaborate on the allegorical significance of Alceste, especially in her descent into the underworld, as the courage of the soul in facing death, even though rescued by virtue (Hercules). The First Vatican Mythographer, after briefly describing Admetus's petition to marry Alceste, the aid of Apollo and Hercules, who helped battle the lion and the boar, the illness of Admetus, and his replacement at death with his wife Alceste, concludes with a Fulgentian moralizing gloss on Admetus as *mentis* and Alceste as *praesumptio* (Bode, p. 31 [myth 92]).

Continuing the elaboration on the second part of the fable, the Third Vatican Mythographer introduces the fable of Admetus and Alcestis (a portion of the larger section on Hercules) with the idea that the Herculean rescue of Alceste manifests her strength, *virtus* ("Nam quod Alcesten liberaverit, ad virtutem spectare videtur")—a change in emphasis from the

Fulgentian focus solely on Admetus. In 13.3, after he again recites the portion of the fable concerning Admetus's petition for Alceste's hand, Tertius carefully elaborates on the second and more important portion, the Herculean descent into the underworld to rescue Alceste, and its Fulgentian moralization (in particular) of Alceste as *praesumptio* or *animositas*: Admetus as *mens* (etymologically, *adire metus*) represents the mind, which, because of its timidity, needs Alceste, *alce* in Greek, in Latin, *praesumptio*, in order to live; in conjunction, and guided by two necessary beasts, the virtue of the soul in the lion and the virtue of the body in the boar, they propitiate Apollo and Hercules, *sapientia* and *virtus*. Therefore, as *praesumptio*, boldness, confidence, Alceste figures forth that virtue which aids the soul in fear of death and the underworld, or *animositas*. Thus, Hercules calls back strength (*uirtus*) from inferior things (*de inferis*) when the vigor of the soul is endangered with spiritual death.[25] This interpretation of Alceste as *praesumptio* continues with the equally Fulgentian glosses of Walsingham in the fifteenth century, who concludes with a nearly verbatim repetition of Tertius on Alceste as "presumptio semetipsam ad mortem."[26]

Thematically and imagistically, Chaucer's poem celebrates spring and reflowering associated with the myth of descent and return with which Alceste is linked in medieval commentaries. The relationship between sun and daisy—on the natural level—represents the visual evidence of the co-existence of male and female principles, whose interrelationship reflects the marriage of heaven and earth, the causal relationship between the warmth of the sun and earthly grasses. Of the mythological references, the first, the particular conjunction of Europa with Jupiter, ultimately signifies that the full literary significance of Alceste within the poem must be explained in conjunction with the God of Love, just as the daisy refers to Alceste but means "eye of the day," or of the sun (presumably not of Alceste, although it is the God of Love and not Phoebus Apollo who appears with her). The remaining two mythological references in the *Prologue*, to Zephirus and Flora (F 171) and Cybele and Mars (F 531, 533), underscore the analogous relationship between Alceste and Amor. Interestingly enough, they also echo rather spectacularly the fact of the daisy as a flower. Finally, they all represent pairs of lovers or rulers who together combat death and mutability, on the literal level, through natural fertility and reproduction; on a more figurative level, they express the spiritual flowering of virtues that occurs through the loyalty and steadfastness of the soul married to God. Hence flower mythography drawn from mostly Latin treatises colors their associations throughout.

For these reasons, the first reference, to Europa, or "Agenores doghtre" (F 114), occurs in the context of a long paean to the daisy, "clernesse and the verray lyght / That in this derke world me wynt and ledeth" (F 84–85). On the first *morwe* of May, the narrator kneels in reverence before the daisy in order to witness the "resureccioun" of the flower as it opens up to reveal the "sonne" within, "that roos as red as rose," meaning the sun or day's eye, but also that which had been concealed, in the form of Jove or son of God, in the breast of the beast "That Agenores doghtre ladde away" (F 110–14). Hence the reference to Agenore's daughter literally invokes Europa, raped by Jove in the guise of a bull, to denote the constellation of the bull, Taurus, and thereby signal the first of May as the time of spring, in the middle of the astrological sign. More figuratively, the reference to Europa foreshadows the entrance of Alceste: just as Alceste represents that *prae-sumptio* of the soul that allows it to withstand death—and winter—so also, according to Bersuire in his moralization of Ovid 2.858, Europa signi-fies the rational soul, spiritual daughter of God the king who "changed Himself into a beautiful bull—that is corporeal, mortal man by assuming human flesh and coming personally to the world—in order to have this virgin—that is the rational soul—he loved."[27]

Zephirus and Flora (F 171) appear in May when flowers have forgotten winter and birds (who have escaped the fowler) sing of love—"welcome, somer, oure governour and lord" (F 170). This reference, like that of "Agen-orcs doghtre," transcends the conventional springtime notation of the dream vision: Flora, Roman goddess of flowers, originally named Chloris, changed her name after being raped by the West Wind Zephirus. Her rites are celebrated during the Roman festival of the Floralia, according to Ovid's *Fasti*, from May 1 to 5.[28] During this festival, erotic activities signal the ad-vent of spring—indeed, the marriage of heaven (the West Wind Zephirus) and earth (Flora, goddess of flowers). An appropriate couple who together "gentilly / Yaf to the floures, softe and tenderly, / Hire swoote breth" (F 172–73), this "god and goddesse of the floury mede" (F 174) encourage the rejuvenation of flowers ("made hem for to sprede" [F 173]) in a metonymy for the rebirth of spring—and the propagation of virtues in "Love's saints," who imitate the passion of Christ.

Finally, in the last mythological image, Cybele and Mars (F 530), Chau-cer provides the key to Alceste's significance. First the narrator signals his learning process by recognizing this unknown queen as Alceste, the daisy he adores: "'Yis, / Now knowe I hire. And is this good Alceste, / The dayesie, and myn owene hertes reste?'" (F 517–19). Upon his recognition, affective understanding follows: "Now fele I weel the goodnesse of this wyf, / That both aftir hir deth and in hir lyf / Hir grete bounte doubleth hire renoun" (F 520–22). It is because of her goodness, he declares, that she was stellified by Jove (F 524–26); her sign, the daisy for whom he has held such affection, was made by Cybele: "In remembraunce of hire and in honour / Cibella maade the daysye and the flour / Ycrowned al with whit, as men may see"

(F 530–32). Within this crown, Mars donated the red in place of rubies (F 532–33).

The reader at this moment also understands that all four levels of Alceste—natural, historical, moral, artificial—converge in her divine alter ego, Cybele, also known as Ceres, Ops, Rhea, and Berecynthia.[29] Perhaps Chaucer names his Ceres "Cybele," the mother goddess and procreatrix of all on earth, in order not to diminish Alceste, whose Berecynthia-like reflowering and accompaniment by the Attis- and Phoebus-like God of love (and poetry) on a more tropological level presents her as *praesumptio*, or *animositas*—a female Hercules.

Allegorically, Cybele, "procreatrix of all on earth," functions as a type of divine alter ego for the mortal Alceste. For such a reason, daisylike Alceste might be more suitably allied with Cybele in her role as Berecynthia, the equivocal goddess described by Fulgentius in the same passage. Her name etymologically reveals her nature as "spring flowers," although it is her husband Attis rather than herself whom she cuts down: "Berecynthia flourished on the mountains like spring flowers (*uernaquintos*), for *quintos* in the Attic tongue is called a flower, whence the hyacinth is for *hiocintos*, which in Latin we call the solitary flower because it is more beautiful than all others.... So, too, whoever loves a flower cuts it, as Berecynthia did to Attis, for *antis* is the Greek for flower" (Fulg. *Mit.* 3.5, trans. p. 86).[30] Attis, the equivalent of Mars to Cybele, or Cupid to Alceste, is named, according to Fulgentius, for *flos* or the sun, *causa omnium florum*, who for this reason loves earth (also known as Cybele-Berecynthia).

If Chaucer were aware of the definition of Cybele's role as one of earthly power, he might very well have added Mars to represent her bellicosity— although Alceste, whom she typifies, hardly seems bellicose, despite her mythographic signification as *animositas*. Leaving aside for a moment Cybele's appearance with Mars (who donates the red corona apparently because of the planet Mars's red color), the name Cybele rather than her other equivocations applies here. Perhaps this "mother goddess" donates the crown because Cybele, according to Fulgentius (*Mit.* 3.5), often appears with towers, "for all elevation of power is in the head"; appropriately, her name etymologically renders her desire to be placed in a position of power: "Cibebe, for *cidos bebeon*, that is, firmness of glory; whereby Homer says: 'To whom Jove vouchsafed renown'.... Thus the renown of power is always both aflame with love and devoured by envy, and speedily cuts off what it delights in, while it also severs what it hates" (trans. pp. 86–87).[31]

The God of Love can be interpreted as a Phoebus Apollo or sun-god, like Attis, linked with Alceste as a twofold Cybele. Critics have cited the God of Love's bright face ("me thoghte his face shoon so bryghte / That wel unnethes myghte I him beholde" [F 32–33] in support of the idea that, like the sun, he represents truth, as Alceste represents the daisy (day's eye, the sun), or poetry.[32] Certainly, the unnamed God of Love is dressed in silk embroidered with green leaves, with a "fret" of red rose leaves, his golden (*gilt*) hair crowned with a sun, and in his hand two fiery darts (F 226–31, 234–35). His angelic wings and arrows (F 235, 236), part of the apparatus of the usually naked medieval Cupid, can hardly be construed as "deadly weapons and a torch," in the words of the Carolingian poet Theodulf of Orleans, who drew on Isidore's definitions, "Ferre arcum et pharetram, toxica, tela, facem," nor does he seem to be winged because he is fickle, naked because of his open crimes, or boylike because of his lack of skill and reason.[33] Chaucer fails to reveal Cupid's quiver and bow (for Theodulf, his depraved mind and his trickery), although he does mention fiery darts (for Theodulf, the arrows are poison, the torch, the ardor of love). Truly, Chaucer's god more closely resembles Berecynthia's Attis, or else Phoebus Apollo (the "sonne" and prototype of Christ, also the god of poetry, rather than the God of Love), than the "daemon fornicationis" of Isidore and Theodulf.

Although Chaucer couples Alcestis with the God of Love, this association was not usual and therefore suggests pointedly our poet's specific purpose in bending the mythographic conventions. In contrast, the fifteenth-century French court poet Christine de Pizan links Alcestis-as-Cybele with Minerva and Isis, the three principal goddesses aiding human civilization, in *Le Livre de la Cité des Dames*. In this dream vision, with which the *Legend of Good Women* has come recently to be compared, Ceres introduces to civilization the art of cultivation, as Minerva introduces the art of armor making and Isis the art of planting.[34] In addition, Ceres is called the goddess of grain because of her great knowledge, for she taught us how to gather together in communities and cities to develop a more rational means of life.[35]

Chaucer's immortalized Alceste does seem to occupy the same role for all women in the *Legend* as Ceres, Minerva, and Isis do in the *Livre*. Chaucer the narrator's ballad to Alceste in 249ff. honors her as the perfect woman, exemplar of all virtues; she becomes the heroic standard against which all women must be measured—including a long list of classical examples. The narrator praises her as a queen "So womanly, so benigne, and so meke, / That in this world, though that men wolde seke, / Half hire beaute shulde men nat fynde / In creature that formed ys by kynde" (F 243–46). The qualities listed here center on her excellence as a wife, her *wifhod* (F 253; specifically, her loyalty, as exemplified in Penelope and Marcia Cato [F 252]) and on her beauty (Helen, Isolde, Lavinia [F 254, 257]—normally wisdom in the *Aeneid* commentaries). Alceste is similarly cast in the *Franklin's Tale* (1442) as an exceptional wife, within a very similar catalog of martyred women recited by Dorigen, but viewed as a mirror image of Dorigen in her chaste loyalty and sacrificial choices.

Accordingly, Alceste also appears here as a model for women who have suffered for love, for in the words of the refrain, she is the lady who "al this may disteyne" (F 255; "make pale, dim"). Among them are those whose tales follow in the *Legend* and who are introduced in a long catalog (F 257–69): Lucretia, the loving Polyxena, Cleopatra, Thisbe, as well as Hero, Dido, Laodamia, Phyllis, Canace, Hypsipyle, Hypermnestra, and Ariadne. Of this list, Lucretia, Cleopatra, Thisbe, Dido, Phyllis, Hypsipyle, Hypermnestra, and Ariadne are represented in the individual legends; Canacee reappears in the *Squire's Tale*; Polyxena plays no central role in a Chaucerian tale. Unlike Alceste, who appears in Chaucer's vision accompanied by the God of Love and in whose mortal life she remained married to Admetus, these women are cataloged here singly, even women who are frequently known as part of a couple (for example, Cleopatra, not Antony and Cleopatra; Thisbe, not Pyramus and Thisbe; Dido, not Aeneas and Dido). They are also perhaps selected from those in Ovid's *Heroides* precisely for their singleness—because in the *Heroides* their lovers do not respond to them with letters.[36]

If Alceste in the religion of love is a saint, or likened to the Virgin Mary as an intermediary between the human and the divine, then her antithesis would be Chaucer's Criseyde, whose very existence as a character instantiates Chaucer's sins against women. In Chaucer's portrayal, Criseyde implicitly signals a lack of *praesumptio*, loyalty: "And of Creseyde thou hast seyd as the lyste, / That maketh men to wommen lasse triste, / That ben as trewe as ever was any steel" (F 332–34).

The individual women whose "legends" are recited may have died for love, and may have represented individual virtues like so many beads on the rosary we call Alceste. For this reason, retelling their tales might be seen as appropriate penance in the religion of love for Chaucer's "crime" of narrating the story of Criseyde—if it were clear these women were generally regarded as positive and not negative examples of women in love.[37] Most likely, given Chaucer's changes in the mythographic Alceste, he had intended for them to be saintly and admirable exemplars. But for Chaucer, their disappointment and suffering in what might be termed *courtly* love links them with the suffering and distraught Alcyone in the *Book of the Duchess*—figures whose emotionality, delusion, denial of reality have in some way led to their martyrdom. For Chaucer, it is neither enough to love (a modern romanticism) nor to destroy oneself out of frustrated love—nor is it necessary to look back at the underworld, which is to say, to regard temporal good too highly, as did Orpheus. In the Middle Ages, Alceste's virtue of *praesumptio* or *animositas* linked her with the hero Hercules, prototype of *fortitudo*—and *sapientia.* Like him, she successfully weathered the underworld of irrationality, temporal good, the earthly—in order to "awaken," daisylike, to the light of the greatest good, God Himself. A *wonder thing,* indeed, this fable of Alceste, and in contrast to the complex figure of Dido, to whom Chaucer will return in the *Hous of Fame.*

CHAPTER 2

"Geffrey" as Dido, Ganymede, "Marcia"

Mythographic and Gender Parody in the *Hous of Fame*

Of the two meetings of Aeneas and Dido in the *Aeneid*, Chaucer in the *Hous of Fame* is more interested in the meeting of the hero and the shade in the gloomy sixth book rather than in the passionate fourth book. Chaucer witnesses Eneas descend into hell to see his father Anchises, but while there, Eneas finds Palinurus, Dido, Deiphebus, "And every turment eke in helle" (445). Among these torments is Dido's worry about her loss of reputation because of Eneas's treachery and how she will be viewed by posterity. Movingly recited before she kills herself, this important speech helps the reader to see the connection between love (Venus and Ovid) and fame (the House of Fame and Virgil), or between book 1 and books 2 and 3. If the major critical question about the *Hous of Fame* concerns the incongruity of setting these three books side by side, then the question might well be rephrased to read, What does the love vision[1] have to do with the jibe at fame,[2] or, by metonymy, what does Ovid[3] have to do with Virgil?[4] How do we read Dido and Aeneas?

In her apostrophe to Fame, Chaucer's Dido attributes to the goddess the loss of her reputation as a result of her "actes" (347), apparently known ("wyst"), even if initially covered by a "myst" ("Though hit be kevered with the myst" [352]). And worst of all, her future, no matter what the reality, will be colored by what people have heard about her role in this past affair:

> "Eke, though I myghte duren ever,
> That I have don rekever I never,
> That I ne shal be seyd, allas,
> Yshamed by thourgh Eneas,
> And that I shal thus juged be:
> 'Loo, ryght as she hath don, now she
> Wol doo eft-sones, hardely'—
> Thus seyth the peple prively.
> But that is don, is not to done;
> Al hir compleynt ne al hir moone,
> Certeyn, avayleth hir not a stre." (353–63)

And yet fame can also cover up vices, by obliterating them as if they have never existed.

This infernal meeting of Dido and Aeneas in *Aeneid,* book 6, is connected in the mythographies to the initial meeting of Dido and Aeneas in book 4 through her concern about her fame and reputation after death. The Third Vatican Mythographer suggests that fame frees (*liberat*) Aeneas and Dido from their folly (*a turpi*) and so it follows (in the words of Virgil) that the lovers can afford to become "forgetful of their nobler fame": "et oblitos famae meliores amantes."[5] Despite this cover-up, her fate will differ from that of Aeneas: after her death, according to Dido in the *Aeneid,* she will become an *imago* passing beneath the earth (4.654), while, according to the Third Vatican Mythographer, Aeneas continues on his journey, guided by Pallas.[6]

Once Chaucer delineates the episode from book 4 of the *Aeneid,* he must contend with the interpretation of Aeneas's sojourn with Dido as a flirtation with the active life, or the pursuit of Fame, dominated by Juno and the city of Carthage. Because "Geffrey" is transported to the castle of Fame through the air, Juno's cosmic realm, in the second book, and because Aeolus, god of winds under Juno's rule, plays a major role in the third book, it is possible that "Geffrey" here rewrites the medieval *Aeneid* to gloss the underworld meeting of Dido and Aeneas, with Dido reconceived as a figure for the poet and Carthage as a figure for the active life he seeks—fame and fortune governed by Juno, as all three books are—in the underworld of life on this earth.

The poet counseled by wisdom should identify with the Virgilian Aeneas, whose ultimate goal is Pallas Athena, but instead he identifies with the Ovidian Dido as passive victim, whose passions and anxieties are connected with the realm of Juno and controlled by fate and Fame—"Geffrey" journeys on to the House of Fame. From the scholastic and mythographic point of view, Dido becomes a site for wrongful choice and adaptation who must be abandoned in order to achieve wisdom. The court poet, however, is often by necessity feminized, or committed to the active life represented by the figure of Juno and her city of Carthage and therefore to the pursuit of fame; unlike Aeneas, he cannot abandon "Dido." He is stuck in the desert, for Chaucer perhaps ultimately more like Ariadne than the suicidal Dido and her fellow martyr Phyllis. All three women, according to the *Heroides* glosses, share *amor stultus,* foolish or irrational love. One might therefore also see the narrator, in his foolish praise of Venus, like Dido, *stultus;* if Aeneas is counseled to depart Carthage by Mercury bearing Jove's decree (with Mercury signifying wisdom in Fulgentius's exposition on the *Aeneid*), his counsel is by definition wise.

The Jovian Eagle rescues Chaucer from the barren desert of Carthage and the scene of passion and suicide and transports him through the air to what appears to be a better, loftier place—the House of Fame—which of course is no better or loftier than the Temple of Venus or the desert on which it is built. In Dante's *Commedia,* whose tripartite allegorical structure the *Hous of Fame* imitates, the *magister* Virgil leads Dante through the underworld and, with aid from Saint Lucia, Statius, and Beatrice, through purgatory; he cannot continue at all into paradise. Chaucer's *Hous of Fame* (also like the *Troilus* in its first three books)—structured like the *Commedia,* with a first book set in an underworld, a second book in a transitional purgatory, and a third book reminiscent of our spiritual home, paradise[7]—is a house of cards that only pretends to be a secure edifice. "Geffrey" never really leaves Carthage (or the earthly underworld of life on this earth); "paradise" exists only as a dreamy illusion.

Chaucer's three mythological invocations in the three parts—to Morpheus, Venus, and Apollo—set the tone and establish the theme for each part relative to the parody of the Virgilian journey and the Dantesque spiritual dramatization of the stages of underworld, purgatory, and heaven.[8] Morpheus, god of sleep, in his psychological and secular underworld, corresponds to the sterility of the Libyan desert (and the emotional effects of Aeneas's desertion of Dido). Cipris (Venus), the mother of Aeneas interpreted by Bernardus Silvestris in his commentary on Martianus Capella as a star "monstrante la viam" ("showing the way"), is invoked at the beginning of the second part; because Cipris dwells on Parnassus, the similar mountain of Dante's purgatory, the hope of penitential change for the secular "sinning" poet is underscored by the inquisitive ascent of "Geffrey" into (Juno's) air guided, if not by knowing Venus, then by Jove's knowing Eagle. Finally, the invocation to Apollo at the opening of the third part is explicitly indebted to the opening cantos of Dante's *Paradiso,* and the Chaucerian narrator's plea for wisdom in helping him compose that part most heavenly, most removed from human ability and understanding— what is actually the palace of Fame and the wicker house of Rumor in the earthly underworld, and not paradise at all.

To knit together his three Dantesque parts, Chaucer changes Dante's spiritual geography to suit his theme. In place of the *Inferno* of sinners, he gives us the "underworld" for lovers reflected in Aeneas's Carthaginian sojourn with Dido (*Aeneid,* book 4), an ingenuity perhaps influenced by medieval glosses on Aeneas's reencounter with the *shade* Dido during his own descent into the underworld (*Aeneid,* book 6). He will transform this more figurative interpretation of the underworld and the *descensus ad inferos* into what twelfth-century commentators called the "artificial descent," *descensus artificii,* in some cases linked to the artificial nature of poetry. Such a linkage will allow a similarly fanciful reinterpretation of the *Purgatorio* and the *Paradiso* in the light of the journey of the poet as hero.

Chaucer's second, but related, change in overlaying the *Inferno* with the

47

sixth book of the *Aeneid* (and amplifying the meeting of Dido and Aeneas by explaining their story, from book 4), then, is to focus on the victim Dido, with whom Chaucer identifies, rather than on the hero Aeneas. The identification of the narrator with the victim is an idea hinted at but not developed by John Fyler: the narrator is "more closely akin to Dido than to Aeneas, as one in 'the daunce' of those whom Love 'lyst not avaunce'" (639–40). Unlike the Queen of Carthage, "Geffrey" does at least get Jupiter's (or his Eagle's) attention; but instead of the rewards for the travails of the soul, his reward for his poetic travails is not Rome, nor, again in Fyler's words, "(as it might appropriately have been) an affair with the lady next door."[9] Chaucer here substitutes the poetic process, what might be called the winnowing of the poet, for the spiritual process, or the winnowing of the soul.

This chapter will therefore reveal how tightly unified this seemingly unfinished poem actually is, its frame based on the *Commedia* but its mythological references, which critics have examined individually, forming a pattern that can be fully understood by reference to the glosses on Virgil and Ovid and the handbooks of the mythographers. It is of course possible that Chaucer used more than one source in weaving its parts into a coherent whole.[10] Because the date of the poem has recently been revised to 1374, earlier than the previous 1379 date, the poem must have been written after Chaucer's first visit to Italy rather than after the second.[11] This earlier date links it much more definitely with the *Book of the Duchess* and Chaucer's French phase than was previously thought. However, the *Commedia* and the *Aeneid* commentaries are certainly equally important as influences on the *Hous of Fame*, as B. G. Koonce has thoroughly demonstrated;[12] Boitani, in his study of fame in Chaucer, explains this by noting that the major images and sources for each part differ, with Fame from Virgil, the Eagle from Dante, the House of Rumor from Ovid.[13]

The *Hous of Fame* carefully traces a satire on medieval literary theory[14] by providing us with a buffoon poet who allies more with the victim (Dido) than with the hero (Aeneas), with whom the other poets, musicians and harpers, magicians and augurs mentioned in the three books ally in their failure, presumption, and childishness, and whose puerile pursuit of Fame results in abandonment by the goddess and subsequent loss very like that experienced by Dido upon Aeneas's departure. Put another way, the hero Aeneas comes to occupy the role of the goddess Fame, against whose power the Carthaginian queen (Chaucer the poet) declaims. As a model for our poet "Geffrey" as narrator, Alan of Lille's Virgil in the *Anticlaudianus* — an important source for the *Hous of Fame* — as both buffoon and liar has been suggested by John Fyler.[15]

In each of three parts, the poet's desire for fame is met with frustration, symbolized by the lack of conclusion in this so-called unfinished poem. Chaucer parodies the mythographies by identifying himself, as reader and poet, with Dido as victim of the power of Aeneas (and the authority of the scholastic literary tradition, of Fame). Because "Geffrey" is eventually seduced by his own text, that is, by reading Dido, he takes her place in a Carthage-based dream in which he participates as a character and which he also dreams and writes. The first part of the *Hous of Fame,* in its reworking of Ovidian and Virgilian material, acts as a mythological key to its other two parts.

"Geffrey" as Ovid's Dido in Virgil's Underworld

Inside the Temple of Venus "Geffrey" meets Cupid and Vulcan, then reads, on a Table of Brass, the engraved story of Eneas—more particularly, of Eneas and Dido. Chaucer's recounting of the *Aeneid* (as Chaucer scholars have attested) derives from medieval redactions of the *Aeneid* story, which focus chiefly on the Dido and Aeneas story from book 4 of the *Aeneid,* coupled with the opening of the seventh letter of Ovid's *Heroides.*[16] By focusing on "Geffrey" reading Dido and on this sympathetic Ovidian Dido as victim of Aeneas, within the overall structure of the Virgilian journey of the heroic founder of Italy, Chaucer also draws attention to the mythographic significance of the domination of Venus over Aeneas in the *Aeneid* from the time of Troy to the sojourn in Carthage.

Chaucer portrays the love between Eneas and Dido as youthful, with boyish Eneas depicted as especially irresponsible and deceitful from the point of view of Dido in her moving complaint about the fickleness of men and their need for multiple women. Indeed, her gloss on Eneas's underlying, or secret, motivations suggests that he was impelled by a desire for fame, friendship, or singular profit. Specifically, the effects of Eneas's falsity have been drawn from *Heroides* 7, to counter the narrator's false excuses:

"Allas," quod she, "what me ys woo!
Allas, is every man thus trewe,
That every yer wolde have a newe,
Yf hit so longe tyme dure,
Or elles three, peraventure?
As thus: of oon he wolde have fame
In magnyfyinge of hys name;
Another for frendshippe, seyth he;
And yet ther shal the thridde be
That shal be take for delyt,
Loo, or for synguler profit." (300–310)

These unusual reasons she attributes for the most part to the deceptive artistry of false men (almost in echo of the falcon's denigration of false lovers in the *Squire's Tale*):

"O, have ye men such godlyhede
In speche, and never a del of trouthe?
Allas, that ever hadde routhe
Any woman on any man!
Now see I wel, and telle kan,
We wrechched wymmen konne noon art;
For certeyn, for the more part,
Thus we be served everychone.
How sore that ye men konne groone,
Anoon as we have yow receyved,
Certaynly we ben deceyvyd!
For, though your love laste a seson,
Wayte upon the conclusyon,
And eke how that ye determynen,
And for the more part diffynen." (330–44)

Sympathizing with her moving tale, Chaucer buttresses this sad and deceitful story with a catalog of equally deceived lovers from the *Heroides* we have seen elsewhere in his poems—Demophon deceived Phyllis, who then hanged herself (388–96; also cited in Chaucer's *Legend* of Phyllis and in the *Book of the Duchess*), and then, much more abruptly, "how fals and reccheles" Achilles was to Breseyda (398), Paris to Oenone (399), Jason to Isiphile (Hypsipyle) and Medea (400 and 401), Hercules to Deianira (402–4), and finally Theseus to Ariadne (405–26). Chaucer will use all of these lovers (except for Breseyda and Achilles, although her letter appears in the *Heroides*) in other tales to signify various kinds of deceit and trauma in loving.[17] The references to the tales of Phyllis and Demophon (388–96) and of Theseus and Ariadne (405–26), while longer, serve to frame the briefer references to similar pairs (398, 399, 400, 401, 402–4). But the way they frame the briefer references undercuts the narrator's emotional response to them, and to Dido.

In the twelfth-century *Epistulae heroidum* (to which Chaucer most likely refers in line 379, without appropriating the more pejorative attitude toward Dido), Dido, like Phyllis, exemplifies foolish love, as does Ariadne.[18] Love is classified as either tripartite or quadripartite, with foolish love identified as one type in both classifications, in the *Accessus* (literary introduction) to the *Epistulae heroidum*. The quadripartite was frequently presented under two rubrics, chaste and unchaste (*castus* and *incestus*), but in *Epistulae heroidum* II there are three kinds of love: legitimate (represented by connubial love, Penelope), illicit (Canacee), and foolish (Phyllis).[19] In yet another division in a twelfth-century manuscript of the commentary, there exists a tripartite division of unchaste love: the foolish (*stultus*, Phyllis), unchaste (*incestus*, Helen), and insane (*furiosus*, Canacee).[20]

In the *Aeneid* the astrological signs are ominous for the couple because the planet Venus has moved into Virgo, the Virgin.[21] The glosses on this episode reveal that Venus represents unchaste love, which affects in particular the early stages of man's life. Chaucer's "portreyture" of Venus in *Hous of Fame* (131–39), derived from Pierre Bersuire and copied by Robert Holkot and John Ridevall,[22] contains all the well-known iconographic signs of lust: she is naked (130); she carries a comb (136), as did Oiseuse (Luxuria) in Jean de Meun's Garden of Deduit in the *Roman*; her son Cupid is blind (138); and Vulcan, her husband, has a brown face because he is a smith (138–39).

Venus as a wily goddess whose influence on Aeneas is vicious and who pursues us more keenly in the *tempus vitae medium* (in the "middle of our life") appears in Petrarch's Latin letter about the fictions of Virgil, "De quibusdam fictionibus Virgilii." Here, too, she materializes "habitu demum venatricis, quia venatur miserorum animas, arcum habet & comam ventis effusam, ut & feriat & delectet [in the garb of a huntress, because she hunts for the souls of miserable mortals, and she has a bow, and has flowing hair, in order that she may smite us and charm us]."[23] Her deceptive nature in *Secretum meum* is expressed as passion clouding Aeneas's sight with love of the things of this earth, when he passionately desires battle during the fall of Troy (nationally representative of drunkenness and the body).[24] Because of his parentage, Aeneas (according to Petrarch in "De quibusdam fictionibus Virgilii") can evolve into the Perfect Man only when aided by Aeolus, the god of winds who represents "ipsa ratio regens frenans que irascibilem & concupiscibilem appetitum animae [our reason, which curbs and controls these headstrong passions]."

The entire episode in Carthage represents adolescence in another tradition of *Aeneid* commentary, the Fulgentian, in which the twelve-book epic overall is interpreted allegorically as the three stages of human life. According to Fulgentius, in his *Expositio continentiae Virgilianae,* in the fourth book Aeneas represents the spirit of adolescence, inflamed by passion as it hunts, and driven by storms (that is, confusion of mind) to commit adultery. But Aeneas, with Mercury's counsel, gives up passion; Mercury is "deus ... ingenii [god ... of the intellect]" (p. 94, trans. p. 127 [no. 16]). Appropriately for this tropological allegorization, when Aeneas sees Dido in his descent into the underworld (book 6), as a shade she is "antiquae libidinis ... iam uacua [void of passion and its former lust]" (p. 99, trans. p. 131 [no. 22]). Thomas Walsingham uses the love of Aeneas for Dido as an example of the puerile and imperfect love reflected in Amor. Depicted as a boy because cupidity (*cupiditas*) reflects the folly of turpitude (*turpitudinis stulta*), and because Amor is imperfect in lovers, likewise the speech of boys (*pueris sermo*), whence Virgil said about Dido loving Aeneas, "she essays to speak and stops with the word half-spoken" (*Aeneid* 4.76).[25]

Chaucer, in his version of the three lives topos (he stops at the second life in the other two parts of this poem), for the first phase of Eneas's journey described in the *Hous of Fame* downplays the spite and deceit of Juno and the role of Mercury in leading Aeneas to Italy to pinpoint the range of Venus's domination over Eneas as the voluptuous life—from Troy through the affair in Carthage. In these nearly two hundred lines on the Dido and Aeneas episode in the first book, Chaucer takes care to emphasize the lack of responsibility of Eneas: it is Venus who brings him to Dido's grace (239–44), although it is Mercury as Jupiter's messenger who instigates his departure (429–30). As Eneas's mother, she appears responsible for all that befalls him of a positive nature, whether the flight from burning Troy (162–73), during which he fled with his father Anchises on his back (173), or the escape from Juno's treacherous storms to Carthage (198–208). Further, Venus, determined to protect Eneas and his army, "Syth that he hir sone was" (218), encourages Dido to fall in love with Eneas when he and Achates meet Venus disguised as a huntress (225–52). Finally, at the end of the *aventure*, the respite from downfall occurs because of the "prayer of Venus" (461–67), which convinces Jupiter to withstand Juno's hostility against Troy, "For al hir sleight and hir compas" (462).

Love is a dream, or illusion, Chaucer argues through the shade Dido and the idea that dreams represent illusions and fantasies with the narrator's petition for dreamers who are lovers. Deceit in love resembles the artifice, illusion, *fantome* of bad dream and bad poem. The poet (Chaucer), a type of Theseus/Aeneas, tells lies to the reader, cast as Ariadne/Dido. The artifice of tale-telling, the deceit and lies of poetry, will be the glue connecting the mythological references in books 2 and 3, in that the poet hungering for fame lies even to himself, as the examples drawn from the mythographic tradition will testify.

Throughout the *Hous of Fame* Chaucer refers to works of art, books, tables of brass, stories, and tales. The levels of artifice are three, forming a kind of Chinese box containing smaller boxes, or what Penelope Doob has identified as a labyrinth:[26] first, there is the dreamer, a character in his own dream poem who finds the wall with its table of brass on which are written a Middle English version of Virgil's opening lines. Chaucer's language emphasizes the role of the poet—*writen, synge, story, telle.*

> I fond that on a wall ther was
> Thus *writen* on a table of bras:
> "I wol now *synge*, yif I kan,

The armes and also the man
That first cam, thurgh his destinee,
Fugityf of Troy contree,
In Itayle, with ful moche pyne
Unto the strondes of Lavyne."
And tho began the *story* anoon,
As I shal *telle* yow echon. (141–50; my emphasis)

The tale "Geffrey" will relay to his audience concerns a second "tale-teller," Eneas, who, in parallel to Othello to Desdemona, "Tolde Dido every caas / That hym was tyd upon the see" (254–55) and thereby seduced her into loving him. In response, Dido

dide hym al the reverence
And leyde on hym al the dispence
That any woman myghte do,
Wenynge hyt had al be so
As he hir swor; and herby demed
That he was good, for he such semed. (259–64)

Aeneas's speech, like all speech, according to Bernardus Silvestris's commentary on book 2 of the *Aeneid,* is understood to mix truth and falsity, which we might say emblematizes the nature of poetry (specifically, the *Aeneid* as history and fable). Here, too, as in Bernardus's commentary, Aeneas's supposed heroic integrity is denigrated as a fiction because of his betrayal of Troy (as Dares Phrygius also noted).[27]

Eneas's tale-telling in the *Hous of Fame* epitomizes the nature of poetry with its lying fictions and its secret truths. Those pretty words that convince Dido of his goodness metonymize his passionate but shallow love for her. Chaucer as reader, moved by the pathos of Dido's own seduction, moralizes on the harmfulness of deceptive appearance, on the glittering of gold-like things only apparently good but in reality evil (265–75): " 'Hyt is not al gold that glareth.' / For also browke I wel myn hed, / Ther may be under godlyhed / Kevered many a shrewed vice" (271–74).

Third, the remembering, awake scholar-poet Chaucer himself echoes all of these deceitful heroes—Virgil's character Aeneas (as glossed by the commentators), Chaucer's own character of Eneas portrayed as a tale-telling seducer of Dido, and the late antique and medieval topos of the lying poet. As a scholar apparently interested in "truth," "Geffrey" acknowledges the sources for the affair of Dido and Eneas engraved on the table of brass and in particular how she died and what she said (as relayed in Ovid's "Epistle" [375–79]). He also notes in an *occupatio* that if it were not too long to "endyte" he would write it here (380–82). For the sources of Eneas's descent into hell, where Eneas meets Dido again, and a description of the torments of the damned, Chaucer refers the reader to Virgil, Claudian, or Dante (447–50). But, simultaneously while he reworks material from these sources he also decries the "harm, the routhe," even a "tene" (vexation, trouble) that has ensued ("betyd") because of the "untrouthe," "As men may ofte in bokes rede, / And al day sen hyt yet in dede" (385–86). It is as if he refuses any responsibility for the harm he himself has caused because he draws on a dangerous book or else observes similar harm in the world itself.

The desert on which Venus's temple stands symbolizes aspects of love, poetry writing, and the soul's journey common both to the *Aeneid* commentaries and the *Hous of Fame*. The desert therefore links both the temple (love) and the flight (fame): Chaucer as narrator enters a temple from a kind of beach or waste desert, at first glance rather like Aeneas landing on the beach of Carthage. Further, Aeneas met his mother Venus in the Libyan wilderness, where she instructed him to find Dido; Libya was the scene of Dido and Aeneas's affair; and Mercury there brought to Aeneas Jupiter's message to depart. However, when Chaucer leaves the temple, he will experience a terrible abandonment like that of a lost soul—Dido, or Ariadne—rather than the eagerness to flee of the hero Aeneas or Theseus. The Libyan-like desert outside the Temple of Venus from which Chaucer is rescued by the Jovian Eagle (just as Bacchus was rescued by Jove's ram) is appropriate because Jupiter was mythologically linked with the Libyan sands and Venus with the Libyan wilderness.[28] More figuratively, the sand, like the glass of Venus's temple and the wind, signals vainglory, as the wasteland signals disillusionment with love.[29]

The setting of the story in Carthage, whose destiny was so dominated by Juno, was, in the *Aeneid* commentaries, often associated (along with Juno) with the active life, just as Troy (along with Venus) was associated with the voluptuous life, and Italy (along with Pallas Athena) with the contemplative life. The emphasis here on Carthage and the desert serves as a warning (understood certainly by the literate audience of Chaucer's time) that the hero—Eneas, and Chaucer, who surely must identify with him—ought to scurry onward to Italy and the goal of the contemplative life, Pallas Athena (wisdom). This allegorization was widely known in the Middle Ages: the earliest sources for the concept of the three lives, amplified through the myth of the Judgment of Paris, belong to a tradition of mythography extending from the sixth-century Fulgentius in his *Mitologiae* (2.1) to the Carolingian Second Vatican Mythographer. Like Fulgentius, the Second Vatican Mythographer identifies the three goddesses in terms of the three lives (contemplative, active, and voluptuary), and also in terms of three kinds of knowledge—*theorica, practica,* and *philargica* ("fond of ease," Epicurean).[30]

Of the three Carolingian and twelfth-century commentators who moralize the Judgment of Paris, the first two Vatican Mythographers and Bernardus Silvestris, only Bernardus applies the Judgment myth directly to the *Aeneid* (on 6.64–66) and offers interpretive clues that may have later affected Chaucer. And, while Bernardus analyzes the Judgment of Paris in the light of the three lives topos, he does not use this interpretation as a frame for his entire commentary on the *Aeneid*, as does Chaucer for his poem. What Bernardus does, instead, is to identify Aeneas's goal in his epic journey as that same golden apple that Paris offers to Venus — as the summum bonum:

> The golden apple is the greatest good because of both its matter and form: because of its matter, since, as gold, it surpasses all metals, and thus this good exceeds all other; and because of its form, since that form lacks beginning and end, and thus it is the highest good. It is properly called an apple, since fruit is expected from honest labor. But which of these goddesses should have the apple is debatable. For certain people such as philosophers prefer the contemplative life over the others; certain people such as politicians, the active life; certain people such as the Epicureans, the life of ease over the active and contemplative. Venus seems more beautiful to Paris, because sense places contemplation and action below pleasure, and therefore Pallas and Juno take revenge upon Troy. Because it is pleasing for sense to wallow in pleasures, it is very painful to the flesh to contemplate or act. ([Bern. Sil.] *Aen.*, p. 46, trans. pp. 46–47)

But Chaucer's narrator resembles his hero Eneas less than he does Dido, or one of the two other female victims of deceitful if amorous men, Phyllis and Ariadne. Of the three, the narrator actually most resembles foolish Ariadne, because, deserted on the beach, she departs for a better life with Bacchus instead of killing herself like Dido; that is, when Chaucer leaves the temple of brass, he seems to have been abandoned like Dido in "the desert of Lybye" (488) where "Ne no maner creature / That ys yformed be Nature / Ne sawgh I, me to rede or wisse" (489–91). Compare Ariadne's plight: Theseus "lefte hir slepynge in an ile / Desert allone, ryght in the se" (416–17). Chaucer, womanlike, a passive victim, calls on Christ "that art in blysse, / Fro fantome and illusion / Me save!" (492–93). Instead, Jove's Eagle rescues him, and that rescue — that real journey undertaken by the narrator, which mirrors Eneas's journey to Italy — is the subject of the second book.

This first, Dido-centered, part suggests that the phantoms and illusions of the poet, like the integumental figures of Virgil's fiction, derive from his own folly — the pursuit of fame offered by the active life associated with Juno. Appropriately, this wintry (December 10) dream has been summoned from the underworld (the air beneath the moon governed by Juno?). The iconography depicts an underworld of sleep, sadness ("unmerie"), forgetfulness ("Lete" [71]) similar to those of Bersuire and the *Book of the Duchess.* "Geffrey" has begun, after all, by invoking Morpheus (Sleep), just as he has invoked Morpheus and Eclympasteur (demons of the Cave of Sleep) in the *Book of the Duchess.* In the latter poem, as we saw in chapter 1 from the glosses by Bersuire on Ovid, *Metamorphoses* 11.633 (repeated by Robert Holkot and Thomas Walsingham), "sleep" becomes a metaphor for sin and his sons the demons, for specific vices. Drawing on the Bersuire gloss on the first, Morpheus, for *honores* and *dignitates,* the second, Icelos, for *voluptates* (pleasures), and the third, Phantasos, for *cupiditates* (desires), Chaucer chooses to focus in the *Book of the Duchess* on the second son, Eclympasteur (Icelos), because his specific role in transmitting cares to worldly sleepers centers on lust and other animal desires appropriate to a love vision.[31] In contrast, in the *Hous of Fame,* Chaucer selects Bersuire's characterization of the first son, Morpheus, because the god governs human characterization and the desire for renown. As well as taking the place of Somnus, or Sleep, Morpheus here is a "god unmerie" (74) with "slepy thousand sones" (75) who "slepeth ay" in a stone cave situated on a Lethean stream (70). And the Chaucerian *moralitas* provided for the story of Dido and Aeneas — that appearances deceive — might very well apply to the pliant narrator who sympathizes with the shade Dido and this underworld equivalent to the *Inferno,* with its description of the deceptive Temple of Venus.

Clearly, creating and interpreting dreams carries a grand and powerful responsibility, for dreams are freighted with anxieties and desires we dare not admit in our waking moments. Morpheus in particular is invoked here in signification of that desire for honor and renown reflected throughout the *Hous of Fame* in the anxieties of the narrator; Morpheus's cave is also a source of dreams. The narrator prays to Morpheus to "me spede / My sweven for to telle aryght, / Yf every drem stonde in his myght" (78–80) — prays to him, in short, for help in relaying his dream, presumably to tell "aryght" (meaning "correctly" and "vividly"). Finally, the narrator also asks Morpheus that dreamers be given joy, to stand in their loves' favor, to shield them from poverty and disease and mishap. Upon those who "mysdeme hyt," that is, misinterpret (92), through malicious intention, presumption, hate, scorn, envy, despite, jape, villainy, should fall the whole history of human harms (begged of the "mover ys of al" [81]). But in addition Morpheus's role in transmitting cares "into the hearts of worldly sleepers" in particular aids the poet, who needs images for characters and visions: "Morpheus has the task of not portraying [*non effigiat*] anything in a sleeper's head except for a human representation [*effigieum humanam*] with the carriage and speech and other qualities which pertain to human nature."[32]

Chaucer's immediate source here (for all three related "boxes") may very well be Fulgentius or his glossator and imitator, the Carolingian Theodulf of Orleans, who himself draws upon Macrobian and Fulgentian ideas of poetry. Like Chaucer in his persona as the passive "Geffrey," Fulgentius identifies himself as "homunculus" ("little man") and plays with the idea of secrets concealed by a fictional cover to prevent "base men" from perceiving the truth of secrets. Like Chaucer a lover of classical poets such as Virgil and "wordy Ovid," Bishop Theodulf (750–821) treats the pagan lies of (love) poetry as similarly connected with the infernal.

In the prologue to the *Mitologiae,* Fulgentius describes himself as not "explaining myth away" but instead revealing its secrets in the best Macrobian manner: "What I wish to do is to expose alterations away from the truth, not obscure what is clear by altering it myself … I look for the true effects of things, whereby, once the fictional invention [*fabuloso commento*] of lying Greeks has been disposed of, I may infer what allegorical significance [*misticum cerebrum*] one should understand in such matters" (p. 11, trans. p. 45). Fulgentius models his approach, so he says, on that of Cicero in his own *Somnium Scipionis,* but more likely he means Macrobius's commentary on the *Somnium Scipionis,* with its explicit discussion of dreams and the fictional cloaks of *narratio fabulosa:* Fulgentius declares that he will provide "ita somniali figmento delusam," or "dreamlike nonsense expounding trifles suited to sleep," specifically, "such things as those of which our Academic orator Cicero has given a lively account, almost making the sleeping Scipio into a citizen of heaven—but what Cicero achieved his own *Republic* may show" (*Mit.,* pp. 3–4, trans. p. 41). If so, it is ironic that he is himself addressed as "homunculus" ("little man") by the Muse and character Calliope (*Mit.,* p. 11, trans. p. 45), as he also was by the character Virgil in his exposition on the *Aeneid* (*Expos.,* p. 86, trans. p. 121).

Theodulf distinguishes between the falsity of the poets and the truth of the philosophers: in "De libris quos legere solebam et qualiter fabulae poetarum a philosophis mystice pertractentur," or "Books I Used to Read," he acknowledges that "much truth lies hidden under a deceptive surface [*sub falso tegmine*]. / Poets' writing is a vehicle for falsehood [*Falsa poetarum stilus affert*], philosophers' brings truth [*vera … sophorum*]; / they transform the lies of poets into veracity" (20–22, Theodulf, p. 169). Theodulf associates paganism and lying poetry with the underworld by depicting the infernal gates of ivory and horn, from *Aeneid* 6.893–96, through which true and false souls pass. Here they are transformed into the gates of sleep (the mouth and the eye) through which false and true dreams pass, reinterpreted in the light of Servius's commentary on the *Aeneid* and Macrobius's commentary on the *Somnium Scipionis,* 1.3.17–20:

Sleep has two doors, so poetry relates,
one bears the truth and the other falsehood.
The gate of horn draws in truth, the ivory gate brings out falsehood,
the eyes see the truth and falsehood passes through the lips.
For horn is smooth, and the eye is also tender and translucent,
while the opening of the mouth bears a barrier of ivory.
The eye experiences no light, and horn feels no cold,
the tooth and ivory alike have strength and colour.
Those two gates do not have the same properties,
the mouth bears falsehoods, the eye sees nothing but the truth.
(49–62, Theodulf, p. 171)

Theodulf's association of sleep, visions, and the underworld is echoed by Chaucer's invocation of Morpheus at the opening of his poem as the god of sleep.

Most dangerous is the gate of ivory, the portal through which poetry— and especially love poetry—may be said to issue, because of its appeal to the senses and its description of the pleasures of the flesh. Theodulf indeed pays especial attention to Cupid as the "demon of fornication" who drags us into an underworld because of loose living. "The demon of fornication [*moechiae daemon*] is terrible and wicked, / it drags wretches down to the brutal purgatory [*saeva barathra*] of loose living. / It is prompt to deceive and always ready to do harm, / since it has the Devil's force [*daemonis vis*], resources and experience at its command" (49–52, Theodulf, p. 171).

For Cupid as a daemon, or figure, of fornication, Chaucer substitutes Venus's other son Eneas, who leads both Dido and the reader into a dark underworld, or *barathrum*, by means of his sweet lies—a figure also for the poet and poetry. Eneas himself is cloaked like the truth of a poem: as a *figura* he *is* a lie, a fiction. Thus "he betrayed hir, allas, / And lefte hir ful unkyndely" (294–95) in violation of his "trouthe" (297). When, at the opening of the *Aeneid,* Aeneas washes up on the shores of Libya after a shipwreck caused by Juno and is concealed by Venus in a protective cloud with Achates, Fulgentius explains the cloud as a symbol of the poet's integument: "Then his mind is taken up with pictures [*picturis*]" (*Expos.* 11, p. 91, trans. p. 124). This clouding of the mind with pictures on a Libyan beach resembles the Chaucerian narrator's double clouding, his dream vision and his confused anxiety as he emerges from the Temple of Venus into a desert in the *Hous of Fame.* Further, throughout his poem Chaucer also associates winds, clouds, disguises, Venus, or *cupiditas* with poetry, as in Bernardus's summary of the first book of the *Aeneid*: Aeneas arrives at Carthage after being buffeted by *storms* caused by Juno's giving of her nymph Deiopea to Aeolus; Aeneas, hidden under a *cloud*, sees his companions but does not speak until his mother, the goddess of love, or Venus, removes it. Entertained at a welcoming banquet with Iopas's *songs,* Aeneas is welcomed by Dido along with *Cupid* in the *disguise* of Ascanius ([Bern. Sil.] *Aen.,* p. 4, trans. p. 6).

Chaucer's repudiation of what might be termed the mythographic line in the Bernardus commentary on the *Aeneid* is only apparent in book 1 of the *Hous of Fame.* The allegorical overthrow of Juno (the active life) by Venus (voluptuous life) and Jupiter (acting through Mercury) seemingly re-enacted here is deceptive: in truth, the *narrator,* like his character Eneas blinded by Venus's mists, cannot see clearly. This idea suggests that "Geffrey"'s emotional reaction to Dido's complaint must be read as a reflection of the narrator's disordered state and poor judgment, for in the other (Virgilian) tradition of moralized Dido, this queen is portrayed negatively. In a scholastic sense, Dido, like "Geffrey" here, represents the disordered soul, or the kingdom of the soul ruled by passion rather than reason. In his comment on 1.496 of the *Aeneid,* Bernardus notes that

> In this city he finds a woman ruling [*mulierem regnantem*] and the Carthaginians enslaved [*Penos servientes*], because in this world such is the confusion that desire rules [*quod imperat libido*] and virtues are oppressed [*virtutes opprimuntur*]. We understand the Carthaginians, brave and upright men, as virtues, and thus men serve [*servit vir*] and a woman rules [*imperat mulier*]. Therefore in divine books the world is called the city of Babylon, that is, the city of confusion. (P. 12, trans. pp. 13–14)[33]

We might paraphrase Bernardus to note that in the *Hous of Fame* here too "imperat mulier"—Dido "rules" over this Dante-like poet "Geffrey." As in the *Commedia,* the misdirected will of Dante must now be instructed by the reason of the pedantic Virgilian Eagle. Or, to recast the frame, we might note that this Eagle, Bacchus-like, rescues the abandoned Ariadne-like victim and carries him through the air on a journey to a type of Babylon—the palace of Fame and the whirling house of Rumor, both places feminized by Chaucer.

"Geffrey" as Dante's Ganymede

In the second part, equivalent to the *Purgatorio,* Cipris or Venus (who dwells on Parnassus) is invoked, along with the Muses and Thought, as she is in the first eighteen lines of canto 1 of Dante's *Purgatorio,* because in a secular and mythical sense the star "monstrante la viam" corresponds to the overarching idea of Mount Purgatory in this second *cantica;* that is, in the poet's eyes, Venus no longer functions as *voluptas scelestis,* specifically manifested through the adolescent love of Aeneas for Dido, as she was in the first book, but now Cipris, a loftier form of love consonant with the elevated setting and regarded as Boethian harmonious and cosmic love in the *Parlement of Foules*. However, as the reader by now knows, Chaucer's journey through the air (province of Juno, signifying fame and victory) will end not in paradise or in Italy (province of Pallas Athena, signifying wisdom) but in Juno's air, where the castle of Fame remains. In parodying the literary tradition, Chaucer also mocks the scholastic tradition of exegesis.

It is significant that book 2 of the *Hous of Fame* takes place, for the most part, in the air high above the earth but beneath the Milky Way: of the four regions of the world, air is governed by Jupiter's sister Juno, as ether or fire is governed by Jupiter, water, by Neptune, and earth, by Pluto, in Bernardus's commentary on the *Aeneid*: "Their sister is called Juno, that is, air, because material things derive from air" (p. 4, trans. p. 6). Juno has fourteen handmaidens, seven aerial storms and seven aerial natures (p. 8, trans. p. 10). As if aware of this scientific definition of Juno, Chaucer chiefly mentions the ally of the cruel wife of Jupiter, Eolus, god of "wyndes," whose help she invokes to "drenche / Lord and lady, grom and wenche, / Of al the Troian nacion, / Withoute any savacion" (205–8). We will meet Aeolus again in book 3—facetiously and capriciously aiding the goddess Fame in her treatment of poets.

If the *Hous of Fame* is a parable about the deceptive nature of poetry and of the poet's quest for fame, just as book 1 could be said to reflect the importance of the trivium and the use of schoolbook texts like the *Aeneid* in the composition of poetry, so also this scientific and philosophical discourse by the Eagle in book 2 is intended to illuminate a second component in the composition of poetry, the role of the quadrivium in the information of philosophic truths that poetry conceals. Drawn from Dante's *Purgatorio*, Jove's Eagle, who transports "Geffrey" on his "flight of Thought," may either metonymize flight or else synecdochize air itself; more figuratively, it may signify the flight of poetic fancy, achieved through Ciceronian rhetoric.[34] In either case, poet "Geffrey" occupies center stage. In this book, the mythological references to males who fly— Ganymede, Phaethon, Daedalus and Icarus—gloss not so much the role of the Eagle as the role of the transported poet "Geffrey." These mythological references reveal that each youth was carried into the heavens by an eagle, the chariot of the sun, or wax wings, and met with some awful fate—ravishment by Jupiter in the case of Ganymede, or death by a disastrous cosmic fall in the cases of Phaethon and Icarus; that is, the seduction of the artist by his own artistry (if that is what this series of equivalences implies) implies that art is fraud and deceit, fantasy and illusion. In addition, several references gloss the role of "Geffrey" as a captive or passive poet-artist whose situation resembles that of the victimized Dido in the first book. Imprisoned Daedalus is an inventor, and in the well-known source passage from Dante's *Purgatorio*—the inspiration as well as source for some of these references, as we shall find—Ganymede is linked with a tapestry maker, the raped Philomela.

In book 2 (and book 3, as we shall see), the pose of the poet as a Dido-like victim of rape, ravishment, and abandonment is constructed by means of mythological references primarily to gods also mentioned or invoked in Dante's *Commedia*; that is, the poet appears to be presumptuous, fraudulent, fallen, false—and certainly unrewarded. The half-failed poets (and related artists and inventors) who aspire to fame, or to the heavens, include cupbearer Ganymede, inventor Daedalus and his lost son Icarus, and the sun's own son, the chariot-driving Phaethon. Ganymede, Icarus, and Phaethon—all humans who attempted to ascend into the heavens—represent the artist's desire to transcend the limitations of this world. In Dante, or in mythographic handbooks, many of these figures reflect the fraudulent and presumptuous, and are meant to gloss the type of the poet represented by the carried "Geffrey." Of these four, only Ganymede is associated with an eagle (like Chaucer), only Ganymede derives exclusively from classical mythology, and only Ganymede plays an important symbolic and figural role in the *Purgatorio*. In parody of Dante's self-deprecating "Io non Enëa, io non Paulo sono" of *Inferno* 2.32, "Geffrey" declaims, " 'I neyther am Ennok, ne Elye, / Ne Romulus, ne Ganymede, / That was ybore up, as men rede, / To hevene with daun Jupiter, / And mad the goddys botiller.' / Loo, this was thou my *fantasye!*" (588–93; my emphasis). In place of Virgil (the Empire, exponent of classical poetry) and Paul (the church, exponent of the Word of God), each of whom was famed either to descend into the underworld or ascend into heaven, Chaucer substitutes biblical and classical figures who have attained apotheosis either through stellification (Ganymede), deification (Romulus), or ascent into the heavens (Enoch and Elijah).[35] With his identification with Ganymede, however, he simultaneously invites us to think about how he is in fact like the character of Dante whose words he echoes, and therefore to look more closely at the use of Ganymede in the *Purgatorio*. That Ganymede served Jupiter, but was raped by him, is a point Dante wishes to make about the nature of grace as violent and penetrating, the role of the sinner as passive and submissive. In canto 9, when Dante is being transported physically by Saint Lucia through the gate of purgatory but spiritually by the grace of God, to signal the motion of grace achieved by means of penitence, the poet interlaces a series of images in a long epic simile to describe what in fact is a profound mystery. While he dreams that he is being lifted up by an eagle, as if he were Ganymede being transported to Jupiter, he first identifies the time of day as that hour when the swallow (into which Philomela metamorphosed) sings its woes:

61

Nell'ora che comincia i tristi lai
   la rondinella presso alla mattina,
   forse a memoria de' suo' primi guai,
e che la mente nostra, peregrina
   più dalla carne e men da' pensier presa,
   alle sue vision quasi è divina,
in sogno mi parea veder sospesa
   un'aguglia nel ciel, con penne d'oro,
   con l'ali aperte ed a calare intesa;
ed esser mi parea là dove foro
   abbandonati i suoi da Ganimede,
   quando fu ratto al sommo consistoro.
Fra me pensava: 'Forse questa fiede
   pur qui per uso, e forse d'altro loco
   disdegna di portarne suso in piede.'
Poi mi parea che, poi rotata un poco,
   terribil come folgor discendesse,
   e me rapisse suso infino al foco.
Ivi parea che ella e io ardesse;
   e sì lo 'ncendio imaginato cosse
   che convenne che 'l sonno si rompesse. (9.13–33, Dante, 2:119)

[At the hour near morning when the swallow begins her plaintive songs, in remembrance, perhaps, of her ancient woes, and when our mind, more a pilgrim from the flesh and less held by thoughts, is in its visions almost prophetic, I seemed to see in a dream an eagle poised in the sky, with feathers of gold, with open wings, and prepared to swoop. And I seemed to be in the place where his own people were left behind by Ganymede when he was caught up by the supreme conclave; and I thought within myself, — perhaps it is used to strike only here and disdains, perhaps, to carry off any in its claws from elsewhere. Then it seemed to me that, after wheeling a while, it descended, terrible as lightning, and caught me up as far as the fire; there it seemed that it and I burned together, and the imagined fire so scorched that perforce my sleep was broken.] (Dante, trans. 2:118, 120)

The image of Philomela used to gloss the major role of Ganymede reminds us of another violent rape, performed by a more human member of the family, in this case, a brother-in-law (Tereus), but without love or joy. The fact that Philomela, in life bereft of her tongue, sings wordlessly of her woe after metamorphosis, reminds us of her artistry in *Metamorphoses* 6.578ff., when she transcribes her complaint onto a tapestry: the hour of

Dante's spiritual transportation, in short, depends on a ravishment that is inarticulate, its awareness of the divine incommunicable except by dream or swallow's cry.

Dante mitigates the harshness of this simile by coupling it with the more tender and maternal one attached to his awakening: he compares himself to Achilles carried to the centaur Chiron by his mother for protection from the Greeks and for education; it is his *conforto,* Virgil, who will act the role of Chiron, supplementing the more spiritually maternal role of Saint Lucia, who has actually borne him there. Achilles was first nurtured by Chiron, then concealed as a girl by his mother until Ulysses found him and made him fight in the Trojan War. This reference to Chiron, known for his music, will actually be invoked in book 3 of the *Hous of Fame:*

> Non altrimenti Achille si riscosse,
>   li occhi svegliati rivolgendo in giro
>   e non sappiendo là dove si fosse,
> quando la madre da Chirone a Schiro
>   trafuggò lui dormendo in le sue braccia,
>   là onde poi li Greci il dipartiro;
> che mi scoss' io, sì come dalla faccia
>   mi fuggì 'l sonno, e diventa' ismorto,
>   come fa l'uom che, spaventato, agghiaccia.
> Da lato m'era solo il mio conforto,
>   e 'l sole er'alto già più che due ore,
>   e 'l viso m'era alla marina torto. (9.34–45, Dante, 2:119)

[Even as Achilles started up, turning his awakened eyes about him and not knowing where he was, when his mother carried him off sleeping in her arms from Chiron to Scyros, whence later the Greeks took him away, so I started, as soon as sleep left my eyes, and turned pale, like one that is chilled with fear. Beside me was my comfort alone, and the sun was already more than two hours high, and my face was turned to the sea.] (Dante, trans. 2:120)

When Chaucer reminds us that he is not Ganymede, he reminds us also that he is *not* Dante, whose travels mirror the process of penitence in the *Purgatorio* and, in the *Paradiso,* the process of salvation. In short, he reminds us, rather plainly, that he is sinful, garrulous (as is the Eagle), and traveling literally through the air, unlike Dante; but like Dante, Chaucer the poet is dreaming and his ravishment is educational and symbolic. Certainly the Eagle's mention of Daedalus and Icarus, followed shortly thereafter by Phaethon, occurs within a digression on antique or medieval works whose authors or their characters, like "Geffrey" and Dante, have been privileged to see the larger workings of the cosmos, what the bird terms "Helle and erthe and paradys" (918). The Eagle's examples include the medieval romances of Alexander in which griffins convey the conqueror through the air in a chariot (911–15), and the *Somnium Scipionis* of Cicero (or Macrobius?), in which dream Daun Scipio is shown the other world (916–18).

Given the company of Alexander the Great and "Daun Scipio," the fictional images of Daedalus and Icarus seem inappropriate, and even insensitive, additions: is "Geffrey" supposed to identify with them, and if so, does he feel comfortable, knowing that Icarus fell to his death because of his inability to fly with wax wings? The Eagle reminds "Geffrey" that no one in the past has flown as high as he,

> "Ne eke the wrechche Dedalus,
> Ne his child, nyce Ykarus,
> That fleigh so highe that the hete
> Hys wynges malt, and he fel wete
> In myd the see, and ther he dreynte,
> For whom was maked moch compleynte." (919–24)

Unlike Icarus, Scipio, and Alexander, Chaucer has thus far not fallen. In line 942, the Eagle mentions another celestial traveler, Phaethon, when he asks Chaucer if he can see the Galaxy, or Milky Way, now white but once burned with heat as a result of the fall of "the sonnes sone the rede / That highte Pheton" (941–42). Like the myth of Icarus, the myth of Phaethon in Chaucer illustrates overreaching one's limits.

The Eagle deploys poetic artifice to explain medieval science, and both for the purpose of moral understanding: "Loo," the Eagle glosses his own fable, "ys it not a gret myschaunce / To lete a fool han governaunce / Of thing that he can not demeyne?" he asks and abruptly departs "Geffrey" (957–59). Phaethon certainly fails to master his horses by failing to discipline himself. Phaethon

> "wolde lede
> Algate hys fader carte, and gye.
> The carte-hors gonne wel espye
> That he koude no governaunce,
> And gonne for to lepe and launce,
> And beren hym now up, now doun,
> Til that he sey the Scorpioun,
> Which that in heven a sygne is yit.
> And he for ferde loste hys wyt
> Of that, and let the reynes gon

Of his hors; and they anoon
Gonne up to mounte and doun descende,
Til bothe the eyr and erthe brende,
Til Jupiter, loo, atte laste,
Hym slow, and fro the cartre caste." (942–56)

All these figures—Daedalus, Icarus (919–20), and Phaethon (941–59)—present "as celestial travelers the presumptuous ones," in Fyler's words.[36] In the mythographies, including those of Pierre Bersuire and Robert Holkot (in a passage based on Ovid, *Metamorphoses* 8.203ff.), Icarus represents the disobedient and presumptuous son whose folly resides in thinking himself better than he is, particularly in attempting deeds beyond his ability. The labyrinth "of sins and goods of this world [*viciorum et bonorum huius mundi*]" from which he wishes to escape can be transcended, for Bersuire, by contemplation (*Ovidius*, p. 127, trans. p. 307). "If he raises himself through presumption or pride more than is just and believes himself better than others or seeks a higher position beyond the sufficiency of his person, the interior wings—virtues—are burned and the exterior wings—that is nobility and worldly power—are loosed and destroyed little by little" (*Ovidius*, p. 129, trans. p. 310).[37]

Phaethon, taken from Ovid, *Metamorphoses* 2.198–200, in the Ovid commentaries of John of Garland and Pierre Bersuire and the Bible commentaries of Robert Holkot also signifies pride, ambition, vainglory, and thereby glosses the *superbia* of "Geffrey" the ignorant artist. John of Garland notes that "Pheton" represents the untaught, in contrast to the wisdom of the philosopher signified by his father the sun: "Light is called *phos*, and Phaeton takes his name from that; so the splendor of the sun is his son. Wisdom begets the crown of the philosopher, whose car it leads, but the untaught falls [by the wayside]."[38] Similarly, Bersuire, in an unconventional gloss, relates Phaethon to the imprudent and ambitious prelate without a call whom the Pope sets over the church; Holkot appropriately attaches the myth to a gloss on fatuity and presumption.[39]

The unique myth of Phaethon and the four horses of the sun dramatizes how Phaethon as Everyman can choose to act wisely or let the four horses pull him toward death, in a myth from a different mythographic tradition, from Boethius. The four horses represent the four ages of man through which we all pass: Eritheus, "red," signifies birth and infancy; Acteus, "beautiful," the beauty of boyhood; Lampus, "shining," man in his prime; Filogeus, "loving earth," old age, and hence bent toward the earth. These horses, representing ignorance, belong to Apollo, "perditio," in contrast to the true sun, Christ, whose light signifies truth. The true sun Christ gave his son, the human race (Phaethon), the four virtues of temperance, prudence, fortitude, and justice, plus four ages to rule earthly life, but Phaethon, "quasi fanon dicitur, id est apparens," every day moves toward death. The etymology of Phaethon from *fanon,* Greek for "is appearing," physically extends the figure's meaning in a way ingeniously suited to Chaucer's purpose in defining poetry as illusion and fantasy, as he has throughout the *Hous of Fame* up to this point. The base word for those creatures is *fanontens,* or apparitions, because they appear to bound up from earth when sun unites with water. For the commentator on Boethius, the myth admirably contrasts the wisdom of Christ (the son/sun) with phantasms and illusions (the ignorance of Phaethon): the gloss ends with a Boethian moral stressing the value, once again, of wisdom.[40]

Chaucer, however, aware of the appearance of both Phaethon and Icarus together in the *Inferno,* and using Dante as he would any other medieval mythographer, as he did with Ganymede, constructs a parallel in the seventeenth canto between "Geffrey" and Dante, who is transported from one circle to another by the beast of fraud, Geryon. Although "Geffrey" in the *Hous of Fame* is not Ganymede, even if borne through the air by an eagle, but is an artist who succeeds where Phaethon and Icarus failed, at least temporarily and tentatively, as the Eagle in a sense reminds him, the Dantesque context with its emphasis on fraud and pejorative artifice suggests that he is self-deluded about his goals and his worth; that is, he knows he is not on his way to heaven to be ravished by Jupiter, like Ganymede, but the fact that he has not fallen yet, like Phaethon and Icarus, does not mean that he will not. Steering his middle course through the air, he is very much like Dante riding the beast Geryon through hell. What Chaucer the poet wants us to see is that "Geffrey" is a victim of his own illusions; he has been transported by his own fantasy, his desire for success, which is itself fraudulent. Chaucer thus conjoins Phaethon with Icarus in his poem as a gloss on his narrator "Geffrey." Aside from the mythological definition given to an experiential situation in Dante, the simile also glosses the significance of the spiritual journey and the failings of the hero himself.

The use of wings or chariot—a contrived or divine invention or machine normally used by gods and not available to humans—as a symbol suggests the power of art. When is art created in the service of God, and when against? When does art become fraud? This fine line is summed up by the descent from one circle to the next by Geryon, "foul image of fraud" (*sozza imagine di froda*), whose very being reflects artifice; he is tied to Phaethon and Icarus in their attempts to fly (circumvent nature and God through artifice) by Dante's epic simile of a predatory falcon.

> Come 'l falcon ch'è stato assai su l'ali,
> che sanza veder logoro o uccello
> fa dire al falconiere: "Ohmè, tu cali!",

discende lasso onde si mosse snello,
per cento rote, e da lunge si pone
dal suo meastro, disdegnoso e fello;
cosi ne puose al fondo Gerïone
al piè al piè della stagliata rocca
e, discarcate le nostre persone,
si dileguò come da corda cocca. (17.127–36, Dante, 1:220)

[As the falcon that has been long on the wing and without sight of
lure or bird makes the falconer cry: "Alack, thou stoopest!" descends
weary, with a hundred wheels, to where it set out swiftly, and
alights, angry and sullen, at a distance from its master, so Geryon set
us down at the bottom, close to the foot of the jagged rock, and,
relieved of our weight, vanished like an arrow from the string.]
(Dante, trans. 1:221)

Most significantly, the iconography of Geryon's appearance mirrors the
nature of fraud in its dependency on art or the artistic process—perhaps
the fraud of artifice—in the knots and embroidery of the imagery used in
17.10–27:

La faccia sua era faccia d'uom giusto,
tanto benigna avea di fuor la pelle,
e d'un serpente tutto l'altro fusto;
due branche avea pilose infin l'ascelle;
lo dosso e 'l petto e ambedue le coste
dipinti avea di nodi e di rotelle:
con più color, sommesse e sopraposte
non fer mai drappi Tartari nè Turchi,
nè fuor tai tele per Aragne imposte.
Come tal volta stanno a riva i burchi,
che parte sono in acqua e parte in terra,
e come là tra li Tedeschi lurchi
lo bivero s'assetta a far sua guerra,
così la fiera pessima si stava
su l'orlo che, di pietra, il sabbion serra.
Nel vano tutta sua coda guizzava,
torcendo in su la venenosa forca
ch'a guisa di scorpion la punta armava. (17.10–27, Dante, 1:214)

[His face was the face of a just man, so gracious was its outward
aspect, and all the rest was a serpent's trunk; he had two paws, hairy
to the armpits, and the back and breast and both the flanks were
painted with knots and circlets—Tartars or Turks never made stuffs
with more colours in ground and embroidery, nor were such webs

laid by Arachne on the loom. As boats sometimes lie at the shore, part in the water and part on land, and as there among the German gluttons the beaver settles itself to take its prey, so the vile brute lay on the rim that bounds the great sand with stone. All his tail was quivering in the void, twisting upwards the poisonous fork that armed the point like a scorpion's.] (Dante, trans. 1:215)

What is most devastating about this compressed portrait is that the chief adversary here is not some outside predator but an inner part of one-self—the pride of Arachne, like the pride of Adam and Eve, leads us back to the destructive pride of Phaethon and Icarus. Unfortunately, the ability to see oneself clearly is difficult, if not impossible. Here Dante piles image upon image, like Pelion upon Ossa: hirsute Geryon reminds us of the beast, and bestial natures beneath the natural, rational, state of human-kind; the serpent harks back to Eden, and the Fall of man. Arachne, a type of the artist, nevertheless in her pride attempted to compete with Minerva, and like Phaethon and Icarus lost. The predatory image of the spider (Arachne was transformed by Minerva into a spider), beaver, and scorpion will be reinforced later by that of the falcon: in an increasingly dangerous series of images—from nonlethal spider to lethal scorpion, most dangerous because deceptively small—Dante makes clear that fraud leads to spiri-tual, if not literal, death.

The special applicability of the figure of Geryon to Chaucer, given the fact that Geryon does not at all appear in the *Hous of Fame,* concerns what might be termed the self-deceit, the doubleness or two-headed nature of "Geffrey" borne by the Eagle. Dante's beast of fraud in the *Aeneid* names a winged three-bodied monster who took the oxen of Hercules; the mythog-raphies transform him into a three-headed king of Spain bested by Hercules in one labor, whose figurative importance was gradually transferred to Ca-cus, a monster Hercules battles in the succeeding labor. Although Dante uses the centaur Cacus in canto 25, on the seventh *bolgia,* of the thieves, nevertheless some of Cacus's fraudulence and evil remains with Geryon as fraud, in that Cacus comes to represent the idea of two-faced, or multi-form, evil clearly applicable to "Geffrey"'s self-delusion in this part of the *Hous of Fame.* Cacus, in Labor ten, having stolen the cattle of the sun from Hercules by dragging them into his cave backwards (to cover their tracks), is killed by Hercules to pacify Evander when Hercules, returning from Spain and the strife with Geryon, hears them mooing. For the literal recita-tion of the Geryon story, commentators on the *Aeneid* and then Boethius 4m7 rely on Servius's commentary on 8.190 and the First Vatican Mythog-rapher (myth 68), but for the figurative signification, of both Geryon and Cacus, they rely on Fulgentius in his *Expositio* on the *Aeneid* and the

Mitologiae 2.3, respectively. The K-Reviser of Remigius of Auxerre on Boethius explains that this son of Vulcan belching smoke derives his name Cacus from *kakos* in Greek, which means "evil," as evidenced from the dark smoke he belches, which is contrary to the light and hence the truth (Remigius, *Boeth.*, p. 76). Cacus's particular form of evil is deceitful and two-faced, *dupplex*: in leading away the cattle, he drags them so that he reverses their tracks; later he hides them in his cave so no one will see them. The two-faced nature of Cacus for the K-Reviser is truly more applicable to the three-headed Geryon: "Ideo et dupplex quod malitia multiformis sit, non simplex triplici etiam."

Geryon ferries Virgil and Dante downward from the Seventh Circle, where those lodge who were violent against God, to the Eighth Circle, where lodge those of the Fraudulent who were panderers or seducers. In an epic simile, Dante likens his own persona's fear (of the beast Geryon, of the steepness of the descent) to that of both Phaethon and Icarus at the moment they begin to fall (106ff.):

> Maggior paura non credo che fosse
> quando Fetòn abbandonò li freni,
> per che 'l ciel, come pare ancor, si cosse;
> nè quando Icaro misero le reni
> sentì spennar per la scaldata cera,
> gridando il padre a lui: "Mala via tieni!",
> che fu la mia, quando vidi ch'i'era
> nell'aere d'ogni parte, e vidi spenta
> ogni veduta fuor che della fera. (17.106–14, Dante, 1:219)

> [No greater fear, I think, had Phaeton when he let go the reins and the sky was scorched as it shows still, nor wretched Icarus when he felt his sides losing their wings by the melting wax and his father cried to him: "Thou takest the wrong way", than was mine when I saw that I was in the air on every side and saw everything lost to sight except the beast.] (Dante, trans. 1:218, 220)

Phaethon and Icarus, then, represent violence against a god, or a patriarchal authority figure such as their fathers: in the former's case, Phoebus; in the latter's case, Daedalus. Phaeton arrogantly demands the chariot from his father because he wishes to test his paternity (his wish itself is a questioning of authority), but he achieves his desire by means of fraud, according to Ovid's version of his story in the *Metamorphoses*, when he asks for a favor and only reveals what he wants after his father has promised it. Icarus, escaping from the labyrinth on wax wings with his father, similarly does not heed his warnings, flies too close to the sun, and melts his wings.

If Phaethon in a sense also expresses a violence against nature (Phoebus naturally guides the chariot in its diurnal course through the skies), then in contrast Icarus succumbs to the seduction of using artifice to be more than human—to rebel against those constraints that God has decreed belong to the human race.

Their fall because of pride mirrors the descent of Dante to the Malebolge by means of Geryon—fraud. By citing these references in canto 17, on violence against God, or a god, Dante identifies them as the most heinous of the three violent types (against others, oneself, and God, nature, and art). In cantos 15 and 16, Dante has met the sodomites, those who are violent against nature, and in canto 17, those whose usury perverts art. Therefore, in the spiritual architecture of the underworld, those who are violent against God are placed lowest of the group.

Dante descends with the help of Virgil and Geryon to understand both the underworld and himself. The process inverts the transportation by grace (Saint Lucia) in *Purgatorio* 9. If Phaethon and Icarus rely on their own wits to defy God/god (as do both the violent against God, nature, and art and also the fraudulent), then sin rests on pride; both of them attempted to ascend into the heavens (= God). Humility means that real understanding— of oneself, of the world—depends on someone or something other than oneself: God, or God's Providence, a descent into oneself (= underworld). The pilgrim Dante, frequently described in imagery as son to Virgil's parent, is not carelessly linked with the rebellious sons Phaethon and Icarus. The use of father and son images mirrors the relationship between Virgil as Reason and Dante as Will in the first two *cantiche.* In another sense, Virgil "fathers" Dante because he wrote a classical epic and represented the Empire just as Dante is writing a spiritual and medieval version of that same epic and represents the emergence of New Italy. Therefore, this passage appropriately presents art as a kind of fraud, extreme manipulation and control of others, through the description of Geryon. In contrast, Phaethon and Icarus, in their attempts to defraud or manipulate, ultimately manifest a lack of control, in that neither could control chariot or wings created by the father. Because the persona Dante often reflects in his own speech, posture, and behavior whatever sin is revealed in the sinners of the particular circle of hell through which he is passing, or the penance ascribed to the penitent of a particular terrace in purgatory, here, clearly, the fear that links him with Phaethon and Icarus (and inversely with Ganymede, who ascended rather than descended) also suggests that his ability as a poet may be linked as well with their fraud, their violence against nature, art, and God, and with their failure.

So also "Geffrey" descends (finally) to the House of Fame with the aid of the well-educated Eagle and his instructional fables of Icarus and Daedalus.

A Ganymede penetrated by wisdom and divine grace in the figure of Jove's Eagle, he is ready to enter heaven—or hell.

"Geffrey" as Dante's "Marcia"

In the third book, Apollo and his contest with Marsyas, and the final fixed image of Daedalus's labyrinth, typify the frustration of the artist ever attaining Paradise: if we are given Ariadne in book 1, abandoned by Theseus, in book 3 we are left with the labyrinth after Theseus's departure. The gods, chiefly Apollo and Aeolus, may appear successful, but the mythological poets, musicians, and inventors in this book, whether Marsyas, Chiron, Orpheus, or Daedalus (most borrowed, ironically, from Dante's *Paradiso*) pale—or fail—in comparison. Many such figures are fraudulent and presumptuous artists—again, types of "Geffrey." Further, Chaucer includes a series of successful mythological magicians, mostly female, such as Medea, Circe, Calypso, as if to suggest that art, like love, is mostly magic, illusion, fantasy, deceit; to them we might then add the augurs Theodomas and Misenus, among others (also linked with the *descensus artificii* as defined in Bernardus's commentary on the *Aeneid*). It is no accident that Juno's sublunary god Aeolus, ruler of winds, governs this book.

It is also no accident that "Geffrey" once again identifies with a victim whose gender is significant in the unfolding narrative: he allies himself with "Marcia," feminizing Dante's "Marsyas," who was reft of his own skin after he challenged Apollo to a musical competition and lost. Like the image of Ganymede, the ravished figure of "Marcia" suggests, on one level, the possibility of Chaucer's homosexuality, on another, his psychological identification with and insistence on female or feminized texts and textuality, and on yet another, his understanding of the passive, feminized role of the contemporary vernacular poet who must bear the weight of Latin tradition.

This third part, with the actual visit to the House of Fame and the whirling wicker house of Rumor, parallels Dante's Paradise—although, because the House of Fame literally occupies the air and not the translunary realm described in the *Paradiso*, it is *analogous* to the setting of Dante's third book, with its iconography indebted to Ovid's description of the palace of Rumor in the *Metamorphoses* 12.39–63 and 12.1588–97.[41] In terms of Chaucer's analogy, the "paradise" of the poem would be a "heaven" of the fame controlled by the goddess Juno ruling the sublunary realm. Apollo is here invoked (appropriately) to remind us of Dante's invocation at the opening of the *Paradiso*, but we might better consider the differences between the beginning of Dante's third *cantica* and Chaucer's third book.

At the opening of the *Paradiso,* Dante twice in the same passage alludes to Apollo's pursuit of Daphne, who was transformed into the laurel to save her from his embraces, and therefore to the meaning of that pursuit as the desire for fame—in his invocation of Apollo after an introductory section stressing the limitations of the mind to understand His light. Clearly the poet openly reflects his own quest for fame in writing the *Commedia.* Although Apollo—often identified *in bono* as the mythological equivalent of Christ in commentaries and interpreted by Fulgentius in the *Mitologiae* as wisdom (or science, or philosophy), in a tradition echoed by the Martianus commentators—also represents the goal of the contemplative life in the *Aeneid* commentaries, equivalent to Pallas Athena in the myth of the Judgment of Paris, in Dante and in Chaucer Apollo plays a different role. Superficially, Apollo would seem in both to be functioning in the Fulgentian role as god of poets or as tenth Muse, and therefore signifying a type of divine illumination, a role similar to the one he plays in the *Manciple's Tale.*[42] But Apollo is also glossed *in malo,* in the Ovid commentaries on *Metamorphoses* 1.474ff., as a type of those who glory in their virtues for his role in the pursuit of Daphne, or those who desire worldly glory—the exact Apollo myth used by both Dante and Chaucer. Bersuire sums up a long gloss on this myth by delineating the charms of Daphne, ultimately the human soul, pursued by Phoebus, the Devil:

> This worldly glory has several different parts, all desirable: head—that is the height of honor; arms—that is the embrace of love; belly—that is desire for pleasure; eyes—that is disposition for knowledge; hair—that is the prosperity of wealth. For these are pleasing to Phoebus—that is the vain-glorious who desire and seek them. But because of God's direction it happens that Daphne—that is the glory of the world—flees and despises such immoderate lovers. Ecclesiasticus 11:10: "If you pursue you will not overtake." Hugo says that this is the glorious property of glory, that it flees those who desire it and chooses those who despise it. (Bersuire, *Ovidius,* p. 41, trans. p. 138)

Dante underscores the ironic doubleness of his invocation to a god whose most positive incarnation suggests the *sapientia Dei* that should truly inform any depiction of Paradise, and whose most negative incarnation suggests the temptation of God's chief enemy, particularly as it concerns the pursuit of worldly glory by the poet who hopes his contribution will merit some earthly recognition.

The myth of Apollo's pursuit of Daphne frames two other Apollo myths, that of the two peaks of Parnassus, sacred to Apollo and the Muses, respectively, and that of Apollo's contest with foolish Marsyas. The doubleness is reinforced symbolically by the two peaks, of Apollo and of the Muses, from whom Dante specifically requests help, especially that of Apollo, because he has already invoked the aid of the Muses at the beginning of the *Purgatorio*:

> O buono Apollo, all'ultimo lavoro
> fammi del tuo valor sì fatto vaso,
> come dimandi a dar l'amato alloro.
> Infino a qui l'un giogo di Parnaso
> assai mi fu; ma or con amendue
> m'è uopo intrar nell'aringo rimaso.
> Entra nel petto mio, e spira tue
> sì come quando Marsïa traesti
> della vagina delle membra sue.
> O divina virtù, se mi ti presti
> tanto che l'ombra del beato regno
> segnata nel mio capo io manifesti,
> venir vedra' mi al tuo diletto legno,
> e coronarmi allor di quelle foglie
> che la matera e tu mi farai degno.
> Si rade volte, padre, se ne coglie
> per triunfare o cesare o poeta,
> colpa e vergogna dell'umane voglie,
> che parturir letizia in su la lieta
> delfica dietà dovria la fronda
> peneia, quando alcun di sè asseta.
> Poca favilla gran fiamma seconda:
> forse di retro a me con miglior voci
> si pregherà Cirra risponda. (1.13–36, Dante, 3:18, 20)

[O good Apollo, for the last labour make me such a vessel of thy power as thou requirest for the gift of thy loved laurel. Thus far the one peak of Parnassus has sufficed me, but now I have need of both [Cyrrha— one of two peaks of Parnassus, sacred to Apollo, as the other is to the Muses], entering on the arena that remains. Come into my breast and breathe there as when thou drewest Marsyas from the scabbard of his limbs. O power divine, if thou grant me so much of thyself that I may show forth the shadow of the blessed kingdom imprinted in my brain thou shalt see me come to thy chosen tree and crown myself then with those leaves of which the theme and thou will make me worthy. So seldom, father, are they gathered for triumph of Caesar or of poet— fault and shame of human wills—that the Peneian bough must beget gladness in the glad Delphic god when it makes any long for it. A great flame follows a little spark. Perhaps after me prayer will be made with better words so that Cyrrha may respond.] (Dante, trans. 3:19)

Most revealingly, Dante uses this Daphne myth to envelop the myth of the contest between divine Apollo and human Marsyas, a contest doomed from the start and representative of the poet's attempt to duplicate the Word of God in writing the *Paradiso*.[43] Assuming the role and posture of Marsyas, Dante here requests Apollo to use and inspire him—make him better by excoriating him, that is, to so inhabit Dante's skin that the resulting poetry will seem divine. The poet accordingly adopts a feminine position—note the use of the vessel (*vaso* [13]) and scabbard (*vagina* [21]) images—in relation to the masculine, swordlike power of God infusing and ravishing him. Because the "skin" (the human part of him) will therefore be removed, left behind, Dante appropriately returns to the figure of the laurel, to signal the victory he will then achieve over human flesh.

While Dante is to a large extent serious in pleading for God's help in composing the *Paradiso*, Chaucer is much more ironic and playful. Like Dante, he invokes Apollo's help, here to describe not Paradise but the House of Fame. He cites specifically Apollo's signification as "God of science and of lyght" (1091), promises to kiss the next laurel he sees because it is Apollo's tree (1107–8), and includes an untutored, Marsyas-like request to "helpe me to shewe now / That in myn hed ymarked ys" (1102–3). However, it is not until after he has resumed his dream narrative, described the outside of the House of Fame, and listed the "mynstralles / And gestiours that tellen tales" (1197–98) huddling in the *habitacles* on each of the pinnacles without, as well as those lesser pipers standing behind them, that he encounters Marsyas, "that loste her skyn," whom he renders as "Marcia" (1229). By separating Apollo and his laurel from Marsyas, Chaucer allows the reader to see "Geffrey"'s full self-deceptive folly in invoking the laurel-seeking Apollo, who pursued worldly glory: this pejorative god becomes a prototype for the vainglorious and presumptuous "Geffrey" who seeks the House of Fame. In addition, "Geffrey" resembles the lowly feminized satyr-musician "Marcia" because of his envy of Apollo (he competes with the god by writing poems), because he is not *doctus*, not learned (unlike the instructive Eagle we have just left): in his invocation, he has specifically asked for help in rhyming and other minor metrical matters: "But for the rym ys lyght and lewed, / Yit make hyt sumwhat agreable, / Though som vers fayle in a sillable; / And that I do no diligence / To shewe craft, but o sentence" (1096–1100).

But "Marcia" is the appropriate name also because he has assumed the feminine role at least figuratively (if not sexually) through his identifications with Dido and Ariadne in the process of reading the *Aeneid* and *Heroides* accounts and in the process of rewriting them. He has also more allegorically adopted that role in his posture as poet—whether abandoned by Eneas or Theseus on the Libyan desert, or rescued, like Ariadne, by the Eagle (hardly a Bacchus-like figure, however), or abducted, perhaps for rav-

ishment, as was Ganymede by the Jovian Eagle. He will once again be aban-
doned (or taken, or interrupted, let us say) at the end of the *Hous of Fame*.
By changing the name from Marsyas to Marcia, Chaucer emphasizes the
poet's Dantesque and feminine role in relation to Apollo (Bacchus, Jupiter,
and so forth): it is neither a scribal error, nor a misreading of the text.[44]

The hierarchy of magicians whom he meets outside the castle provides
a rich gloss on the nature of *ars poetica* as a *descensus artificii,* a descent
into the underworld of artifice that might include consultation with demons
or visions of the future. Of the minstrels and storytellers he hears, the
most distinguished are the classical harpers and musicians Orpheus (1203),
Orion (actually Arion [1205]), Chiron (1206, whom we have seen previ-
ously in Dante, *Purgatorio 9,* in an informative passage for book 2 of the
Hous of Fame), followed by the Briton bard Glascurion (1208). The lesser
pipers, playing on "cornemuse and shalemyes, / and many other maner
pipe" (1218–19), include Atiteris and Pseustis, piping shepherds, the latter
from Virgil's *Eclogues,* who with Alithia plays a central role in the school-
book mythography of the *Ecloga Theoduli* (1227–28), the satyr Marsyas
(1229), and others unnamed. They are succeeded by trumpeteers: the Tro-
jan Messenus (1243), the Old Testament Joab (1245), and the Theban augur
Theodomas (1246). Finally, jugglers, magicians, and *tregetours* (sleight-of-
hand artists) appear, including the classical mythological Medea (1271),
Circe, and Calypso (1272), the classical legendary Hermes Ballenus (1273),
and the New Testament Limote (Elymas) and Simon Magus (1274), as well
as the contemporary English Colle (1277).

Of the classical mythological figures, a dark, deceptive, and even self-
destructive similarity undercuts this "paradise" of fame. Orpheus descended
into the underworld to retrieve his lost wife Eurydice and then lost her
when he looked back; he was also torn apart by angry women, after he re-
turned to life on earth, because of his refusal to remarry. Even on the figu-
rative level he represents flawed artistry: as a poet he represents skill or
eloquence—from *oreaphone*—but without profound thought, or Eurydice,
from *profunda iudicatio.*[45] Chaucer in fact expressly notes his craft of harp
playing, that "sowned bothe wel and sharpe" (1202), and also his craftiness
(he plays "ful craftely" [1203]). Poet Arion seated next to Orpheus is favor-
ably mentioned in the Prologue to John Gower's *Confessio Amantis* (1053ff.)
as an ideal uniter of the three estates, the microcosm and the macrocosm,
because of his ability to bring predator and beast victim together, and mu-
sician Chiron, who reared Achilles, in Dante's *Purgatorio 9* represents the
analogue to educator Virgil in the image used to depict the transportation
of Dante through the gate of purgatory. But their poetry making is under-
cut by the "smale harpers" beneath them (1209), whose imitation is con-
strued as both apelike (1212; and therefore unthinking, bestial) and imita-
tive, counterfeit, "as craft countrefeteth kynde" (1213). And the female

magicians Medea, Circe, and Calypso (1271–72), according to the mytholog-
ical tradition, either destroy their male companions and partners or trans-
form them into beasts. In this sense, they ally with Dido, who, according
to the Third Vatican Mythographer, used sacred magic to obtain Aeneas's
love.[46] The augur Theodomas (Thiodamas [1243], also mentioned in the
Merchant's Tale 1720ff.), who in the *Thebaid* 10.552 blew his trumpet at
Thebes the midnight before the Argive attack on the city, is coupled in
1243 with Messenus (Misenus), trumpeter to Hector and Aeneas, who sig-
nifies praise or worldly glory in *Aeneid* commentaries (and whose use of a
trumpet allies him with Aeolus, who blows either the clarion of Clere
Laude or Sklaundre arbitrarily in response to the petitions of poets to
Fame).[47] Both suggest the often oracular nature of poetry and music (at
least for poets weaned on Macrobius's chapters on dreams and *narratio
fabulosa* early in the commentary on the *Somnium Scipionis*).

If these musicians and magicians surround the exterior of the castle
(iconographically suggesting the external—sensuous, physical—nature of
music and magic), then inside the House of Fame it is appropriate to find
famous epic poets—Homer, Virgil, Ovid, and then Claudian, the poets Vir-
gil and Ovid much glossed in schoolbook commentaries—standing atop
metal pillars. Primarily pillars of lead (common to Saturn, god of melan-
choly) or iron (common to Mars, god of war and discord), they again appro-
priately designate gods for epics that rehearse battles of human and divine
proportion (only Ovid stands upon a pillar of copper, perhaps because he is
"Venus clerk" [1487], and Claudian, who writes of hell and Pluto, upon a
pillar of sulfur; neither poet truly writes epic poems, even in the looser me-
dieval sense of the form that would label a work like the *Commedia* as
"epic"). Claudian—to whom Chaucer alludes by means of a reference to
Pluto and Proserpina, the subjects of his *De raptu Proserpinae*—because of
this work (which treats of the underworld governed by Pluto) reminds us
(again) of the *descensus ad inferos* common to so many epic poems (the
Odyssey and *Aeneid* among them, and the subject of Dante's *Inferno*);
these gods also appear in Dante, *Inferno* 9.44, and in Ovid, *Metamorphoses*
5.507–8. The epic heroes Hercules and Alexander (1413), about whom
these poets write, stand rightly upon the shoulders of Calliope, the Muse
of epic poetry, and the last in the series of nine Muses, according to the
Fulgentian topos.

Calliope appears in line 1400 as representative of the nine Muses (asso-
ciated with Apollo in Fulgentius, who is tenth and chief Muse in his role
as wisdom), singing harmonious songs—"hevenyssh melodye" (1395)—for
the goddess Fame. Her name is glossed in the Martianus commentaries by
Bernardus Silvestris (the fullest and most mainstream of all of the Mar-
tianus commentators) as meaning "optima vox" ("best voice"), that is, as
"celestial harmony." This celestial harmony is investigated appropriately

by philosophers (*philosophi* [3.75, p. 51]). Interestingly, Bernardus's succeeding discussion focuses on scientific principles of sound waves, in a mirror image of the subject matter of the Eagle's lecture in book 2 of the *Hous of Fame* (p. 51). In 3.288, in a discussion of *semina* (presumably the Stoic cosmic seed, part of the world soul), Bernardus notes that "It refers to Calliopea not with reference to the worldly [*ad mundanam*] but instead to the instrumental [*ad instrumentalem*]" (p. 58). Finally, in 10.294, in a discussion of the Muses, associated, respectively, with each of the planets, Bernardus repeats the etymology of Calliope as "optima vox" and adds that "Hec est in Mercurio, id est in eloquente." Mythographically, Calliope is the mother of Orpheus (from *Orea* and *phone*, "pleasing sound"). In short, she represents the cosmic "harmony of the spheres," tying in with the idea that book 3 is a "Paradise" analogous to Dante's in the *Commedia* and the transmitter of "Fame" (sound waves in book 2), as well as the divine source of human melody and poetry.

Further, as Muse of epic poetry, Calliope is especially important not only because of the prestige connected with this kind of poem but also because mythography developed in the Middle Ages primarily through glosses on epic poems. Indeed, Calliope appears before the narrator Fulgentius in the prologue to his *Mitologiae* to discuss the "lying fictions" of the pagans. Having advised the "homunculus" ("little man") Fulgentius to receive the teachings of the Muses in his home (she has heard that barbarians ban literature in their houses), Calliope warns him, "'If such recondite and mystical matters [*secretis misticisque rebus*] are to be vigorously studied, the full approval of the authorities must be sought; for no trifling must be pursued, whereby we find ourselves patching up correct styles of verse with some frivolous lines'" (p. 12, trans. p. 45).[48] So she endows herself with Philosofia and Urania to help with rhetorical matters and gives Fulgentius a mistress, Satyra (satire or comedy), for consolation. It is this genre to which many integumental (fabulous) poems belong in the Middle Ages, including the *Hous of Fame.*

King of the trumpeting augurs we have met earlier, Aeolus, too, is a musician, his music a gloss on, or arbitrary judgment of, the eight companies who appear before him (representing the eight spheres through which the descending soul must pass before being born?). First mentioned in book 1 and here termed "Eolus the god of wynde" (1571), he serves Fame, sister to Fortune, by helping to hear poets' petitions to her. This Thracian god's ability to control and bind the winds humorously reflects the poet's ability to shape and order the windy nature of the poems whose claim to immortality Aeolus must judge (1586–90). In responding to petitions, he appears to blow one of two clarions, either Clere Laude or Sklaundre (1571), to suggest the future life (or destruction) of poems, in a parody of his function as god of birth in Bernardus's commentary on the *Aeneid*, book 1. The parody reminds us, again, of the Augustinian definition of a written text as having a "body" (its *littera*) and a "soul" (its *sensus* or *sententia*):

We read that Aeolus is the god or king of winds who stirs up the sea with winds. By this we understand childbirth [*nativitatem pueri*] which is called Aeolus, as if *eonolus,* that is, the destruction of the real world [*seculi interitus*], since when a man is born, the world (that is, the life of the spirit dies, as long as it is oppressed by the heaviness of the flesh [*dum gravedine carnis oppressa*], descends from its divinity [*a divinitate sua descendit*], and assents to the passions of the flesh [*et libidini carnis consentit*]. ([Bern. Sil.] *Aen.,* pp. 4–5, trans. p. 7 [book 1])

This descent from divinity, for Bernardus on the *Aeneid,* aided by Aeolus, represents the astrological effect on the body:

This Aeolus stirs up winds, since a person's birth suffers disturbances of vices according to the constellations. Thus philosophy teaches that the birth of a child stirs up vices according to the constellations, that is, the powers of the stars. It calls 'constellations' those powers which the stars have when they are ascendant in their houses, which are called *abisides.* Thus, if a child's birth occurs in the constellation of Saturn (that is, while that star is ascendant in Cancer and far from other stars which inhibit its nature), then the vices of torpor, of laziness, and of negligence result. If, however, the birth occurs in the constellation of Mars, then the vices of ire, madness, and temerity result; if in the constellation of Venus, lust. Thus, Aeolus (that is, birth) brings forth winds (that is, the excitement of vice). With these he attacks the sea, the human body which is a deep whirlpool of ebbing and flowing humors. (Ibid.)[49]

After this "last judgment" of the best remains of poets, "Geffrey" is accosted by a "Frend" who asks him his purpose; when the "Frend" has determined that he is interested in learning "Somme newe tydynges" (1886), he directs him to the whirling house of wicker lodged in a valley outside, and under, the castle. It is this house to which our journeying Aeneas-poet "Geffrey" aspires, the equivalent of Italy, as the contemplative life, according to the three lives topos. The whirling house of wicker does move incessantly, like thought: "And ever mo, *as swyft as thought,* / This queynte hous aboute wente, / That never mo hyt stille stente" (1924–26; my emphasis). But, in its insubstantial twig-timbered cagelike structure, the house of wicker reflects iconographically the petty nature of rumor and gossip that provides the rough subject matter of the poet. So this large wicker house (sixty miles in length [1979]) is appropriately timbered with material "of no strengthe, / Yet hit is founded to endure / While that hit lyst to Aventure, / That is the *moder* of tydynges, / As the see of welles and of sprynges" (1980–84; my emphasis). It is, after all, *aventure* that "mothers," or gives birth to, "tidings," a crude oral version of the poetry that, specifically in romance, celebrates in fixed form that same *aventure*.

Chaucer's description of the birth of tidings is analogous to the Neoplatonic process of human birth in Bernardus's commentary on the *Aeneid*, over which the god Aeolus, with Juno's permission, rules. However, in the Neoplatonic schema described earlier, and derived most probably from the famous account in Macrobius's commentary on the *Somnium Scipionis*, the soul descends from the Milky Way through the fixed (eighth) sphere and down through the planetary spheres until it is incarcerated in the prison of human flesh; the equivalent beginning of the poem, however, is in the *aventure* that mothers the tidings, of which this whirling house of wicker is full in its *chirkynges* (1943) and workings. This designation seems appropriate in terms of the Neoplatonic descent of the soul at birth derived from the *Aeneid* commentaries from which Aeolus and Juno are taken, and also given the nature of *aventure* mothering tidings. But the gloss is also appropriate if we consider the future of the rumors, which fly directly out to Fame, who then names each of them and gives them a "duracioun" (2114; similar to a life span), after which they are blown about by Aeolus: "Wynged wondres faste fleen, / Twenty thousand in a route" (2118–19)—part of the winds that also apparently affect human birth and events (and, very like the lecherous souls of canto 5 of the *Inferno*, whirled about eternally like the passions that controlled them).

Termed *Domus Dedaly*, or *Laboryntus* (1920, 1921), "labyrinth," the house of wicker belonging to Daedalus suggests the prison created by the successful artificer introduced in part 2 through the reference to his son Icarus, a type of the failed artist. An appropriate figure in book 2 because of his creation of wings, which suggest to Bersuire contemplation as a means of ascent, here his "Domus" suggests the prison of mortality from which artists attempt to escape but which provides a model nevertheless for the lying and fictional portion of fabulous narrative, according to medieval literary theory espoused by Macrobius in the commentary on the *Somnium Scipionis*. As a "Domus" it also signifies the prison of the world, or sin, as we have previously seen in Bersuire's Ovid gloss, echoed and amplified by Holkot; it has been designed by a Daedalus who, according to Holkot, is the Devil. Such a prison is associated with work and the sins that result from work, including fear, negligence, and so on, deriving from the etymology of "labyrinth" from "labor intus, quia in egrediendo et in ingrediendo maximus labor fuit"; these sins can only be purged by confession and the process of penance.[50] To escape the labyrinth, unless one is Theseus, requires transcendence by means of contemplation ("Unde propter verecundiam sui generis excogitavit Dedalus labyrinthum, in quo Minotaurus vitam finivit")—or, as Holkot has declared elsewhere, by confession, "sed omnia pandit et ostendit nude et aperte." Whether such confession occurs to a priest or, for Chaucer, within art, it is escape from a prison housing a monster.

Chaucer's label of the "House of Daedalus" (1920) underscores the nature of the beast imprisoned within the labyrinth—the Minotaur, half-beast (or half-god), half-man, product of Pasiphaë's lust for Neptune—unless the monster has already been killed by Theseus and this hero will instead soon emerge. In a sense, the Minotaur within may be those worldly tidings or jangles, mothered not by Pasiphaë but by *aventure,* "Of werres, of pes, of mariages, / Of reste, of labour, of viages, / Of abood, of deeth, of lyf," continuing, for some twelve lines, until Chaucer concludes with the final tidings, "Of fyr, and of dyvers accident" (1961ff., 1976). Certainly this verbalized Minotaur summarizes all of human activity, not just passion, although the implicit passion of Pasiphaë, which resulted in the conception of the Minotaur, might indeed reflect backwards in this poem on the passion of Dido and Aeneas. The Minotaur in Robert Holkot's commentary on wisdom (212) represents a man in nature, a demon in pride, and a bull in lechery ("talis debet monstrosus reputari utpote qui est homo per naturam, demon per superbiam, et taurus per luxuriam"); so that it will not deprive citizens of life, this monstrous sinner either must be killed or imprisoned perpetually in the labyrinth ("monstrosus [*sic*] peccator occidi debet civiliter, ut videlicet vita civili privetur, vel in labyrintho perpetuo conservetur" [p. 697, in Allen, "Mythology," pp. 367–68]).

If one does not wish to escape the prison (by contemplation or confession), how does one then slay the Minotaur, if it results in *aventures,* the tidings of which will form the basis for further poems? Originally, the hero Theseus performed this task and emerged from the labyrinth by following Ariadne's advice, that is, by unwinding the ball of string as he descended. Theseus would be an appropriate hero to meet at this moment, a figure echoed in Aeneas, Hercules, and Orpheus, all of whom are mentioned as heroes in the poem, the subject of epic poems, and all of whom, like Theseus, descended into the underworld. "Geffrey," like Ariadne, rather than Dido, was abandoned on the beach at the end of the first book. Rescued by the Eagle, as Ariadne was by Bacchus, he may be looking for that Theseus (wisdom, in the commentaries) who seems to have abandoned him in a more figurative sense.

The question we are left with, at the end of the poem, then, pertains to "Geffrey"'s final vision, as he peers voyeuristically (but obediently, following the Eagle's instruction) into the windows of the Domus Dedaly at the folk passing along tidings from one to another. When the "man of gret auctorite" (2158) enters at the end of the poem, apparently in the great hall of the House of Rumor, is this Theseus, exemplar of wisdom, coming to quell

the Minotaur? Or is the poet who depends upon tidings as the stuff of po-
ems mistaking the personification of tidings, the Minotaur himself, for "a
man of gret auctorite"? Or is the man who appears another "frend," signi-
fying in reality what the mythological images of ravished women and raped
men have hidden, "Geffrey"'s acknowledgment of his own homosexuality?

I would argue that this poem is finished, that Chaucer deliberately wants
the question left open, and that there is no viable answer. The philosopher
would never identify the Minotaur as having great authority—nor would
the poet, who depends upon lying fictions, on pagan fables, on the tidings
of *aventures* to compose his *narratio fabulosa,* identify the "man of gret
auctorite" as Theseus, destined to kill what "Geffrey" most depends upon.

At the end of the *Hous of Fame,* then, "Geffrey" is back in the under-
world of Morpheus, plagued by phantoms and images, capable of being so
moved by the passionate tale of Dido that he identifies with her, and the
poem begins again, as fixed as the cyclical process that fuels the winds of
Aeolus with tidings, and which Juno's (and Fame's) chief god then uses to
blast the petitions of poets, eternal, incessant, and finite. The *Hous of Fame,*
a wondrously learned poetic joke, parodies nearly every extant epic com-
mentary tradition, from Virgil, to Boethius, to Ovid, and including even
Dante.

Chaucer may even intend this inconclusive ending to parallel that of
Dante's *Commedia,* when the poet sees God in a final, blinding, ineffable
vision, with God represented much more humbly by the "man of gret auc-
torite" (the archetypal poet?). In the course of its complex interweaving of
mythological references, the poem twists and distorts the mythography of
each source to fit into the overall fictional frame. Further, "Geffrey," as the
Fulgentian "homunculus," is no little man but the most grotesque image
imaginable of the poet in his bumbling ignorance, presumption, and portly
girth, a dreaming Alice in the Wonderland of poetic integument, a Dante
traversing the cosmos of poetic fame. Because both the Minotaur and The-
seus will resurface in Chaucer, in the Boethian tale told by the Knight on
the Canterbury pilgrimage, Chaucer does not intend for us to take his mytho-
graphic parody, this imitation of Dante's epic, this conjoining of Ovid with
Virgil, too seriously here. Or perhaps the "man of gret auctorite" "Geffrey"
meets here *is* Theseus, the Theseus who represents his own character in
another poem. Chaucer's self-irony, and his sense of humor, are in no other
poem as willful or as learned, as densely mythological, as opaque—or as full
of pagan wonders.

In addition to casting himself as poet in the guise of an abandoned Dido
in Carthage (or Ariadne on the beach) in the *Hous of Fame,* Chaucer identi-
fies himself as what appears to be a more conventional unhappy (but inap-
propriate) lover in other poems. The image of the lover out of harmony
with his surroundings, both social and natural, dominates many Middle

English lyrics (for example, "Foweles in the frith," "Lenten ys come with love to toune"); John Gower's Amans reflects this image at the opening of the *Confessio Amantis*. For Chaucer, *The Complaint of Mars*, "The Envoy a Scogan," and the *Parlement of Foules* similarly document an entire moment of interruption, alienation, and frustration for the human microcosm within the larger social and natural macrocosm. In each of these, Chaucer provides a philosophic context different from that of the scholastic and literary, which he favors in the more complex *Hous of Fame*, but equally gendered, and centered on the goddess Venus.

CHAPTER 3

Venus Contextualized
The Mythographic Authority of the Body in
The Parlement of Foules

The center of the *Parlement*—and the most vexing problem, in relation to its complex subject, love[1]—concerns the depiction of Venus in the temple within the garden, whose apparently negative description in lines 260–73 has engendered critical opprobrium. Lying on a golden bed (265) in a "prive corner" (260) of a "derk" place (263) and dallying with her porter Riches (261) "in disport" (260), Venus is "naked from the brest unto the hed" (269). The semiotics of the description reveal a lustful sign of aroused masculinity in the rising of the sun after Venus "lay to reste" (265)—"Til that the *hote sonne* gan to weste" (266; my emphasis). Similarly, Venus herself is vulnerable, accessible, without defense, as signified by her bound but uncontrolled golden hair: "Hyre gilte heres with a golden thred / Ibounden were, untressed as she lay" (267–68). In addition, the lower portion of her body was "wel kevered to my pay" (the narrator remarks facetiously), "Ryght with a subtyl coverchef of Valence— / Ther was no thikkere cloth of no defense" (271–73).

On the basis of the physicality of description in this passage, Venus has been identified as evil and lustful, or as double in nature, lustful and charitable. In a very influential interpretation based on this passage involving Venus, J. A. W. Bennett distinguishes her signification based on place—between the Temple of Venus dominated by sexual desire, viewed as corrupt in various sources, and the outside garden;[2] other British scholars, such as Derek S. Brewer, Derek Pearsall, and Elizabeth Salter, have supported this position.[3] Interpreting this scene more positively, several American scholars familiar with Alan of Lille and other Chartrian poets and philosophers, including Dorothy Bethurum Loomis,[4] Charles O. McDonald,[5] and George D. Economou,[6] have argued for a unified conception of Venus, or love, in the poem—as Chartrian, that is, derived from a system of philosophy associated with the twelfth-century School of Chartres and therefore Platonist, allegorical, and mediated by Nature. This view can be corroborated in large part by the sources used by Chaucer, although none of these scholars pushes the argument far enough to do so.

Such dualities and contrarieties some years ago convinced scholars that this poem lacked unity;[7] more recently, with the burgeoning of poststructuralist thought involving deconstructive strategies, this duality has been regarded, anachronistically, as itself Chaucer's point.[8] However, there exists a *tertium quid*: if the poem's multiple parts, its "medium," reflect its message, and its subject concerns "varying types of love experience," then to understand how those love experiences are linked—if they are—is to understand how the segments of the poem are linked, and therefore how Chaucer has unified the poem.[9]

Clearly, the issue of the "two Venuses" has much misled Chaucer scholars, for in fact Venus's various facets can be explained by the Chartrian allegories associated with her, whether in conjunction with her birth, her marriage and adulteries, or her children. The key to understanding Venus is the contextual allegory in which she appears with her mythological companions, whether father, husband, lovers, or sons. The signification, then, of Venus depends upon what the narrator learns from the tour of the garden and temple in which Venus appears with Priapus, Bacchus, and Ceres. The interrelated mythographic glosses on these figures view love as driven by the laws of nature and the need to reproduce—the concept of fertility, whether physical, sexual, or divine, and linked with the continuation of the species and the workings of the cosmos. The god Chaucer leaves out of his tableau—a god that in other mythographic contexts has rationalized this interrelationship from a spiritual and philosophical perspective—is Hymen, god of weddings.

Rarely is Venus associated with weddings, or Hymen as god of weddings, in Chaucer. Chaucer utilizes the figure of Venus over the course of his career, drawing on a variety of traditions, whether mythographic and scholastic, philosophical, astrological, or courtly. As we have just seen, Venus is parodied in the *Hous of Fame* as a literary figure associated with Fortune and glossed in the *Aeneid* commentaries; in the *Knight's Tale,* as we shall later see, Chaucer philosophizes her role in order to contextualize human desire within divine Providence. As a planet or star, Venus also is employed in the *Prologue to the Wife of Bath's Tale* and in the *Merchant's Tale* (discussed in chapters 5 and 6). And she appears in many guises, from many traditions but beginning with the courtly and most superficial and culminating in her planetary role as "fair chain of love," in the complex drama of *Troilus and Criseyde.*

In the love poems, some of them quite early, the goddess has her genesis. Chaucer's earliest Venus appears in a courtly context, the Valentine poem of the *Parlement* (dated in the *Riverside Chaucer* as late 1370s or early 1380s), but with the gods of natural fertility and regeneration, Priapus, Ceres, Bacchus. Thereafter, as goddess and star, the character Venus distresses her courtly lover Mars in the later Valentine poem of *The Com-*

plaint of Mars (dated as probably 1385), which serves both as a second draft of the *Parlement* and as an anticipation of the similar triangle of characters and views of love in the *Troilus*. She is also used as goddess, star, and philosophical concept in the much later epistolary "Envoy a Scogan" (dated as probably 1393), primarily to reflect the natural law of plenitude through her mythic association with Adonis.

It may come as a surprise in these poems to find that the goddess of love, from a mythographic perspective, is more anticourtly than courtly in her literary role — that she functions less as the mother of Aeneas or of Cupid than as the handmaiden of Nature. Chaucer's philosophic view of Venus in these love poems may be indebted to the twelfth-century Chartrian poet and philosopher often called "Bernardus Silvestris" for convenience, although his identity has been the subject of some dispute.[10] Possibly the same scholar whose commentary on the *Aeneid* informed the mythographic parody at work in the first section of the *Hous of Fame*, "Bernardus" also wrote a syncretistic commentary on Martianus Capella (with mythographic definitions found also in the works of many of his contemporaries). This commentary outlines not two but four equivocations for Venus (3.226–60, pp. 56–57), related through the Chartrian idea of the literal planet whose light guides the way and of the goddess as underdeputy of Nature, or the governor of sexual reproduction, earthly fertility, cosmic plurality.

First, as literal planet or star (*ad stellam*), Venus represents the mother of Aeneas as guiding light, leading him out of Troy and into exile; she is, according to "Bernardus," "Matre dea monstrante viam," "The goddess as mother showing the way" (from *Aeneid* 1.382; lines 228–34, pp. 56–57; 3.234). Second, as earthly beauty and natural fertility (*ad pulchritudinem terre*), Venus is born from Saturn's severed testicles, or from heat and moisture, Saturn's virility, because time governs these. Earthly beauty is therefore linked with autumn, a time of contraries, for this time of year is neither hot nor humid, "cum contrarias habeat naturas" (lines 235–41, p. 57). Third, as human carnal desire, or will (*ad voluptatem carnis*), companion of Ceres and Bacchus (Liber), she represents "Aphrodite" born from the severed testicles of Saturn cast into the sea; she is depicted naked either because desire is concealed minimally or because reason strips naked desire (lines 248–51, p. 57). Fourth, as the plurality of things (*ad pluralitatem rerum*), she signifies the plenitude of the four elements, the qualities of the seasons, the humors of the body, and the faculties of the soul and is called "Cipris," "because she is interpreted as a mixture" (lines 251–55, p. 57).

The relationship between Venus and Nature in all four significations is tightly interwoven: as goddess of love, the Chartrian Venus always associates with the principles of hierarchy and plenitude characterizing the Great Chain of Being, but frequently cheapened and demeaned by errant human choice. To this end, whatever interferes with Nature's program to regenerate and revitalize, be it selfishness, isolation, courtly love, homosexuality, or age, interferes also with that of Venus, whose role it is to trigger that process of regeneration.

Just this point is made in the twelfth-century *De planctu* of Alan of Lille. Venus, wife of Hymen and mother of Cupid, consorts with Antigamus (Anti-Marriage, whether in relationships involving homosexuality or courtly love, it is not clear which, but in either case, those from which sterility rather than procreation results), or Antigenius (Anti-Genius, the priest of Nature, god of human nature, and agent of sexual reproduction). As a consequence, Venus produces Jocus, an illegitimate son:

> To Dione, then, were given two sons, divided by differences in kind [*discrepantia generis disparati*], unlike [*dissimiles*] by law of their birth, dissimilar [*discrepantes*] in the marks of their qualities, ill-agreeing in the variance of their occupation. For Hymen, who is related to me by the bond of brotherhood from the same mother [*uterinae fraternitatis in affinis confinio*], and whom a stock of excellent worth produced, begot [*propagat*] to himself from Venus a son Cupid. But Antigamus, scurrilous and descended from a race of ignobility, by his adultery with Venus [*adulterando*] has lightly become the father of an illegitimate son, Mirth [*adulterinum filium jocum sibi joculatorie parentat*].... The former dwells by gleaming springs, silvery in white splendors; the latter continually frequents places cursed with perennial barrenness. The latter pitches his tent on the desert plain; the former is pleased with the wooded valley. (P. 56; col. 460)[11]

The metaphor of marriage sanctions the union of the former coupling: "A solemn marriage accounts for the birth of the former; a low and notorious concubinage [*divulgati concubinatus ... vulgaritus*] denounces the descent [*propaginem*] of the latter" (p. 56, col. 460). It is not, then, Venus who is responsible for such excesses, but the scurrilous, ignoble Antigamus, father of an illegitimate son, who "frequents places cursed with perennial barrenness" ("loca perenni ariditate damnata indefesse concelebrat" [p. 59, col. 460]).

Further, Venus bears a special relationship to Nature and Genius as gods of spiritual fertility in *De planctu*. Nature as "vicar of God" ("sui vicariam" [col. 453]) regenerates all things by stamping out copies from images of the original (she is portrayed as a coiner); her priest Genius, god of human nature, is responsible for maintaining the idea of humankind as rational animal, and ensuring human reproduction (he is depicted as a scribe with a pen and parchment);[12] Venus as her underdeputy ("operationis subvicariam" [col. 454]), along with her husband Hymen and son Cupid, actually forms the living things on earth. She metaphorically hammers out new individuals on her anvil; Nature also grants her a reed pen so that she might, "according to the rule of my orthography [*juxta meae orthographiae normulam*], trace the natures of things [*rerum genera figuraret*], and might not suffer the pen to stray [*divagari*] in the least measure possible from the path of proper description [*a propriae descriptionis semita*] into the by-track of false writing [*in falsigraphiae devio*]."[13] Chaucer of course, in the *Parlement*, acknowledges his indebtedness to the "Pleynt of Kynde" for "Aleyn"'s portrait of Nature, if not for his own portrait of Venus (line 316).

In the three courtly-love poems examined in this chapter, it is not Venus at fault but her deficient lover or husband or son who cannot accommodate feminized sexual desire as part of natural law. Chaucer tells the same anticourtly story three times, each time dependent upon Chartrian allegories of Venus as the subvicar of Nature and agent of the body, but each time differently. Of the two short poems, the *Complaint* paints an astrological allegory in which Venus's benevolent and ennobling effect cannot withstand Mars's corrupting *malitia* in his adultery; the "Envoy a Scogan" paints a psychological allegory in which the inability of the schoolmaster Scogan to love makes Venus cry as she did when her lover Adonis was slain by the boar, a hyperbolic allusion to the interruption of natural regeneration during winter, according to the Martianus commentaries. Finally, the "Envoy a Scogan," only rarely compared with the *Parlement*,[14] nevertheless glosses Venus in that earlier poem, for the *Parlement* depicts Venus as Genetrix through her mythographic relationship with Priapus, Bacchus, and Ceres.

What remains the same in each poem (once we understand the figure's multiple, Silvestran significations) is Venus; what changes slightly in each, as the poet's craft evolves over time, is the narrator, from the bumbling courtly lover Chaucer in the *Parlement*, to the knowledgeable bird singing the aubade in the *Complaint*, to the aging (53 years old), wise poet Chaucer in the "Envoy." What also changes is the errant lover: the persona and the self-centered, aristocratic eagles as courtly lovers in the *Parlement*, the selfish, complaining, myopic Mars, or the jibing but influential middle-aged, portly Scogan. In each case, the lover who affronts Venus affronts married love, love as a fair chain that binds together the universe and individuals through the accommodation of the body.

The Body of Venus in *The Complaint of Mars* and "Envoy a Scogan"

The first Silvestran signification of Venus—as star, mother goddess lighting the way—may appear to have dictated the role of the planetary Venus in *The Complaint of Mars*, but closer examination reveals the other significations masked by nonmythological guises. Mars's carnal desire unleashes *cupiditas*, in a critical portrait of the courtly lover corrupting married love

(Venus) through an adulterous affair with the spouse of Vulcan. In addition, the more philosophical and Chartrian principles of love—as natural plenitude and as *concordia*, the fair chain of love—emerge in the role of the bird as a foil for Venus singing the aubade at the opening.

In this poem, Chaucer conjoins the mythological and Ovidian tale of the affair of Venus and Mars with the astrological explanation of the motions of the planets Venus, Mars, and Mercury.[15] His purpose, once again, is to criticize the self-centeredness of courtly love—its inability to incorporate sexual desire into virtuous and charitable concern for the other; Chaucer may be using topical allegory (parallels between Mars and Venus and aristocratic lovers of his time),[16] but he also uses the gods as planets to comment through the devices of humor and irony upon the deficiencies of courtly love and its conventions.[17] Chaucer also gently corrects this view of love through the "voice" of the Valentine poem's initial speaker, the bird singing the aubade to the lovers at the beginning of the poem, who is parallel to the persona of Chaucer the narrator in the *Book of the Duchess*, the *Parlement*, and the *Troilus*.

The story of Mars and Venus has been characterized by Melvin Storm as chiefly the corruption of manly strength by lust, or "mollification of violence and belligerance by love," and serves as an index to the gods' appearance together in other Chaucerian poems. To the basic frame of the story of the adultery of Venus and Mars (from Ovid, *Metamorphoses* 4.171–89, when Vulcan surprises the lovers with his net, and the *Ars amatoria* 2.561–98),[18] Chaucer adds, in his complaint, the planets Venus, Mars, and Mercury as characters, understood in the light of the glosses of the astrologizing mythographers, such as Hyginus, especially on Venus and Mars.[19] To flesh out their characterization, Chaucer also provides mythographic glosses on the relationship of Venus and Mars, inspired by *Amores* 1.929–30 and Statius, *Thebaid* 3.269,[20] as well as by Plutarch, Fulgentius, Arnulf of Orleans, and Walter Map.[21]

Yet Chaucer reverses this misogynistic reading of Venus as lust in his treatment of the story, despite the critics who seem to want to blame her for the affair, by showing that Mars—astrologically speaking—corrupts Venus by means of his adultery, a paradigm found in a commentary on Macrobius by William of Conches. This twelfth-century Chartrian philosopher explains the astrological conjunction of Venus as "benivola stella," benevolent star, and Mars as "stella horribilis et malivola," malevolent star, expressed by means of his depiction as an adulterer committing adultery with her ("Item Mars fingitur fuisse adulter et adulterasse cum Venere") signifies his corrupting ("corrumpit") of her benevolence, "eius benivolentiam," that is, her virtue or strength, through "sua malitia," his "malice": *virtus corrupta libidine*, that is, Mars is said to "lie with her in adultery [*Mars dicitur eam adulterare*]."[22]

In the narrative or middle section (30–42) of *The Complaint of Mars*, the goddess Venus ennobles courtly Mars by means of their "marriage" of love:

And she hath take him in subjeccioun,
And as a maistresse taught him his lessoun,
Commaundynge him that nevere, in her servise,
He nere so bold no lover to dispise. (32–35)

Consequently, she forbids him jealousy, cruelty, boasting, tyranny, pride (36–38). Their binding of vows suggests the "marriage made in heaven" between Troilus and Criseyde. His binds him to "perpetuall obeisaunce" (47), hers, to "loven him for evere," unless, that is, "his trespas hyt desevere" (48–49).

Unfortunately, as in the *Troilus*, despite Venus's positive influence on Mars's character, his love for her degenerates into a much more earthy and even erotic "bond" ("Ther is no more but unto bed thei go" [74]) that leads to even more negative consequences. Once the "marriage" is consummated, Phoebus the sun (truth) frightens Venus from Mars into the safe arms of Mercury, eloquence: Mercury "salueth [Venus] and doth chere, / And her receyveth as his frend ful dere" (146–47). Although disillusioned Mars in his own *compleynt* in the third part of the poem concludes that love—*all* love—lasts "not the twynkelyng of an ye, / And somme han never joy til they be ded" (222–23) and he wishes to affix some cause for his suffering in love, yet Mars does not blame Venus. Venus, like the valuable Broche of Thebes desired by the avaricious, is not to blame for this "confusioun" (258), but instead, the maker of Venus, like the maker of the Broche—God. "And therfore in the worcher was the vice, / And in the covetour that was so nyce" (261–62), he declares, adding himself and his own concupiscence-of-the-eyes. Logically, he reasons that of the two, the *worcher* and the *covetour*, the former is far more culpable: it is not Venus's fault that he succumbed to her beauty and allowed her physical attributes to bedazzle his reasoning so that he could not see her shallow character, nor is it God's fault for creating this bedazzling beauty that leads to his "death." Far worse is his spiritual death—his blindness to his own pride, avarice, and lechery—than the physical death he imagines will overtake him in typical courtly fashion as a result of his suffering over loss of lady (266–71). The blindness of Mars anticipates that of Troilus in his Digression on Predestination, just as the seeming fickleness of Venus anticipates the conventional criticism of Criseyde after she leaves Troy and Troilus.

Note that Chaucer signals Mars's hostility to marriage and his negative influence on Venus, not only in the *Knight's Tale*, when Arcite's victory at the altar of Mars becomes an antithetical position to Palamon's victory at the altar of Venus, but also in the *Wife of Bath's Prologue*, wherein she identifies Mars and Venus as belonging to the same horoscope but with

Mars creating certain antipathies to marriage, and in the Man of Law's tale of Constance. The Man of Law addresses the "Crueel firmament" (295) whose "crowdyng" has so adjusted the heavens, at the beginning of this voyage, "That cruel Mars hath slayn this mariage" (301). The Man of Law exclaims against the clearly negative influence of Mars upon the voyage of Constance to marry the sultan: "Infortunate ascendent tortuous / Of which the lord is helplees falle, allas, / Out of his angle into the derkeste hous! / O Mars, o atazir, as in this cas!" (302–5). Astrologically, according to Walter Clyde Curry, this reference means that the horoscope is in Aries, Mars in *casus ab angulo,* and it is in Scorpio, the eighth house.[23] Luna is *cadent,* that is, just passing from Libra, the seventh house, into the unfavorable succeeding sign, which is Scorpio. And therefore, given the conjunction with malefic Mars, either the voyage or the marriage will lead to great misfortune.

In questioning God's plan and refusing to accept responsibility for his own actions, Mars reveals a pejorative dependency on fortune and fate; the poem assumes Boethian appositeness. For these lovers are also planets without free will to direct their astral paths; they are guided by the transmission of Providence through the translunary spheres. Mars was destined to meet Venus but did not have to fall in love with her, sleep with her, let her slip out the back door, or blame her beauty and God's craftsmanship for his work; his attitude and his values toward these events are his own to determine. At the end of this poem there is no transformed and understanding Troilus looking down from the eighth sphere and laughing; there remains only blind Mars immersed in his own "hevynesse" and complaining to knights, ladies, and all other courtly lovers to learn from his example and to be kind to one another. He has neither learned from his experience nor changed.

But the actual speaker of the poem—the bird—glosses Mars's complaint against love as itself incomplete and selfish. His role helps to explain the complicated tripartite structure of *The Complaint*—lyrical *prohemium,* dramatic narrative concerning Venus and Mars, and concluding didactic complaint by Mars—each with its own style and "voice." The bird's beginning aubade (1–28) is lyrical; the narrative in the second part (29–154) relates the story of Mars and Venus in highly dramatic fashion; the complaint of Mars (155–298) is moralistic and didactic. Of course the bird is singing the narrative " 'in my briddes wise' " (23) as well as the " 'sentence of the compleynt' " (24) made by "woful" Mars upon the departure of "fresshe Venus" (26) so that his voice actually predominates at the poem's end. Further, behind the bird is the poet Chaucer, inviting his audience to agree with the interpretation of love most convincing in the tale, in a brilliant display of authorial Providence set against the reader's literary free will.

In itself, neither bird nor planet is free to choose, for neither is human, but together as symbols of the sides of man they tug him first one way, then the other, striving for dominance, and aptly mirror the doubleness of humanity as both beast and angel. The bird, embodying the natural order, surprisingly celebrates supernatural and even cosmic love, just as the planets, also embodying the natural order, lament their too human and physical love. The calm wisdom of the bird who sings the aubade at the poem's beginning provides a dramatic contrast to Mars's bitter and woeful cynicism in the third section of the poem. The bird notes two possible reactions to the rising of the sun: the joy of the mated pairs of birds as obeisance offered to the light of God, and the fear of the adulterous lovers that they will be caught. This representative of the natural order advises other birds (and more human lovers) on Saint Valentine's Day to "cheseth yow your make" (17). Those who have already chosen he advises to "renoveleth your servyse. / Confermeth hyt perpetuely to dure, / And paciently taketh your aventure" (18–20). The perpetual bond of service to another exists in marriage intended for procreation in order to renew the natural world; the counsel is Macrobian, Boethian, Chartrian, and identical to that of Nature in the *Parlement*. The admonition to have patience in confronting the adversity brought by Fortune is both Stoic and Boethian: whatever ill luck befalls the lover will have less effect on him if he values the spiritual (virtue, wisdom) rather than the physical and material (sexual pleasure, wealth, status). The bird thus points to the microcosmic mated love as an ideal that the great "fair chain of love" reflects in macrocosm.

Criticism of the courtly lover voluntarily separated from his lady and therefore from any fruitful union (Venus)—and from the society in which he lives, whose community equally depends on concord—resurfaces in a very late Chaucerian poem whose dramatic tension similarly derives from a philosophically conceived moment of sexual and natural frustration. "Lenvoy de Chaucer a Scogan" (1393) is not just a begging poem requesting assistance from the royal court through a friend, as its literal meaning seems to suggest: Chaucer also asks his important friend Scogan, whose actions are apparently closely scrutinized by royal as well as divine observers, to remember him at court. Nor, given its topical situation involving a conventional courtly-love problem,[24] is it merely Chaucer's refusal to pacify the anger of his friend's lady. Once again, in the psychological drama of this epistle to Scogan, the lover's inability or refusal to love—to take part in a social ritual that might lead to marriage—is condemned. Its underlying level, however, concerns secular and religious means of circumventing the power of mutability and spiritual death.[25] The goddess of love signifies (through the mythological image of her tears) the regenerative power of natural plenitude and *concordia*.

In reality, this miniature *De planctu Naturae* complains not about homosexuality interfering with reproduction in married love, but instead about pride that results in psychological isolation from the lady, society, and ultimately nature and the cosmos. Chaucer's complaint concerns Scogan's disdain of love (Venus: "in blaspheme of the goddis" [15]), out of pride or recklessness, in saying things forbidden under "the lawe of love" (17). Apparently Scogan failed to serve his lady faithfully and, worse still, because she did not recognize his "distresse" (18), gave her up on *Michelmesse* (September 19, a quarter day). In defying Cupid with his "rebel word," Scogan, along with Chaucer, will "have neyther hurt ne cure" from the god (28) because the god will "nat with his arwes been ywroken / On the, ne me, ne noon of oure figure" (26–27)—not because of some mechanical failure, like a broken bow (which, it is clearly stated, it is not [25]), but because of "oure figure." Here, as in the *Troilus*, Cupid does not need to punish a defiant and proud lover like Scogan with an arrow from his bow to make him fall in love with a lady against his will because his figure—his shape and his nature, his "meaning"—is his own punishment and his own cure: the hefty Scogan will not now be able to consummate the union with the lady he no longer serves and will certainly not marry. Chaucer is included in this punishment for reasons developed in the next two stanzas: as Scogan's friend, he believes he is too fat and old to fall in love, marry, and procreate in obedience to the eternal law of love and nature.

As a result of Scogan's infraction of law, "Tobroken been the statutz hye in hevene / That creat were eternally to dure" (1–2): these "statutz" belong not to courtly love but to the law of Nature represented as a "fair chain of love" in Boethian terms, of which earthly love partakes. A hyperbole conveys the consequence of Scogan's courtly crime: because the gods, especially Venus, are so disturbed, she weeps a deluge of tears through heavy rains that fall upon the earth: "But now so wepith Venus in hir spere / That with hir teeres she wol drenche us here" (11–12). Thus, Scogan's infraction appropriately involves not just Cupid and the realm of courtly love, but also Venus as one of the "bryghte goddis sevene," or planets who "Mowe wepe and wayle, and passioun endure" (4). For this reason the flood of tears overreaches the fifth "sercle" (Venus's sphere, counting outward from the edge to the center), in violation of the "word eterne," to "drenche" us on earth. This word is God's, expressed through the law of Nature, which structures the cosmos and is broken now in consequence of man's breaking of God's word. The remainder of the poem explains why Scogan's fall from the lady's grace so shakes the entire universe. The moral is clear: in the envoy, Chaucer warns his friend, "loke thow never eft Love dyffye" (49).

Behind the drama of the poem looms the myth from which is drawn the hyperbole of Venus's tears threatening to drench us all. Commentaries on Martianus help to explain this puzzling exaggeration, actually based on a humorous turn to the myth of Venus and Adonis. Adonis's death is likened by Martin of Laon and John Scot, in commenting on Martianus, to the descent of the sun into the lower hemisphere during the advent of winter, which brings on Venus's tears as terrestrial rivers of plenty when she calls out for him in the forest—as if she were the source not only of all beauty but also of all abundance ("quasi Venere totam pulchritudinem et copiam lacrimarum fundente").[26] Elsewhere in Martianus commentaries—specifically by Remigius of Auxerre in the early tenth century and by the Florentine in the twelfth—Venus and Adonis are linked with other mythological couples whose union suggests cosmogonic harmony, including Isis and Osiris and Berecynthia and Attis.[27] Scogan's rebellion against courtly love—the laws of Cupid—severs him ultimately from Venus as much so as the departure of Adonis, the "sun." Note also that in a different mythographic tradition—that represented in the *Metamorphoses*—Adonis initially spurned Venus's advances out of pride, just as Scogan spurned the lady on the earthly level, and by analogy Venus on the heavenly level; Venus crying in the forest is echoed in this poem by the image of Chaucer decrying Scogan's offense from the isolation of his own "solitary wilderness."

The Chaucerian persona, like Scogan, here reasons mistakenly: he assumes that love must be only courtly and sexual and therefore confined to youth, that lovers must be gallant and attractive, not "hoor and rounde of shap" (31), and that poetry, especially courtly poetry, with such love as its subject, belongs only to the young poet ("thow wolt answere and saye, / 'Lo, olde Grisel lyst to ryme and playe!' " he imagines Scogan scoffing at his love poems in lines 34–35). Certainly Chaucer believes that he is too old to write about courtly love, whether on his own or on Scogan's behalf, as the fifth and sixth stanzas testify: "in no rym, dowteles, / Ne thynke I never of slep to wake my muse, / That rusteth in my shethe stille in pees" (37–39). His swordlike pen rusty from disuse reminds one of the phallic and explicitly unbroken Cupid's arrow of stanza four. The young poet can use his sword "in battle" as the young lover can his phallus, whether in writing about love or in heroically aiding other lovers by writing lyrics to ladies: "While I was yong, I put hir forth in prees" (40). But the old poet, like the old lover, in his decaying ability shares in that earthly mutability to which we are all prey: "But al shal passe that men prose or ryme; / Take every man hys turn, as for his tyme" (40–42).

The envoy fully reveals their errors about love and art and their need to atone for their crimes against Venus, Nature, and God. Chaucer warns against being "Forgete in solytarie wildernesse" (46)—possible consequences for Scogan's defiance of the God of Love and even God Himself, even though in his youth (at 32) he kneels "at the stremes hed / Of grace, of alle honour and worthynesse" (43–44), that is, at Windsor, the head of the Thames,[28] where he has in the past received the king's grace and may so again, especially if he does not offend ladies of the court. If not, if he rebels again, he may be destined to finish his life away from court, like old Chaucer, "In th'ende of which strem I am dul as ded" (45)—that is, at Greenwich, Chaucer's residence at the end of the Thames. The wilderness as a wasteland where natural life does not "fructify" is an appropriate place of exile for the lonely rebel against love, or the aging poet. In another sense, the wilderness can be seen as this earth on which humankind is forced to wander during life, in exile from Eden because of Adam and Eve's Fall.

To be forgotten, to be turned away from the brightness at court and spiritually turned away from God, leads to "dullness" and ultimately death, at least spiritual death. Chaucer clearly hopes his friend will help him be remembered at court—"Mynne thy frend" (48), he begs—revealing at the end of the poem the more selfish (and limited) purpose behind his ostensibly helpful advice to Scogan. The one kneeling and the one "dull as dead," the one at stream's head, at court, and the one at stream's end, in exile, cannot share fully in the vitality of that stream whose nature image suggests physical and sexual life. Both men, having avoided love courtly in nature for reasons of pride, shame, or age, do not sufficiently realize that the stream of grace, honor, or worthiness cannot "fructyfye" (48) or bring forth fruit if they do not themselves obey the law of God by reproducing their own kind through married love and their virtues through a higher form of love—the Augustinian concept of *caritas*. Because the persona Chaucer himself longs for grace and remembrance from the king and court, he views the "stream's" head and end too literally; he thus fails to understand the true nature of love and spiritual grace and the more awful possibilities inherent in the isolated "wilderness" he inhabits away from court.

To remember and to be remembered is kindness; to use reason and thereby learn how to "fructyfye," or renew himself, in virtue and in love, Chaucer thus ironically reminds Scogan of the varied nature of love through words that seem to beg for favor: "thenke on Tullius kyndenesse; / Mynne thy frend, there it may fructyfye" (47–48). This "kyndenesse" may refer to the natural law that enforced the reproduction of kind; it may also refer to the abstraction of kindness characteristic of the love and friendship described in Cicero's *De amicitia* (if the Tullius involved refers to Cicero).[29] Such "kyndenesse" on both levels can lead to a relationship that culminates in marriage rather than courtly love; further, love that transcends the sexual and approaches the love of neighbor is Christian. Such "fructification" is not sexual and transcends any limitation of age or physical attributes; and it applies as well to the poet Chaucer, friend of Scogan. In his case, the "fructification" will result in the writing of the tales of the Marriage Group after the period of lying fallow that culminates in the writing of this poem.[30]

The implicit biblical allusions—cosmic upheaval and suffering at the time of the Fall, the Flood, the fall of Scogan out of pride, his and Chaucer's exile to a solitary wilderness—place the courtly love infractions within a larger philosophic and religious context in which redemption can occur through recognition of and obedience to higher cosmic laws, specifically those of Cupid's mother, Venus, subvicar of Nature, the vicar of God. The concept of friendship and love transcends the game of courtly love, and Ciceronian "kyndenesse" serves as a classical and secular model for that Augustinian *caritas*, or "commune profyt," which Chaucer advocates throughout his works, especially in the *Parlement*.

The Bodies of Venus in the *Parlement*: Bacchus, Ceres, Hymen, and Priapus

The fourth Silvestran equivocation of Venus, of plenitude married to divine love, resulting in harmony, figures forth an aesthetic principle that controls the *Parlement*. "Bernardus," we recall, adapted the Martianus allegory to Chartrian purposes, one no doubt familiar as well to Alan in *De planctu Naturae*: Bacchus (Liber) begets Hymen from Venus, with Bacchus understood as divine love (*divinus amor*), and Hymen, god of marriage, as that *concordia* which results from the unification of plurality and the "fair chain of love" (lines 255–60, p. 57); that is, harmony, or concord, promotes consensus over differences—differences from Venus, consensus from Bacchus ("Unde diffinitur concordia dissentientium consensus. Dissensus ergo a Cipride, consensus a Baco" [259–60; *Mart.*, p. 57]). Appropriately, Venus appears in the *Parlement*'s garden scene with Bacchus, Ceres, Hymen, and Priapus in the fairly short passage (211–94) describing both the temple and the garden outside. Also outside the temple, under a tree beside a well (211), Cupid, his arrows sharpened and his bow at his feet, waits with his daughter Will for lovers-to-be. The *Parlement* truly focuses on all the forms of Venus, at that moment just before the world is regenerated in spring, before the various species are reproduced, before human lovers consummate their desire within marriage, before the Aeneas-like poet Chaucer, guided by the planetary Venus, completes his poem.

Such harmony resulting from plurality and dissonance may be seen as the fourth signification of Venus, as *concordia*. But Chaucer also uses the four Silvestran significations of Venus separately and structurally in the *Parlement*. The guiding star Cytherea—"thow blysful lady swete" (113)—functions as the planet Venus "showing the way" (but in Chaucer, "That with thy fyrbrond dauntest whom the lest" [114]). She manifests the way to "Aeneas" in his journey, that is, to the narrator Chaucer traversing the dream journey of the love vision ("And madest me this sweven for to mete"

[115]). In another sense, Cytherea shows the way to the artist as epic hero seeking help from the goddess as muse, or mother: "Be thow myn helpe in this, for thow mayst best! / As wisly as I sey the north-north-west, / Whan I began my sweven for to write, / So yif me myght to ryme, and endyte!" (116–19). Finally, Cytherea operates here as a "guiding light" for the Aeneas-like reader in that she supplies the connections for this apparently disconnected, tripartite puzzle. Note at the end of this section that after reading about heaven, hell, and earth in Cicero's *Somnium*, Chaucer literally requires a guiding light, perhaps from the bright planet Venus, to see, and more figuratively to understand what he has read about "commune profyt" (47) in order to write about Venus in his dream vision: "The day gan faylen, and the derke nyght, / That reveth bestes from here besynesse, / Berafte me my bok for lak of lyght" (85–87).

Most of the midsection of the poem, the garden scene with its problematic temple and the troubling depiction of Venus, can be explained through the second and third equivocations of Venus from "Bernardus"'s passage, as cosmic fertility and corporal desire. The two meanings are clearly linked in "Bernardus," for the severing of Saturn's testicles (a mythological version of the Fall from Paradise) caused the advent of autumn and then winter, whose deadening of the world's greenery and darkening of its light requires spring to regenerate the macrocosm. Similarly, desire in the microcosm triggers the regeneration of the human race, in despite of the penance of mortality incurred at the time of the Fall. The Chartrian gloss on the birth of Venus suggests a cosmological signification dependent upon fertility: the castration of Saturn by his son Jupiter led to the birth of Venus from his cut genitals, explained in the Macrobius commentary of "Bernardus"'s contemporary William of Conches as, first, the ripening of fruits by the warmth of the upper element, which makes them ready for harvesting, related to the regeneration of the earth, and second, the casting of the fruits into the sea, that is, the human belly, from which Venus or *luxuria* (sensual delight) is born, related to the microcosmic urge to regenerate, which is the mirror image of that in the macrocosm.[31]

In the *Parlement*, the undraped Venus hidden away in a dark corner, her son Cupid with his bow and arrow, and her companions Bacchus, Ceres, and Priapus explicitly suggest both microcosmic and macrocosmic versions of sexual desire leading normally to the regeneration of nature—the reparadising of the garden park. The references to Bacchus, "god of wyn" (275) who sits beside Ceres, "that doth of hunger boote" (276), stress their visceral and earthly and earthy connections. Amid the odor of the flowers ("The place yaf a thousand savours sote" [274]), these deities satisfy the hunger of the stomach as Venus does the desire of the sexual organs; thus Venus lies in the middle ("amyddes lay Cypride" [277]). Specifically, Bacchus is interpreted by the Chartrians as both the vine and the wine, because he is "twice-born," and interpreted more figuratively as the faculties of the human soul in the microcosm and as the World Soul; "Bernardus," in his Martianus commentary, also provides four related significations for him, as he has for Venus.[32] Ceres (the earth) is the mother of Proserpina (the moon), who was raped by Pluto (the shadow that sometimes obstructs the moon) in a myth glossed as a pagan version of the Fall in William's commentary on Macrobius: when Proserpina disappears or is obstructed, earthly growth fails.[33]

In Chaucer, Venus appears inside the temple with Ceres and Bacchus to symbolize the human body's role within the garden of Nature: the sexual organs—Priapus, Venus—are located in a dark corner of the body (= temple). Literally, the belly must be full to love—one must survive to reproduce, or, one must replenish the earth in order to enjoy its fruits, and so such body work prefaces the recreation of reproduction. Bacchus and Ceres are coupled in "Bernardus"'s long *integumentum* on the goddess—in the Martianus commentary, in the Terentian passage from *Eunuchus* 732, "'Sine Cerere' enim 'et Libero friget Venus'" ("'Without Ceres [bread],' indeed, 'and Liber [wine], Venus grows cold'").[34] Put in a more sophisticated and courtly way, good wine and fine food enhance romantic pursuits. These more practical interpretations of the Terentian quote are given a scientific and philosophical twist by "Bernardus" (3.241–48) when he notes that "Venus" is so called because she comes to all (from *venire*, to come, 3.247–48); thus her sea birth from Saturn's cast-off testicles, in the light of humors theory, represents the moist origin of all life (within the microcosm or macrocosm). In short, without the material stuff of earth, life (from the heavens) cannot occur: "Without Ceres and Liber, Venus grows cold."[35]

Venus and Bacchus, according to the fourth definition in "Bernardus" on Martianus, beget Hymen, god of weddings: the plenitude of the created world, structured and organized by the principle of hierarchy, creates the "fair chain of love," or the Great Chain of Being, familiar to us from Lucretius's *De rerum naturae*, Macrobius's commentary on the *Somnium Scipionis*, and Boethius's *De consolatione Philosophiae*. Bacchus also fathers Hymen in the Florentine commentary on Martianus Capella, which has been attributed, at least indirectly, to William of Conches: as the Anima Mundi, who has replenished the earthly orb ("qui replevit orbem terrarum"), he has generated divine love in each single thing ("et amorem divinum singulis generavit") (see William, *Macrob.*, p. 174 [fol. 50v]). Hymen as the natural power of propagation ("vim propagationis naturalem"), the Chartrian World Soul, or Spiritus Sanctus, inculcates the ardor of *caritas* in all things ("qui quendam caritatis ardorem omnibus rebus infundit") (in William, *Macrob.*, p. 174 [fol. 50v]).

Note, however, that Hymen is missing in the garden description. In his place, Chaucer substitutes the god Priapus (253), ready to begin the sexual act but depicted as solitary and "in sovereyn place" (254). Priapus in the Martianus commentaries occasionally plays a role related to that of Venus and Hymen. That Chaucer intends us to perceive the garland-bedecked Priapus (257–59) as a surrogate for Hymen, god of weddings, but frustrated at the moment of consummation, is clear from the details of his portrait.[36] Within the temple (full of sighs caused by the sorrows of Jealousy), Priapus is depicted "In swich aray as whan the asse hym shente / With cri by nighte, and with hys sceptre in honde" (255–56)—presumably with an erect penis. It is possible, given the fourteenth-century context, that Priapus's aroused moment has been blocked from consummation by the strictures of courtly love.

Priapus as a type of scarecrow defended his flowers against birds, thieves, and evildoers by holding a willow hook or sickle (rather than a scepter or a penis), according to Virgil's *Georgics* 4.109–11 and Ovid's *Metamorphoses* 14.640—and as a patron of fertility defended the human race against diminution because of his large virile member, in the eighth-century Berne scholia on the *Georgics*, and thereafter in glosses on the *Fasti* and in the mythographic compendia. He is called "lord of the Hellespont," according to Adanan the Scot, probable author of the scholia, because he was born in a town thereon and because he is believed to control all magic arts (this ability apparently accounts for the great size of his phallus); other commentators note that, because of this phallus, he was ejected from the Hellespont, no doubt by the husbands of admiring women.

Deified by mothers and called the god of gardens because of his fecundity,[37] Priapus, for the medieval commentators on Martianus, came to be associated with Hymen, *deus nuptiarum* (god of weddings), as the god of sexual intercourse (therefore, a type of Alanian Genius, priest of generation opposed in *De planctu* by Antigenius, or Antigamus). Because Hymen is *deus nuptiarum*, the rules of Hymen, Hymeneia, are marriage rites, just as Venus is associated with the *operae nuptiarum*, in Remigius's commentary on Martianus;[38] Priapus is also "deum nuptiarum quem nuptae colunt," the god of weddings whom nuptial rites cultivate (Remigius, *Mart.* 2:175 [par. 725, 363.22]). The phallic gifts of Priapus are celebrated by means of the sacrifice of an ass, according to medieval commentators, because in Ovid's *Fasti* the braying of Silenus's ass awoke Lotus during the Bacchic festivals at the moment Priapus was preparing to assault her sexually (1.391–458).[39] Although the *Fasti* was not well known in the Middle Ages, and was rarely commented upon, this particular passage concerning Priapus was frequently copied in the mythographic commentaries of others, especially on Martianus Capella and later in mythographic manuals. In the latter commentary tradition, Priapus joins Venus, Bacchus, and Ceres, as he does in the *Parlement*, and also Hymen, in the *Merchant's Tale*.

Priapus is linked in function with Bacchus in both the *Fasti* and *Georgics* passages: the incident involving Silenus's ass in the *Fasti* occurs during the triennial Greek festivals in honor of Bacchus; Priapus is identified as the minister of Liber Pater (or Bacchus) in the *Georgics* commentary of Servius, as repeated by the Second Vatican Mythographer (probably Remigius of Auxerre), "deus libidinis" because of his role in sacred rites ("sacris"): for (once again) "without Ceres and Liber, Venus grows cold" (without bread and wine, ardor cools).[40] Priapus is also known as Adonis, "the son of Venus who is cultivated [*colitur*] by females" (Bode, myth 38). This connection between Venus and Adonis-Priapus may have struck Chaucer when he came to write the "Envoy a Scogan" much later in his life.

In the *Parlement*, however, while Priapus's member (or the willow hook) remains erect ("hys sceptre in honde" [256]), he is nevertheless depicted alone (without Lotus or Silenus's ass); half-dressed Venus does not in fact consummate her dalliance with her porter, and so reproduction halts. This moment of delay, sexual frustration, suspension, matches neatly the conclusion of the debate among the birds — the formel's decision to postpone her choice of tercels for a year (fortunately, the other birds do choose mates on this Valentine's Day, despite the growing dark). We might imagine a cinematic continuation of the scene in the garden after the birds signal their harmony in the poem's concluding roundel — the separation of these personifications might end, Venus might join Bacchus and Ceres, Priapus might finish his work.

Chaucer the poet stresses the falsity of the perception of all love as contrarious and difficult, through the viewpoint of the dull and perplexed narrator who complains about courtly, cupidinous love in particular. As a type of Alanian Jocus or Antigamus primarily interested in the game of courtly love and therefore opposed to the goals of marriage, the "dul" narrator of the *Parlement* reveals his fundamental misunderstanding of the God of Love before his dream instructs him otherwise: it is "dredful joye alwey that slit so yerne: / Al this mene I by Love" (3–4); he offers "myrakles and his crewel yre. / There rede I wel he wol be lord and syre; / I dar nat seyn, his strokes been so sore" (11–13). This subjective construction of the God of Love anticipates the details of the portrait of Cupid outside the temple of Venus (212), who, with his daughter Wille (214), on the one hand articulates the faculty of the human will as it relates to desire (*cupiditas*); on the other, the iconography of the god suggests the false Cupid, or rather Alan's Jocus, product of Venus's adulterous union with Antigamus, and what Isidore (and later, Theodulf) denigrates as "daemon fornicationus."[41]

With his bow and arrows, Cupid, who lingers near a well (the well of Narcissus, *amor sui*, drawn from the *Roman*?), perhaps *has* fathered Wille, Voluptas (or Voluttade, according to Chaucer's source in the *Teseida*).[42] His bow and arrows may also represent the weapons of the winged, nude boy described by Theodulf of Orleans (750–820); to him we likened the other son of Venus, Eneas, of the *Hous of Fame,* in chapter 2. Theodulf's Cupid carries arrows and a bow, "deadly weapons and a torch," "Ferre arcum et pharetram, toxica tela, facem" (34), to signal the process of falling in love, in this scholar's influential Ovidian mythological poem "De libris quos legere solebam et qualiter fabulae poetarum a philosophis mystice pertractentur" ("The Books I Used to Read," pp. 168–71). But these implements allegorize in fact the destructive psychology of the predatory (Ovidian) lover; that is, "[Cupid's] depraved mind is symbolised by the quiver, his trickery by the bow, / the boy's arrows are poison and his torch is the ardour of love" ("Mens prava in pharetra, insidiae signantur in arcu, / Tela, puer, virus, fax tuus ardor, Amor") (p. 171 [37–38]).[43] Even Theodulf's description of the dangers of love, changeable, irrational, wicked, hurtful, seems to echo that of the narrator at the opening of Chaucer's *Parlement*:

> For what could be more changeable or fickle than lovers
>   whose minds wander and whose bodies are lascivious?
> Who can conceal the crimes passionately committed by Love [Amor]
>   whose evil deeds will always be exposed?
> Who with the coils of reason could bind
>   that boy who is uncontrollable and irrational?
> Who could see into the wicked darkness of his quiver
>   to count how many cruel weapons lie in the evil womb
> whence shoots its blow, poisoned and mingled with fire,
>   which soars, deals a deadly wound, burns, and hounds us on.
>   (39–48, p. 171)

Chaucer may have been drawn from this Isidorian description of the God of Love as a "demon of fornication" who "drags wretches down to the brutal purgatory of loose living" ("Est scleratus enim meochiae daemon et atrox, / Ad luxus miseros saeva barathra trahens" [49–50]; discussed in chapter 2) in this poem about himself suffering in the hell of courtly love. Just as Theodulf adapts the Virgilian *descensus ad inferos* to the descent of the lecherous wretches, Chaucer borrows Theodulf's adaptation of the two gates into the underworld for his own poem: the gate into the garden park of love and nature has that twofold inscription derived from Dante's *Inferno* to suggest that the way humans treat desire on earth will determine whether they enter "that blysful place / Of hertes hele and dedly woundes cure" (127–28), or else a sterile hell of barren trees, dried-up weirs, dominated by "Disdayn and Daunger" (136). In Chaucer's model for these two inscriptions, Theodulf transforms the god of desire, Cupid, into a *daemon*, a demon from hell. Cupid's appeal to the flesh, rather than to the soul, links him to the underworld with the false gate of ivory, of nightmares, and surface reality (the gate of the mouth), rather than with the true gate, the gate of horn that provides wise dreams (the gate of the eyes, but both gates adapted from *Aeneid* 6.893–96; Theodulf, 53–62, p. 171). If the god of desire had his way, Chaucer the narrator would pass through the false gate of ivory, and his "sweven" (118) would result as a nightmare. Fortunately for Chaucer, unlike Aeneas — who, we recall, was guided by his stellar mother Venus — the narrator passes through the true gate, of horn, of the *somnium* with its enigmatic figures, and, we hope, learns how to love wisely, in accordance with natural law.

These gates, of mouth and eye, are glossed by Theodulf's contemporaries, the first two Vatican Mythographers, more macrocosmically in terms of earthly fortune (the "underworld" of the sublunary realm), or the false gate of ivory through which Aeneas passes, and the translunary realm, or the true gate of horn.[44] For Macrobius in his exposition on dreams (1.3), true dreams are indeed conveyed from the heavens (the *oraculum* by an oracle, the *visio* as a prophetic vision, and the *somnium* as an enigmatic dream), as opposed to the nightmare (*insomnium*) sent by *manes* from the underworld and the *visum* or apparition (*phantasma*) of the *succubus*. In Chaucer's *Hous of Fame*, Theodulf's gloss that "Sleep has two doors, so poetry relates, / one bears the truth and the other falsehood" (53–54, p. 171) explains the dream visions sent by the infernal god of sleep, Morpheus (invoked by Chaucer at its beginning). The problem there involves the false gate of ivory (for Theodulf, the mouth) as a source for love poetry — no doubt the repository also of infernal pagan imagery drawn from classical sources. Here in the *Parlement* the problem may also be said to be "the eye" — Theodulf's true gate of horn — in that through the eye Cupid shoots the disarming arrow of libidinous love.

In Chaucer those who break the law, "likerous folk" (79), whirl around the earth in pain, unlike those who strive for "commune profit" (75), who enter heaven. These "likerous folk" resemble Theodulf's wretches dragged down by the "demon of fornication" to the "brutal purgatory of loose living." The dream-frame opening of the *Parlement* adapts to a medieval understanding the "hevene and helle / And erthe, and soules that therinne dwelle" (32–33) described in the fragmentary version of Cicero's *De re publica*, on the *Somnium Scipionis*, preserved in copies of Macrobius's commentary on the work.

In support of this gloss in the *Parlement*, the narrator's posture as frustrated courtly lover mirrors that of the separated, dying, unfortunate lovers painted on the temple walls in lines 281–92. These figures pervert the ideal of natural (that is, married, or procreative) love. They do so either by virtue of time wasted in serving "Dyane the chaste" ("Ful many a bowe ibroke heng on the wal" [281–82]), or because of excessive (libidinous, often adulterous) infatuation and fornication that led to death (293–94). Among

Diana's troupe are those who lost their virginity in disastrous affairs, including Calyxte and Athalante (286). Calyxte was transformed into a bear for sleeping with Jupiter, and Athalante first lost her chastity, to Meleager, and then lost Meleager. In the next, truncated, group (288–94), four mythological lovers are listed in Chaucer who, according to myth, die because of their love: Hercules (288) burns to death because he trusts Deianira's gift of a cape, which has been poisoned by his enemy Nestor; Biblis (289) unnaturally loves her brother and is turned into a fountain; Dido (289) fornicates with Aeneas and, after he abandons her, commits suicide; Thisbe and Piramus (289) die because of the limitations of their unconsummated but blind love—loving in the dark, so to speak. In this same catalog (288–94) appear another four mythological lovers who (outside the text) die for reasons related to love, often in wars engendered by passion: Paris (290) started the Trojan War by abducting Eleyne (Helen [291]), wife of Menelaus; Achilles (290), who loves Polyxena and who kills Hector in this same war, is killed by Paris; Silla (Scylla [292]) destroys her father Nisus and her country out of love for the Cretan king Minos.

In the drama of the third part of the poem, when the narrator recedes momentarily from the text, his alter ego is feminized (= naturalized, embodied) through the formel eagle who refuses to serve Venus or Cupid as courtly-love facilitators. She defers reproduction of kind by delaying her choice of suitors for one year in a bird parody of the frustrations brought on by the game of courtly love: "I wol not serve Venus ne Cupide, / Forsothe as yit, by no manere weye" (652–53; note that she identifies the ever-propagating sparrow as "Venus sone" in 351). Whether the narrator has understood the harmony that should derive from married love by poem's end is unclear. But the roundel sung by the chorus of birds in welcome of summer shaking off winter's storms suggests, by metonymy, the resolution of poem *and* lover's quandary—in "Bernardus"'s terms, Hymen, *concordia*, produced by Venus and Bacchus. It suggests also the bird singing an aubade in the *Complaint of Mars*.

In the *Parlement*, the narrator, like Theodulf, has been guided in his journey by books he likes to read ("On bokes rede I ofte, as I yow tolde" [16]). He also subscribes to the aphorism that "out of olde books, in good feyth, / Cometh al this new science that men lere" (24–25)—as if asking, Is there nothing new under the sun?—and he confesses, rather plaintively, by the last line of the poem that he will continue reading until "I shal mete som thyng for to fare / The bet" (698–99). Why he has not fully profited from what he has read remains unclear, although his complaint was also anticipated by Theodulf. The Carolingian scholar reads these pagan authors, "Although there are many frivolities in their words" (19), because "Plurima sub falso tegmine vera latent" (much truth lies hidden under a deceptive surface [20]). Perhaps Chaucer's narrator has been misled or confused by the frivolities he has encountered in his own dream vision.

Mendacious classical poetry that conceals truth as a concept informs medieval poetic, at least as understood by Theodulf and later, Chaucer in the *Parlement*. The Augustinian and Macrobian idea that truth hides beneath a false outer layer or cloak traditionally justifies reading classical poetry and reappears at every Renaissance, in the twelfth century in Hugh of St. Victor's *Didascalicon* and Alan of Lille's *De planctu Naturae*, in the fourteenth century in Italy in Dante, Petrarch, Boccaccio, Salutati, and in England in Chaucer, Gower, and others. Theodulf, in fact, seems to mark this unsettling effect as part of the nature of poetry rather than of philosophy, like the false gate of ivory rather than the true gate of horn, and therefore analogous to the underworld of our sublunary world: "Poets' writing is a vehicle for falsehood, philosophers' brings truth; / They transform the lies of poets into veracity" ("Falsa poetarum stilus affert, vera sophorum, / Falsa horum in verum vertere saepe solent" [21–22]). The subtitle of Theodulf's poem, "De libris quos legere solebam et qualiter fabulae poetarum a philosophis mystice pertractentur," is explained at the end. If poets hide mystical secrets in their fables, we can see how and why. Theodulf's poem contrasts the virtues of poetic figures and heroes — Proteus, Virgo, as Justice, the good Hercules versus the evil Cacus — so that a thousand lies are made manifest: "A thousand lies blatantly attempt to pervert the truth; / when it is plainly revealed, it returns in its previous beauty. / The untainted power of justice shines like a virgin, / the foulness of injustice cannot corrupt it" (25–28). For Theodulf, such figures are associated with (covered by) the smoke of the underworld: "Madness walks backwards, stepping like cunning thieves, / from its mouth belching foul smoke and denying what is right" (29–30).

In the model provided by Theodulf and imitated by Chaucer, the bookish love poet should emulate Aeneas in his heroic descent into the underworld by consulting the Sibyl (or even emulate Hercules against Cacus) — that is, understand the truth concealed by these underworld figures: "But forceful resolve [*Vis ... mentis*] exposes, destroys and crushes them / and so their wickedness is starkly revealed" (31–32). Like Theodulf, the Chaucerian narrator wishes to strip the new corn, the truth (also paradise, concord, the light of day) from old fields, falsity, lies, suffering (also hell, chaos, darkness). As Theodulf has suggested, the light shines through; Chaucer began his poem at night, in the dark, begging Cytherea for light to guide him in his journey. At the end, in the celebratory roundel of the birds, spring returns after winter's dark. From the cycle through the heavens, in the journey of Africanus through the heavens, to the musical circle, and harmony, of the birds' roundel — the answer to the questions voiced by the narrator at the beginning is that life continues, a new day dawns, and poetry marks the fact of new life. The journey *is*, "Th'assay so hard" (2), and, as Chaucer concludes, the journey will continue, without end: "and yit I rede alwey" (696), he will always keep reading, in the hope of faring better, "and thus to rede I nyl nat spare" (699). To cease journeying, to arrive, is to end life and hope: to become perfect is no longer to live. Therefore, "Now welcome, somer, with thy sonne softe," as the refrain goes.

Venus, the star Cytherea, has indeed offered her light for guidance at night in this dream and is matched by the strong truthful light of the sun and the promise of summer. The fourth Silvestran signification of Venus — as that concord binding different things, of plenitude harmoniously married to Hymen, divine love — truly dominates the imagery and structure of what has previously been considered a disjointed and disunified poem. The image of marriage — joining together with another to produce children — depends here upon the idea of fructification, fertility, the Silvestran Venus married to Hymen as god of weddings, in contrast to singleness and wilderness, and even in contrast to the courtly games of Cupid, or the sterility of homosexuality. If homosexuality becomes a metaphor for the disordered soul in Alan, then human nature's real role, Chaucer suggests, is to find that normal place in the universe, that part of nature that is defined as human — to be a rational animal. Finding this place in the natural order involves meshing with that "fair chain of love" — resolving discordances harmoniously.

The image of the alienated lover marked the beginning of this chapter, and with it the idea of interruption, disjunction, and frustration as it affects sexuality, reproduction of the species, and natural order. This image will be writ large in the mythological tapestry of the *Troilus*, but with much more devastating results. In the dream visions, Chaucer uses the mythographic tradition to gloss his own characters, that is, to explain their motivations. In the *Troilus*, wherein the mythological images and references move backward in time or forward, to foreshadow later narrative developments, they gloss the characters' actions often ironically, as in a commentary, like the epic digressions in *Beowulf*, and cast the Chaucerian narrator into the double role of tale-teller and scholiast.

PART 2

Mythographic Cross-Gendering in the *Troilus*

CHAPTER 4

The Narrator as Mythographic Glossator

The Rape of Criseyde

The romance of the *Troilus* represents Chaucer's first extended use of classical fable — fable that even Macrobius would have regarded as inappropriate — as a gloss on his own narrative, an approach to the narrative (like that to the narrator) that has received surprisingly little attention from scholars.[1] The first two lines of the poem proclaim that it plans "The double sorwe of Troilus to tellen," meaning Troilus's suffering before and after Criseyde grants him her favors, and also the suffering caused by the fall of Troilus's nation, Troy (if we note the "eye-rhymes" throughout between "Troilus," or "Troylus," and "Troy"), as a result of the rape of Helen.[2] In both cases, Chaucer uses mythographic glosses to mock the excessive suffering of the two-dimensional courtly lover Troilus and to remind his readers of the dark backdrop — rape, the imminent fall of Troy, death, destruction, conquest — against which this drama takes place. He also uses them to vindicate the choices made by Criseyde, to counter the mythographic and misogynistic perception of woman as a type of Eve, responsible for the fall of Troy and Troilus, a point Chaucer labors throughout the *Troilus* to refute by affixing responsibility for this complex sequence of events to the choices of various individuals and the power of the stars.

By the end of the romance, in the Epilogue, when the hero is brought to the eighth sphere after death, looks down on this "wrecched world," laughs at those mourning his death, and damns our "blynde lust" (5.1814–27), because of the accumulation of mythological comparisons, the pagan Troilus's moralized judgment (1807–69) seems more appropriate to the Christian narrator, who specifically denigrates the "payens corsed olde rites" (1849) and such "rascaille" (1853) as the gods Jove, Apollo, and Mars. And, despite the echoes in these lines and those following (1840–41) of Chaucer's short poem "Truth," Troilus's moralization (and the narrator's following exhortation to "yonge, fresshe folkes" to repair "hom fro worldly vanyte" to God [1838–39]) also seem out of keeping with the pagan background (thereafter "forth [Troilus] wente, shortly for to telle, / Ther as Mercurye sorted hym to dwelle" [1826–27]) and the characterization of the narrator as bumbling and Criseyde-struck.

Recent justifications for the Epilogue have, rather surprisingly, mostly ignored the pagan machinery per se as well as Chaucer's pointed dedication to John Gower, whose moralized and Christianized use of classical fable in the *Confessio Amantis* Chaucer surely admired and intended to honor by means of his dedication to Gower. Although critics find precedents in Dante, Boccaccio, Boethius, and Statius for Troilus's apotheosis,[3] only Chauncey Wood rationalizes the moralizing of the poem by invoking the Gower of *Vox clamantis* and thus similarly casting the poem as a warning to "New Troy."[4]

The judgmental narrator Chaucer who moralizes his own poem at the end can be perceived as mirroring the judged and judgmental Trojan hero who pauses in his afterlife journey at the eighth sphere. That Chaucer intends to identify the two is bolstered by literary and theological antecedents for apotheosized Troilus as a virtuous pagan[5] and for the Epilogue in a previously unacknowledged source (or parallel) in Dante's *Paradiso* 22:133ff.[6]

At first glance, the *contemptus mundi* of Troilus at this place in the cosmos draws attention more to its difference from Dante's passage than to its similarity. The eighth sphere has been identified superficially as that of the fixed stars and not of the empyrean region, and Troilus's guide is neither Saint Peter, the Virgin, nor even Beatrice. Also, while Troilus's laugh resembles Dante's smile, his markedly gloomy, even bitter, attitude contrasts with Dante's joyous acceptance of the world below. When Beatrice tells Dante, so near to final blessedness (*ultima salute'* [124]), that he should look down before going any farther to see how much she has put beneath his feet, he obeys: "With my sight I returned through every one of the seven spheres, and I saw this globe such that I smiled [*sorrisi*] at its paltry semblance; and that judgment [*consiglio*] which holds it for least I approve as best, and he whose thought is on other things may rightly be called just [*probo*]" (3:322 [3.22.133–38]).

The difference between the two passages, in fact, depends on the difference in religious faiths of the two heroes and therefore the final outcome of their own cosmic journeys: Dante will continue his journey upward, to God, but in contrast, pagan Troilus will be sent to a place that his guide Mercury deems appropriate (most likely in the underworld), "Ther as Mercurye sorted hym to dwelle" (1827). They share the eighth sphere, or the sphere of the fixed stars (the signs of the zodiac), as they look down upon the world, or upon the earth as an *under*world in the Ptolemaic cosmological system, because this sphere affixes individuality upon the soul as it descends through the planetary spheres into the body at the moment of birth and retracts it at the moment of death.[7] Appropriately, according to Macrobius's commentary on the *Somnium Scipionis*, the soul returns to the Milky Way, the place from which it has descended through the gate of Cancer, through a gate in the fixed stars, the gate of Capricorn (1.12.1–2).

Yet perhaps this difference in religious context can aid in answering the question of whether or not the narrator (if not Chaucer the poet) has violated the rules of medieval fabulous narrative by so explicitly (and so literally) stripping off this veil of pagan Troy and Troilus (or Troylus, as he is sometimes called), as a consequence of what might be read as his "seduction" by the (female) text—Criseyde—and in an attempt to control what Carolyn Dinshaw has termed female disorder. This chapter will show that the judging by and of Troilus—of Troilus's love, by the disapproving narrator at the end, and also by Troilus, about the God of Love, at the beginning—explains the reason for the Epilogue, the moralizing of the narrator, and the pagan machinery, and serves as a structural frame for the five books of the *Troilus* and their interrelated mythological invocations.

The macrocosmic invocation at the beginning of each of the five books is keyed to the specific book's mythological references, which reveal psychological insights into the principal characters. The pattern of mythological references works throughout to undercut the narrative and puncture the delusions or illusions of the central character(s). Further, the references foreshadow and anticipate (like the legendary and heroic digressions in *Beowulf* and other epics) the details of the history of the fall of Troy generally known to scholars and poets in the Middle Ages. As Chaucer critics have known for some time, the *Troilus* narrator, Dante-like, recounts the voyage of his protagonist Troilus through a literary cosmos structured similarly to that of the *Commedia*. Overlaying the five-part drama of this *Commedia* is a Boethian structure—the concept of medieval tragedy as the fall of a good man.[8] The poet specifically innovates by gathering various and varied references in clusters within each book as commentary on what might be regarded (from the mythographer's perspective) as the "scandalous" or "base" activities of his characters. But for humanist Chaucer, what these mythological references teach us (set within the overarching myth of the Judgment of Paris appropriated by the poem) is that, like Paris, Pandarus and Troilus are condemned, and Criseyde, like Helen, will be victimized. Each cluster is controlled within each book by the opening invocation of a Fury, Fate, Muse, or god within some specific cosmological situation, usually the underworld (books 1, 4), or the earth (books 2, 5) viewed morally as an underworld, or a heaven that ironically is hell (book 3). Thus, Thesiphone the Fury (book 1) matches the three Furies (book 4) for the two *Inferno* books, with Cleo the Muse of History (book 2) matched with the Parcae (Fates, book 5) for the two *Purgatorio* books, and with Venus the planet and Calliope the Muse of epic poetry designating the *Paradiso*.

Within this mythological context of judgment, the narrator's own seemingly inappropriate and judgmental Epilogue violating tone and narrative unity[9] is an inappropriate reader's response to the use of pagan materials within the poem—but follows from Chaucer's conscious use of a scholastic persona in parody of the normally moralistic mythographer. In all five books the narrator interweaves mythographic paradigms from the various scholastic traditions—Virgilian, Ovidian, Homeric, Statian—on which to set his characters acting and interacting, eventually in gendered and what might be termed "cross-gendered" ways. This cross-gendering of diverse mythological traditions, put in sexually figurative terms, attempts to "kis the steppes where as thow seest pace / Virgile, Ovide, Omer, Lucan, and Stace" (5.1791–92): the "kiss" a metonymy for the sexual relationship enjoyed by Criseyde and Troilus, the path of the great poets the narrative structures Chaucer uses to unify the poem. As Troilus is effeminized by courtly love, so Criseyde is emboldened and masculinized, becoming more and more powerful imagistically as the external situation diminishes and effaces her political, "real" power.

Specifically, in book 1 Troilus repeats the Virgilian myth of the Judgment of Paris in his choice of Venus (Criseyde) over Juno (fame) and Pallas Athena (wisdom); he is aided by Mercury (Pandarus), who also presided over the wedding of Peleus and Thetis, into whose celebration the uninvited Discord rolled the golden apple that caused the ensuing rivalry among the goddesses.

In book 2 a different Trojan myth frames the action: Criseyde, her heart barricaded against assault, learns from the song of Antigone, granddaughter of Laomedon who founded Troy, to love again and tear down her "walls." Unfortunately, Laomedon, who built Troy's walls to begin with, incurred the wrath of the god Neptune and the hero Hercules for refusing to pay them for their aid in building those walls; Antigone, whose lechery was well documented by the mythographers, therefore forecasts the treacherous future of Criseyde's relationship with Troilus, who will at the last minute refuse to aid her by allowing her to leave Troy. Finally, Janus, "god of entree," functions as patron of Pandarus in his so-called seduction of his niece in books 1 and 2. Chaucer overlays a variety of images from the underworld (specifically, Dante's *Inferno*) and from the overworld (Dante's gateway to the *Purgatorio*) to show Pandarus's two faces as Cerberus and as Saint Peter when he introduces Criseyde (compared with Philomela, Antigone, Ganymede) to two kinds of love. The "seduction" is seen as a mock rape, a ravishment, and hinges the first two books together through their infernal imagery.

The climactic third book of the *Troilus* traces the deeply ironic Ovidian metamorphosis of Venus from cosmic *genetrix*, at the beginning, to Venus *scelestis*, perversely enamored of her son Cupid at the end, in a macrocosmic parallel to the "marriage" of Criseyde to the puerile Troilus, a Chaucerian version of Shakespeare's "Venus and Adonis." Chaucer links various relationships between mothers and sons in this book to undercut the sexual and emotional wedding of the older Criseyde to the younger Troilus.

In the fourth book, underworld (Virgilian and Homeric) references define the earthly, temporal, and immature love of Troilus for Criseyde—beginning with the invocation of the Furies, and followed by references to Proserpina and Pluto, Orpheus and Eurydice, Minos, judge of the underworld, the three Fates, Atropos as a kind of death, Athamas in the Styx. Then, given Troilus's failure to act like a man, which in a perverse way psychologically "rapes" and victimizes Criseyde, Criseyde "changes" or metamorphoses, in an Ovidian sense, as witnessed in her reification (as incestuous Myrrha) and madness (as the imbalanced falsifier Athamas), and her promise to return, which has been sealed by her vows on the goddess of childbirth and the fickleness of the moon (Juno, goddess of childbirth; Lucina, Cynthia the moon).

In book 5, Criseyde, who has "mothered" Troilus, destroys their relationship when she cannot bear its loss; as a destructive mother, she takes on a new "son," Diomede, whose ancestor was Meleager, destroyed by his mother and the Fates. The (primarily Statian) mythological references in book 5 of the *Troilus* thus cover two very broad groupings, linked by the three Fates and Theban genealogy: in addition to the Diomede-Meleager connection, the cosmic underworld, which they are said to govern, both as pain and suffering in this world and as in the afterlife, therefore associated with death and the Wheel of Fortune, through the framing references to the Parcae in the invocation as well as to Ixion, Aesculapius, the Manes, and Alceste and to other signs of the turn of Fortune's Wheel (Zephirus, Ixion, Phaethon, Charybdis, Lathona) to show that Troilus/Troy must fall, having once subscribed to earthly values. The book ends with the final mock-Virgilian guide Mercury, cunning god of traders who leads the dead Troilus into the heavens, foil for the Trojans who do trade women—Helen, Criseyde, and, earlier, Hesione—an ironic emblem of eloquence and deceit in place of wisdom (Pallas Athena).

In each book, the invocation (or its absence) marks the mythographic "trace" of interest to Chaucer and therefore to his narrator as scholastic glossator. The literalism of the narrator's condemnation of paganism and his appeal to Christian authority, his condemning judgment of the stripped fable, and his very role as a foil for the pagan Troilus all mark him as the imprudent philosopher criticized by Macrobius and later by William of Conches commenting on Macrobius. This role of the narrator has not received critical recognition even by A. J. Minnis, who views the narrator as a "compiling historian" rather than a "prudent (or imprudent) philosopher": "Chaucer's narrator professes to be dependent on *auctores*, and so he cannot be praised or blamed for what (it is implied) he is merely repeating.... An historian must allow the pagans to think and act as pagans—a perfectly acceptable procedure providing one's own Christian standards are asserted." This approach, dependent on the views of medieval historians like

Ralph Higden and John Trevisa, unfortunately ignores the role of medieval literary theory in the poem and the probably ironic use of the narrator's literalism in accounting for the Chaucer persona's skewed perceptions and critical opaqueness.[10]

Is Chaucer's Macrobian narrator guilty of imprudence in openly revealing, and reveling in, Criseyde's two sexual encounters, one beginning within her uncle's house and the other within her father's own tent? Macrobius's "prudent philosopher" shuns the use of fables detailing immoral activities — indeed, these are excluded from his concept of fabulous narrative altogether because "the presentation of the plot involves matters that are base and unworthy of divinities and are monstrosities of some sort (as, for example, gods caught in adultery, Saturn cutting off the privy parts of his father Caelus and himself thrown into chains by his son and successor)" (1.2.11). If the wise philosopher should openly reveal these holy truths or "secrets of Nature" (as did Numenius when he interpreted the Eleusinian mysteries), he would debase and offend the gods (1.2.19) and allow vulgar and ignorant men to see Nature "openly naked" (1.2.17). Apparently narrator Chaucer is guilty of such a revelation largely because as a "character" separate from the poet he allows himself to be seduced by the text he relays. About the gods' adulteries, William of Conches glosses Macrobius 1.2: "the words are base [*turpia*], and yet by that adultery [*adulterium*] something honorable and beautiful must indeed be meant: as can be read in the case of Jupiter's adulteries with Cybele, and Semele, and other things of this kind which will be expounded in due course" (William, *Macrob.* 7a, p. 71). As long as these truths are not interpreted literally, they remain "honorable and beautiful truths" for William, even if his interpretations center primarily on the natural or physical truths about the universe (as we have seen, in relation to Jupiter as ether, Juno as air, Semele as earth, and the twice-born Bacchus). Chaucer's narrator, blind to his own desires, forgets himself as a "historian" and philosopher and reads the female text literally, insensitively. The mythological shorthand in that text — the veil — provides a very different, and more gendered, key to the truth in what is more Criseyde's story than Troilus's. Whatever the narrator's judgmental literalism, the actual mythological images warn of danger at the moment of the central characters' "fall," so to speak, as it occurs in book 1 in relation to Troilus and in book 2 in relation to Criseyde, and place the greater responsibility for what happens on the shoulders of the Trojan prince.

Actually, *two* great myths warn the reader, if not Troilus, of the danger ahead. First, Dante descends into the underworld, which becomes a model for Troilus's fall — into sexual love; second, Paris judges the three goddesses, which becomes a model for Troilus's own errant decision — to love Criseyde. The two myths converge in the prototype of the initiation and consequences of the Trojan War—the monomyth of the *Aeneid*. Dante's descent, of course, itself expands Aeneas's descent into the underworld in the sixth book of the *Aeneid*, which came to dominate allegorical interpretations of the epic early on, in the twelfth century, as a descent into the underworld that occurs at birth, in vice and virtue, and through magic arts, and later, as a journey of life represented by three stages paralleling the three lives. Finally, Troilus's commitment to the God of Love duplicates the Judgment of Paris, in which the golden apple was awarded to Venus— thereby precipitating the rape of Helen, the Trojan War, and ultimately the fall of Troy in an event analogous to the Fall of man in classical terms, as we are reminded by means of the symbol of the apple.[11]

Throughout the poem, Chaucer compares Troilus with several mythological figures who descend into underworlds or who suffer fatal falls. Troilus is Ixion, whose lust for Juno spins him on an ever-whirling wheel (for Troilus, the Wheel of Fortune), and also Orpheus, who descended into the underworld to retrieve his wife Eurydice but looked back, disobeying the infernal judge's injunction, and in his excessive love for temporal things lost her a second time. He is also Phaethon, whose lack of understanding led to his fall. And, of course, he is like his brother Paris, whose faulty judgment led him to betray Oenone and abduct Helen—and to choose Venus as most beautiful instead of Juno or Pallas Athena.

Book 1, The "Judgment of Troilus" and Mercurial Pandarus

The "Judgment of Troilus" links the central themes of the overall journey of Troilus through this world and in the afterlife, although of course it is the first book in which Troilus "judges" the God of Love and "chooses" Criseyde. The guide and god Mercury unites both of these different levels: within pagan mythology he serves as the messenger of the gods (like the Greek Hermes and the Egyptian Thoth) and therefore as an appropriate guide for the soul of Troilus traversing the underworld after death. As the "divine go-between," *internuntius furiatrinusque deus* (Fulg. *Mit.* 1.18), he is "said to pass through both realms, the upper and the lower [*superna atque inferna*], because now he rushes aloft through the winds, now plunging down he seeks out the lower world [*inferna*] through storms," his name Hermes in Latin meaning *ermeneuse*, or "translating"—an analogue for the earthly go-between Pandarus in the other world (trans. p. 30).[12] In addition, within the myth of the Judgment of Paris, Mercury originally led the three goddesses Venus, Juno, and Pallas Athena to the wedding of Peleus and Thetis, to which Discord had not been invited and into the midst of whose festivities she threw the golden ball that confused Paris enough to choose Venus (and the promise of loving the most beautiful woman in the world) instead of Pallas. Paris's poor judgment, unfortunately, led to the fall of Troy. Therefore, Mercury's appearance at the poem's end provides a kind of closure for Chaucer's version of the story in the *Troilus*.

But within the mythographic tradition the god Mercury also stands for two contradictory values that typify the double levels of much of this poem. On the one hand, in Fulgentius's commentary on the *Aeneid* (*Expos.* 16) he signifies the *deus ingenii*, the god of memory, or imagination, even the intellect, who appears when youth quits the straits of passion (as does Aeneas in book 4 when he gives up Dido). This faculty is lacking in the irrational, love-dazzled characters of Troilus (until he damns lust in the Epilogue) and Criseyde (until her swoon in book 4) and therefore suggests a goal within the moral journey of Troilus. On the other hand, in Fulgentius's *Mitologiae* 1.18 he signifies deceit, theft, and cunning, and, as the god of traders and merchants, reminds us that the Trojans traded Criseyde for a traitor—Antenor—which led to the ruse of the Trojan horse and the downfall of Troy. In this sense, too, Mercury continues the role of cunning Pandarus, whose stratagems win Criseyde for Troilus.

In book 1 the mythological references all in some way forecast doom or underline the infernal spiritual associations of Troilus's choice. The underworld references, keyed to the invocation of the Fury Thesiphone (line 6), include the reference to the proud Troilus as a type of Tityus (786), who falls—into vice, into the underworld—and to the go-between Pandarus as a type of the guardian Cerberus (859), who opens the gate to hell.

Surely Thesiphone fosters the "Discord" that will similarly mar the "Judgment" of Troilus in the first book. An inhabitant of Pluto's underworld, the Fury Thesiphone, who weeps as Chaucer writes, is invoked at the beginning of book 1 for aid in shaping this "woful vers" (6–7). This scanty characterization nevertheless echoes her Fulgentian signification as the second stage in contention, "bursting forth into words" (*in uoco erumpere; Mit.* 1.7). The three Furies—Alecto, Tisiphone, and Megaera—together signify the process of sinning. They are leaders of the vices that attack the New Man in Alan of Lille's *Anticlaudianus*; in Bernardus Silvestris's commentary on the *Aeneid* 6.273–81, they are glossed as stages in sinning. The daughters of Night (ignorance of spirit) and Acheron (Sorrow), they represent disturbed thought (Alecto), voice applied to wicked thought (Tisiphone), and wicked deed (Megaera).[13] Tisiphone alone, however, represents that intermediate stage prior to action, when wicked thoughts (associated with libido in Nicholas Trevet's glosses on Boethius, according to D. W. Robertson, Jr., p. 474) have been felt and voiced but not acted upon. Her specialized function characterizes Troilus's situation in this book, where his wicked thoughts are given voice during the debate between Pandarus and Troilus (but perhaps articulated by Pandarus rather than Troilus). Note also the reference to the damage to lovers by wicked tongues mentioned in the narrator's bidding prayer (38–39). Such a fear of wicked tongues motivates Criseyde in all of her decisions throughout the poem—the fear, in fact, of Thesiphone, a Fury who pursues her endlessly.

Although Chaucer generally shies away from heavy moralizing, he may be doing it here under mythological cover for ironic purposes, to show how inappropriately Troilus chooses and why the narrator judges so severely. Troilus's courtly love for Criseyde, like Tityus's for Latona and Orpheus's for Eurydice, valorizes temporal good, therefore characterizing his love as a descent into the hell of suffering lovers. Temporal love, for the narrator, can be understood as "infernal" if one accepts the Neoplatonic designation of this earth as an underworld, that is, one marking Pluto's realm. According to Pandarus, Troilus suffers "As sharp as doth he Ticius in helle, / Whos stomak foughles tiren evere moo / That hightyn volturis, as bokes telle" (1.786–88). The infernal sufferings of the giant Tityus as punishment for his desire for Latona comes from Boethius's *Consolatio* 3m12.41–43—on Orpheus's descent in pursuit of Eurydice—and provides a clear gloss on Troilus's moral position at this moment.

In Chaucer, Tityus's "stomak" must endure the eternal torture of the vulture's beak (785–88). The more usual site of punishment is the liver, identified in the Remigian glosses on Boethius 3m12 as appropriate because of his lecherous attempt to rape Latona, mother of Diana and Apollo. That this specialized site was intended is reinforced by Remigius's Servian gloss on *Aeneid* 6.596 to explain that the liver is the seat of lechery, as the spleen is the seat of laughter and the gall is the seat of anger.[14] The love from which Troilus suffers is, if not lecherous, at least unfortunately physical in its focus. Chaucer may have changed the liver to "stomak" to heighten the irony of Troilus's seeming anxiety and impotence in the consummation scene of the third book (for example, 3.1247–53, 1531, 1546–47, 1650–52).

There is at least a double significance in Chaucer's use of the underworld in book 1 because of the fourfold interpretation of such descents in medieval commentary, outlined in chapter 1 of this study. Bernardus Silvestris, as we have witnessed in his commentary on Aeneas's descent into the underworld (*Aeneid* 6), and William of Conches, in his comment on Orpheus's descent into the underworld to retrieve Eurydice in 3m12, both describe these four as natural, virtuous, vicious, and artificial, of which this descent might be described as vicious, *into* vice.[15] And in general, so does Remigius's comment on 3m12 of the *Consolatio* that the hell to which Orpheus looked back represented earthly vice in the soul, as opposed to "sovereign day" (the truth of God).[16] Orpheus is bound to earth by "chains," which Boethius implies are earthly cupidity. To look back, for Orpheus or Troilus, means losing what might be termed, on the psychological level, the kingdom of God—the beloved.

The go-between Pandarus, in a similar ironic and inadvertent reference at the end of the book, allies himself with the gatekeeper of hell, Cerberus, because of his immoral willingness to offer Criseyde to his friend. The guardian for the gate by whom Pandarus swears is no authority at all, but the changeable, fickle nature of the underworld known as earthly life. Attesting to his good intentions, Pandarus swears by Cerberus ("To Cerberus yn helle ay be I bounde") that if Criseyde were his sister, she would be Troilus's, "to-morwe" (859–61). The oath defines the nature of the cosmos to which Troilus's friend will introduce both of the lovers; that is, the kind of love Pandarus means to suggest, a paradise of joy, by romance's end becomes hell. Pandarus's invocation of the three-headed monster as guarantor of his sincerity should have revealed the true nature of the love that he promises. Its slippery ambiguity harks back to the doubleness of the two-gated garden of love in *Parlement of Foules*. The only protection against Cerberus, according to the Orpheus myth, is the sweetness of the poet's singing, which momentarily mesmerizes the monster. Glossed by Bersuire as the new song of Christ, used against human mortality ("Cerberus," from *creosboros*, "flesh-eater," *carnem vorans*), the weapon assumes a spiritual cast unavailable to the all-too-human (and all-too-pagan) Troilus. The canine monster's three heads additionally represent the ages of man (infancy, youth, old age) through which death enters earth, according to Fulgentius.[17] Chaucer uses this infernal, mutable authority to gloss the "Judgment of Troilus."

Love and treachery always seem to be mixed in Chaucer. The myth of the Judgment of Paris provides a catalyst and explanation for Troilus's changes, his fall: as Paris abducted Helen (62–63), in consequence of his Judgment awarded to Venus, one of three goddesses (Venus, Juno, Pallas Athena), so also Troilus similarly chooses "Venus" (Criseyde), or, in a homosocial sleight of hand, her son Cupid, to whom he declares fealty. Just as Helen's abduction leads the Greeks to besiege Troy, so also Criseyde's leaving Troy allows Antenor to enter Troy and therefore betray it. Unfortunately, just as Paris's choice led to the Greeks' desire to avenge Helen's "ravysshyng" (62), by means of the Trojan War, so also does Troilus's choice lead to his ultimate fall, into pride and then into death. Paris's choice of Venus has been glossed by the mythographers to signify the voluptuous life (to be distinguished from the active and contemplative lives).[18] Although Venus is not directly involved in the first book of the *Troilus*—as she is in the usual mythographic source for the Judgment of Paris, Virgil's *Aeneid* (which also details the fall of Troy)—nevertheless the God of Love (Cupid in the medieval guise of Amor) is credited with Troilus's falling into love (206). Further, in Chaucer's presentation of this second judgment, of Troilus, Criseyde is described as fairer than Helen or Polyxena, Troilus's sister loved by Achilles (454–55). Troilus's judgment, like his brother Paris's, seems skewed: his golden apple should have gone to Pallas Athena.

Chaucer does not explicitly invoke the Judgment of Paris, although he does refer to Paris's love for the shepherdess and nymph Oenone in line 654. The youthful shepherd Paris abandoned this nymph of Mount Ida for Helen when Oenone recognized him as Priam's son; bitter Oenone will later refuse to heal the wounded Paris, and when she changes her mind, it will be too late—Paris will die—for which delay she kills herself. Pandarus compares his own love-longing for his mysterious beloved with Oenone's suffering at Paris's hands, as expressed in a "compleynte of hir hevynesse" (652–55; presumably a reference to Ovid's *Heroides* 5). Pandarus wishes Troilus to use her letter of complaint as a model to convince Criseyde of the sincerity of his pain and to stir her pity for him. His counsel seems ironic, both because of its insistence on rhetorical strategy to convince and manipulate, and because it foreshadows the abandonment of Troilus by Criseyde and his subsequent Oenone-like suffering. The role-reversal paints Troilus as passive, somewhat effeminate, and Criseyde as heartless, aggressive, more masculine—as indeed both characters will prove to be, at least from the other's perspective, in the well-known lovemaking scene of book 3, and in the exchange and its aftermath in books 4 and 5. Finally, as a negative interpretation of Paris's character it also sheds light on those later actions of Criseyde: it reflects badly on Paris in a double sense, in that he has abandoned Oenone when his identity is known (as Criseyde abandons Troilus when she worries about wagging tongues) and that he has ravished Helen—an act of violence, of *raptus* (an act, ironically, that Troilus can perform neither in book 3, at the moment of sexual consummation, nor in book 4, before the exchange of Criseyde).

Troilus has the opportunity to "read" a female text in Pandarus's partial recitation of the contents of Oenone's letter of complaint about Paris's abandonment of her, but he appears unaware of the specifics of Oenone's letter and of her situation, and uninterested in learning more. Familiarity with its contents might at least have made him more wary of love outside of marriage and the suffering that might befall *him*, in the place of abandoned Oenone; at best it might have sensitized him to the gender problem in loving. What Pandarus does relay of the letter in itself might have instructed Troilus in the need for Apollonian remedies for love:

> "Phebus, that first fond art of medicyne,"
> Quod she, "and couthe in every wightes care
> Remedye and reed, by herbes he knew fyne,
> Yet to hymself his konnyng was ful bare,
> For love hadde hym so bounden in a snare,
> Al for the doughter of the kynge Amete,
> That al his craft ne koude his sorwes bete." (659–65)

Oenone calling on Apollo Phoebus, god of medicine (and again, god of wisdom), reminds us of the lack of rational restraint in the actions of Paris and

Troilus—and that Oenone's plea for his help also becomes ironic, given the god's own inability to cure his lovesickness for the daughter of Admetus.[19]

Troilus and the Trojans appear unwise in many ways, primarily because they seem to neglect Pallas Athena, goddess of wisdom, whatever the city's supposed allegiance to its patron. Certainly the one person who could have predicted the city's fall has fled. The "lord of gret auctorite" (65) who knows Troy will be destroyed is Calkas, which he knows "By answere of his god, that highte thus: / Daun Phebus or Appollo Delphicus" (69–70, again in 72). His name puns on calculating, as vocation and as moral flaw, at least in astrological terms, for this priest of Phoebus Apollo and student of the movements of the stars is absorbed in "calkulynge" (line 71). Phoebus, father of the Muses, exemplar of wisdom and divination, suggests right reason—and when Calkas flees Troy, so in a sense does wisdom. What remains is passion, excess, Troy, Paris—and Troilus. After all, the first book begins during, and Troilus falls in love with Criseyde at, the Feast of the Palladium (153, 161), of Pallas Athena, associated with wisdom, at least in the myth of the Judgment of Paris. Ironically, Troilus's choice is garnished with adjectives suggestive of pride and blindness: in the simile of the proud peacock (210), in the simile of the "proude Bayard" (218), and in the blind world apostrophized by the narrator (211).

Troilus's pride—and his "astonishment"—are fixed by the female image of proud, enmarbled, weeping Niobe, in line 699, and again in line 759. Pandarus first uses the image after exhorting Troilus to trust him, because he who remains alone will have no one to help him rise when he falls (694–96). Because Troilus *does* have a friend to help him, he should leave off weeping like Niobe—"For this nys naught, certein, the nexte wyse / To wynnen love—as techen us the wyse" (697–98). It is a curious example for Pandarus to use—Niobe's tears result from her proud disobedience of the gods, and not from design to win favor or love from anyone. Enmarbled Niobe weeps perpetual tears, in *Metamorphoses* 6.147ff., because her children were all slain by Latona and her son Apollo as a result of Niobe's refusal to believe in their divinity.[20] She is mentioned again in line 759, when Troilus says he knows no cure for himself, that he will die: "What knowe I of the queene Nyobe? / Lat be thyne olde ensaumples, I the preye" (759–60). The references to Niobe are, of course, important to the reader in understanding Troilus's real problem, which is pride.

This second female mythological reference to Troilus underscores his effeminization, or at least the effeminizing results of courtly love. Proud Troilus like Niobe defies a god—not Latona but the God of Love. And in a sense he will turn to stone—he will be so paralyzed throughout this love affair that he cannot act, much less act like a man, so that Pandarus must arrange trysts, throw him into bed with Criseyde, arrange letters of exchange once she leaves, and counsel him. In book 4 he will be the "man who sits" in his predestination digression. Even Criseyde will be "still as stone" and "astoned," when she falls in love and later swoons, at his refusal to act. (Troilus at this moment in the narrative "ley as stylle as he ded were" [723].) Indeed, Pandarus scoffingly compares him with the ass who hears sound when men play the harp, but because he is a beast cannot recognize the sound as melody and thus be gladdened by it (731–35).

Troilus, like the errant judge Midas, also wears asses' ears. Pandarus alludes to Midas's judgment of the contest between Pan and Apollo, which in this context represents a mythological foil for the Judgment of Paris — and the Judgment of Troilus. Because Midas stupidly preferred Pan's earthly music to Apollo's heavenly music, he was awarded asses' ears. Similarly, Troilus represents a beast who cannot hear true "music," true words, an idea conveyed through the equine images associated with Troilus (the proud *bayard*) as well as the absence from Troy of the god of music, the archetype of the poet, wise Apollo. The mixture of the two different myths, both associated with making manly and prudent choices, and especially false choices of earthly over heavenly good, shows Troilus inhabiting an underworld already — of temporal temptations uncontrolled by reason — that will lead to his own "fall," a repetition of the fall of Paris, a parallel to the fall of Troy.

Book 2, Criseyde's Seduction: Pandarus as Gatekeeper Janus and Laomedon's Granddaughter

Chaucer tips his hand about his intentions in this book by invoking Cleo, "O lady min" (8), the Muse of history, for mythographically the Muses signify the stages of learning and knowledge assigned to Apollo, god of wisdom and divination, himself a tenth Muse. Clio is identified as the first conception of learning in a gloss established by Fulgentius in *Mitologiae* 1.15 and repeated by the Third Vatican Mythographer and various commentators on Martianus Capella, as well as by Robert Holkot in his commentary on the Twelve Prophets: she is so named because "cleous" is Greek for fame or rumor, and "no one seeks knowledge except that by which he can advance the honor of his reputation" (*Mit.*, trans. p. 56).[21] In this book, if the characters begin to understand, then their knowledge is impelled by their concern with fame or rumor, the fear of loss of reputation, rather than real wisdom. It is not clear, however, with this early invocation of the first Muse, that the characters understand that the goal of the entire process remains Apollo, wisdom — for his priest, as the first book has explained, who is Criseyde's father, has fled the city of Troy. For Chaucer's audience, the lessons of the past are clear, at least in relation to Troy and its walls, and its lovers. Criseyde will succumb to Pandarus's entreaties, his verbal rape, be overcome by a flood of emotion, enter a hell of temporal good, and lose her self. There are other ways of overcoming walls besides storming them—Chaucer has reminded us many times in his use of mythological images that there are gates that can be opened, and, as we know from the familiar story of Troy's fall, even though they are not mentioned, there are also Trojan horses. But that is a different myth—and a different poem—altogether.

What the characters learn hardly constitutes a virtuous descent into the underworld, in terms of the system of four descents. Criseyde falls in love with Troilus at the moment she sees him passing through the adoring crowds—falling in love, it would seem from the surface, with his fame, his glory. Worse, Troilus has been stirred to the heroic exploits rewarded by the crowd's adulation precisely because of his imaginary love for Criseyde— he wants to perform for her, to let his fame win her approval, and, indeed, by the end of book 1 he has become the friendliest creature and the most gentle, generous, thrifty, and best of knights (1079–85). But the way to fame is false, at least in terms of the myth of the Judgment of Paris, wherein Juno represents Fame—a way spurned by Aeneas and also, ultimately, by Troilus, in his elliptical journey toward Apollo (or else Pallas), wisdom.

Because of their focus on knowing and beginning to know, both the beginning invocation and a group of oaths sworn by the three major characters throughout book 2, particularly at the end, provide a frame for Criseyde's falling in love with Troilus and therefore also for the blindness and self-indulgence of Chaucer's lovers and their guide Pandarus. This invocation foreshadows the ultimate end of Troilus in book 5 and his death, and what he learns in looking down from the eighth sphere—that his past trials and tribulation seem petty indeed in contrast to what one finds on the way up to eternity. The last group of mythological references in book 2, minor oaths on various gods, in general emphasizes the frailty of human knowing and therefore also the need for education and enlightenment suggested by Cleo. The swearing of oaths upon the gods by various characters occurs after all the important and initial mythological references and, most significantly, if ironically, begins with Minerva (or Pallas Athena [232]).[22] This calling on the gods to act in human affairs seems self-centered— Troilus assumes that the gods would stop their cosmic duties to help him compose a letter.

They also frame other mythological references, occurring primarily at the beginning of book 2, that center on the "seduction" of Criseyde, set against the backdrop of the Trojan War (itself attendant on the "seduction" of Helen). Chaucer, conscious of the Greeks' need to storm the walls of

Troy, by force or stratagem, uses the political story as a context for the more intimate story to remind us of the many parallels between macrocosm and microcosm. The building and storming of walls in the myth remind us in the *Troilus* of the god of gates, Janus, and the need to keep some gates closed—again depicted through the characters Pandarus and Criseyde, respectively. The narrator, apparently aware of some dark significance in the date of May 3 when the go-between makes his way to his niece's house early in the morning to convince her to love Troilus, appeals to Janus as "god of entree" to guide him (77).[23] The time of Pandarus's coming, "Whan Phebus doth his bryghte bemes spred / Right in the white Bole" (54–55), and the book Criseyde is reading when he bursts in upon her, gloss the nature of her seduction: Criseyde herself can be viewed as "walled," enclosed—and, despite her reading of Statius's "historical" *Thebaid,* deliberately blind and lacking foresight. These references establish her choice as a gateway, either into hell or heaven, but monitored by Pandarus as a Janus figure, in one respect like the gatekeeper Cerberus, in another like gatekeeper Saint Peter.

Janus as the "god of beginnings" will indeed aid Pandarus in initiating the relationship of Criseyde and Troilus; the image also connects others, of doors and walls, throughout book 2—and the very end of book 1. According to Cicero (*De natura deorum* 2.68), Janus as god of doorways for a house derives his name from *ire,* to go, in that *jani* are archways and *januae* are portals in secular buildings; he leads in every sacrifice because the beginning and end are most important.[24] Macrobius in *Saturnalia* adds that Janus, god of doors, or of beginnings and endings, rules gates and doors; his name comes from "janua," door, and relates to the month of January as the "gate" of the new year (1.7.9); his two faces, or Janus and Jana, represent the knowledge of the past and the future, or Apollo and Diana as the sun and the moon (1.7.9). Macrobius explains such an identification through the sun's control of the heavenly gates of day and night. He notes that the Greeks worshiped Apollo as the god of the door and Diana as the keeper of the city streets. Originally, Janus, who along with Cameses ruled Italy, allowed Saturn to share the rule; therefore the months named after them or their festal celebrations are contiguous and succeed one another, with December and the festival of Saturn, called the Saturnalia, preceding January and the "portal" of the new year (1.7.26). Janus allowed such generosity because the newcomer Saturn taught Janus the laws of husbandry in using the fruits of the earth. Later commentators will use this historical interpretation to enrich Janus's signification as a catalyst of cosmic fertility. Janus's double knowing, of things past and future, is responsible for his signification as wisdom by the twelfth-century Florentine commentator on Martianus Capella: out of the past, indeed, the future ought to be known.[25]

121

The Third Vatican Mythographer, also in the twelfth century, glosses Janus in a similar fashion.[26]

In general, medieval mythographers preferred the more figurative interpretation of Janus as a cosmic gatekeeper, *deus anni,* who opens the gate of the year.[27] Macrobius also understands Janus as the universe, the heavens, his name taken from "eundo," since the universe is always in motion, wheeling in a circle and returning to the point at which it began. The emphasis on "beginnings" and "endings" in the second book of the *Troilus* takes on an anagogical significance in this Neoplatonic interpretation (life and death) of the two-faced keeper of heaven and hell—for the Phoenicians the *ouroboros,* which images forth the universe. Capricorn and Cancer, the portals of the universe, according to Macrobius's commentary on the *Somnium Scipionis*—as we remember from the discussion of Troilus's ascent to the eighth sphere, the Aplanon—represent the two gates over which Janus rules, in the twelfth-century Arnulf of Orleans's glosses on Ovid's *Fasti.*[28] Through these two gates souls descend into life on earth and ascend after life on earth.

As gatekeeper, Pandarus will literally open the gate to Criseyde's house on the city streets and, through the stratagem devised later on—the dinner at his house, the favorable rain, the hiding of Troilus in a closet—he will open other, figurative, doors and gates, such as those to Criseyde's heart and arms, and to the bedroom, to ensure that the couple winds up in the same room. Pandarus, like Janus, also presents two faces, one nocturnal, secretive, pandering, to Troilus, the other diurnal, public, wise, to his niece and public officials. In this sense, Chaucer's casting of wise Janus as patron for the "knowing" Pandarus becomes bitterly ironic. If, like Janus, he controls the gates of heaven, or knowledge of the past and future (Apollo and Diana), his actions are appropriately enhanced by Phoebus Apollo moving into Taurus, on May 3, when he opens the door to Criseyde's house. In a larger narrative sense, Pandarus (and his opening of Criseyde's door) represents Chaucer's cosmic Janus. Like the *deus anni* the *Troilus,* through its invocations, "starts over" again in book 4; there exist other cycles it duplicates, such as the disastrous cycle of sensual love, repeated in the relationship of Troilus and Criseyde, and the annual cycle of nature—or the Wheel of Fortune. The image also works ironically—Troilus does enter the heavens, but not until the fifth book—and not the way he anticipates beforehand.

If Pandarus is aided by Janus, it is the woeful face of the gatekeeper of hell and not the gatekeeper of heaven who aids him—that is, the classical and mythological figure of Cerberus guarding hell and not the Christian and theological figure of Saint Peter opening the gate to Dante's purgatory. In the first book, Pandarus has sworn his fidelity to Troilus by the gatekeeper Cerberus (859), that is, sworn by human mortality, or death; Criseyde's *em* anticipates the spiritual death that both lovers will experience, or, alternatively, her uncle foreshadows Troilus's literal death at poem's end. Chaucer's point here, as in the *Parlement of Foules*, centers on love (particularly its courtly variety) as either infernal and purgative or paradisal in nature; that is, by layering these gatekeepers and gates, Chaucer reinforces the pivotal nature of this episode, in which Pandarus as Cerberus, Janus, and Saint Peter has the option of opening the gate to either hell, purgatory, or heaven — or perhaps all three — for the lovers.

The emphasis on gates and gatekeepers visually depicts the choices or opportunities to exercise free will and suggests the poem is therefore about free will, a tragedy caused by bad choices. Chaucer's emphasis culminates in the use of the myth of Philomela and Tereus in line 64, in a passage indebted to Dante's second *cantica*.[29] The swallow Procne, Philomela's sister, sounds the mournful "lay" about her transformation ("Whi she forshapen was" [66]) that awakens Pandarus for his day's quest. It is the consequences of the rape of Philomela that Chaucer draws attention to in his clustering of three mythological images with Pandarus's visit to Criseyde on May 3. Before Pandarus arises,

> The swalowe Proigne, with a sorowful lay,
> Whan morwen com, gan make hire waymentynge
> Whi she forshapen was; and ever lay
> Pandare abedde, half in a slomberynge,
> Til she so neigh hym made hire cheterynge
> How Tereus gan forth hire suster take,
> That with the noyse of hire he gan awake. (64–70)

Chaucer's source for this image of the swallow in *Purgatorio* 9 (13–33) identifies that point at which God ravishes the contrite sinner with grace, although the mournful cry of the swallow Procne — and the implicit warning of imminent rape — becomes ironic here. In Dante, Saint Lucia lifts the dreaming Dante to the gate of Purgatory guarded by Saint Peter, or one of his angels (2:119–20), a passage used previously by Chaucer as mythographic gloss on Ganymede in book 2 of the *Hous of Fame*. Criseyde, unlike Dante the pilgrim, will not be ravished by God, and unlike Ganymede, she will not be taken up to heaven, but like Philomela, she will be "seduced," in a manner of speaking, by her relative and "guide," her older, presumably wiser *em* Pandarus. Dante compares his pilgrim self with Ganymede, also ravished but by Jove's eagle, to be the cupbearer of the gods, and with Achilles, carried by his mother to Scyros to be instructed by the centaur Chiron, just as Dante is to be later instructed by Virgil and ultimately Statius (34–42). Whereas Ganymede's rape by Jove's eagle implies anagogically transcendental ravishment, the necessary penetration and violation of self involved in divine grace as well as the ineffable, wordless nature of the experience for the sinner, in contrast the rape of Philomela—also bereft of her tongue by the violent Tereus—is neither spiritual nor interior in nature, but destructive, carnal, and manipulative. Thus the mythological references undercut the intentions and roles of Pandarus. Further, the allusion to the rape of Philomela also works backward, to the rape of Helen that initiated the Trojan War, and forward to the ravishing of Criseyde by Diomede. It also anticipates the ironically bold ravishment of Troilus by Criseyde (in an unconventional role-reversal) in book 3.

The very specific and telling date on which Pandarus's assault on Criseyde occurs, May 3—represented in Chaucer through the sun as Phoebus Apollo, the god of truth, passing through the zodiacal sign of Taurus, the bull—designates in other poems either a time of epiphany, or else of misfortune and discord due to blindness. Yet this roundabout way of introducing May 3 as the time of Pandarus's first "assault" on Criseyde ironically highlights the folly of Pandarus, despite his "wise speche," acting supposedly under the guidance of wise Janus. On this date in the *Nun's Priest's Tale* (3190) Chauntecleer meets the fox, and in the *Knight's Tale* (1463) the escaped prisoner Palamon overhears Arcite's confession of love in the wood, which leads to their tournament. But because May 3 marks the date on which Saint Helen discovered the Cross and the end of the Roman fertility festival of the goddess Flora, it also fixes this occasion of Pandarus contemplating methods of seducing his niece as an "epiphany" with ironic and allegorical significance.[30] The invention of the Cross anagogically signals the manifestation of the promise of resurrection, epiphany, and therefore the reaffirmation of Christian truth. By analogy, within this ostensibly pagan poem, the designation of Phoebus Apollo "in the bull" signals this moment as the opportunity for understanding, special insight. And yet such understanding will be impossible: Criseyde's father Calkas has fled, leaving his daughter and his city behind so that Criseyde and Troy lack a seer, or foresight. In addition, the Palladion, emblem of Pallas Athena, goddess of wisdom, is missing. Such a lack will permit Pandarus as doorkeeper to open the gate to her heart more readily because it remains unguarded.

At that hour of morning when the swallow Procne sings, the soul is more occupied with thinking than with the needs of the flesh, according to Pietro Alighieri's comment on these lines in *Purgatorio* (9.13–33). Appropriately, when Pandarus first opens the door to her house this May 3 morning, Criseyde appears more interested in thinking than in playing: she is listening to Statius's *Thebaid*, trying to learn from the past. And that Procne gloss leads Bersuire to discuss the three functions of the soul: to live, to sense, and to understand. But at this hour Criseyde and not Pandarus contemplates intellectual matters, trying to understand herself, whereas Pandarus instead mulls how best to put Troilus's case to Criseyde. What causes her to shift her attention from thinking to sensing? Is she in reality contemplating the lessons of history, or only pretending to? The mythographers do provide insights into her behavior, although such insights remain in some cases intriguing possibilities rather than probabilities. For example, Chaucer's actual reference to Procne in line 64 may be indebted to Bersuire on Ovid's *Metamorphoses* 6.430ff., which suggests that the story of Philomela is an allegory of incest under the cover of family relationships.[31] Even if Chaucer does not intend Pandarus to be guilty of incest, the mythographer's gloss bolsters the pejorative image of the voyeur who vicariously delights in Troilus's consummation of his love for Criseyde.

The "romance of Thebes" that Criseyde is reading to improve herself when Pandarus enters appropriately frames the events that occur in Chaucer's romance, especially two mythological references that Chaucer uses at this point in the narrative (and again in book 5). At least initially, Criseyde refuses Pandarus's entreaties to put off her widow's garb and dance; more interested in the frequently glossed school-text epic of Statius's *Thebaid* (or more likely, the vernacular version, the *Roman de Thèbes*) when the cunning Pandarus first opens her door and begins his seduction, Criseyde does not fit the mythographer's misogynistic typing (Bersuire glosses Philomela as a type of evil woman more accustomed to play and sing) even though Chaucer seems to agree with moralist Bersuire that evil men like Tereus—or Pandarus—are hoopoes who build nests in a dungheap.

Chaucer pinpoints the blindness of his characters, that their attempt to "know" will lead them into the underworld, by references to the self-blinded, doomed Oedipus and the damned diviner Amphiaraus, who descended into hell. Criseyde innocently tells her uncle that "we han herd how that kyng Layus deyde / Thorugh Edippus his sone," but that they have stopped reading at the beginning of a new chapter ("at thise lettres rede"), at the point that "the bisshop ... / Amphiorax, fil thorugh the ground to helle" (100–105). The references work in two ways. First, Oedipus and his blindness are reminiscent of Troilus's blindness[32]—the narrator has made a point of showing that our hero is blind in book 1—and second, Oedipus sleeping with his mother and killing his father is reminiscent of Pandarus's own voyeuristically incestuous violation of his relationship with his niece. These references together illustrate what the family should be by what it is not. Chaucer may intend to confuse the reader, given both Laomedon's and Oedipus's blindness to the consequences of their proud and willful acts for their descendants and heirs. Although the story of Oedipus's killing of his father Laius and then his self-blinding may have been familiar to a medieval audience, mythographers infrequently glossed the myth of Oedipus in the Middle Ages: in one unusual reading, in Fulgentius's *Thebaid*, Oedipus represents licentiousness and Laius is sacred light; Oedipus's two sons from Jocasta are greed and lust. The introduction of the Greek diviner, Argive hero, and seer Amphiaraus (line 105)—one of the Seven against Thebes—underscores the ironic lack of foresight in Chaucer's major characters. Amphiaraus fell living into Hades as he had predicted he would, so that he had the satisfaction of being ultimately right, according to Fulgentius and Bernardus Silvestris, both commenting on *Aeneid*, book 6. But he also descended, unfortunately, into hell. As an example of a damned diviner, he turns up in the eighth circle, of the Fraudulent, in Dante's *Inferno*. Because "hell" in the mythographers refers to the earth, the choice of Troilus and Criseyde—and the reference to Amphiaraus—means that they have wrongly chosen temporal good, or the good of this world. A measure of their blindness, such a choice reflects the absence of Apollo; knowing past and future, or seeking the help of those who do know, constitutes an important theme in this book. Appropriately, in a gloss on Martianus (67.17), Remigius couples the knowing but fraudulent Amphiaraus with the diviners Mopsus and Apollo and treacherous Calchas (1:187). With his reference to Calkas, Chaucer returns to Criseyde's dilemma—the absence of her knowing father and her decision to love Troilus on May 3.

The correspondence between Troy and Criseyde, and their betrayals by Calkas and Pandarus, is strengthened primarily by Pandarus's invocation of Neptune (443), who, once deceived by Troy's founder, Laomedon, in the building up of the walls of Troy, intends now to overcome them, so to speak, in revenge—and by the framing character of Antigone (840ff.), possible daughter or granddaughter of the founder of Troy.

In order to convince Criseyde to love Troilus, Pandarus swears by Neptune of his trustworthy intentions and of the reliability of his word (442–45), both qualities undercut through this oath in seeming ignorance of Neptune's past damaging enmity toward Troy. The oath by Neptune simultaneously foreshadows the future of Troy—and of Criseyde; later, in book 4, even the narrator (but not the poet) seems unaware of the hostility of Neptune and Apollo toward Troy and of Laomedon's original, unfortunate, role in its building. In that book, when the traitor Calkas begs the Greeks for his daughter, knowing that Troy's walls will fall, the narrator acknowledges the continued enmity of Phoebus Apollo and Neptune, "That makeden the walles of the town," toward the "folk of Troie" that they will "brynge it to confusioun,"

> Right in despit of kyng Lameadoun;
> Bycause he nolde payen hem here hire,
> The town of Troie shal ben set on-fire. (120–26)

It is Neptune's role that the Trojans in general (and Troilus and Criseyde in particular) should recall in choosing how to love, as Laomedon, builder of

Troy's walls and grandfather of Antigone, did not when he requested the help of the sea god and Apollo in building Troy's walls and then refused to pay them. As a consequence of Laomedon's refusal of payment, Neptune flooded the city until Laomedon's daughter Hesione was given to the sea monster, according to Bersuire, commenting on Ovid's *Metamorphoses* 11.202ff. Even after Hercules aided Laomedon by freeing Hesione, Laomedon betrayed *him* by refusing to pay him in horses (as promised), and Hercules therefore repeated history by storming the walls and overcoming the city. As a prize, his helpers Telamon took Hesione and Peleus won Thetis—at whose wedding Discord threw her golden ball and Paris made his infamous judgment. The image of horses in Trojan history affecting important turns of event culminates, of course, in the use of the ploy of the Trojan horse.

Past and future assaults on Troy, then, become both a context and a metaphor for the assault on Criseyde. Pandarus, like Laomedon, deludes himself as well as the "city" under his protection, that is, in microcosm his niece Criseyde; as punishment Neptune might "flood" (destroy) him, Criseyde, or Troy, might overcome these "walls." The fall of Troy is framed by the history of its building and the consequences of its fall as documented in the *Aeneid* in the founding of Italy. Bersuire also treats the fall of Troy as a classical parallel to the Fall of humankind: Troy, the city of the world, falls because the king (Adam) refuses to pay the promised gold to those who helped build the city (those gods representing God and the angels); the king is vexed by sea waves (tribulations) and his daughter Hesione (human nature) is granted to monsters (demons) until she is freed by Hercules (incarnated Christ), who hopes for a reward of fast horses (loyal and pure men). Again, because this payment will not be made, the city will be destroyed and its pieces scattered in judgment. In addition, in application to the *Troilus,* the idea of a prize (Hesione) both looks back to Helen and ahead to Criseyde as prizes—this city both prizes and uses women. The idea of storming the walls because of nonpayment also looks backward and forward: although Helen is not a payment, let us say that Paris breaches his honor to steal his host's wife, which will result in the overcoming of Troy's walls, not by force but by stratagem.

The character Antigone, possibly the granddaughter of Laomedon, connects the stubborn "walls" of Criseyde's heart and the walls of Troy: one of the reasons Criseyde falls in love that night after Pandarus's argument derives from Antigone's song of soulful submission to the God of Love (827–30). Even though Criseyde refers to her as her niece, nevertheless her name invokes Laomedon's presence—and the founding of Troy. According to the glossators, in particular the First and Second Vatican Mythographers, she is either the daughter or granddaughter of the original builder of the walls of Troy—Laomedon, father of Priam—or the daughter of Oedipus of Thebes, which provides a link with the earlier reference to the blind Oedipus about whom Criseyde read in her "romance."[33] Like her grandfather Laomedon proud and stubborn, Antigone serves as a warning to Criseyde to avoid any course that might be described as lecherous; the indirect reference to her grandfather's deceit and betrayal of his city warns against the machinations of her protector Pandarus. Of Antigone, mythographic glosses emphasize her lechery and pride—an understanding of which undercuts the almost masochistic submission implied by her song to Love. According to the twelfth-century Digby mythographer, she is the daughter of Priam who sleeps with Jupiter: in myth 62, when castigated by Juno, she responds "contumaciter," after which Juno, irate, turns her first into scorpions, then into a stork, a double punishment that fits her double crime of lechery and pride.[34] Alternatively, according to the First Vatican Mythographer (myth 179), Juno changes her hair into snakes because Antigone wished to imitate Juno's form; in the Second Vatican Mythographer (myth 69), Juno turns Antigone into a stork because Laomedon preferred his arrogant daughter, pleased with her form. What appears in the First Vatican Mythographer (myth 179) Bersuire essentially repeats, on *Metamorphoses* 6.424ff. Antigone's consistent lechery and pride perhaps anticipate a misogynistic view of Criseyde's later actions with Diomede, if not with Troilus.

Chaucer signals the consequence of Pandarus's verbal seduction and Antigone's song of submission to love—enamored Criseyde—through a complementary image from the rape myth of Procne and Philomela, that of the nightingale into which Ovid's Philomela was transformed and who echoes Dante's Jovian Eagle transporting him to Purgatory proper. After debating long over whether she should or should not fall in love with Troilus, in line 918 Criseyde falls asleep while the nightingale sings of love under the chamber wall. But in her dream, an eagle feathered white as bone, not a nightingale, sets his long claws under her breast and tears out her heart, putting his own back into her breast instead. In its violence, this heart exchange reminds us once again of the ravishment of Dante by Saint Lucia and of Ganymede by the eagle (the grace of God on the Christian and classical levels) in canto 9 of the *Purgatorio.*

At this point, Criseyde's resistance to her uncle's wiles, her defensiveness and closed heart, the embattled and barricaded Troy, and penetration by a phallogocentric, human or divine, predatory force somehow fuse together through Chaucer's ingenious artistry in relating mythological images. The "rape," however, is hardly fruitful: in book 3, when Pandarus actually throws the bumbling Troilus into bed, sowing might occur, but apparently encounters "barren" ground. The "marriage of bliss" that the lovers enjoy will not result in propagation, given its form as a heavily sensual courtly love. Pandarus's ironic role as agent of ravishment is reinforced once again by the mythographic Janus figure, in Macrobius also known by the name of Roman Consivus, from "conserendo," to identify him as the patron of sowing or propagation of the race. We now turn to the "heaven" that Troilus imagines he will enjoy.

Book 3, "Venus and Adonis": Unnatural Mothers and Blind Sons

From the invocation of Venus and Calliope, Venus and images related to her describe lovemaking or the so-called marriage of Troilus and Criseyde through her relationship with her son Cupid or other sonlike figures, such as Adonis, in this third book. Unfolded through them is a pattern of unnatural (incestuous) love—mothers prefer their sons to their husbands, with Adonis, a key mythic image here, himself the result of such unnatural love between his sister-mother Myrrha and their own father. Such love is defined in mythological terms of blindness, lasciviousness, rape, child-oblation rather than as that fair chain of love that marries heaven to earth. Women characters prefer chastity to heterosexual relationships; to protect themselves against rape, they reify themselves—transform to stone or bark. Their choices in loving are limited and dangerous. Such images are, more often than not, used to describe the plight of Troilus rather than Criseyde, who is identified with the aggressor—Venus.

The double invocation to Venus (1–44) and Calliope, Muse of epic poetry (45), identifies the structural position of the third book of the *Troilus* within the Dantesque frame as a lover's putative "Paradise," the equivalent of Dante's third *cantica*. Yet this cosmic and astrological invocation is drawn from Troiolo's song in Boccaccio's *Filostrato* 3.74–79, itself derived in part from the otherworld descriptions in Boethius, *Consolatio* 2m8, and Dante, *Paradiso* 8.1–15.[35] Chaucer intentionally links the doomed character Troilus to the narrator "Chaucer" by echoing the narrator's formal invocation of Venus in the Prologue and "Epilogue" to this book in Troilus's private invocations of Venus in lovemaking, which become equivalent or analogous to the narrator's task in summoning sufficient inspiration to write about this joy, deceptive as it apparently is. By such a strategy, Chaucer also undercuts as delusion the idealistic view of love shared by lover and narrator and its analogue in romance, this romance, as a "divine comedy."

To hint at the dramatic climax to the unnatural relationship of Troilus and Criseyde that will occur in this book and to underscore the image of Venus as *mater*, at the end of the forty-four-line paean to Venus Chaucer tacks on a second invocation, to the mother of Orpheus and *bona vox*, "best voice" of all the Muses—Calliope.[36] As mother of Orpheus, Calliope anticipates the dominant Orpheus images used to describe Troilus in book 4, the latter of which suggests that Troilus seeking the return of Criseyde, like Orpheus wishing to retrieve his lost wife Eurydice, will descend into the underworld. As a type of Orpheus, in this respect Troilus also represents a son to Calliope—whatever such a tie may mean in the larger context of the whole poem. Calliope, as Orpheus's mother, is *bona vox*, "excellent voice," as if Troilus mistakes the voice, the style, for the substance—the "blisful Venus" for the white, shapely form of his mistress, whose image also merges with that of Fortune. In addition, as mother of Orpheus Calliope appears in other classical or medieval epic or dialogic poems frequently glossed in the schools, such as the *Aeneid* (9.525), Statius's *Thebaid* (4.34–35), and Boethius (3m12.24). Perhaps Calliope represents epic poetry incarnate, especially in the hiding of secrets beneath false integument, attributed to her by Fulgentius.[37] Certainly the hiding of secrets, whether adulterous or incestuous, is paramount in this book for reasons of courtly love, fame, and civilization.

In addition, the narrator's invocation of the chief Muse suggests an apex, a climax, a goal toward which the lovers have been moving. Within the context of the whole *Troilus*, the drama climaxes in "Paradise" (or Parnassus?) with the "marriage" of the lovers. Calliope as chief Muse recalls the invocation of Muse Cleo in book 2 and therefore ties the process begun in that book—Criseyde's falling in love with Troilus, and his woeful ignorance and need for education—with its culmination in this book. If Clio, first of the Muses, in that book signifies the first stage in the search for knowledge, specifically, fame, then in this book Calliope, the last and ninth Muse, as "optimae uocis" ("she of the excellent voice"), represents what appears to be the culmination of that search, in Fulgentian terms her function to "bene proferre quod elegeris" ("make known in attractive form what you select"), or the final polishing of the communication of knowledge and memory, or rhetorical ability (Fulg. *Mit.* 1.15, p. 27, trans. p. 56).[38]

Venus's planetary role in the invocation, as the "blisful light" whose clear beams adorn the third heaven (or the third sphere), is expanded optimistically by the narrator to become "Joves doughter deere" (1–7), or the "fair chain of love," a Boethian cosmic genetrix whose plenitude is sealed with "vapour eterne" to bind together the orderly hierarchy of all created things, "man, brid, best, fissh, herbe, and grene tree" (10), throughout "hevene and helle, in erthe and salte see" (8). As "unitee" itself, or concord that binds together the discordant, she represents wisdom hidden from most mortals, the "sothfast cause of frendship" (30). Her bright cosmic plenitude and "benignite" (39) ensure the reproduction of the species, a Chartrian idea whose final effect represents a law "set in universe" (36), that is, obeyed by humans as well as animals, and known to the narrator in microcosm, by those who are lovers (37).

Yet at the end of this book, the narrator adds simultaneous blind and foolish praise of Cupid, personification of *cupiditas*, both cupidity and avarice (1808), to his invocation of Venus and the Muses ("Yee sustren nyne ek, that by Elicone / In hil Pernaso listen for t'abide" [1809–10]), in echo of the beginning invocation of the celestial Venus and Muse Calliope. By so doing, he also reintroduces the warped and unnatural relationship of mother and son characteristic as well of the relationship between Criseyde and Troilus:

> Thow lady bright, the doughter to Dyone,
> Thy blynde and wynged sone ek, daun Cupide,
> Yee sustren nyne ek, that by Elicone
> In hil Pernaso listen for t'abide,
> That ye thus fer han deyned me to gyde—
> I kan namore, but syn that ye wol wende,
> Ye heried ben for ay withouten ende! (1807–13)

The narrator also changes his Venus by humanizing the reified and distant star into a "lady bryght" (1807), the "doughter to Dyone" rather than Jove's daughter (according to Hyginus, Praef., both Jupiter and Dione were her parents), with a son both blind and winged (1808)—"daun Cupide" (1808).

That Venus could be both the third planet, symbol of the fair chain of love, and mother (or daughter) figure can be explained through the Virgilian Venus, the bright star described as the "Matre Dea monstrante viam," the mother goddess literally showing the way to the journeying Aeneas as well as counseling him at every turn, as we saw in chapter 3 in relation to the reference to "Cytherea" in the *Parlement of Foules* drawn from Bernardus Silvestris's commentary on Martianus Capella. Cupid, described in this same Isidorean-Theodulfan mode as the blind and dangerous demon of fornication in *Parlement of Foules*, denigrated the irrational, destructive, and narcissistic aspects of courtly love; to defy him, Scogan, in Chaucer's "Envoy" of the same name, spurns a lady; and to him Eneas in the *Hous of Fame* has been likened, as we recall from chapter 2. Chaucer deliberately chooses Venus's filial relationship with Dione over that with Jove, even though the latter would appear to be more appropriate here: as Jove's daughter, that is, as if the classical Anima Mundi, to be sure, she would perpetuate the world again and again (15–17); but also as that libidinous force she would empower the mythological deity Jupiter in Ovidian tales of metamorphosis to consort adulterously with human women so that (we surmise) new genealogies and nations may be created: "And in a thousand formes down hym sente / For love in erthe, and whom yow liste he hente" (20–21). Venus as cosmic desire ordinarily derived from the Silvestran myth of Cipris married to Bacchus and engendering Hymen, god of weddings; she is often coupled in glosses with Ceres (bread) and Bacchus (wine) (see [Bern. Sil.] *Mart.*, p. 57, 3.237–60).

By emphasizing her little-glossed relationship with mother Dione, the narrator in the "Epilogue" inadvertently asserts the primacy of the maternal relationship for this particular daughter—her relationship *as* a mother, the influence of her own mother upon her—"inadvertently" in that Venus is so attractive and so dangerous here because of her maternal and familial role as mother of Cupid and also of his half brother Aeneas, her son by the human Anchises. In the Troy story, Anchises is the brother of Priam, Antenor, Hesione, and Antigone (they all share Laomedon as father, according to the genealogy found in myth 204 of the First Vatican Mythographer), which makes his son Aeneas cousin to Troilus, Hector, Cassandra, and Paris. When Paris chooses Venus as the most beautiful, he is choosing, in effect, his future aunt. And similarly, when Venus rescues her own son Aeneas from the devastation of Troy (caused by Juno's enmity toward Paris after his Judgment), she reveals her power not only as a goddess but also as a mother, while repudiating other human kinship bonds. Troilus, half brother of Aeneas, may psychologically adopt Venus as his own stepmother here, and therefore yearn for maternal Criseyde, but it is Aeneas's half brother Cupid who provides the paradigm for Troilus, specifically in his more sexual relationship with his mother Venus.

Cupid is therefore depicted as blind in this end stanza (1811ff.) as a foil for blind Troilus in an analogous role (unlike Aeneas, he cannot see the way) and to characterize the relationship and climactic "marriage in heaven" between Troilus and maternal Criseyde in mythological terms as perverse, excessive, incestuous—a union more reflective of the underworld of Pluto than of the heavens and their inhabitants. Such blindness is evident both before Troilus gets into bed with Criseyde, when he entreats the planetary Venus, "Now, blisful Venus, thow me grace sende!" (705, again in lines 712 and 715), and in Troilus's joyous paean, after he has Criseyde in his arms, to Cupid as "O Love, O Charite" and his "moder ek, Citheria the swete" (1254–56; meaning Venus, the "wel-willy planete" [1257]). Like Cupid, he deliberately blinds himself:[39] he follows Cupid's behests, although, as courtly lover, he in fact offers himself as servant to "blisful" Venus (705, 712) "ful of myrthe" (715) and begs her to "enspire" him (712–14). Ironically, after this double invocation Troilus names another son of Venus, the medieval Hymen (1258), fathered by Bacchus. Hymen as the love that is equivalent to the cosmic wedding, the "holy bond of thynges" (1261), is invoked then by Troilus in echo of the narrator's voice at the beginning of book 3—in other words, he asks for the possibility of love without wings ("his desir wol fle withouten wynges" [1263]), love that is not Cupid. Ironically, it is love *with* wings that will actually dominate his relationship with Criseyde.

That Criseyde is older than Troilus, even by a few years,[40] widowed and already adept in matters of love, marks her as a Venus to his Cupid, a relationship underscored by her own libidinous uncle, Pandarus, whose voyeurism and kissing of his niece hints at incestuous feelings:[41] he pries under her sheet the morning after the "wedding of bliss"; then "thriste / Under hire nekke, and at the laste hire kyste" (1574–75). Other signs throughout the book portray this relationship between Criseyde and Troilus as a mirror of that of Venus and Cupid/Venus and Adonis: in line 186, at Deiphebus's house, Pandarus invokes Cupid as "Immortal god ... that mayst naught deyen" (185), after Criseyde has accepted Troilus as a lover and "hym in armes took, and gan hym kisse" (182). Further, after this initial meeting, they hope that Cupid will aid them in bringing them time to speak more fully instead of engaging in the hurried queries and addresses secret lovers must (460–62).

The incestuous relationship between mother Venus and son Cupid presents a foil for a perverse relationship between older Venus and youthful Adonis in Ovid's *Metamorphoses* and glossed by Bersuire (10.503ff.). Bersuire explains that Venus was wounded by her son Cupid one day when, *incautius*, he was kissing her. She therefore "burned with love [*exarsisse*]" when she first saw Adonis and neglected her duties to make love with him (Bersuire, *Ovidius*, p. 154, trans. p. 360). "Cupid kissing his mother signifies relatives who kiss other relatives too familiarly [*consanguineos qui nimis familiariter consanguineos osculantur*] with the result that because of it the latter are wounded [*vulnerantur*] by the desire of luxury [*per appetitum luxuriae*]."

Chaucer's Venus in book 3 in reality is she who nuzzles Cupid and burns for Adonis after being accidentally hit by her son's own cupidinous arrow. Chaucer's reference to Venus's love for Adonis occurs as part of Troilus's request for help from Venus in lovemaking. Before hiding in the closet to meet Criseyde for their first union (712–18), he asks that Venus use her harmonious stellar influence with her father, Saturn, to counter the malign aspects of Mars and Saturn (713). But he does so by appealing to the goddess's unhappy and besotted love for the ill-fated Adonis: "For love of hym thow lovedest in the shawe, / I meene Adoun, that with the boor was slawe" (720–21). Although it appears as if Troilus seeks her celestial help as "fair chain of love" (naively and in part ironically, as if his potential sexual failure may equally affect the natural workings of the cosmos), it is her role as daughter of Saturn (signifying the voluptuous life in the *Aeneid* commentaries, the beautiful goddess wrongly chosen by Paris in his Judgment, as cited in [Bern. Sil.] *Mart.*, p. 57, 3.226–37), that is specifically mentioned, in remembrance of her love for youthful slain Adonis: the valiant warrior, in "drede" (707), needs Venus's help in getting through this long night of lovemaking (705–7, 712–14). This realistic assessment becomes clear in the kneeling and swooning scenes when he is assisted by the impatient bawd Pandarus (962–66 and 1092), who scoffs, "O thef, is this a mannes herte?" (1098) and tears off his "bare sherte" (1099). Earlier, it is true, Troilus's desires have been advanced by Fortune, specifically through the conjunction of the moon, Saturn, and Jupiter under the sign of

Cancer that made a "smoky reyn"[42] so terrifying that Criseyde must sleep at her uncle's house (617–30).

Like Troilus, Adonis has been glossed as *luxuriosus*, who flees love as too much work; appropriately he is transformed into a flower that perishes each year in memory of the sadness of his death and his sin against Venus, in Giovanni del Virgilio's comment on *Metamorphoses* 10.13.[43] Further, when Adonis metamorphoses into a flower (the hyacinth) after his death, he follows in his mother's path, for Myrrha was changed into the myrrh tree who weeps tears of myrrh. Myrrh, according to Arnulf of Orleans in his commentary on *Metamorphoses* 10.10–11, does not enhance virility, as Sutrius so fallaciously broadcast in his comedies, for the Adonis killed while hunting is transformed into a flower either to show the sweetness of love, the labor of hunting, or (as Ovid notes) the sloth that results from the piercing of Cupid's arrow (referring apparently to the grazing of Venus by her son's arrow that pricked her love for Adonis). Adonis's death and resurrection as a flower of the same name therefore also is moralized to represent the sweetness of hunting in place of work, or libidinous love (*amor venereus*) as deceptively sweeter than charitable love (*amor caritativus*).[44]

In one sense, the image of Adonis's sloth that keeps him from work characterizes Troilus's behavior, in that his courtly love removes him from the business of the Trojan War. In another, the image of Adonis's flight from loving Venus that leads to his death and metamorphosis forecasts Troilus's own future—Troilus's inability to act virilely with Criseyde leads to his own death and apotheosis later after her departure. In this respect may be useful, if ironic, the Ovidian advice (10.543–44)—mixed with kisses of careful Venus to the hunter Adonis, glossed by Bersuire—to be bold with timorous beasts but cautious with bold ones, like lions and boars. Adonis, "mindful of his own power [*propriae virtutis memor*]," unfortunately ignores this advice (*Ovidius*, p. 156, trans. p. 359). Interestingly, in the myth a fierce boar will kill Adonis just as Troilus will be "overcome" by a boar—the heir of Calydon, Diomede. Troilus also relates to Criseyde as if he were Adonis fleeing the maternal Venus. Criseyde is exhorted by Pandarus to "save" Troilus (1100–1101) by pulling out the "thorn" in his heart (1104–5), presumably because he fears that she has another lover. Venus-like, Criseyde takes the initiative "And therwithal hire arm over hym she leyde, / And al forgaf, and ofte tyme hym keste" (1128–29), chastising him by asking, "Is this a mannes game? / What, Troilus, wol ye do thus for shame?" (1126–27).

The myth of the incestuous union of Myrrha and her father is in fact more frequently glossed in the mythographies than that of her son Adonis, the product of that union, although the passion motivating both Myrrha and Adonis, at least in the gloss of Giovanni del Virgilio, is *cupiditas*. This mythological identification of mother and son by means of their cupidity or lechery (or lack of it; the glosses are ambiguous), is linked by common imagery. This imagery may also explain the salacious image of the Trojan couple's lovemaking in 1230–32 in terms of the "swote wodebynde" twisting and writhing about the tree:[45] Myrrha metamorphosed into the myrrh tree, just as Adonis metamorphosed into the flower of the hyacinth. Appropriately, Troilus's day-after-the-night-before reaction to the affair signals his own lechery: "I hadde it nevere half so hote as now; / And ay the more that desir me biteth / To love hire best, the more it me deliteth" (1650–52). In addition, Criseyde resembles Adonis's mother Myrrha, who excessively loved her father Cinyras (Calkas, responsible for negotiating her entry into the Greek camp).

Other incestuous, uncaring relationships between parents and children, particularly mothers and sons, or relationships in which birth is stressed, dominate this book. These mythological references help to define the relationship between Criseyde and Troilus: Is Criseyde attracted to Troilus because of his boyishness and timidity, because of her misplaced maternal urge? Further, what of the question of children, from the previous marriage, and possibly from this union? Such references to birth and nativity begin with Pandarus's oath by "natal Joves feste" (150) in an attempt to cheer up the lovelorn, bed-bound lover Troilus: Pandarus swears by "natal Jove" that if he were a god, he would be angry enough to make her die if Criseyde did not yield to Troilus out of pity for his suffering and his honorable intentions toward her (148–54). The reference is ironic because the festival of "natal Jove" celebrates fertility and conception, or, in other words, Jove's function as a generation god.[46] If marriage is out of place in a courtly love affair, then indeed it would be ironic for Pandarus to swear by the "god of procreation."

Other references center on indifferent and uncaring parents, to gloss either the irresponsibility of uncle Pandarus offering up his niece Criseyde to his friend Troilus, or Calkas's irresponsibility in leaving behind his daughter Criseyde in a town famous for its adulterers. Again, such references also reflect back on the maternal-filial relationship of Criseyde and Troilus. For example, Pandarus swears to Criseyde by the gods in heaven (590) that, if all is not well when she comes to dinner that night, he would prefer being "soule and bones" with King Pluto, "as depe ben in helle / As Tantalus" (589–93). The casting of Pandarus as Tantalus evokes the indifference and greed of the unnatural parent willing to sacrifice his son (or niece, or friend) out of pride.[47] Tantalus was condemned to hell because he offered up his son Pelops to the gods during a dinner as a test of their divinity, to see if they would detect his humanity; of the gods, only Ceres ate part of his shoulder, after which Pelops was eventually restored to life with his shoulder replaced by ivory. Pandarus similarly will offer up, if not his son, then his niece, not to the gods but to Troilus, for lovemaking: he has asked

Criseyde only thirty lines prior to his oath to "Come soupen in his hous" that evening (560). And yet the reference also works in an opposite way, to suggest that Pandarus in fact will offer up the timid and boyish Troilus to the friendly arms of earthy Criseyde, rather than Ceres.

More figuratively, the reference to the punishment of Tantalus in hell foreshadows the effects of the lovers' blissful matchmaking (and subsequent lovemaking) as infernal and inferior rather than, as they imagine when they "wed," paradisal, spiritual, conjugal. Their lust-of-the-flesh is appropriately matched by their lust-of-the-eyes when they exchange rings, and when Criseyde gives him the ruby brooch of gold and azure (1370–71) later that night: the exchange of gold symbolizes, instead of the sacrament of marriage, the erotic and acquisitive nature of their illicit, dark, and therefore infernal (earthly) love. And when Pandarus seeks out each of them the next day to satisfy his own curiosity, he truly becomes a Tantalus-like figure epitomizing and mirroring back their love: Fulgentius and other mythographers identify Tantalus as covetousness of sight.[48] Just as Tantalus is punished by having food and water that he cannot eat, despite his earthly riches, so also voyeuristic Pandarus is punished for his coveting of his niece (and other women) by his proximity to the ripe fruit of Criseyde that he cannot "eat." Tenth-century glosses on Ceres in the Tantalus myth found in Boethius's *Consolatio* 3m12 project onto the figure earth that eats up the body—the idea of earthly existence as a consumption of the physical and the spiritual,[49] which pervades this third book of the *Troilus* as a dark undercurrent to the blissful, doomed union of the lovers. Indeed, Bersuire notes that the infernal punishments of Tantalus, Ixion, Sisyphus, Belides, and Tityus represent "five sins which in the hell of this world give many evils to their possessors," specifically, parsimony or avarice, ambition (Ixion), unquiet state of mind (Sisyphus), the insatiability of avarice (Belides), wanton desire (Tityus) ("De formis," pp. 49–50, trans. pp. 110–12).

The mythological images used in the single long prayer of Troilus to the gods for help (722–38), just before he sees Criseyde that night, similarly undercut the "marriage in heaven" by means of the Ovidian freight they carry into the poem with them: because they stress rape, victimization, and the reification of the victim—changed to stone, bark, or some other thing—they gloss pejoratively the excessively physical nature of the lovers' long night together. In many of these instances, the image of the female, and passive, victim anticipates the inactivity of Troilus rather than Criseyde that night—boyish Troilus will later (in book 4) symbolically kneel on a cushion while he discourses about predestination by using the example of a man sitting on a cushion, and will do nothing to prevent Criseyde's exchange with Antenor because he is philosophically committed to the idea that he cannot act, is paralyzed. The passage of violent and tragic images (in 722–35) therefore bears closer scrutiny.

At first glance, the list of mythological resources in Troilus's petition more or less seems to match the most conventional hierarchy of the translunary and helpful planets,[50] starting with the outermost planet Jupiter (722), then Mars and Venus (724), the sun Phoebus (726), Mercury (729), and concluding with Diana as the moon (731) and the Parcae (733). The frame for Troilus's petition thus appropriately mirrors the fair chain of love invoked by the narrator at the beginning of book 3 through the figure of Venus. From Boethius's *Consolatio* 2m8 we know that the fair chain of love linking all of the world in harmony derives from God, so that pagan Troilus here requests God's help in loving Criseyde this particular night.

But a closer reading reveals the disintegration of the "fair chain of love" into a fragmented and destructive bond more like the chains of hell than any heavenly tie. Chaucer couples each planetary god with an Ovidian myth of metamorphosis that characterizes sexual union in the most perverse ways—as rape, violence, and dehumanization. Certainly the petition brilliantly conveys Troilus's own ambivalence about the upcoming meeting.

Because in fact Jove, in the form of a bull, raped an unwilling Europa, Troilus's petition to Jupiter seems ludicrous: is he so timid that he must encourage himself by means of images of rape and violence? The penultimate planet Jupiter (called "Jove" in the first part of Troilus's prayer) "for the love of faire Europe" appeared "in forme of bole" to fetch her away (722–23). Alternatively, if we understand the invocation on a more figurative and mythographic level as a request for a more firmly based spiritual relationship (Bersuire interprets Jove and Europa as the soul and Christ, the former riding on a foundation of faith, glossing *Metamorphoses* 2.833ff. in *Ovidius*, p. 61, trans. pp. 176–77), then, given the actual later physical relationship the lovers will enjoy, the invocation is intended by Chaucer ironically. Psychologically and literally, the myth suggests rape as trust betrayed, which indeed the next few moments will echo, given Pandarus's invitation to both of them, especially to Criseyde, to stay the night safely in his house.

An ironic reference to adultery, bloodshed, and betrayal appears in the summoning of the help of the next planet moving inward, Mars. With his "blody cope" (or cloak [724]), Mars—invoked through Troilus's appeal to his "love of Cipris" (Venus [725])—reminds us of the similarly illicit love between planetary Venus and Mars (outlined in *The Complaint of Mars* in chapter 3) that ended in scandal when Vulcan caught the two of them with his net. The union of Venus and Mars yokes power with lust to reveal the ideal inner workings of courtly love; here she appeases the "ire" of Mars and makes hearts "digne" in order to ennoble lovers, that is, so they "dreden shame, and vices they resyngne" (22–28); all the while, however, the lovers are those "ye [Venus] wol sette a-fyre" (24) with desire—cupidity. In addition, the reference to the bloody cloak presents Mars in his more customary role as god of war rather than as lover. Unfortunately, as god of war, no doubt accustomed to the bloodshed of the Trojan War, Mars will be responsible for the later exchange of Criseyde with Antenor that severs the relationship between the two lovers, and therefore will ultimately be no help at all to the petitioning Troilus. In fact Mars may be said to end Troilus's pain, in that he dies in battle.

The violence of the rapist and the fear of his victim are staged through the myth of Apollo's desire for Daphne in Troilus's invocation of the sun, Phoebus, who wished to love Daphne (726) but whose desire was frustrated by her concealment "Under the bark" and transformation into laurel "for drede" (727). Phoebus's aggressive pursuit may seem less like the course followed by Troilus than by Criseyde once they meet and Pandarus tears off Troilus's shirt. Also, Daphne's metamorphosis into laurel psychologically traces the defensive reaction of the individual unable or unwilling to love, because of the fear of being hurt. In this sense the image of the nymph's metamorphosis anticipates the "change" of Criseyde in book 4 as a result of Troilus's inability to act in the face of her possible exchange, when she swoons and then awakens, as a calmer, less feeling, and more accepting, if withdrawn, pawn in the war between Troy and Greece. The more figurative mythographic signification of the myth in Bersuire does not at first glance appear to apply here, although understanding it casts a wickedly ironic light on the erotic coupling of the lovers later that night. The myth signifies the pursuit of the Christian soul by the devil because Phoebus represents those who glory in their virtues, and Daphne, worldly glory (on *Metamorphoses* 1.452–567, in *Ovidius*, p. 40, trans. p. 137). It concludes (on *Metamorphoses* 1.543ff.) with Daphne's appropriate retreat into the shelter of a laurel to allegorize religious transformation into a virtuous penitent. "And so she should become the laurel—that is a religious person, virtuous and perfect—by attaching the feet of a good course as roots, by putting on the bark of penitence, by acquiring the branches of good desires, and by never putting off the greenness of an honest life" (*Ovidius*, p. 41, trans. p. 139). In light of the detailed tree image, the later woodbine image used to characterize the lovemaking of Criseyde and Troilus (1230–32) must demonstrate a solely physical rather than spiritual transformation, whatever the lovers' illusions. Such plant-growth imagery associates with the equally ironic echo of the transformation of Myrrha into the myrrh tree and Adonis into the hyacinth in myths of this third book discussed earlier. All of them equate the metamorphosis of lovemaking with tragedy, violence, fear, rape, and death.

The planet Mercury (with whom Pandarus was compared in book 1) projects Troilus's sexual fantasy of power because he is a raping, violent god; taking his place is Pandarus, who performs Troilus's role for him, or Criseyde, who reverses the gender roles and performs the part of the aggressor with Troilus. Once again a mythological image portrays love as violent and leading to death or reification. Mercury's desire for and rape of Herse (with the help of angry Pallas Athena) engendered the envy of her sister Aglauros in *Metamorphoses* 2.708ff.; when Aglauros tried to thwart that love, Mercury turned her to stone. Passive Troilus ironically glosses over the rape by characterizing it as Mercury's "love of Hierse" (729) and merely acknowledges that "Pallas was with Aglawros wroth" (730) without noting the resultant reification into stone. Criseyde, too, a divided self combining encouraging Herse/sullen Aglauros into a single figure, will turn to stone in book 4, dead to Troilus's ineffectual love. Because Aglauros functions as a go-between, although an avaricious one who demands gold from Mercury, and because Herse's sister is named Pandrosus,[51] she therefore reminds us of covetous (and envious?) Pandarus in bringing the two lovers together.

The last invocations cast an ominous underworld pallor over Troilus's requests. He invokes the aid of Diana the moon (731; also the goddess of chastity) and then the "fatal sustren which, er any cloth / Me shapen was, my destine me sponne" (733–34) in finishing the "viage," or "this werk that is bygonne!" (735), although whether he means by this "voyage," or "this work," the relationship with Criseyde, the night's anticipated lovemaking, or the course of his life, remains ambiguous. In the first image, although requesting help with sexual performance from the goddess of chastity may appear to be a non sequitur, Troilus may also associate Diana as the moon with Fortune, as is true of the goddess in the *Knight's Tale*; further, Diana as the triple goddess Hecate, Luna, and Proserpina, together with the Fates, often appears in mythographies in conjunction with Pluto, ruler of the underworld, and therefore suggestive in general of the powers of mutability swaying the sublunary realm.[52] Troilus's request, given these mythographic and Neoplatonic associations, remains ironic and thus consonant with the earlier examples of irony, for the Fates Clotho, Lachesis, and Atropos will indeed spin his destiny to its final length before snipping it off by poem's end, a destiny in great measure determined by their help in his meeting with Criseyde on this rainy night.

If this long prayer of Troilus undercuts the subsequent culmination of the lovers' relationship in bed as primarily sexual, verging on rape, a reification of the other, the remaining mythological references in book 3 similarly gloss the consequences of their "wedding" later that night and the following day. Normally procreation follows weddings, but the lack of procreation after *this* wedding is ominous; instead of racial immortality and continuation, the references stress competition, limitation and hoarding, disruption, fall, tumescence, death.

Midas—a figure used by the Wife of Bath in her tale as a subtle gloss on her old rich husbands and perhaps her most recent younger husbands, as we shall see in a later chapter—in his covetousness antithesizes the generosity of the lover, which the narrator wants to acknowledge in the ceremonial gifts of Troilus and Criseyde. After the exchange of rings and Criseyde's gift of the brooch (1371–72), the narrator digresses on Midas (1387–89) in castigation of the avaricious who despise the service of lovers and blame love (1373–77). The narrator fantasizes such "wrecches" with "erys also longe / As hadde Mida, ful of coveytise" (1388–89) and drunk "as hoot and stronge / As Crassus did for his affectis wronge" (1390–91) as an appropriate lesson in their vice.

More broadly, however, a second Midas in the mythographies provides a gloss on Troilus and Criseyde's gift giving that once again defines their relationship as excessively sensual and thus destructive. In Bersuire, Midas epitomizes poor judgment arising from ignorance because he prefers the rustic music of Pan to the universally admired music of Apollo, for which folly he is punished by the addition of asses' ears. Such a choice underscores the temporal rather than the celestial, and therefore the errant judgment of Troilus and Criseyde, who wrongfully choose *voluptas* over *caritas* in an exhibition of their own *stulticia*. Bersuire cites 1 Cor. 2:14 and Prov. 23:9 in this gloss on *Metamorphoses* 11.100ff. to prove that rude and bestial men such as Midas deserve the ears of an ass because they appreciate "rural Pan" and the "words of terrestrial advocates" more than "heaven-dwelling Apollo" and "heavenly doctors" (learned men): "The sensual man [*animalis homo*] does not perceive those things that are of the Spirit of God" and "Do not speak in the ears of fools [*in auribus insipientium*]; because they will despise the instruction of your speech [*doctrinam eloquii tui*]" (*Ovidius*, p. 158, trans. p. 368).[53]

Finally, because the narrator interjects this exemplum into his narrative, wagging his finger reproachfully at his listeners and applauding the generosity of Troilus and Criseyde, the figure of Midas reflects back on the speaker's own untrained and limited judgment: not only does the narrator mistake the quality of love expressed by the exchange, but also the exchange of rings anticipates two later exchanges in *Troilus* that will define the covetous and physical underpinnings of this relationship. First, Criseyde will be exchanged, brochlike, for Antenor; next, she will accordingly, and appropriately under the rules of exchange with which she has been living, give to Diomede a brooch that Troilus gave her on the day she left Troy (1661–62). The narrator also expresses Midas-like ignorance by mixing explicit moralizing with the fictional integument of his poem, although mythographer Bersuire feels comfortable in glossing the Midas myth as an example of "truth will out": "Allegorize [*allega*] the rest and say that there is nothing secret [*occultum*] that will not be revealed [*reueletur*]" (*Ovidius*, p. 158, trans. p. 368).

After the exchange of rings and gifts, Criseyde continues to play the dominant role in the relationship—Venus to Cupid, or to Adonis—when she sings the courtly *aube* in lines 1422–42. If Criseyde had longed differently, or else tempered her desires with contemplation, she might have achieved a renown different from the one she earns by the end of the *Troilus,* as Troilus might have exhibited a different valor. In this dawn song, she wistfully wishes that the night would last as long as it did when Alcmena lay with Jove in *Metamorphoses* 9.280ff., who lengthened it to three times its normal length, and conceived Hercules: "'O nyght, allas, why nyltow over us hove / As longe as whan Almena lay by Jove?'" (1427–28). Conventionally, a male courtly lover sings this song, and the hope for the night to lengthen springs from a masculine and antifeminist tradition of songs of deception, which anticipates Criseyde's later infidelity to Troilus.[54] Further, to applaud night, associated with darkness, pleasure, and ignorance, and dislike day, associated with light and truth, turns the normal order upside down, stretches the natural length of the night to perversity. Because Troilus and Criseyde create a similarly upside-down wedding, one unnatural because it is not intended for procreation, unlike the result of Alcmena's long night of lovemaking, perhaps appropriately the mythographers say that the union of "Alcmena" (from *salsum,* salt, the "saltiness of wisdom" in the Third Vatican Mythographer) and Jove is "virorum fortium nascitur gloria," glory born from strong men, meaning Hercules, who withstands the temptation of *temporalia* through contemplation.[55]

Troilus follows her *aube* with his own Donne-like apostrophe to the "Busy old fool," "O cruel day" (1450), whom he identifies as "the sonne, Titan" (1464), in an unusual mythographic merging with Tithonus, the lover of Aurora, or the dawn. Like Criseyde, Troilus prefers darkness (and all that it signifies) to light (and all that it signifies). "O fool, wel may men the dispise, / That hast the dawyng al nyght by thi syde, / And suffrest hire so soone up fro the rise / For to disese loveris in this wyse" (1465–68). Indeed, Troilus imagines Tithonus as a bad lover, an antitype of his own love for Criseyde, because Tithonus allows Aurora to leave his side so early in the day and thereby make lovers like himself so miserable. This irony deepens when we learn that Aurora, in *Metamorphoses* 9.421ff., granted Tithonus immortality to have him by her side always, an exemplary and eternal love not limited by the measure of days and nights which does contrast with Troilus's flawed love, which lets Criseyde slip from his side without resistance, which contrasts also with Criseyde's measured love for the Trojan that ends shortly in the Greek camp with Diomede in her bed. Finally, the controlling role of Aurora in charge of obtaining immortality for her lover recalls dominant Criseyde's role throughout this third book.

After the lovers separate, the remaining mythological images continue to define their love as erotic and therefore infernal rather than paradisal, and to define Troilus as a blind lover whose failure to see his love and himself clearly will lead to his downfall. In line 1600, Troilus thanks his friend Pandarus for rescuing him from Phlegethon — a reference to one of the four rivers of hell clearly drawn from canto 12 of Dante's *Inferno.* In that canto the seventh circle of hell included those violent against others, to be followed in the next canto by those violent against themselves, the suicides. "Thow hast in hevene ybrought my soule at reste / Fro Flegitoun, the fery flood of helle" (1599–1600), Troilus gratefully acknowledges, while the reader realizes that Chaucer's use of other mythological references in this book has already characterized the culmination of his desire as infernal, temporal, earthly, and that the next book of the *Troilus* will plunge our hero into a despair truly underworld in nature that nearly leads to his suicide. The reference to his rescue from a river of hell reminds us that he is already a man disordered, unstable, clearly part of hell in terms of his destructive, earthly, and infernal choices.

Troilus imagines that the four horses of the sun rise deliberately to spite him, in a novel twist to the conventional image of horse and rider to show not only Troilus's skewed and irrational perception of external reality as a manifestation of his own immaturity and adolescent self-gratification but also to show his inability to keep the course of his own life on track. By blaming one of the horses drawing the sun's chariot instead of the charioteer, Troilus shows that he misunderstands the proper relationship between charioteer (or rider) and horse(s):

> Quod Troilus, "Allas, now am I war
> That Piros and tho swifte steedes thre,
> Which that drawen forth the sonnes char,
> Han gon som bi-path in dispit of me;
> That maketh it so soone day to be;
> And for the sonne hym hasteth thus to rise,
> Ne shal I nevere don hire sacrifise." (1702–8)

First, as if truly blind, myopic, he mentions only one horse, Piros, rather than four; in addition, "Piros" is probably in fact Eritheus, whose name means "red" and who stands for the first of the four ages of man — "birth" (Remigius, *Boeth.*, pp. 73–74). The four horses as the four ages of man that rule earthly life thus suggest ignorance, according to the K-Reviser of Remigius's commentary on Boethius's *Consolatio* 4m7; all belong to Apollo the sun, *perditis,* instead of the true son, Christ, with the specific human ages defined: Eritheus, birth (red); Acteus, "beautiful," boyhood; Lampus, "shining," man in his prime; Filogeus, "loving earth," old age (that is, bent toward earth). In a sense, because Troilus cannot guide Piros and the chariot of the sun, he resembles Phaethon in *Metamorphoses* 2.153, a man who can either act wisely or let the four horses pull him toward death, according to the K-Reviser, which in fact Troilus allows them to do by preferring night to day.

Troilus's blindness to the natural order, hinted by his angry apostrophes to the sun, will deepen into despair over the loss of Criseyde in the next book, when he descends into the underworld like Calliope's son Orpheus, who wanted to retrieve his beloved Eurydice. Accordingly, the narrator's invocation of all three Furies at the beginning of book 4 will emphasize the narrative return to the underworld explored in book 1, when Tisiphone alone was invoked. The Wheel of Fortune is already turning, and happy but blind Troilus is already beginning to fall from that warm place he thought so secure.

Book 4, The *Descensus ad Inferos* of Troilus and the Metamorphosis of Criseyde

The narrator's invocation of the three Furies, the "Herynes, Nyghtes doughtren thre, / That endeles compleignen evere in pyne" (22–23), and of "cruel Mars ek, fader to Quyryne" (25), cruel because god of war and discord, sets the scene for the dramatic action in book 4. The two narrative "pieces" of book 4 seamed together by the image of the Furies in the invocation include the dramatized perturbations of Troilus's soul as his fear and hopelessness deepen into despair and the macrocosmic backdrop of the walled city of Troy as an infernal landscape similar to the walled City of Dis separating lower hell from upper hell in the *Inferno*. Troilus here descends into the underworld, blind and self-divided from an internal civil war caused by conflicting loyalties to nation, family, and Criseyde. Although the mythographers gloss the underworld as earthly, temporal, and spiritually inadequate, Chaucer, in modeling Troilus's descent on the Homeric and Virgilian epic descent of the hero into the underworld, defines the psychological and spiritual state of Orpheus-like Troilus (791) and the nature of his love for Criseyde, perhaps following a note introduced by the glossators on the descent of Orpheus in Boethius's *Consolatio* 3m12. Although Ann Astell has identified the beginning of the descent into vice with the time when Troilus-Orpheus falls in love with Criseyde in the Temple in book 1, and has interpreted Criseyde as a type of Eurydice who also descends into vice, she does not consider the possibility of book 4 instead as the narrative moment when the choices made, especially by Troilus, result in an "afterlife" in hell.[56] Here begins the "double sorrow" promised at the poem's opening, one that depends more on anger, guilt, and anxiety than real sadness, and one whose Boethian infernal associations are filtered through Dantesque and Ovidian mythological and mythographic lenses.

143

Because the overall structure of the *Troilus* is predicated on that of Dante's *Commedia*, Chaucer returns in this fourth book to the *Inferno*, a *cantica* from which several key mythological references (to the Furies and Athamas) may have been drawn as a gloss on Troilus's psychological situation.

In addition to these Boethian and Dantesque infernal references to the descent of Troilus, there also exist Ovidian references to the metamorphosis of Criseyde, who is a type of Eurydice who "dies," bitten by a phallicized serpent. The whole dramatic description of the effects of the exchange on the lovers (218–1414)—the mirror image of books 1 to 3 with the falling in love of first Troilus and then Criseyde, followed by the consummation—is bracketed by two mythological references symbolizing metamorphosis and revealing psychological aspects of the lovers' motivations. In line 1138, Chaucer compares Criseyde's tears to those of Myrrha, the lover of her father Cinyras and mother of Adonis; in line 1459, Troilus refers to Calkas as a type of hundred-eyed Argus, implying that Criseyde resembles the watched Io; and in line 1539, Criseyde swears by mad Athamas in hell (and Juno who put him there) that she will remain faithful to Troilus. The transformations of Myrrha and Io are physical, the transformation of Athamas is psychological, both changes glossing the "change" of Criseyde. Let us first examine Troilus, then Criseyde.

The narrator's previous references to the Furies—or at least to Tisiphone—have glossed Troilus's danger as mere evil thoughts. In the invocation to book 4, the inclusion of all three Furies (24) deepens and intensifies the process of anger to include despair, the sin of wrath Dante depicts as part of the Fifth Circle, and accompanying rage. Mythographically, the process of manifesting anger begins internally and privately and ends externally and publicly, according to Fulgentius in his *Mitologiae* and later, in the twelfth century, John of Garland in his *Integumenta Ovidii*, although each defines the process differently. For Fulgentius, the Furies serve Pluto, the first, Alecto, who "means unstoppable [*inpausibilis*], while Tisiphone is *tuton phone*, that is, the voice of these same ones [*istarum vox*], and Megaera for *megale eris*, that is, great contention [*magna contentio*]. The first stage, therefore, is to create rage [*furiam*] without pause; the second, to burst forth into words; the third, to stir up a quarrel" (*Mit.* 1.7, pp. 20–21, trans. p. 52). In contrast, John of Garland notes that the Furies "sully [*sordent*]" the mind, speech, and hands in a process beginning with thought (Alecto), transforming into words (Thesiphone) and finishing as deeds (Megera) (p. 52, trans. p. 135).

Dante extends the psychological allegory further still by differentiating between a more physical wrath and a more intellectual fury, to mark the transition from sins of the flesh, sins of weakness, to sins of the will. Thus, the Furies appear in *Inferno 9*, at the gate to lower hell, just after the circle of the wrathful, which has included the appearance of angry Phlegyas, who ferries souls to places in the Stygian marsh associated with this sin, and just before the Sixth Circle, of the heretics. In Dante's passage in canto 9, Virgil forces him to turn his back and close his eyes to the Furies, which advice succeeds in moving them past this barrier. The danger is that the Furies, along with Medusa, will turn sinners to stone, and therefore Dante closes his eyes so that he cannot see. More psychologically, fury (wrath) becomes the entryway into despair. In other words, fear and hopelessness lead to insanity, the punishment of those of guilty conscience in classical myth, as evidenced in the *Oresteia*. Accordingly, Dante sees

> tre furïe infernal di sangue tinte,
> che membra femminine avìeno e atto,
> e con idre verdissime eran cinte;
> serpentelli e ceraste avean per crine,
> londe le fiere tempie erano avvinte. (9.38–42, Dante, 1:123)

[three hellish, blood-stained Furies that had the parts and bearing of women and were girt with hydras of bright green, and for hair they had little serpents and horned snakes twined about the savage temples.] (Dante, trans. 1:122)

The snake, an important symbol of the devil and of carnality in the Garden of Eden, appropriately adorns the locks of the Furies. In an image suggesting the marshy nature of the Styx and a reworking of Fall into Redemption, the angel of grace scatters the Furies like frogs and also "più di mille anime distrutte" ("a thousand ruined souls"). Their chaotic movement contrasts symbolically with the orderly and directed progress of souls from terrace to terrace in the *Purgatorio*.

Chaucer invokes that Dantesque distinction here by summoning all three Furies, for in the relationship between Troilus and Criseyde their carnal sins will now lead them, willy-nilly, to behavior that signifies a sin of the will, treachery and deception and cold-heartedness signaling the lowest reaches of Dante's hell. Just as Virgil has counseled Dante to pass by the Furies with eyes closed and back turned, the rational man might arm himself with this advice to withstand nights of despair. Laomedon, founder of Troy, experienced such nights as these, and Troilus soon will, when the workings of Apollo's revenge are made manifest. In the discussion of the myth of Laomedon as founder of Troy in book 2, we established that the walls he had built with the help of Neptune (and, in Chaucer, of Phoebus Apollo) represented both the city's safety and its curse, for Laomedon twice neglected to pay for the help he had promised; the second time, he offended Hercules. The fury of those betrayed, gods and hero, will result in the flaming destruction of Troy (117–19), as the prescient priest of Apollo, Calkas, has revealed:

"For certein, Phebus and Neptunus bothe,
That makeden the walles of the town,
Ben with the folk of Troie alwey so wrothe,
That they wol brynge it to confusioun,
Right in despit of kyng Lameadoun." (120–24)

The god Phoebus Apollo, according to Calkas, is thus responsible for shedding light on the future, through astronomy (115), "By sort, and by augurye ek, trewely" (116). This nice overlay of the legendary, astrological, and mythographic traditions reinforces the association of Apollo, god of wisdom whose planet is the sun, with light and truth; for Hector's capture of Antenor when the sun is in Leo—"Byfel that, whan that Phebus shynyng is / Upon the brest of Hercules lyoun" (30–31)—probably in July (according to the note in Benson), will spark Calkas's proposed exchange of Antenor for Criseyde.

The reference to the sun's astrological position in the constellation of Leo, the Nimean lion defeated by Hercules, recalls the anger of both Hercules and Apollo over Laomedon's treachery. Because Laomedon nearly lost his own daughter out of covetousness, Calkas's apparent generosity and love for Criseyde (despite his own treachery to Troy) stand in relief. But Laomedon, like Troilus, was blocked from the light of truth, of day, and instead lived through nights of despair. Further, Laomedon was motivated by fury, a soul perturbed (as Holkot would have it) by desire for riches, if not carnal pleasure. Later medieval mythographic glosses on the Furies single out their serpentine locks to particularize the nature of the sins represented in the stages of fury, adding to the glosses a desire for riches and carnal delight that will join together two different pieces of narrative in the fourth book. The fullest gloss on the Furies as illustration of the process of rage, by Robert Holkot, borrows from the lexicographer Papias in its equation of the Furies with Fortuna and in its iconographic gloss on the serpentine locks of the three as the three effects of fury (that is, Alecto, Tisiphone, Megaera) on the soul, namely, it begets many perturbations and desires for riches and the fulfillment of *voluptas*.[57]

As if transfixed by the Furies, paralyzed into stasis, metamorphosed to stone, Troilus compounds his fury turned inward, his despair, by rationalizing his paralysis, in the famous solipsistic Digression on Predestination (958–1078) later in the book, a rational man's scholastic acceptance of predestination.[58] Ironically, unlike Laomedon, and instead of arming himself for "war"—even in a metaphorical sense, as the invocation of Mars suggests he might well do—Troilus does nothing but sit passively on a cushion. Caught between his desire for Criseyde and his obligation to his nation, in temperament yielding and pliant, and opposed by the configurations of the stars (or fate), Troilus resembles the doomed but self-blinded hero Oedipus, with whom he compares himself: "But ende I wol, as Edippe, in derknesse / My sorwful lif, and dyen in distresse" (300–301). According to Robert Holkot, in his commentary *In librum duodecim prophetas,* the Sphinx whose riddle is solved by Oedipus can be interpreted as worldly wisdom, but *stulticia* before God, and Oedipus, therefore, who makes the Sphinx perish, can be interpreted as a type of the good Christian who lives well, knowing the danger predicted for the future.[59] Yet, unlike Oedipus, Troilus too frequently appears stupid or stupefied, so overwhelmed by his understanding of the political and familial machinery dominating his life that he neither acts nor thinks well. For example, he identifies his despair as so infernal that he informs Pandarus of his intention to descend after death "down with Proserpyne" (473) (rather than Pluto, king of the underworld) where he will "wone in pyne" (474) and bewail his painful separation from Criseyde (476–77). In the classical myth, Pluto abducted Proserpina from her mother Ceres and imprisoned her in his underworld until the judge of the dead, Minos, decreed, after Ceres's long search for her ended, that Pluto could keep her in the underworld for six months each year (winter), and that Proserpina could return to earth for six months each year (spring).[60] Ironically, passive Troilus will in a sense join Proserpina after death, but only after failing to abduct his own beloved, the maternal and Ceres-like Criseyde ("Ceres-like" if we remember the Tantalus myth and its application in book 3).

Chaucer characterizes the love of both Troilus and Criseyde as infernal, temporal. Chaucer also links the lovers with the planet of change and fickleness, associated with Pluto and Proserpina in the mythographies. Troilus's appeal to the Fates can be read as ironic if we understand the frequent mythographic linking, as early as Fulgentius and continuing as late as Bersuire, of the Fates with the underworld ruled by Pluto — evidence of his imminent death of heartbreak as well as his passive acceptance of Fate.[61] Troilus appeals to the third Fate, Atropos, charged with snipping off the thread of individual destiny, to "make redy thow my beere" (1208), although it is he who stands with sword at his heart preparing to die (1211). Criseyde echoes Troilus's appeal to Atropos, except that she demands that the Fate "my thred of lif tobreste" (1546) if she is false (an ironic oath if the Fates owe allegiance to Pluto, king of hell). The underworld of temporal good on this earth is governed by Fortune and mutability, with which Criseyde has been increasingly identified, by herself and others.

In several places, the infernal and unstable relationship of Troilus and Criseyde is tied to the moon through the characters' appeals to Juno, the ruler of air, and Lucina, goddess of childbirth, with whom Criseyde is linked; both Juno and Lucina[62] were associated with women and childbirth as well as with the moon and upper air. First, when Pandarus counsels grieving Troilus to visit Criseyde that night and "make of this an ende," he also begs "blisful Juno thorugh hire grete myght" to send her grace to them (1116–17). Second, in line 1539, Criseyde herself will pledge her fidelity to Troilus by Juno, swearing to return in ten days "as helpe me Juno, hevenes quene" (1594). Turned mad like Athamas, in her failure to return, Criseyde will reveal the failure of Juno to aid either lover. She illustrates the passage of ten days through the astrological image of "Lucina the sheene," or the moon, identified as Phoebus's sister, as she moves from Aries to Leo (1591–92). Like the moon, Criseyde too will pass from one house (the city of Troy) to another (the Greek camp). Criseyde compounds the association by swearing by "the love of Cinthia the sheene" (1608) once again in the face of Troilus's continuing fear that she will not return.

Criseyde's helplessness, her despair, may overlay her desire for Troilus-Orpheus to rescue her from this hell, or even from the Greek camp, if the Orpheus myth is interpreted as a foreshadowing of their imminent separation. Misguided Criseyde, imagining their eternal reunion in "the feld of pite ... /That highte Elisos" (789–90) at some later time, ironically casts her lover delivering them "out of peyne" (789) to Calliope's son Orpheus in his descent to retrieve "his fere" Eurydice (791). This descent (and its lack of success) have been explained by commentators on Boethius's *Consolatio* 3m12, among the many mythographers who have glossed the descent, as the gaze of wisdom (signified by Orpheus, and therefore here, ironically, by Troilus) misdirected toward the dark underworld of *temporalia.* Those earthly delights have misled concupiscence (Eurydice, and therefore Criseyde) away from the light of the "summum bonum" (Remigius, *Boeth.,* p. 71). Criseyde's reassurance that they will meet again, therefore, also smacks of rationalization and self-delusion. In this sense, the "death" of Eurydice, or her separation from Orpheus, because of a serpent's bite (according to Bernardus Silvestris, the desire for temporal things),[63] is translated by Chaucer into the exchange of Criseyde to the Greek camp, followed by her psychological distancing from Troilus, her "death" to him, because of the intervention of serpentlike Diomede and his large tongue. As she says, rightly, in line 793, she soon will be "chaunged," changed as the moon changes, another kind of lunacy, as well as exchanged, for Antenor.

Given Troilus's failure to prevent Criseyde from leaving, a failure specifically gendered as masculine, which in a perverse way "rapes" and victimizes her, she "changes" or metamorphoses, in an Ovidian sense, as witnessed in her reification (as incestuous Myrrha [1139]) and madness (as the imbalanced falsifier Athamas [1538], husband of Ino, father of Meleager, and ancestor of Diomede). Criseyde's metamorphosis begins with her realization that Troilus can and will do nothing to prevent her departure, however

much he grieves over her imminent loss, followed by the concomitant real-
ization that she must think rationally and act for both of them. After hear-
ing the news of the exchange, Criseyde undergoes the same emotionally
wrenching experience as her lover (743–98), complaining of the "synne" of
her father Calkas in causing the exchange and the woeful responsibility of
her mother Argyve[64] in giving her birth (761–63). But gender vindicates
Criseyde's passivity in a way that it cannot Troilus's. Just as he had to
summon cosmic energy (in his invocation to the planets, in book 3) in or-
der to initiate the first night's "labor," that is, his sexual performance, here
he requires outside assistance—which Pandarus, and Criseyde, fail to sup-
ply as they did on that auspicious early occasion. Instead of forceful deter-
mination, Troilus expresses weak rationalization for his lack of action
(marriage, kidnapping, etc.): he castigates Fortune, the God of Love, his soul,
his eyes, Calkas, as responsible for this sorry turn of events (260–336).
Troilus also worries about another war ensuing after a ravishment, much
like the Trojan War after Helen's abduction, and the consequent harm to
Troy, so damaged after the present war (547–53); he accordingly worries
about darkening Criseyde's name and her honor, and causing her anxiety,
given the violence and slander that would accompany an abduction (561–66).
Even after Pandarus's spirited argument in favor of Troilus's taking her
with him, at whatever the cost (582–630), Troilus insists on abduction—
raptus—only with Criseyde's consent (632–37), an oxymoronic logic. Pan-
darus colludes with his inaction by arguing for the option of finding
another woman to take his niece's place (400–427); after Pandarus has en-
treated Criseyde to control her grief in her lover's presence, to prevent
Troilus from dying, the go-between once again attempts to cheer up Troilus
by counseling him to forget her (1093–99) and then to go to her to "make of
this an ende" (1115), that is, presumably, to prevent her from going ("Myn
herte seyth, 'Certeyn, she shal nat wende' "[1118]).
   It is at this crucial point in the narrative that Criseyde abruptly and by
necessity "changes": her swoon marks a kind of death of her love—and a
protection against pain, for which she has no resources. After kissing and
hugging her lover, woeful Criseyde in broken voice cries "I deye" (1149)
and beseeches mercy from Jove and help from Troilus (1149–50), then lays
her face upon his chest and "loste speche" (1151). Ironically, Troilus, as a
deluded Pyramus, imagines Criseyde as dead during this Thisbe-like faint-
heartedness, and nearly kills himself in order to follow her soul, wherever
"the doom of Mynos wolde it dighte" (1188). Perhaps he hopes that Minos
as the judge of souls in the underworld would decide to send them to the
circle of lechery, the place in hell of the famous adulterers Paolo and
Francesca in Dante's *Inferno*. Once she has awakened and spied his naked
sword, his confession of his near suicide and her maternal enfolding of him

in her arms (1230) somehow give her the resolve to act for him—to lay out their alternatives rationally and decide for both of them the best, most practical course of action. Her reasoned and organized deliberations (the parliament has decided their future; she will return in ten days, a doubtlessly painful but endurable space of time; the war will end; she will persuade her father to allow her to return, etc.) reassure both of them, in the best maternal fashion, that her "change" will be temporary.

In book 4 the narrator's glosses of Criseyde as a type of Myrrha and Athamas are borrowed from Dante, who uses them in canto 30 of the *Inferno* as mythological examples of impersonators, although in book 3 Chaucer has used primarily Myrrha's son Adonis to characterize Troilus mythographically by drawing on Ovidian glosses. In addition, Criseyde's psychological anesthesia against the pain that results from a love too carnal, too temporal, is described in terms of the Ovidian image of reified Io, the heifer guarded by the hundred-eyed Argus (her watchful father, in line 1459) against further adultery with Jupiter.

The reference to the incestuous Myrrha, transformed into the myrrh tree weeping tears of myrrh after her father spurned her continuing advances, characterizes Criseyde's reification as a punishment and a protection against pain:

> The woful teeris that they leten falle
> As bittre weren, out of teris kynde,
> For peyne, as is ligne aloes or galle—
> So bittre teeris weep nought, as I fynde,
> The woful Mirra thorugh the bark and rynde—
> That in this world ther nys so hard on herte
> That nolde han rewed on hire peynes smerte. (1135–41)

The bitterness and pain of Criseyde are most obviously in focus here, pain continued in the classical myth when the tree must burst open upon the birth of Myrrha's son Adonis. The underscoring of Criseyde's maternal reactions to the ineffectual Troilus is heightened by the incestuous relationship between Myrrha and her father: her excessive love for her father ironically foreshadows the reason for Troilus's separation from Criseyde—so that she can return to her father Calkas, who knows Troy will fall and who loves his daughter enough to plead for her exchange. Finally, the mythological incest also reflects back on the earlier question of the avuncular role of Pandarus toward his niece. When Criseyde exchanges Diomede for Troilus, she also exchanges a paternal relative—Calkas for Pandarus—and the question of his collusion in whatever is happening in the tent in which he also sleeps is never answered.

Criseyde's numbing of herself—dulling sensation, or vitality, in order to protect herself against pain—becomes equivalent to metamorphosis and reification as expressed by Myrrha in Ovid's tale. Robert Holkot notes that such pain is caused by carnal pleasure, *voluptas*:

> Following sexual pleasure is the accumulation of pain or grief and discontent: because naturally after pleasure follows discontent.... In this figure Ovid depicts *Metamorphoses* 10.312ff. That virgin by the name of Myrrha who desired unchaste relations [*incaestum*] with her father obtained her desire, having been aided by her nurse; after this was discovered, she was put to flight by her father, and fell into such great sadness that, altered by the weeping of tears and sighs, was transformed into a tree of her name, which still pours from itself bitter drops as if tears, as a sign that perpetual pain of mind follows illicit bodily desire.[65] (My translation)

Chaucer's point is that Criseyde's love for Troilus is skewed toward temporal pleasure, the loss of which leads to dolor and discontent and which can be ameliorated only by such numbing and "change."

Chaucer reinforces Criseyde's excessive *voluptas* (even on this night of woe they discuss matters in bed, enfolded in each others' arms) by Troilus's end-bracket reference to her father Calkas being "in sleght as Argus eyed" (1459). Voyeurlike, Calkas will be exchanged for the voyeurlike Pandarus. Perhaps bearing a hundred eyes, watchful Calkas is capable of being blinded by the appropriate Mercurial ruse of eloquence so that this Io-like Criseyde can escape to Troilus once again. But Chaucer wants us to see Calkas's cunning, his "calkullynge," too, coupled with his avarice—he can be bought:[66]

> For al Appollo, or his clerkes lawes,
> Or calkullynge, avayleth noght thre hawes;
> Desir of gold shal so his soule blende
> That, as me lyst, I shal wel make an ende. (1397–1400)

Io's transformation into a "vaccam bestialem concupiscentiam et voluptatem" in Holkot resembles Myrrha's transformation into a tree. And Argus, interpreted morally as the "clericus litteratus" because he has a hundred eyes, or "considerationes multas, idest cautelas," becomes analogous to Calkas in Chaucer: when Argus's watchfulness is subverted through an appeal to his worldly appetites, through the adulations of friends, he sleeps and his negligence leads to death, specifically defined as his avarice.[67] Troilus is aided by Mercury here (as in the myth of Argus and Io), perhaps to be interpreted as the devil, or "medius currens," "running between," in Holkot's words, "who runs asking whom he devours," and also at the end of the *Troilus*, when the messenger of the gods leads Troilus away from earth.

Such anesthesia ultimately so changes Criseyde that she becomes mad—she loses her reason, her judgment, her ability to act prudently. Chaucer notes this final process in her grief over the loss of Troilus by means of her pledge of loyalty, sworn upon the might of "Saturnes doughter, Juno," to make her dwell "As wood as Athamante" (1539) in "Stix, the put of helle" (1540), should she be false to her lover. Criseyde here responds to Troilus's final, but delayed, offer to steal away with her (1499–1526)—however, it comes too late, and is offered too quickly; Criseyde, caught up in her own fantasy of bribing her father and returning in ten days, and insulted by his suggestion that she might find a "lusty knyght" among the Greeks in response to her father's imagined request for a husband (1471–91), swears by all the gods and goddesses, nymphs, infernal deities, satyrs, and fauns (1541–45) that she will remain true.

The figure Athamas in the oath she swears, like Io and Myrrha, describes the metamorphosis in Criseyde, given Troilus's failure to meet her needs, although Troilus has just voiced his fear that she will also fail to meet his (as indeed she will). In addition, these images all represent aspects of Criseyde's doubleness, her self divided in order to protect her against further hurt from the hero she loves. Athamas, the husband of Semele's sister Ino, grows mad as a result of Juno's anger against Semele, a Theban woman like Europa to whom her husband Jupiter has been attracted: when he sees his wife carrying their two children, he cries, in Dante's *Inferno*,

> "Tendiam le reti, sì ch'io pigli
> la leonessa e'leoncini al varco";
> e poi distese i dispietati artigli,
> prendendo l'un ch'avea nome Learco,
> e rotollo e percosselo ad un sasso;
> e quella s'annegò con l'altro carco. (1.7–12, Dante, 1:370)

["Let us spread the nets to take the lioness and the whelps as they pass!", then stretched out his pitiless claws, taking the one that was named Learchus, and whirled him round and dashed him on a rock, and she drowned herself with the other burden.] (Dante, trans. 1:371)

Athamas, like Myrrha, appears in canto 30 of Dante's *Inferno*, Athamas in line 4, Myrrha in line 37, both suggesting mythological examples of impersonators—the falsifiers of persons, coins (counterfeiters), or words—as part of the fraudulent who occupy the ten *bolge* of the Eighth Circle, just prior to the treachery of the Ninth Circle. The falsifying of a person occurs either in Athamas's madness, or Hecuba's, in this same passage. Hecuba's barking like a dog when she sees her children dead—Polyxena is sacrificed on Achilles' tomb; Polydorus, on the beach, is murdered by his guardian

Polymnestor[68]—defines madness as change, splitting of personality, self-destruction, reification. The classical madness of Athamas and Hecuba, inflicted by the gods, contrasts with the moral insanity of Schicchi and Myrrha later in the same canto—all involving madness within the family. In his craziness, Athamas fits in with those who are magicians, falsifiers, or impersonators in the tenth *bolgia*, sinners who perverted the physical (and therefore the moral) world, beginning in the Eighth Circle with the panderers and seducers (1), and continuing with the flatterers (2), simonists (3), diviners (4), barrators (5), hypocrites (6), thieves (7), fraudulent counselors (8), makers of discord (9), and falsifiers (10). Their use here accentuates the necessary fraud of Criseyde that will deepen into treachery in book 5.

The falsity and cunning of the traitor Calkas are visited upon the false and perhaps slightly mad Criseyde, the child he has sacrificed in the past and will again. Her oath upon Athamas in hell ironically foreshadows her future, both in terms of Calkas's sacrifice of her to Diomede in the immediate future, and in terms of her sacrifice of the boyish Troilus and her afterlife in hell, as a traitor. In book 2, falling in love with Troilus, for Criseyde, involved the violent wrenching of her heart from her breast by the eagle. Literally, Chaucer suggested by that symbolic action that falling in love changes one's self, when the lover cares more for the emotional well-being of the beloved than for one's own, which the lover has granted to the beloved, in this case Troilus. The violence of this kind of romantic (and highly carnal) love, according to Chaucer, can madden and split the lover into two, can make Criseyde deny her own feelings, deaden herself to pain, in order to ensure what she perceives as her beloved's own well-being. That her concern for Troilus is maternal, continuing the pattern of imagery set in book 3, crops up in the mythological identification that she makes with mad father Athamas, and that Chaucer makes with her and daughter Myrrha. The change of Criseyde, the psychological transformation she experiences upon the news of her imminent exchange for Antenor, naturally results when her father, rather than her lover, "abducts" her.

The mythological backdrop of the Trojan War, caused by the abduction of Helen by Paris, when conjoined with the infernal backdrop of Dante's *Inferno*, reveals the perversity of her "exchange" and transformation. It is because the Trojans insist that they do not trade women, when in fact they have, because Troilus insists that he cannot ravish Criseyde, when in fact Paris has ravished Helen, that makes Criseyde's bitterness all the keener, her anomie all the more striking, and her metamorphosis all the more sympathetic—like the victims in Ovid's *Metamorphoses.* In book 5, her mourning, like Myrrha's, will continue, but more important, Troilus will experience firsthand the effects of a tribe, family, love, or beloved divided and turned against itself.

Book 5, Criseyde's Flight from Troilus: Atalanta and the Fate of Theban Meleager

Book 5 has two parts, a body and an Epilogue, which reverses the "prologue plus body" structure of earlier books. This narrative reversal mirrors the reversal of fortune suffered by Troilus, to actualize this Boethian tragedy defined as reversal. Further, because only this last book lacks an invocation—read by previous critics as testimony of Chaucer's carelessness in completing the romance[69]—the invocation for book 4 serves also for book 5, as if it were a continuation of the furious changes initiated by the exchange of Criseyde.

Book 5 does open with a truncated announcement of the inexorable progress of the workings of fate, as if also in continuation of Troilus's conclusions regarding predestination in book 4—and as if in symbolic reflection of the final snipping of Atropos, who seems to have cut away the invocation for book 5 as she will later with Troilus's life. The three fatal sisters whom the narrator pauses to address ("yow, angry Parcas, sustren thre" [3]) recall the imminence of the fall of Troy, and of *Troy*lus; the ending of the relationship of Troilus and Criseyde, largely through the advent of Diomede, will precede the ending of the life of the hero and of his nation. To these endings Chaucer will tie the myth of the Fates (insofar as they control both these microcosmic and macrocosmic relationships) and the Theban myth of the Calydonian boar defeated by Meleager, who also loves Atalanta and as a result dies—a myth in which the Fates figure greatly. "To fall" implies, as it has earlier, in a psychological and Boethian sense, a figurative decline and deterioration, characterized as a descent into the underworld in book 1 and true as well for both Troilus and Criseyde here.

Although Chaucer's use of the *Thebaid* (and Theban mythology) has been carefully examined by scholars, the relationship between this particular Theban myth of Meleager and the role of the Fates therein has never been singled out for examination in relation to book 5.[70] The Fates play an important role in the myth of Meleager: at the time of his birth, they gave his mother a brand that, when lit, burned until consumed—like his life, which ends with the brand.[71] That his mother chose to end Meleager's life by relighting the brand is a portion of the myth Chaucer will find especially attractive, given Criseyde's new and distinctly unmaternal reactions to Troilus—and her exchange to the hands of the heir of Calydon, descendant of Meleager's family. The misanthropomorphic Fates and the misogynistic treatment of Criseyde exist as an overwritten text, or palimpsest, for reading the poem. Fulgentius's definition of the Plutonian-ruled Fates in *Mitologiae* 1.8 emphasizes the apparent chaotic and therefore whimsical process of their control of human life, one in which the summons at birth (Clotho) is linked with destiny (Lachesis) but ends with the lack of order

(Atropos) that typifies the abrupt completion of each individual's life.[72] Bersuire's gloss on the Fates in the Meleager myth appropriately identifies them as the *deae infernales* who govern the fate of each single person in the earthly underworld, to emphasize the three parts of the sensitive soul — natural, vital, and animal — or therefore the life fluid, which runs as long as life lasts.

The key to the fall of Troy as well as the fall of Thebes is (as we might expect from the misogynistic mythographers) the mother, who seems to be missing in both the Trojan and Greek camps, both literally (Hecuba, for example, is never seen; Criseyde seems not to have a mother) and figuratively (there is neither gentleness nor nurturing in the private domestic and sexual scenes or the public political ones). Bersuire unintentionally provides an interesting link between the stories of the birth of Paris and the birth of Meleager in his interpolation into the gloss on *Metamorphoses* 12.4–6 of Hecuba's dream of the burning brand (*Ovidius*, p. 162, trans. p. 377). According to Bersuire, pregnant Hecuba's dream is interpreted as the future burning and destruction of Troy because of baby Paris, which results in her hiding the child to prevent the death decreed by his father. Bersuire concludes that this maternal pity is inferior to the kinder paternal pity that would have killed an evil man quickly and saved the country. This maternal pity toward a son whose judgment will lead to the burning brand of war contrasts with the maternal anger toward a homicidal son whose life is controlled and destroyed by a burning brand — Meleager. And yet Meleager's mother also is responsible for his demise.

Early in book 5, Chaucer has reminded his reader of the importance of the myth of the Judgment in the fall of Troy by Troilus's reference to Pallas Athena — at first glance, a suggestion that the protagonist has achieved that wisdom that the goddess signifies in the mythographies and in which, like Aeneas, he has suffered deficiencies up to this point. Troilus declares his last will and testament: at his vigil, Mars should receive his horse, sword, helm (306–7) and Pallas, his shield that "shyneth cleere" (308). Most probably Chaucer here invokes that Pallas Athena associated with Mars as a goddess of war, *dea bellorum,* in Robert Holkot's commentary on Wisdom, because in battles wisdom is more necessary than strength,[73] and therefore once again casts Troilus ironically in the role of the warrior, in contrast to the role of the lover he has played since book 1. Troilus will, unfortunately, achieve true perspective, true wisdom, only after death when he looks down on the petty goings-on of earth and laughs. Further, he will die in battle, a reminder of the discord with which the Trojan problems started. Discord, who was not invited to the wedding of Peleus and Thetis, offered the golden ball to Paris and the challenge of the judgment as a means of creating enmity between the Trojans and the Greeks.

Chaucer similarly conjoins two different myths — one from the *Aeneid* and involving a revised Judgment of Paris, one concerning the moon and thus connected with the previous lunar images—in a mythological sequence on Latona-moon to suggest that the ultimate goal of Troilus as he navigates the dark seas is the sublunary underworld marked by the concealing triple goddess (Lucina, Diana, Proserpina) and not at all Italy (or the contemplative life). In Troilus's address to Latona (655), the identification of the moon as Latona instead of the more conventional Lucina reveals the changeability of the moon and its phases. The two myths are joined through a curious interwoven Fulgentian etymology for Latinus-Latona-Lucina (respectively, the father of Aeneas's wife Lavinia, the mother of Apollo and Diana, and the moon). The logic of the conjunction works this way: the correct choice of Paris should have been Pallas Athena, goddess of wisdom, rather than Venus, a choice fulfilled instead by his half brother Aeneas, according to the mythographic allegorization of the *Aeneid,* when he arrives at the contemplative life, which has been his journey's goal, geographically designated as Italy.[74] So far, so good; but then the mythographer links Latinus, father of Lavinia (Aeneas's final wife, in Italy), with Latona and Lucina, through *latitando* and the idea of concealment: "Now Latinus is from *latitando,* being concealed, because toil [*labor*] is always concealed [*latitet*] in various places; wherefore Latona is also called *luna,* moon, because now she hides [*celet*] her upper parts, now her lower, and now is entirely concealed [*latitet*]" (Fulg. *Expos.,* p. 104, trans. p. 133 [chapter 24]). Troilus is moving in the wrong direction.

Troilus follows the path down to the underworld, not upward to the contemplative life: at this moment in the narrative, suspended between a "double sorrow," Troilus projects his unhappiness, if not his madness, through his angry sequential cursing in response to Criseyde's departure; in this denunciation of the entire universe, Troilus also renounces this world for the other world of hell, a self-destructive form of suicide. He curses the gods Jove, Apollo, and Cupid, or God, the sun, or god of wisdom, and the personification of desire, *cupiditas,* coupled with the gods of natural plenitude, Ceres, Bacchus, and Venus, and then a myriad of other forces, including his nativity, himself, his fate, Nature, and all creatures (206–10). Then he goes to bed—chooses paralysis once again—where he "walwith ther and torneth / In furie, as doth he Ixion in helle" until dawn (211–13), the night of despair likened to the underworld in which Ixion suffers. Troilus's prayers will do no good because the die is cast, his fate is predetermined, and changing what has been set rests with him, not with Cupid. As in book 1, Troilus must judge wisely in order to pacify the gods, the power of Cupid notwithstanding—and once again he does not.

Because he has chosen Venus instead of Pallas Athena, Troilus endures the most Ixion-like of punishments, whirled around on the Wheel of Fortune in the underworld of temporal care—on earth. Chaucer's comparison of Troilus with Ixion serves multiple purposes, not least of which is the infernal link between the two: like Ixion, Troilus is lecherous, manipulated by a changing Fortune, and doomed by wrong choices. Troilus, immersed in a hell of despair and suffering because of his desire for Criseyde, suffers because he has just relinquished her to Diomede. Ixion, literally condemned to an eternity of suffering as punishment for his lechery, originally so desired Juno that when he attempted to make love with a cloud shaped in her likeness, his falling semen resulted in the birth of the centaurs; therefore, Ixion signifies lechery, in the glosses on Boethius 3m12 by Remigius of Auxerre, William of Conches, and Nicholas Trevet.[75] Further, Troilus is turned by Fortune's Wheel and manipulated by the Fates; so also Ixion forever turning on his wheel is the type for the traveling peddler, the runaway fugitive, and the wayfarer who now stands and who now falls, in John of Garland's brief gloss in his *Integumenta* (p. 53, trans. p. 36). Ixion's desire for Juno (the active life, or temporal care, "que consistit in curis temporalium") signifies the desire for heavenly joy ("in ea querit delectacionem beatitudinis") in Nicholas Trevet's continuation of the allegory, which echoes that of William of Conches (p. 510).[76] In place of herself, Juno substitutes clouds because through this active life man incurs the darkening of reason ("per hanc uitam incurrit homo obscuritatem racionis"). Hence the centaurs are the product of this intercourse, part man and part horse, that is, part rational and part irrational (pp. 510–11). Thus Ixion spins on an eternal wheel of temporal cares, elevated by prosperity and falling by adversity ("Qui apud inferos in rota uoluitur quia deditus curis temporalibus continue eleuatur prosperitate et deprimitur aduersitate" [p. 511]). The wheel stops whirling only when man, instructed in wisdom, condemns it. The mythological context of Ixion's desire for Juno as the active life — the choice of the three goddesses made by Paris at the wedding of Peleus and Thetis, that framing myth for all of the *Troilus* to which Chaucer returns again and again in his mythological images in the *Troilus* — is recited only by William of Conches, of all the Boethius commentators.[77]

Troilus's obsessive desire for Criseyde — rather than an external and misogynistic projection of that desire in her identified as "carnal delight" — is responsible for his plight. So he blames Cupid, his own *cupiditas*, appropriately, as he has previously — but he curses the other gods and forces, including Jove, Apollo, and Ceres, Bacchus, and Cipride, or Venus, and his birth, his fate, his nature, and every creature (207–8), without understanding the role of his desire in creating his unhappiness. In this regard, his apostrophe to Cupid in front of Criseyde's empty palace (582–85) seems most consistent, as does his plea to his "blisful lord" Cupid (599) not to be as cruel to "the blood of Troie" (600) as "Juno was unto the blood Thebane" (601) because of Jove's adulteries with various Theban women, including Europa (sister of Cadmus, founder of Thebes), Semele, and Io. Ironically, those women frequently represent carnal delight in the mythographies and appear in conjunction with Criseyde (as Europa, *Troilus* 3.722; as Io, 4.1459, 5.808). Further, and also ironically, Juno's enmity toward Thebes because of Jove's adulteries connects the fall of Thebes with the imminent fall of Troy: her anger toward the ancestors of Cadmus, including Diomede as heir of Calydon, as we shall see, resulted in the Theban civil war in which Eteocles and Polynices perished, leading to the Athenian Theseus's victory over the nation. Her anger toward Troy because of Paris's false choice of Venus instead of Juno or Pallas Athena will eventually result in the triumph of the Greeks over the Trojans.

In the sequence of the three Fates typifying the limits of human life, from birth (Lachesis), to the span of life (Clotho), followed by its ending (Atropos), its snipping off, it is no accident that Chaucer replaces Atropos—lack of order—with Lachesis (line 7)—destiny—to emphasize the power of the Fates over the underworld of earth. The Fates appear to control events in this book, whether suggested by natural forces or a luminary such as the moon (Fortune, who dominates the aerial underworld). In line 638, part of his *canticus*, Troilus bewails the possibility that he will lose his bearings and the light of his star (Venus, Aeneas's guiding mother?) in the night as he journeys toward his goal of Criseyde, and that death will ensue ("My ship and me Caribdis wol devoure" [644]) on the tenth night after Criseyde's departure, or the eve of her proposed return. A whirlpool off the Sicilian coast that sucks in ships to their destruction, Charybdis represents the Wheel of Fortune, or the swallowing up of those who love inordinately the riches and honors of this world, in Robert Holkot's commentary on Ecclesiasticus.[78] Troilus's reference veils the destructive power of Fortune, its dependence on the ship image recalling the invocation of book 2, wherein the narrator described his protagonist as a ship on the black waves of despair, whose tempests will be ameliorated by the skill of his Creator and the help of the Muse Clio.

The mythographic overlay of the silenced or unheard prophet Cassandra with traitor Calkas works to underscore the doom imminent for both Troilus and Troy. During Troilus's sleepless and fear-filled nights, he imagines that the owl "Escaphilo" has "after me shright al thise nyghtes two" (319–20), as if the owl calling Troilus's name were an ironic image for Calkas, the astrologer who summons his daughter to the Greek camp because he knows that Troy (and with it Troilus) will fall. By giving the owl the name of Ascalaphus (son of Orphne, dark bride of Acheron), Troilus evokes the mythographic treatment of the bird as a tattletale motivated by envy and malice.[79] Although no such detractor exists in book 5, Troilus's great fear of scandal and of the revelation of indiscretion aids his continued paralysis—at least until Criseyde's affair with Diomede is uncovered for him by Cassandra's interpretation of his dream. It is Cassandra, too, who

functions as a prophet hated by others, largely because of her own fate—
and perhaps because she reveals insights that the Trojans, like Troilus,
would prefer not to know. Rather interestingly, earlier interpretations of
Ascalaphus by the twelfth-century commentators Arnulf of Orleans and
Giovanni del Virgilio typify the owl as the *philosophus* or *astrologus* whose
knowledge of the moon explains his noctural predictions.[80]

The overlay also deepens the double understanding of the underworld as
both the afterlife to which Troilus will in fact be led by Mercury and the
temporal pleasures associated with his relationship with Criseyde; for "As-
calaphus" also evokes the underworld, given Ascalaphus's transformation
into an owl by Proserpina, in *Metamorphoses* 5.533. This owl's role, like
that of Mercury, is to guide the soul back to the underworld, presumably
after death, and therefore this remarkable summons foreshadows the end
of Troilus's life to enhance the mood of doom and finality. The myth of As-
calaphus and Proserpina is also glossed by Ovid commentators, including
Bersuire, as a misogynistic comment on the bad woman, who becomes hell
itself: "Or say that hell is a bad woman [*mala mulier est infernus*]. If some-
one tastes her fruits—that is delights—he will escape only with difficulty
from her snares" (*Ovidius*, p. 96, trans. p. 242). In this reading, Proserpina
represents the underworld of fleshly desire, with the three pomegranate
seeds she eats as the pleasures of desire, sight, and touch taken "from the
garden of her delights" because of love, and the garden of hell itself, the
prosperity of the world:

> Or say that hell is the world where it seems customary that, if
> someone has tasted some of its fruits—that is some of its goods—for
> pleasure, he will not go from there. Those who in the garden of
> hell—that is in the prosperity of the world—eat three seeds—that is
> pleasures, riches, and honors—will be so pleased that they will not
> be able to be drawn from its love. Wisdom 2:1: "No man has been
> known to have returned from hell."

In the light of this Neoplatonic reading, Bersuire's allegorization of Pros-
erpina as fleshly pleasure easily slides into the *in malo* interpretation of
Criseyde in Chaucer's fifth book, an interpretation that will develop into
Criseyde's portrait as a lecherous leper in Robert Henryson's *Testament of
Cresseid* and a prostitute in Shakespeare's *Troilus and Cressida*. Like Pros-
erpina, Criseyde is led away from her own safe world by a male with whom
she experiences, at worst, rape, and at best, an eventual furtive pleasure—
in Proserpina's case, Pluto, in Criseyde's, Diomede. In the latter case, the
reader is reminded, once again, of Paris's abduction of Helen and Hector's
solemn (but ironic) declaration that the Trojans do not trade women—just
before Criseyde is exchanged for Antenor, in the fourth book. Also like
Proserpina, who eats the pomegranate seeds, Criseyde, perhaps because she

will dally with Diomede in her father's tent, cannot leave from hell (or the Greek camp).

Troilus equates the advent of the new moon with the bliss of seeing Criseyde again, as her departure was equated with the waning of the old moon; the horn images anticipate his cuckolding by Diomede, and the association of the changes of the moon with changed, exchanged, and changeable Criseyde underscores the earlier doubling of the goddess Fortune with Criseyde; that is, the help for which Troilus alone begs must come from the moon, "The gydyng of thi bemes bright an houre" (643) upon the seas that he traverses on his lonely journey on the tenth night. Even if her light is restored to the hapless Troilus, it will unfortunately prove to be as fickle and unfortunate as that destructive whirlpool Charybdis (= Criseyde) that he will confront in ten days. Hoping for the time "whan thow art horned newe" (650), he awaits the new moon with the promise that he will be "glad" a few lines later "if al the world be trewe!" (651):

> "I saugh thyn hornes olde ek by the morwe
> Whan hennes rood my righte lady dere
> That cause is of my torment and my sorwe;
> For which, O brighte Latona the clere,
> For love of God, ren faste aboute thy spere!" (652–56)

The light he longs for will certainly not foster his sea journey but instead lead him straight to Charybdis and destruction.

In the association of Latona and Criseyde is concealed the recurring maternal image. Latona, of course, gave birth to Apollo (sun) and Diana (the moon). The image also applies to Criseyde in that Troilus—if not as Apollo himself, then as Apollo's son, Phaethon, with whom the Trojan identifies in line 664—bears to her a filial regard. Worrying that the ten days until Criseyde returns will not pass because Phaethon rather than the sun will drive the sun's chariot ("Ywis, me dredeth evere mo / The sonnes sone, Pheton, be on lyve, / And that his fader carte amys he dryve" [663–65]), Troilus reveals a mistrust of the son/sun, of himself, and of natural law, or, in other words, of external reality. Phaeton, according to glossators of Boethius who base their interpretations on the original Fulgentian signification in the *Mitologiae,* represents apparition, fantasy, delusion—exactly that distortion of perspective now afflicting our hero.[81] In another sense, that hallucination of what might happen *does* happen: Criseyde does find another lover, and Troilus's hallucination deepens into his dream of the boar, glossed by his sister Cassandra as the Calydonian heir, Diomede. Finally, as the distortion of reason, Phaethon, according to the K-Reviser of Boethius, represents the soul who will either wisely control the four horses of the sun (meaning the four ages of man), or else will allow them to pull him toward death, swayed by the pull of Apollo's four unmanageable horses (that is, ignorance), or perdition, in contrast to the true Son, Christ as wisdom.[82]

In terms of the human microcosm, Criseyde, who, up to this point, has "mothered" Troilus, allows their relationship to die when she cannot bear its loss; from Troilus's perspective, a destructive mother (Lathona [655] versus the good wife Alceste [1527, 1778]), she takes on a new lover, Diomede, the heir of the Calydonians and Meleager, who was destroyed by his mother and the Fates. The book ends with the final mock-Virgilian guide who leads the dead Troilus into the heavens (1827)—Mercury, cunning god of traders and therefore foil for the Trojans who do trade women (Helen, Criseyde, and, earlier, Hesione) and ironic emblem of eloquence and deceit in place of wisdom (Pallas Athena [308]).

In the Greek camp, Criseyde fares as ill with Diomede as she has with Troilus, the new relationship compared at various points in the narrative with the myth of Calydonian Meleager and Atalanta, or Meleager and his vengeful mother (1474, 1482). The comparison is intended to remind Chaucer's readers that Criseyde has exchanged self-indulgent Troy, destined to fall, for cunning Greece, which conquered the divided city of Thebes, the nation to which Diomede is related by blood (805). But in exchanging Trojan Troilus for Greek Diomede, Criseyde is compared with Scylla (1111), who sacrificed her father Nisus out of love for Cretan Minos, after which Scylla in Ovid was transformed into a Ciris.

The mythological sameness of the familial betrayal—Meleager's vindictive mother destroys her own son to avenge the loss of her brothers and Scylla sacrifices her father and her nation to her own desire—undercuts all of the familial and personal relationships in this book. Criseyde occupies the role of both vindictive mother (to boyish Troilus) and unloving daughter (to traitor Calkas) in her acceptance of Diomede's advances. In both cases, her behavior can be explained as repressed fury over her losses and over her exploitation by family and nation, a self-destructive course apparently intended to wound those who have wounded her and reflective of the madness and imbalance ("change") characterizing her behavior since her exchange for Antenor was proposed in book 4. As with the infernal references used to describe Troilus's reactions, the references to Criseyde's response to Diomede tie in with the power of the Parcae, the Fates, who gave the burning brand to Meleager's mother at his birth. They also tie in with references to the Judgment of Paris, the framing story for the *Troilus* as a whole and the explanation for what goes wrong with Trojan relationships.

Aware of Theban history (unlike Criseyde, who was interrupted by Pandarus while reading aloud a vernacular version of Statius's *Thebaid*), Cassandra interprets Troilus's dream by relaying the adventures of Diomede's father Tydeus, who "Unto the stronge citee of Thebes, / To cleymen kyngdom of the citee, wente" (1486–87) on behalf of "his felawe, daun Polymytes"

(1488) and whose brother "daun Ethiocles, / Ful wrongfully of Thebes held the strengthe" (1489–90).[83] Of the two references in book 5 invoking for the reader the myth of Meleager and establishing Diomede's Theban lineage, the first begins with the narrator's description of Diomede ("And heir he was of Calydoigne and Arge" [805]), and the second, hidden by the boar figure in Troilus's mysterious dream (1445–49), is revealed to the Trojan by Cassandra (whose curse is that no one will heed her prophecies) as Calydonian Meleager's heir Diomede (1513–15). She concludes that "Tideus sone" Diomede is the boar in Troilus's dream ("down descended is / Fro Meleagre, that made the boor to blede" [1514–15]).[84] She also relays a portion of Hyginus's fable in her detailing of the deaths of Archimoris, Amphiorax, Hippomedon, Parthenope, and Tydeus (1499–1512).[85]

In the older Theban "history," the competition between Tydeus and Polynices for the daughters of Adrastus and their mutual antipathies toward kin, especially the fratricide of Tydeus, anticipate the rivalry of Troilus and Diomede for Criseyde, although in a sense Criseyde's father has already "given" her to Diomede. And the destruction of the Calydonians (and the brothers Eteocles and Polynices) also foreshadows in particular the deaths of the rivals Troilus and Diomede. But the symbolism of Diomede as a boar, linked with the more distant Calydonian ancestor Meleager through his father Tydeus, remains unexplained thus far.

The boar-draped Tydeus who relates to Meleager, Calydon, and Argus must be clarified by reference to Ovid's *Metamorphoses* 8.271 and the story of the Calydonian boar rather than to Statius's *Thebaid*. Because King Oeneus of Calydon refused to sacrifice to Diana, she unleashed on that country a ravaging boar successfully hunted by the Argonaut Meleager, son of Calydonian queen Althea. However, having fallen in love with the Arcadian Atalanta, Meleager gave this Diana-like huntress who spurned contact with men the spoils of the hunt in which they engage and which he wins, an act that angered his uncles. When Meleager was compelled to kill his uncles, his furious mother Althea, who had possession of the fatal log controlling the length of his life, chose to avenge the deaths of her brothers by sacrifice of her son; therefore she threw the fatal log—controlling the length of his life—into the fire.

The Ovidian mythography on the boar in the Meleager myth misogynistically clarifies the source of all of Meleager's woe—not his genes or his nation, but his love for Atalanta, which easily collapses in the *Troilus* into a model for Troilus's love for Criseyde. Cassandra's more "historical" gloss—actually mythological—stresses two major aspects of the Meleager story: first, the actual hunt and Meleager's love for Atalanta, and second, the consequences of the hunt and that love in Althea's burning of the brand. Of the first aspect, Cassandra notes that Meleager as "lord of that contree" (1476) loved the free maiden Atalanta so much that "with his manhod"

(1478) he slew the boar and sent to her his head. But she dismisses the second aspect ("But how this Meleagre gan to dye / Thorugh his moder" [1482–83]) with an *occupatio*: "al to longe it were for to dwelle" (1484). What she conceals is the role of the mother in his death. According to Bersuire, the two portions of the myth focus on the power of the strong women involved in the myth—the three Fates, the maiden Atalanta, and Meleager's mother Althea. Characteristically misogynistic, Bersuire blames the entire wretched sequence of events on Meleager's love for a woman:

> Note how endless evils came to be because of the love of women. Meleager's love of Atalanta was the reason why his uncles were killed, the son burned, the mother killed, the kingdom of Calydon lost, and his sisters turned into birds—that is into flight. Ecclesiasticus 25:31: "A wicked woman makes a wounded heart [*Plaga mortis mulier nequam*]," and Ecclesiasticus 25:33: "From woman came the beginning of sin, and by her we all die." (*Ovidius*, pp. 130–31, trans. p. 313)

Certainly Troilus rather than Diomede suffers from an obsessive concern with a woman, losing his life as a result of his pain. Certainly, too, Criseyde might have educated herself sufficiently to be able to identify Diomede's heritage, and hence her role in that heritage, if Pandarus had not interrupted her reading of a version of the *Thebaid*, possibly the *Roman de Thèbes*, in book 2. From Troilus's point of view, she is guilty of "untrouthe": "He thought ay wel he hadde his lady lorn" (1445) and that Jove's "purveyaunce" has demonstrated to him "in slep the signifiaunce / Of hire untrouthe and his disaventure" (1447–48). But Chaucer takes care not to blame Criseyde for what she does not understand and over which she has incomplete control—what is in part a type of consensual rape, of favors exchanged on demand.

In contrast to the violent rape of Criseyde's heart by the Eagle in book 2, this exchange, of a lady's glove for a warrior's sexual favors, presses for a dehumanized equality in which the woman offers the thing, the token, or sign—her glove—instead of her hand in consent. After she grants this sign to Diomede, he leaves, only to return to the tent later that night. The actual moment when Criseyde offers herself to Diomede the boar—or the devil, in mythographic terms—is heralded by an astrological conjunction of the signs most appropriate to the specific exchange, that is, Venus, Phoebus, and Cynthia:

> The brighte Venus folwede and ay taughte
> The wey ther brode Phebus down alighte;
> And Cynthea hire char-hors overraughte
> To whirle out of the Leoun, if she myghte. (1016–19)

Cynthia the moon is leaving the Lion (Leo): that is, Criseyde (the moon) leaves the lion (Troilus) for the boar (Diomede), which recalls the dual symbols of lion and boar in the fable of the competition between Theban Polynices, heir of Hercules, and Calydonian Tydeus, heir of Meleager. Figuratively, Phoebus, the sun (and the god of wisdom) is subverted by the (false) brightness of Venus, goddess of love: at this moment, all rationality (Phoebus) is subverted by what passes for "love" (the offering of the glove).

Diomede's "instruction" of Criseyde manipulates, if not subverts, rationality: in plying Criseyde, Diomede perceives her sorrow, surmises that she loves a Trojan, and uses her father's predictions to assure her that the Trojans will be punished, by the Greeks even more so than the Manes, for having stolen Helen away (so much so "That Manes, which that goddes ben of peyne, / Shal ben agast that Grekes wol hem shende" [892–93]). These spirits of the dead are defined by Remigius of Auxerre in his commentary on Martianus Capella as gods of the underworld, *diis infernalibus,* associated with Discordia (1:119 [1.29.2]; 1:105, 138 [1.38.20])—Discordia being the troublemaker in the myth of the Judgment of Paris, of course. In another sense, Diomede establishes a bond between the Greeks and the underworld spirits, as if Criseyde, duplicating the role of Eurydice fleeing from Aristaeus, or of Proserpina fleeing Pluto, or of Alceste rescuing her husband Admetus, had already descended into hell—the Greek camp.

Chaucer twice compares Criseyde with heroic Alceste. First, Troilus defends Criseyde from Cassandra's negative gloss in her explanation of his dream by suggesting that Criseyde is beyond reproach and that she might as well lie about Alceste, "kyndest and the beste" of creatures (1529). Alceste, wife of the Admetus who faced death, "ches for hym to dye and gon to helle / And starf anon" (1532–33). But in other myths Alceste was rescued from hell by Hercules; her role as the good woman, symbolized by the daisy, suggestive of the Resurrection, resurfaces in Chaucer's *Legend of Good Women* (as we saw in chapter 1). Ironically, Troilus's idealized image of Criseyde-as-Alceste works by antithesis: Criseyde will not take Troilus's place at the moment of death; her failure to return to life in Troy will in fact propel him into a self-destructive heroism; and after his death, his soul will not be reborn in Paradise but merely transported to the sphere of fixed stars. Second, the narrator next mentions Alceste in line 1778 when he refuses to write of Criseyde's guilt—an echo of Troilus's defense of Criseyde:

> Ye may hire gilt in other bokes se;
> And gladlier I wol write, yif yow leste,
> Penelopeës trouthe and good Alceste. (1776–78)

Both Penelope and Alceste demonstrated loyalty to their husbands, unlike "disloyal" Criseyde to her lover Troilus—and yet these comparisons also emphasize the missing bond of marriage, which would have countenanced loyalty, fidelity, and self-sacrifice on Criseyde's and Troilus's part. Through this reference, Troilus, Chaucer now reminds us, has failed Criseyde in sending her to the "hell" of the Greek camp. Criseyde may also be perceived as entering hell in exchange for Antenor—out of love for her father Calkas, and therefore as a loyal daughter like heroic Alceste.

Late in book 5 Criseyde's duty to her father and fatherland is glossed by reference to her antithesis Scylla, Nisus's daughter who so loved his enemy Minos that she destroyed her kingdom and her father. Chaucer introduces this myth on the morning of the tenth day after Criseyde's departure, when Troilus and Pandarus eagerly look from the walls for some sign of her approach as the day progresses, "The laurer-crowned Phebus with his heete / Gan, in his cours ay upward as he wente, / To warmen of the est se the wawes weete" (1107–9). Despite the promise implied by the appearance of "laurel-crowned Phoebus" (who unsuccessfully pursued Daphne, transformed into the laurel by Diana for protection from rape), the interjection that "Nysus doughter song with fressh entente" darkens the moment Troilus has so eagerly anticipated. According to Ovid, in *Metamorphoses* 8.11ff., Scylla fell in love with the Cretan king Minos, who made war on Alcathous to avenge the murder of his son by the Athenians; she cut off the purple lock of her father Nisus as a gesture of her love, thereby ensuring the downfall of her country. Thereafter she was spurned by Minos and transformed into a bird named a *ciris*. In Bersuire's comment on this myth, Nisus represents intellect or reason, *ratio*, with his hairs the virtues that safeguard the kingdom of the soul from capture by the devil:

> Say that Nisus signifies the intellect or the reason which is known to rule in the city of the soul. His hairs are virtues; most importantly, the gold or purple hair is charity which is a golden virtue and which is certainly fatal. While it is on the head of our intention neither does its father—that is reason—die through sin nor is the kingdom of the soul captured. The daughter is concupiscence [*concupiscentia*] or will [*voluntas*]; Minos is the devil [*diabolus*] or the world [*mundus*]. When King Minos of Crete—that is the devil, the king of hell— besieges the city of the soul through temptations, it often happens that the will or concupiscence voluntarily plots to hand over its country and its father—that is reason and the soul—to the devil through sin and to consent to copulation with him through enjoyment of sins. It is she who cuts off the fatal hair—that is charity—and because of this the king—that is reason—dies and Minos—that is the devil—seizes the kingdom of the soul through sins. 1 Corinthians 13:2: "If I do not have charity I am nothing." (*Ovidius*, p. 123, trans. p. 299)

Scylla is opposite to Criseyde, who must believe that she protects her "head" (her father) by giving in to Diomede, the enemy captain, and therefore that she also saves Troy (as she must believe she does in cooperating with the exchange for Antenor). Chaucer's point may also be that Troilus's love for Criseyde, like Scylla's for Minos, will destroy him: he has lost his head, his reason. In yet another sense, Calkas the father inverts the myth by sacrificing his own daughter to save his own life: inviting her into a hostile all-male camp knowing what happens to female prisoners.

The myths of Nisus, Scylla, and Minos and of Meleager and Atalanta appear in the same book of the *Metamorphoses*, separated only by the myth of Daedalus and Icarus, and linked by a common Athenian tie: the war of Cretan Minos with the Athenians is resolved by the Greek Theseus, whose help is also sought in quelling the Calydonian boar. Although Theseus will not appear in the *Troilus*, he will in the *Knight's Tale*, written about the same time as the *Troilus*. In that context he offers harmony to a world troubled by discord, division, and war, by families split asunder, their members betraying one another, whether brother by brother or father by daughter, daughter by father. In such a world heroes become boys looking for mothers and the women who love them always betray them. The baby Paris, separated from Hecuba to protect him from his father's decree of death, grows up not knowing his real parents or understanding familial ties and therefore, we surmise, willing to disrupt or sever the ties between man and wife, in the case of Helen and Menelaus; it is no accident that his brothers act accordingly, with Deiphebus taking Paris's place after his death and Troilus secretly loving Criseyde. The underlying mythological imagery in the *Troilus* proclaims its real significance, not as a poem about a love affair so much as a poem about broken families, missing mothers, impotent fathers.

It is no wonder, then, that Troilus laughs as he looks down at the squabbling of earthly life, the darkness of the temporal underworld from which he has been led by the wisdom of Mercury. As a pagan, he cannot enjoy that spiritual renewal promised to Christians by the Resurrection—a renewal of which the didactic narrator pompously reminds us in the Epilogue and which has been hinted at at the beginning of book 5 in a reference to the natural rejuvenation heralded by Zephirus, the West Wind.[86] Like the Retraction to the *Canterbury Tales*, this Epilogue serves as a schoolmaster's gloss on his own work, and therefore also serves as an *integumentum* or fictional cloak concealing Chaucer's real intentions. Morally true, the Epilogue, like the Retraction, is rhetorically necessary by convention, yet aesthetically reprehensible, a violation of Macrobian dicta concerning the use of pagan fable. Looking down at his troubled little characters, the creator-narrator cannot resist the impulse to play God; unlike Troilus, he fails to see earthly life, in the Dantesque and Christian sense, as a divine comedy crowned by the promise of eternity in Paradise. Like Troilus on earth, he succumbs to the temptation offered by earthly goods — not the erotic delights of Criseyde, but the delight of manipulating his characters, or being manipulated by them. And he insists on telling his audience what he intended when he created them. Chaucer's final word, in the *Troilus,* is no word at all, unlike his narrator's homilizing — like Troilus's, it is a laugh we do not hear.

The power of the narrator to manipulate his characters at the end of the *Troilus* transmogrifies into the reportorial subjectivity of pilgrim Chaucer as guide and interpreter in the *Canterbury Tales,* just as the angry characters in that "little tragedy" might be said to metamorphose — or degenerate — into realistic and contentious approximations of figures contemporaneous with Chaucer the poet, like the Miller and Reeve. The difference between the two works, for mythographic purposes, depends upon a shift in narrative style and context: Chaucer will continue to use mythographic imagery to conceal the sexual politics of a character's situation within a tale that dramatizes the psychological moment of his or her subjectivity. That subjectivity is constantly tested against the overall purpose of the Canterbury pilgrimage and the group dynamics of the pilgrims themselves. Both purpose and dynamics are set out in the *General Prologue,* whose unifying principle, as "Idea of the *General Prologue,*" can be used as touchstone in examining this more complex mythographic imagery.

PART 3

Subversive Mythography: The Speaker as Feminized Subject in the *Canterbury Tales*

CHAPTER 5

Zephirus, Rape, and Saint Thomas à Becket

The Political Vernacular

The tension between pagan and Christian forms what might be termed the idea of the *General Prologue* as it functions on its two levels, literal (natural, physical, pagan, feminine) and figurative (supernatural, spiritual, Christian, masculine). Although Chaucer refers to many classical gods throughout the dream visions, the *Troilus*, and some of the tales of the *Canterbury Tales*, he mentions only one pagan figure in the whole of the *General Prologue* — the West Wind, or Zephirus, in line 5. The dependent clause in the first half of the *reverdie* indicating the time when Zephirus most influences the natural world (5–9; that is, "*Whan* Zephirus eek with his sweete breeth / Inspired hath in every holt and heeth / The tendre croppes, *and* the yonge sonne / Hath in the Ram his half cours yronne, / *And* smale foweles maken melodye") is succeeded in the second half (12–18) by an independent clause indicating the temporal consequence of Zephirus's influence on humankind ("*Thanne* longen folk to goon on pilgrimages, / *And* palmeres for to seken straunge strondes" [12–13]).

For the alternation of Christian and classical, Chaucer may have drawn on the idea of the Latin pastoral debate poem *Ecloga Theoduli*, which similarly juxtaposes classical myth with Old Testament story to create an effect similar to that which he achieves here and elsewhere in his poems, including the classical epic parody in the moralistic *Nun's Priest's Tale* and the conjunction of the mythological fable in the *Manciple's Tale* with the Christian homily in the *Parson's Tale* at the end of the *Canterbury Tales*. Chaucer's political interest in veiling "abominations" through the use of classical mythology in his composition of narrative "chaff," particularly as filtered through his own subjectivity, is also embedded in his only short poem with a mythological image — like the *General Prologue*, an image seamed with scriptural (and Old Testament) referentiality. Chaucer contrasts Roman Jupiter and Assyrian Nimrod in the Boethian lyric "The Former Age." The "abominations" are those of castration of the father and rebellion against God — the moral and religious dangers, in short, of abusing or undermining authority. Chaucer compares lecherous Jupiter ("Yit was not Jupiter the likerous, / That first was fader of delicacye, / Come in this world" [56–58]) with Nimrod, the proud builder of the Tower of Babel ("ne Nembrot, desirous / To regne, had nat maad his toures hye" [58–59]). Although Nimrod was not lecherous, he did contend with God the Father by build-ing his heaven-reaching towers, just as Jupiter did overthrow his father Saturn; Jupiter, in castrating his father, and Nimrod, in building his tower, are attempting the same goal, the subversion of perfection and authority through insurrection and pride. Chaucer inherits glosses on both figures from the mythographic tradition, which are used, in the spirit of the *Ecloga Theoduli*, to define the nature of sin, lower and higher, and the Fall, defined as the turning of created against creator. By means of these over-laid figures, the poet invites reading with double vision—classical and biblical: "Jupiter the likerous" represents by synecdoche the bodily, earthly natures of giants, and Nembrot represents the more intellectual sin of pride and heresy.

How Jupiter and Nimrod are parallel in "The Former Age" does not become clear until the effects of their errors are examined—in the sinful state of contemporary England (60–63): "Allas, allas, now may men wepe and crye! / For in oure dayes nis but covetyse, / Doublenesse, and tresoun, and envye, / Poyson, manslawhtre, and mordre in sondry wyse." It is not clear who has committed these crimes and sins (the commons? the aristocracy?), but Chaucer may also be warning against the repressive and harmful tendencies of an autocratic government. If Jupiter, as J. Norton-Smith has argued, is derived from Jean de Meun's *Roman*, lines 20095ff., then Chaucer's Jupiter may, like Jean's, promote his unlimited appetite as "law" and thereby contradict most medieval authorities on the duty of the monarchy.[1] Jupiter's arbitrary appetite (*voluntas*) exercised, he would be a tyrant. As human prototype of Jupiter, Chaucer's Nimrod, for Norton-Smith, represents the first monarch; if Nimrod represents Richard II, then it was probably written after May 1389—when Richard declared he wished to be free of tutelage and to take the place of monarch—or in 1398–99, toward the end of Richard's life.

For this mythological reading of English regal indulgence and irresponsibility in imagery and theme, Chaucer most likely borrowed from a tenth-century Old High German gloss on Boethius by Notker Labeo, given the source of this Boethian poem, in poem 5 of book 2 of the *Consolatio Philosophiae*.[2] The glosses reveal Chaucer's warning against heresy (Nimrod) as well as tyranny (Jupiter). In Notker's gloss on prose twelve of book 3, Nimrod is compared with the giants Otus and Ephialtes.[3] But Chaucer's specific contrast of contentious Nimrod with "likerous" Jupiter probably stems from a conflation of two mythological parallels in the important twelfth-century commentary on the *Ecloga Theoduli* by Bernard of Utrecht. The first mythological parallel compares the expulsion of Saturn from paradise with that of Adam, and the second compares the Titans who warred against the gods with the tower builder Nembroth (Bernard's version of the name resembles Chaucer's, "Nembrot"). Because of the association of the post-Saturnine reign of Saturn's son Jupiter with turpitudinous giants, Bernard glosses the Titans as brothers of Saturn, also a Titan, and children of Caelus (Uranus) and Gaea (Heaven and Earth); like his brothers, Saturn in some accounts tried to castrate his own father Caelus and thereby overcome him. The Titans, who, after Saturn died, tried to overcome Jupiter by piling mountain atop mountain, were said to have piled "Pelion on Ossa" — the names of the chief mountains.

Bernard's related moralizations, of the Titans' battle with Jupiter and of Nimrod's battle with God, differ in that the former battle illustrates the earthly tangling with the heavenly, whereas the latter battle illustrates devilish and tyrannical pride, in an allegorical sense interpreted as heresy and disputation of Christ's divinity. In the first instance, the giants are said to fight against nature, or the earthly, by building "machines" (mountains) to ascend into the air. Perhaps Bernard drew here on Remigius's ninth-century Boethius commentary, in which the idea is also found: the giants fighting against heaven represent the bodily contending with heaven, or fighting with the clouds.[4]

In the second instance, rebel Nembroth allegorically represents pride and the Devil. Nembroth, in the high place of "Babylon" (rather than Babel), built towers, to see what was in the heavens, or in fear of floods; as the Devil (hence interpreted as a tyrant), he builds a tower to the heavens out of pride, wishing to compare his power with that of God, and therefore God fells the tower and divides language, "quia potestatem eius precipitavit, reservatis nouem ordinibus angelorum in celis" ("because he cast down his power, having reserved the nine orders of angels in the heavens").[5] Alternatively, by Nembroth is meant both him and his companions, who, by building the tower, accept heresy and question Christ's divinity. God destroys this work, and therefore divides languages, because heretics lack effectiveness, and their dogma is always discordant, Ecclesia preserving unity.[6]

Chaucer's deployment of Zephirus in the *General Prologue* also warns against heresy and tyranny, through a series of mythological and literary associations chiefly drawn from Dante's *Paradiso* but similarly linked with the rebellious Titans. Both Chaucer and Dante bend the conventional mythographic significations of Zephirus as the West Wind: classical Zephirus is associated with the *Aeneid* and other works such as that of Apuleius wherein, as personification of the West Wind and as metonymy for spring's fructifying breezes,[7] he is a harbinger and messenger, a fructifier of the world in spring. In many of the earliest medieval mythographic poems and tracts, Zephirus as a rejuvenating force is also linked with the World Soul, in which the individual human soul was believed, in microcosm, to share. From this early association, the figure of Zephirus gradually accumulates a potency suggestive of psychological and then Christian renewal. In the *General Prologue* especially, but also in most of his other works, Chaucer's use of Zephirus depends upon the conception of the fructifying West Wind as a masculinized poetic correlative for spiritual renewal, as developed in the Latin mythographic tradition and in Dante. In Christianizing his role, Dante, a vernacular and poetic source, reveals his association with the soul and good works within the context of the birth of Saint Dominic, warrior for God against heresy. Only Boccaccio, in his humanistic collection of the *Genealogia deorum gentilium*, retrieves an Ovidian Zephirus whose violent rape of Flora, undercutting the many positive significations, suggests a gendered power within nature.

Chaucer draws on both these Italian interpretations in his use of a classical ("pagan") image within a Christian context, to defuse artistically that dramatic tension between the desires of this world and those for the next from which humankind suffers and which is amply demonstrated in the pilgrims on the Canterbury journey. In addition, Chaucer here demonstrates how the vernacular poetical context subverts and colors, controls, the rigid clerical Latin mythographic tradition. Chaucer lifts from the patristic mythographic tradition a much-glossed figure, Zephirus, to use within a passage about an English martyr; he also borrows, I am arguing, from contemporary vernacular imagery associated with the birthplace of the author of the Dominican Inquisition. The English rebel-martyr Thomas, in helping to protect the hegemony of the church, is, in this sense, like the Spanish Saint Dominic.

The beginning as well as the ending of life for the soul is linked with Zephirus in several classical and medieval literary texts by means of the Greek concept of Zephirus as the breath of human life, in part because the World Soul, according to Stoic belief, was a macrocosmic equivalent of the human soul and responsible for its engendering. Zephirus's power over life translates into psychological and spiritual power over the human microcosm and within the cosmic macrocosm. According to Boccaccio's *Genealogia,* "life" or *vita* is the meaning of the Greek "Zephs" from which the West Wind's name derives.[8] Similarly, when the First Vatican Mythographer discusses Zephirus in myth 183.6, he cites a line from the *Aeneid* at the time of Dido's death, noting that the winds (Zephirus is not singled out) bring and take away life. In this passage, Iris the rainbow, Juno's messenger in the region of air ruled by the goddess, descends to Dido's head to free her from the flesh: "Dilapsus calor, atque in ventos vita recessit" ("With that she cut the wisp; at once all warmth / dispersed, and life retreated to the winds").[9] And in a narrative exposition in the Fulgentian *Mitologiae* (3.6), Zephirus seems to be associated with life, again in relation to the soul as represented by the character of Psyche;[10] that is, Zephirus, in the myth of Cupid and Psyche, initially comes after her marriage to carry Psyche into the golden mansion of her new husband Cupid, a role denoting trans-portation and communication as well as beginnings — as in the beginning of a new relationship, particularly here one of marriage, which might her-ald creativity, fructification. This particular marriage, of Cupid — love, lit-erally from *cupiditas*, cupidity, desire, concupiscence — and Psyche, the human soul, argues for spiritual renewal as well, or for what could be inter-preted as a change in consciousness as a result of falling in love. The sec-ond time Zephirus appears it is to carry Psyche to her worried sisters, who fear she is dead because of her love for Cupid. Here the passage communi-cates reassurance of the continuance of life, or rather, the attempt to pre-vent worry and death. In all cases, Zephirus serves as a messenger who an-nounces the beginning of life, or at least a kind of beginning, symbolized in the wedding of Cupid and Psyche (to be understood on the literal and figu-rative levels), and also the ending of life (or its possibility), symbolized by the fear of Psyche's sisters that she is dead.

Such a connection between beginnings and endings also occurs in other, later works. Zephirus, as Favonius, is declared by Boccaccio in the *Ge-nealogia* to control beginnings and endings, particularly of germination, beginning in spring and ending in summer, through the sweet and gentle nature of his influence and his complexion.[11] In Chaucer's *General Pro-logue,* too, the West Wind appropriately signals the return of life to the English countryside, awakening it from the "death" of winter and human mortality and suffering. Thematically, the arrival of the West Wind in the *Prologue* also signals a "marriage" — of the body and the soul, Cupid and Psyche, or, within the eighteen lines of the *reverdie,* the natural urge of the birds to mate, in the first eleven lines, so to speak, coupled with the super-natural urge of the pilgrims to travel for penance, in the last seven.

Prior to Chaucer, the association of Zephirus with spiritual life in a specifically Christian context involving renewal of the soul occurs in a ninth-century passage from Rabanus Maurus's *De universo.* Rabanus uses as a base for his allegorical reading the more usual associations of Zephirus with the West Wind as fructifier of seed and flowers ("Occidentalis autem ventus, Zephyrus Graeco nomine appellatur eo quod flores et germina ejus flatu vivificentur") and the name Favonius because he warms (*foveat*: liter-ally "warms," figuratively "cherishes, embraces") that which is born ("Hic Latine favonius dicitur, propter quod foveat quae nascuntur").[12] In addi-tion, Zephirus's appearance in spring, the time of year in which Christ died, carries with it the seeds of all virtue and good works that are born in the world ("Tunc autem hic ventus in bonam partem positus reperitur, cum mortis Christi et veri solis occubitum significat, unde omnium germina virtutum et bonorum operum in mundo nascuntur"). Rabanus, however, focuses only on the tropological interpretation of Zephirus as a rejuvenator of the human soul, an idea used by Chaucer in the *Book of the Duchess* to suggest psychological renewal of the soul without any necessary and explicit Christian renewal, in contrast to the more explicit relationship celebrated in the *reverdie* of the *General Prologue.*

In the *General Prologue* and at the end of the *Canterbury Tales,* Chaucer seems to use Zephirus anagogically, within the church militant, to typify Saint Thomas as a catalytic rejuvenator of the church in his empowerment of male sanctity—ironically, one that is achieved through a feminizing posture, of martyrdom as political "rape," or else one that subverts hierarchy and order through its displacement of secular authority. But this image evolves into the rich and complex vernacular treatment of Zefiro by Dante in the twelfth canto of the *Paradiso,* a text that I believe Chaucer was familiar with and that he used in part as a model for the literary roles of Zephirus in the *General Prologue.* The Dantesque association of Zefiro with the Spanish-born Saint Dominic also acts as an analogue, in Chaucer, for the English martyr Saint Thomas à Becket, whose resistance to the king's secular authority led to his homicide and whose shrine, symbolically as well as literally and anagogically, is the pilgrims' goal—the "thanne"—of the syntactical diagram in the opening lines.[13] Such syntactical patterning invites an identification of the inspiration of the tops of leaves by Zephirus's "sweete breeth" with that of the pilgrims traveling to Canterbury, to echo the natural process of growth suggested by the mythic action with a more supernatural one—the "inspiration," or longing, of the pilgrims to visit Canterbury.

Although the contemporary Dante commentaries have little significant to add about Zefiro, the reference within the text richly illuminates a nexus of ideas and images that Chaucer may have anglicized and politicized in his *reverdie.* Chaucer's interest in Dante and other writers of the Italian trecento may have been whetted by several trips to Italy, the most important of which (in terms of Dante's influence on his poetry) occurred in 1378,[14] some years after the writing of the *Book of the Duchess.*[15] Various studies have demonstrated his use of and familiarity with Dante, in particular, whose status as an *auctor* was made manifest before Boccaccio's death through a series of public lectures delivered by the scholar and poet on the early cantos of the *Inferno* and in the fourteenth century generally through scholarly commentaries.[16]

For Dante in the early fourteenth century, Zefiro was associated with the birth of a saint who revitalized the church by battling ignorance and heresy. The chief champion of Christ's army is the "holy athlete" Saint Dominic, founder of the order of the Dominicans (canto 11), who provide a counterpoint to the faithful Franciscans; the rigorous scholasticism and rationality of the former order is exemplified by Saint Thomas Aquinas (canto 10), as the revelation, mysticism, joy, and love associated with the latter order is exemplified by Saint Bonaventure. Both exemplars, and both orders, belong to the Sphere of the Sun, that of the theologians, and are harmonized and reconciled in Paradise, a perennially springlike otherworld symbolized by the Celestial Rose.

Saint Dominic serves as the Christian analogue of the classical, and even Stoic, figure of Zephirus. To begin with the natural, literal, and macrocosmic level, it has been noted that Spain is the country nearest the source of Zephyr, the West Wind, and that Saint Dominic was born in Spain, which underscores the vitality of the region and the saint. Dante accordingly describes Saint Dominic's birthplace as touched by the masculinized power of the sweet wind Zephirus in *Paradiso* 12.46–52: literally, it "fructified" Castile to give birth to Dominic:[17]

> In quella parte ove surge ad aprire
>   Zefiro dolce le novelle fronde
>   di che si vede Europa rivestire,
> non molto lungi al percuoter dell'onde
>   dietro alle quali, per la lunga foga,
>   lo sol tal volta ad ogne uom si nasconde,
> siede la fortunata Calaroga
>   sotto la protezion del grande scudo
>   in che soggiace il leone e soggioga.
> Dentro vi nacque l'amoroso drudo
>   della fede cristiana, il santo atleta
>   benigno a' suoi ed a' nemici crudo.
> E come fu creata, fu repleta
>   sì la sua mente di viva virtute
>   che, nella madre, lei fece profeta. (Dante, 3:176)

[In that part where sweet Zephyr rises to open the new leaves in which Europe sees herself reclad, not far from the beating of the waves behind which the sun, after his long flight, sometimes hides himself from all men, lies favoured Calahorra under protection of the great shield in which the lion is subject and sovereign. In it was born the loving liegeman of the Christian faith, the holy athlete, gracious to his own and pitiless to enemies; and his mind, as soon as it was created, was so full of living power that in his mother's womb it made her prophetic.] (Dante, trans. 3:177)

More figuratively, Saint Dominic himself acts as a type of Zephirus in tending Christ's garden, understood as that teaching which kept the vineyard of the church vital; that is, figuratively, Dominic then restored the vineyard of the church by planting new seeds of faith (the Dominican order) and creating future means of revivification (streams feeding saplings):

Domenico fu detto; e io ne parlo
sì come dell'agricola che Cristo
elesse all'orto suo per aiutarlo.
Ben parve messo e famigliar di Cristo;....
Non per lo mondo, ...
ma per amor della verace manna
in picciol tempo gran dottor si feo;
tal che si mise a circüir la vigna
che tosto imbianca, se 'l vignaio è reo.
E alla sedia che fu già benigna
più a' poveri giusti, non per lei,
ma per colui che siede, che traligna, ...
contro al mondo errante
licenza di combatter per lo seme
del qual ti fascian ventiquattro piante.
Poi con dottrina e con volere inseme
con l'officio apostolico si mosse
quasi torrente ch'alta vena preme;
e nelli sterpi eretici percosse
l' impeto suo, più vivamente quivi
dove le resistenze eran più grosse.
Di lui si fecer poi diversi rivi
onde l'orto cattolico si riga,
sì che i suoi arbuscelli stan più vivi. (70–73, 82, 84–90, 94–105;
Dante, 3:178)

[He was called Dominic, and I speak of him as of the labourer whom Christ chose to help Him in His garden. He seemed indeed a messenger and of the household of Christ.... Not for the world ... but for love of the true manna, he became in a short time so great a teacher that he began to go round the vineyard, which soon withers if the keeper is at fault; and to the seat which is now less kind to the upright poor than once it was—not in itself, but in him who sits there degenerate [Boniface VIII]—he appealed ... for leave to fight with the erring world for the seed of which twenty-four plants encircle thee [i.e., the twenty-four saints that whirl around Dante in two circles, one representing the Franciscans and love and the other representing the Dominicans and knowledge].... Then, with both learning and zeal and with the apostolic office, he went forth like a torrent driven from a high spring, and on the heretic thickets his force struck with most vigour where the resistance was stubbornest. From him there sprang then various streams by which the Catholic garden is watered, so that its saplings have new life.] (Dante, trans. 3:179)

Saint Dominic planting seeds of faith in his vineyard resembles the English Zephirus producing seeds and flowers with his breath—Saint Thomas à Becket empowering pilgrims drawn to his shrine. Instead of the world reclad in flowery new garb, however, Dante images forth rebirth in the new leaves of the reclad and feminine Europe. The point (as we shall see later in the canto) is that from Saint Dominic came the streams by which the gardens of the church were watered, so that saplings had new life. In the *Legenda aurea*, "Dominicus" denotes the keeper of the vineyard of the Lord (from *domus* + *canes*, "watchdog of the house").[18] Thus the "new leaves" that regenerate the saplings come from the gardens we see emphasized in line 106: "From him there sprang then various streams by which the Catholic garden [*l'orto cattolico* (104)] is watered, so that its saplings have new life [*i suoi arbuscelli stan più vivi* (105)]." Earlier in this passage, Dominic is described as the "labourer" (*l'agricola*) whom Christ picked to help in his garden (*l'orto* [71]). As teacher, Dominic went around the "vineyard" (*la vigna* [86]), "which withers if the keeper is at fault" (*che tosto imbianca, se 'l vignaio è reo* [87]). The point is that his scholastic work kept the garden alive, the garden being the Christian faith: he appealed in 1216 to Pope Honorius III for authorization for his order and thereafter preached against the Albigensian heresies. He appealed specifically "for leave to fight with the erring world for the seed of which twenty-four plants encircle thee" ("thee" is Dante [96]), that is, for the faith that culminates eventually and perfectly in saints. Then follows the line, "From him there sprang then various streams by which the Catholic garden is watered, so that its saplings have new life."

Dante's reference to Zefiro sums up the wind's associations with macrocosmic and natural regeneration and microcosmic life, the latter understood spiritually and psychologically as well as naturally. Dante uses all of the other classical associations of Zephirus with regeneration and vitality, both of the external world and of the little human world, but to these he adds the idea of Christian renewal ultimately typified in the figure of Christ and his Resurrection. In terms of the political macrocosm of the church, then, Dante's association of the Zephirus and garden images with the birth of Dominic marks an allegorical rebirth like that of spring in the natural world. The earlier mythological contrast between winter and spring (Boreas and Zephirus, if we use the names of the North and West Winds) traced from late antique writers like Boethius thus becomes, in Dante's hands, a typical allegorical contrast between spiritual death and life—and between Fall and Redemption. The image of the garden reminiscent of the Fall indicates, on the tropological level, how humankind's progress in the wilderness should lead to that earthly Paradise at the top of Mount Purgatory, which Dominic's activities attempt through knowledge. For the microcosm, the association marks a tropological rebirth of human nature like that expressed through the resurrection of the second Adam, Christ, to which we may aspire in our search for purgation and redemption. Man has descended from Adam, and like him is condemned to labor in the wilderness after the Fall. The gardening imagery used by Dante to describe Dominic's life reminds the reader that this saint is a model of human perfection in emulation of Christ. Thus Saint Dominic is likened to the ultimate source of spiritual renewal in the Christian faith.

For Chaucer, much of his opening passage focuses on an unfolding of new life in a gardenlike setting thematically and imagistically reminiscent of Dante's passage—the emphasis on seeds, gardening, and the vineyard parallel Chaucer's heaths and holts, the burgeoning plant and animal life. And just as the "sweet wind" fructifying human nature for Dante brings Dominic, so also what was important for Spain initially and, later, Europe (that is, the saint Dominic) was equally important for England (that is, the saint Thomas à Becket). In addition, the sweet wind (traditionally cause of revivification of life in the human soul) in England fructifies the human process of need for purgation so that pilgrims wish to journey toward Canterbury (more figuratively, the heavenly Jerusalem, as the Parson points out).

The reference to Zephirus may also exemplify the underlying satiric theme contemporary with Chaucer of corruption—impotence—in the church fighting against the state and thus the need for renewal: just as Zephirus announces what might be seen as a pagan "marriage," in the first eleven lines, of a feminine and passive earth, or the roots, sap vessels, and flowers of lines 2–5, to the masculine and active heavens, or the showers and Wind of April of lines 1, 5–6,[19] so also Zephirus anticipates the analogous analogical revivification of the church, not by her ostensible leaders, the Prioress, Monk, or Friar, but by the truly Christian Parson and his brother the Plowman, in echo of Saint Thomas.

The power of Zephirus to transform the church through his anthropomorphized "breath" has been explained by Boccaccio in *Genealogia* through the sexual relationship of Zephirus and Flora, goddess of flowers—the gendering of Nature. To clarify, Boccaccio primarily draws upon Ovid's *Fasti* 5.183–371, Lactantius Firmianus's *Divinae institutiones* 1.20.6, and Arnulf of Orleans's commentary on the *Fasti*. Resembling other pagan figures and personifications, such as the female Aurora, Daybreak, frequently associated with spring openings in dream visions, Zephirus, according to Ovid's *Fasti*, raped the nymph Chloris (a Greek name relating to "green," later changed to the Roman Flora, a Latin name relating to *flos*) in the spring and later married her. Her name—and action—implicitly explain her diluted and gentle function as goddess of the flowers, her enjoyment of perpetual spring, and her dowry, a fruitful garden nourished by a breeze and irrigated by flowing water. But her festival, the Floralia, which extended from April 28 to May 3 (the date recurs in Chaucer for moments of violence and seduction, such as the angry chance meeting of Palamon and Arcite in the woods, or Criseyde's seduction), is described by Lactantius Firmianus as involving lascivious games and concupiscence of all sorts, perhaps because of her identification in late antiquity with the Magna Mater (Bona Dea, Cybele, Ops, Juno, etc.).[20]

In its harsh emphasis on masculine violence, the rape belies the seeming gentleness of Chaucer's Zephirus and his "sweet breath." The gender associations in the mythography on the figure assume, in Chaucer, a more politicized role involving church and state, a signification that can be teased out through Zephirus's genealogy and his kinship with the Titans. According to the First Vatican Mythographer, the Greek Zephirus is one of four winds, including the North Wind Boreas, the East Wind Eurus, and the South Wind Auster, who, according to the Second Vatican Mythographer, were born as a result of the mythological coupling of Astraeus, one of the Titans who bore arms against the gods, with Aurora the dawn, and who are (according to John of Garland in his *Integumenta Ovidii*) ruled by the king Aeolus, father of the winds.[21] The mythological family connections of the winds reveal ties to those same Titans conjoined in Bernard of Utrecht in his gloss on castrating Jupiter and tyrannous Nimrod—both involved in political and cosmic subversion, a social rape.

But Zephirus's patristic mythography is employed by Chaucer to suggest a *remedium* for social rape, for the violence of Henry II toward Saint Thomas, by means of the healing of England through pilgrimage, or the marriage of Zephirus and Flora (which, of course, does not actually happen on this pilgrimage). Within other vernacular poems, and within Chaucer's other poems, the rejuvenation offered by Zephirus is ironic counterpoint to the narrative. Zephirus is mentioned in the description of the passing of the seasons in *Sir Gawain and the Green Knight* to signal the year Gawain must wait before setting out on his quest; in "þe sesoun of somer wyth þe soft wyndez" (516) rather than that of spring, "Zeferus syflez hymself on sedez and erbez" (517) so that "Wela wynne is þe wort þat waxes þeroute, / When þe donkande dewe dropez of þe leuez / To bide a blysful blusch of þe bryȝt sunne" (518–20).[22] But the natural image of growth does not tally with the collective and spiritual image: Gawain, still taking himself far too seriously when he breaks out into an angry, misogynistic diatribe in front of the Green Knight and upon his return to court, insisting rather pompously on his many character flaws by wearing the green girdle as sign of failure, is matched in his immaturity by the court, which, in its first age, greets Gawain's story with laughter. Similarly, the appearance of Zephirus and Flora, in the *Book of the Duchess* within an idealized and verdant spring-meadow setting, acts by metonymy to suggest the psychological goal of both narrator and grieving Black Knight—the healing or renewal of self and soul—which, of course, neither achieves until, perhaps, the abrupt ending/waking. In the "floury grene," which the narrator imagines as the domain of Flora and Zephirus because of the thick grass and many flowers abloom there (398–409), the poet specifically contrasts the rich plenitude of spring with the meager poverty of winter: "Hyt had forgete the povertee / That wynter, thorgh hys colde morwes, / Had mad hyt suffre, and his sorwes" (411–13). If "All was forgeten" (414), it is because the "swetnesse of dewe" has made the wood "waxen grene" (413–15).

And, as we have seen, although Zephirus's yearly advent, in *Troilus* 5.10, marked by the arrival of tender green leaves, harks back to the narrator's prefatory paean to the fair chain of love and the heavenly Venus and the harmonious music of Calliope in the third book, Zephirus does not convey a rebirth of spiritual love for Troilus, despite the echo of the harmonious love theme in his postcoital song in the third book. In book 5, "gold-tressed Phebus heighte on-lofte" (8) is said to have melted the snows "with his bemes clene" (9) and Zephirus, to have brought "the tendre leves grene" (11) for three years of the relationship between Troilus and Criseyde—a superficially happy rejuvenation that will end with her imminent departure to the Greeks, a sort of permanent winter. This cyclical repetition heightens the dramatic contrast between the ending of the relationship in this fifth book (and the literal as well as spiritual death of Troilus, as well as the striking lack of fertility indicated by the "marriage") and the continuing new beginning of the natural world—and the advent of superior understanding after Troilus's death, a kind of rebirth as well as apotheosis, when he looks down from the eighth sphere on the wretched world beneath him and laughs aloud.

Zephirus and Flora "gentilly" (if ironically, given their initial meeting through rape) rejuvenate flowers in the *Prologue* to the *Legend of Good Women* by means of "Hire swoote breth" when they appear in May, a month of revivification in nature and in human love (and also, if we look at May 3, of Flora's lascivious festival). Their appearance together marks what might be termed superficially the marriage of heaven (the West Wind Zephirus) and earth (Flora) as "god and goddesse of the floury mede" (F 174). Such natural rejuvenation underscores the spiritually defined role of loyal Alceste in the *Prologue* to the *Legend* in choosing to die for her husband, descending into the underworld, and returning; she also appears in the form of a daisy, with similar behaviors and meanings.

Chaucer also uses Zephirus to describe, in a rough image, the destructive and crazed—psychologically speaking, wintry, cold, barren—power of father over daughter in a brilliant inversion of the normal associations of the classical figure, and of the revivifying power of spring, in the legend of Hypermnestra later in the *Legend of Good Women* (2681). There the reaction of the central figure to her father Aegyptus's command to slit her husband's throat when he sleeps (Aegyptus has been forewarned that one of his nephews will kill him, and so commands all his daughters), or else die by her father's hand, is likened to the influence of Zephirus, as if her father had the same paternalistic power over her as the West Wind over his feminized nature. On the night her husband sleeps, "dredfully she quaketh / As doth the braunche that Zepherus shaketh" (F 2680–81). Thereafter, "As cold as any frost now waxeth she; / For pite by the herte hire steyneth so" (F 2683–84). The image of Zephirus shaking the branch invokes the genealogical cycle that normally renews the family by means of succeeding generations, in contradistinction to Aegyptus's frosty attempt to foreshorten that natural cycle in order to extend the duration of his own life. In what other sense does a cold frost "waxeth" (F 2683)?

The association of a powerful, masculine Zephirus with weak, passive, abducted or raped female figures in all the sources—Dido in the *Aeneid*, Flora in Ovid, Psyche in Apuleius, Europe in Dante ("dressing" herself, being reclad), the latter who, through the birth of Saint Dominic and his work, will be reborn both politically and spiritually, given his many gifts to the church—culminates here in the images of a passive feminized Nature and a potent masculinized English church, but a church whose power springs from its independence, its rebellion by martyrs, its vernacularism, and not its tradition, its obedience, its Latinate ties. This model is one that Chaucer will find especially congenial in those mythologized Canterbury tales whose sexual politics demand the concealment afforded by such fabulation. To Canterbury the rebels of 1381, led by dissident preacher John Ball, also headed, according to Jean Froissart's *Chronique* account, where they damaged Christ Church Cathedral and whose archbishop, Simon Sudbury, they later beheaded.[23]

CHAPTER 6

Feminizing Theseus in the
Knight's Tale
The Victory of Pallas Athena over Mars

In the *Knight's Tale*, the enmity between Theban cousins Palamon and
Arcite may project a masculine imbalance also characteristic of the "lord
and governour" of Athens (861) and ruler of Thebes, Duke Theseus. If The-
seus is wise, then his is a wisdom diverted and distracted by excessive mar-
tiality, a narrowly focused masculinity. When he first appears, he seems
more interested in besting "olde Creon," lord of the city of Thebes "Fulfild
of ire and of iniquitee" (940), to enhance his own reputation than to rid the
country of a "tiraunt" (961) offensive to war widows. Theseus pledges his
might, the skills of Mars, so that "al the peple of Grece sholde speke / How
Creon was of Theseus yserved / As he that hadde his deeth ful wel de-
served" (962–64), and indeed he "slough hym manly as a knyght / In pleyn
bataille" (987–88). It is true that Theseus was credited with using "wysdom"
and "chivalrie" (865) in his recent conquest of "the regne of Femenye." But
his insistent martiality (coupled with his forced marriage of the captive
Hippolyta and the apparent imprisonment, or at least control, of her niece
Emelye) advances, through the mythological signs in this tale and their
glosses, the idea of ominous and pervasive lechery, perhaps more aptly
characterized as rape.

   To describe Theseus's homecoming after the hero's victory over the
Amazons at the beginning of the *Knight's Tale*, Chaucer cites *Thebaid*
12.519 as an epigraph: "Iamque domos patrias, Scithice post aspera gentis /
Prelia laurigero, etc." (later paraphrasing the Statian lines in 859–74). By
this means, the significance of Theseus's homecoming and its function as
legitimized rape become more apparent, for Chaucer does not in fact use the
classical epic of the *Thebaid* directly in the tale as heavily or frequently as
this epigraph might imply. He did probably combine Statius with Boccac-
cio in lines 893–996, a practice he followed frequently in "translating"
Latin originals, that is, using the vernacular translation or adaptation con-
currently with the original Latin.[1] And Statius's *Thebaid*[2] was itself used
by Boccaccio in his *Teseida*, a poem adapted by Chaucer to his more philo-
sophical purpose, the symmetry of the Knight's medieval, Boethian world[3]
superimposed on the Renaissance world of Boccaccio's *Teseida*.[4] Chaucer,

however, has in fact reduced Boccaccio's *Teseida* from 10,000 to 2,250 lines, with only 800 lines of the English poem corresponding to Boccaccio's Italian. Of these, 270 have been directly translated, 374 have a general likeness, and 132 bear slight similarity.[5]

What Chaucer has added in his own 2,249-line poem, and how he shaped it, must be sought from other sources, including Chaucer's own "first draft" of the *Knight's Tale,* the fragmentary *Anelida and Arcite,*[6] which must have been written before the *Knight's Tale* but after the *Hous of Fame.*[7] A poem dismissed as inconsequential by critics because of its hodgepodge of sources,[8] the *Anelida* itself is a puzzle, with its double invocations, to Mars and Bellona and again to the nine Muses, and its description of the triumphal procession of Theseus leading home the defeated Amazons, coupled with Anelida's complaint.

This Statian homecoming of Theseus after the civil war and after the war with the Amazons is key to both the *Anelida* and the *Knight's Tale.* *Thebaid* 12.519 is also used directly in lines 22–42 of the *Anelida,* with line 38, on Emelye, taken from the *Teseida* (lines 22–70 were indirectly influenced by the introductory story in Boccaccio).[9] Appropriately, Chaucer claims, in this 357-line epic-complaint, that "First folowe I Stace, and after him Corynne" (21), with "Corynne" referring possibly to a Theban woman poet, or more likely, to Boccaccio, from "wry face," or to Ovid, as the author of the *Heroides.*[10] Of the three possibilities, the last may be most important, given the significance of Ovidian influence in both the *Anelida* and the *Knight's Tale,* even though other parts of the poem are taken from other sources.[11]

In the fragment of the *Anelida,* Chaucer uses the homecoming of Theseus to contrast the Amazons (Hippolyta) and their god Pallas Athena (wisdom) with the Thebans (ruled now by Theseus) and the goddess of war, Bellona (female counterpart to Mars). But in the long philosophical romance of the *Knight's Tale,* the homecoming acts as a springboard for the expansion of the arena from Thebes or Athens to the cosmos. The gods are increased from Statius's two (Pallas Athena, Mars) to three (Diana, Mars, Venus), changed (as is the unmarried Pallas of the Amazons) to Diana, goddess of chastity, and supplemented, by means of the higher tier of decision-making and problem-solving, unifying gods, Venus's father Saturn and his son Jupiter.

The *Anelida,* as a first draft of the *Knight's Tale,* thus sketches in the ideas of tension and conflict developed and resolved in the four parts of the *Knight's Tale,* especially as embodied in the central figure, whether Arcite or Theseus. Arcite, as a prototype for Theseus (or Palamon-Arcite), is described in the *Anelida* as "double in love and no thing pleyn, / And subtil in that craft over any wyght," for it is through his "kunnyng" that he won this "lady bryght" (87–89). Later, he is described several times as "fals

Arcite," so much so that he attempts to cover his falsity (155ff.). Understanding how Theseus, modeled on the double Arcite of the *Anelida,* evolves from the martial victor of part 1 to the ruler who augments justice with the more civilized virtue of mercy in part 2 will help to explain the problem of Theseus for Chaucer critics, when in part 4 he becomes truly wise and just at the time of his Prime Mover speech.[12] Because Chaucer's Knight is perhaps interested in demonstrating to his listening son, the Squire, the long educational process of becoming a truly ideal knight, he stresses here the *process* rather than the *product* of that education.[13] The problem is also mythographic: commentators interpret Theseus *in malo* and *in bono,* conflicting interpretations that Chaucer inherits in rewriting the Ovidian (*Heroides*) story of the betrayer Theseus in the *Legend of Ariadne* on the one hand, and the Fulgentian moralization of the wise ruler in this continuation of the *Thebaid* on the other.[14]

Whereas Theseus does learn, by the end of the *Knight's Tale,* to perpetuate the double role of Pallas Athena and Minerva, that is, chivalry and wisdom, as we shall see, in the first two parts of the *Knight's Tale* Theseus shows faulty judgment and behavior influenced more by Mars than by Pallas Athena—or even by Venus and Diana. It is his feminine side—the side of wisdom, Minerva—that he must learn to allow expression. Such wisdom assumes a divinely subjective cast in part 2 but throughout is linked with female characters—the Theban widows; Hippolyta, Emelye, and their ladies; Venus and Diana. From Mars, Venus, and Diana to Pallas Athena is a dialectic anticipated in the twin themes of the *Anelida,* of the war between the Athenians and the Amazons and of the love of Anelida for Arcite, explicable, then, by the *Anelida*'s two major sources, specifically, Statius's homecoming of Theseus coupled with Boccaccio's Arcite story. These two very different emphases, sources, forms, styles ally perfectly well with the puzzling twin invocations supposedly drawn from the *Teseida* in lines 1–21 that focus on Mars and Bellona and also the Muses.

Conflicts between the Theban and Amazonian Gods: Mars, Bellona, and Pallas Athena in the *Anelida*

As we have observed, Chaucer changes Boccaccio's invocation in the *Anelida*: whereas Boccaccio invokes Mars, Venus, Cupid, and the Muses, Chaucer invokes only the deities of war. He summons not only "Thou ferse god of armes, Mars the rede" (1) but also "thy Bellona, Pallas, ful of grace" (5), whom Chaucer apparently misunderstands as Pallas Athena.[15] This first summons is followed by a second, to the nine Muses, especially Polymnia (15), the Muse of sacred poetry who dwells "On Parnaso ... with thy sustres glade, / By Elycon, not fer from Cirrea" (16–17). The invocation, indeed, is based on the description of Theseus's homecoming in the *Thebaid,* in which Mars and Pallas Athena, not Bellona, are the gods affiliated with the principal characters. In Statius, *Thebaid* 12.519ff., Theseus marches in a procession with spoils and virgin chariots of the Amazons reminiscent of *duri imago Marvortis*, "the grim War-God." Yet the unafraid warrior-maids, termed "dominae," seek the shrine of the unwed Minerva ("innuptae ... delubra Minervae"). This strange means of describing the wise Minerva, the goddess associated with Athens and a virgin who sprang intact from Jupiter's head, enhances Statius's tension between wisdom (Minerva, Athens) and war (Mars, Thebes).

As if Chaucer intended for the gods of war to predominate in place of absent Pallas Athena, or wisdom, the poet, in addition to coupling Mars literally with Bellona in place of Pallas in the invocation, also emphasizes war, dissension, and enmity throughout the narrative portion of the *Anelida.* The backdrop for the love story of Anelida and Arcite is Theseus's victory in Scythia and his return to Athens after "werres longe and grete" (22), then Creon's tyranny, during which "the olde Creon gan espye" (64) in the most suspicious way. Further, "The ymage of Mars" marks the Duke's banner "in tokenyng of glorie" (31) during the triumphal procession. Mars reappears a few lines later, "The olde wrathe of Juno to fulfille" (51) by kindling enmity between Athens and Thebes "through his furious cours of ire" (50). Finally, and most curiously, Anelida will offer sacrifices to Mars in lines 354–56, after which she will pray to the god of war.

The human need to knit together, or at least to record the existence of, the fragmentary and discordant (suggested by war making) by means of song and artistry is suggested by Chaucer's second invocation, to Polymnia, who, along with her "sustres glade" (the Muses), sings on Parnassus. Yet Mars and Bellona are linked with the nine Muses by means of the number nine. As gods of war, Mars and Bellona appear together in Martianus's *De nuptiis,* and, in Remigius's commentary on the epic, Mars appears with the number nine (if not the Muses per se) because it is he "by whom all things are brought to an end." Remigius explains that for this reason Mars is either linked with all virtue, or with death, and hence with nine as the sum of all virtue, or death as that by which all things are brought to an end.[16]

Further, in relation to the puzzling misidentification of Bellona with Pallas, Chaucer may be aware of the late medieval mythographies in which wise Pallas is also glossed as a maker of armor and therefore appropriately synonymous with Bellona, goddess of war. In the fourteenth century, Holkot, commenting on the Book of Wisdom, defines Pallas as a goddess of wars (*dea bellorum*), because in wars wisdom joins the goddess with bodily strength ("quia bellis magis confert sapientia quam corporis fortitudo" [p. 380 (113)], in Allen, "Mythology," p. 365). She is, however, "nova," "new," because wisdom experiences neither debility nor old age. And the Book of

Wisdom 5 (6:1) teaches that Wisdom is better than force ("Melior est sapientia quam vires"), a prudent man greater than a strong man ("vir prudens magis quam fortis"). Further, the peace she brings—Pax de Minerva—is the peace of God:

> First I say Peace is generated by Minerva because Minerva is the goddess of Wisdom born from Jove. The wisdom of God through miseries made flesh generating and making peace for us—I give up peace to you, all my peace I give to you. Grace and peace of God our father Jesus Christ be with you.[17] (My translation)

Holkot, however, also distinguishes Pallas from Minerva, *dea sapientie* whose name, "Min" or "not" plus "erva" or "mortal," denotes "immortal":

> That same goddess is depicted as if a decorated virgin [*virgo decora*], having three vestments, and depicted as carrying the head of the Gorgon on her shoulders, according to Alexander Neckam in *Scintillarius poetarum*: she is said to be born from Jove's head, and without mother, and is called Tritonia, Pallas, and Minerva, to whom the number seven is sacred, and is the goddess of wisdom, and of all arts [*et omnium artium*], and of wars. The same virgin is depicted as goddess of wisdom, because she never endures the corruption of vices [*vitiorum corruptionem*], but always enjoys the integrity of (their) perpetual death. Three vestments she has on account of the three literary arts [*tres scientias sermocinales*], by which she is covered up and decorated, which are grammar, rhetoric, and dialectic. (P. 380 [113], in Allen, "Mythology," pp. 363–64; my translation)

Arms and wisdom are again linked with the goddess in Christine de Pizan's *Epistre d'Othéa* (1399; translated into Middle English by Stephen Scropes in the late fifteenth century): Othea, as a mythical goddess of prudence, addresses her "Pistell" to fifteen-year-old Hector, who is "The son of Mars, the god of bataile, / That in deedis of armes which will not faile" and of "myghti Mynerve, the goddes, / The which in armes is hiȝ maistres" (myth 1, 33–35).[18]

But Christine parts company with Holkot by distinguishing between the functions of two separate goddesses, for she glosses Minerva in myth 13 and Pallas in myth 14. Minerva is "a ladi of grete connynge and fonde the crafte to make armure, for a-foore the pepill armed them not but with cuirboille" (pp. 23–24), and Pallas, from the "ile that is callid Pallaunce," is "goddes of connyng" because of her wisdom. Further, of the two names, Minerva "is callid thus in that the which longeth to knyghthod, and Pallas in alle thinge that longeth to wisedome; and therfore it is seyde that he scholde ioyne wisedome to knyghthode, the which is ful wel according therto, and that armes scholde be kepte may be vnderstanden be feith. To this purpos seith Hermes: Joyne the loue of feith with wisedome" (pp. 24–25). Allegorically, the joining of Pallas (wisdom) to Minerva (knighthood) means that the virtue of hope should join with faith, or the "good vertues of the knyghtli spirite, withoute the which he may not availe" (14, p. 25).

Chaucer's invocation in the *Anelida* thus draws attention to the reduction of Pallas Athena to Bellona as goddess of war and agent of discord. Both Minerva, goddess of wisdom, and Pallas Athena, maker of armor and goddess of war who signifies strength—but not literal warmongering, brutality, violence, and strength without wisdom—for true harmony to exist are needed. Theseus, ruler of Athens, and later, of Thebes, is thus associated with Mars and domination, conquest, and therefore with the perfidy of Arcite in Anelida's complaint. Anelida does not yet see the perfidy of Arcite sufficiently to acknowledge that Pallas Athena, not Mars, is the appropriate god to whom to pray. Like Hippolyta, Anelida is too vanquished and therefore too accepting of her fate. Wisdom and fortitude, Minerva and Pallas, have been subjugated, the world reduced, not made more harmonious.

The bulk of the *Anelida*—a longer section than the introductory portion of the *Anelida*, which will be most echoed and used in the *Knight's Tale*—is most likely transmogrified into the story of Criseyde and Troilus in the *Troilus*. Here the *Anelida* outlines the conventional story of a lover's betrayal of the beloved (lines 78–219), followed by the lady's conventional complaint, consisting of Strophe, Antistrophe, and Conclusion (220–350), and ending with the seven-line continuation of the story (351–57). The most specific link between the two poems exists especially in Criseyde's long soul-debate about love in book 2, lines 694–903, including Antigone's apostrophe to Love in lines 827–75, which seems to mirror the Strophe and Antistrophe of Anelida's complaint.

What appears most problematic about the *Knight's Tale*, unlike the *Anelida*, even though both poems use as a catalyst for the narrative Statius's description of Theseus's homecoming, is the difference in their sources, especially the heavy dependence in the *Knight's Tale* on Ovidian use of myth. As Richard Hoffman has documented, "There are several explanations to account for the striking fact that, while the *Knight's Tale* is based upon the *Teseida*, it contains more allusions or parallels to Ovidian passages than any other of the *Tales*," perhaps in large measure because so much of the classical material in the tale concerns mythology.[19] It is possible, Hoffman suggests, that Chaucer may have gleaned some of his mythological material either directly from Ovid, or from Boccaccio, who may have read Ovid himself; it is also possible that Chaucer's understanding may have derived from other sources, including commentaries on Ovid, as well as from the classical source for the story of Thebes, in Statius's epic.

This source material is important because Chaucer's treatment of the gods in the *Knight's Tale* has long troubled critics: are they primarily planets or gods? Answering this question means turning to the specific Ovidian sources Chaucer used to effect changes (for example, in relation to Venus's *citole*), chiefly Bersuire and John Ridevall.[20] Walter Clyde Curry suggested years ago that "it appears that Chaucer had not *confused* the gods and the planets but that he is with painstaking accuracy calling attention to the fact that, in the action of the story, they will function as planets alone."[21] Not all critics have agreed with this statement, whether or not they have turned instead to "pagan" mythology or mythography to explain the role of the gods in the poem: altars are built to the gods, statues sculpted, and their effect may be more than astrological.[22] These Ovidian sources provide a key to the Knight's mythography, although the theme of the *Knight's Tale* (as reflected in the dramatic conflict of its characters, human and planetary or mythological), derives from the *Anelida,* and earlier still, the *Thebaid* through the *Teseida.*

Given Chaucer's changes in his sources, one change not satisfactorily explained by critics is Chaucer's addition of Saturn as a problem solver and resolver specifically of the quarrel between Venus and Mars (the latter two also appear in Boccaccio). The issue of the role of the gods in the *Knight's Tale* hinges in particular on the ambiguous role of Saturn: is his influence on the world positive or negative? Dorothy Bethurum has argued that Chaucer's change of Boccaccio is responsible for Saturn's role in the *Knight's Tale,* in that Boccaccio's conflict between Venus and Mars is not fully or explicitly resolved. She declares that his real source is the twelfth-century cosmographic poem of Bernardus Silvestris, *De mundi universitate (Cosmographia),* which synthesizes many of the details found in Chaucer's portrait. She focuses the problem on the traditions associated with Saturn: in the Fulgentian tradition of Saturn as a god, his influence is beneficent and he signifies wisdom; in the astrological tradition of Saturn as a planet, his influence is malign and he signifies melancholy and the passing of time. "Chaucer's poem," Bethurum concludes, "in the end converts Saturn's act to good in the marriage of Palamon and Emelye. He does not really solace himself with anticipation of heaven, whether Christian or pagan, but with the succession of the generations on the earth."[23]

In contrast, Saturn and Mars are linked in the commentaries on Martianus through their malevolence and discord, in a passage that Chaucer may have had in mind in constructing the *Knight's Tale.* Remigius of Auxerre conjoins the significations of the two gods in glossing book 5, on Rhetoric. Death resulting from war between nations (or tropologically, between body and soul) resembles Saturn's similarly destructive effects. In Martianus's text, because the deities imagine war is on its way, Silvanus begs for the bows of the Delians, the arms of Hercules, Portunus's (Neptune's) trident, but does not dare to request the spear of Gradivus Mars.

"Being used to rustic warfare, he was considering the scythe of Saturn and, distrusting his own strength, was eyeing the missiles of the Thunderer" (Martianus, trans., 211.2, pp. 155–56). Saturn's scythe is glossed in 211.7 (Remigius, *Mart.* 2:65) as that weapon with which he castrated his father Caelus, for which reason Saturn is the god of years, because they run back upon themselves like a scythe ("Et ipse est deus temporum quae in se quasi falx recurrunt"). Then Remigius adds a line from Virgil's *Georgics* 2.402, no doubt anticipating line 406 in which the farmer uses Saturn's knife to prune the vine during the winter: "'Atque in se qua per vestigia volvitur annus'" ("as the year rolls back upon itself over its own footsteps"). Remigius thereby ties Saturn, god of time, to Mars, marcher in steps. Literally, Mars as "deus bellorum" is also termed "Gradivus," from *cratos divus*, the god of power, or because he marches in steps to war, or from the spear that is called a *gradein* in Greek. Figuratively, Mars signifies death, that is, the separation of soul from body ("Mars autem dicitur quasi mors, id est separatio animae a corpore")—which might indeed be imagined as the result of a war: Remigius adds, "Mors autem effectus est belli" ("death is caused by war").

As in the *Anelida,* Mars in the *Knight's Tale* appears as god of war, with Arcite, and to a certain extent, Theseus, as his exponent. Mainly the idea of war—discord and division—will predominate throughout the poem's conflicts, beginning with the war between Athens and Scythia, then Athens and Thebes, next the conflict in love between Palamon and Arcite, and then the disputes among Venus, Mars, and Diana, who is linked with Emelye. The human and societal discord we witness is thus repeated in the discord of the gods Venus, Diana, Mars, and summed up not by Mars—but by Saturn, father of Venus and chief god, with whom he is linked in Martianus's *De nuptiis.* The narrative structure of the first two books of Martianus Capella's *De nuptiis* as an *ascensus ad Deum* is here used to mirror the ascent to God, Jupiter (and is analogous to the ascent to God provided at the end of the *Canterbury Tales* in a more Christian form by the purgative *Parson's Tale*).

What of Pallas Athena as wisdom and fortitude, or peace, harmony, which emerges from miseries, from wars? Initially, in the *Knight's Tale* the place of the "unmarried" Minerva to whom the Amazons are devoted will be arrogated to Diana as goddess of chastity and the hunt, with Emelye as her exponent. But the idea of Minerva as wisdom will be arrogated to Jupiter, less Saturn's son than the Boethian Prime Mover, or God Himself. The principle of Stoic cosmic order, Jupiter subsumes and incorporates all the other gods (and planets) as a kind of one God, divine order, within himself. Jupiter is defined as the Stoic "iuris pater" in Bernardus Silvestris's alleged commentary on Martianus 3.107: "Dicitur enim Iupiter quia iuris pater est: Apollo quia sapientia; Bachus quia opulentia vel gaudium; Mars quia in conflictu spirituali iuvamur ab eo" ("Jupiter is called so because he is *iuris pater,* father of law; Apollo because he is wisdom; Bac[c]hus because he is opulence and joy; Mars because in spiritual conflict we are aided by him" [pp. 52–53]). The passage cites the famous lines from the lost work of the Stoic Valerius Soranus ascribing six different roles to Jupiter:

Iupiter omnipotens, regum rerumque repertor,
Progenitor genitrixque deum, deus unus et idem.

[Jupiter Omnipotent, creator of kings and things. Father and mother of gods, the one god and the same.]

It is toward this end—of Jupiter as the one God summing up, encompassing, the other gods and their respective concerns and disputes—that the romance moves as it works through conflict and war.

Thus the late mythographic bifold view of Pallas Athena (Minerva), summing up the ideal of *sapientia et fortitudo,* of peace emerging out of conflict, will evolve through the four parts of the *Knight's Tale,* out of, and subsuming, the familial, societal, national, and cosmic conflicts of the characters and the planetary gods. If the gods are planets, they represent as well a place in the universe through which the message of human desire passes as it is translated, step by step, from an earthly need into one reconcilable with fate and providential order.

The very fragmentedness of the *Anelida* mirrors important Chaucerian ideas used later in the *Knight's Tale*: that Chaucer wants to have some truth presented both ways—that he wants to praise the warrior but criticize the unfaithful lover, both of whom are the same person, Arcite—suggests the same attitude toward truth and toward human beings witnessed in the Retraction, when our poet, on his deathbed, retracts those stories of love; and yet do we believe him, given the context in which he retracts? While the *Anelida* may be unfinished and the Retraction, ironic, nevertheless, the *Knight's Tale* details step-by-step how love and individual desire fit into a universal pattern of cosmic harmony through Arcite's deathbed renunciation. The way to Pallas Athena is through Mars, as the *Anelida* teaches. The idea of the *Anelida,* then, can be used to gloss the *Knight's Tale* and its Statian frame of homecoming.

If doubleness marks *Anelida* and the first three parts of the *Knight's Tale,* then singleness—oneness, harmony, resolution of conflict, indeed, Pallas Athena herself—marks the concluding fourth part of the *Knight's Tale.* In the first part, devoted to human blindness to his own mortality, the Minotaur demonstrates the divided self of Palamon and Arcite. In the second part, the union of Theseus and Hippolyta suggests the justice and mercy of the monarchy as a paradigm for the human spiritual kingdom, body guided by reason. The third part, with its altars to Venus, Mars, and Diana, projects the deities' conflicting value systems onto the cosmos through the three planets. The fourth part, beginning with the strife among the gods, ends with the counsel of the last planet, Saturn, and the ultimate wisdom of Jupiter as the Stoic one God.

In part 1, as has been shown, Theseus settled disputes with martial energy and boldness more than with wisdom. In part 2, after his victor's marriage to Amazon Hippolyta, who like her niece Emelye worships Diana, he practices the art of Diana, hunting, rather than that of Mars, warfare and battle: "For after Mars he serveth now Dyane" (1682). This exemplar of virility, this martial ruler who has defeated Creon and Thebes and also captured and married Hippolyta, normally swears by "myghty Mars" even in part 2, when he comes upon the battling brothers and promises death for violating the peace (1708). And after he inadvertently overhears Palamon's confession that he loves Emelye and hates Theseus, he damns both Palamon and Arcite, swearing by "myghty Mars the rede!" (1747). But his ability to accommodate and learn from other points of view results from that initial decision to marry the captive Hippolyta. He will thus accede to the widows' request to bury their husbands, in despite of the tyrant Creon's edict, and he will also soften his command to the cousins after Hippolyta pleads with him. In other words, by marrying Diana's representative he assimilates Diana's point of view, not only by hunting rather than by battling but also by tolerating others who are different. This broad-mindedness is necessary in the rational soul and the wise king. Eventually he will inculcate the knowledge of, and practice the values and behavior associated with, the gods Mars, Diana, and perhaps also Venus (or Minerva).

Arcite versus Palamon in the *Knight's Tale*, Part 1: The Image of the Minotaur

As a first stage in this philosophic process, Palamon and Arcite represent individual will, or human desire, whose conflict is figured in the emblem of the Minotaur defeated by Theseus and borne on the hero's banner in ironic forecast of his solution to their enmity in part 2. Specifically, when Theseus in *Thebaid* 12.665–74 waves the large shield bearing the image of himself victorious over the Minotaur, he invokes his own past power to aid him in this new battle with the ruthless tyrant Creon of Thebes. Since the figure of the Minotaur is not found in Chaucer's direct source for the *Knight's Tale,* Boccaccio's *Teseida,*[24] Chaucer uses the Statian description in this first part of his romance. The beaten image of the Minotaur, "which that he [Theseus] slough in Crete," appears on a *penoun* of gold in a description of the white banner bearing the red statue of Mars and his spear and shield (975–80). The colors of Theseus's banner—red for Mars, and white for Venus—recur in the later description of the lists in association with their respective champions, Arcite and Palamon (2581–86).

The association of the Minotaur with the two cousins therefore also suggests self-division, or individual rupture between soul and body; the symbol of the Minotaur as half man, half beast, enhances that significance in its mythographic recapitulation of the conflict between Athens and Scythia, Theseus and Hippolyta.[25] And Theseus's other conflicts—mainly with Thebes, with the two Theban cousins Palamon and Arcite—take on some of the coloration of those earlier battles. Once he has defeated the monster Minotaur, he continues to rely on the symbolism of that victory for help in quelling other disturbances. Because the Minotaur, as Pasiphaë's son, directly emblematizes her lechery in sleeping with the bull of Neptune, according to Richard H. Green he also represents that passion that leads to broken friendships, treachery, madness, and bloodshed—here, the passion of Palamon, echoed by Arcite, which divides and separates the two cousins and leads eventually to Arcite's death. That familial division mirrors the original Theban conflict between the sons of Oedipus, Eteocles and Polynices, that blossomed into a civil war, as David Anderson has noted.[26] The mythographers also understand the Minotaur as a monster, "semibos, et semivir," whose combined natures—man, demon, bull—suggest a variety of sins, chiefly pride and lechery. In his commentary on the Book of Wisdom, Holkot echoes Bersuire in implying that the monster signifies civil disorder, controllable either by depriving the monster of life or imprisoning it perpetually in a labyrinth.[27] The thematic clash between order and disorder in the *Knight's Tale* has fascinated critics, who have plotted characterization and structure in reflection.[28]

The two brothers, who emblematize the discordant will of the individual, summed up by the sinful Minotaur, literally epitomize their nation's inability to work together in peace. Among the mythographers, Hyginus, who in the *Fabulae* provides a model for Chaucer's construction of the characters of Palamon and Arcite, tells the story in two parts, both times stressing the one brother's dispute with the other as a violation of natural, social, and divine order. In the second part of the story (narrated first in Hyginus), which describes the war and its outcome, the heavens and the earth together help to defeat the Seven against Thebes and thereby signal cosmic dissatisfaction with fratricide: "Capaneus, who said he would take Thebes against Jove's will, was *struck by a thunderbolt of Jove* while scaling the wall, and Amphiaraus was *swallowed by the earth* in his four-horse chariot. Eteocles and Polynices, fighting against each other, killed each other. When a common funeral offering was made to them at Thebes *the smoke divided* because they had killed each other. The others perished" (my emphasis).[29] In the first part, told second in order and more fully delineated (and used in part by the First Vatican Mythographer, in myth 80), Hyginus explains the reason for the civil disorder in the errant political decisions of two fathers. The first, Oedipus, unknowingly and unnaturally slept with his mother to conceive two sons who were also his brothers, Polynices and Eteocles, which split the kingdom. The second, Oeneus, married to a captive, drove out his own son Tydeus (soon-to-be father of Diomede), for fratricide. The disinherited son Polynices and Tydeus, marrying sisters and joining forces with their new father-in-law, storm a city that more closely approximates a prison.[30]

The summary might have suggested a number of narrative similarities in the story of Palamon and Arcite: like Polynices, Palamon must compete with a rival (here, Tydeus) for the same woman (here, Adrastus's daughter, although Adrastus solves the problem by giving him the older daughter); like Polynices separated from his brother, Palamon is separated from Arcite (although in Polynices' case Eteocles drives him out of the city); however, like Polynices, Arcite is exiled from his city; finally and most importantly, the walled and seven-gated city of Thebes that Polynices must attack in its circularity resembles the four-gated amphitheater built by Theseus (rather than Amphion) for the lists—and is anticipated by the prison that dominates parts 1 and 2.

Chaucer overlays his Theban story with the Ovidian myth of Theseus's battle with the Minotaur. Indeed, what seems usual in all of these usages—Statian, Chaucerian, mythographic—is that the myth of the Minotaur is Ovidian in origin and that the medieval commentators most intrigued by it are in fact glossing Ovid. The Minotaur appears both in the *Metamorphoses* 8.155–56 and *Heroides* 10; the gloss on the Minotaur in Bersuire (copied by Holkot) appears in a commentary on the *Metamorphoses* that Chaucer will use extensively and repeatedly throughout the *Knight's Tale*, especially in the descriptions of the three altars and their gods in part 3. Further, the imprisonment of the Minotaur in the Labyrinth—also glossed by Bersuire and Holkot as this world—refracts throughout the *Knight's Tale* in the repetition of the word "prison" and the prison setting.[31] Perhaps of greatest significance for the present reading of the *Knight's Tale* is the equivalence between Polynices-Eteocles and Palamon-Arcite and the Minotaur. What may appear only implicit in Hyginus is made explicit by Fulgentius: the latter mythographer moralizes the brothers, in his commentary on the *Thebaid*, like Holkot glossing the triple nature of the Minotaur. Eteocles signifies *avaritia*, Polynices, *luxuria*, with Creon, Jocasta's brother and the sons' uncle, representing *superbia*.[32] In Chaucer, in echo of Holkot's prescription to society for the civil disorder represented by the Minotaur, "in labyrintho perpetuo conservetur," the closely knit cousins ("of sustren two yborn" [1019], but "Bothe in oon armes" [1012]), after defeat by Theseus, are to Athens to "dwellen in prisoun / Perpetuelly" (1023–24). The fact

195

that they come to disagree because they share an inability to decide who most deserves a woman, Emelye, may forge a link with some of the stories discussed earlier. Both cousins perceive her as reified: Palamon, loving her as if she were a goddess, possibly Venus (1101), establishes him as an exponent of what Holkot would term lechery; indeed, it is Venus to whom he prays for release from their prison. Arcite, equally smitten, but perceiving her as if she were a paramour or a creature (1155), allies himself with Mars by quarreling with his cousin over her—by refusing to accede to Palamon's prior commitment, by disputing the superiority of his attachment ("For paramour I loved hire first er thow.... And therfore, at the kynges court, my brother, / Ech man for hymself" [1155, 1181–82]). His position is not only contentious but proud, and self-willed—he is the incarnation of that minotaurish pride from Holkot's gloss. Hence together, as lechery and pride, bull and demon, they duplicate the figure of the Minotaur that Theseus is most famous for besting. Both Palamon and Arcite are sons of the wrong father.

If the cause of the discord in the Statian, Ovidian, and Chaucerian cases originates outside mere youthful rivalry, then what emerges is a history of familial and national discord resulting from adultery and consequent enmity. Palamon derives his name from that of Palaemon in *Thebaid* 1.12–14, 115–22, as the son of Ino and grandson of Cadmus, founder of Thebes, and therefore he inherits Juno's hostility toward Thebes. Her antipathy stems from her anger over Jupiter's adulteries with Theban women, especially Cadmus's daughter Semele, Alcmena, mother of Hercules, and Cadmus's sister Europa.[33] Juno's dislike of Venus may in part be attributed to Venus's role as mother-in-law to Cadmus, grandmother of Semele and Ino, and mother and foster mother of Bacchus. The later enmity of Juno toward this nation and toward Venus is explained in the genealogy of the Theban First Family in myth 151 of the First Vatican Mythographer. Hermione (Harmonia elsewhere), born of the adulterous union of Mars and Venus, marries Cadmus, founder of Thebes; these first parents produce offspring that include Agave, who killed her son Pentheus; Semele, whose adultery with Jupiter burned her to a crisp but produced Bacchus, god of Thebes; Jocasta, mother and wife of Oedipus, and grandmother and mother of Polynices and Eteocles—those feuding brothers upon whom Palamon and Arcite are modeled.[34] The family founder and origin of its present woe, Cadmus, will play a prominent imagistic and mythological role in part 2 of the *Knight's Tale*.

In accord with the genealogy above, much of what occurs to Theban Palamon and Arcite stems from a family (or even tribal) flaw. Juno, "jalous and eek wood" (1329), is responsible more generally for the predicament of the Theban royal cousins because she "hath destroyed wel ny al the blood / Of Thebes with his waste walles wyde" (1330–31), even though as individuals they attribute their woes differently. Palamon explains that "I moot been in prisoun thurgh Saturne" (1328) and also Juno (1229), whereas his present woeful circumstances seem carved out by Venus (1332). Saturn is responsible for the cousins' imprisonment because of his malign astrological influence. Finally, Venus "sleeth me on that oother syde / For jalousie and fere of hym Arcite" (1332–33)—lechery, in short.

Lechery crops up in one other significant mythological reference, in line 1191, in the role Theseus played in aiding his friend Perotheus, in the latter's descent into the underworld to rape Proserpina. The Knight especially recasts the friendship of Perotheus and Theseus as an ironic gloss on the enmity of Palamon and Arcite, whose sworn "brotherhood" has ended as a result of their acquisitive desire for Emelye. Perotheus, "That felawe was unto duc Theseus, / Syn thilke day that they were children lite" (1192–93), comes to Athens to visit his friend, "For in this world he loved no man so, / And he loved hym als tendrely agayn" (1196–97)—lines that rather glowingly describe a friendship that in the old books led even to possible rape. The Knight abruptly stops in recounting the depth of their love, as if reminded of the reason they descended into the underworld previously:

> So wel they lovede, as olde bookes sayn,
> That whan that oon was deed, soothly to telle,
> His felawe wente and soughte hym doun in helle—
> *But of that storie list me nat to write.*
> (1198–1201; my emphasis)

Pirithous, not mentioned in the *Teseida*, does appear in Statius's *Thebaid* 1.474ff., Ovid, and the *Roman de la Rose* 8186ff.[35] Apparently when Pirithous descended into the underworld to rape (or marry) Proserpina, and Theseus attempted to aid him in what Lactantius in his Statius scholium terms an "evil plan," Pluto bound both of them and Hercules rescued only Theseus.[36] Although Theseus and Pirithous appear together three times in Ovid (in the Calydonian boar hunt in *Metamorphoses* 8.4–6, the fight between the centaurs and Lapiths (12.226–29), and *Heroides* 4.109–12), the descent into hell to rape Proserpina appears only in the Ovid commentators on *Metamorphoses* 8.4.[37] The Knight's sudden desire not to tell the story reflects a cronyistic collusion with Chaucer's Perotheus, even what might be termed a pale affirmation of Perotheus's original infernal desire. In line with the spirit of cronyism, *duc* Perotheus (1191) himself later favors Arcite, whose love for Emelye is creaturelike and whose own martial passions so resemble those of mythological Perotheus. Perhaps it is no coincidence, in these terms, that Proserpina's mate Pluto plays a role in the accident that leads to Arcite's death.

When the two friends attempt to carry off Proserpina, the abduction, according to Bernardus Silvestris glossing *Aeneid* 6.393, implies what appears to be a class perversion, or contamination, of the ideal of medieval education. The communal desire shared by Pirithous and Theseus that perverts medieval education means that merchants love to philosophize about mundane matters, but that their flawed understanding drives out true wisdom (or that garrulity defeats eloquence). That ideal comprises the seven liberal arts, or the quadrivium and trivium. Unfortunately, whereas Theseus, part mortal, part divine, may allegorically signify wisdom, in contrast Pirithous signifies a kind of false eloquence. That is, Theseus derives his name from the Greek, *theos* and *eu* (in Latin, *Deus bonus*)—the good god, divine because of his theoretical knowledge of the divine, good because of his practical knowledge, which teaches the human good (pp. 83–84).[38] Pirithous is the god of circumlocution (*peri, circum,* round about, and *theos, deus,* god), with "circumlocutions" defined as wandering merchants who are eminently eloquent. Because merchants are themselves linked with Mercury, Pirithous is established as wholly mortal, because words and deeds are transient. This commentary coupling of Pirithous and Mercury (god of eloquence and of merchants) seems to foreshadow the dream of Arcite in part 2, in which Mercury appears before him with a message.

Arcite, the Theban Founding Mother, and Theseus's Initial Feminizing in Part 2

If Palamon and his vision of Emelye have dominated part 1, by catalyzing the dramatic conflict between the cousins, in part 2, in contrast, Arcite and his dream vision of Mercury, messenger of the gods, provide the dramatic conflict, their dispute and recapture by Theseus. The dream occurs close to the beginning of the part and is significant for the narrative action because Mercury instructs him to return to Athens after he is released from prison. Accordingly, after Palamon escapes from prison, he is situated so as to overhear Arcite confessing his false identity, resumes the fight with his disguised cousin, and together with Arcite is discovered by Theseus on a hunting trip. Because of this encounter, Theseus will allow the cousins to settle their differences through the lists—a judicious and orderly decision on the duke's part. This dream vision does not appear in Boccaccio's *Teseida;* the myth of Argus's blinding, of course, appears in Ovid's *Metamorphoses* 1.671–72.[39] Further, the dream changes Arcite: after he sees Mercury, Arcite will return to Athens literally disguised as "Philostrate" to serve Emelye in her own household.

How the dream vision is constructed will provide the mythological focus for this part: in it Mercury is garbed as he was when he blinded Argus and rescued Io. The Theban connection between Io, Arcite and Palamon, and Cadmus (1546ff.) unifies this part and provides a mythological backdrop for the feud between the cousins—one of national as well as personal and familial discord that will broaden into cosmic discord in Part 3. The "wynged god Mercurie" (1385) appears before Arcite with a "slepy yerde in hond" (1387) and a hat upon his "heris brighte" (1388), to bid him "to be murie" (1386). He is "arrayed," we are given to understand, as he was "whan that Argus took his sleep" (1390). The reference to Argus implies Mercury's cunning murder of Argus, the guard's many watchful eyes lulled to sleep by the messenger's music, so that Io, transformed into a heifer by jealous Juno, might escape. Mythologically, either Argus or Io may be fruitfully used to gloss Arcite, the first in the sense that he is deceived or blinded by Mercury, the second in that he is imprisoned and then released by Mercury.

Mythographically, Arcite in his blindness resembles Argus put to sleep because eloquence (Mercury) always circumvents the prudent man and reports victory over the same: "quia eloquentia viri sepe prudentes circumvenit et reportat victoriam de eisdam," according to Thomas Walsingham in *Archana deorum* (p. 44). This deception is especially disturbing because Argus, "one who is full of eyes [*qui plenus ocellis*]," is usually glossed as "clear-sighted," as the etymology of his name ("ab arguto") reveals. But in Chaucer, Arcite, blinded by his own distress, will be similarly deceived by Mercury into returning to Athens, for the god has assured him that "'Ther is thee shapen of thy wo an ende" (1392); that is, he will be able to *see* Emelye and presumably cure his lovesickness. In this sense, Mercury colludes with the visual panacea articulated by Arcite after his release from prison and exile in part 1: "'Oonly the *sighte* of hire whom that I serve, / Though that I nevere hir grace may deserve, / Wolde han suffised right ynough for me'" (1231–33; my emphasis). At that earlier moment, because Arcite cannot literally see her and because his materialism creates great suffering, he discourses on human blindness, in seeking false felicity while dwelling on earth. This "dronke man" (1261), sightless, irrational, cannot find the "righte wey" (1262) home although he knows he has one (1260–67). This metaphor suggests the spiritual somnambulance of Arcite-Argus and the darkening of human reason that will prevent him from seeing clearly. But it also suggests that this mythographic explanation, laying the blame as it does for his deception on the god Mercury, may be insufficient.

The fact that Mercury appears to Arcite in a dream, presumably sent from the heavens above, places Arcite's desires within a larger, more cosmic plan that will result in harmony eventually, despite the present discord resulting from Arcite's stubbornness. In another mythographic tradition, based on *Metamorphoses* 1.670 and flowering in Bersuire, Mercury *in bono* represents Christ, with Argus instead the devil with many eyes who keeps in his power sinful souls—specifically Io, and now Arcite. Mercury's blinding of Argus therefore frees Io, as human nature, from the devil's power, changing her from a sinner to a just woman.[40] In a sense, this does represent an act of grace, because Arcite's stubbornness will be turned to good.

As if signifying discord, divided physically by his love malady and perhaps also spiritually by his separation from his brother, Arcite will adopt a second self, or personality: as Philostrate he can safely return to Athens and serve as one prostrated by love—which he truly has been. Indeed, his malady has "so disfigured" his face (1403) that he is unrecognizable. His melancholic humor (1375) has made him lean and "drye as is a shaft" (1362), "His eyen holwe and grisly to biholde, / His hewe falow and pale as asshen colde" (1363–64): he has "died" spiritually if not literally, has succumbed to the devil, has been transformed, like Io, but also blinded and killed, like Argus—and he will, eventually, die literally. The dream, however, in which Mercury appears before him, offers a solution, a remedy, for his sickness—and therefore it is no accident that Mercury bears in hand a "slepy yerde" (1387). This staff or rod (*virga, baculus*) in Holkot's commentary on the Twelve Prophets explains his role as god of medicine, but is used by the classicizing friar to suggest a remedy for sin, through the consolation provided by the "rod and staff" of God in the Psalms (fol. 59v, in Allen, "Mythology," p. 151).

Arcite can also be literally compared with Io, this great-grandmother of the founder of Thebes who was also imprisoned and guarded, although, ironically, his greatest "imprisonment" occurs after he has been released from watchful eyes. Figuratively, in this reading, Arcite signifies, if not the *voluptas* of the Theban, then concupiscence, in insisting on having his own way. Io, often glossed as a figure for both concupiscence and *voluptas* by the Ovid commentators, and in Holkot as the purity of innocence in conscience, is transformed, by the negligence of Argus, into a cow: bestial, concupiscent, and desiring. This *clericus litteratus* is prevailed upon by blandishments of worldly pleasures and the adulations of friends, with Mercury a figure for the *Diabolus* (*In librum Sapientiae* 37, p. 130, in Allen, "Mythology," pp. 228–29). The signification works for Arcite, especially upon his return to Athens, for as Philostrate he appropriately rises to do his May observances on May 3. This date represents part of the Roman festival of the Floralia in which acts of rampant eroticism took place, according to the *Fasti* account. But in the Middle Ages, May 3, coinciding with the advent of spring and the resurgence of courtly love, was also notable because on that date Saint Helen discovered the Cross, in a temple of Venus.[41] Perhaps it is significant that, later in the *Knight's Tale*, during the "lusty seson of that May" (2484), the citizens of Athens enjoy the rites of a Floralia-like festival by jousting and dancing all Monday, intending to "spenden it in Venus heigh servyse" (2487). The May 3 occasion is marked by lightness and brightness images associated rather conventionally with the dawn rising of "firy Phebus" as sun and god of truth; so bright is he "That al the orient laugheth of the light, / And with his stremes dryeth in the greves / The silver dropes hangynge on the leves" (1494–96). But the images are also used here ironically; in the early hours of May 3—preceding Arcite's dawn rituals—Palamon escapes from his prison, meets Arcite in the woods, and precipitates their "discovery," as an inversion of the True Cross, by a mock Saint Helen, Theseus. The discovery should (and will eventually) lead to insight, revelation, and true wisdom—true rescue—but the initial reaction of the cousins is anything but happy.

Even more important here is the connection of Io, the great-grandmother of Cadmus, founder of Thebes, and his sister Europa, with the rise of the Theban nation. As we have seen, Juno's enmity toward Theban women like Io who, in her eyes, committed adultery with Jupiter, resulted in her frequent punishment of Thebes. Accordingly, Arcite, in the woods on May 3 observing the rites of Venus, complains of Juno's "crueltee" (1543) toward his family line and the city of Thebes:

"The blood roial of Cadme and Amphioun —
Of Cadmus, which that was the firste man
That Thebes bulte, or first the toun bigan,
And of the citee first was crouned kyng." (1546–49)

Even greater shame than his poor position as a squire to his enemy is the loss of his own identity caused by Juno (1555), "For I dar noght biknowe myn owene name" (1556)—as Philostrate he is "noght worth a myte" (1558). In his appeal to Mars later, it becomes clearer why he is so anxious to restore his name and the dignity of his family line and nation through demonstrations of his prowess. Such motivation would help to vindicate Io and her descendant and founder of Thebes, Cadmus.

Cadmus and Thebes are often interpreted by the mythographers as a type of disorder, or an abrogation of natural and even divine order. This gloss is continued in the *Knight's Tale* through the conflicts of the Theban royal cousins. For Holkot, in his commentary on the Book of Wisdom, Cadmus represents that *discordia*, which is augmented by detraction, specifically through poisonous words ("verba venenose detractiones") among those who ought to be friends ("inter illos qui debent esse amici" [10, p. 38, in Allen, "Mythology," p. 248]). This gloss of *Metamorphoses* 3:31ff. begins with Cadmus's pursuit of his sister Europa, who had been seized by Jove and transformed into a heifer, which led him to Boeotia and his successful battle with a serpent. When he sowed its teeth, soldiers sprang up fighting—the new nation of Thebes. For Holkot, the sowing of poisonous words leads to hostility, enmity, and eventually battle ("quia verba detractoris concepta in cordium hominum ad effectus hostilitatis et inimicitiae procedunt, quandoque ad pugnam"). Cadmus, "Iste seminator," is regarded by Holkot, citing Proverbs, as one of the seven whom God hates (the future kings of Thebes), that is, who sows discords among brothers ("quos odit Deus, qui videlicet seminat discordias inter fratres, Prover. 6 [6.19]"). Arcite especially, who upholds the power of Mars in his dispute, as a descendant of these hated Thebans bears a connection with the diabolic: in Bersuire's commentary on *Metamorphoses* 3.31ff., the serpent defeated by Cadmus, from whose teeth future Thebans spring, signifies the devil, termed Martian because "quia marti deo belli id est ad bellandum cum fidelibus a principio deputatus fuit" ("he had been delegated to Mars the god of war— that is, to war with the faithful—from the beginning").[42] Just as Theseus has defeated Thebes in the *Thebaid,* so too will he resolve the present discord between Palamon and Arcite, but instead of using his martial skill, he relies on cosmic peacemaking, linked in Fulgentius's *Super Thebaiden* with God (p. 186).

The Feminization of the Gods: From Diana to Minerva in Part 3

In part 3, the most important section of the *Knight's Tale* thematically, astrologically, and mythologically, the desires of the human characters transmitted to their corresponding deities must be translated into heavenly law and order. Chaucer accomplishes this within his narrative by a careful repetition of the dramatic cycle enacted once already in parts 1 and 2: first he describes the specific amphitheater temples of the gods—Venus (1918–62), Mars (1969–2050), and Diana (2051–89)—assigned to each character. Next he relays each character's petition to that planetary god at the appropriate astrological hour, Palamon to Venus in 2215–72, Emelye to Diana in 2274–2346 (out of place in the chronological order established by the first cycle), and Arcite to Mars in 2367–89. It will be the duty of Saturn, the last planetary god in part 3, to resolve the conflicting desires of the human characters and their divine agents, in lines 2431–80. The human characters and their planetary deities appear to be joined in some significant pattern, perhaps a moral or allegorical schema, a reflection either of the Four (or Three) Ages of Man,[43] an astrology-based theory of humors, or the faculties of the soul.[44]

Chaucer clearly intends to relate the microcosm to the macrocosm through some type of astrological correspondence; in addition, he attempts to reconcile astrology with mythography, the Boethian and Macrobian with the Ovidian in particular, in an admirable synthesis of frequently discordant systems. How appropriate, though, for a fourteenth-century poet to resolve philosophical discord in a poem by celebrating, through its narrative drama, the amalgamation of disorderly desires within orderly macrocosmic systems. In the case of each character, the value of the human appeal and the planetary deity corresponding to that appeal are undercut either by the mythological characters or the description of the statue of the god included in the temple. Even Saturn, who as a planet and a deity sums up and re- solves the conflicts of both the human and the divine petitioners, sounds a negative, discordant tone in the way he translates desire into action, for his resolution leads to the death of Arcite even while it satisfies to the letter all the human and divine petitions.

A planetary equivalent of Theseus, Saturn, as ruler of the outermost, seventh sphere, appropriately resolves the conflicts of those planets closer to the earth—Mars in the fifth sphere, Venus in the fourth sphere, and Di- ana, or the moon, in the first sphere.[45] The astrological placement of each planet in the cosmos—and its position in a circular world—is reflected in the directional iconography of the altars within the amphitheater. Thus, at the eastern gate, Theseus constructs the altar and oratory for Venus, at the western gate, the altar and oratory for Mars, and in the north, "in a touret on the wal" (1909), an alabaster white and coral red oratory for Diana. The white and red duplicate the colors of Theseus's banner and the gods of Pala- mon (Venus) and Arcite (Mars), as if suggesting synthesis in this "touret" to a goddess marginalized in the ensuing narrative action. She may be marginalized iconographically because she incarnates the feminine princi- ple, as Susan Crane has recently demonstrated.[46] But there may be other explanations.

Of the deities, only Diana does not correspond exactly to her planetary function, for the moon governs change and mutability rather than chas- tity and hunting, and signals the line of demarcation between the sublu- nary and translunary realms. Perhaps because of this disjunction, Chaucer places Diana third in the description of the three temples within the am- phitheater (related to mythological and mythographic signification), but second in the order of petitioners' visits (related to astrological and plane- tary signification). Because only her temple is wholly invented by Chaucer and is not based on a source description in the *Teseida*, her placement in the narrative, and his description of her temple, become unusually inter- esting in assessing the significance of the gods' meaning in part 3. Perhaps Chaucer uses this original description so fraught with unhappiness to ex- press the gulf between heaven and earth.[47] And perhaps he combines the mythological and astrological significance of Diana to show that all human interactions and relationships under the moon's sway reflect change, mu- tability, fickleness, including the wars of nations and the longings of lovers.

In each of the temples, the wall paintings gloss each deity negatively by means of the effects of each upon their human devotees and by means of the mythological antecedents of those devotees portrayed in the wall paintings (except for Mars, who lacks any mythological antecedents). In addition, the iconography of each deity's statue reveals the equally pejorative nature of the attitude and temperament represented by the deity, whether love (Venus), war (Mars), or chastity and hunting (Diana).

Appropriately, within the Temple of Venus, love is defined in the wall painting as the most courtly of activities, full of "sikes colde," "sacred teeris," "broken slepes," and unfulfilled sexual desire and longing "That loves servantz in this lyf enduren" (1923). Rather curiously, instead of the garden of *Teseida* 7.51–56, the wall painting mirrors the Garden of Deduit from the *Roman de la Rose* 1323–1416 of Guillaume de Lorris, a work also translated by Chaucer;[48] it is peopled by the same abstractions, including these personifications of the courtly love process: Plesaunce, Hope, Desir, Foolhardynesse, Beautee, Youth, Bauderie, Richesse, Charmes and Force, Lesynges, Flaterye, Despense, Bisynesse, and Jalousye. This catalog duplicates some of the personifications found within the Garden of Sir Myrthe — specifically what might be termed Gladness, Swete-Lokyng, Compaignye, Beaute, Richesse, and Youthe (in Chaucer's *Romaunt*)—but, in a degenerative and increasingly pejorative sequence, they appear toward the end as Bauderie, Lesynges, Flaterye, Despense, Bisynesse, and Jalousye, emphasizing the lies and fictions more common to the Ovidian than to the courtly lover. Further, the cuckoo sitting on Jalousye's hand, the musical instruments, carols and dances, and the garden all suggest, again negatively, adultery, leisure, aristocratic pursuits, as well as the literary convention of the *hortus conclusus*.[49]

In the *Romaunt*, however, Chaucer links the personified abstractions of the twelfth-century French love poem with mythological characters from Ovid's *Metamorphoses* through the porter Ydelnesse (1940), who opens the door to the enclosed garden of Sir Myrthe (Deduit in Old French); she opens the door to the kind of changing, mutable love signified by Venus and celebrated in Ovid's text through the formal changes experienced by his various characters. Ydelnesse's self-description mingles honesty and irony simultaneously as she declares herself "Ful myghty and ful riche" (595) but her sole purpose that of advancing "my joye and my pleying, / And for to kembe and tresse me" (598–99). The Old French personification Oiseuse (Idleness) often appears in manuscript illuminations with a mirror, like Venus,[50] a topos reflected in the combing and tressing of Idleness in the *Romaunt* and the depiction in the wall painting of the Temple of Venus next to Narcissus. The latter figure, signifying *amor sui* and found in *Metamorphoses* 3.339–510 but not in the *Teseida*,[51] also plays an important role in the *Romaunt* because of his well, the fountain into which he plunged to his death and whose two "cristall stonys" (1568) probably mirror the lover's (or the beloved's) eyes. For this reason, the well is called a "mirror perilous" (1601) and Narcissus, who spurned Echo out of love for his own image, is termed "proude" (1602).

The conjunction of the two figures in Chaucer's wall painting seems to indicate that leisure (Oiseuse, Idleness) leads to selfishness (Narcissus). But, in addition, self-love and pride in loving truly respect neither wise nor strong heroes such as the Old Testament Solomon with his many wives (1944) or the classical Hercules, whose love for Deianira led to his death (1945), nor female mythological magicians and sorcerers like Medea and Circe (1946) or the male historical examples of the angry and rich, like Turnus and Croesus (1947–48). In a gloss on his own mythological references, the Knight, rather smugly, concludes that the "wo" that befalls lovers respects neither "wysdom ne richesse, / Beautee ne sleighte, strengthe ne hardynesse" (1947–48). Venus, like fortune and the world, acts capriciously (1951–52).

In a well-known passage, the statue of Venus, much analyzed by modern commentators, reveals the attributes of Luxuria borrowed from the Third Vatican Mythographer, as repeated by Bersuire, Holkot, and later Ridevall. Saturn's daughter, born from the foam (literally, his severed testicles), is naked (1956), "fletynge in the large see," and covered with "wawes grene" (1956–58), bearing a *citole* in hand (1959), wearing a rose garland (1961), her doves flickering about her (1962), accompanied by her son Cupid (1966). Holkot's very long gloss on Venus describes her as "Luxuria," surrounded by doves, born from the sea, bearing a *concha* (rather than a *citole*), and similarly adorned with roses.[52] Her doves are "wanton people" and Cupid, "concupiscence of the flesh," wounds Apollo, "just men," with the "arrow of temptation."

Like the wall painting in the Temple of Venus, the one in the Temple of Mars portrays the changeable, mutable—here, defined as murderous, destructive, death-inducing activities appropriate to the god and summed up by the idea of the sublunary. Unlike the paintings in the other temples, however, this painting omits mythological figures altogether in favor of infernal iconographical details—"frosty," dark, "grisly" iron features and horrible sounds ("a rumbel in a swough, / As though a storm sholde bresten every bough" [1979–80]). The temple is set within a northern forest that resembles the wood of the suicides in Dante's *Inferno*, canto 13:[53] it contains neither human nor animal inhabitants, only "knotty, knarry, bareyne trees olde, / Of stubbes sharpe and hidouse to biholde" (1977–78). The lack of greenery in this barren landscape suggests the primacy of death, enhanced by the imposing temple of "burned steel" (1983) with its iron pillars, the "northren lyght" (and therefore diabolic?; 1987) shining in only at the adamant door because the temple lacks windows.

An echo of Palamon's seven-year stay "In derknesse and horrible and strong prisoun" (1451), the description of the Temple of Mars primarily combines *Teseida* 7.29–37 with details from *Thebaid* 8.34–73.[54] In addition, its personifications, unlike those in the Temple of Venus drawn from the *Romaunt*, exemplify that division and discord we have seen previously in the *Anelida*. The personifications Felonye, Ire, Drede, Contek, Meschaunce, Woodnesse, Armed Compleint, Outhees, Outrage, and Conquest trace the psychological and social process not of falling in love, but of falling into war. Beginning with wickedness ("the derke ymaginyng / Of Felonye, and al the compassying" [1995–96]), the process is initiated through the internal stages of anger ("crueel Ire, reed as any gleede" [1997]), fear ("pale Drede" [1998]), and strife (a very long section, including both agent and victim, "The smylere with the knyf under the cloke" [1999] and "The shepne brennynge with the blake smoke" [2000], along with "mordrynge in the bedde" [2001], "The open werre" [2002], Contek [2003], and the "colde deeth" [2008]). Thereafter ensues Meschaunce (or misfortune; 2009), Woodnesse (or madness; 2011), culminating in the action of Armed Compleint (2012). This external event, into which the earlier emotions and actions are channeled, is itself followed by the external stages of outcry (2012), violence (many examples [2013–2027], and including a corpse with its throat cut [1213], thousands slain [1214], a tyrant [1215], a destroyed town [1216], and most grotesquely, "The sowe freten the child right in the cradel" [2019]), and the ultimate act of Conquest—ironically depicted as ready to be conquered himself, in that a sharp sword hangs above his head by a "soutil twynes threed" (2030). It is no accident that the Knight exemplifies the process by means of the "slaughtre" (2031) of emperors Julius Caesar, Nero, and Mark Antony (2031–32), all of whose deaths were anticipated by the stars and their association with the "manasynge of Mars" (2035). Chaucer lists no mythological figures in the wall-painting depiction of Mars, perhaps because history rather than fable literally records the sin of *discordia* that he epitomizes and that kings and tyrants perpetrate. (Martian guise befits even Emetreus, king of India, who "Cam ridynge lyk the god of armes, Mars," along with Arcite [2159].)

As with the statue of Venus, Chaucer turns to Bersuire and Holkot for iconographic details to describe the statue of Mars, Discord incarnate. Mars's statue stands upon a "carte" (2041), taken from Bersuire's chariot, the *currus*, or evil soul, turned by four wheels (the vices of avarice, pride, detraction, and injustice, or the four evil dispositions, or the four types of pride), which support Mars (or discord, quarrels, wars, and controversy; "De formis," p. 16, trans. p. 55). Two stars, Puella and Rubeus, shine above his head (2045) and a wolf stands before him at his feet, "With eyen rede and of a man he eet" (2048). According to Bersuire, the ancients consecrated the wolf to him, an animal that emblematizes the cruel, wicked princes, tyrants, officials, soldiers, and rulers who "have the knowledge [*sciant*] and the desire [*velint*] to ravage [*rapere*] the sheep—that is to afflict their rulers' subjects [*subditos ledere*]—so that they can have the opportunity to wage war [*opera bellicosa exercere*]" (pp. 15–16, trans. p. 54).

If Venus intimates the power of individual desire to destroy and harm and Mars reflects the more macrocosmic power of the tyrant able to destroy by waging war (although rendered in Chaucer by the more homely vocations of butcher and smith), then the third and last god, "Dyane the chaste," in the way she is described here, exemplifies the mutability of the prisonlike underworld in whose dark region the human race is condemned to play out both desire and power. Actually, the Temple of Diana is summed up in two sentences—"Depeynted been the walles up and doun / Of huntyng and of shamefast chastitee" (2054–55)—whereas the figures who suffer for their association with, or allegiance to, her reveal far more than hunting or chastity. Aside from the thematic link of metamorphosis, these figures image forth the idea of mutability, change, and underworld ambience. The mythological figures inscribed on the walls include the metamorphosed Callisto (2056), Daphne (2062–64), Actaeon (2065), and dead Meleager (2071), lover of Atalanta (2070). Of these, the hunters Callisto and Actaeon bear the brunt of Diana's anger for their violation of her rule of chastity, as hunters Meleager and Atalanta also suffer for their violation of her hunting rules. Only chaste, hunted Daphne benefits from her protection from rape, "yturned til a tree" (2062) and somehow perceived by Chaucer as a foil for Diana, given his patient explanation that "I mene nat the goddesse Diane, / But Penneus doghter, which that highte Dane" (2062–63).

What these four have in common, aside from their placement in the Temple of Diana, may have been prompted by Ovid moralizations by Bersuire and Holkot, given their appearance in the *Metamorphoses*: Daphne, 1.452–567; Callisto, 2.401–530; Actaeon, 3.158–252; and Meleager and Atalanta, 8.260–444. Of the four figures or pairs, only Daphne and Actaeon appear in the *Teseida* (and Actaeon appears in the petition of Emelye to Diana there, which Chaucer will also repeat in the *Knight's Tale*); Callisto's broken bow, if not Callisto herself, also appears in Boccaccio's poem, along with the arms of Atalanta, but in the Temple of Venus, in 7.61.[55] Bersuire's elaborate glosses on the four in his *Ovidius moralizatus* connect them (in part) through the role of Diana (or another god posing as Diana) as Fortuna, afflicting both good and bad individuals. For Bersuire, the nymph Daphne signifies worldly glory, pursued by those who love her very much, including soldiers, hypocrites, and the ambitious (p. 40, trans. p. 137). Similarly, the nymph Callisto, transformed from woman to bear as a result of Juno's jealousy of her rape and impregnation by Jupiter (who duped her by pretending to be Diana), is allegorized as a person whose station is changed from high to low as a result of Fortuna; she forgets what she is in her proud desire to associate with the rich (p. 52, trans. pp. 162–63). Actaeon, who inadvertently witnesses Diana and her nymphs bathing, is transformed by the goddess into a stag torn up by his unrecognizing hounds; his transformation reflects the rule over the forest of this world by Fortuna, who often turns the rich into poor no longer recognized by friends and family (p. 66, trans. p. 186).

The reference to Meleager and Atalanta may be the richest of all four: linked with Diana through the Calydonian boar, who ravaged the kingdom because of her anger over its lack of sacrifices to her, Meleager dies because his mother vengefully, in return for his killing of her brothers, burns the brand (signifying his life) given to her by the Parcae, or Fates, whom Bersuire terms "deae infernales quae singulorum fata dictare dicuntur," or "infernal goddesses who are said to dictate the fate of each man" (p. 130, trans. p. 312).[56] Bersuire chastizes Meleager's love for Atalanta, which led to this sorry pass; Chaucer may have selected Meleager here not only because he killed the boar she intended as punishment for the Calydonians, and because his inordinate love violated Diana's rule of chastity, but also because of Meleager's indirect tie with the subsequent history of Thebes. (His killing of the Calydonian boar reminds us that the Calydonian king at that time was an ancestor of Tideus, rival of Polynices for the daughter of Adrastus; Adrastus gives the loser Tideus another daughter in marriage and then himself aids the exiled Theban Polynices to reclaim his kingdom from his brother Eteocles, before Theseus felled the city—in short, Chaucer brings up once again the issue of fraternal and national discord.)

In all these cases, Diana's connection, likened to the power of Fortuna in Bersuire, in some way leads to horrible death and destruction, transformation, rape, self-punishment, a concept underscored by the mythographies. This power of Fortuna recurs in Chaucer through her connection with Pluto, to whose "derk regioun" (2082) the statue of Diana casts "ful lowe adoun" (2081) her eyes; she also sits on a hart, her hounds at her feet and the moon under them, "Wexynge it was and sholde wanye soone" (2078). In Bersuire and early Parisian mythographic commentators, Diana embraced three separate personalities—as Proserpina, wife of Pluto in the underworld; as Luna, or the moon, the seventh planet (counting outward); and as Diana, in her virginity equated with Mary.[57] This triple function is mentioned a little later in Emelye's petition to the chaste goddess Diana, queen of Pluto's realm (2299), "For tho thre formes that thou hast in thee" (2313). Diana's infernal roles are also invoked in the Stygian rites of Tiresias and his daughter Manto used to predict the Theban War, in *Thebaid* 4.443ff., when they light three fires for Hecate, then for the Furies, one for Pluto, and one for Persephone, after which they burn entrails and invoke Hecate, Pluto, Tisiphone.[58] This triple function explains the somewhat puzzling wall-painting description of women in labor during childbirth calling upon Lucina, the goddess of childbirth also associated with the moon but often linked with Juno as goddess of women:

A womman travaillynge was hire biforn;
But for hir child so longe was unborn,
Ful pitously Lucyna gan she calle
And seyde, "Help, for thou mayst best of alle!" (2083–86)

Emelye's invocation of Diana as the "chaste goddesse" "To whom bothe hevene and erthe and see is sene, / Quene of the regne of Pluto derk and lowe" (2298–99) broadens her role to include the entire "underworld," interpreted by mythographers—especially Parisian glosses on the *Aeneid* and *De nuptiis Philologiae et Mercurii*—as our earth.[59] As the moon, ruler of the sublunary realm identified with Fortune, and ruler of Pluto's underworld, in the *Knight's Tale* Diana sums up the earthly region swayed by mutability and change and therefore is last in the series to suggest the arbitrary, irrational, discordant events and desires dominating human behavior, whether prompted by the goddess Venus or the god Mars.

The cosmic region from the moon to the the eighth sphere, of the fixed stars, however, transcends that mutability and change of the sublunary realm and was often identified as Fate in the Middle Ages, or mythologically, the three Parcae, or Fates, whose role it was to assign and control human life, as just noted in Bersuire's gloss on Meleager's brand in *Metamorphoses* 8.260–444. Because, in astrological terms, Fate is represented by the workings of the planets, Chaucer repeats the planetary hierarchy through the respective petitions of Palamon, Emelye, and Arcite.

The interconnected mythological roles in each of the petitions blend mythological and planetary functions within Chaucer's larger cosmic interpretation of the interaction between earth and the heavens—a secularized *ascensus ad mentis Deum*. When Palamon, on Sunday at the hour of Venus, goes on a "pilgrymage" to Citherea, in his prayer (2221–26; derived from *Teseida* 7.43)[60] he refers to her positively as Jove's daughter and Vulcan's spouse (2222), but also negatively, given her adulterous affair with Adonis (2224). This inadvertent denigration of the kind of love she represents also blends the role of Venus with that of Diana: Adonis was killed by a boar during a hunt, an activity associated just prior to this and just after, in Emelye's petition, with the goddess of hunting. In a similar confusion of divine functions, when Emelye prays to Diana her interpretation of the goddess of chastity characterizes Diana's Martian, or bellicose, reactions to violations of her rule through the "vengeaunce" and "ire" "aboughte cruelly" by Acteon (2302–3). The petitioners come full circle, literally and figuratively, when Arcite offers his prayer to "fierse Mars" (2369) during his hour at the end of part 3. Referring to Mars's love for the wife of Vulcan, Venus, Arcite echoes the petition of his cousin Palamon to Venus, in which he alludes to Vulcan's wife. Further, if Mars is god of war, then why does Arcite remind him of his losing adultery with the goddess of love

(2383–92) and suffering "thilke peyne and thilke hoote fir / In which thow whilom brendest for desir, / Whan that thow usedest the beautee / Of faire, yonge, fresshe Venus free, / And haddest hire in armes at thy wille" (2383–87), as well as the sorrow he felt when he and Venus were caught by her husband Vulcan (2389–91)? Because Chaucer here merely elaborates on a similar petition in *Teseida* 7.25, complete with damning reference to the adultery with Venus, he therefore reveals the nature of Arcite's true feelings for Emelye — lust.[61]

In his attempt to answer the very human question of why God allows unfortunate events to occur to the best of humans, Chaucer's Knight patiently constructs an explanation of the individual's role in the universe, the relation of the human will to Providence. Does human choice exist? Are human desires ever assimilated into providential reality? If we are blind to the reasons calamities occur, whom should we blame? The Knight explains calamity as if he — and we — had God's foresight and could understand the relationship between heaven and earth — could see that a universal order exists. But normally we cannot, our vision having been darkened by the Fall.

At the end of part 3, Saturn, outermost planet, with the widest course, is introduced "to stynten strif and drede" (2450) among the planets, in lines 2338–2480. In this case, mythological Saturn, as Chronos, or Time, will "remedie fynde" (2452), although not in the most happy of ways for all parties involved. Because Saturn castrated his father Caelus, he is often depicted iconographically with a scythe and interpreted as Chronos (his name in Greek), Time, because he mows down the years — and because he devoured (almost all of) his own children; mythographically, given Jupiter's castration of his virility, he represents *sapientia* or *prudentia,* and is accordingly depicted as a *senex.* However, Chaucer here has to balance the astrological malignity of the outermost planet with this more positive interpretation of the god.[62] He resolves his own dilemma by describing Saturn as Chronos, mutability epitomized, Discordia, that figure who incarnates the discord of Mars that we first saw in the *Anelida.*[63] Note the grinding, malign texture — image, sound, feel — of his self-description in lines 2456–69, enhanced by the relentless reiteration of "myn":

> "*Myn* is the drenchyng in the see so wan;
> *Myn* is the prison in the derke cote;
> *Myn* is the stranglyng and hangyng by the throte,
> ....
> *Myn* is the ruyne of the hye halles,
> ....
> And *myne* be the maladyes colde" (2456–58, 2463, 2467; my emphasis)

More than human or national discord, Saturn expresses global, or cosmic, catastrophe, whether geological, or epidemic; his is the gaze of the executioner, the traitor, the murderer—the anarchist: "My lookyng is the fader of pestilence" (2469). In one figure, with one brilliant stroke, Chaucer adds the idea of the "Temple of Saturn" (it is not described explicitly at all)— the entire sublunary realm, if we permit the deities to convey human or earthly attitudes and behaviors. By connecting this Neoplatonic reading of mythological Saturn to his malign astrological influence, Chaucer brings together the two elements of sublunary and translunary discussed from the beginning of this chapter in the *Anelida*: once again, Mars and Bellona are set against Pallas Athena, rewritten in much more complex guise here as Mars-Saturn (sublunary realm) confronting Pallas Athena-Jupiter (translunary realm).

If Saturn's daughter is Venus, that generative principle whose promptings ensure the reproduction of the human race, then it comes as no surprise that Saturn's sons project both the polar extremes of the workings of natural and divine order, dark Pluto, god of the underworld—and the radiant, beneficent Jupiter, God Himself, Wisdom Incarnate.

Jupiter's Castration of Saturn in Part 4

Saturn, as Venus's father, authors the fateful calamity of Arcite's accident, but simultaneously fulfills the "wills" of Venus and Diana, or, put another way, translates the providential response to human prayers through the effect of earthly situations like the "accident." Venus, seeing that Arcite has bested Palamon in the lists, resorts to tears (2665; in other poems and treatises a mythographic image of plenitude) and then turns to her father, Saturn, for help, in a reminder of their genealogical and mythographic bond. He chides her, "Doghter, hoold thy pees! / Mars hath his wille, his knyght hath al his boone, / And, by myn heed, thow shalt been esed soone" (2668–70). Now that Arcite has won, and therefore Mars has had "his wille," Saturn will instruct his son Pluto, god of the underworld, as we have just seen, to send "a furie infernal" (2685) to startle Arcite's horse into a fatal leap and foundering (2688) that helps to "ease" Venus's shame (2670). Because Pluto, king of the dead, in Bersuire's "De formis figurisque deorum," is armed with the Furies and helped by the Parcae, the Fates (p. 43, trans. p. 108), in effect here he issues the fatal termination of Arcite's life through the "accident"; that is, the planets themselves do not move on their own, by their own willing, but are in fact moved by the Primum Mobile, outside the outermost, eighth, sphere of the fixed stars (the zodiac). But by whose authority does the Primum Mobile move—who authorizes Saturn to send the "furie"?

That higher authority belongs to Jupiter, "maximus deorum," in Holkot's words, an equivocal name for God's Providence, or, to Bersuire, in his role as "Deum, ipsi[u]s celi principem & magistrum" ("God, lord and ruler of heaven itself").[64] Indeed, concord, rather than discord, prevails in this fourth part, in which the enmity between couples and cousins is resolved in terms of both macrocosm and microcosm by analogy with part 2, in which Theseus brought just order to the human and social realms. To this king Theseus, in his famous "First Mover" speech (2987–3074), attributes the finitude and death of all things, *"prince and cause of alle thyng,* / Convertynge al unto his propre welle / From which it is dirryved, sooth to telle?" (3036–38; my emphasis). Accordingly, the point of Theseus's long dissertation is to turn the woe of the assembly to joy ("But after wo I rede us to be merye" [3068]). Further, on the national and earthly level, Theseus inculcates the values represented by Mars and Diana by the end of Part 2, being able to see other points of view, although the order he brings more closely resembles that just, terrible consequence determined by Saturn rather than the true, wisely ordained harmony offered by Jupiter. So also Jupiter, Prime Mover, sums up, influences, and controls all the other planets on the cosmic level. The grace of Jupiter is the last note sounded by (and literally the last word of) the tale (3069).

In terms of the development traced thus far from the *Anelida* to the *Knight's Tale,* Jupiter here represents the equivalent of Pallas Athena in that unfinished poem, his daughter who sprang fully grown from his head. Depicted as wise, mostly through abstract epithets and the long speeches of Theseus, Jupiter occupies the most conventional of his mythographic roles.[65] Even Arcite on his deathbed begs wise Jupiter (rather than the messenger of the gods, Mercury) to guide his soul—"And Juppiter so wys my soule gye" (2786, also 2792)—although it is Mars, according to the Knight, who actually conveys his soul (2815).

Perhaps that correction on the part of the Knight is not a slip of the tongue but a reflection of his own interest in making wars (an activity documented in his *General Prologue* résumé). In his martial vigor like the youthful Arcite, now an old man whose age reflects saturnine influence, upon his homecoming the Knight may very well present his tale as a rationalization of a life-long devotion to war rather than peace to settle disputation: it is reassuring to know that Arcite's "accident" catalyzes the final harmony of Theban and Athenian, male and female. If the Knight identifies with Saturn, pale and cold (2443)—a plausible identification if he agrees that "elde hath greet avantage" and "In elde is bothe wysdom and usage" (2448)—does he then fear "castration" by his own son, the jovial Squire who loves love, like the Ovidian Jupiter, and if so, what does that castration involve? Being proved wrong in his choice of vocation? Being cut short as a tale-teller? Or does he hesitate to name Pallas Athena as wisdom of Jupiter because he identifies with Jupiter's father and not the son himself?

In a very secular and classical way, the Knight is pointing to the divided, fallen, discordant nature of humankind, as the myths of the rape of Proserpina and the castration of Saturn by Jupiter both disclose in the mythographies, and as we saw in chapter 5 in relation to the short poem, "The Former Age." Surely every rationalization issues from some guilt, some doubt, some ambivalence. Doubleness pervades this poem—in the dispute of the cousins, the nations, and finally, the gods themselves. Certainly this division, divisiveness, has resurfaced from the early draft in the *Anelida*, with its twin gods, of the victor and vanquished, male and female oppositions, the double invocation, the appeal to Mars and Bellona as apparently double gods of war. What is missing is the peace associated with the feminine— Pallas Athena.

Or perhaps Chaucer is using the Knight's ambivalence, in his tale of discord made concord, to present the *Knight's Tale*, first of the *Canterbury Tales*, as a philosophical and classicized answer to the question of the human place in the universe that will recast our Knight as a Saturn figure. The last of the *Canterbury Tales*, the *Parson's Tale*, provides a Christian and homiletic answer to the same question, a response still hinging on the human relation to God. In a broader sense, the most unlikely of Jupiter figures, the Parson, may seem to fulfill the Knight's worst fear and does—in a manner of speaking—"cut short" the old Knight. Even more ironically, it is the knife-bestudded Miller whose obscene and scatalogical *fabliau* will "cut short" the wisest pilgrim. Finally, it is the Wife of Bath whose experiential wisdom undercuts the learned Latin mythographic tradition from whose authority the old Knight has spoken his tale.

CHAPTER 7

Maister Alisoun's Feminist Self-Mythography

Chaucer's friar, a "leeve maister," appears in his *Prologue* to praise the Wife of Bath for touching "in scole-matere greet difficultee" (1272), although he simultaneously advises her, as if afraid of some Wycliffite inclinations on her part, that she should speak instead "of game" and "lete auctoritees ... / To prechyng and to scoles of clergy" (1275–77).[1] For him to perceive her as mimicking a "leeve maister" introduces for the reader a different interpretation of the much-debated issue of "maistry," one that involves the school*master*'s method of peering beneath the veil of classical artifice to see truth (in the Macrobian sense). Although Alisoun clearly uses the fruits of patristic exegesis for her own "up-so-doun" purposes, she also demonstrates her "mastery," that is, her understanding of the allegorical glossation of classical mythology found in medieval glosses and commentaries.[2] Because medieval schoolmasters were in fact male, her use of the characters and gods of classical mythology casts her in the incongruous role of what might be termed a protofeminist (rather than an antifeminist) mythographer who inverts and subverts the conventions generally in use within that patriarchal tradition. Like a "leeve maister" addressing his clerks, Alisoun's pagan alter ego, the Fairy Queen in the *Tale*, lectures the recalcitrant Knight on the subject of true "gentilesse." That she does so by invoking Christ's true nobility as a paradigm recasts Alisoun's tale of rape as a veiled sermonizing forbidden to women by the church.

Unlike the schoolmaster, however, Alisoun lectures in a school of marriage: "Diverse *scoles* maken parfyt *clerkes*," she asserts, and acknowledges her perseverance and endeavor in this school: "And diverse practyk in many sondry werkes / Maketh the werkman parfyt sekirly; / Of fyve husbondes *scoleiyng* am I" (44c-f; my emphasis). In this school she teaches from experience, rather than from authority, of woe in marriage and of the nonsense produced by the figurative methods of the (male) glossator in relation to biblical texts like the parables of the wedding at Cana and Christ's meeting with the Samaritan woman. Here she firmly distinguishes what has been described as patriarchal discourse involving glossation or allegorization of a text literally conceived of as "feminine" (to be inscribed, or read) from the kind of literal "glossation" of the carnal text of her "joly body."[3] "Men may devyne and *glosen*, up and doun," Alisoun declares (26; my emphasis), expressing through her words "devyne" and "up and doun" the lack of focused intellectual direction of this masculine activity, but the truth she has learned ("withoute lye" [27]) directly from *divine* authority invites men *and women* ("us") to "wexe and multiplye" (28).

This more balanced reading of a divinely sanctioned text (the Book of Genesis) is gender-complete in its directions, for Alisoun essentializes the highest Christian ideal, despite its Old Testament nature. Using a term ("gentil") that will resonate throughout her tale with Christian implications, she concludes, "'That gentil *text* kan I wel understonde'" (29; my emphasis). She is literate, can read, can understand, needs no additional help from the cleric to know that it means what it also means in the *Pardoner's Tale*:[4] apparently, having had no children, she knows that to "wexe and multiplye" connotes multiplying virtues for the Christian, words for the tale-teller, cloth for the cloth maker. This honest and truthful text implies living usefully in the world in preparation for the next, by marrying, working, obeying God, sharing with others what she has.

Ironically, her clerical husband Jankyn—not to mention those frequent visits to Mass—has taught her well those methods of exegesis she decries, both patristic and mythographic, by reading to her his book called "Valerie and Theofraste" (671), compiled from various medieval sources glossing earlier biblical and classical examples.[5] As preacher, Alisoun may also alter and manipulate her recollection of Jankyn's reading; his recitation functions for Alisoun in exactly the same way that her re-creation of classical myths functions for her audience—as a self-gloss, on himself and his motives in regard to their relationship. Further, her mythological "tale" of her marriages has supposedly been recorded on the pilgrimage by Chaucer the pilgrim and then recited by Chaucer the poet to his courtly audience. This labyrinthine complexity vies with the narrative structure of the *Book of the Duchess*, raising the question of *whose voice* is speaking—Alisoun's? Jankyn's? Chaucer's?—and how reliable she/he is. Is she truly feminist, as contemporary critics have argued, or is she still a tool of the misogynist, a projection of male fantasy?[6] *Is* she responding to the ultimately antifeminist mythographic discourse of the Knight, who substitutes Jupiter for Pallas Athena, as the highest (and therefore feminine) ideal of wisdom? Or is her expression of the authority of carnal experience itself imbued with the patristic identification of woman with the body?[7]

Instead of offering a tale to the pilgrim audience from her extensive knowledge of homilies and misogynistic texts about a wicked wife, Alisoun spurns such patriarchal glossation as a distortion of the truth and tells instead an honest and balanced tale of husbands, *her* husbands: "now wol I telle forth my *tale*" (193), she declares, promising to tell "sooth" (195), or the truth, about three good, old, rich husbands and two bad, young, attractive husbands (196). And the tale she tells in her *Prologue* is her own, as both a young and then an old wife, the tale of her experience as she speaks "after my *fantasye*" (190; my emphasis).[8] Her desire, however, is to tell the truth, without "gloss"—adornment, dressing up, interpretation[9]—as if her use of the male concept of "fantasy" needed to be redressed with an honest female equivalent.

Like the "autohagiographer"[10] Margery Kempe and other medieval female mystics and lay ecclesiastics, Alisoun relays her own truthful tale of her "joly body"; but in addition she inverts the usual mythographic process—of glossing a classical, poetic story by means of medieval didactic prose often allegorical in nature—by using two mythological references in her *Prologue* to gloss her own life and experience, her "tale," as text. And she tells her tale to rectify what she sees as an ecclesiastical learned (gender) imbalance—the perception of wives as wicked, whether rich and therefore proud, or poor and therefore expensive, fair but unchaste, homely but lecherous, manifesting their vices only after marriage (248–301)—a paraphrase of Jankyn's recitation from the "Book of Wicked Wives" (711–85). Whatever Jankyn intended when he read to her on the day of their awful quarrel, in her re-creation of the truth Alisoun's recollected examples of mythological wicked wives reflect pejoratively on him—and her other husbands—*just as* the mythographer's disapproving glosses on wicked women created and reflected a monumental cultural prohibition against the value of the female. Examples of wicked classical wives from Jankyn's homily (725, 733, 737, 743) represent jealousy, lechery, wrath, avarice—all vices that she sees in Jankyn rather than in herself. Thus she learns from him the method as well as the product of medieval mythography, which, in her cleverness, she learns to apply for her own purpose—to show that vicious *husbands* need to be taught by their wives.[11]

The short tale Alisoun appends to the tale of her wicked husbands seems an afterthought, an addition spurred by the scoffing words of the friar—who, as representative of that exegetical and classicizing group, might well reject her literalism and realism. And yet, as we shall see, Alisoun reverses text and gloss so that the "parable"—the short romance she tells—in its fictional narrative and its Ovidian digression concerning Midas, actually glosses (or interprets) the literal "tale" of herself and her husbands in the *Prologue*. What emerges is a skillfully woven fabric of experience *and* authority (despite Alisoun's disclaimers) that knits together the sexes in a natural and convincing garment.

Alisoun's "Joly Body": Venus, Ceres, and Io

Because she desires youth and its pleasures and opportunities—evident in her memories of a younger self—Alisoun continues in her autobiography to identify especially with an astrological and mythographic Venus (lines 464, 604, 611, 618, 697, 700, 704, 705) associated with desire or sexuality as an adjunct to fertility, a necessary part of natural law: she reveals that she has a birthmark—the print of Saint Venus's seal—in a certain place (604); she confesses that she is Venerian in feeling (611). In focusing on her past history and many marriages, at two points she mentions her love of venery—personified by Venus, to which wine is able to lead her. The first instance occurs when she talks of her fourth husband: "yong and ful of ragerye" (455), she liked to dance and sing "Whan I had dronke a draughte of sweete wyn!" (455–59). The second instance uses the present tense: now older, when she drinks, her thoughts still turn not just to song and dance but also to "Venus." "And after wyn on Venus moste I thynke, / For al so siker as cold engendreth hayl, / A likerous mouth moste han a likerous tayl" (464–66). At first glance, Alisoun's reference to wine and Venus serves as an apparently casual modification of what must have seemed a trite adage in the Middle Ages—the ubiquitous proverb, "Venus without Ceres and Bacchus grows cold" ("Sine Cerere et Libero friget Venus"), interpreted in the *Aeneid* glosses as lechery—[12] but strangely enough, Alisoun does not personify wine through Bacchus here. The Wife just says, "and after wyn on Venus moste I thynke" (464), with Bacchus reduced here to mere "wine" and with Ceres mentioned neither as goddess *nor* as bread, although a pale and vestigial sign of her fertile influence may be present in the use of "engendreth" in the meteorological observation that "cold engendreth hayl" (465).

That Chaucer intended to invoke this proverb and to change it deliberately in this context of the "tale of Alisoun" is corroborated by references in two other poems: after Criseyde has gone to the Greeks, Troilus first curses Jove, Apollo, and Cupid, then "He corseth Ceres, Bacus, and Cipride [Venus]" (5.208), and finally his brothers, himself, fate, and nature, as if to affix blame to the gods who control the universe, earthly love, and individual, familial, and racial will. Also, in the *Parlement of Foules*, in the description of the courtly love garden (253–76), the narrator witnesses, in addition to Venus and Priapus, Bacchus and Ceres: "Bachus, god of wyn, sat hire besyde, / And Ceres next, that doth of hunger boote" (275–76).

Here Chaucer, through the Wife, feminizes the meaning of the proverb: in the Wife's confession of "after wyn on Venus moste I thynke," she glosses the meaning of this diluted mythography, which omits Ceres, by noting from her own experience that inebriation dismantles female defenses against lechery: "In wommen vinolent is no defence— / This knowen lecchours by experience" (467–68). Of course, in the mythographies on Martianus's *De nuptiis*, Venus and Bacchus together arouse desire and conceive the god of weddings, Hymen, or "of natural conception" (Remigius,

Mart. 1.3.5, 1:67), who is given the duty of garlanding thresholds abloom with the flowers of spring "because after abundant stimulation, desire becomes aroused" ("quia post nimiam petulantiam solet excitaria libido" [1.3.5, 1:69]).

Similarly, according to Alisoun's *Prologue,* desire (Venus) frequently became aroused in Alisoun's past from such inebriation (Bacchus), and weddings (Hymen) followed, but bread, grain (Ceres) apparently played no part whatsoever in this process. Yet throughout, Alisoun describes her sexuality through images of bread and flour, as, for example, when she recalls that "the flour is goon ... /The bren ... now moste I selle" (477–78). The Wife's omission of Ceres—or a depersonalization of the goddess to a bread image—suggests an anxiety, perhaps subconscious, about her own fertility and what she has (or, more important, has not) done with it during her life, or, better still, an unfulfilled desire, a hunger. In making her argument against virginity, Alisoun constructs a feminine allegory of virginity in which virgins are represented by wheat ("Lat hem be breed of pured wheteseed" [143]) and wives by barley bread ("lat us wyves hoten barly-breed" [144]). Since Alisoun is neither a virgin nor apparently a mother and possibly no longer a wife, it seems an odd analogy to use; odder still is her sense of barley bread as refreshing to men—used here first in the secular sense just observed and then in a spiritual sense: "And yet with barly-breed, Mark telle kan, / Oure Lord Jhesu refresshed many a man" (145–46). She normally thinks of sexuality in terms of food and drink: she refers to sexual intercourse as refreshment, rejuvenation, and she refers to her first three husbands as "old bacon." For example, she introduces Solomon, who used to "refressh" his many wives sexually (38), and she mentions that Christ "refresshed" many a man with barley bread (146). These two references, to the Song of Solomon and then to Christ, couple the Old and New Testaments, as if to suggest that this symbol of physical and spiritual need works in two ways—literally, on the materialistic level, and figuratively, on the Christian, symbolic level. The sustenance she suggests that we all seek derives both from bread or from Ceres and perhaps also from the Eucharist, and both from the "refresshment" of literal wine or Bacchus and from the inebriating wine of Christ glossed by D. W. Robertson, Jr., in the two biblical passages used by the Wife.[13] But that hunger and thirst experienced by Alisoun within marriage—for natural conception, for the generation of children—have not yet been satisfied.

This latter underlying psychological and sacramental need becomes clearer when the mythographic glosses on Venus, Bacchus, and Ceres are considered together. Each of the three mythological figures exemplifies fertility, whether that of nature—grape or grain—or that of human nature. The mythographers' gloss of Venus, Bacchus, and Ceres to exemplify fertility myth reflects ironically on Alisoun as a barren *wife* (given her many marriages and the canonical medieval insistence on marriage for purposes of procreation) who talks about the grades of virginity in terms of bread imagery. In relation to Venus, for example, William of Conches, in a twelfth-century commentary on Macrobius, perceives her as a cosmic fertility force, a *genetrix*: he explains the castration of Saturn by his son Jupiter, from which act Venus was born, first, as the ripening of fruits by the warmth of the upper element, which makes them ready for harvesting, and second, as the casting of the fruits into the sea, that is, the human belly, from which Venus or *luxuria* (sensual delight) is born—or, to paraphrase Bersuire, reproduction occurs only on a full stomach (p. 26, trans. p. 70, on 1.2.10).[14] Similarly, William of Conches explains Bacchus as the "vines," product of human and divine intercourse;[15] the true role of Ceres involves "earth's natural power of growing into crops and multiplying them," just as Bacchus's involves "earth's natural power of growing into vines"; Bernardus Silvestris, glossing the four significations of Venus in his commentary on Martianus Capella, cites the Terentian adage in conjunction with her third signification, as the natural catalyst of regeneration.[16] The Wife of Bath lacks both physical and psychological or spiritual "fertility," although she has frequently enough "refreshed" herself carnally with that bread and wine so necessary for Venus's presence and activities.

That Alisoun was unable to have children and therefore suffers from both a physical and psychological hunger may not have been her fault, not only because of conflicting stellar influences by Mars and Venus in her own temperament[17] but also because of marital ones. In the mythological allegory that follows, old Alisoun reveals that she has been married to two young clerks, neither of whom, apparently (unlike the rich old husbands to whom she was first married), has felt sufficiently urgent the performance of those "Venus werkes" in marriage that might have led to procreation. And they displace any guilt they may feel over this onto her as wife, the conventional clerical target for error and wickedness. She identifies herself primarily as a child of Venus at war with a child of Mercury—her clerical husband, the "ful contrarius" (698) children of Mercury and Venus (697) at odds, with Mercury's love of "wysdam and science" (699) countering Venus's love of "ryot and dispence," her vitality (700, 703, 705). Astrologically, Mercury is desolate in Pisces, where Venus is exalted. But for mythographic reasons she links the clerk and his patron god Mercury with cunning, manipulation of language, and barter—full of words, but not so physically responsive after all. Mercury is *eloquentia* in Martianus but the "divine go-between and thief" in Fulgentius (and the Third Vatican Mythographer, 9.3, Bode, pp. 214–15), his name derived from *mercium-curam* because he is the "complete trader" (*Mit.* 1.18, trans. p. 59). He is also called Hermes (from *ermeneuse,* translating) because a trader needs fluency in languages. Alisoun also associates Venus's child with youth and Mercury's child, the clerk, with old age: the clerk regards "Venus werkes" as "worth his olde sho" (708), but when old and presumably impotent, "Thanne sit he doun, and writ in his *dotage* / That wommen kan nat kepe hir mariage!" (709–10; my emphasis). Mythographically, a marriage of the children of Venus and Mercury takes place in Martianus's *De nuptiis,* the result of which is Hermaphroditus. This monster signifies lascivious speech in which truth is neglected and embellished with unnecessary words.[18] In Martianus's *prosimetrum* it is no accident, then, that Juno, goddess of childbirth and, with Jupiter, co-ruler of the created world, wants Mercury to marry Philology rather than procreate another unnatural Hermaphroditus by marrying Venus. From a misogynistic perspective, surely clerical Jankyn's speeches on wicked wives and the loquacious *Prologue* of Alisoun reveal these same consequences of marrying Venus and Mercury—lascivious speech, a sterile bond, and a sterile marriage.

Once again, however, Alisoun feminizes the mythographic tradition by using, within her own "tale," the myth of Argus and Mercury, also invoked by the Knight in relation to Arcite's dream vision of Mercury, to distinguish her old jealous husbands from her most recent, young, clerical husbands, or jealous young clerical husband four from clever young clerical husband five, or, best of all, all of her husbands from her own clever self. She identifies the former with the hundred-eyed Argus and the latter with Mercury, Jupiter's son, who blinds Argus and thereby helps to rescue poor Io transformed into a cow. The myth in Ovid relates to the jealousy of Jupiter's wicked wife Juno, who asked Argus to guard Io. This approach is reversed by Alisoun, who relates it (in line 358) to her old husbands' jealousy, who might ultimately "preye Argus with his hundred yen / To be my warde-cors, as he kan best" (358–59), however ineffectual in containing her, for "In feith, he shal nat kepe me but me lest; / Yet koude I make his berd, so moot I thee!" (360–61). The identification reflects more pejoratively on the "old bacon," her old husbands, than on Alisoun, for Ovidian commentaries associate Argus with vanity, stupidity, avarice, crafty cunning, concern for the mundane, and worldly wisdom.[19] The Argus myth, as glossed in Fulgentius's fable of Mercury (*Mitologiae* 1.18), can also be used to explain the former husband(s) as Argus-like, artful guardians, overcome because they were idle (or *uacuus*) by the cunning (*astutia*) of the Mercurial clerk, that is, her fifth husband.[20] Clever Mercury blinded Argus, a mythological anticipation of another "blinding" (deluding), of her fourth husband by the clerk Jankyn. The latter dallies with Alisoun while husband four is gone (550ff.); husband four's death permits Alisoun to escape a bad marriage.

Or instead of representing one or the other husband, Argus includes all Alisoun's artful guardians, even Jankyn, "slain" by herself as a Mercurial trader. In this respect, it is interesting that Holkot, in his commentary on the Book of Wisdom, links the morally literate clerk always on guard against concupiscence not with Mercury but with Argus. The identification suggests that Jankyn's sermonizing on wicked wives results in his "blinding" by the eloquent Alisoun, who then plays the role of wily Mercury who blinds Argus when she provides him with exactly the right response to his blow.[21] The identification additionally suggests that she is an Io to her husbands' Argus, a type of *voluptas* imprisoned by their Junoesque jealousy, in Holkot's little allegorization. Further, Io's metamorphosis into a heifer equates with the metamorphosis of the Fairy Queen in Alisoun's tale, not into a heifer but into a beautiful and faithful spouse—a reclamation of the *voluptas* of the self, into the desiring self—and again suggests Alisoun's deep-seated desire to be transformed, young once again, and able to have children.

The mythological examples Alisoun uses to describe her own self and her husbands—Venus and Mars, Venus without Bacchus and Ceres, the children of Venus in opposition to the children of Mercury, but figuratively producing a monstrous child, Hermaphroditus, when they do couple—project a powerful image of the Wife's physical and psychological hunger, thirst, emptiness, need. Chaucer continues to chart the exact dimensions of this desire in the mythological examples used in the *Prologue* through Alisoun's clever and subversive "reading" of Jankyn's "Book of Wicked Wives."

The Book of Wicked Husbands

Late in her "tale" of her self, Alisoun concludes her story of five marriages with the climactic event of her altercation with Jankyn. This conflict between the Mercurial clerk and the child of Venus hinges on how "wicked wives" should be read; truly it epitomizes the product of the union between Mercury and Venus as a monster, Hermaphroditus—eloquence manipulated by clerical cunning, whether his, initially, or hers, by mimicry.

Jankyn recites from his "Book of Wicked Wives" in lines 725 to 743 not only to taunt Alisoun but perhaps also to convince her to function as a better wife; they are examples *Alisoun* recounts, however, for her own purposes. These classical women, if they did not murder or cause the downfall of their husbands, at least embarrassed them considerably and, according to Jankyn, resemble Alisoun. In mythographic terms, like Deianira, Pasiphaë, Clytemnestra, and Eriphyle, Alisoun manifests the lechery, wrath, and avarice of the adulterous, homicidal, and greedy wife bent on betraying her husband. But if these wicked wives are read more figuratively and less literally, the wives also explain something about the psychology of her husbands, especially the fifth—usually negative husbandly aspects of Jankyn's own personality and his motivations.

Alisoun's recounting of Jankyn's first example—that of Deianira whose gift of a poisoned cloak to her husband, Hercules, unintentionally resulted in his death—emphasizes the culpability of Deianira. She "caused hym to sette hymself afyre" (726), to escape from the poison disintegrating his flesh. Implicit within this sketchy reference is the reason for her culpability: jealous of her husband Hercules' apparent passion for the captive Iole, Deianira inadvertently kills him by sending him a robe she thinks has been marked by a love potion. Instead, it has been dipped by the lecherous centaur Nessus (who has unsuccessfully tried to rape her and has been killed by Hercules for his efforts) in his own death blood from Hercules' poisoned arrows and therefore burns the hero alive.[22] Such jealous love *is* death—Hercules dies, symbolically demonstrating that Deianira loves him in the wrong way, at least according to the ecclesiastical interpretation.

The blame for Hercules' death, which Jankyn may have wished to lay on Deianira as a foil for jealous and possessive Alisoun, is interpreted differently elsewhere in the *Canterbury Tales.* The Monk attributes Hercules' death to Fortune: "who may truste on Fortune any throwe?" (2136). And whereas the Monk does reveal that "thise clerkes" (2121) have mentioned that Hercules' "lemman" Deianira was responsible for sending the "noble champioun" a "sherte" that "Envenymed was so subtilly withalle / That er that he had wered it half a day / It made his flessh al from his bones falle" (2124–26), he also exonerates Deianira, as do "somme clerkes" (2127), by identifying Nessus as its maker (2128).

Of all these details included in standard mythological treatises and which Jankyn may or may not have read to her that particular day, Alisoun selects only the causal relationship between Deianira and the fire, as if to illustrate the ambiguity in affixing responsibility for Hercules' fate: was it Deanira's fault, or was it Hercules', whose love for her led him to his own demise, "That caused hym to sette hymself afyre" (726)? The jealousy of Deianira (725), even if omitted in Alisoun's recounting, parallels that of Alisoun's old husbands, not of Alisoun. And in Alisoun's edited reference, the cause of Hercules' death is actually *Hercules'* love for Deianira, which made him too trusting; in the book altercation that follows his reading to her, after she tears three pages out of the book and hits him, he strikes her so hard she is deafened and believes she is dying—and asks him for a last kiss (800–802). Hercules is like Alisoun in her own faithful love for Jankyn, which nearly resulted in her death.

Jankyn's second mythological exemplar, Pasiphaë, "that was the queene of Crete" (733), is equally useful to him as a gloss, this time on difficult, deceptive Alisoun: "For *shrewednesse,* hym thoughte the tale swete" (734;

my emphasis). In the classical myth, Pasiphaë gave birth to the Minotaur after her adulterous relationship with Neptune in the form of the bull; as in the *Knight's Tale*, her passion mythographically reinforces the misogynistic attribution of *voluptas* to women. It is curious, then, that Jankyn, suspicious of Alisoun's having chosen paramours within marriage, did not refer to Pasiphaë's lechery and deceit as an echo of Alisoun's.

Alisoun seems to be familiar with this clerical reading of Pasiphaë, for she uses *occupatio* when she cries in disgust, "Fy! Spek namoore—it is a grisly thyng— / Of hire horrible lust and hir likyng" (735–36). The cry, however, seems so sincere that it truly helps to dissociate Alisoun from any accusation against her of being lecherous. And Jankyn's charge of "shrewednesse," in terms of Alisoun's later self-mythography, as we shall see, might more appropriately characterize the eloquent, tricky, or cunning clerk, guided by Mercury. Indeed, Alisoun declares of her fourth husband, who died so abruptly, "'And yet was he to me the mooste *shrewe*'" (505; my emphasis), meaning "scoundrel" but also conveying the idea of the "scold" and the cunning associated with wicked deeds. Finally, in the *Knight's Tale* discussion of the Minotaur produced by Pasiphaë's union, the Minotaur emblematizes the sins of the fathers being visited on the sons, namely the Theban cousins Palamon and Arcite. For Chaucer to use such a reference here, in a tale so emphatically anticlerical and so directly responsive to the Knight, invites us to compare the usages: the alleged "shrewednesse" of the bookish clerks to whom Alisoun has been married has resulted in no offspring at all, not even a monster like the Minotaur. It is a recurrent theme in many of the glosses inherent in the mythological references. And Jankyn's "shrewednesse" to Alisoun—his arrogant reading to her from this "Book of Wicked Wives"—results in violence that causes deafness in her and near death.

Jankyn appears particularly pleased with his third example, "'Of Clitermystra, for hire lecherye, / That falsly made hire housbonde for to dye'" (737–38), at least in Alisoun's recapitulation: "He redde it with ful good devocioun" (739). In one mythological figure, Jankyn can address both the lechery of women, especially Alisoun, and perhaps her own homicide of husband four.[23] Clytemnestra kills her husband Agamemnon when he returns from the Trojan War. Her wrath over his departure and his sacrifice of their daughter Iphigenia to gain for the Greeks good sailing winds motivate her adultery with Aegisthus.

Again, however, the "devocioun" with which Jankyn reads so subjectively and with such relish hints, in Alisoun's retelling, of significant omissions, or at least of her own disregard for Jankyn's slanted clerical reading. For one thing, it is Jankyn who nearly kills her with his deafening blow. But in another tradition, Agamemnon's sacrifice of their daughter is weighted more seriously than in this antifeminist reading. According to the glosses on 4m7 of Boethius's *Consolatio* beginning in the twelfth century and continuing to the fourteenth, Agamemnon was an antihero who killed his daughter in pursuit of vainglory.[24] Deliberate sacrificing of one's progeny, even for heroic and national reasons, would have violated most natural, social, and moral values of a medieval audience. Its indirect invocation here reminds us that Alisoun's marriages to old or clerical husbands had been barren and empty, a "sacrificing" of progeny for reasons of economic and social survival by the younger spouses.

Jankyn may have chosen his last mythological exemplar, Eriphyle, as a gloss on Alisoun's avarice and marital treachery, but, like the other examples, it refracts back on him and her other husbands in her retelling. Eriphyle was married to Amphiaraus, a Theban diviner who foretold his own demise in a forthcoming war and therefore tried to hide from the conscriptors who came to his house to gather warriors. Out of avarice for a gold necklace, she betrayed her husband to the authorities so that he had to fight — and die — in the Theban War. For Jankyn, the avarice of Eriphyle, "that for an ouche of gold / Hath prively unto the Grekes told / Wher that hir housbonde hidde hym in a place" (743–45), reflects back on young Alisoun in her marriages to the "old bacon" for their treasure. The ultimate in treachery of Eriphyle results in a death, "sory grace" (746), for "Amphiorax at Thebes loste his lyf" (741), that can be likened to the death of husband four, *if* it occurred as a result of the treachery of either Alisoun or Jankyn.

As with the other references, Alisoun reveals as much about her husbands as herself. The hiding and deceit of the farsighted Amphiaraus ("Wher that hir housbonde hidde hym in a place" [745]) might also hint at Jankyn's secret meetings and plottings with the still-married Alisoun (550ff.). And after Jankyn — believing she is dying, or wanting him to think she is — strikes her, in the altercation over the book, the Wife accuses him of of these same sins, of treachery and theft, of having killed her for her possessions. Finally, Eriphyle's revelation to the authorities about her husband's whereabouts (even if motivated by greed) echoes Alisoun's present confession about the sins and other secrets of all her husbands: she's garrulous, but she's also honest and open about her own desires.

Why, in his "homily" to Alisoun, does Jankyn select classical examples of wicked wives who kill, betray, or cuckold their husbands, and why does he feel it necessary to homilize on this issue to his wife? Whatever his role, Jankyn may have believed that she primarily engineered her last spouse's death and therefore his catalog warns her of public incrimination if she does not obey him like a proper wife. Or, if both of them conspired to murder him, it plays the antifeminist trick of laying major blame on her.

There exist disturbing if unlikely hints of such a murder, whether by her acting alone, by him acting alone, or by conspiracy.[25] In her recapitulation of the stages in her relationship with Jankyn, Alisoun tells us that she met with Jankyn and her gossip Alys, with whom he lodged, while her husband was away in London one Lent (543–53); that when the couple walked alone in the fields, dallying together, she promised him marriage, should she be widowed (564–68); that she enticed Jankyn into a relationship by telling him her (manufactured) dreams about his killing her in her bed (but that the blood signified gold [577–84]); that husband four died when she returned from a pilgrimage to Jerusalem (495); that when Jankyn followed the bier she noticed his well-shaped legs (596–99). Even if husband four died of natural causes, the misogynistic catalog might also have served as a means of distancing himself from her and avoiding intimacy, physical or psychological. Certainly the homily initially affects her and their material goods negatively: the blows they exchange damage his (no doubt expensive) book and cause her (as his "property") irreparable damage, although the end result, from her point of view, is positive—the transfer of sovereignty in the marriage to her, deciding the issue of "maistry" once and for all.

And why does Alisoun now retell this shocking incident to this audience of Canterbury pilgrims? Perhaps she expects, through her selection of details, that the audience will recognize the clear misogyny of her clerical spouse and thus exonerate her from any blame of lechery, avarice, treachery, homicide. Or, as mythographer she may be using the wicked wives in her reconstruction of the incident to reveal his true motives: *he* was avaricious, lecherous, even homicidal, wanted money and, in striking her, determined to obtain it. If he had murdered once for money—as may have been the case with her fourth husband—he might well have done it again. And so he acted out her made-up "dream," of finding blood in her bed, once in fantasy, once in threatened reality. If he is still alive and still her husband, such a threat of a public "hue and cry" effectively functions as a deterrent to future violence and treachery and also labels him in advance as potential suspect should any foul play occur.

But perhaps more appropriate still is the incident's existence as a "homily" in this preacher's repertoire of sermons. Her authority springs from the "wo that is in mariage" (3) and, like a friar who preaches, she educates the public in what she knows best. The tale of her "joly body" is itself a lesson and continues in the actual tale, of a wise woman who educates an ignorant pupil. The violence by the clerical exegete will be transformed into the rape by the inarticulate knight in the *Tale*, a Jankyn-like husband who must "study" under the tutelage of a new Alisoun-like schoolmaster. This wise and eloquent Fairy Queen constructed from a non-Latinate, non-learned, nonmythographic tradition better understands true "gentilesse" than the well-educated cleric who was Alisoun's husband. In this dream fantasy, another tale of her self, Alisoun also depends upon a mythological fable—of Midas and his wife—that, in topsy-turvy fashion, continues to "gloss" the story of wicked husbands presented in her *Prologue.*

Midas's Wife and Minerva's Flute

The Wife's celticized tale of a figure who, in a patriarchal and learned context, might be regarded as a "Loathly Lady" (or a Wicked Wife) in fact celebrates the wisdom of a beautiful and good Fairy Queen. Embedded within it is a mythographic mirror digression about an invented truth teller who, in a patriarchal context, might also be interpreted as a wicked wife—the wife of Midas (951–82). In these cases, Alisoun functions, respectively, as storyteller and as mythographer, in particular in her reference to Midas's wife, to continue her "autohagiography." When Alisoun wishes to reverse Jankyn's role as clerk and mythographer by telling a tale of a wicked husband—the errant knight—it is logical and appropriate that her digression on Midas's wife also, probably intentionally, reveals as much about her as it does about her spouse.[26] In her tale, she adds to her Ovidian source the figure of Midas's wife to justify her truth telling (possibly Jankyn's murder of her fourth husband, although more likely the flaws of her various husbands and the candid truths about herself) and therefore to justify also her clerical and mythographic tour de force on the pilgrimage, her demonstration of her "maistry." But an examination of glosses on details of the Midas myth perhaps deliberately omitted from her presentation continues to expose the poor judgment and avarice of her former husbands, while returning to the Canterbury dialogue the missing goddess Minerva, exemplar of wisdom.

From the beginning, Alisoun inverts the patristic method of homilizing and mythographizing. The wife of Midas digression is inserted into Alisoun's gendered "homily" on what women love most (925–49) as a negative example, to counter the claim that " 'somme seyn that greet delit han we / For to been holden stable, and eek secree, / And in o purpos stedefastly to dwelle, / And nat biwreye thyng that men us telle' " (945–48). But this "homily" that cannot essentialize female experience appears within a tale (rather than a tale appearing as illustration within a homily); the homily is on what women want most (rather than on what men want most); the homily is not predominant and focused but varied, diverse, tangential, and mainly, as we can tell from the wife of Midas digression, untrue. The mythological reference is not used as exemplification but as antithesis. The source is apparently conventional—Ovid's *Metamorphoses*—a classical authority in itself, especially for poets, until it becomes clear that Midas's wife is made up by Alisoun. Whatever "somme" may say about women and what they want, the only real authority here is a woman—Midas's wife, who does not exist, or the Fairy Queen, who belongs to vernacular legend, or to Alisoun, a woman given a voice by an English poet. How appropriate that the truth has to be made up—there is no given feminine authority able to reveal it, and the ones that exist, whether patristic or mythographic, have been written down by clerics and are therefore suspect.

Midas's wife is Alisoun's main character here, not her disfigured husband with his two long ass's ears. Midas functions, like the examples in Jankyn's "Book of Wicked Wives," as a brief example of the masculine need to conceal embarrassing truths about himself: "He preyede hire that to no creature / She sholde tellen of his *disfigure*" (959–60; my emphasis). His tale (we assume the tale of how he acquired his ears) may interest Ovid and the mythographers, but it does not especially interest Alisoun. She assumes perhaps that her audience is familiar both with the tale of acquisition and failure as well as with its mythographic explanation so that she can proceed with her subject, his wife. Her silence would not necessarily convey approval, for in the mythographies Midas is castigated for his poor judgment and his avarice; indeed, greater attention to the details of the myth might have allowed her yet another opportunity to suggest Midas as a type of her husbands, who have failed her in so many ways. And yet, by focusing on this invented wife, she draws attention to *herself* as wife and truth teller, which by association leads to an implicit comparison of disfigured Midas and those husbands.

Midas's wife is substituted for Midas's slave barber, or *famulus*, in Ovid's fable (*Metamorphoses* 11.172–93).[27] The wife, however, essentially performs the same role as the barber: to reveal Midas's transformation only to a hole in the marsh covered by reeds. In her fantasy re-creation of the myth, she first adds Midas begging his wife not to reveal his disfigurement (959–60). The very act of his request implies equality of position, or even the subordination of the husband, if power over him lies with the perfectly whole and nondisfigured wife. Next, Alisoun gives Midas's imaginary wife a voice, whose first utterance is a denial, followed by a promise of obedience out of a desire to protect her own reputation:

She swoor him, "Nay"; for al this world to wynne,
She nolde do that vileynye or synne,
To make hir housbonde han so foul a name.
She nolde nat telle it for hir owene shame. (961–64)

Midas's wife actually keeps her promise, for she has not indeed sworn to conceal the news of his failure and disfigurement but instead not to tell it in any way that would bring shame to her. Thus she runs to the most private spot she knows, the marsh, and puts her mouth down to the water to beg:

"Biwreye me nat, thou water, with thy soun,"
Quod she; "to thee I telle it and namo;
Myn housbonde hath longe asses erys two!
Now is myn herte al hool, now is it oute.
I myghte no lenger kepe it, out of doute." (974–78)

Only from a masculine and clerical point of view might a reader identify Midas's wife as resembling other wicked wives of Alisoun's *Prologue* and *Tale* who, like Alisoun, disobey and betray their husbands. This antifeminist response would be to characterize the female as unstable, wavering, unable to keep counsel, a garrulous tattler and gossip. Instead, Alisoun glosses the need of Midas's wife to reveal the truth: she essentializes as female openness and lack of deception. "Heere may ye se, thogh we a tyme abyde, / Yet out it moot; we kan no conseil hyde" (979–80), she cheerfully asseverates, thus essentializing deceitfulness as male.

Alisoun also justifies herself: her *Prologue*, after all, the longest in the *Canterbury Tales*, seems to expose too much about her and her flaws—and about her husbands'; for if Midas's wife resembles Alisoun, then Midas's secret hints at the secrets of Alisoun's husbands old and young, their physically unappealing nature as "old bacon," their jealousy, adulteries, and even violence and possibly (in Jankyn's case) murder (or, if we accept the implications of the mythological references, his asininity). In addition, by means of this digression she exonerates wives, including herself, of hidden crimes: because of their inability to keep secrets, they would eventually reveal to the world any perfidy they themselves had committed, including homicide. We might infer that, if wives were male, this need to reveal, to explain, to teach ("conseil"), would compel them to become morally astute clerks.

If men did not need to hide embarrassing secrets about themselves (what Virginia Woolf termed "that dark place at the back of the head" so difficult to see), they would not blame women for their garrulity. The truth about men implied by this amazing "digression" is that they do not tell the truth, whatever the clerical misogynists have claimed, either because they fear the truth or because they are ignorant of it. The mythographic glosses on Midas so carefully omitted by Alisoun from her digression establish stupidity, or asininity, as the basis for Midas's poor judgment in the music contest that resulted in Apollo's punishment, of ass's ears. In myth 116 of the Second Vatican Mythographer (like myth 90 of the First Vatican Mythographer), Midas, King of Lydia, judges the music competition between Apollo and Pan and awards the prize to Pan, only to have the irate Apollo exchange Midas's ears for those of the ass. In relation to the contest and the two choices offered to judge Midas, John of Garland says that

> Music is meant by the contest of the pipe and the lyre; the pipe, which is more joyous, soothes the ears, but the lyre is sweeter if the proper scheme (proportio), is known — or else I would say that *you* had the ass's ears. And so whoever attends the senses and does not show rational judgment, is an ass ["Sic quisquis, sensus et non rationis acumen, / Iudicat, attendit, est asininus homo"]. (P. 69 [11], trans. pp. 149–50)

More important still for Alisoun's tale, Holkot specifically glosses this Midas myth as an exemplum of the prelate's asinine stupidity, transformed from his initial wisdom through evil habits.[28] Midas, in short, becomes a type of the clerk to whom Alisoun was married (and not necessarily a foil for Alisoun, because of her errant judgment and her wandering by the way, her supposed "deafness" to Truth, or the Word of God).[29] In other myths of Midas, his stupidity grows out of his avarice, which might well characterize the chief flaw of Alisoun's husbands, whether old and rich or young and clerical.[30] Yet John of Garland perceives Midas's avarice in this story as a kind of barrenness, or need: "Midas who grasps after gold signifies the greedy man who, although rich, wretchedly lacks fertility" (p. 149). The golden touch of Midas, in the hands of the Second and Third Vatican Mythographers, applies especially to the avarice, and also, perhaps, impotence, of Alisoun's old rich husbands.

Midas's wife's tale-telling, her truthfulness, thus mirrors Alisoun's own truthfulness and her ability to weave this tale of her "joly body." In the mythographies, the Midas myth is generally associated with a context involving artistry and wisdom that supports this construction of Alisoun as poet and alter ego for the wise Fairy Queen. For example, in place of the Ovidian barber transformed into Midas's wife by Alisoun, the Second Vatican Mythographer adds two characters, the Fulgentian servant who has helped Midas's barber successfully "bury the secret" in the ground and another who performs the Midas's wife role, a shepherd who sings out the secret when he plucks a reed growing in that spot. Not only do all the Midas myths bear some connection with music contests, but indeed the instruments (pipe and lute) involved in the competition were invented by Minerva, goddess of wisdom. The earliest part of the Midas mythological sequence, according to the Vatican Mythographers, involves Minerva's invention of the double flute from a bone. This preface to the fable of the musical competition between Apollo and Marsyas also relates to the musical competition between Apollo and Pan judged by Midas.[31] In the first part, when the gods ridicule flute-playing Minerva because of her blown-out cheeks, she goes to Lake Tritonia, where, seeing from her reflected image in the water that she does indeed appear ridiculous, she discards her flute. Marsyas then finds it, challenges Apollo, and, in the Second Vatican Mythographer's version, is flayed for his temerity in challenging the god. The actual music contest between Apollo and Pan judged by Midas, as we have seen, turns out badly for him because he prefers Pan's music to Apollo's.

Just as Minerva dislikes her distended face, Midas dislikes his *disfigure-ment*—and both of these ugly truths ("the dark at the back of the head") can be understood as changes, metamorphoses. Such metamorphosis is key to the mythographies on Midas, in relation to the golden touch of Midas's hands and his donkey ears. Such metamorphosis is also part of the me-dieval storyteller's craft, of *poesis* as a process of changing the story to fit one's purposes. It fits the personal needs of Alisoun as wife and her narra-tive needs as storyteller—and also her conception of her husbands. From one, slightly misogynistic perspective (because it privileges beauty and youth as necessary for sexual attractiveness to men), the metamorphosis of the old woman into the young, fair bride at the end of the tale epitomizes the Wife of Bath's psychological desire for restored youth, that she will somehow be physically rejuvenated or changed (perhaps, as if by homeo-pathic magic, as a result of the "refresshment" by her young husbands). But from a more feminizing perspective, one that acknowledges the attrac-tiveness of young men for older women, the theme of transformation in-herent in both of Midas's changes relates as well to Alisoun's desire for young husbands—as if any aged husbands who might wish to wed her, like her first three, might be exchanged for young ones, like her last two. Al-isoun prays to Christ in lines 1258ff. to send her and other women "Hous-bondes meeke, yonge, and fressh abedde" (1259), and the metamorphosis of the rude and dominating knight in her tale into the meek, "gentil," and obedient husband of the Fairy Queen. Ultimately, the change she most desires—all women desire—is social and cultural revolution so that women can be allowed a voice in their own stories, can be respected for their wis-dom. After all, Alisoun changed Midas's wife from the *famulus* or slave in Ovid, someone supposed to obey a master, to a wife—another kind of metamorphosis.

The "disobedience" of Midas's wife and Alisoun serves to remind the reader of the debate over "maistry," which has been important not only in the Wife's own life but in the tale she tells, of a knight errant who learns to respect a queen's—and wife's—wishes. Husbands should want to please their wives, Alisoun tells us at the end of her tale. A clever and adept tale-teller and mythographer, she bends many of her myths and tales (even the nonmythographic ones) to the same end. But she also remains an honest and truthful glossator. Her homily and her tale establish female authority and hegemony as legitimate, sanctioned by law. Alisoun's emphasis on Midas's wife fits in with the tale's emphasis on Guenevere rather than Arthur, the

Fairy Queen rather than a King, the Fairy Queen as Wife rather than the Knight as Husband, and, bound by the *Prologue's* context concerning the issue of "maistry," with Alisoun's self-identification as a child of Venus rather than of Mercury.

Throughout both *Prologue* and *Tale*, Alisoun may, in the Augustinian sense, read her texts literally and therefore carnally, but she also insists rather brilliantly that fable and parable gloss, or interpret, the truth of her own "tale," her autobiography. By using the mythographic tradition to understand or at least dramatize the complexities of her self, the Wife is most conventional, most clerical, most the schoolmaster—as the friar acknowledges in his interchange with her. Perhaps the issue of "maistry" deserves another look—perhaps what Alisoun most wants, if she cannot have children, is not dominance over her husbands but respect for her "maistry"—her wisdom and memory, if not her literacy and judgment, and the literal honesty of her own *tale*.

CHAPTER 8

The Merchant's *De Nuptiis Maii et Januarii*

The dark tone of the Merchant in his *Prologue* has convinced many critics that his tale reveals an equally cynical view of marriage and courtly love.[1] Certainly the tale's mythographic emphasis on the underworld—its domination by Pluto, god of riches, and by Mercury, cunning god of traders and merchants—appropriately mirrors the character of the speaker, the Merchant; Mercury is associated with merchants because of the necessity of using speech to bargain in commerce, according to the tenth-century commentary on Martianus by Remigius of Auxerre.[2] But, unlike his characters Januarie and Pluto, the Merchant is not in fact rich ("Ther wiste no wight that he was in dette" [A, 280]) and he has been, finally, unhappily married these past two months (1234), although he veils his own sorrow: "of myn owene soore, / For soory herte, I telle may namoore" (1243–44).

Judging from Chaucer's mercantile pilgrim, what works best in the underworld of this world is not the human ideal of wisdom and eloquence as the goal of individual perfection and as symbol for ideal conjugal unions, but instead the practical ingenuity of May's response to Januarie's accusation of adultery. May's eloquence satisfies Januarie's desire, his need for her, and is magically blessed by its proponents, the rulers Pluto and Proserpina. According to the Merchant's view of marriage, this union of eloquence and desire is especially important for social and economic survival and the preservation of the species. As fantasy, the union is most attractively packaged in the fabulous lies of the poets, and in particular those of Martianus Capella.

In line 1732 of the *Merchant's Tale*, Chaucer breaks into the Merchant's narrative with an apostrophe to "poete Marcian" to "Hoold thou thy pees" (1733) in describing the marriage of Januarie and May, for "Whan tendre youthe hath wedded stoupyng age, / Ther is swich myrthe that it may nat be writen" (1738–39). Addressing Martianus Capella because of his fame in writing of "that ilke weddyng murie" (1733) of "hire Philologie" and "hym Mercurie" (1734), and also "the songes that the Muses songe" (1735), Chaucer admits that the Roman North African's pen and tongue are "To smal" (1736) to "descryven" this marriage. Most difficult is the description of the "myrthe"—happiness, and also hilarity, absurdity—associated with the joining of the "tendre" with the "stoupyng": "Assayeth it youreself; thanne may ye witen / If that I lye or noon in this matiere" (1740–41); that is, if marriage is naturally intended for procreation, then the marriage of the aged and the young might well seem absurd and the rhetorical skills necessary to describe such a marriage as happy might also seem inadequate even in a "lying poet" like Martianus. Martianus's *De nuptiis Philologiae et Mercurii* allegorically presents the marriage of Wisdom and Eloquence (which follows a protracted search for the best bride), explained (after the two-book frame in which the marriage is described) by elaborate book-length expositions on their handmaidens, the seven liberal arts of the trivium and quadrivium. Although the metaphor of marriage in the allegorical epic signifies the bond of the two qualities that should inhere in good writing, namely, eloquence and wisdom, it also suggests the ideal marriage of the body and soul.[3]

So also marriage dominates the *Merchant's Tale*, itself part of the so-called Marriage Group: here too there exists a protracted search for the best bride for the groom Januarie, complete with a "debate" between his brothers Placebo and Justinus, followed by the spectacular wedding night—and, breaking with its source, its less than spectacular consequences, the night-long "lovemaking" attempted by turkey-necked Januarie. Further, within the first paragraph or two of *De nuptiis* appear most of the major mythological references and characters in the *Merchant's Tale*—Hymen, the Muses, Venus, Bacchus, Pluto, and Janus—figures accordingly glossed in the Remigius commentary early in his significant and influential first book, which, in addition, glosses other figures important to the *Merchant's Tale*: Proserpina, Amphion, Orpheus, and Priapus.[4]

Chaucer knew Martianus's *prosimetrum* about the marriage of Philology and Mercury through the tenth-century commentary of Remigius of Auxerre or the twelfth-century commentaries of Bernardus Silvestris and Alexander Neckam, which remained current until Chaucer's time. *De nuptiis* offered Chaucer a veritable cornucopia of material concerning the gods as planets: for the ascent in Chaucer's *Hous of Fame*, as well as that of Dante in the *Paradiso*, Philology's ascent through the spheres and her subsequent apotheosis provided an influential paradigm, as it did also for the ascents in Alan of Lille's *Anticlaudianus* and Bernardus Silvestris's *Cosmographia*. Chaucer's Apollo in the *Manciple's Tale* was colored by Martianus's emphasis on his major character, Apollo, as the god of divination. More specifically, the puzzling hyperbole of Venus's tears in the "Envoy a Scogan," as seen in chapter 3, is explained by glosses on Venus and Adonis in the commentaries on Martianus. Like the petitions of Emelye, Arcite, and Palamon to Diana, Mars, and Venus, followed by the debate among the gods, and settled by Saturn and Jupiter in the *Knight's Tale*, bride Philology's petition to the gods for divinity in the first book of Martianus provides a mythological antecedent for the situation in which the gods consider and grant or deny a mortal's petition after a debate. For example, Januarie's silent "petition" at the end of the *Merchant's Tale*, to justify his wife's apparently adulterous behavior and therefore keep her instead of drowning her, is overheard by the nearby Pluto and Proserpina and granted, one might argue, by Pluto.

But Chaucer transforms Martianus's allegorical (read: unrealistic) fable of Mercury and Philology into a more practical vision of marriage by the Merchant, who deceives even himself. The reference to Philology and Mercury (1734) appropriately marks the literal scene as one of celebration, replete with wine, music, festivity, to invite comparison of Chaucer's vernacular skills with Martianus's Latin rhetoric, and, most important, to signal what should be the tropological significance of Januarie's marriage to May, or the ideal relationship between the body and soul in the microcosm man. Chaucer's fable, however, does not celebrate the marriage of Wisdom (Philology) and Eloquence (Mercury), but instead that illegitimate coupling of Desire (Venus) and Eloquence (Mercury) that results in the bastard of Fantasy, Lascivious Speech (Hermaphroditus)—the lies of the poets. Chaucer proclaims this union as magically blessed by Pluto and Proserpina—meaning, ironically, that this marriage *can* work "happily" in the *real* world, if not in the afterlife. Given the importance of Januarie's "fantasye" and the genre of allegory in reading this tale,[5] I would argue that the Mercurial Merchant projects his fantasy of marriage in this world onto the characters of Januarie and May, who provide a mythographic solution to Chaucer's Marriage Question: when Januarie (Venus's knight) marries May (who, as Mercury's child, communicates eloquently), the marriage results in the monster Hermaphroditus (Hermes plus Aphrodite), as witnessed in the adulterous fusion of Damyan and May in the pear tree. Januarie's "ideal" perverts and subverts the natural order through all the deceptions practiced, not only by the pagans but by the central characters Januarie and May and by the Merchant. Through this fable of what might have been for the Merchant, an alter ego for Chaucer, in response to the Wife's feminist mythography, marriage works in fact when a husband, Argus-like, does not see so clearly as the Merchant and is lulled by a (bought) wife more eloquent in fulfilling her husband's desire than the Merchant's wife, "a shrewe at al" (1222).

In this tale, Chaucer uses three consecutive groups of mythological references, figures, or characters, to undercut ironically the character of Januarie and his actual marriage to May. Each group is associated with marriage, read on a different allegorical level in each case, and most of the references relate to Martianus's allegorical epic.

The mythological references in the first group characterize "wedding" in the tropological sense as a marriage of body and soul, eloquence and wisdom, in denigration of the marriage of Januarie and May (whose personified names invite figurative readings): "If thou lovest thyself," advises Januarie, "thou lovest thy wyf; / No man hateth his flessh, but in his lyf / He fostreth it" (1385–87). Here, the references appear in the description of Januarie's wedding night to invoke the more figurative marriage celebration in *De nuptiis* through the figures Philology and Mercury in line 1734.

The second group helps to define the ironic limitations of Januarie's actual marriage in its inversion of the traditional three goods of marriage, *fides, proles, sacramentum* (faith, offspring, and the sacrament of marriage), as identified by Hugh of St. Cher in the thirteenth century.[6] These inversions are reflected in his motive for marrying: first, in buying a young wife as he would any other piece of property, he views her primarily as a carnal good and thus ensures that she will wander (a subversion of *fides*). A second inversion is manifested by his choice of a partner: he disregards nature and his advanced age in desiring an heir (a subversion of *proles*). A third inversion exists in his reaction to May on his wedding night and his purpose in limiting the world of the marriage to a garden in which he daily dallies with May: because he regards marriage as paradise on earth and thereby repeats the Fall of our first parents, he subverts *sacramentum*, or the sacramental relationship between Christ and the church mirrored in marriage, even though Januarie warns, "Love wel thy wyf, as Crist loved his chirche" (1384).[7]

Chaucer deploys mythological references from Martianus's *De nuptiis* to extend the range of ironic inversion of these goods of marriage on the allegorical level. On this level, the unnatural wedding of Januarie and May displays the uxorious relationship of Adam and Eve, the tableau of May's adultery with the serpentlike Damyan ("O servant traytour ... / Lyk to the naddre in bosom sly untrewe" [1785–86]), and the triumph of the Devil over Adam in Januarie's acceptance of May's Eve-like justification of her actions, in a reenactment of the Fall.[8] In this group, mythological references overlap those in other groups (Venus, in the first group, Pluto and Proserpina, in the third group) to suggest the interrelatedness of all the figurative senses, and the nature of wedding.

Finally, in the third group, when the spouse is viewed as a treasure, or paradise, to be enjoyed in this world (like Proserpina, "riches")—the anagogical level—the result is abduction to the underworld (Pluto, spiritual death): Januarie declares his fervent belief that a "wyf is mannes helpe and his confort, / His *paradys terrestre*" (1331–32; my emphasis). In this group, mythological references to figures from Martianus, Boethius, and Ovid commentaries, primarily the underworld rulers Pluto and Proserpina, gloss the ugly adulterous consequences of the marriage of Januarie and May as well as its ultimate practical success in this world—through Januarie's deliberate self-blinding to reality and May's continuing skill in articulating what her husband wants to hear.

The Wedding

The references in the first group, consisting of various classical deities and personifications, duplicate those involved in the wedding of Mercury and Philology while darkly foreshadowing the later bawdy adultery in Januarie's enclosed garden. Illustrating the material splendor of Januarie's wedding reception, including its music (poets Orpheus and Amphion of Thebes), food and drink (the gods Bacchus and Venus [1722–23]), and dancing (Hymen, god of weddings, and son of Venus and Bacchus [1730]), the references invite comparison with the literary model of weddings, that of the personification of wisdom, Philology, and the god of eloquence, Mercury (1734), in whose description the Muses had a hand (1735). But in each case the figures, which all appear significantly in Martianus commentaries, darkly gloss the mirth in Chaucer's text to show that this wedding, in its attention to material flash and show, contrasts with the celestial pomp of the wedding of Mercury and Philology. Chaucer subtly conveys the macrocosmic harmony (and the fair chain of love) normally blessing microcosmic marriage through the Muses in line 1735, mentioned just after Philology and Mercury (1734) and Hymen (1730). They appear in a Remigian gloss on *copula*, used of Hymen as the sacred bond among the gods, in the plural used for those who sing songs. As *copula* we accept the nuptial gods, or *proles deorum* (offspring of the gods) as a second meaning, or the nine Muses born from Jove and Juno (3.6, 1:67).[9]

But in this incongruous marriage, the very old knight who needs to increase his "corage," or sexual energy, by means of aphrodisiacs to use his "instrument" (1807–8), is counter to the paired musicians, Orpheus and Amphion (1716), whose instrumental excellence Januarie's musicians duplicate. To undercut Januarie's excessive age as a groom, his disordered spiritual kingdom—in that what he desires rules what he should do and think—and his uxoriousness, Chaucer uses the two poets together and separately to show that neither "Orpheus, ne of Thebes Amphioun, / Ne maden nevere swich a melodye" (1716–17) as occurred in the "loud mynstralcye" during every course (1718). (Even Theodomas, insists Chaucer, did not play his music "half so cleere" during the siege of Thebes [1720–21].) The emphasis on their music making, in Thrace (for Orpheus) and Thebes (for Amphion and Theodomas), recalls their extraordinary and supernatural skill in the Martianus commentaries in controlling nature, in taming wild beasts, in the case of Orpheus, or in bringing life to stiffly cold

bodies, animating mountains, and making rocks feel, in the case of Am-
phion—power over flesh and stone, power to regenerate that Januarie badly
needs at this moment.[10]

More tropologically, Orpheus is the antitype of the foolish, irrational
Januarie because the Theban poet represents the superiority of the rational
faculty over the sensitive faculty.[11] This latter facility is manifested when
he calms trees and animals, according to the commentators, whereas the
folly of Januarie is revealed when he is "ravysshed in a traunce / At every
tyme he looked on hir face" (1750–51). In another myth glossed in the
commentaries, that of Orpheus's descent into the underworld to retrieve
Eurydice,[12] the fretful and insecure love of Orpheus for Eurydice hints at
the uxoriousness of Januarie, so inclined to believe May that he loses *his*
wife a second time (after losing her first time to the serpentlike Dam-
yan); that is, after he is granted a moment of insight when he can see
clearly what his wife is doing in the pear tree with Damyan, he then "looks
back" (so to speak) and loses her again. He chooses to be blind, to accept
her explanation that indeed she was arguing with a man in a tree to re-
trieve his lost "eyesight." Further, in the commentaries this marriage of
Orpheus and Eurydice, interpreted in the light of the arts, duplicates and
mirrors the relationship between Mercury, or eloquence, and Philology, or
wisdom. If Orpheus represents the poet, etymologically his name means
"sweet voice" (*orea phonu*), and Eurydice represents the most profound un-
derstanding (*inventio*, imagination) of the art of music; because her hus-
band has neglected the art, he loses his ability as a poet and must descend
into the underworld of profound study or discipline to retrieve this art.[13]

The mythographic contrast between Amphion, as builder of the walls of
Thebes, and Januarie, as builder of the enclosed garden, establishes the old
knight's selfish intentions toward his wife. Like Amphion, Januarie delib-
erately creates a world of his own—but a fantasy world—in the walled
garden in which he imprisons May. Amphion, poet and king, built Thebes
by playing so beautifully with his lyre that, with the aid of the Muses, the
mountain stones leapt into place of their own accord. Although not a poet,
Januarie plays questionably on his wedding night: the Merchant acknowl-
edges that he does not know what May thought about the groom's love-
making, except that, as if paralyzed by trepidation or repugnance, "The
bryde was broght abedde as *stille as stoon*" (1818; my emphasis). Januarie's
hortus conclusus built of stones encloses a world figuratively closed off
from others that allows him to fulfill his fantasies with her, a locked gar-
den symbolic of his own possessiveness, toward which he remains blind. A
model for Januarie, Amphion not only appears in Martianus;[14] he is also
mentioned in Dante, who asks the Muses who aided Amphion in building
Thebes to help him describe truthfully the last and most difficult circle
in the *Inferno*.[15] In Dante's epic the Theban poet typifies *amor civium*,

according to Guido da Pisa in his commentary on the *Inferno*,[16] which in the Augustinian sense contrasts with the *amor sui* of Januarie in building his walled city. Dante's Amphion is the antithesis of those treacherous to kin, country, or cause in the Ninth Circle, such as Chaucer's treacherous Damyan, who invades Januarie's little city, his *hortus conclusus*, and violates his role as serving squire to knight Januarie.

Januarie's concupiscent, irrational motives in marrying fresh May are also bolstered by the remaining references in this first group, to Bacchus, god of wine, his consort Venus, goddess of love, and their son Hymen, the nuptial god, all three characterizations borrowed from Martianus's *De nuptiis*. In the reference to Bacchus and Venus ("Bacus the wyn hem shynketh al aboute, / And Venus laugheth upon every wight" [1722–23]), Januarie pays allegiance to the two gods through the food and drink that stimulate good fellowship, in the light of the aphorism, "Venus without Bacchus and Ceres grows cold." The expression is used here by the Merchant ironically of his alter ego's pathetic attempt at love, just as Alisoun used the proverb, in the previous chapter, to justify her own search for love and to castigate both her old and her clerical husbands for their deficiencies in lovemaking. "Januarie was bicome hir knyght / And wolde bothe assayen his corage / In libertee, and eek in mariage" (1724–26), as if he is challenging the limits of nature and male potency. Because of Venus's association with cosmic love, in Martianus she represents Venus Genetrix, what Martianus terms the "mother of conception." In a reflection of the difficulty of Januarie's challenge, Venus appears to do what she can to help: "And with hire fyrbrond in hire hand aboute / Daunceth biforn the bryde and al the route" (1727–28). Chaucer uses this Venus ironically, given Januarie's less than holy regard for May, to reveal the old knight's inversion of the marriage good: Januarie appears to desire to serve Venus Genetrix, heavenly love that he wants to enjoy on earth (1723), the Remigian Venus of chaste, honest love, indeed the mother of all conception, who gave birth to Hymen, "deus ... nuptiarum," the god of weddings, or for Remigius, "naturalium conceptionum" (3.5, 1:67). Of the several Venuses appearing in the same passage in Martianus commentaries, chaste and unchaste love (in Remigius, made fourfold in Bernardus Silvestris), the more clearly negative definition better serves to develop Chaucer's characters here.[17] The role of the unchaste Venus derives from her Greek name "Aphrodite," because of her birth from foam (that is, *spumea*, or in Greek *afro* plus *spuma*, resulting from the amputation of the virile member of her father Caelus);[18] through illicit pleasures, the gifts of Venus subvert the rational soul and lead to vice, a result of original sin (the sin of origin: hence Remigius emphasizes her origins).[19]

The references to both Bacchus (Liber) and Venus also connect inebriation and madness[20] with the dark side of love in the late Martianus commentaries, explained in the light of the Terence quotation—the lascivious desires of "Venus Scelestis" that subvert the rational soul and culminate in death, both physical and spiritual.[21] Januarie is not only physically inebriated (from the aphrodisiacs on his wedding night), but also spiritually: "O Januarie, dronken in plesaunce / In mariage" (1788–89). According to Bernardus, Martianus's reference to Bacchus signifies "opulentia vel gaudium," temporal good or joy, understood (as is usual in his glosses) to have four meanings, based on the literal, tropological, allegorical, and anagogical levels of signification.[22] Venus also represents the lascivious goddess associated with courtly love at that same celebration when she so severely burns Januarie's squire and servant Damyan with her brand that he takes to his bed in courtly ardor (1777), suffering from "Venus fyr" (1875). Her union with Mercury resulted in the bastard Hermaphroditus, lascivious discourse, meaning that such eloquence neglects the reason of truth and requires instead ornate and superfluous speech.[23] This type of decorated and even bombastic rhetoric is used by Chaucer to describe the awful wedding night of the aged Januarie and fresh May, and in a sense is repeated in the gift of Proserpina to May, who artfully answers her blind husband when he momentarily sees her struggling in the tree. This surprising link of wedded Januarie's Venus with courtly Damyan's—Damyan's Venus is clearly the unchaste, adulterous goddess—suggests that Chaucer is using Venus Genetrix ironically, to expose Januarie's confused actual allegiance to Venus Scelestis.

Ymeneus, Chaucer's "god of weddyng" (1730), is depicted as gazing on Januarie: he "Saugh nevere his lyf so myrie a wedded man" (1731). In Martianus, Hymen also is summoned by Calliope, the Muse of epic poetry, to bless the beginning of the *prosimetrum* (4.1), either because dancing pleases him (Bacchus is his father), or because he sings at weddings such as the one between Mercury and Philology (and weddings are the province of his mother Venus), or because his duty is to garland thresholds blooming with flowers provided by the three Graces. His role in both of these wedding celebrations is linked with his genealogy and its figurative significance: Remigius notes that Bacchus is his father and Venus is his mother, or, in other words, "after excessive excitement comes the agitation of desire" ("post nimiam petulantiam solet excitaria libido" [4.1, 1:69]), presumably followed by Hymen—the sign of union. Hymen was often understood as god not only of weddings but also of cosmic weddings, and therefore represents that harmony between body and soul, Christ and his church, this world and the otherworld, which should have resonated in microcosm in Januarie's marriage to May; that is, Hymen suggests the fair chain of love that knits together the whole of the universe ("Hymeneum ... amorem illum et concordiam qua elementa omnia et universitas subsistit creaturarum" [Remigius, *Mart.* 3.14, 1:69]).[24] Hymen serves as the "main object of the Cyprian's care" (3.13), "the Cyprian" denoting Venus on account of her association with the island of Cyprus, which means "mixtura," "copulation." Thus the desire inflamed by Venus that glows on Hymen's face in Martianus's text (p. 3) should be that of *cupiditas honesta,* the good Cupid, not that of *cupiditas turpis* (Remigius, *Mart.* 3.14, 1:69).[25] *Cupiditas turpis* has instead inflamed Damyan, although Januarie's lecherous behavior toward his wife within a *hortus conclusus* imported straight from Guillaume de Lorris's *Roman de la Rose* suggests that the *cupiditas honesta* within lawful marriage merely masks that same *cupiditas turpis* of Damyan — that Januarie also consorts with Venus Scelestis, mother of Hermaphroditus, and in a sense betrays himself as *sponsus.*

Ceres — most important of these three deities, Bacchus, Venus, and Ceres (as she was in the Wife of Bath's employment of the mythological proverb) — is missing in the Merchant's reference to the two gods, Bacchus and Venus. Literally signifying grain, bread, but more figuratively fertility, the absent Ceres dominates the denouement of the *Merchant's Tale.* Januarie certainly hopes for a son from this marriage ("Thanne sholde he take a yong wif and a feir, / On which he myghte engendren hym an heir" [1271–72]; "And on hir wombe he stroketh hire ful softe" [2413]), an overweening desire that fosters his self-delusion. Procreation was one of the three goods of marriage, as becomes clearer in the second group of references.

The Marriage

During the same wedding celebration, other mythological references ironically undercut Januarie's paradisal concept of marriage by showing the harsh reality. These references center on the antithesis of faith, that is, adultery — Paris and Helen in 1754, Venus and her brand in 1777, and her fire in 1875, which, as we have just seen, burns Damyan, her courtly love servant. With regard to Paris and Helen, Januarie imagines that he "that nyght in armes wolde hire [May] streyne / Harder than evere Parys dide Eleyne" (1753–54), as if Paris, son of Priam, represented *sensus* (in echo of Bernardus on Martianus).[26] In fact he relies on aphrodisiacs to harden his "corage" — although if anyone is raped this night, it is probably Januarie, "ravysshed in a traunce."

After the wedding night and with the passage of time, the lack of fertility in the marriage is also ironically signaled by the presence of Priapus, "god of gardyns" (2035) and fertility, in the lush garden scene drawn from the *Roman de la Rose* (2034). Reminiscent of the Garden of Eden, this garden contains a "laurer alwey grene" that stands over a "welle" (2036–37) — of fertility. Around that well dance the underworld rulers, Pluto and Proserpina, "and al hire fayerye" (2039), instead of Deduit or the angels. The disporting, melody making, and dancing of the gods (2038–41) echo the previous wedding celebration of Januarie and May attended by Venus, Bacchus, and Hymen, to draw the reader's attention to other similarities between the wedding night that followed and the days of dalliance that mark the progress of the marriage. Priapus has been identified as a phallic deity, Januarie's "true patron saint of his old age and the proper tutelary deity of his garden,"[27] whom Januarie resembles and wishes to obey, and also, in his connection with the satyrs, as a "comical figure of frustrated and embarrassed lust" that seems to suggest old Januarie.[28] Although Priapus does not appear in Bernardus's commentary on Martianus, in the glosses of Remigius he represents the god of fertility and hence is rightly used by Chaucer as the patron of the second good of marriage, *proles,* or offspring, in that he is linked with the *opera nuptiarum* of Hymen and Venus (363.17, 2:174) and termed "deus nuptiarum quem nuptae colunt" (par. 725, 363.22, 2:175).

Because Priapus protects *this* garden, May's deceits and Januarie's blindness will most likely result in the desired heir. Certainly Januarie desires "corage" sufficient to beget an heir—given Priapus's other associations, especially his presumed magical powers and the enormous size of his phallus, in classical texts and their commentaries, it is possible Priapus externalizes Januarie's fantasy of hardy "corage," formerly aided on his wedding night by aphrodisiacs, into an entire magical garden overseen by "Pluto and his queene, / Proserpina, and al hire fayerye" (2038–39). This "god of gardens"—also found in the *Parlement of Foules* (253–59), as we saw in chapter 3—was regarded in *Georgics* 4.109–11 as a scarecrow who holds a willow hook and guards a garden whose flowers attract bees. In the Berne scholia on the *Georgics,* Priapus's role is to protect and ensure fertility; he holds a willow hook to guard against thieves as well as birds; he is called "lord of the Hellespont," according to Adanan the Scot, probable author of the scholia, because he was born in a town therein and because he is believed to control all magic arts (this ability apparently accounts for the great size of his phallus).[29]

In addition, the final outcome of Priapus's protection ensures all couples that happiness in marriage depends, if not upon offspring, then upon a necessary blindness, a little lying, the fictions of harmony. For this reason, the outcome is also furthered by those fairy gods who are key to understanding the entire tale, Pluto and Proserpina. Januarie's final blindness is witnessed by those whose own magic projects Januarie's earlier fantasy, delusion, hallucination.

For couples to be happy in marriage they must give in to their delusions—they must become myopic. Januarie's initial fantasy—his blindness, if you will—centers on a wife as a treasure, a savior, a paradise on earth: although no man can have "parfite blisses two," meaning in earth and in heaven, "Yet is ther so parfit felicitee / And so greet ese and lust in mariage ... / That I shal have myn hevene in erthe heere" (1642–43, 1647),

Januarie concludes. He merely puzzles over how he will "Come to the blisse ther Crist eterne on lyve ys" (1652). For him to be happy in his marriage after his monstrous vision of May and Damyan *swyving* (making love) in the pear tree, he must close his eyes — a gift, in fact, from the gods witnessing this act. That this delusion is indeed an answer to Chaucer's alleged Marriage Question becomes clearer after examining the layered mythological images in the tale relaying other examples of blind seers and psychologically blind lovers of whom Januarie represents one instance.

Januarie's name, first of all, suggests the two-faced Janus married to Argione, who weeps; he is a type of double-sexed Hermaphroditus resulting from the wrong union of Mercury and Venus (rather than Mercury and Philology), and the antitype of the knowing but blind prophet Tiresias, both male and female, found in the Boethius commentaries. His blindness to May's adultery and to her cunning in continuing to hide it is mirrored in the images of the blinding of Io's guard Argus by the eloquent Mercury (2111) and in the destructive blindness of the separated lovers Pyramus and Thisbe (2128), which leads to their mutual deaths. Note that the reference to Pyramus and Thisbe comes in the narrator's invocation of Ovid (as author of *Metamorphoses*) — as if Chaucer were again drawing our attention to the classical authors and their commentaries, as indeed he does with these myths of Janus and Argione, double-sexed Hermaphroditus, Tiresias, Argus and Mercury, in the Martianus and Boethius commentaries.

If Januarie's name derives from Janus, then he is two-faced (his two sides expressed by Placebo and Justinus), and he wants eternal life[30] — as if he guarded the cosmic gate to heaven, he watches over his future life. But in the Martianus commentaries, in addition, he has a relationship with his wife that suggests that love is similarly blind. This god of the year, "deus anni," is called Ianus for an etymological reason, that is, because he opens the gate of the year: "IANUS dictus est quod ianuam pandit anni"; thus the month January is said to have two faces, because it is a month of ingress and egress for the year — sometimes four, because of the four seasons or the four regions of the heavens (Remigius, *Mart.* 6.1, 1:73 [1.4]). The reference to a weeping Argive (her name linked with Argos) in Martianus leads Remigius to identify her as Janus's wife, who weeps because "Ubi amor, ibi oculus; ubi dolor, ibi manus" ("Where love, here the eye; where dolor, here the hand"), that is, to wipe away tears. The blindness of Janus here — and the emphasis on love — makes the equation with Januarie possible.

In a sense, when self-delusion prompted by desire (Januarie) marries eloquence (May), the result is Hermaphroditus, who fused with Salmacis into an androgynous figure in Ovid. In the Martianus commentaries, Hermaphroditus is the monster produced from the adulterous union between young Mercury and Venus and therefore, during Mercury's search for a bride, she is rejected as unsuitable (unlike May). This union, and its final outcome, are allegorized by Remigius as eloquence (Hermes) used for perverse or concupiscent ends (Aphrodite).[31] This fused figure in Chaucer can be seen in the adulterous union of May and Damyan (the equivalent of Salmacis) in the tree above the head of the aged and blind Januarie. But it is Januarie himself who allows eloquence (Placebo's, his own, or May's) to be used for concupiscent ends—Hermaphroditus.

An echo of Januarie in a figure combining male and female also exists in blind, double-sexed Tiresias, similarly bandied about by deities, if not by Pluto and Proserpina, then by Jupiter and Juno. Tiresias the prophet is struck blind by Juno for confessing, after his experience as a woman, that women enjoy sex more than men, but he is granted divinity for his answer by Jupiter. The ironic connection between the blind Januarie and Tiresias—one who can see and refuses to do so and one who chooses to see too much—appears in the twelfth-century Erfurt commentary, which refers the reader back to the Boethian context for the gloss. The moralization of the Anonymous Erfurt commentator on Boethius book 5 prose 3 provides the butt of the joke in the figure of Tiresias as an example of man's unknowing, analogous to Januarie's uncertainty about what he saw—in contrast to the full knowledge of God, or, in the *Merchant's Tale,* the gods Pluto and Proserpina. In the *Consolatio,* in 5p3, when the persona Boethius has trouble understanding the idea of divine foreknowledge and free will, he asks what knowledge is worth, if it is not certain: "But if he sees that those future things are just as indeed they are, so that he knows that they can equally either happen or not happen, what sort of foreknowledge [*praescientia*] is this, that grasps nothing certain, nothing stable? Or how does it compare with that ridiculous prophecy [*vaticinio illo ridiculo*] of Tiresias?—'Whatever I say will either happen or not'?" The ambivalence of this "ridiculous prophecy" is related by Erfurt to the change of Tiresias's sex after he had separated two copulating serpents with a rod; the ambivalent answer of Tiresias is linked to his dual sexual nature, whose ambivalence reflects the uncertainty of man's knowing in contrast to God's certainty.[32] Chaucer embodies the two sexual natures of Tiresias in Januarie and May, just as the punishment and reward bestowed upon Tiresias are both granted as gifts to Januarie and May. Tiresias's copulating snakes are transformed into the serpentlike Damyan and the subtle May *swyving* in the pear tree above Januarie's head, and Tiresias's rod can be visualized quite literally as the pear tree that Januarie embraces. It can be seen symbolically as a symbol of the virility Januarie yearns to demonstrate through May's illusory pregnancy, and also as a rod that joins the lovers.

Another gloss on Tiresias was available to link the prophet directly with hermaphroditic Januarie through the fable of his double-sexedness, as explained through a Stoic myth of the changing seasons of the year. In "The Fable of Tiresias," Fulgentius, in his *Mitologiae* 2.5, understands the seer as "an allegory of time, as for *teroseon*, that is perpetual summer," although in Ovid Tiresias became expert in human sexuality from actually experiencing each sex himself.

> Thus in springtime, which is masculine because at that season there is a closing and immovability of plants, when he saw before him the creatures coupling and struck at them with his staff—that is, in the heat of temper, he is turned into the feminine gender, that is, into the heat of summer. They took summer to be in the form of a woman because at that season all things blossom forth with their leaves. And because there are two seasons for mating, spring and autumn, having stopped their conceiving he returned again to his former appearance. (Fulg. *Mit.* 2.5, pp. 43–44, trans. p. 70)

Unfortunately, when Tiresias is summoned as a judge between Jupiter (fire) and Juno to decide the true meaning of love (Fulgentius does not reveal the Ovidian parameters of the debate, which have to do with which sex enjoys intercourse the more), the prophet answers honestly and is blinded by Juno. Fulgentius again decorously conceals the true answer by providing a natural explanation of plant regeneration that depends upon a greater amount of air (Juno) than fire (Jupiter) to produce leaves and "impregnate the shoots" (that is, women [Juno] do enjoy intercourse more than men). For Fulgentius, the sun's role (in Jupiter's ether) is negligible, and thus it is appropriate that Tiresias loses the ability to see the light ("for the reason that wintertime grows black with dark clouds in the air") even while Jove grants him foresight (that is, "assists with the conceiving of future growth by granting inner forces"). Fulgentius concludes the fable with an amazing (for Chaucerian purposes) link between Tiresias, who used the parable of the annual cycle, and Januarie, the first month: "for this reason January is depicted with two faces, so that it can see both what is past and what is to come."[33]

The blindness of Januarie to May's adultery because of his desire to believe her eloquent explanation is also glossed within the tale by another, a reference to Argus's blinding by Mercury—that deity who functions as the protagonist bridegroom of *De nuptiis* who has also appeared in this same myth in the *Wife of Bath's Tale*. Mercury's blinding of "Argus, which that hadde an hondred yen" (2111), after the guardian had been lulled to sleep by the god of eloquence's music, allowed Mercury to rescue Io, transformed into a heifer as a result of Juno's punishment for her alleged adultery with Jove. The Merchant lingers over Argus in a moment of astonished self-recrimination: "For al that evere he koude poure or pryen, / Yet was he blent, and, Got woot, so been mo / That wenen wisly that it be nat so" (2112–14). Argus's name is explained by Bernardus (in a gloss on *Metamorphoses* 1.625) from the Greek *argos* (*oculus* or eye in Latin), an etymology that reveals why Argos was linked with Greek civilization (the Argives), which he was said to rule (*Mart.* 5.860, 862, 863, p. 122); the etymology also explains Chaucer's choice of the blinded Argus as a mythological image for the self-deluded Januarie.

Finally, the reference to the lovers Pyramus and Thisbe, who fell in love while communicating through a chink in the wall (2128), has reminded many critics of the stratagems of Damyan and May,[34] but not of Ovid's thematic emphasis on the barriers preventing the lovers from knowing each other and consummating their love—the wall, the darkness, the night, the mistaken reasoning concerning the lion's actions—all of which point to an identification with blind Januarie and the May he knows not at all. Chaucer, like the "noble Ovyde" he addresses directly (2125), stresses the "sleighte" (2126, 2132) that borders on ingenuity to which all lovers will turn to gain the object of their desire, even using a hole in the wall like Pyramus and Thisbe. Because Januarie knows May very little, he loves in darkness, if at all—as if through a chink in the wall. Hence the outcome of the "love" of Januarie for May mirrors the love of Pyramus and Thisbe, tragicomic rather than tragic: as May declares, "He that mysconceyveth, he mysdemeth" (2410). Further, despite the sleight of Pyramus and Thisbe, the relationship ends literally, horribly, in death, whatever more positive outcome is signaled by its allegorical meaning (the Incarnation and Passion of Christ, according to Bersuire, for whom Pyramus, in *Metamorphoses* 4.67–69, represents the son of God and Thisbe the human soul [*Ovidius*, pp. 202–3]). The outcome of the marriage of Januarie and May inverts spiritual life, although the relationship survives.

Procreation

Specifically, Januarie imagines that he will attain the otherworld, the treasure of the heavenly Jerusalem, in his wife; in fact, his preference for temporal over spiritual good will, ironically, win him hell. But marriage can also be understood figuratively, so that the consequences of Januarie's inversion of marriage focus on the inversion of body and soul. Thus, Januarie's blindness in picking May and misunderstanding the nature of marriage becomes permanently damaging: in choosing *temporalia*, things of this world, riches, an heir, he chooses the underworld rather than Paradise, the body rather than the soul, not only this world rather than the otherworld, but the promise, in the afterlife, of the *Inferno* rather than the *Paradiso*. He therefore solves the problem of his mis-"marriage" of body and soul in the sense intended by Alan of Lille in the *De planctu*.

Within the third group of mythological references, which comment on the consequences of marriage specifically for Januarie, and which generally respond to the Marriage Question, marriage is treated from the anagogical perspective, as in the "Envoy a Bukton" and the *Wife of Bath's Prologue.* In the "Envoy," marriage becomes the "cheyne / Of Sathanas" in prison, although Alisoun claims of herself, in relation to her fourth husband, "in erthe I was his purgatorie" (489). In the *Merchant's Tale,* marriage appears to be paradise on earth for Januarie. However, his actual purchase of the underworld (the goods of this world) is bolstered especially by the references to Pluto and Proserpina, the rulers of the underworld, who witness his "exchange." The gods are introduced twice in the tale — in lines 2038–39, in conjunction with Priapus, and again, as characters, in lines 2227ff.

Clearly, the underworld associations of Pluto and Proserpina attracted Chaucer in changing from his sources the supernatural figures Saint Peter and God, or Jupiter, Venus, and Mercury, who aid the protagonists.[35] Identified as the ruler of the underworld in the Boethius commentaries (on 3m12, in which Orpheus also appears), Pluto represents one of three brothers who govern the major regions of the cosmos — as Jupiter rules the air and Neptune, the water, so Pluto rules the earth and the underworld, the region defined by Bernardus on Martianus as the earth underneath the moon.[36] In Chaucer, Pluto, "kyng of Fayerye" (2227), and his "wyf," "the queene Proserpyna" (2229), as similar "gods of the underworld," rule *earth* as opposed to the heavens or the waters and hence judge mortals who choose foolishly and with concupiscence in the "underworld."

Chaucer, however, dismisses the conventional interpretation of the myth of Proserpina's rape, with its hint of violence and imprisonment, as interpreted by Claudian ("In Claudyan ye may the stories rede, / How in his grisely carte he hire fette" [2233–34]), although he preserves the "ravishment": Proserpina is still "ravysshed out of [Ethna] / Whil that she gadered floures in the mede" (2230–31). Usually, the abduction of Proserpina to the underworld by Pluto is interpreted by glossators as a classical version of the Christian Fall; Proserpina's six months on earth with her mother Ceres (spring) and six months in the underworld with her husband Pluto (winter) are explained as the natural cycle of the year resulting from the Fall. Chaucer focuses instead on the psychological aspects of "ravishment" — how a couple survives a marriage of economic or political necessity — in the postmarital relationship between Pluto and Proserpina. The key for the powerful spouse *is* myopia, which we have already seen developing in Januarie and which certainly exists in Pluto, just as sleight is the key for the powerless spouse.

More pertinent still to this marriage is the specific mythographic information concerning Pluto and Proserpina. The coupling of Pluto (avarice) and Proserpina (procreation) yokes Januarie's motive for marriage (and therefore the necessity for his myopia in not seeing May's adultery) with May's motive for marriage (and therefore the necessity for her myopia in not seeing aged Januarie). In Remigius's commentary on Martianus, Pluto is not the god of sensuality, as one critic has termed him,[37] but instead, the *inferorum deus*, the god of the dead in the underworld (5.18, 1:72 [1.4]) and, more importantly for Chaucer, of material riches: his name "Dis" derives from *dives* because nothing is richer indeed than the depths of the earth, which receives everything ("quia infernus omnia recipit" [35.20, 1:133]). The etymology explains the connection between Pluto and avarice, a form of spiritual death.[38] As competitive and unsuccessfully married spouses, Pluto and his abducted Proserpina (2038ff.) serve as foils for Januarie and the "bought" but unravished (at least by Januarie) May. However, as a gloss on the rich Januarie, the figure Pluto suggests that the economic motive in marriage is infernal: Januarie has "bought" May. Hence, he declares, when an old man takes a wife — and we know avarice is an old man's sin — "Thanne is a wyf the fruyt of his tresor" (1270). Consequently, it is no accident that he thinks about possibilities ("Many fair shap and many a fair visage / Ther passeth thurgh his herte nyght by nyght" [1580–81]), says Chaucer, "As whoso tooke a mirour, polisshed bryght, / And sette it in a commune market-place" (1582–83) — as if he were shopping for a wife: "Thanne sholde he se ful many a figure pace / By his mirour" (1584–85). May accordingly becomes "His paradys terrestre" (1332) and, ironically, within his paradise a ripe fruit in deed if not in fact when she becomes a part of the pear tree itself, a young, fair, and pregnant wife braced against the branches.

In Remigius's commentary on Martianus, May's analogue, Pluto's mate Proserpina, represents growth, fertility — a bolstering of the powers of Priapus on the cosmic level. She is called so from *proserpendo*, that is, *porro* and *multum crescendo*, who accepts the life of herbs and all that grows from the seeds of earth.[39] Called "Echate" in Greek (Hecate) and connected with the growth of trees in particular[40] — an important symbol in the narrative outcome of the *Merchant's Tale* — Proserpina is also related to human procreation by Pietro Alighieri, in commenting on Dante's *Purgatorio*, cantos 27 and 28.[41]

The specific appearance of Pluto in the *Merchant's Tale* also suggests a kind of literal uxoriousness common both to worldly Januarie and to the hero Orpheus, who functions in both this world and in the underworld. Like Orpheus intent on retrieving Eurydice, Januarie descends into the underworld, a descent similarly marked by the entry of Pluto and Proserpina, god and goddess of the underworld, to show that his descent is a vicious one. Indeed, glosses in the Martianus commentary of Bernardus relate the system of four descents into the underworld to the myth of Pluto and Proserpina.[42]

The material riches of Pluto relate, then, to those of Januarie buying his young wife, but they also relate to the trader Merchant. The underworld (and mercantile) emphasis in the tale is finally not as pejorative as it seems if the modern reader relaxes her anachronistic sentimentality about medieval marriage. In reality, May retains her uxorial status (rather than being cast into the river as a harlot) through her Mercurial eloquence and her implied pregnancy (Priapus, Proserpina)—that is, she survives and retains her economically advantageous marriage (she comes, after all, from the commons), also her young lover (Venus), and certainly her riches (Pluto). In addition, Januarie, who wants an heir (Priapus, Proserpina) and Paradise on earth (Venus) through a young wife, also attains his desires—triumphs through and in spite of his blindness (Argus, Tiresias, Pyramus), and despite Damyan's union with May (Hermaphroditus).

All these rhetorical flourishes, the invocation of Martianus, suggest tricks and dazzle, sleight of hand—fantasy, in short, Mercury without the wisdom of Philology, but Mercury allied with Venus to produce Hermaphroditus. Unlike Martianus's fable, the Merchant's fable applauds the "marriage" of Venus (Desire) to Mercury (Eloquence) because it will result in the fulfillment of fantasy, lascivious speech, and what we want to hear—the bastard Hermaphroditus.

Mercury and Venus, therefore—the perspective of the Merchant and his silent, adulterous young wife—can be said to triumph in this tale, the triumph of nature and this world over the otherworld, the triumph of Pluto over Saint Peter. The fertile prosperity of Proserpina, coupled with her gift of eloquence (from Mercury) to the disempowered wife, donates a voice to the silenced and disenfranchised "bargain." The wife speaks—in other words, young Alisoun is restored from the past and is granted her ultimate desire, for a child.

The question that one might ask now of the Merchant, or of Chaucer, is, Are marriages ever founded on honesty and fidelity? Do couples only buy and sell one another—is marriage merely an economic and political imperative? Is marriage ever more than earthly imprisonment governed by blindness and deceit? Another response, that of the upwardly mobile and Epicurean Franklin, counters this practical concept with one more liberal, more equal—more modern, to the contemporary reader—and more homosocial.

CHAPTER 9

The Franklin's *Derke Fantasye*

Squire Aurelius as Ekko, Lady Dorigen as Narcissus's Image

The Franklin responds to the Wife of Bath's marriage question by visualizing the consequences of Alisoun's desire for sovereignty in marriage: ideally, neither man nor woman should be sovereign ("Love wol nat been constreyned by maistrye" [764]), because love is a "thyng as any spirit *free*" (767; my emphasis) and cannot be constrained "as a thral" (769). "Free," according to the glosses in the *Oxford English Dictionary*, literally denotes "free, not servile (having the social status of noble or freeman)"—clearly an issue not in question for these aristocrats. But when, at the end of his tale, the Franklin, referring to his principal aristocratic and clerical characters, asks, "Which was the mooste fre?" does he mean something other than the conventional class construction privileging the aristocracy in this puzzling adaptation of the *demande d'amour* (1622)? Does the Franklin mean to imply that love should be free of class ties?

"Fre" defined as "noble," "generous of spirit," "unrestrained," "unconstrained (as of the will), without obstruction," and "generous, as in liberal in spending" applies more accurately to the Franklin's characters as aristocrats familiar with courtly and chivalric behaviors. *Liberalitas*, a classical virtue, was identified in the Middle Ages with the ideal knight, according to Eustache Deschamps in his late fourteenth-century ballade, "Du bachelier d'armes" ("Show generosity" [line 23]); the knight was also enjoined in Honoré Bonet's *Arbre de batailles* (1387) to avoid purchasing land or vineyards, largely because worldly riches might cause him to leave arms.[1] The explicit link between the theme of liberality and the chivalric obligation in particular is less focused in Chaucer's tale than in the source for the *Franklin's Tale*, Boccaccio's "Tale of Menedon" in *Il filocolo*, in which each of the suitors is a *cavaliere* and in which the word "fredom" appears as *liberalità*.[2] If Boccaccio's concerns were Chaucer's, then the Franklin would be asking, "Who is the best knight (or gentleman)?" in a clear reflection of his own interest in and desire for upward mobility.[3] But the Franklin's desire is to deconstruct chivalry and courtly love and to disengage rigid class hierarchies that prevent fluid intersections. As a franklin, he has no desire to learn who is the best *knight* in his story.

Leaving aside for the moment the definition of "fre" as "unconstrained," in a more figurative and even spiritual sense the Franklin is asking, "Who is most generous of spirit (who gives up the most)?" From a medieval point of view, none of the characters seems "fre," or "gentil," in terms of the exemplar of "gentilesse" in Christ espoused by the Wife of Bath's Fairy Queen (*Wife of Bath's Tale* 1117).[4] When each character is explained by what s/he sacrifices, or gives up, in Boccaccio's *moralitas* for this tale (but not in the tale itself), the analogue for Chaucer's clerk of Orleans reveals the flaw of avarice, the analogue for the squire Aurelius, lust, and the analogue for the knight Arveragus, pride or honor. These flaws are described in 1 John 2:16 as lust of the eyes, lust of the flesh, and pride of life, the three motives of the world known as the world, the flesh, and the devil. Within the moral hierarchy of these vices in the Middle Ages, a medieval audience would guess correctly that the knight appears most guilty, as representative of the chief of the seven deadly sins, and therefore least "fre" in his behavior, whether in a courtly, Christian, or socioeconomic sense.

Unlike Boccaccio's tale (the chief source for the tale), which argues for the social and natural superiority of all of the characters, and more in keeping with his *moralitas*, Chaucer creates socially, morally, and naturally flawed characters involved in a superficially attractive, modern-seeming courtly-love marriage, in which the lord presents himself in public through his seemingly conventional roles as dominant husband to subservient wife, but plays in private the aristocratic and courtly role of subservient lover to dominant beloved.[5] Like the rocks substituted for Boccaccio's winter garden, Arveragus's courtly-love marriage is Chaucer's innovation in his other major source, Geoffrey of Monmouth's brief excerpt in the *Historia regum Britanniae*, in which the Briton Arviragus deeply loves the Roman Genuissa, daughter of Claudian.

To stress the primary class responsibility of Arveragus as lord and husband and therefore his most significant failure in the tale, Chaucer uses legal, contractual, and even martial language to describe the knight's enterprising victory over Dorigen. Because of the "labour" and "greet emprise" (732) of Arveragus—his "worthynesse" and his "meke obeysaunce" (738, 739)—the knight convinces Dorigen in the best courtly fashion "To take hym [Arveragus] for hir housbonde and hir lord, / Of swich lordshipe as men han over hir wyves" (742–43), even though courtly love theoretically could not exist in marriage, according to the rules of Andreas Capellanus. Arveragus promises to overcome this obstacle by attempting the impossible task of continuing his courtly service to his lady in private, which makes him a class aberration, a monster. He forswears mastery and jealousy, except for "the name of soveraynetee, / That wolde he have for shame of his degree" (751–52) and becomes "Servant in love, and lord in mariage," or in other words, "bothe in lordshipe and servage," except "in lordshipe above, / Sith he hath bothe his lady and his love" (792–96).

In addition, the love of Aurelius, serpent-in-the-garden, for Dorigen is a thinly disguised homosocial bonding with the knight achieved through imitation of Arveragus's private role, as courtly lover-servant, when, in terms of his social relationship with both knight and lady, he might very well serve them both in fact, as a squire would a knight and his liege lady. Even the Franklin's language in the description of his love echoes that courtly and chivalric language used by Arveragus to describe his love for her: as "servant to Venus" (937ff and also 1303–5), he had "loved hire best of any creature / *Two yeer and moore, as was his aventure,* / But nevere dorste he tellen hire his grevaunce" (939–41; my emphasis), just as the knight had worshiped her for a year and a half (806). Aurelius's role as courtly lover is itself predicated on the absence of a married lord, without which he could not petition the lord's wife for her sexual favors; as recent studies have shown, courtly love developed as a socioeconomic construct *by the lords themselves* primarily intended to keep satisfied—and peaceful—second sons.[6]

As if to underscore his character as Arveragus's double, or alter ego, Aurelius compares himself, in expressing his love to Dorigen, to Ekko dying of love for the indifferent and selfish Narcissus, thereby "echoing" the earlier vow of Arveragus as courtly lover. Although Echo plays an important role in the myth in the *Metamorphoses*, Narcissus, the beautiful river nymph's son, occupies center stage; Echo's inability to find her own voice and assert herself leads her to choose the wholly inappropriate, self-absorbed Narcissus as lover. Echo's bad habit of never starting a conversation or failing to respond causes Juno, whom Echo delays in her search for her adulterous husband, to curse her with a permanent inability to initiate conversation and to repeat the last words of others; next, after she falls in love with the proud Narcissus during a hunt, her unfulfilled desire for him leads to a living death, sleeplessness, loss of appetite (and weight). Eventually she becomes an echo of herself: "Only her voice and her bones remain; then, only voice; for they say that her bones were turned to stone" (Ovid, 3.395–99). Clearly it is this antecedent of the malady of courtly love and not her blocked perception of reality and lack of self that Aurelius intends in comparing himself with Echo: he will die "as dide Ekko / For Narcisus, that dorste nat telle hir wo" (951–52). In a reversal of the genders involved in the usual courtly-love process, Aurelius's imagery ironically suggests a disastrous future for both of the incipient lovers: in Ovid the *female* Echo pursued Narcissus relentlessly and died because of her inability to accept his indifference to her. Like Echo, Aurelius wishes to serve his beloved and, like her, remains so insensitive to Dorigen that he fails to perceive the depth of her pain, both before and after he falls in love with her ("Ne dorste he not to hire his wo biwreye" [954]).

Elsewhere in Chaucer, however, Ekko serves as a symbol of female empowerment. Ekko, in fact, was employed by the Clerk as a paradigm to empower "noble wyves"—to give them voices instead of silence them—in a possibly ironic apostrophe at the end of his tale: "Folweth Ekko, that holdeth no silence, / But evere answereth at the countretaille" (1189–90). As a dual emblem in that tale, Ekko also accurately reflects Griselde in her echolalic rhetorical responses to her cruel, testing husband: she offers an opportunity to make trouble through mimesis, deliberately exaggerated gender behavior that subverts and therefore empowers. By appropriating Ekko for use as a foil for the Squire and also for Dorigen in his own tale, the Franklin disgenders the myth and makes it serve his own response to the marriage debate—he suggests that *gender* prevents Dorigen from acting independently, just as the rigidity of gender and class obligations keeps the squire "echoing" the knight.

The better-known myth of Narcissus in the Middle Ages had become popular with poets, including Chaucer, concerned with describing the psychological and social dangers of courtly love for the (male) lover, whether in the courtly-love lyric, the *Roman de la Rose,* or John Gower's *Confessio Amantis,* perhaps because of its clearly defined bond in Ovid's *Metamorphoses* with *amor sui,* clouded perception, and frustrated desire.[7] Chaucer mentions "Narcisus the faire of yore" elsewhere only in the *Knight's Tale,* in description of the "mount of Citheroun" portrayed on the wall in the Temple of Venus (1941), and together with Ekko in the *Book of the Duchess,* in description of other courtly lovers who have wasted away and died because of their obsessions (735). The former example of the destructive aspects of courtly love iconographically depicts a garden similar to that of Deduit in the *Roman,* complete with courtly-love personifications, the porter Ydelnesse, and a naked statue of Venus over which doves flicker. The parallel between the Narcissus images used of the courtly lover Palamon in the *Knight's Tale* and implied of Dorigen by the suffering Aurelius as Ekko in the *Franklin's Tale* invites the reader to imagine Palamon married to Emelye—or the idea of courtly love within marriage to a woman who has formerly espoused chastity as an ideal. This fantasy is exactly the situation of Arveragus and Dorigen in the *Franklin's Tale.* In this way the Franklin "quits" the Knight, by undercutting the aristocratic male characters of Arveragus and Aurelius. (Interestingly enough, the link in the *Book of the Duchess* between the Black Knight and Echo reinforces the overlay with the socially ambitious Franklin here because of the Black Knight's social role as knight; the Black Knight's excessive grief over the loss of Blanche, depicted as irrational and Alcyone-like, anticipates the gender switching found in the *Franklin's Tale.*)

Chaucer exposes the danger of pursuing courtly love within marriage through the limitations of the conflicting and double roles played by Arveragus and Aurelius. The resultant selfishness and irresponsibility of the two principals—especially Arveragus as husband, but including his social and courtly "echo," Aurelius—undercuts the novelty of their original contract and reverses their initial apparent humility and selflessness. Arveragus's autocratic and irresponsible decision to depart for England for two years publicly places his chivalric duties above his courtly and marital duties, signaling his failure both as subservient courtly lover and as protective procreator and guardian. Thereafter, Aurelius echoes the courtly Arveragus by falling in love with the knight's distraught wife. Dorigen, caught in the middle between two men whose social roles exclude any real place for a woman except as pawn, can be said to "fail" first by qualifying her refusal, its contingency opening the door to Aurelius's request and thereby violating her courtly vow of obedience, and second by making public to Aurelius her private courtly sovereignty within conventional marriage (because she meets Aurelius finally at the instigation of her husband), thereby shaming the knight as husband. But because of her voicelessness within her class and her husband's signal irresponsibility in leaving her, these "failures" are insignificant: she is the pale reflection of the desire of her husband, whose existence is predicated on patriarchal constructions. Indeed, Arveragus's honoring of his vow of obeisance to her, although she has broken hers to him—and his insistence that she uphold what he terms her honor, but which smacks of chivalry—underscores his selfishness in assuming that his pride and honor are more important than hers, should she commit adultery with Aurelius.

The Franklin's use of the Echo myth inverts the gender of this figure to show that Arveragus, failing to maintain courtly love within marriage, also inverts, as it were, the social hierarchy, natural order, and cosmic law. By focusing on Echo and not Narcissus and in feminizing Aurelius as Echo to a Narcissus that may be interpreted as Arveragus rather than Dorigen, the Franklin correctly interprets the nature of Aurelius's "love" as social appropriation and masculine rivalry, "lust-of-the-eyes," *invidia*, envy of Arveragus. Such an interpretation of Echo appears in the gloss of the fourteenth-century moralizer of Ovid, Pierre Bersuire, about the quarrelsome servant who wants to have the last word,[8] a type that Aurelius certainly fits: one might characterize his refusal to accept Dorigen's first "no" as quarrelsome. And he represents an Echo to her imaged Narcissus in that he repeats her last words, for she agrees to love him if the rocks disappear. "If the rocks disappear" becomes his echo, his refrain, and he becomes obsessed with removing them, his existence contingent on her words. He defines himself in terms of her refusals, and in a negative way, psychologically, he gives up his own identity, his will, his own self. Thus the fantasies and hallucinations the clerk presents to Aurelius include his social fantasy of images of courtly and chivalric life beginning with the hard hunt (forests, parks of wild deer, hundreds of harts slain by hounds or wounded by arrows, falconers slaying herons with hawks, knights jousting) and, given the play on words in hart/heart, and the wounding by arrows, the soft (Ovidian) hunt (the image of Aurelius's own lady dancing with the squire himself [1190ff.]).

Because Narcissus in Dante's *Inferno* (canto 30) is a Falsifier (the *bolgia*, described in canto 29, includes magicians), associated with the counterfeiting, or distortion, of reality, the clerk can be construed as yet another example of Narcissus. In this particular canto (very close to the end circle of treachery), the falsifiers and magicians join with counterfeiters, falsifiers of words, and so forth. A falsifier in his making of images, the clerk of Orleans is nevertheless engaged by "Echo"—Aurelius—to further deceive "Narcissus." The clerk of Orleans creates an *apparence* (or fantasy) in order "to maken illusioun, / By swich an apparence or jogelrye" (1264–65), which the Franklin identifies as "astrologye" (1266).

How, then, would Chaucer answer the Franklin's *demande*? One clue exists in Chaucer's change of character from that in his source relating to Dorigen. Whereas Boccaccio omits Dorigen from his moralization, perhaps because liberality, or generosity, chiefly characterizes the knight or *cavaliere* rather than the lady, Chaucer, in contrast, once again disengaging his tale from aristocratic sychophancy, names Boccaccio's unnamed *donna* "Dorigen" (called "Genuissa" in Geoffrey of Monmouth, his source for Arveragus's name).[9] Further, Chaucer changes the *donna*'s whimsical request for a blooming garden in January to Dorigen's more wifely (but still fantastic) request for the removal of the rocks on the coast to protect her returning husband's life, and he merely refers to the January date of Aurelius's visit to the clerk of Orleans. Through this change, Chaucer focuses more clearly (if unconventionally) on the essentially courtly nature of the marriage of Dorigen and Arveragus.[10] Finally, Arveragus's wife should play some role in Chaucer's social and moral allegory if the tale is understood as a reflection of the teller, primarily because the Franklin appears not to have a wife—at least he does not mention one, even though he mentions his son—and because this tale at least superficially ends the so-called marriage debate.[11]

In her lack of traditional role models, her own identity mediated by masculine desire, Dorigen rather ironically represents the character potentially most "fre," although she is not the character most responsible for their predicament—with the centuries of chivalric valor and duty at his back, Arveragus is. But she projects (also ironically) the urge of the Franklin to be "fre," perhaps in his marital, social, or religious relationships with his wife, his superiors, or God.[12] The Franklin may identify with Dorigen in her unfettered "fredom" rather than with Arveragus the knight, whose "fredom" is contingent on unbending, rigid social obligation. The gender reversal here signals—as it does elsewhere in Chaucer—social imbalance reflective of the changes in fourteenth-century culture.

Once gender is removed from the conventional rigid role definitions, Chaucer's myth of Ekko continues in this tale as it has in the *Clerk's Tale,* as an assertion of the need for female voice and individuality, for a female heroism based on its own separate cultural tradition. Dorigen appears to suffer more like Echo than the Narcissus with whom Aurelius inadvertently equates her. Overwhelmed by grief over her husband's departure, she fixes obsessively on the rocks as a possible danger to him upon his return. And when she sees no way out of her disastrous agreement with Aurelius, she turns, for models of appropriate female behavior in this situation of conjugal violation, to literary examples of classical women martyred to love. As the image of Narcissus reflected back to him, she is a shadowy figure left out of the Ovidian myth altogether who cannot exist without his presence.

The classical myth of Narcissus alone, without any mythographic gloss, provides for this interpretation of Dorigen as the image of Narcissus who does not know himself—that is, does not know the true identity of the reflected beloved. Tiresias prophesies that Narcissus will live long "si se non noverit," if he never knows himself (3.348); his inability to know himself springs from the pride that keeps him from others. Meanwhile, because Narcissus spurns a boy who loves him, the boy's curse is made reality by Nemesis: "sic amet ipse licet, sic non potiatur amato!" ("So may he himself love, and not gain the thing he loves!" [3.405]). Thereafter, Narcissus falls in love with his own image while he drinks from a pool, and "visae correptus imagine formae / spem sine corpore amat, corpus putat esse, quod umbra est" ("He is smitten by the sight of the beautiful form he sees. He loves an unsubstantial hope and thinks that substance which is only shadow" [3.416–17]). Self-knowledge of a sort eventually arrives: in 3.463–64, he thinks he loves himself ("uror amor mei"), and eventually dies by suicidally pursuing that false image into the pool. Most interestingly, the self-love and the images and shadows marking fantasy also characterize Narcissus: "That which you behold is but the shadow of a reflected form and has no substance of its own. With you it comes, with you it stays, and it will go with you if you can go" ("ista repercussae, quam cernis, imaginis umbra est: / nil habet ista sui; tecum venitque manetque; / tecum discedet, si tu discedere possis" [3.434–36]). Dorigen is Arveragus's shadow.

In other late medieval poems (French, English, and Italian), Narcissus similarly figures forth destructive fantasizing that derives from the inability to see clearly. Most significantly, in Guillaume's *Roman* (1560ff.), Amaunt as a courtly lover and a type of Narcissus (whose story is recited in this section) gazes into the Mirror Perilous (the fountain into which Narcissus plunged) at two crystals (the lover's own eyes, or the lady's reflecting back the lover's) that reflect only half the garden (i.e., half of reality) at one time. Will, at the beginning of *Piers Plowman*, gazes into a burbling stream, seemingly hypnotized by its sound, and, overcome by a lethargy, a kind of noonday demon often termed *accidia* or sloth in the Middle Ages, he succumbs to the magic of this *ferly*—the dream visions of the poem, in particular the morally instructive Visio. Like Arveragus, in effect he represents the untutored Will who does not know himself enough even to differentiate between magical *ferly* and visionary instruction; for, like Narcissus, Will "lay and lened and loked in the wateres, / I slombred in a slepyng it sweyued so merye" (9–10).[13] According to the thirteenth-century John of Garland, Narcissus represents "a greedy [*cupidus*] boy whom the glory of material things deceives [*fallit*]—things which bloom, and which float off as mere shadows [*umbra*]."[14]

The shadowy Dorigen needs a stronger sense of herself so that she will not depend so on her husband for reassurance, self-confidence, and validation. But, like Narcissus reflected in the pool, she is a shadow, the appearance of reality rather than the reality itself, very much like the abhorrent rocks.[15] The "dark fantasy" that comes to obsess her derives first from a hope that her lord will return, symbolized by the permanence of the rocks, and then from a fear that he will not, because of the rocks. To drive away this "derke fantasye" (844), her friends beg her to join them "in compaignye." And yet at other times, when alone, she succumbs to her fears and fantasies, Narcissus-like casting "hir eyen dounward fro the brynke" at "the grisly rokkes blake" (858–59). Preoccupied with her husband's absence, she questions God's "purveiaunce" (865) for allowing these "feendly" rocks to exist as a "foul confusion" rather than "any fair creacion," what seems an "unresonable" work by a "parfit wys God" (868–72).

Elsewhere, images of stone convey her emotional reactions, as if she had become the rocks about which she worries, or the obstacle separating him from her—the fantasy of her need for him in order to survive. These images converge with the blind pride of Narcissus here, although Ovid uses them as part of the process to reduce Echo from a person to bone and then stone and finally to voice alone. For example, when her friends console the distraught Dorigen after her husband's departure, gradually the emotional support wears away her rage and her determination to grieve; the "emprentyng of hire consolacioun" (834) is described through the analogy of men engraving stone over a long period (829–31). For her to cling to her rage, despite her friends' help, suggests that her rock-hard stubbornness, her fear that Arveragus may die or not return, stems from a lack of self-confidence caused, presumably, by the lack of social support from the class to which she belongs. Later, when Aurelius reveals to her that the rocks are "aweye," she appears "astoned" (1339). For Dorigen, the image of the departed rocks portrays exactly the desire of her husband, and it is upon this desire that she nearly founders.

Men imitate other men within the social structure because their roles are public and powerful, especially within the aristocracy. The aristocratic life Aurelius wishes to emulate—serving a knight's lady, providing her with what he sees as her desires, participation in a courtly relationship during a husband's absence—is a masculine sexual fantasy. When Dorigen is faced with fulfilling this male fantasy, she balks and instead resorts to a female literary tradition for an example of appropriate behavior in the face of what, from her point of view, can only be construed as adultery, or even rape. In her "Book of the City of Ladies," in a long catalog, she identifies as models martyrs resisting incest, rape, lechery, and defilement by men (1379–1456). The digression, appearing where it does in the narrative, suggests that the contemporary society (of Roman Britain)—or reality—has failed her, and that she must resort to the feminizing traditions of classical antiquity for answers. Here she introduces twenty-two classical mythological and legendary women, mostly drawn from Saint Jerome's *Adversus Jovinianum*, in positions she sees as similar to hers.[16] In all these extreme and hyperbolic situations, loyal wives or virgins choose death rather than dishonor or life without their spouse. Dorigen's changes all portray the women as gaining greater fame as the result of their conscious decision to die for principle. These heroic women are empowered in sexual situations outside their control.

Dorigen's example of the virgin Stymphalides and her desire to "hente" (hold on to) the image ("ymage") of Diana (or the image of herself—Chaucer merely says "the ymage," whereas the Latin source reads "simulacrum ejus") inside the Temple of Diana types the distraught wife as searching for an appropriate image of herself. In this sense, Dorigen resembles, at least in part, the selfless virgin Emelye, who also worships the image of Diana in the *Knight's Tale*. Stymphalides, who takes the image of Diana into her own hands in the goddess's temple, does not, however, release the image until she is slain: "No wight ne myghte hir handes of it arace" (1393). According to Saint Jerome (F 1387), the lines emphasize not so much the image of Stymphalides—or her insistence on retaining a divine image, which she projects as her own, given her virginity—but her wooing by a tyrant, Aristoclides, and her avenging by Arcadia.[17] Dorigen, although not a virgin, is a wife similar to Stymphalides whose problem has been a fixation on a false and limited self-image rather than on the strong woman she is in resisting Aurelius. Because she fears not rape but adultery with Aurelius, in a sense it can be said that Dorigen does not wish to leave the Temple of Diana.

Dorigen glosses the wife Alcestis as exceptional ("Lo, which a wyf was Alceste" [1442])—but here Chaucer strengthens the bond between Alcestis and Dorigen as exceptional wives by mentioning her immediately before "goode Penalopee" (1443). Because Alcestis exchanged her life for that of her husband out of love or duty (the Latin reads only that Alcestis died in place of her husband), Dorigen perceives suicide as self-sacrifice for an appropriate cause, although Alcestis's sacrifice has nothing to do with her chastity. In the example of the faithful wife Penelope, Dorigen mirrors her own loyalty to Arveragus, who like Ulysses has left her for some time, but she colors her image to make her chaste, just as Saint Jerome presents her: "Al Grece knoweth of hire chastitee" (1444).[18]

In the last mythological example, of Laodomya, who killed herself at Troy after her husband Protheselaus (Protesilaus) was slain because she feared what would then happen to her, Dorigen slightly alters the Latin's emphasis to project herself into the image of Laodomya: "Ne lenger wolde she lyve after his day" (1447). Mulling possibilities, Dorigen is not faced with the death of her husband, but she will certainly lose control over her own body and is contemplating suicide as a result. Dorigen here changes her source: Saint Jerome stresses the authority of the poets who "writen thus" rather than that of the determined Laodomya; they sing only that she would not survive after Protesilaus's death ("noluisse supervivere").[19]

Thus, Dorigen, cast off by her Narcissus-like husband, clings to these famous projections of the chaste wife to empower herself through female heroic exempla rather than male expectations of sexually desirable behavior. As the reflection of Narcissus gazing into the pool at himself, such expectations are centered on the male gazer and have no other reality. Dante's other depiction of Narcissus, in canto 3 of the *Paradiso*, in the realm of the moon, stresses both the poet's and the youth's misperception, the mistaken judgment of the latter, in loving. Dante looks into the glass (mirror) of the moon's spheres and thinks that the very real shades are not real—the obverse of Narcissus, who thought his unreal reflection was in fact another real boy:

> Quali per vetri trasparenti e tersi,
>   o ver per acque nitide e tranquille,
>   non sì profonde che i fondi sien persi,
> tornan di nostri visi le postille
>   debili sì, che perla in bianca fronte
>   non vien men tosto alle nostre pupille;
> tali vid'io più facce a parlar pronte;
>   *per ch'io dentro all'error contrario corsi*
>   *a quel ch'accese amor tra l'omo e 'l fonte.*
> Subito sì com'io di lor m'accorsi,
>   quelle stimando specchiati sembianti,
>   per veder di cui fosser, li occhi torsi;

> e nulla vidi, e ritorsili avanti
> dritti nel lume della dolce guida,
> che, sorridendo, ardea nelli occhi santi. (10–24; Dante, 3:48; my
> emphasis)

[As through smooth and transparent glass, or through limpid and still water not so deep that the bottom is lost, the outlines of our faces return so faint that a pearl on a white brow does not come less quickly to our eyes, many such faces I saw, eager to speak: *at which I ran into the opposite error to that which kindled love between the man [Narcissus] and the spring.* The moment I was aware of them, taking them for reflected semblances, I turned my eyes to see whose they were, and saw nothing, and turned them forward again straight into the light of my sweet guide, whose holy eyes were glowing with a smile.] (Dante, trans., 3:48)

Dorigen's desire for virtuous behavior is heroic, as illustrated in her catalog of exemplary wives and virgins, and her posture as Narcissus's image reflects her need for a self outside the construction of masculine desire. Pietro Alighieri, writing on this passage, finds Narcissus allied with the moon, Luna, Dante's Lucina, through its population of water-colored shadows or shades—and *mulieres*—who incline to lovelessness, frigidity, coldness, virginity.[20] Their will reveals a sublunary connection with earth very like that of Dante's Piccarda, who wished to be chaste, and Dorigen's virgins and wives, whose Dante-like chastity becomes her image—a female tradition of moral strength. She needs a self outside the symbiotic relationship of Narcissus and Echo. Pietro glosses Narcissus as arrogance and Echo as good fame who loves and extols the arrogant, unless she is contemned by him.[21] Further, the use of the Narcissus image in Dante's phrase "amor fra l'omo e 'l fonte" ("love between the man and the spring") reminds of their unnatural and inhuman relationship.

The moon—not as chastity but as Diana—as an emblem of the female, is instrumental in making the rocks appear to disappear and thereby empowering Dorigen to reconstruct herself. The importance of the rocks to Dorigen has all along remained within her power to control and does not depend on masculine largess by squire, clerk, or knight. She merely needs to think less about her husband and more about herself, for which she needs the help of Diana. However, because it is Aurelius who acts to make the rocks appear to disappear, he calls upon the help of Lucina or Diana the moon, who controls the tides and whose movements are themselves controlled by the sun, her brother Apollo. Despite Aurelius's courtly and conventional allegiance to Venus, he petitions not just the moon and the sun but their pagan equivalents, Lucina and Apollo—sister and brother—in their natural roles as governors of the tides and the seasons, that is, astrologically, growth and vitality, for help in transforming the landscape. Chaucer is careful to establish the appropriate hierarchy: "Lucina the sheene" is "chief goddesse and queene" of the sea: "Though Neptunus have deitee in the see, / Yet emperisse aboven hym is she" (1045–48). Further, within this hierarchy, one "follower" of a regional governor is itself a ruler of other followers; for example, the moon follows and obeys the sun, but the moon also rules the seas. Note the underlying Echo/Narcissus relationship of Lucina and Apollo: Lucina's "desir" is "to be quyked and lighted of youre fir, / For which she folweth you ful bisily," but it is also natural and right that the sea "desireth" "To folwen hire, as she that is goddesse / Bothe in the see and ryveres moore and lesse" (1050–54). To request a flood, Aurelius therefore appeals to Apollo as the sun who dominates the moon, bypassing the ruler of tides. Once again Aurelius demonstrates his insensitivity to female desires.

This unusual invocation involves several levels of meaning for the tale. First, the relationship between the moon and the sun, as sister and brother, may initially suggest that Diana echoes or mirrors Apollo, in exactly the way Echo mirrored Narcissus, that Neptune, the sea, obeys Diana, the moon, and Aurelius the lover obeys and "echoes" the beloved, whether Dorigen or in some more profound sense, the patriarchal image of woman for Arveragus. Thus Pietro, in the same passage, states that as the moon she resembles a light, similar to the sun in size and beauty.[22] The invocation of a great flood here is also ironic, given the reason for Narcissus's spurning of Echo (his falling in love with his own image in the pool) and the means of his eventual death (drowning in that pool in an attempt to be joined with the beloved) and therefore the end of her love for him. While the cover that veils the rocks will indeed end the proposed love affair of Aurelius and Dorigen, it also reveals the extent of his falsity.

Second, Aurelius appeals to Apollo (1036–37) because the distraught lover is, like Amans in John Gower's *Confessio Amantis,* out of harmony with the vitality of nature. Lucina and Apollo also represent lord and lady of the universe, or Juno and Jove, who, in addition to Neptune (1047) and Pluto (1075), in the medieval schema of the cosmos represent the four rulers of the elements: air, fire, water, and earth.[23] Aurelius accordingly, but ironically, addresses Apollo as Lord and Governor of All Plants and Flowers in 1031–1245, somehow controlling the Chain of Being and in charge of all growing things, to alter the natural order and thereby fulfill the lover's sexual desire for another man's wife (1031–35). It is no wonder that Apollo fails to meet Aurelius's needs.

Third, the invocation is associated on a more cosmic level with the reference to fork-bearded Janus at the end of the tale, a reference that epitomizes the double standards, double vows, and double worlds of the principal characters. According to Macrobius, Apollo and Diana as the sun and the moon control the heavenly gates of day and night, and are therefore linked with the cosmic gatekeeper Janus.[24] Apollo was worshiped by the Greeks as the god of the door and Diana as the keeper of the city streets. These two planetary deities also represent knowledge of the past and the future, as if in echo of Janus's two faces. His name responsible for the month of January (as seen earlier in discussion of the role of Pandarus in *Troilus*, book 2), Janus looks back to the past and forward to the future and was regarded as the god of the door in both antiquity and the Middle Ages.[25] Invoked in the *Franklin's Tale* as a personification of the new year, Janus plays a role as god of beginnings and cosmic gatekeeper, spring and winter, the sun and moon as Apollo and Diana, at the moment the squire Aurelius travels to Orleans to obtain the clerk's help:

> Janus sit by the fyr, with double berd,
> And drynketh of his bugle horn the wyn;
> Biforn hym stant brawen of the tusked swyn,
> And "Nowel" crieth every lusty man. (1252–55)

Chaucer has apparently modified a detail contained in his chief source, the "Tale of Menedon," in which the anonymous lady's impossible request centers on a garden blooming in January ("del mese di gennaio, in quella terra, un bel giardino e grande, d'erbe e di fiori e d'alberi e di frutti copioso").[26] Chaucer's depiction of Janus emphasizes winter, as if the figure represented a kind of icon for the snowy-bearded Franklin himself as he was described in the portrait in the *General Prologue*.

But doorkeeper Janus sitting before the fire—inside—also reminds us of Dorigen sitting before the rocks—outside, alone, gazing into the sea, which contains the reflection of her husband's loss—her dark fantasy. Indeed, her name "Dorigen" might in part derive from the Anglo-Saxon *dor* ("door"), nominative plural and accusative *duru*, as if identifying the exit from the *hortus conclusus* in which Dorigen has been imprisoned by her gender for so long. Just as Janus keeps gates, so does she—for the garden of delights in which Aurelius wishes she would frolic and in which the compact between Dorigen and Aurelius was made. And Janus's double visage, looking backward and forward, is suggested by the forked beard of the Franklin's Janus; Janus's doubleness relates to the double vows and roles of Dorigen—wife and beloved, but like Echo without a self, or selfless, when she swears obedience to her husband but commands over her lover—and to the marriage within which those double vows apply that looks backward to the spouses' premarital courtly love but also forward to their married future. Or is their relationship meant to suggest beginning over and over again, in its emphasis on romance within marriage (where are the children, one might well ask?). Finally, within the description of Janus sitting before the fire singing

Noel, Chaucer implies a season cold and inhospitable to nature, an under-tone that may very well underscore the frigidity of Narcissus, but also the lack of children in the marriage because of Arveragus's absence.

Chaucer may wish to present the Franklin, who desires to achieve a so-cial position similar to that of the pilgrim Knight, as like the Squire, at-tending to an absent and irresponsible aristocracy for leadership that never comes. The image of Narcissus and Echo undercuts the aristocratic exposi-tion of a kind of free love—love without constraint—which becomes, like Dorigen's anxiety over her husband's departure and her selfless fantasy con-cerning the rocks, a "derke fantasye" impossible to maintain. Ultimately, Arveragus is a blind and self-deluded Narcissus echoed by Aurelius, an im-age constructed by the Franklin in the role of Dorigen, whose inquiry into "fredom" reflects frustration with masculine constraints in marriage, so-cial rankings, and art. It is interesting that the Franklin's own wife is ab-sent from the *Prologue*, like Arveragus from Dorigen, while the son about whom he complains remains unknowing, undisciplined. What of the Frank-lin's helplessness to reform his own son? The Franklin claims to be undis-ciplined and untutored in the techniques and backgrounds of rhetoric and the schools when he reveals his lack of familiarity with Parnassus and the language sacred to the Muses while repeating his desire for freedom: "I sleep nevere on the Mount of Pernaso, / Ne lerned Marcus Tullius Scithero. / Colours ne knowe I none, withouten drede, / But swiche colours as growen in the mede, / Or elles swiche as men dye or peynte" (721–25).

It is similarly no accident, one might conclude, that Chaucer undercuts even the Franklin's artistic motives in his tight, precise use of his sources, as he makes "fre" only with those changes most likely to point to Dori-gen's generosity toward others—and her freedom in constructing an iden-tity for herself outside the patriarchal binarism of the myth of Echo and Narcissus.

CHAPTER 10

Conclusion
The Artist Pygmalion, the Subject Chaucer,
and Self-Seduction

At the end of the *Canterbury Tales*, the Manciple warns the reader against telling the truth, for the sake of literal lives and friendships. The Parson, in contrast, insists on the need of the eternal soul to understand the truth. The necessary lies of the former, unfortunately, seem to have no place in the stripped-down clarity of the latter. The problem posed at the end of the *Tales* has been articulated at the beginning through the classical image of Zephirus, as the West Wind associated with fertility and renewal (the surface entertainment of *fabula*) and as the rapist of Chloris associated with violence (the underlying "abomination" of "arcana, veritas"). But even in the dream visions, mythological characters such as Venus and Priapus, Alceste or Alcyone, or Dido, pass through artificial landscapes removed from the reality of sexual frustration, rape, impotence, death, heresy and/or misogyny, in reality the actual subjects of these poetic narratives, or else within that sordid territory, as in the *Troilus*, the mythological images bejewel the text to describe the major characters and their world, but whose complex mythographies Chaucer uses as an invisible thread to join the underlying terrible meanings of the romance.

How, then, should the reader interpret the Retraction? Is Chaucer sincere, confessing as a result of his own Parson's homily, and suggesting therefore the power of his own word — Word — art over nature, or is even the Retraction a fable, a cloak for some unpleasant truth that Chaucer wants the reader to see as honorable and beautiful? As if stymied by conflicting counsel — the Manciple's Mother warns of the secular and political danger of loosing one's tongue and the Parson of the spiritual need to loosen one's tongue in confession — Chaucer rhetorically repudiates his lecherous love poetry for the sake of the Parson while presumably concealing his real feelings, whatever they are.

Toward the end of the *Canterbury Tales*, Chaucer moves ever closer to an explicit poeticized commentary on the theoretical nature and political necessity of the "lies of the poets." In the Ovidian-based tales — of the Physician, Pardoner, and Manciple — Chaucer explores the nature of poetic and especially fabulous poetic as counterfeit, fiction, and lie. This study

263

having begun with an examination of the *Manciple's Tale* and the political necessity of holding one's tongue, it appropriately ends with an examination of the other two Canterbury tales with sources in Ovid, and especially, given its crucial mythological image, the *Physician's Tale*, as a prologue to discussion of Chaucer's truthfulness in the Retraction. The Physician's image of counterfeiting, in nature and in art, and the shape changing of the con man Pardoner extend ever so slightly the "dark fantasy" of the Franklin and his characters, just as the Franklin's tale-telling extended ever so slightly the fairy-tale fantasies of both feminist Alisoun of Bath and the more cynical Merchant. Their tale-telling, however subversive of the traditional mythographizing of the old Knight, has concealed, as has been the case with all of the tales examined in this study, sexual secrets and politically difficult truths that fabulous narrative was originally intended to veil. Rape, especially, but also impotence, misogyny, violence, adultery, bastardy, narcissism, lust, homicide, incest, homosexuality—whatever the dark secret, the speaker's manipulation of classical fable and allusion has masked them, just as the reader's understanding of their mythographic signification has helped to reveal them.

For both the Pardoner and the Physician, the use of counterfeit—of God or of nature—helps them to achieve their worldly and selfish ends, unfortunately, the less than Augustinian love of neighbor turned back to oneself. The counterfeiting, more deception than imitation, ultimately undermines self-knowledge, if any, in the case of each: the Physician's wealth is a poverty, as his learning and use of classical sources (Livy) are literalistic, impoverished; the Pardoner's confessed duplicity and evil are turned to good, despite his intentions. The artistry with with each pilgrim plies his trade (and tells his tale) is similarly mixed, more self-consciously in the case of the Pardoner, who in his confession provides his homily as an exemplum of the kind of deceit he normally practices and not as entertainment for the other pilgrims. And a larger joke is rehearsed by Chaucer, in taking the prototypes for both Physician and Pardoner from mythological figures found in the *Roman de la Rose*—a poem about courtly love. If there exists a kind of lust in greed, in deception of others, and in artistry, Chaucer may be saying, the Physician, the Pardoner, and the Poet all may need to seduce their victims, as in a sense each has seduced himself.

The tales of the Physician and Pardoner in Fragment VI, like their tellers, have occasionally been linked as a miniature, unified group sharing a source in the influential thirteenth-century satire of Jean de Meun, *Le Roman de la Rose*.[1] From this work Chaucer takes passages on Appius and Virgine (5589–5658) as well as on nature and art (16177–90) to help mold his characters and structure their relationships in the *Physician's Tale*, and from the confession of Faus Semblant (11065ff.) to create his Pardoner.[2] In addition, Chaucer likens the tales' tellers: both the "healing" Physician and the

Pardoner profit from the sickness of others, love gold, and literalistically view death as a terminus; both accordingly tell tales exhibiting spiritual sterility and the power of death.[3] Both tales also probe the nature of evil, despite the Physician's moral deficiency and inability to understand its cause, so that the two tales can be read together with the *Franklin's Tale* as a triad:[4] the perception of sin, like the understanding of poetry in the Middle Ages, involved seeing beneath the surface reality and therefore constituted a problem for all three of these pilgrims.

If it is true, as Katherine Trower argues, that the *Physician's Tale* functions as a "prelude to the Pardoner's entire performance,"[5] then the mythological references in the first tale may also relate to those in the second, although at first glance there appears to be no mythological reference at all in the *Pardoner's Prologue and Tale*, whereas five references exist in the *Physician's Tale* (Pigmalion [14]; Phebus [37]; Pallas [49]; Bacchus [58]; and Venus [59]). Just as the reference to Pygmalion in line 14 of the *Physician's Tale* can be traced to the *Roman*, however, so also in the source for the Pardoner, in the confession of Faus Semblant in the *Roman*, there exists a reference to Proteus (11181) that Chaucer omits, but that controls the image of inside and outside that dominates the Pardoner's character in both the *Prologue* and *Tale.*

Further, both of these Ovidian mythological figures, Pygmalion and Proteus, bear some relation to counterfeiting, a major theme in the pilgrims' deceptions of others and of self and to a lesser extent manifested in their tales. In the Physician's case, he creates or counterfeits astrological images for his patients to counteract malefic influences, as the reader learns from the *General Prologue* ("Wel koude he fortunen the ascendent / Of his ymages for his pacient" [417–18]); so too does Virginius's daughter Virginia counterfeit the excellence of Nature, and Pygmalion sculpt a statue so beautiful that it is given life by Venus. In the Pardoner's case, he openly admits, "I wol noon of the apostles *countrefete*" (447; my emphasis). In Chaucer's main source for the Pardoner, however, the deceitful figure Faus Semblant compares himself with the shape-shifting Proteus. Mythographic commentary on this god, in fact, may have shaped Chaucer's characterization, given his own "confession" (like that of Faus Semblant) and his abrupt, protean changes in behavior (particularly his sales pitch at the end).

Chaucer's interest in "lying fictions," fables, fantasies, stories, and parables explains his selection of a Roman historical tale about justice—in which Virginius, father of Virginia (609), justly defends her virginity—for the Physician, and of a Gospel-like parable about morality told by the dishonest, protean Pardoner. Most interesting of all, Chaucer may have linked these two tales, their pilgrims and their sources, because of a significant literary connection in the Carolingian Latin poem by Theodulf of Orleans on "Books I Used to Read" known to Chaucer (as we saw in chapter 3), in which two mythological figures in the same line, Proteus and the Virgin, epitomize the chief mythological images in these two tales. Theodulf, after giving examples of the lying fictions of his favorite classical poets, Ovid and Virgil among them, in a conjunction of images drawn from Virgil's *Georgics* 4.387ff., mentions Proteus, who signifies truth ("Sic Proteus verum ... repingit"), and Virgo (Erigone, the Virgin), who signifies justice ("sic iustum Virgo repingit" [23]). One tale literally prefaces the other, in the single line from the famous poem by Theodulf.

The Physician as Pygmalion and Virgin Artistry

As glosses for his characters, the Physician uses two medieval strands of signification on Pygmalion—on the virginity of the statue brought to life and on the artistry of the sculptor. The first, on its virginity, characterizes Virginia, the "ivory girl," as physically and spiritually ideal, an icon whose character is rigidly fixed and essentialized as unchanging in her perfection (like the perfect self Sylvia Plath wishes to create in "Edge," the last poem she wrote before her death). The second, on the artistry of the sculptor, helps to darken the selfish motivation of the paternal and judicial authorities, Virginius and Apius, who ape the *artifex* Pygmalion by falling in love with their own images—and who cannot abide change in or loss of what they love. Pygmalion also typifies the ideal physician, one who might bring the dead back to life, and thus projects the Physician's heroic and self-justifying fantasy of his vocation.

The Physician refers to Pygmalion in a hyperbolic description of the handiwork of Nature, the perfect Virginia: "For Nature hath with sovereyn diligence / Yformed hire in so greet excellence, / As though she wolde seyn, 'Lo! I, Nature, / Thus kan I forme and peynte a creature, / What that me list; who kan me countrefete?'" (9–13). No one else can "countrefete" as well as Nature, she boasts, even renowned artists and engravers such as Pygmalion: "Pigmalion nought, though he ay forge and bete, / Or grave, or peynte; for I dar wel seyn / Apelles, Zanzis, sholde werche in veyn / Outher to grave, or peynte, or gorge, or bete, / If they presumed me to countrefete" (14–18). Pygmalion's gifts as an artist in creating a realistic and beautiful statue resulted in Venus's endowing it with life, but unlike the *artifex* Nature, who creates for God ("I made hire to the worshipe of my lord" [26]), he foolishly falls in love with his own creation. The difference between the two artist-creators grows out of their motivations and therefore their attitudes toward their art, one of worship of God or of self—the pleasure of the body.

In Ovid's misogynistic fable, Pygmalion disdains to choose a wife from the Propoetides, who deny the divinity of Venus by sacrificing guests (and who therefore incur the goddess's wrath and, as punishment, are transformed into bulls). Pygmalion "had seen these women spending their lives in shame, and, disgusted with the faults which in such full measure nature had given the female mind [*offensus vitiis, quae plurima menti / femineae natura dedit*], he lived unmarried" (*Metamorphoses* 10.243–46). After he creates, and falls in love with, a truly beautiful statue of a woman, he prays to Venus to have as wife "similis mea ... eburnae" ("one like my ivory maid" [276]), and his request is granted. Paphos, the daughter of their union, gives birth to Cinyras, and Cinyras fathers the incestuous Myrrha, mother of beautiful Adonis.[6]

Chaucer's description of Virginia is without that misogyny so prevalent in Ovid and in some of his commentators. Fourteen-year-old Virginia's perfect virginity on the literal, or natural, level allies her with the ivory statue because of her skin's incarnation of the whiteness of the lily and the redness of the rose. In addition, the sun is identified as the god whose rays suggest Samson-like locks (and who, like Nature, occupies the role of *artifex* here in relation to the "ivory girl"): "Phebus dyed hath hire tresses grete / Lyk to the stremes of his burned heete" (37–38). On the figurative level, her singular purity endows her with discretion in answering (48) and the wisdom of Pallas Athena (49), but also "alle hire wordes, moore and lesse, / Sownynge in vertu and in gentillesse" (53–54). Most important, her wisdom is natural and not fabricated, the result of what Jean de Meun has identified as the only way human nature can reproduce itself: "No countrefeted termes hadde she / To seme wys, but after hir degree / She spak" (51–53). Because of her virtue and self-control, she avoids Bacchus (wine), who, like youth, is drawn to Venus (lechery):

> Bacus hadde of hir mouth right no maistrie;
> For wyn and youthe douth Venus encresse,
> As men in fyr wol casten oille or greesse. (58–60)

The Terentian aphorism, "Venus without Bacchus and Ceres grows cold," used by Alisoun and the Merchant (and also appearing in the *Parlement of Foules*) to convey the sterility of sexual love that does not reproduce, is perhaps echoed here to suggest the coldness of Virginia's chaste and singular perfection.

What most intrigues Chaucer (in the Ovidian text) is the creation of the statue as an image of chaste and singular beauty at a time of great lechery among women on Paphos, but an image granted life as a result of Pygmalion's desire for her—life as Pygmalion's wife and as the great-grandmother of Myrrha, whose incestuous love for her father Cinyras mirrors, in a sense, Pygmalion's "incestuous" love for his own creation.

Ovidian glosses on Pygmalion, whose story appears in *Metamorphoses* 10.243ff., initially highlight the virginity of the statue and only later the sculptor's incomparable artistry in this fable of moral transformation. But all the commentators, whether the twelfth-century Arnulf of Orleans, the thirteenth-century Giovanni del Virgilio, or the fourteenth-century Bersuire and Boccaccio, stress Pygmalion's motivation as illicit desire, even though the later glossators establish this catalytic love as responsible for her miraculous transformation into flesh.[7] Later Ovidian commentators prefer to delineate the role of the creator, whether regarded as a forger, a fabricator, or more figuratively and importantly for the Physician, a preacher. In the fourteenth-century *Ovide moralisé*, the artist occupies a Neoplatonic role as one of nature's forgers ("ses forgierres" [10.3564]) whose creation metamorphoses into a woman in response to his passion and avarice—that is, for all the wrong reasons ("Et tant l'ama qu'il la fist dame / De son regne et de son avoir" [10.3565–66]).[8] Bersuire similarly adapts the Arnulfian portrait of the artist to that of the *praedicatores*, or preachers, who "know how to sculpt and paint a soul with corrections and virtues" in the manner of Pygmalion (*Ovidius*, p. 152, trans. p. 355). Although his ivory girl therefore typifies the *sanctimonialem*, or holy woman, ivory because she is said to be chaste, frigid, weighty, and honest (p. 152), the statue's transformation into life illustrates a pejorative fall into carnality and vice for both preacher and holy woman. The preacher, who attempts to make an ivory image—to form holy women in chastity and spiritual habits—sometimes slips, desiring the transformation of the good person (the nonliving statue) into a foolish, living one. If the "goddess of wantonness," Venus,

> causes that chaste woman to feel the goads of the flesh and changes her from a good person into a foolish one, then Pygmalion—the preacher—himself seeks and desires this alteration from Venus. When they return in the customary manner to their colloquies they find themselves so changed that she who had been ivory becomes flesh and he who abhorred women begins to desire the filth of the flesh. These carnal people then take one another and sometimes produce sons (Bersuire, *Ovidius*, p. 152, trans. pp. 355–56)

Bersuire's incestuous relationship of preacher and the holy woman he is teaching presents a situation very like the one Virginius seeks to avoid by his drastic measure.

Chaucer apparently seized upon the original typing of Pygmalion as artist to use as a foil for the father who created Virginia and for the Physician who tells the tale in part because of another source, for Nature, in Jean de Meun's *Roman*. There it is the poet Jean de Meun who confesses his inadequacy in reproducing Nature as a *figura*, a Pygmalion-like personification rather than Nature boasting of ability unmatched by human equivalents:

> Bien la vous vousisse descrire,
> Mais mes sens n'i pourrait soufire.
> Mes sens! Qu'ai je dit? c'est du meins.

Non ferait veir nus sens humains,
Ne par voiz vive ne par notes.

[I would willingly describe her to you, but my sense is not equal to it.
My sense! What have I said? That's the least one could say. No
human sense would show her, either vocally or in writing.]
(16165–69; 4:135; trans. p. 274)

Philosophers such as Plato, Aristotle, Algus, Euclid, and Ptolemy, despite
their great reputations as writers, were unable to describe Nature; nor could
well-known sculptors and painters describe her beauty. "Ne Pygmalion
entaillier" (16177), "Nor could Pygmalion fashion her" (trans. pp. 274), or
Parrasius, Apelles, Miro, and Polycletus (16178–84, 4:136). For Jean, Na-
ture's handiwork can be duplicated only by regeneration and reproduc-
tion of kind rather than by poets; even the alchemist, who understands
how to transform base metal to gold, fails to duplicate Nature. Jean de
Meun's metaphor, however, for the natural ability to regenerate—in the
Book of Nature—centers on the human activity of book copying and
writing. Following this digression, Nature's priest Genius recites "Les fig-
ures representables / De toutes choses corrompables / Qu'il ot escrites en
son livre, / Si con Nature les li livre" ("the representative shapes of all cor-
ruptible things that he had written in his book, just as Nature had given
them to him" [16282–84]). Yet Pygmalion also appears elsewhere in the
Roman, to describe the moment when the lover has fallen in love with the
rose (when Venus will shoot a hot arrow into the image) and his fantasies
create an image for him to love.[9] The *Roman* version, however, does not
stress the statue's virginity, of which Ovid and medieval glosses on his
tale make much, unless in the idea and existence of a virgin that op-
poses the work of Nature in perpetuating the species. Chaucer is clearly
more interested in Virginia's exemplary excellence here than in Nature's
artistry.

Instead, Chaucer emphasizes the fraudulence of the fatherly authorities
in this tale by utilizing the *Roman*'s image of "counterfeit" in increasingly
pejorative ways. First, Virginia also copies or counterfeits the father genet-
ically, as does Nature who copies (we think of Genius reading from her
"Book" in the *Roman* passage). Second, whereas Chaucer introduces the
word "counterfeit" as artistic imitation when it first occurs in line 13, in
echo of Alan of Lille's counterfeiting and coining imagery in *De planctu
Naturae*, gradually Chaucer exchanges the abstract role of the *artifex* for
that of the coiner, and finally the counterfeiter, agent of fraud:

For Nature hath with sovereyn diligence
Yformed hire in so greet excellence,
As though she wolde seyn, "Lo! I, Nature,

Thus kan I forme and peynte a creature,
Whan that me list; who kan me *countrefete?*" (9–13; my emphasis)

"Counterfeit" appears again in images of jewelry making, coining, and painting in line 18 in which Nature contrasts herself as *artifex* with the artist Pygmalion:

Pigmalion noght, though he ay forge and bete,
Or grave, or peynte; for I dar wel seyn
Apelles, Zanzis, sholde werche in veyn
Outher to grave, or peynte, or gorge, or bete,
If the presumed me to *countrefete.* (14–18; my emphasis)

Finally, "counterfeit" conveys the idea of reproduction as fraud, deceit, untruth, in line 51 in the description of Virginia's inner, natural purity, as noted earlier: "No *countrefeted* termes hadde she / To seme wys; but after hir degree / She spak" (51–53; my emphasis).

The counterfeiting image in this last usage conveys clearly the idea of falsity, deceit, alien to Virginia but not to Claudius and Apius, or to the Physician in his greed for gold (like Pygmalion's love of ivory) and in drug arrangements with the apothecaries. The Physician may wish to convince other pilgrims of his honesty by telling this rigidly moralistic tale, but his reference to Pygmalion as a counterfeiter of Nature—a type of the artist who turns ivory into flesh, in an unusual inversion of the alchemist's goal in transforming base metal to gold—may remind the reader that the Physician profits from the plague, that is, turns dying flesh into gold. He joins Apius, Claudius, and even Virginius (some would add Chaucer himself) as types of Pygmalion—those fraudulent and counterfeiting "fathers" who reify others, exchanging life for imagery and abstraction.

Virginia's involvement with her father, the false judge, and the lying "cherl" who petitions this judge for the return of his thrall, supposedly lost since birth, leads the reader back to the role of Pygmalion in the story—leads to the false preachers described by Bersuire. In a sense, the father who protects her best self, or image, her physical and spiritual purity, by cutting off her head so that Apius will not exercise his carnal appetites, grants her eternal life, like Pygmalion who gave his ivory statue life. In another, opposite, sense, this destruction reverses the process of Pygmalion (and of Nature), whose love for his statue compels his prayer to Venus for life: he brings life to the nonliving, whereas Virginius brings death to the living—even on the spiritual level, for he commits a deadly sin. Virginius, who has originally given his child life, then withdraws it; however, it is questionable whether his murder of her counts as love at all. Finally, Apius's desire to possess Virginia may be Pygmalion-like in that as judge he represents the literalist who demands the letter, the body, without love and marriage—

accident without essence, like the lover violating the rosebud at the end of the *Roman de la Rose* (where the Pygmalion passage appears). The association of Pygmalion with the false preacher, of course, calls up the character of the con man Pardoner, to whom we now turn.

The Pardoner as Protean Fals-Semblant

The Pardoner, who counterfeits a religious man through his humble appearance, his "false seeming," is very like the Physician in his fraud and greed. In terms of the patristic implications of his character, he can be seen as an exemplum of sin, a scriptural eunuch, or an Augustinian Old Man.[10] Given his apparent external appearance and role as a pardoner and his true disfigured inner nature, the metaphor of outside versus inside seems to dominate his *Prologue* and *Tale*.[11] Given the disparity between inner and outer, the model for the Pardoner exists in Faus Semblant (False Seeming) from Jean de Meun's *Roman de la Rose*, who appears as Fals-Semblant in a long passage that comprises Fragment C of the Middle English translation occasionally attributed to Chaucer.

On the basis of this correspondence, Carolyn Dinshaw has argued provocatively for a "eunuch hermeneutics" to show in both characters a similar "breakdown of interpretive stability" illustrated through the change of clothing of Fals-Semblant.[12] Approaching patristic exegesis from the stance of gender and psychoanalytic theory, Dinshaw notes that "The hermeneutic I have identified as heterosexual discards the surface of the text, the letter and its wanton seductions, for the uncovered truth, but the eunuch suggests that the passage between the letter and any sentence within is not so smooth, is not guaranteed" (pp. 158–59). Dinshaw's rhetorical strategy here unfortunately makes literal the metaphor of body and soul while retaining the figurative medieval analogy with letter and sentence, or meaning, gloss. She interprets the Pardoner's literal body, maimed and "other" in its alleged homosexuality, both as a literal "text" to be read (or glossed) and, impossibly, as the "truth" beneath the false, integumental cloak of fiction. His "unclassifiable body" points to the possibility of an unmediated poetics, of the incarnate Word, or the obviation of "all difference," even though the construction of the Pardoner literally demands a poetics of absence.

Given the Augustinian concept of reading used as the basis for Dinshaw's version of this poetic, Fals-Semblant's change of clothing also compares with the Pardoner's counterfeiting. In Chaucer's *Romaunt* passage, the personification's "false seeming" depends less on boxes, chests, or doors (all images in the *Pardoner's Prologue* and *Tale*) than on clothing, particularly religious habits and robes used as signs of ecclesiastical titles and social positions, and hence, more figuratively, as signs of identities and roles whose continual changing Fals-Semblant adopts, in the manner of the sea-god Proteus, in order to gain his avaricious ends. Chaucer first transforms this clothing imagery in his *Prologue* and *Tale* into the more Christian emblem of body as a cover for the soul and then adapts the shape shifting of Fals-Semblant into the many faces of the Pardoner revealed in his confessional, his homiletic tale, and his concluding sales pitch. The purpose of this analysis is to locate the key to the Pardoner's "poetics of absence" in a mythological figure absent from the *Pardoner's Prologue* but present in the *Romaunt*—Proteus.

In his "sermon" (*Romaunt* 6136), Fals-Semblant continually uses clothing imagery to convey the idea that, because he can deceitfully manipulate his outer appearance as an ecclesiast, he can conceal his nefarious intentions. This concealment is more facile, in fact, for the religious than the secular person: "And certeynly, sikerest hidyng / Is undirnethe humblest clothing. / Religiouse folk ben full *covert*; / Seculer folk ben more *appert*" (6147–50; *Roman* 11011–16; my emphasis). This tension between closed and open, when used by the deceptive religious, allows a perfect cover-up ("I mene of fals religious, / That stoute ben and malicious, / That wolen in an abit goo, / And setten not her herte therto" [6157–60; *Roman* 11023–26]), for the world assumes that appearance reflects reality: "'I have a robe of religioun, / Thanne am I all religious'" (6188–89; *Roman* 11054–55). Of course, Fals-Semblant continues, "Abit ne makith neithir monk ne frere" (6192; *Roman* 11058). Virtuous actions and faith ("clene lyf and devocioun" [6193]), not words, clothing, or estates (6207–10, 6215–18), remain key to intentions (*Roman* 11079–80). Conversely, says Fals-Semblant, those who wear worldly clothes do not necessarily lead a wicked life or lose their souls (6227–30; *Roman* 11091–94); it is possible for worldly clothing to hide a good soul: "Men may in seculer clothes see / Florishen hooly religioun" (6232–33; *Roman* 11096–97). It is the intention that affects the thought and the deed: "Good herte makith the goode thought; / The clothing yeveth ne reveth nought" (6253–54; *Roman* 11117–78).

Fals-Semblant uses a conventional image often employed in discussions of letter and figure—on how to read biblical texts—to explain his use of disguise. This metaphor of kernel and husk, also frequently used by Chaucer (for example, in the *Nun's Priest's Tale*), suggests the worthlessness (hence, falsity) of the outer husk as opposed to the value of the true kernel, in an apt analogy for poetry. The image has also been used by theologians to suggest the Incarnation. However, Fals-Semblant reverses the dialectic, boasting: " 'But to what ordre that I am sworn, / I take the *strawe*, and lete the *corn*'" (6353–54; *Roman* 11216–17; my emphasis). He means that he takes the false, worthless straw and leaves the true corn by adopting the outer garment of the religious: " 'To gyle folk I enhabit; / I axe nomore but her abit. / What wole ye more in every wise? / Right as me lyst, I me disgise'" (6355–58; *Roman* 11218–21). His true desire is concealed by the false outer "cover," but his intention to deceive subverts any real truth: " 'Wel can I wre me undir wede; / Unlyk is my word to my dede' " (6359–60; *Roman* 11222–23). Later in the fragment, in a passage interpolated into the *Roman* by the C translator, Fals-Semblant will connect the literal text with the body, which could be cleansed (absolved) more readily (so he argues, falsely) if it had no gloss (soul): " 'And if men wolde ther-geyn appose / The *nakid* test, and lete the glose, / It myghte soone *assoiled* be' " (6555–57; my emphasis).

Chaucer's depiction of the Pardoner as a false seemer also involves items of clothing, or accessories, or covers—for example, the mitten he attempts to sell (372); his "male," or bag (920), containing relics and pardons; and, in the *General Prologue* portrait, the careful description of his head covering (or lack of hood), carried in his wallet, the veronica sewn on his cap, the veil of Our Lady. But, in addition, the Pardoner remains aware of the idea of divestiture of sin as if sin were clothing: in requesting pilgrims to purchase pardons, he asks the Host, whose tavern might be likely to foster the kinds of tavern sins about which he has been homilizing,[13] to come forth first, "For he is moost *envoluped* in synne" (942; my emphasis). He also asks him to "divest himself," not of sin, or wolf's skin, but by opening a money bag that is both clothing and symbol of avarice: "Unbokele anon thy purs" (945). As if the Host understands his "clothing," the "skin" of the old man, as false, unholy, deceitful, that which the snake leaves behind (to recall the Pauline metaphor), and therefore a remnant or relic of his existence in contrast to the relics of saints (bones, rings, sails), which often do not perish, or become corrupted, he exclaims, "Thou woldest make me kisse thyn *olde breech,* / And swere it were a relyk of a seint" (948–49; my emphasis). Further, as if the Pardoner's best "relic" were his masculinity, the Host insists that his "coillons" "shul be shryned in an hogges toord" (955).

In place of the extensive clothing and disguise imagery used by Fals-Semblant to emphasize the outer garb as a frequently deceptive cover for intention and spiritual state of the soul, the Pardoner primarily portrays the body as an appropriate cover for, or reflection of, the soul. For example, in his sermon to the pilgrims at the opening of his tale, the Pardoner suggests that sin—specifically, drunkenness, a type of gluttony and a metonymy for the loss of reason—disfigures the soul's cover, the body, so that one may rightly read the body to understand the state of the soul. He cries, "O dronke man, *disfigured* is thy face" (551; my emphasis), for example: through the figure of the evil Pardoner, Chaucer wishes the reader to see disfigurement as unnatural and evil. The clothing metaphors of which Fals-Semblant is so fond here become metaphors for the relationship between body and soul, with the Pardoner homilizing, "For dronkenesse is verray *sepulture* / Of mannes wit and his discrecioun" (558–59; my emphasis); that is, if the best of man, his rationality, succumbs to drunkenness, dies, he therefore appears a fool and his behavior (external appearance) becomes a sepulcher, or cover, for his dead wit (= corpse). But, in addition, the Pardoner denigrates the outer covering of the body—and organs within the body, which themselves cover and shelter—because of their temptation to sin: "O wombe! O bely! O stynkyng cod" (534).

The literalistic materialism of Fals-Semblant is mirrored in the Pardoner's emphasis on outer as inner, on body as a reflection of soul, on body as itself text. Unfortunately, the drunken Pardoner, like Fals-Semblant, also understands the carnal literally as the basic text, one to be read without gloss—without spiritual understanding, which, as Saint Augustine notes in *De doctrina Christiana* 3.5, leads to the death of the soul.[14]

Thus, within the tale, the Old Man whom the rioters meet not only longs to be inside the cover of earth, safe (" 'Allas, whan shul my bones been at reste?' " [733]), but also laments the loss of his body (" 'Lo how I vanysshe, flessh, and blood, and skyn'" [732]), which, as the covering for his soul, constitutes his earthly life and his human identity. For the Old Man, the body *is* the soul: he takes the analogy literally, to understand that the fact of carnality, the outer cover, ensures life; when it goes, one must add another, as in the Old Man's request for a shroud: "Ye, for an heyre clowt to wrappe me!" (736).

As with the Pardoner and the Old Man, the sin of the rioters is one of literalism, anticipated by Fals-Semblant: they understand the spirit carnally, and therefore attempt to slay death as if it were mortal,[15] swearing by "Goddes armes" (692) and "I make avow to Goddes digne bones" (695). There is, of course, one way to slay death (or diminish its importance), as the moral of the tale makes clear: by belief in Christ, who died for love of man, one attains eternal life, by means of valuing the soul, spirit, above temporal good, the body.

Throughout his tale, the Host and the rioters illustrate well the Pardoner's homily on the sin of swearing (Male Bouche?), but, in addition, their oaths often center on an anomaly, that is, God's body, God's bones. If the body truly reflects the state of the soul, where is God's body? Christ, God incarnated in human shape, can be said to be a shape shifter, and therefore for Christians to swear by his outer covering, his "garment" of flesh, is to affirm the paradox of his birth, or therefore belief in Christ. And yet, to swear without meaning it, to swear by God's body while demonstrating singular sinfulness (as do the rioters, and the Host), is to seem falsely, to imitate Fals-Semblant. In the Introduction to the *Prologue,* the Host swears "by nayles and by blood" (288), and "By corpus bones" (314; he means Corpus Domini, By our Lord's body); in the *Pardoner's Tale,* the rioters swear "By Goddes precious herte," "By his nayles" (651), "By the blood of Crist that is in Hayles" (652), "By Goddes armes" (654), and in general the company of young folk in Flanders therefore tatter their faith in Christ: "Our blissed Lordes body they totere" (474).

The problem of faith in a world in which God's body is torn and scattered is crucial to the meaning of the *Pardoner's Prologue and Tale* and its antecedent in the *Romaunt*. Fals-Semblant's favorite "disguise," of sheep masking the wolf, probably echoes the shepherding image of Gregory's *Cura pastoralis* drawn from Matt. 7:15 and commonly used to designate the relationship between pastor (literally, shepherd, from *pastorus*) and flock, whose ideal exemplar is Christ, Jean de Meun's Bon Pasteur. Chaucer, whose Fragment C does not continue that far in its translation, does include the image in lines 6259–68 when he envisages the likely but grim consequences of a false wolf disguised as a sheep among sheep (*Roman* 11123ff.). Further, as a predator, Fals-Semblant confesses that he even prefers to pray and recite the Pater Noster and thereby cover ("wrie") his foxlike nature ("foxerie") "Under a cope of papelardie," hypocrisy (6793–96; *Roman* 11523–24).

Jean de Meun and later Chaucer connect the chief ecclesiastical sin in the Middle Ages, avarice, with the conventional image of the wolf as a type of the Devil, when they identify the Antichrist as the father of Fals-Semblant. Fals-Semblant declares about himself that he is "Of Antecristes men," those who wear the "abit of hoolynesse" but live in wickedness, appearing to be "lambren" but "inward we, withouten fable, / Ben gredy wolves ravysable, / We enviroune bothe lond and se; / With all the world werreyen we" (7013–18; *Roman* 11716–19). The image, and the role, might very well have been created for Chaucer's Pardoner, a wolf masquerading as a sheep. (It is an image also used, incorrectly, by the Physician.)

Most interesting, given the Pardoner's insistence on shriving the other pilgrims, Fals-Semblant suggests skinning as the only means of divesting the wolf of his false but simple garment of the religious—although once divested of his skin the wolf would die (7311–20; *Roman* 11995–12001). Is the wolf's "unskinning" equivalent to Fals-Semblant's (or the Pardoner's) confession? Or is his (their) apparent sincerity in confessing only another cover-up? Probably so—Fals-Semblant, like the Pardoner, not only reveals, but revels in, his perfidy; contrition is absent. And because Love needs—in fact, has already begun—to learn the tricks of False Seeming to win the rose, in Jean's *Roman,* after this alarming confession the Lover swears he believes the thief Fals-Semblant, who, in Jean de Meun, "with the face of treachery, white without and black within, knelt down on the spot and thanked him" (Guillaume, *Roman,* trans. p. 209).

How then does this "dialectic" affect our understanding of the Pardoner's pitch to the pilgrims—an analogue for Chaucer's similar Retraction at the end of the *Canterbury Tales*? In Jean's *Roman,* Faus Semblant, after his confession/sermon, uses the trick of apparent sincerity to beguile Male Bouche; this convoluted allegory may help to explain the curious shift of the Pardoner from apparent openness and sincerity to professional slickness, followed by manufactured sincerity. In the *Roman* the fraudulent man disguised as a religious seems sincerely to aid (but in fact exploits for his own ends) Love, in gaining Fair Welcome for the lover and overthrowing Reason. His goal instead is the triumph of falsity, disorder, itself: False Seeming *is* the son of the Antichrist. Apparently pledging his loyalty to Amor, Faus Semblant then joins the rest of Love's Barons in aiding Amaunt by attacking Male Bouche, who holds Bel Acueil (Fair Welcome) inside the castle and thereby prevents Amaunt from capturing the rose by foul-mouthing his intentions. To overcome Male Bouche, Faus Semblant and Astenance Contreinte (Lady Constrained Abstinence) disguise themselves as pilgrims, Astenance Constrainte as a Beguine and Faus Semblant as brother Seier, and use their apparent sincerity, but in fact cunning eloquence—particularly the reinterpretation of the young lover as a friend of the slanderous Male Bouche—to urge the latter's confession, after which Faus Semblant treacherously, horribly, strangles Male Bouche.

In a sense, the Pardoner's sincerity at the end of his tale tests the pilgrims' belief in God and their spirituality. The Pardoner admits that his saints' bones are those of sheep, but if the spirit and not the body is important, then buying them is neither relevant nor helpful. And if the bones *are* saints' bones, to buy and sell them would be dishonest, blasphemous. Saints' relics, like God's body, represent symbols, or signs, of faith: the Eucharist, God's body, is literally God's body and also a sign of renewing grace. (It is no accident that the rioters' drink kills, unlike the wine of the Eucharist that enlivens; they also "kill" Christ with their literalism: "And Cristes blessed body they torente" [709], although the young hasarder swears "By God and by the hooly sacrement!" [757].)[16] Thus, the Pardoner here appears to offer the pilgrims absolution, or cleansing, when he asks to "assoille" them, divest them of dirt, as if they wore dirty clothing (= sinful bodies):

> "Looke which a seuretee is it to yowe alle
> That I am in youre felaweshipe yfalle,
> That may *assoille* yow, bothe moore and lasse,
> Whan that the soule shal fro the body passe." (937–40; my emphasis)

But is this absolution valid if the Pardoner's intent is warped? Can a soiled pardoner cleanse others?

One other explanation of the Pardoner's final pitch to the pilgrims occurs through the image of Proteus, which Fals-Semblant employs in the long passage ending with his shocking admission that he takes the straw and leaves the corn. Projecting a godhead attainable despite constantly changing forms and identities, Fals-Semblant suggests that one shape will never be sufficient once deceit is the goal, which makes the constant changing of garments (or therefore roles, estates, external identities) very like that of the sea-god and shape shifter Proteus:

> "For Protheus, that cowde hym chaunge
> In every shap, homly and straunge,
> Cowde nevere sich gile ne tresoun
> As I; for I com never in toun
> There as I myghte knowen be,
> Though men me bothe myght here and see.
> Full wel I can my clothis chaunge,
> Take oon, and make another straunge.
> Now am I knyght, now chasteleyn,
> Now prelat, and now chapeleyn." (6319–28; *Roman* 11181–91)

As a religious, Fals-Semblant appears to be divorced from the world, but in fact remains part of it, deeply immersed in it, through his super-Protean shape shifting. One Proteus image he uses later suggests that the garment he puts on, or the shape he changes into, is the world itself:

> "My paleis and myn hous make I
> There men may renne ynne openly,
> And sey that I the world forsake,
> But al amydde I bilde and make
> My hous, and swimme and pley therynne,
> Bet than a fish doth with his fynne." (7003–8; *Roman* 11709–12)

Proteus's shape shifting as well aptly characterizes our Pardoner in his abrupt and hypocritical changes in behavior. This classical sea-god — who appears in Horace, *Epistles* 1.1.90, Virgil, *Georgics* 4.388, and Ovid, *Metamorphoses* (various passages, but especially 2.9 and 8.731), and in a recapitulation of the *Georgics* passage in *Fasti* 1.378, as a wily shape shifter and sea-god able to change form from that of lion, to boar, to snake, to bull, and then to stone, tree, stream, and flame — represents, in Bersuire's glosses on the *Metamorphoses* 2.9, false and vain men in the home of the sun of justice who have a false rather than a real existence ("ficti & vani homines qui pictam habent apparentiam non realem existentiam") ("false and empty men who have a feigned appearance, not a real existence"), including hypocrites, false friends, and flatterers, very like our Pardoner. "Such men can be called changeful gods because their shape or their goodness are not known; the reason for this is that they easily change themselves into different shapes (*in diuersas figuras*). Therefore they are properly called changeful gods (*Dii ambigui*) — that is, uncertain men, changeable and inconstant. About such men, it is said in Ps. 77:41, 57: 'They turned back and tempted God and were turned aside as a crooked bow'" (*Ovidius*, p. 47, trans. p. 152).

In another tradition, Proteus is glossed by medieval mythographers Servius and Giovanni del Virgilio and handbook compilers Third Vatican Mythographer and Thomas Walsingham as a type of the soul incarcerated within the body whose vices must be purged. Virgil depicts Proteus in the *Georgics* as an old man whose prophetic ability and understanding of medicine make him valuable — if one can fetter him strongly enough that his "wiles" shatter themselves in vain, that is, his ability to assume various shapes ("vim duram et vincula capto / tende; doli circum haec demum frangentur inanes" ("With stern force and fetters make fast the captive; thereon alone his wiles will shatter themselves in vain" [4.399–4.400]). This shape changing is therefore interpreted by Servius (in a passage quoted directly by Thomas) as various vices from which men should cut themselves off, presumably in order to emulate divinity, which in Proteus is his *prudentia* (or, as Theodulf of Orleans would have it, his truth;[17] in the Third Vatican Mythographer, he is glossed in the long chapter on Saturn, Prudentia).[18] Accordingly, Giovanni del Virgilio, in his glosses on *Metamorphoses* 8.11, concludes that "Protheus est animus tenebroso in carcere clausus / Cuncta videns formas concipiensque novas" ("Proteus is the mind shut up in a dark prison / seeing all things and taking on new forms").[19] Giovanni glosses these "new forms" more prosaically as changes that oppress the soul as if immersed in the Egyptian sea, that is, the sorrows of our world: "Understand our soul, which remains in the Egyptian sea because in that world which is full of bitterness like the sea. But by Proteus very changed understand our soul shut up in the body and oppressed by the very changing into diverse forms because he includes all forms in himself" (my translation). Even more specifically, Thomas says (in *Archana deorum* 8.8) about the changes in form, from lion to bull to stone in the Servian passage, that each represents a different vice that must be removed (or bound up) in order for Proteus to assume divinity. The eunuch Pardoner can only become spiritual by cutting off his vices: "Servius says man similarly has within himself desire [*libidinem*], boredom [*stultitiam*], ferocity [*ferocitatem*], and cunning [*dolum*]. And so while they are in him the part which is closest to divinity does not appear, which is prudence [*prudentia*]. And so men can then hold them fast, when those have been bound, that is, when a man has been freed from all vices [*id est cum quis omnibus carueret vitiis*]. Hence therefore we read that Protheus can foresee and assume divinity, when desire [*cupiditas*] has been bound in him, like wild hares in the wood, a slipping of the mind, which is like fluidity of water" (my translation).[20]

Like Proteus, the Pardoner's model Fals-Semblant in Fragment C wishes no priest to "constreyne" him in "shrift" (6403), nor shall he be "compelled" ("streyne" [6406]) to make a double confession, for one is enough:

"This latter assoilyng quyte I thee.
I am *unbounde* — what maist thou fynde
More of my synnes me to *unbynde?*
For he, that myght hath in his hond,
Of all my synnes me *unbond.*" (6412–16; my emphasis)

He is "unbounde" — free — and does not need to be unbound from any other sins. Yet, if sin captures by binding, then absolution, or unbinding, or cleansing, will indeed free the soul. Ironically, to control Proteus and free the Pardoner from sin, we must bind his "changes," his sins — confess him, absolve him.

Our Pardoner, like the Proteus-like soul, becomes a figure for the soul bound by the prison of the body. In another passage, whose source I have not located although it sounds Isidorean, Thomas etymologizes "Protheus" as "distant from God" ("procul a theos, id est procul a deo"). Clearly, he would be distant from God because, in the Neoplatonic sense, God is one, unity itself, divine reason, and Proteus is many, diversity itself, multiple forms. In this same passage, this figure alienated from God is said to be turned to stone, or into a eunuch by Perseus when he sees the Gorgon Medusa, that is, a tyrant is overcome by the good man, made impotent by fear of virtue.[21]

Chaucer may have used many of these rich Proteus-linked images in his *Pardoner's Prologue* and *Tale* — the concept of the god as an "old man"; the image of his wiliness expressed by means of his face changing (found especially in Horace, *Epistles* 1.1.90); and, most important, the idea of fixing, binding, limiting of identity and form (as apprehending), for the polyform Proteuses among us. Such binding is opposed to the idea of shape shifting, or changing of identity, which is apparently mystifying to others and therefore liberating to the deceiver. Thus, to fix Proteus or his alter ego, the Pardoner, that is, to control him, it is necessary to "hold" him, in other words, to understand his nature — to see, beneath the surface, the similarity in his various disguises, or what might be termed the consistency of his false seeming (to identify him *as* Fals-Semblant). For the Pardoner, abrupt behavior shifts seem to free him, or else allow him to manipulate others by misusing his understanding of human nature. Hence he can shift personae as often as he does in his tale in order to profit handsomely. On another level, however, he must be fettered, or his vices understood: despite his many guises, his many covers or "bodies," as it were, manifested through *his* drinking, swearing, avarice, nevertheless he is capable of pardoning sinners, and, by means of his single, homilizing vocation, capable of rousing and testing their faith in a virtue analogous to Proteus's prudence. From a more providential (and authorial) point of view, this nefarious Pardoner, like the wily goddess Fortune whom slippery Fals-Semblant also resembles, and like the many-masked Devil-bailiff in the Friar's tale, also works *for* God: by testing what the reader most values—and, like the Devil-bailiff, by giving the reader the correct answers ahead of time. Jean's God of Love, in contrast, will fail to see under the surface because he remains blind and cupidinous—by definition; as will the worldly Host.

A little like an inverse George Herbert in "The Collar," the Pardoner thinks he is most free to display his evil inner nature when most bound by his role, his vocation. In short, his very shape shifting *is* False Seeming, Fals-Semblant—but to him, not to us. Despite his avaricious intention in telling this moralistic tale, he should inspire the pilgrims to reform and thereby overcome the old Donatist heresy once more.[22] Like Faus Semblant in the *Roman*, the Pardoner seems to pledge his loyalty to God (not the God of Love but the Christian God) to overcome Male Bouche (the Host?), in order to gain Bel Acueil (Fair Welcome), for the Lover—not Christ, but his own *cupiditas*. He thinks he gains access to the Fair Welcome of the pilgrims in order to win not the Rose, but gold; indeed, this bound Proteus who relinquishes his many shapes gains access to the Fair Welcome of the pilgrims for peace and social harmony, if not for God and eternal life—note, at the very end, that the jeering Host and the wrathful Pardoner, as instructed by the pacifying Knight, "kisse," "drawe ... neer," "laughe," and "pleye" (956–67). It is then no accident that cunning Proteus in related medieval literary texts (for example, the fifth book of John Gower's *Confessio Amantis*)[23] appears in contexts stressing erotic love as avarice—or cupidity as desire and greed; the reader thinks of the Pardoner's less secular moral, "Radix malorem est cupiditas," as well as the Physician's love for gold ("Therefore he lovede gold in special"). Nor is it an accident that Chaucer, whose Pardoner imagines that he seduces his audience while in fact tricking himself, omits any reference to Proteus in his tale while retaining the shape of all the ideas and images with which he is linked in his source—or, might the reader say of the text in which he appears, by which he is bound? In his "poetics of absence," it is what is not said that determines what is meant, a noetic symbol for the idea of *fabula* and an appropriate determinant for Chaucer's purpose in the fabulous Retraction.

Fabulous Chaucer

After the Ovidian-based tales glossed by the intermediary *Roman* leading up to the *Parson's Tale*, Chaucer moves toward the Retraction and what it means, at the moment of death, to have spent one's life writing poetry of a somewhat morally dubious nature. In ending his most important work with the fictional Retraction and therefore his own supposed voice in the "character" of the poet and not just the pilgrim, Chaucer parodies the na-

ture of fabulous narrative by making himself his subject.²⁴ Whether or not
Chaucer is serious in his Retraction—whether he mindlessly echoes the
kind of Retraction provided in the third book of Andreas Capellanus, for
example, or the entire work of Ovid's *Remedia amoris,* or instead pokes
fun at the rhetorical practice and at himself by playing yet another learned
joke—may be clearer after examining one other "autobiographical" com-
ment in his work. Although there are two such segments in Chaucer's works
(aside from the pseudobiographical narrative frames for the early dream vi-
sions and the two tales of the pilgrim Chaucer, *Sir Thopas* and the *Melibee*):
one, the Retraction at the end of the *Canterbury Tales* (and presumably at
the end of Chaucer's life), and the other, the recitation of Chaucer's literary
biography in the *Man of Law's Prologue,* outlined in the Introduction. In re-
lation to this biography, an astrological digression early in the *Man of Law's
Tale* (190–203) functions as a gloss on Chaucer's poetic practice, and there-
fore, along with the *Manciple's Tale,* can serve as a key to the Retraction.

The Man of Law's point is that fate is fixed and can be read in the stars,
although in fact it is poet Chaucer writing this fiction, believing that the
reader is free to exercise choice in making decisions—as is the medieval
author confronting the weight and authority of the mythographic tradition.
The Man of Law's astrological image suggests that God, like human poet-
scholars, also "writes" in his various books of the heavens and nature.
Such writing would include the setting down of his own "character" of the
historical poet Chaucer. In the book of the stars, one can read predisposi-
tions in character and in events that will enable the wise individual to
act appropriately; God, and his Providence, provide the authority for this
"text"—that is, the stars can be read at nativity and therefore used for
election, for at nativity there is a certain configuration of the stars that de-
termines the life and destiny of the individual, and at election, one can, for
example, determine an auspicious time for beginning a journey; from the
planets' conjunctions and squares the classical astrologer and prophet (im-
plicitly, Cassandra, Calchas, Tiresias, Amphiaraus) could have determined
the time of death of various heroes—Hector, Achilles, Pompey, Julius Cae-
sar, Hercules, Samson, Turnus, and Socrates (198–201)—before their actual
demise. It is ironic that the Man of Law as Chaucer's fictional character,
pretending to be real, discusses *auctoritas* (authority and that which au-
thors) as a gloss on the historical poet Chaucer, and equally interesting
given Chaucer's treatment of himself in the Retraction.

The Retraction supplies another version of the character of the Man of
Law (or the Manciple). The prolix literalist, the liar, the base man never-
theless tells a moral and figurative tale in his legend of incest, the tale of
Constance who triumphs over adversity. She provides a clear role model
for Princess Marie, daughter of Edward I of England and a nun at Malmes-
bury for whom the source for the *Man of Law's Tale,* the *Chronicle of Nich-*

olas Trivet, was written in 1335. So the Man of Law as *figura* glosses (and rationalizes) Chaucer, the man accused of *raptus* who nevertheless gives women a voice in his tale-telling and tells the truth about their rapes and exploitations and strength through mythological images.

If the reader pursues the idea of the Retraction as itself integumental, fictional, cloaked, then perhaps at the end of the *Tales* Chaucer truly reveals the nature of poetry, how earnest is made game and game earnest. The three sons mythographically established in the *Manciple's Tale* together provide a definition of Chaucerian purpose in the construction of fabulous narrative—Bacchus (Dionysius), god of the vine and restorer of social peace, the omitted Aesculapius, god of (physical) healing, and Jesus Christ (God who permanently heals man's soul). In a sense, Chaucer as poet-Manciple, purveyor of classical fable and morality, obeys both Host (who demands game and entertainment in his story telling) and Parson (who demands instruction in his biblical morality); put another way, the poet as Manciple speaks in response to the Host (the need for social harmony) and in anticipation of the Parson (the need for spiritual rejuvenation)—but in either case always guided by his mother, who, in her practical wisdom and shrewd perception of human nature, assumes the role of the patriarchal and ecclesiastical mythographer, continually inverting the tradition while preserving and adapting it. Chaucer wants it—and has it—both ways. The Retraction retracts and mimics and retains, simultaneously, everything Chaucer has written, especially of an immoral nature. What the reader sees, finally, about Chaucer's concealing mythographic aesthetic, is not that Chaucer has obliterated himself from the text out of a concern for political survival, or that poetic subterfuge necessitates the adornment of the naked truth with classical and integumental fictions. What the reader learns, finally, is that the book *is* the man, or this man at least, the fourteenth-century English middle-class, middle-aged Controller of Customs and courtly poet, a "naked text" in whose rich and complex mythological images can be read pederasty and rape, impotence, illusion, failure, desire—"my giltes."

Notes

Preface

1. For the antiessentialist view of women, see, for example, Faye Walker-Pelkey, "Gender Nominalized: Unmanning Men, Disgendering Women in Chaucer's *Legend of Good Women*" (Diss., Rice University, 1991); and Marilynn Desmond, *Reading Dido: Gender, Textuality, and the Medieval* Aeneid (Minneapolis: University of Minnesota Press, 1994). But see also the essentialist view, in Carolyn Dinshaw, *Chaucer's Sexual Poetics* (Madison: University of Wisconsin Press, 1989), esp. chapter 2, " 'The naked text in English to declare': The *Legend of Good Women*." Recent significant treatments of gendered patristic reading in the Middle Ages include Susan Schibanoff, "Taking the Gold Back to Egypt: The Art of Reading as a Woman," in *Gender and Reading*, ed. Elizabeth A. Flynn and Patrocinio P. Schweickart (Baltimore and London: Johns Hopkins University Press, 1986), pp. 83–106; R. Howard Bloch, "Medieval Misogyny," *Representations* 20 (1987): 1–24; and Elizabeth Robertson, *Early English Devotional Prose and the Female Audience* (Knoxville: University of Tennessee Press, 1990), esp. chapter 3, pp. 32–43. Contemporary theorists have probed the problem of men reading women: see, for example, Jonathan D. Culler, "Reading like a Woman," in *On Deconstruction: Theory and Criticism after Structuralism* (Ithaca, N.Y.: Cornell University Press, 1982); Robert Scholes, "Reading like a Man," in *Men in Feminism*, ed. Alice Jardine and Paul Smith (New York: Methuen, 1987), pp. 204–18; and, as corrective, Diana Fuss, "Reading like a Feminist," *Differences* 1 (1989): 76–92; repr. in *Essentially Speaking* (New York: Routledge, 1989), chapter 1.

2. See Anne Hudson, *The Premature Reformation: Wycliffite Texts and Lollard History* (Oxford: Clarendon Press, 1988), esp. chapter 9, "The Context of Vernacular Wycliffism," and the related book by Margaret Aston, *Lollards and Reformers: Images and Literacy in Late Medieval Religion* (London: Hambledon Press, 1984), esp. pp. 30–45, "Lollardy and Sedition, 1381–1431." On language and reading, see Janet Coleman, *Medieval Readers and Writers, 1350–1400* (New York: Columbia University Press, 1981), esp. chapters 2 and 3; and the excellent essay by Russell Potter, "Political Chaucer: Heresy, Sedition and the Vernacular Tradition of Dissent: 1400–1550," *Hwaet!* 1 (1989): 15–30.

3. Derek Brewer, ed., *Writers and Their Background: Chaucer* (London: Bell, 1974), p. 18.

4. David Aers, "Reflections on the Allegory of the Theologians: Ideology and *Piers Plowman*," in *Medieval Literature*, ed. David Aers (Brighton, Sussex: Harvester Press, 1986), p. 61 (but see also pp. 58–73). See also the excellent analysis of the veiled sedition of the rebels' letters during the Peasants' Revolt of 1381 in Susan Crane, "The Writing Lesson of 1381," in *Chaucer's England: Literature in Historical Context*, ed. Barbara

Hanawalt, Medieval Studies at Minnesota, vol. 4 (Minneapolis: University of Minnesota Press, 1992), pp. 201–21. For allegory and its modern theoretical usefulness, see, for example, the collection edited by J. Stephen Russell, *Allegoresis: The Craft of Allegory in Medieval Literature*, Garland Reference Library of the Humanities, vol. 664 (New York and London: Garland, 1988 [for 1987]). For the alterity of the Middle Ages and its accommodation of difference in reading and writing—a revision of Robertson—see Charles Dahlberg, *The Literature of Unlikeness* (Hanover, N.H., and London: University Press of New England, 1988). The general reception of the Middle Ages in contemporary criticism in the light of new developments in theory is the subject of a collection edited by Laurie A. Finke and Martin B. Schichtman, *Medieval Texts and Contemporary Readers* (Ithaca, N.Y.: Cornell University Press, 1987).

5. On the general antipathy between Lollard and mendicant, see Richard Firth Green, "John Ball's Letters: Literary History and Historical Literature," in Hanawalt, ed., *Chaucer's England*, pp. 176–200. For Chaucer's friends, see Paul Strohm, *Social Chaucer* (Cambridge, Mass., and London: Harvard University Press, 1989), esp. chapters 1 and 2.

6. See the documents cited in Potter, "Political Chaucer," p. 30 n. 30.

7. See G. L. Kittredge, "Chaucer's Alceste," *MP* 6 (1908): 435–39; J. L. Lowes, "Chaucer and the *Ovide Moralisé*," *PMLA* 33 (1918): 302–25; W. C. Curry, "Astrologizing the Gods," *Anglia* 47 (1923): 213–43; W. C. Curry, "O Mars, O Atazir," *JEGP* 22 (1923): 347–68; and S[anford] B[rown] Meech, "Chaucer and the *Ovide Moralisé*—A Further Study," *PMLA* 46 (1931): 182–204. Three later essays preserve the same astrological (natural or physical) approach: Kemp Malone, "Chaucer's Daughter of Cupid," *MLR* 45 (1950): 63; J. I. Cope, "Chaucer, Venus, and the Seventhe Sphere," *MLN* 67 (1952): 245–46; and Ernest H. Wilkins, "Descriptions of Pagan Divinities from Petrarch to Chaucer," *Speculum* 32 (1956): 511–22.

8. See the broad-ranging analysis of the place of "historical criticism" in the history of medieval studies in Lee Patterson, *Negotiating the Past: The Historical Understanding of Medieval Literature* (Madison: University of Wisconsin Press, 1987), chapter 1. In addition to those scholars listed in the Acknowledgments as influential in shaping the conclusions of this study, see Robertson, *Preface*. In addition to specific essays and books on Chaucer's gods or planets and heroes cited at appropriate points in this volume, see especially Chauncey Wood, *Chaucer and the Country of the Stars: Poetic Uses of Astrological Imagery* (Princeton: Princeton University Press, 1970); John M. Fyler, *Chaucer and Ovid* (New Haven and London: Yale University Press, 1979); and McCall, *Chaucer Among the Gods* (1979).

9. See, for example, Theresa Tinkle, "Saturn of the Several Faces: A Survey of the Medieval Mythographic Traditions," *Viator* 18 (1987): 289–307; Jane Chance, "'Disfigured is thy Face': Chaucer's Pardoner and the Protean Shape-Shifter Fals-Semblant," *PQ* 67 (1989): 422–33, reprinted in different form in this volume; and several essays in Chance, *Mythographic Art*, including Patricia R. Orr, "Pallas Athena and the Threefold Choice in Chaucer's *Troilus and Criseyde*, pp. 159–76; Jane Chance, "Chaucer's Zephirus: Dante's Zefiro, St. Dominic, and the Idea of the *General Prologue*," pp. 177–98 (reprinted in different form in this volume); Janet Levarie Smarr, "Mercury in the Garden: Mythographical Methods in the *Merchant's Tale* and *Decameron* 7.9," pp. 199–214; and Melvin Storm, "From Knossos to Knight's Tale: The Changing Face of Chaucer's Theseus," pp. 215–34.

10. For the first, see Dinshaw, *Chaucer's Sexual Poetics*, and for the second, Elaine Tuttle Hansen, *Chaucer and the Fictions of Gender* (Los Angeles and London: University of California Press, 1992).

11. Bert Dillon, "A Dictionary of Personal, Mythological, Allegorical, and Astrological Proper Names and Allusions in the Works of Geoffrey Chaucer" (Diss., Duke University, 1972), p. 18 (pp. 14–25 on Chaucer's use of the classics), published as *A Chaucer Dictio-*

nary: Proper Names and Allusions, Excluding Place Names (Boston: G. K. Hall, 1974). See also N. Dean, "Studies of Chaucer's Use of Ovid in Selected Poems" (Diss., New York University, 1963); and Jacqueline de Weever, *A Dictionary of Classical, Mythological and Sideral Names in the Works of Geoffrey Chaucer* (Diss., University of Pennsylvania, 1971), published as *Chaucer Name Dictionary: A Guide to Astrological, Biblical, Historical, Literary, and Mythological Names in the Works of Geoffrey Chaucer* (New York: Garland, 1987), which provides the etymologies for classical, myth, and sideral names but which includes few mythographers. Finally, a similarly Renaissance treatment of Chaucer's use of the ancient poets (that is, without recourse to the medieval mythographic tradition) can be found in Winthrop Wetherbee, *Chaucer and the Poets: An Essay on Troilus and Criseyde* (Ithaca, N.Y., and London: Cornell University Press, 1984). See the corrective vision of John V. Fleming, *Classical Imitation and Interpretation of Chaucer's "Troilus"* (Lincoln: University of Nebraska Press, 1990).

12. See Robert Pratt, "The Importance of Manuscripts for the Study of Medieval Education, as Revealed by the Learning of Chaucer," in *Progress of Medieval and Renaissance Studies in the United States and Canada*, Bulletin no. 20 (1949), p. 50; also Shirley Law Guthrie, "The *Ecloga Theoduli* in the Middle Ages" (Diss., Indiana University, 1973), esp. chapter 5, n. 50.

13. To create mythologized poems, a medieval poet would have needed the scholastic mythographic tradition of commentary. See the outline of scholarship on allegoresis, the survival of the pagan gods in the Middle Ages and the Renaissance, the mythographic process during specific historical periods from the twelfth to the fifteenth centuries, the commentary traditions on Virgil, Ovid, Boethius, and Dante, and the development of the mythographic tradition, in Chance, "Introduction," *Mythographic Art*, pp. 6–12, and the bibliography on pp. 33–44; see also Jane Chance, *Medieval Mythography: From Roman North Africa to the School of Chartres, AD 433 to 1177* (Gainesville: University Press of Florida, 1994). Some studies of Chaucer detail his mythologizing without relating his methods to the mythographic process: see, for example, Barbara Apstein, "Chaucer and the Gods" (Diss., City University of New York, 1971), p. 34, which covers primarily the minor poems, the *Troilus*, and the *Knight's Tale* and the *Merchant's Tale*, but without attention to the mediating presence of the commentary tradition. See also Leah Zeva Freiwald, "Chaucer's Use of Classical Mythology: The Myths in the Context of the Medieval Audience" (Diss., University of California-Berkeley, 1983); and Alastair J. Minnis, *Chaucer and Pagan Antiquity* (Bury St. Edmunds, Suffolk: D. S. Brewer; Totowa, N.J.: Rowman and Littlefield, 1982). Some recent studies have allowed that if Chaucer did read the commentators, he read only the most well known fourteenth-century commentators, such as the *Ovide moralisé* (see, for example, Bernard L. Witlieb, "Chaucer and the *Ovide Moralisé*" [Diss., New York University, 1969]). But because mythographers often added their own interpretations to the mythographic tradition for a particular figure, a "bewildering variety of equivalences developed for a single image" (Apstein, "Chaucer and the Gods," p. 6) and the "equivalences" span a history of a thousand years (see "A Chronology of Major Medieval Mythographers"). One purpose of this study is to generalize about Chaucer's use of the tradition while isolating specific indebtedness where possible.

14. See the listing of books in Edith Rickert, "Chaucer at School," *MP* 29 (1931–32): 257–74, esp. 258–70; and her *Chaucer's World*, ed. Clair C. Olson and Martin M. Crow (New York and London: Columbia University Press, 1948), pp. 121–26. According to the latter, Isidore, Hugutio, the *Ecloga Theoduli*, Ovid's *Metamorphoses*, and Virgil's *Georgics* would have been available to Chaucer.

15. See J. A. W. Bennett, "The Men at Merton," chapter 3 of *Chaucer at Oxford and at Cambridge* (Toronto: University of Toronto Press, 1974), pp. 67–69.

16. See Allen, "Mythology." See also the manuscripts described in his "Eleven Un-published Commentaries on Ovid's *Metamorphoses* and Two Other Texts of Related Interest: Some Comments on a Bibliography," in Chance, *Mythographic Art*, pp. 281–89.

17. On the importance of the *Ecloga* as a school text, see George L. Hamilton, "Theodulus: A Mediaeval Textbook," *MP* 7 (1909–10): 169–85. For its influence in the Middle Ages, see George L. Hamilton, "Theodulus in France," *MP* 8 (1910–11): 611–12; and Guthrie, "The *Ecloga Theoduli* in the Middle Ages." For its manuscripts and collections, see Betty Nye Quinn, "ps[eudo]. Theodolus," *Catalogus Translationum et Commentariorum: Mediaeval and Renaissance Latin Translations and Commentaries,* ed. Paul Oskar Kristeller and F. Edward Kranz (Washington, D.C.: Catholic University Press of America, 1971), pp. 383–408.

18. Identified by Christopher Baswell, "The Medieval Allegorization of the *Aeneid*: MS. Cambridge, Peterhouse 158," *Traditio* 41 (1985): 181–237.

Introduction. "Fables and Swich Wreccednesse"

Portions of the Introduction were delivered as papers: "Revising Macrobius on Fiction: The 'Fabulous Cosmogony' of William of Conches," in a session entitled "Mythography and Literature," Fifth Citadel Conference on Literature: The Poetry, Drama, and Prose of the Renaissance and Middle Ages, The Citadel, Charleston, S.C., March 15, 1985; and "Chaucer on *Satura: Tidynges, Integumentum,* and Gender in the *Manciple's Prologue and Tale,*" in a session entitled "Genre: The Limitations of Medieval Literary Theory," Sixth International Congress of the New Chaucer Society, University of British Columbia, Vancouver, August 11, 1988.

1. Generally, scholars have accepted the speculation that this was the original plan for the unfinished *Legend of Good Women.*

2. John M. Fyler, "Domesticating the Exotic in the *Squire's Tale,*" *ELH* 55 (1988): 1–26, discusses as a context the preoccupation with incest in the romance genre. But see also Carolyn Dinshaw's feminist discussion in *Chaucer's Sexual Poetics* (Madison: University of Wisconsin Press, 1989), pp. 88–112.

3. For a discussion of the Parson's Wycliffite traits and the seditious context in which he existed, see Margaret Aston, *Lollards and Reformers: Images and Literacy in Late Medieval Religion* (London: Hambledon Press, 1984), p. 16, but also chapter 1, "Lollardy and Sedition, 1381–1431," pp. 1–47; and, for the argument that Chaucer "has deliberately chosen to surround his Parson with a suggestion of Wycliffism," see Anne Hudson, "The Context of Vernacular Wycliffism," chapter 9 of *The Premature Reformation: Wycliffite Texts and Lollard History* (Oxford: Clarendon Press, 1988), esp. pp. 390–94.

4. These influential theoretical concepts (influential at least for the Middle Ages) are discussed in my introduction, "The Medieval 'Apology for Poetry': Fabulous Narrative and Stories of the Gods," in Chance, *Mythographic Art*, pp. 5–6, 14, 31–33.

5. "Alia causa quare scribit satiram, scilicet gulositas imperatoris. Sed quia non est ausus reprehendere illum notat per integumentum sic." See Bradford Wilson, ed., *Glossae in Iuvenalem,* Textes philosophiques du Moyen Âge 18 (Paris: J. Vrin, 1980), p. 108. But *satura,* according to William, is also a rustic, pagan, *and* earthly mode used to cloak scandalous stories of the gods that personify aspects of the natural process of harvesting because the art form in which they are used, satire, is intended for the rustic or *paganus* (country dweller). It is therefore logical to expect agricultural meanings in satire, whether pertaining to land or to farmers. See the Accessus, in Wilson, p. 91: "id est ab agrestibus dicta est."

6. Analyses of Chaucer's sources in the tale include, among others, Gardiner Still-well, "Analogues to Chaucer's *Manciple's Tale* in the *Ovide Moralisé* and Machaut's *Voir-Dit*," *PQ* 19 (1940): 133–38; and Hoffman, *Ovid*, pp. 193–202, who carefully notes medieval Ovidian mythographic explanations for many of the details of the Manciple's tale. For the major texts, but without much analysis, see James A. Work, "The Manci-ple's Tale," in Bryan and Dempster, pp. 699–722.

7. For the tale as an exemplum, see J. Burke Severs, "Is the *Manciple's Tale* a Suc-cess?" *JEGP* 51 (1952): 1–16. For the tale as comic, see Richard Hazelton, "The *Manci-ple's Tale*: Parody and Critique," *JEGP* 62 (1963): 1–31. For the tale as ironic, see Earle Birney, "Chaucer's 'Gentil' Manciple and his 'Gentil' Tale," *NM* 61 (1960): 257–67. Jack-son J. Campbell views the Manciple as a "folksy babbler" whose moralizing is senten-tious, in "Polonius Among the Pilgrims," *ChauR* 7 (1972): 140–46.

8. The *Parson's Tale* has been regarded as the climax of the *Tales*, in that Fragment X emphasizes confession as the greatest good of all. See, for example, Sister M. Madeleva, *A Lost Language and Other Essays on Chaucer* (New York: Sheed & Ward, 1951), pp. 69–79, who interprets the Retraction as Chaucer's repentance (pp. 105–15). Frederick Tupper also views the *Tales* as manifesting the seven deadly sins, with the *Parson's Tale* as a summa, in "Chaucer and the Seven Deadly Sins," *PMLA* 29 (1914): 93–128.

9. For the relationship between the Manciple and Parson as central to an under-standing of the unity (or the disintegration of unity) of the *Canterbury Tales*, see Chaun-cey Wood, "Speech, the Principle of Contraries, and Chaucer's Tales of the Manciple and the Parson," *Mediaevalia* 6 (1980): 209–27; James Dean, "Dismantling the Canterbury Book," *PMLA* 100 (1985): 746–62; and Mark Allen, "Penitential Sermons, The Manciple, and the End of *The Canterbury Tales*," *SAC* 9 (1987): 77–96.

10. For the studies of speech and silencing as a theme in the tale, see the respective studies of Mark Allen, "Penitential Sermons" (pp. 77–96), and Louise Fradenburg, "The Manciple's Servant Tongue: Politics and Poetry in *The Canterbury Tales*," *ELH* 52 (1985): 85–118.

11. See D. S. Bland, "Chaucer and the Inns of Court: A Re-Examination," *ES* 33 (1952): 145–55, who acknowledges that Chaucer's study there may be only a plausible theory.

12. Chaucer's description and use of Apollo here generally follows the sequence found in Fulg. *Mit.* 1.12–17, including sections on his significance, his association with the crow, the laurel, the nine Muses, Phaethon (omitted in Chaucer), the tripod, arrows, and python, and his beardlessness (despite being called "father"). As the god of music, po-etry, and truth in the Middle Ages, he plays an important role in Martianus's *De nuptiis*—in which he is linked with the raven because of his oracular ability and said to be the brother of rhetoric because he represents the philosopher; he is also representative of *consilio* as his brother Mercury is representative of *sermo*, at least in commentaries on the passage. See Remigius, *Mart.* 73.10, 1:197. Dante invokes him in the Prologue to the *Paradiso* (11.13–36) as god of truth associated with the ineffable and therefore indescrib-able: in 11.1–12 Dante has seen things that he is afraid he cannot relate, and so he in-vokes Apollo in his competition with Marsyas, suggesting the competition between hu-man and divine poetry, as that fable was understood (1:19–21). On the association of Apollo with the Muses as a tenth Muse, see Remigius, *Mart.* 286.17, 2:126 (par. 574), which borrows the idea from Fulg. *Mit.* 1.15; because there are ten organs of articulation in the human voice, his subsequent depiction with a cithara (lyre) of ten strings is allego-rized in Remigius (supposedly from Saint Augustine but actually from Fulgentius 1.15) as the way the voice utilizes nine sounds and therefore connects with Apollo as the tenth, representing all of them. Is it possible that Chaucer used this passage in the rather strange metaphor used by the Manciple's Mother in explaining the God-given structure

of the tongue within the mouth? "My sone, God of his endelees goodnesse / Walled a tonge with teeth and lippes eke, / For man sholde hym avyse what he speeke" (322–24).

13. Fulg. *Mit.* 1.17; repeated by Arnulf of Orleans so that the python represents "falsa credulitas," whom Apollo, "sapiens," exterminates by means of "ratione sua." So the wise man exterminates false belief by means of truth, or fallacy, which can be done by killing the false serpent Python: "Sic et sapiens falsam credulitatem exterminat a veritate, vel etiam fallaciam que potest haberi per Phitonem serpentem fallacem" (p. 202). See also the discussion of these mythographies by Hoffman, *Ovid,* pp. 198–99. It is apparently because of this victory that Phoebus becomes so proud that he claims that only he should bear bow and arrow (in Arnulf), not Cupid, who promptly dispenses an arrow that leads Phoebus Apollo to fall (futilely) in love with Daphne (the laurel, interpreted mythographically throughout the Middle Ages as fame).

14. The expanded version of the *Integumenta Ovidii,* cited in Bryan and Dempster (p. 716), derives from MS. Lansdowne 728, *Expositio vel commentarius in libros xv Ovidii Metamorphoseon, cum tabulis genealogicis deorum,* fol. 54r. The actual moral in John of Garland states: "Garrulous est corvus et cornix fert quia Naso: / 'Inter aves albas non habet illa locum'" (p. 46, ll.136–37).

15. Fulgentius explains Apollo's protection of the crow, *cornix* (rather than the raven, *corvus*), in *Mit.* 1.13, for one of two reasons: "either because *contrary to the way of nature* it alone produces its young by laying eggs at the very height of summer heat, as also Petronius: 'So the crow, contrary to the products of the well-known ways of nature, Lays its eggs when the corn is high,' or because according to Anaximander in his books on *Orneoscopics,* or according to Pindar, it alone of all the birds has names bearing sixty-four interpretations" (p. 24, trans. p. 54).

16. Guido da Pisa, *Expositiones et glose super Comediam Dantis* or *Commentary on Dante's Inferno,* ed. Vincenzo Cioffari (Albany: State University of New York Press, 1974).

17. For the "My sone" formula appearing in wisdom literature, see John S. P. Tatlock, "The Date of the 'Troilus': and Minor Chauceriana," *MLN* 50 (1935): 296. The *moralitas* on jangling and holding the tongue appears in passages conveniently collected in Bryan and Dempster from Jean de Meun, *Roman* 7037–57 (true except when praising God [7043ff.]) (Bryan and Dempster, p. 722); from the *Ovide moralisé* 2176–2202 (Bryan and Dempster, pp. 704–5 and 708–9); from Guillaume de Machaut, *Le livre du voir dit* 7986 (Bryan and Dempster, p. 713); from Gower, *Confessio* 3.768–835.

18. See Jane Chance Nitzsche, *The Genius Figure in Antiquity and the Middle Ages* (New York and London: Columbia University Press, 1975), chapter 6.

19. See *Confessio Amantis* 3.768–835, on the sententious passage, in G. C. Macauley, ed., *The English Works of John Gower,* EETS, 2 vols. (1900–1901; repr. London, New York, Toronto: Oxford University Press, 1957), cited in Bryan and Dempster, pp. 709–11.

20. Cited conveniently in Bryan and Dempster, pp. 720–21.

21. In Ovid, Coronis dies from Apollo's arrow after the crow blabs, but before she dies she cries, "'Twas right, O Phoebus,' she said, 'that I should suffer thus from you, but first I should have borne my child. But now two of us shall die in one'" (pp. 102–3 [2.608–9]). It is because of the death of the son that Apollo hates the bird; he tries to bring her back to life and to conquer her fate. Note Ovid's bathetic description of the father's reaction to his lost son when he sees Coronis's pyre, described in terms of a maternal simile: "from his deep heart he uttered piteous groans; such groans as the young cow utters when before her eyes the hammer high poised from beside the right ear crashes with its resounding blow through the hollow temples of her suckling calf" (pp. 102–3 [2.622–25]). After preparing her body for the pyre, he delivers his own son: "But that his own son should perish in the same funeral fires he cannot brook. He snatched the unborn child from his

mother's womb and from the devouring flames, and bore him for safe keeping to the cave of two-formed Chiron" (pp. 104–5 [2.628–30]).

22. After reciting the literal myth of Semele's sleeping with Jupiter, which resulted in the birth of Bacchus, William in his commentary on Macrobius (fol. 7b) explains that Jupiter represents the ether, Juno the lower air, and Semele the earth (p. 71). Chaucer also uses the myth of Bacchus, with Macrobian construction, in the *Parlement of Foules* (see chapter 3 for a fuller exposition).

23. William, *Macrob.*, 7b, on 1.2.10–11, in a passage that describes the base activities of the gods not suitable for fabulous narrative, explains Bacchus, the product of the adulterous (and therefore unacceptable) union of Semele and Jove, "quia vinee inde nascuntur," as "earth's natural power of growing into vines" (p. 71).

24. Note that Martianus's major depiction of Bacchus centers on his signification as god of wine: Liber or Bacchus (36.9) is said by Martianus to be agreeable, drunk, and holding a sickle in his right hand and a "soporific bowl" (82). Remigius notes that lascivious desires are associated with the unstable and the drunk ("Lascivia enim libido vel instabilitas ebriosorum est" [1:134]). Bacchus is glossed by [Bern. Sil.] *Mart.* 3.175–222, as having four significations. See the fuller discussion in chapter 3, on the *Parlement*, and chapter 8, on the *Merchant's Tale*.

25. See Wilson, ed., *Glossae in Iuvenalem*, p. 91.

26. Explicitly contrasting pagan and Christian belief, William declares that we are said to exist between things to be enjoyed and things to be used, which we use not for themselves but for another purpose, just as *temporalia* should be used not for their own sakes but so that we may be sustained and merit the heavens: "quia inter frui et uti dicimur quibus non propter se sed propter aliud utimur, ut temporalibus si bene his utamur non propter se sed ut vivamus utimur et ut celestia promereamur" (ibid., p. 109). Thus William modifies Augustine's distinction between two kinds of love—*cupiditas* that enjoys things for their own sakes, *caritas* that uses things for the sake of love of God—to demonstrate that the pagans cupidinously worshiped earthly things (bread and wine) as if they were divine, or gods (Ceres and Bacchus). See Saint Augustine, *On Christian Doctrine*, trans. D. W. Robertson, Jr. (Indianapolis: Bobbs-Merrill, 1958; repr. 1976), p. 9 (1.3). According to William, this world, and all of its earthy and earthly processes and products, was to the pagans imbued with the divine, just as the otherworld is to the Christian the source of the divine and to the Neoplatonist immanent in this world. Such earthly agricultural activity, in the light of the model disseminated by William in other works and by his contemporaries at Paris and Chartres, is a manifestation of the World Soul, which in the twelfth century was frequently identified with the concept of Natura and depicted so in literary and allegorical form.

Chapter 1. "A wonder thing": The *Descensus ad Inferos* of the Female Heroes Alcyone and Alceste

1. The only treatment of both together is by Robert O. Payne, who views the *Prologue* in relation to the *Legend of Good Women* as the final draft of the poem Chaucer had started in *Book of the Duchess* and continued in *Parlement of Foules* and *Hous of Fame* ("Making his own Myth: the Prologue to Chaucer's *Legend of Good Women*," *ChauR* 9 [1975]: 197–211).

2. In line with Charles Muscatine's "three stylistic phases" (courtly, bourgeois, mixed) in *Chaucer and the French Tradition: A Study in Style and Meaning* (Berkeley and Los Angeles: University of California Press, 1966), critics have noted that they treat their primarily French sources conventionally—for the *Book of the Duchess*, Guillaume

de Machaut's *Dit de la fonteinne amoureuse,* or *Livre de Morpheus.* See, for example, especially G. L. Kittredge, "Chaucer and Froissart," *Englische Studien* 26 (1899): 321–36; G. L. Kittredge, "Guillaume de Machaut and the *Book of the Duchess,*" *PMLA* 30 (1915): 1–24; Constance L. Rosenthal, "A Possible Source of Chaucer's *Booke of the Duchesse— Lii Regret de Guillaume* by Jehan de la Mote," *MLN* 48 (1933): 511–14; Haldeen Braddy, *Chaucer and the French Poet, Graunson* (Baton Rouge: Louisiana State University Press, 1947); J. B. Severs, "The Sources of *The Book of the Duchess,*" *MS* 25 (1963): 355–61; James I. Wimsatt, *Chaucer and the French Love Poets* (Chapel Hill: University of North Carolina Press, 1968); James I. Wimsatt, "Machaut's *Lay de Confort* and Chaucer's *Book of the Duchess,*" in R. H. Robbins, ed., *Chaucer at Albany* (New York: Burt Franklin, 1975), pp. 11–26; and M. M. Pelen, "Machaut's Court of Love Narratives and Chaucer's *Book of the Duchess,*" *ChauR* 11 (1976): 128–55. For summaries of the French tradition, see James I. Wimsatt, "Chaucer and French Poetry," in Derek Brewer, ed., *Writers and Their Background: Chaucer* (London: Bell, 1974), pp. 109–36; and Haldeen Braddy, "The French Influence on Chaucer," in Beryl Rowland, ed. *A Companion to Chaucer Studies,* rev. ed., (New York: Oxford University Press, 1979), pp. 143–59.

For the French sources of the *Prologue* to the *Legend of Good Women,* see the notes to the *Prologue* in Benson's revised *Riverside Chaucer* edition, wherein references occur to Jean Froissart's *Paradys d'amours, Le joli mois de may,* and *Dittié de la flour de la margherite,* Eustache Deschamps's *Lai de franchise, Lay amoureux,* and *Ballades* nos. 532, 539, and Guillaume Machaut's *Dit de la marguerite* and *Jugement dou Roy de Navarre,* among others. For Marguerite poems possibly responsible for Chaucer's paean to the daisy, see the excerpts from Machaut's *Dit de la marguerite* and Froissart's *Dit de la marguerite* in B. A. Windeatt, ed., *Chaucer's Dream Poetry: Sources and Analogues* (Woodbridge, Suffolk: D. S. Brewer; Totowa, N.J.: Rowman and Littlefield, 1982), pp. 145–48, 149–51. See also *Le lay de franchise* by Deschamps in the same edition, pp. 152–55. For the criticism on the French sources of the *Prologue,* see John L. Lowes, "The Prologue to the *Legend of Good Women* as Related to the French *Marguerite* Poems and the *Filostrato,*" *PMLA* 19 (1904): 593–683; and Robert M. Estrich, "Chaucer's Prologue to the *Legend of Good Women* and Machaut's *Le jugement dou Roy de Navarre,*" *SP* 36 (1939): 20–39. More recently, the *Legend* has been examined in the light of French sources connected with the *Querelle des femmes* initiated by Jean de Meun in the *Roman de la Rose* and continued at the end of the fourteenth century by Christine de Pizan in *Livre de la Cité des Dames* (1405). See Ruth M. Ames, "The Feminist Connections of Chaucer's *Legend of Good Women,*" in *Chaucer in the Eighties,* ed. Julian N. Wasserman and Robert J. Blanch (Syracuse, N.Y.: Syracuse University Press, 1986), pp. 57–74; and Sheila Delany, "Rewriting Women Good: Gender and the Anxiety of Influence in Two Late-Medieval Texts," in *Chaucer in the Eighties,* pp. 75–92.

3. Critics for the most part ignore their mythological references, or discuss them only in part, or ignore their connection with the mythographic tradition. The use of the Latin mythographic tradition in the *Book of the Duchess* has not been much examined, nor has the relationship between the French sources and the Latin tradition; certainly its pattern of mythological figures (with the exception of Seys and Alcyone) has only begun to be examined. J. L. Lowes, "Chaucer and the *Ovide Moralisé,*" *PMLA* 33 (1918): 319, suspected that the story of Seys and Alcyone derives from the *Ovide moralisé,* as does Machaut's Ovid (pp. 320ff.). Major articles dealing with this particular reference include Joseph B. Martin III, "The Medieval Ceyx and Alcyone: Ovid's *Metamorphoses* XI, 407–750 and Chaucer's *Book of the Duchess,*" *DAI* 33 (1973): 6318A (Duke); J. Burke Severs, "The Sources of the *Book of the Duchess,*" *MS* 25 (1963): 355–62; James I. Wimsatt, "The Sources of Chaucer's 'Seys and Alcyone,'" *MAE* 36 (1967): 231–41. The other mythological characters and references have received surprisingly little attention. For a

brief analysis of epic sources in relation to the *Book of the Duchess*, see Ann Taylor, "Epic Motifs in Chaucer's 'Tale of Ceyx and Alcyone,'" *Helios* 14 (1987): 39–45. For a general treatment of the classical scene in the *Legend*, see McCall, chapter 4, esp. pp. 113–22, although it focuses on the passive women of the legends.

In relation to the *Legend of Good Women*, most attention has been focused on the *Prologue*, on the characters of Alceste and Cupid, without attention to Europa and Jove (F 114), Flora and Zephirus (F 171), and Cybele and Mars (F 531, 533). Despite a superficial resemblance to the French court of love, which here becomes a "trial of Chaucer as a heretic," the *Prologue* is as indebted not only for its mythological allusions and characters but also its literary sources to specifically non-French materials. In terms of the Latin mythographic background, most promising for this study and for interpretations of the unity of the poem has been the study of V. A. Kolve, with its brief mythographic description of Alceste in the light of Fulgentius and the Vatican Mythographers, in the context of an overall iconographic argument that suggests the pattern of Christ's death and resurrection in the legend of Cleopatra and in the myth of Alceste, and by extrapolation in many of the other legends. See V. A. Kolve, "From Cleopatra to Alceste: An Iconographic Study of *The Legend of Good Women*," in *Signs and Symbols in Chaucer's Poetry*, ed. John P. Hermann and John J. Burke, Jr. (University: University of Alabama Press, 1981). For the example of Boccaccio's *Genealogia* as source, see J. M. Cowen, "Chaucer's *Legend of Good Women*, Lines 2501–3," *N & Q* 31 (1984): 298–99. Most of the acknowledged non-French sources involve the individual legends. On *Metamorphoses* as a source, see, for the legend of Thisbe, James W. Spisak, "Chaucer's Pyramus and Thisbe," *ChauR* 18 (1984): 204–10. On the *Ovide moralisé* as a source, see Lowes, "Chaucer and the *Ovide Moralisé*," pp. 302–25, particularly on Philomela; S[anford] B[rown] Meech, on the legends of Ariadne and Philomela, in "Chaucer and the *Ovide moralisé*—A Further Study," *PMLA* 46 (1931): 182–204; see also Bernard L. Witlieb, "Chaucer and the *Ovide Moralisé*" (Diss., New York University, 1969), pp. 36–154, for line-by-line parallels. On the sources of individual legends in other Latin or mythographic works, see, as a source for the conclusion of *Lucrece*, Robert Holkot's *In librum Sapientiae*, in Martha S. Waller, "The Conclusion of Chaucer's *Legend of Lucrece*: Robert Holcot and the Great Faith of Women," *Chaucer Newsletter* 2 (1980): 10–12. For the historical, Latin sources of the legend of Cleopatra (and the view that the legends invert the ideals of the *Prologue*), see Beverly Taylor, "The Medieval Cleopatra: The Classical and Medieval Tradition of Chaucer's *Legend of Cleopatra*," *Journal of Medieval and Renaissance Studies* 7 (1977): 249–69. For Dido as a deliberate distortion of Ovid and Virgil, see Marilynn Desmond, "Chaucer's *Aeneid*: 'The Naked Text in English,'" *Pacific Coast Philology* 19 (1984): 62–67. For Phyllis's source as Boccaccio's *Genealogia*, see Clarence G. Child, "Chaucer's *Legend of Good Women* and Boccaccio's *De Genealogia Deorum*," *MLN* 11, no. 8 (1896): 476–90; for *Ecloga Theoduli* as source, see [Ferdinand] Holthausen, "Chaucer und Theodulus," *Anglia* 16 (1864): 264–66. Among the legends, Cleopatra has received most critical attention.

4. On current treatments of both poems as handbooks on reading, especially the reading of classical tales, see especially, on *Book of the Duchess*, Robert W. Hanning, "Chaucer's First Ovid: Metamorphosis and Poetic Tradition in *The Book of the Duchess* and *The House of Fame*," in *Chaucer and the Craft of Fiction*, ed. Leigh A. Arrathoon (Rochester, Minn.: Solaris Press, 1986), pp. 121–63. On the *Legend of Good Women* as Chaucer's *ars poetica*, viewed in relation to his other works, see Payne, "Making his own Myth," pp. 197–211; Lisa J. Kiser, *Telling Classical Tales: Chaucer and the Legend of Good Women* (Ithaca, N.Y.: Cornell University Press, 1983), sees its purpose as not just comic but also serious—on how classical fiction should be used. For an analysis of the *Prologue* as an allegorization of the process of imagination within what might be termed

Chaucer's *ars poetica*, see Russell A. Peck, "Chaucerian Poetics and the Prologue to the *Legend of Good Women*," in Wasserman and Blanch, pp. 39–56. See also Peter L. Allen, "Reading Chaucer's Good Women," *ChauR* 21 (1987): 419–34, who notes the similarities between the reader and these women: "the reader is, at least metaphorically, a woman who has given herself over to a deceitful man (in this case, the unreliable narrator)" (p. 420). Hence we as readers must reject the narrator's authority, and reaffirm ourselves and Chaucer's women like Criseyde.

5. The gloss on Ovid's title comes from a medieval commentary on the *Heroides*: "Vnde quidam intitulant eum 'O(uidius) heroum' idest matronarum uel 'liber heroydos'. 'heros, herois' grecum est masculinum et significat grecas mulieres nobiles" (fol. 13vb, Huygens [1970], p. 31), from *Epistulae heroidum* III, in Ralph J. Hexter, *Ovid and Medieval Schooling. Studies in Medieval School Commentaries on Ovid's Ars Amatoria, Epistulae ex Ponto, and Epistulae Heroidum*, Münchener Beiträge zur Mediävistik und Renaissance-Forschung (Munich: Arbeo-Gesellschaft, 1986), p. 160. For Ovid and the *Heroides* as a source for the *Legend of Good Women*, perhaps filtered through the medieval translators, see especially Eleanor Winsor Leach, "A Study of the Sources and Rhetoric of Chaucer's *Legend of Good Women* and Ovid's *Heroides*" (Diss., Yale, 1963); and Sanford Brown Meech, "Chaucer and an Italian Translation of the *Heroides*," *PMLA* 45 (1930): 110–28.

6. For the use of the *Aeneid* in the schools, see the old but still useful Domenico Comparetti, *Vergil in the Middle Ages*, trans. E. F. M. Benecke, 2d ed. (1895; repr. New York, Leipzig, Paris, and London: G. E. Stechert and Co. [Alfred Hafner], 1929). On the use of mythography in medieval schools, see Jane Chance, *Medieval Mythography: From Roman North Africa to the School of Chartres, AD 433 to 1177* (Gainesville: University Press of Florida, 1994). Christopher Baswell's study of the *Aeneid* commentaries and vernacular literature in the Middle Ages, *Figures of Olde Werk: Visions of Virgil's Aeneid in Medieval England*, is forthcoming from Cambridge University Press.

7. At the beginning of the commentary on the sixth book of the *Aeneid*, Bernardus declares that there is nothing lower than the human body, and therefore they call it "the underworld," for which reason it is viewed as a prison for the soul, because of its vices: "Cum itaque nil sit inferius humano corpore, infernum id appellaverunt. Quod autem legimus in inferis animas coactione teneri quadam a spiritibus carcerariis, hoc idem dicebant pati anime in corporibus a viciis" (p. 28).

8. On the four descents see also William of Conches's analysis in his glosses on Boethius, cited in Édouard Jeauneau, "L'Usage de la notion d'*integumentum* à travers les gloses de Guillaume de Conches," *AHDLMA* 32 (1957): 42; and the analysis of their influence in the Middle Ages, in Jane Chance Nitzsche, *The Genius Figure in Antiquity and the Middle Ages* (New York and London: Columbia University Press, 1975), chapter 3.

9. On the Boethius commentaries in the Middle Ages and their history and use, see Diane K. Bolton, "Manuscripts and Commentaries on Boethius, *De consolatione Philosophiae* in England in the Middle Ages" (B. Litt. thesis, Oxford, 1965). For the evolution of the Orpheus figure in the Middle Ages, see John Block Friedman, *Orpheus in the Middle Ages* (Cambridge, Mass.: Harvard University Press, 1970); and John Warden, ed., *Orpheus — The Metamorphosis of a Myth* (Toronto and Buffalo: University of Toronto Press, 1982).

10. See Jane Chance, "Chaucerian Irony in the Boethian Short Poems: The Dramatic Tension between Classical and Christian," *ChauR* 20 (1986): 235–45. Recent views advance the date of the *Book of the Duchess* from 1369 to 1372. See also Francis Xavier Newman's analysis of the parallels between the *Book* and the *Consolatio* in his excellent dissertation, "*Somnium*: Medieval Theories of Dreaming and the Form of Vision Poetry" (Diss., Princeton, 1963), pp. 360–72.

11. Normally, within the very long tradition glossing Hercules in the *Aeneid* and Boethius commentaries, and the Senecan glosses growing out of them, Hercules represents wisdom and fortitude, attributes of the ideal prince. See, for example, the tenth-to-twelfth-century gloss on Hercules by Remigius of Auxerre and his English revisers, commenting on Boethius 4m7 (they attribute this gloss to Ovid) and his name derived from "heroncleus," or the "fame of strong men," in particular the "citadel" of mind that overcomes anxiety and adversity: "Hercules quasi Heracles id est heroncleos dicitur, hoc est virorum fortium fama. Arx mentis esse intelligitur que omnes equanimiter adversitates sustinet et temporalium erumnarum molestia sunt victrici curam. Depugnat ut invisibili creatoris contemplatione quoniam creature possibile est in celestibus delectetur" (Remigius, *Boeth.*, p. 71). For Hercules in late medieval and Renaissance art and literature, see E. Tietze-Conrat, "Notes on Hercules at the Crossroads," *Journal of the Warburg and Courtauld Institutes* 14 (1953): 305–9; Theodor E. Mommsen, "Petrarch and the Story of the Choice of Hercules," *Journal of the Warburg and Courtald Institutes* 14 (1953): 178–92; Erwin Panofsky, *Hercules am Scheidewege und andere antike Bildstoffe in der neueren Kunst, Studien der Bibliothek Warburg*, 18 (Leipzig and Berlin: B. G. Teubner, 1930); and most recently, Lawrence Nees, *A Tainted Mantle: Hercules and the Classical Tradition at the Carolingian Court* (Philadelphia: University of Pennsylvania Press, 1991).

Chaucer's sources for the Monk's legend of Hercules include Boethius's *Consolatio* and its commentary tradition as well as Virgil's *Aeneid*: R. L. Hoffman, "Ovid and the Monk's Tale of Hercules," *N & Q* 210 (1965): 406–9, notes that the list of twelve Labors is modeled on 4m7 of Boethius (13–31) rather than Ovid, *Metamorphoses* 9.101–241; the Monk's focus on Deianira perhaps derived from *Heroides* 9.67–70, wherein Deianira reproaches Hercules for his effeminacy. For a brief examination of Chaucer's indebtedness to Virgil's *Aeneid* 6.268–94 (a description of the entrance to the underworld and the monsters that include centaurs, Scyllas, and the beast of Lerna, in 287) for a misplaced epithet used in describing the Hydra of Lerna in the second of the twelve Labors, see William C. McDermott, "Chaucer and Virgil," *Classica et Medievalia* 23 (1962): 216–17.

12. In the Monk's version, Chaucer follows the order of Labors provided by Nicholas Trevet in his fourteenth-century commentary, except that he reverses the first two Labors, that is, he begins with the Nemean lion and follows it with the battle with the centaurs; however, unlike Trevet, Chaucer's Monk downplays Hercules' extraordinary ability as a wise man. Edmund Silk has transcribed Oxford, Bodleian, MS. Rawlinson G.187.

13. Barbara Nolan, "The Art of Expropriation: Chaucer's Narrator in *The Book of the Duchess*," in *New Perspectives in Chaucer Criticism*, ed. Donald M. Rose (Norman, Okla.: Pilgrim Books, 1981), p. 219.

14. "Thus when the soul, the wife of Christ, sees that her husband the Son of God mounted the ship of the cross where he suffered and died and sees him dead, she should put herself in the sea—that is in the bitterness of penitence and confession through devotion—because of him. She should be renewed together with him who was made a bird in his Resurrection and Ascension and in this way put on the likeness of a bird and ascend and fly through contemplation. In this way Psalm 76:20 may be said to her: 'Your way is in the sea and your paths in many waters'" (Bersuire, *Ovidius*, trans. p. 373; *Ovidius*, p. 161).

15. Chaucer may have used the version in Guillaume de Machaut, *Le dit de la fonteinne amoureuse*, in *Œuvres*, ed. E. Hoepffner, Société des Anciens Textes Français (Paris: 1908–21); trans. B. A. Windeatt, p. 31. Severs, "The Sources," pp. 355–62, acknowledges the similarity of Chaucer's tale to that of Machaut's *Dit de la fonteinne amoureuse*, particularly in its use of Morpheus and what might be termed the middle of Ovid's narrative—the prayer to Juno, Juno's sending of Iris to the Cave of Sleep, Morpheus's appear-

ance in a dream. But Severs finds additional parallels in Statius, *Thebaid* 10, in the description of Juno's visit to the cave; Virgil's *Aeneid* 2.794, in the appearance of Creusa's ghost to Aeneas; the *Ovide moralisé*, Machaut's main source, on the Cave of Sleep. Nolan, however ("The Art of Expropriation," pp. 203–22), while interpreting the narrator as an entirely new creation transcending Chaucer's sources, also points to two main sources for the story, the *Ovide moralisé* 11.3830–31 (instead of Ovid), where the lovers pay more attention to their hearts than to the journey to heaven, and Machaut, *Le dit de la fonteinne amoureuse*, in which Morpheus also appears (p. 214). In addition, note the possible Italian influence on Alcyone and her traditional significance in Petrarch and Boccaccio, in Ellen E. Martin, "The Interpretation of Chaucer's Alcyone," *ChauR* 18 (1983): 18–22. For the citation of the story of Ceyx and Alcione in relation to Somnus and his three sons, within a larger discussion of dreams, see Holkot, *In librum Sapientiae*, pp. 633–34 (192).

16. "The first son is sent to the proud and for them makes representations of human nobility, or dignities and honors, or of worldly pomp in dress, in carriage, in the possession of servants, and in riding. These are the ones who do not care much for riches or pleasure; and the second son is sent to the lustful and does not represent anything except what pertains to brutes.... This son creates in man worry and fleshly care about desires and food and drink and love and rest. These men are not principally concerned with honor or riches but with pleasure. The third son of Sleep is sent to the greedy. He makes a man think about inanimate things, especially gold, silver, and the minerals of the earth" (Bersuire, *Ovidius*, trans. pp. 374–75; see also *Ovidius*, pp. 161–62). The sons of Sleep are sent only "ad reges et nobiles duces," to "kings and noble leaders." Their duties are carefully specified: "Morpheus has the task of not portraying anything in a sleeper's head except for a human representation with the carriage and speech and other qualities which pertain to human nature. Icelos creates likenesses of animals, birds, and serpents with all the characteristics pertaining to beasts. But he has nothing to do with human or inanimate shapes. Phantasos principally creates the figures of inanimate things like stones, mountains, or homes." There is nothing at all on Morpheus in the Ovidian commentaries of Arnulf of Orleans and John of Garland, or in the mythographic compendia of the three Vatican Mythographers and Giovanni Boccaccio; however, Holkot cites the same Bersuire passage (with the sons called Morpheus, Icarus, and Panthesus) in his commentary on *Sapientia* 192, pp. 633–34, cited in Allen, "Mythology," pp. 368–70. Thomas Walsingham, in his fifteenth-century *Archana deorum* 11.7, devotes much of his analysis of the myth of Ceyx and Alcyone to Morpheus, a figure he describes as one of the three sons of Somnus (along with Ithacon, or Icelos, also called Febetonia, or Phobetor, and Panthasos, or Phantasos) (p. 167). Walsingham describes Sompnus as one of the gods of the underworld, "unus e diis infernorum" (p. 166). His differentiation of the functions of the sons is identical to Bersuire's. These glosses will also be important for Chaucer's specific invocation of Morpheus (who governs fame and honors) in the *Hous of Fame*.

17. On Medea, see Joel Nicholas Feimer, "The Figure of Medea in Medieval Literature: A Thematic Metamorphosis," *DAI* 44A (1984): 3057A; through the influence of courtly love, Medea was transformed into a saint of love in both the *Legend of Good Women* and Gower's *Confessio*.

18. See the famous introductory stanza of *Sir Gawain and the Green Knight*, ed. J. R. R. Tolkien and E. V. Gordon, 2d ed. rev. Norman Davis (Oxford: Clarendon Press, 1967), with its Arthurian genealogy traced back to Aeneas. See also the early chapters of Geoffrey of Monmouth, conveniently found in *History of the Kings of Britain*, trans. Lewis Thorpe (Harmondsworth, Middlesex: Penguin, 1966).

19. For treatments of the Judgment of Paris in the Middle Ages, see Jane Chance,

"The Medieval Sources of Cristoforo Landino's Allegorization of the Judgment of Paris," *SP* 81 (1984): 145–60; also Margaret J. Ehrhart, *The Judgment of the Trojan Prince Paris in Medieval Literature* (Philadelphia: University of Pennsylvania Press, 1987). For Chaucer's use of the myth in the *Troilus*, see Pat R. Orr, "Pallas Athena and the Threefold Choice in Chaucer's *Troilus and Criseyde*," in Chance, *Mythographic Art*, pp. 159–76.

20. Paris is glossed as *concupiscencia et amor speciei* by Holkot, *In librum Sapientiae*, p. 520 (156).

21. "We interpret Pallas as the life of contemplation; Juno, the active life; Venus, the life of pleasure.... But which of these goddesses should have the apple is debatable. For certain people such as philosophers prefer the contemplative life over the others; certain people such as politicians, the active life; certain people such as the Epicureans, the life of ease over the active and the contemplative. Venus seems more beautiful to Paris, because sense places contemplation and action below pleasure, and therefore Pallas and Juno take revenge upon Troy. Because it is pleasing for sense to wallow in pleasures, it is very painful to the flesh to contemplate or act" ([Bern. Sil.] *Aen.*, p. 46, trans. p. 47). The Judgment of Paris myth reappears in Holkot's gloss on Paris (cited in n. 20), but without the mythographic weight of the three lives.

22. See F. N. Robinson's note on line F 510 in the second edition of *The Works of Geoffrey Chaucer* (Boston: Houghton Mifflin, 1961).

23. In Hyginus's first-century *Fabulae* appears a fairly literal rendition: Apollo here grants two gifts to Admetus before he marries Alceste—first, a boar and a lion to yoke to a chariot in order to carry her off, and second, the possibility of a substitute at the moment of death. "When neither his father nor his mother was willing to die for him, his wife Alcestis offered herself, and died for him in vicarious death. Later Hercules called her back from the dead" (p. 58 [myth 51]).

24. First, "When Admetus fell ill and discovered he was dying, he sought to avert it by entreating Apollo, who said he could do nothing for him in his sickness unless he found one of his relatives who would voluntarily accept death in his place."

25. For the TVM, 13.3, on Alceste, see Bode, pp. 247–48.

26. After the recitation of the literal fable, Walsingham ends with a moralization repeating TVM almost verbatim: about Alceste he agrees (p. 113 [7.8]). Note that Walsingham identifies the source of the Alceste-Admetus fable as Virgil and "non est huis loci" ("this place" meaning not his major source, that is, neither Ovid's *Metamorphoses* nor a mythographic collection like that of TVM) (p. 104 [Incipit to 7]).

27. "The girl—that is the soul—should touch him because of charity, mount him as a firm foundation because of faith, and grasp him without moving out of perseverance. Thus she will be carried by him because of the austerity of her penance and will enjoy his comfort. Psalm 44:11: 'Listen, O Daughter, and see' " (trans. pp. 176–77).

28. See the discussion of Flora and the Floralia in relation to the *Knight's Tale*, in Lorraine Kochanske Stock, "The Two Mayings in Chaucer's *Knight's Tale*: Convention and Invention," *JEGP* 85 (1986): 206–21. Also see chapter 5 of this study for a more thorough discussion of the mythographic treatment of Zephirus in relation to Chaucer's *General Prologue*.

29. Paul Clogan, in "Chaucer's Cybele and the *Liber Imaginum Deorum*," *PQ* 43 (1964): 272–74, sees Cybele in *Liber imaginum deorum* of the TVM as the source for Alceste, building on Skeat's earlier argument that in Froissart's *Dittié de la flour de la margherite* Heres' tears turned into daisies, which were then made into a garland and sent by Mercury to Serés (Ceres). This interpretation unfortunately ignores the more figurative signification of Alceste as a Christian transformation emblem—in short, the duality of her symbolism on both the classical and Christian levels; see Robert W. Hanning,

"Poetic Emblems in Medieval Narrative Texts," in Lois Ebin, ed., *Vernacular Poetics in the Middle Ages*, Studies in Medieval Culture, no. 16 (Kalamazoo, Mich.: Medieval Institute Publications, 1984), pp. 1–31. In addition, it is difficult to reconcile with Kiser's interpretation of Alceste as poetry, the daisy or day's eye, vehicle for truth (*Telling Classical Tales*). However, note that Holkot links Cybele as the mother of all the gods with bitterness or penitence that follows destruction and ruin in his commentary on the Twelve Prophets—and certainly it is Alceste to whom the narrator "confesses" his literary sins. See *In librum duodecim*, fol. 107r, cited in Allen, "Mythology," p. 264.

30. See also TVM 2.1–2, Bode, pp. 157–58, on Cybele as *gloriae firmitas*.

31. The passage is repeated by TVM 2.3, in Bode, p. 158, and Walsingham, 1.26, p. 34. TVM 2.3 attributes its gloss to Remigius of Auxerre: Cybele, as Ops, wife of Saturn, is said to be a corpulent mother because she is the procreatrix of everything on earth, dressed in a discolored garment ornamented with gems and metals to represent all the species and varieties of herbs and grasses (p. 158).

32. Kiser, *Telling Classical Tales*, pp. 22, 36. Other treatments of Cupid seem unaware of the conventional mythography: for Cupid as a medieval symbol of marital generative love, but nevertheless interpreted as indiscriminate in love in the *Legend*, see Sarah Stanbury Smith, "Cupid's Sight in the Prologue to the *Legend of Good Women*," *Centerpoint* 4 (1981): 95–102; for Cupid's antifeminism and the systematic irony directed at him, see Elaine Tuttle Hansen, "Irony and the Antifeminist Narrator in Chaucer's *Legend of Good Women*," *JEGP* 82 (1983): 11–31.

33. Theodulf, pp. 168–71, is repeated essentially by Walsingham, p. 156 (10.11). See the discussion of Theodulf in chapter 2 for his influence on Chaucer's depiction of the other son of Venus, Aeneas.

34. "Ceres, who was in ancient times queen of the kingdom of the Sicilians, enjoys the privilege of being the first to discover cultivation and to invent the necessary tools," namely, using oxen for plowing (the implement for which she invented), and sowing, harvesting, grinding, and using grain in bread. "Thus this woman taught and instructed men who had been accustomed, like beasts, to live on acorns, wild grain, and haws, to make use of more convenient foods," in Christine de Pizan, *The Book of the City of Ladies*, trans. Earl Jeffrey Richards (New York: Persea Books, 1982), pp. 75–76 (1.35.1). The Old French text is available only in Maureen Cheney Curnow, "'Le Livre de la Cité des Dames' de Christine de Pisan: A Critical Edition" (Diss., Vanderbilt University, 1975).

35. "This lady did even more: for she had the people of that time gather together in communities. They had traditionally lived scattered here and there in the forest and wilderness, wandering like animals. She taught them to build cities and towns of permanent construction where they could reside together. Thus, thanks to this woman, the world was led away from bestial living conditions to a rational, human life. Poets dreamed up the fable that Ceres' daughter was carried off by Pluto, the god of Hell. And because of the authority of her knowledge and the great good she brought about for the world, the people of that time worshiped her and called her the goddess of grain" (Christine de Pizan, *The Book of the City of Ladies*, p. 76 [1.35.1]).

36. Allen, "Reading Chaucer's *Good Women*," p. 419.

37. On the composite "Good Woman" (in fact not good at all, but lecherous, homicidal, etc.), suggested by the famous martyrs whose legends were not finished, see Pat Trefzger Overbeck, "Chaucer's Good Woman," *ChauR* 2 (1967): 75–94. She suggests that the connection between the unfinished nature of the *Legends* and the *Canterbury Tales* may be the Bad Woman, the Wife of Bath. On the three types of literary women in the Middle Ages—chaste wife, "manly" virgin, martyr of love—see Ann Hunter McMillan, " 'Evere an Hundred Goode Ageyn Oon Badde': Catalogues of Good Women in Medieval Litera-

ture," *DAI* 40 (1980): 5437A. See also the introduction to her translation of the *Legend* (Houston: Rice University Press, 1987). Faye Walker-Pelkey has completed a dissertation (at Rice University) that explains the complexity of these legends in terms of contemporary gender theory ("Gender Nominalized: Unmanning Men, Disgendering Women in Chaucer's *Legend of Good Women*" [1991]).

Chapter 2. "Geffrey" as Dido, Ganymede, "Marcia": Mythographic and Gender Parody in the *Hous of Fame*

1. For echoes of French love visions in the *Hous of Fame*, especially Nichole de Margival's *Panthère d'amours*, see W. O. Sypherd, *Studies in Chaucer's "Hous of Fame,"* Chaucer Society 2d series, no. 39 (London: K. Paul, Trench, Tubner and Co., 1907); Howard R. Patch, "Chaucer's Desert," *MLN* 34 (1919): 321–28, esp. 321–26; also Eustache Deschamps's *Lai du desert d'amour*. For the texts of the French sources (de Margival, *Le dit de la Panthère d'amours*, ca. 1300, and his account of a house of fortune, and Jean Froissart, *Le Temple d'Honneur*, perhaps 1363, for a brief description of a Temple of Honor), see pp. 127–38 of B. A. Windeatt, ed. and trans., *Chaucer's Dream Poetry: Sources and Analogues* (Cambridge, England: D. S. Brewer; Totowa, N.J.: Rowman and Littlefield, 1982).

2. On fame and the role of poet, see Piero Boitani, *Chaucer and the Imaginary World of Fame* (Cambridge, England: D. S. Brewer; Totowa, N.J.: Barnes and Noble, 1984), who documents the history of their relationship from Homer to Italian trecento writers; for his discussion of the poem, see especially chapter 4, pp. 159–74. For Chaucer's indebtedness to the views of Froissart and Christine de Pizan on fame, see Laura Kendrick, "Fame's Fabrication," in Paul Strohm and Thomas J. Heffernan, eds., *SAC*, Proceedings, no. 1, 1984 (Knoxville: New Chaucer Society/University of Tennessee Press, 1987): 135–48.

3. For Chaucer's use of Ovid in the poem, particularly for its moral, which stresses flux and mutability, see John M. Fyler, *Chaucer and Ovid* (New Haven: Yale University Press, 1979), pp. 23–64. For an excellent discussion of the indebtedness to the Ovidian model of the character of the Chaucerian narrator as an inept and inexperienced lover in various poems, esp. the *Hous of Fame*, see Fyler, chapter 5, and on the *Hous of Fame*, chapter 2. On Chaucer's use of the *Ovide moralisé* in the poem, particularly for the story of Ariadne, see John Livingston Lowes, "Chaucer and the *Ovide moralisé*," *PMLA* 33 (1918): 302–25. For the concept of fame as a judge, see Sheila Delany, "Chaucer's *House of Fame* and the *Ovide Moralisé*," *Comparative Literature* 20 (1968): 254–64. For other specific mythological references from Ovid, see notes 18 and 19.

4. On Chaucer's overall use of Virgil in the poem, see Edgar Finley Shannon, *Chaucer and the Roman Poets*, Harvard Studies in Comparative Literature, vol. 7 (Cambridge, Mass.: Harvard University Press, 1929), esp. pp. 48ff. for the discussion of the use of the *Aeneid* and Ovid in book 1; Albert C. Friend, "Chaucer's Version of the *Aeneid*," *Speculum* 28 (1953): 317–23; and J. A. W. Bennett, *Chaucer's Book of Fame: An Exposition of "The House of Fame"* (Oxford: Clarendon Press, 1968). For a comparison of Chaucer's "journey" and that of Aeneas, with Aeneas's diversion in Carthage equivalent to Geoffrey's diversion in the court of Fame, see William Joyner, "Parallel Journeys in Chaucer's *House of Fame*," *Papers on Language and Literature* 12 (1976): 3–19.

5. All three of the Vatican Mythographers are contained in Bode, here, p. 161 (TVM 3.34). This gloss, in the section on Jupiter, is followed in 3.4 by a section on Jove's eagle, suggesting a structural paradigm for the sequence of books in *Hous of Fame*. Further, as if in anticipation of book 2, there immediately follows the section on Aeneas and Dido within a discussion of physics, the left, cosmologically associated with adversity, and the right, with the heavenly (p. 161).

6. In another place, the TVM distinguishes between the fates of Dido and Aeneas, the first as an *imago* under the earth, the second led by Pallas on his journey (6.1). Note that Aeneas's fame was important in Christian historiography, although clouded by his betrayal of Dido, according to David Lyle Jeffrey, "Sacred and Secular Scripture: Authority and Interpretation in *The House of Fame*," in Jeffrey, ed., *Chaucer and Scriptural Tradition* (Ottawa: University of Ottawa Press, 1984), pp. 207–28, who nevertheless concludes that the biblical language of the poem brings up the chief questions, not the "story of Troy or its panoply of typologies."

7. B. G. Koonce, *Chaucer and the Tradition of Fame: Symbolism in "The House of Fame"* (Princeton: Princeton University Press, 1966).

8. See Boitani for his succinct description of the differences in source for the three parts (*Chaucer and the Imaginary World*, pp. 118–25).

9. Fyler, *Chaucer and Ovid*, p. 45.

10. For other, little-known, sources, especially Latin (for example, Calcidius), see Joseph E. Greenan, "Chaucer and Chalcidius: The Platonic Origins of the *Hous of Fame*," *Viator* 15 (1984): 237–62; and for the *Ecloga Theoduli*, see [Ferdinand] Holthausen, "Chaucer und Theodulus," *Anglia* 16 (1894): 264–66. Whether or not its parts have different sources may help to resolve the issue of whether or not it is unified, as some earlier critics argued, including Paul G. Ruggiers, "The Unity of Chaucer's *House of Fame*," *SP* 50 (1953): 16–29; repr. in Edward Wagenknecht, ed., *Chaucer: Modern Essays in Criticism* (London, Oxford, New York: Oxford University Press, 1959; repr. 1970), pp. 295–308; and in Schoeck and Taylor, 2:261–74, who see the poem as unified through fortune's changes, fame, and love. For the narrator's progression from fantasy to the reality of experience as unifying, see David M. Bevington, "The Obtuse Narrator in Chaucer's *House of Fame*," *Speculum* 36 (1961): 288–98. For the belief that the conflicting theories about dreams, morals, universe, and literary theory emphasize faith as reconciliation rather than reason, see Sheila Delany, *Chaucer's "House of Fame," The Poetics of Skeptical Fideism* (Chicago: University of Chicago Press, 1972).

11. On its dating, see Howard H. Schless, *Chaucer and Dante: A Revaluation* (Norman, Okla.: Pilgrim Books, 1984), p. 41. For an excellent discussion of "Anglo-Italian Contacts in the Fourteenth Century" focusing in particular on Chaucer's two trips to Italy (between December 1, 1372 and May 23, 1373 and between May 28 and September 19, 1378), see the article of the same title by Wendy Childs, in *Chaucer and the Italian Trecento*, ed. Piero Boitani (Cambridge, London, and New York: Cambridge University Press, 1983), pp. 65–87.

12. Koonce (*Chaucer and the Tradition of Fame*) views the three parts of the poem as Chaucer's equivalent of hell, purgatory, and paradise. For the Eagle as a Dantesque Virgil figure, see Cino Chiarini, *Di una imitazione inglese della Divina Commedia: La Casa della Fama di Chaucer* (Bari: Giuseppe Laterza, 1902), pp. 76–77. On fortune and fate, see John S. P. Tatlock, "Chaucer and Dante," *MP* 3 (1905–6): 367–72; and more broadly, see John Livingston Lowes, "Chaucer and Dante," *MP* 14 (1916–17): 705–35; and Howard H. Schless, "Chaucer and Dante," in *Critical Approaches to Medieval Literature: Selected Papers from the English Institute 1958–9*, ed. Dorothy Bethurum (New York and London: Columbia University Press, 1960; repr. 1967), pp. 134–54; and Schless, *Chaucer and Dante*, pp. 29–76, esp. pp. 41–42, for the well-known allusion to *Purgatorio* 9, plus the first and last cantos of the *Commedia*, and widely scattered "analogous passages." See also J. A. W. Bennett, "Chaucer, Dante and Boccaccio," and Boitani, "What Dante Meant to Chaucer," in Boitani, ed., *Chaucer and the Italian Trecento*, pp. 89–116 and 117–39, respectively. Boitani's essay, esp. pp. 118–25, analyzes parallels (journeys, invocations, eagle symbolism) between the *Hous of Fame* and Dante's three books.

13. In acknowledgment of its disunity, Boitani declares that "Its construction has often given the impression of total disorder. At first sight it is impossible to understand. After reading it the least one can say is that it is puzzling" (*Chaucer and the Imaginary World*, p. 7). The differing images and sources for the three parts are discussed on pp. 118–25. Those critics who believe that it can be examined as a whole poem have nevertheless puzzled over the incongruity of linking what might be summed up by the figures of Venus, Virgil, and Fame (or at least her Palace). Fyler succinctly summarizes the problem (*Chaucer and Ovid*, p. 30).

14. For the poem as a vehicle for literary theory—on how and why stories are believed, as we can see from *sooth* and *trouth* in the poem—see Geoffrey T. Shepherd, "Make Believe: Chaucer's Rationale of Story-Telling in *The House of Fame*," in *J. R. R. Tolkien, Scholar and Story-teller: Essays in Memoriam*, ed. Mary Salu and Robert T. Farrell (Ithaca, N.Y., and London: Cornell University Press, 1979), pp. 204–20. On the poem as an *ars poetica* on speech, sound, and poetic order, with its discussions of love actually veiling discussions of poetry, see Lawrence K. Shook, "*The House of Fame*," in Beryl Rowland, ed., *Companion to Chaucer Studies* (New York, Toronto, London: Oxford University Press, 1968; rev. ed. New York and Oxford, 1979), pp. 414–27. On the address to Thought, in the invocation to book 2, and the emphasis on memory in art and on love tidings, or words from old books, that stimulate new poems, see Beryl Rowland, "The Art of Memory and the Art of Poetry in the *House of Fame*," *University of Ottawa Quarterly* 51 (1981): 162–71.

15. *Anticlaudianus* 8.305 (a work by Alan of Lille mentioned in line 986 of the *Hous of Fame*) has been identified as an important but little-known source, in Fyler (*Chaucer and Ovid*, p. 34): in 1.142–43, Virgil is construed as a liar and historian.

16. See Friend, "Chaucer's Version of the *Aeneid*," pp. 317–23; Louis Brewer Hall, "Chaucer and the Dido-and-Aeneas Story," *MS* 25 (1963): 148–59; Mary Louise Lord, "Dido as an Example of Chastity: The Influence of Example Literature," *Harvard Library Bulletin* 17:1 and 2 (1969): 22–44, 216–32; and Bennett, *Chaucer's Book of Fame*, pp. 27–48 in particular. Most of these accounts show Chaucer's use of the medieval romance version of the *Aeneid* portraying Dido as heroine found in the *Roman d'Énéas* (ca. 1160) and of the *narratio naturalis*. They conclude: the wall painting of the temple of Venus follows the arrangement of Simon Aurea Capra in the twelfth-century *Ilias*, resembling the enlarged version of the poem in *Scriptorium*'s first volume published by André Boutemy (Friend); this version emphasizes Venus, uses the *narratio naturalis*, but Chaucer in contrast stresses Dido more. Shannon in *Chaucer and the Roman Poets* sees the poem as a conflation of the *Aeneid* story and the seventh letter of the *Heroides* so that Dido is extolled; Louis Brewer Hall instead turns to the medieval tradition of *Aeneid* redactions (the *Excidium Troiae*, the redaction in the *Primera crónica general*, Simon Aurea Capra's *Ilias latina*, the thirteenth-century *I fatti d'Enea*, and selections from Guido da Pisa's *Fiore d'Italia*). All these suppress book 2 and most of book 6; use the *ordo naturalis*; add Trojan history outside the *Aeneid*; use contemporary settings and characters; and use various techniques to motivate the story's changes. These result in an emphasis on the story of Dido and Aeneas, to which Chaucer adds a long *amplificatio* emphasizing the theme of desertion (387–427) and a portion of the beginning of the seventh letter of the *Heroides*. Hall compares the Dido of the *Hous of Fame* with the queen of the legend. Finally, Lord examines Dido's role as an exemplum of chaste widowhood for early Christian writers; she traces example literature beginning with the Apologists to show that Dido's desire not to remarry her African suitor Iarbas led to her suicide and recognition of her bravery, versus her Virgilian role as tragic victim of Aeneas's love (in part 1). Grammarians and Virgil commen-

tators such as Servius, Macrobius, Priscian, early Dante commentators (despite the account in the *Inferno*), Petrarch, especially in *Epistolae de rebus senilibus* (4.5), and Boccaccio in the *Genealogia* 2.60 and 6.53 all preserved the figure of the chaste Dido despite the poetic account; some of these commentators defend Virgil against the charge of lying, as Boccaccio did when he indicated Virgil masked her chastity under a poetic veil (14.13).

17. These unhappy pairs appear elsewhere in Chaucer, in the *Book of the Duchess* (Medea and Jason, 330, 726–27; Phyllis and Demophon, 728–31; Dido and Aeneas, 731–34), in the *Prologue* (or the legends) of the *Legend of Good Women* (Dido, Phyllis, Ariadne, Hypsipyle, and Medea), the *Squire's Tale* (Medea and Jason, Paris and Oenone [548]), the *Troilus* (Oenone [1.654]), and the *Monk's Tale* (Deianira [2095–2142]).

18. On Dido, see fol. 25vb, in Ralph J. Hexter, *Ovid and Medieval Schooling. Studies in Medieval School Commentaries on Ovid's Ars Amatoria, Epistulae ex Ponto, and Epistulae Heroidum*, Münchener Beiträge zur Mediävistik und Renaissance-Forschung (Munich: Arbeo-Gesellschaft, 1986), p. 256: "Ex intentione auctoris stultus amans arguitur." Phyllis, in SVM, myth 214, also suffers from impatience and sad impulses. See fol. 27vb on Ariadne (Hexter, p. 270).

19. See fol. 1rb, in Hexter, *Ovid and Medieval Schooling*, p. 157. In terms of the *Heroides* women, then, Penelope (*Heroides* 1) represents legitimate love, and is the most important example, followed by Deianira (9), Medea (12), Laodamia (13), Hypermnestra (14), and perhaps Hermione (8).

20. The commentary on *Epistulae heroidum* (Clm 19475, fols. 16rb-31vb, now in Munich, and twelfth century) is contained in Hexter, *Ovid and Medieval Schooling*, pp. 229–304.

21. Put another way, it may be that Aeneas leaves because Venus has moved into Virgo, the Virgin, according to TVM 11.4, in Bode, p. 230.

22. This portrait of Venus in 131–39 links her in this poem with the description of the statue in the *Knight's Tale* (1955–66), the *Libellus de deorum imaginibus*, and Bersuire's *Ovidius moralizatus*, according to Betty Nye Quinn, "Venus, Chaucer, and Peter Bersuire," *Speculum* 38 (1963): 479–80. For an excellent mythographic survey of Venus in the Middle Ages and in this poem, see Koonce, *Chaucer and the Tradition of Fame*, pp. 89–97, in which Venus appears to represent "carnal delight"; he draws on Boccaccio, the TVM, Bernardus's commentary on the *Aeneid*, Fulgentius, and John Scot's commentary on Martianus. On the iconography of Venus, see Bennett, *Chaucer's Book of Fame*, pp. 15–26. See also Holkot's portrait describing her as Luxuria, who has been depicted as "mulier plena sorde, sine corde, excecata, spoliata, ignita, columbis custodita, cum dampno de mari nata, Vulcano maritata, concha marina honorata, rosis adornata" (*In librum duodecim*, fols. 85v-86v, cited in Allen, "Mythology," p. 383). This passage is essentially repeated by John Ridevall in *Fulgentius Metaforalis, ein Beitrag zur Geschichte der antiken Mythologie im Mittelalter*, ed. Hans Liebeschütz, Studien der Bibliothek Warburg, no. 4 (Leipzig and Berlin: B. G. Teubner, 1926).

23. *Rerum senilium libri*, 4.4, "De quibusdam fictionibus Virgilii," appears in the facsimile edition of *Francisci Petrarchae operum*, vol. 2 [Basel, 1554], repr., Ridgewood, N.J.: The Gregg Press, 1965, pp. 867–74 (the only complete edition of Petrarch's works). There exists a partial translation by James Harvey Robinson and Henry Winchester Rolfe, *Petrarch: The First Modern Scholar and Man of Letters*, 2d ed. (New York and London: G. P. Putnam's Sons and The Knickerbocker Press, 1914), pp. 234–36.

24. See *De secreto conflictu curarum mearum*, in Francesco Petrarca, *Opere*, ed. Giovanni Ponte (Milan: U. Mursia and Co., 1968), pp. 432–597; also, *Petrarch's Secret: or, the Soul's Conflict with Passion: Three Dialogues between himself and S. Augustine*, trans.

William H. Draper (London: Chatto and Windus, 1911; repr. Norwood, Pa.: Norwood Editions, 1978), p. 82.

25. Walsingham takes his description from Isidore and Theodulf, who interpret wings as fickleness, and so on; the passage reappears in *Archana Deorum* 10.11.29–49, pp. 156–57.

26. Penelope Doob, *The Idea of the Labyrinth from Classical Antiquity through the Middle Ages* (Ithaca, N.Y.: Cornell University Press, 1990).

27. Bernardus's gloss on book 2 culminates in his explicit source-mongering for the tale of Dido and Ariadne. See [Bern. Sil.] *Aen.*, p. 16, trans. p. 16. This suspicious view of the Trojan colors other events involving Aeneas outside the Dido episode, mostly connected in some way with Troy, the national character, and Juno's enmity toward the nation, all of which anticipate his perfidy, in the epic story repeated in the *Hous of Fame*. So Chaucer takes care to pile one deceitful, discordant event atop another as he begins his account of the fall of Troy with Sinon's Greek deceit ("his false forswerynge, / And his chere and his lesynge" [153–54]) in pretending to be a traitor so that the Trojans would allow both him and the Trojan horse entry into the city (155–56). This climactic incident is followed by the fall of Troy: the slaying of old Priam as well as his son Polites, the castle burned, the flight of Aeneas (157–61), and, in addition, the death of Creusa, Iulus, and Ascanius, the tempests caused by Juno, the false love of Aeneas for Dido, followed by her suicide (certainly the expanded heart of Chaucer's *Aeneid*), further tempests once Aeneas puts to sea again, followed by the loss of his steersman, his battles with Latinus in Italy, and finally the completion of what Chaucer terms the hero's *aventure.*

28. According to John M. Steadman, "Chaucer's 'Desert of Libye,' Venus, and Jove," *MLN* 76 (1961): 196–201, "Ammon" means "sandy" and represents another name for Jove; Bacchus is also rescued from the sands by Jove's ram just as Chaucer is rescued by his eagle.

29. See Boitani, *Chaucer and the Imaginary World*, p. 165.

30. SVM relies heavily on Fulgentius in his passage in myth 206, on p. 144. This identification occurs within the context of a discussion of free will, as in Fulgentius, but amplified to include a description of the physiological (and, perhaps obliquely, astrological) reasons for such an identification. Created out of a mixture of earth and water, man's parts are joined together by the "nuptial" gods, "nuptial" presumably in the cosmogonic and Stoic sense of which Martianus speaks in *De nuptiis Philologiae et Mercurii,* so that Jove controls the head, Minerva the eyes, Juno the arms, and Neptune the breast.

31. See Bersuire, *Ovidius,* p. 162 (on 9.633), trans. pp. 374–78. The Ovidian commentaries of John of Garland and Arnulf of Orleans, and the compendia of the three Vatican Mythographers and Giovanni Boccaccio, do not gloss Morpheus; Holkot and Walsingham, however, cite the same Bersuire passage (changing the names of the sons). See the extended discussion in chapter 1, n. 16.

32. See Bersuire, *Ovidius,* trans. p. 375; the remainder of the passage elaborates on the three roles (see chapter 1, n. 16).

33. Koonce consults Bernardus's commentary on the *Aeneid,* as well as Fulgentius and Boccaccio, to discover that the Dido episode represents the soul's "triumph over evil concupiscence" (pp. 107–25). Koonce, however, also sees Dido as illustrating a mind destroyed (inordinate love, grief, despair, suicide). Her despair is "hell" to which sloth has led her.

34. Jove's Eagle in Chaucer is drawn especially from *Purgatorio* 9.19–24, 28–30. Further, the "flight of Thought" is initiated with the invocation to the Muses and Thought (in addition to Cipris), drawn from *Inferno* 2.8.524 and *Paradiso* 1.11.528, according to Schless, *Chaucer and Dante.* For the Dantesque parallels and associations of the Eagle,

also in *Purgatorio* 32 as well as *Paradiso* 20, see Schless (*Chaucer and Dante*, pp. 46–47), who also mentions Ovid, *Metamorphoses* 10.155–61. Chaucer also draws on the Eagle in *Amorosa Visione*; see David Wallace, *Chaucer and the Early Writings of Boccaccio* (Woodbridge, Suffolk, and Dover, N.H.: D. S. Brewer, 1985), p. 17. On the Eagle as a symbol of air, see Reginald Berry, "Chaucer's Eagle and the Element Air," *University of Toronto Quarterly* 43 (1974): 285–97. As a traditional symbol for the flight of thought, see John M. Steadman, "Chaucer's Eagle: A Contemplative Symbol," *PMLA* 75 (1960): 153–59. In line with these interpretations, on the Eagle's Ciceronian rhetoric, see William S. Wilson, "The Eagle's Speech in Chaucer's *House of Fame*," *Quarterly Journal of Speech* 50 (1964): 153–58.

35. Boitani, *Chaucer and the Imaginary World*, p. 186.

36. Fyler, *Chaucer and Ovid*, p. 49.

37. Holkot echoes this *moralitas*, compressing the very long gloss in Bersuire to an exemplum about pride of the son and the need to escape sins through contemplation of God (*In librum duodecim prophetas*, fol. 37r, cited in Allen, "Mythology," p. 337).

38. John of Garland, p. 44; trans. p. 129. See also Koonce's discussion, *Chaucer and the Tradition of Fame*, pp. 164–66. On the Eagle's oversimplification of the Ovidian story of Phaethon, with consequent conflicts and deficiencies of meaning, see Joseph A. Dane, "Chaucer's Eagle's Ovid's Phaethon: A Study in Literary Reception," *Journal of Medieval and Renaissance Studies* 11 (1981): 71–82. For Chaucer's use of Ovidian phrasing in "the rede" (referring either to Phaethon or father Phoebus, but probably Phaethon burning), see Carolyn Merlo, "Chaucer's Phaethon: 'The Sonnes Sone, the Rede,' *House of Fame*, II, 941," *ELN* 17 (1979): 88–90. For "Pheton" and Dante's Feton from *Purgatorio* 4.72 connected through phantoms and illusions (except that Dante invokes Apollo at the beginning of the *Paradiso* as an agent of truth), in a larger discussion of idolatry and paganism in medieval poetry, see James S. Whitlark, "Chaucer and the Pagan Gods," *AM* 18 (1977): 65–75, here esp. 71–72.

39. Bersuire compares Phaethon with the "imprudens praelatus" (p. 49, trans. p. 155). See also Holkot, *Super librum Sapientiae 9*, p. 33 (cited in Allen, "Mythology," pp. 376–77).

40. From Fulg. *Mit.* 1.12 and 16, and FVM, myth 113, the K-Reviser of Remigius on Boethius interpolates the myth of the four horses of the sun into a gloss on Hercules' sixth Labor (the conquering of Glaucus, which is a mistake for Diomede and his flesh-eating mares). See Remigius, *Boeth.*, p. 74; discussed at length on p. 46.

41. See Schless, *Chaucer and Dante*, p. 58, on the Ovidian source for the House of Fame and its location; see also Boitani, *Chaucer and the Imaginary World*, esp. the last chapter.

42. For Apollo *in bono* as divine wisdom, both *sapientia* and *scientia* as suggested by the twin peaks of Parnassus, see Koonce, *Chaucer and the Tradition of Fame*, p. 179. For the Dantesque parallels, see also Schless, *Chaucer and Dante*, pp. 68–69. For Apollo as the tenth Muse, see Fulg. *Mit.* 1.15, pp. 25–27, trans. pp. 55–57. For polyform signification (and the fullest set of equivocations), see [Bern. Sil.] *Mart.*: as *sapientia (humana)*, see 3.107, 4.230, 6.1089–96; as *sapientia Dei*, 3.221–22, 6.301–5; as *philosophia*, 6.301–5; as *scientia de creaturis*, 6.301–5, 8.12, 8.141–42, 8.388; as god of medicine, 6.301–5; as *moderator musice sperarum*, 11.81–82; as god of *divinatio*, 6.301–5. Apollo also plays an important mythological role in the *Manciple's Tale*.

43. In the Second Vatican Mythographer, the myth of Marsyas is prefaced by the story of the invention of the double flute from a bone by Minerva (Pallas Athena), whose creation the gods ridicule because of her comic appearance in playing it—with blown-out cheeks. After she sees her foolish image reflected in Lake Tritonia, she casts it away and Marsyas finds it, challenges Apollo, and after he loses, is punished by excoriation

that removes his skin. See myth 115 on Minerva, followed by myth 116 on the competition between Apollo and Marsyas, in Bode, p. 114; the myth comes from Ovid, *Metamorphoses* 6.383–85. Marsyas has been much discussed as a type of the ignorant but vainglorious artist, glossed by the TVM, Giovanni del Virgilio, and others: see Koonce, *Chaucer and the Tradition of Fame*, p. 200. In his comment on this passage in Dante, Pietro Alighieri interprets Marsyas in the manner of other mythographers, as a type of presumptuous or vainglorious artist not aware of his own limitations, specifically as one who is not informed or instructed (*non doctus*), who disputes with a wise teacher (*cum docto et sapiente*), that is, Apollo, knowing nothing of the changes of words—declensions and conjugations, as in grammar and rhetoric; he is stripped of skin, or rather, the external appearance is raised up (or made beautiful) by wisdom (p. 549).

44. Alfred David, "How Marcia Lost her Skin: A Note on Chaucer's Mythology," in *The Learned and the Lewed: Studies in Chaucer and Medieval Literature*, ed. Larry D. Benson (Cambridge, Mass.: Harvard University Press, 1974), pp. 19–29.

45. See Koonce, *Chaucer and the Tradition of Fame*, pp. 199–200, who cites Giovanni del Virgilio, [Bern. Sil.] *Aen.*, and Coluccio Salutati. Orpheus has been much glossed in the Boethius commentaries, particularly in glosses on 3m12, in which he descends into the underworld to retrieve Eurydice; he also appears in Virgil and Ovid. See John Block Friedman, *Orpheus in the Middle Ages* (Cambridge, Mass.: Harvard University Press, 1970), who distinguishes the two traditions of Orpheus, the Boethian and the Fulgentian, in which Orpheus represents wisdom and music or poetry, respectively (pp. 90–91), but also chapter 4. See also John Warden, ed., *Orpheus—The Metamorphoses of a Myth* (Toronto and Buffalo: University of Toronto Press, 1982).

46. See myth 9.11, in Bode, p. 219. Bode indicates that the reference is taken from *Aen.* 4.516, as glossed by Servius; the Pliny reference derives from 8.42 no. 165. For the references to other magicians as expressive of a world of flux and mutability, see Fyler, *Chaucer and Ovid*, pp. 60–61.

47. See Koonce (*Chaucer and the Tradition of Fame*, p. 201), who interprets Messenus as "worldly glory." Thiodamas, after becoming the chief soothsayer for the Greeks, blew his trumpet at Thebes the midnight before the Argive attack on the city, which occurs in Statius 10.552; Chaucer apparently thinks he was the trumpeteer sounding the later attack as well as the earlier, and thus in 1455–63 places Statius on an iron pillar (iron was Mars's metal—and the tiger was linked with Thebes, which saw the animal as sacred). See Boyd A. Wise, *The Influence of Statius upon Chaucer* (Baltimore, Md.: J. H. Furst, 1911; repr. New York: Phaeton Press, 1967), pp. 36–38.

48. For the sources in Dante and Ovid, see Schless, *Chaucer and Dante*, p. 72.

49. See also Augustine, *De doctrina Christiana* 3.5, in which he explains that literal understanding is carnal understanding, as if the text had a body and soul like a human being; this passage can be found along with other texts on medieval literary theory in Robert P. Miller, ed., *Chaucer: Sources and Backgrounds* (New York: Oxford University Press, 1977), p. 55. On various literary terms, such as *sensus* and *sententia*, see also the comprehensive analysis by D. W. Robertson, Jr., "Some Medieval Literary Terminology, with Special Reference to Chrétien de Troyes," *SP* 48 (1951): 669–92.

50. Holkot echoes Bersuire in his gloss on the labyrinth. See *Super librum Sapientiae* 115, p. 387, cited in Allen, "Mythology," pp. 343–45. According to Boitani, *Chaucer and the Imaginary World*, chapter 6, pp. 189–216, the image of the labyrinth derives from the Sibyl's cave and labyrinth in *Aen.* 6.9–27. He notes that Aeneas sees a picture of the Daedalan labyrinth before entering Sibyl's cave: it is linked with the temple of Apollo, because the picture appears on its doors. The labyrinth is an image of art, like the Temple of Venus. See Doob, *The Idea of the Labyrinth*. Daedalus is also connected with the "partridge wings" on Fame's feet, taken from the *Ovide moralisé*, where Perdix or the par-

303

tridge signifies the deceitful but clever craftsman, Daedalus, the wise man; the image conveys the emptiness of fame (and the arts). See Francis X. Newman, " 'Partriches Wynges': A Note on *Hous of Fame,* 1391–92," *Mediaevalia* 6 (1980): 231–38.

Chapter 3. Venus Contextualized: The Mythographic Authority of the Body in *The Parlement of Foules*

Portions of this chapter were delivered as a paper, "Chaucer and Mythology," in the Research-in-Progress Session of the New Chaucer Society Conference, York University, York, England, August 10, 1984.

1. Love implies "an entire spectrum of varying types of love experience which the poet is trying to define and analyze," in Charles O. McDonald, "An Interpretation of Chaucer's *Parlement of Foules,*" *Speculum* 30 (1955): 444–57, repr. in *Chaucer: Modern Essays in Criticism,* ed. Edward Wagenknecht (New York: Oxford University Press, 1959), pp. 309–27, and in Schoeck and Taylor, 2:275–93; all references in this chapter are to the latter collection (this passage, p. 275). On the varieties of love within the poem, exemplified by the dream of Scipio and the dreamer's vision of the garden linked by the *Roman* as source, see A. C. Cawley, "Chaucer's Valentine: The *Parlement of Foules,*" in *Chaucer's Mind and Art,* Essays Old and New, no. 3 (London: Oliver and Boyd, 1969), pp. 125–39. Charles Muscatine finds comic, contradictory attitudes toward love in his seminal *Chaucer and the French Tradition* (Berkeley and London: University of California Press, 1957; repr. 1966), pp. 115–263. On the three episodes, each with a different source and style—involving, first, Cicero's *Somnium Scipionis* and the expository discussion of Augustinian "common profit"; next, the lyrical love garden, drawn from the *Roman de la Rose* and Boccaccio's *Teseida;* and finally, the dramatic parliament of birds, drawn from the *De planctu Naturae* of Alan of Lille—see Wolfgang Clemen, *Chaucer's Early Poetry,* trans. C. A. M. Sym (London: Methuen, 1963), pp. 125ff. Robert Worth Frank, Jr., in "Structure and Meaning in the *Parlement of Foules,*" *PMLA* 71 (1956): 530–39, determines there exist three attitudes toward love in the poem. On the ambiguous symbols and iconography of the poem to express the doubleness of love—the two gate inscriptions, the high and low orders of birds, and most important, given the conflict between courtly love and lawful married love, two Venuses—Cytherea, the star, "thow blysful lady swete" (113), and the partly undressed Venus attended by a porter named Richesse inside a dark temple whose walls portray failed lovers, see Donald C. Baker, "The *Parliament of Fowls,*" in *Companion to Chaucer Studies,* ed. Beryl Rowland, rev. ed. (New York and London: Oxford University Press, 1979), pp. 428–45, and his discussion of Bronson (1935) on the antithesis between the *Somnium* portion as well as the garden, *caritas* as well as passion, Africanus and Cytherea.

2. See J. A. W. Bennett, *Parlement of Foules: An Interpretation* (Oxford: Clarendon Press, 1957), 2d ed., 1965, which analyzes its Christian love and Neoplatonic imagery to conclude that love is the binding force in the universe. For Venus as "a prostitute goddess, not the servant of Nature, but her enemy" (p. 121), and Priapus as "the frustration of sexual desire" (p. 120), with the garden paradise as the church corrupted by man, see Bernard F. Huppé and D. W. Robertson, Jr., *Fruyt and Chaf: Studies in Chaucer's Allegories* (Princeton: Princeton University Press, 1963), pp. 104–48.

3. Derek S. Brewer, in the Introduction to his edition, noted that "The Venus passage in the *Parlement* is clearly a moral allegory, signifying selfish, lustful, illicit, disastrous love" (p. 31); see *The Parlement of Foulys,* Old and Middle English Texts (1960; repr., Manchester: Manchester University Press; New York: Barnes and Noble, 1972), pp.

1–64. This view of evil Venus in the *Parlement* has been so well assimilated that Derek Pearsall's more recent summary of medieval images of the garden, among them the *locus amoenus* of the *Parlement*, echoes it; see "Gardens as Symbol and Setting in Late Medieval Poetry," *Medieval Gardens* (Washington, D.C.: Dumbarton Oaks Research Library and Collection, 1986), pp. 237–51, here, p. 243. Earlier, in another work, Pearsall and his coauthor Elizabeth Salter similarly concluded that "Here, in the temple of Venus, and in the tableaux surrounding it, the theme is mutability, in love, in beauty, and in desire" (*Landscapes and Seasons of the Medieval World* [Toronto: University of Toronto Press, 1973], chapter 4, on "The Enclosed Garden," p. 96). Pearsall does caution in the article, "It would be wrong to simplify the whole scene into a straightforward allegory of the corruption at the heart of sexual desire contrasted with the innocence of the garden: Chaucer has laid too many allegorical traps to allow such a simpleminded encounter with his poem" (*Medieval Gardens*, pp. 244–45).

4. See Dorothy Bethurum Loomis's excellent study, "The Venus of Alanus de Insulis and the Venus of Chaucer," *Philological Essays in Honour of Herbert Dean Meritt*, ed. J. L. Rosier (The Hague: Mouton, 1971), pp. 182–95, here p. 183, also, p. 193. Elsewhere, she argues for the garden and idea of love as central to the poem, in "The Center of the *Parlement of Foules*," in *Essays in Honor of Walter Clyde Curry*, Vanderbilt Studies in Humanities, 2 (Nashville: University of Tennessee Press, 1954), pp. 39–50. Comparing the Venus in the *Parlement* to the Venus described by Alan of Lille in his *De planctu Naturae* and *Anticlaudianus*, Bethurum Loomis maintains that "she is still the handmaiden of Nature, who presides as beneficently over this poem as she did over Alain's *De Planctu*" (p. 192), despite her seeming opposite in the planet Cytherea (113).

5. McDonald has concluded, after examining source materials, that Nature is the "greatest single unifying factor ... the mediator in the poem spiritually as well as physically" (McDonald, in Schoeck and Taylor, 2:291).

6. George D. Economou has suggested that the conflict between Venus as Luxuria (in the temple) and Cytherea, goddess of legitimate love, derives from the *De planctu* portrait of conflict between Natura and Venus, in her bond with Cupid (George D. Economou, *The Goddess Natura in Medieval Literature* [Cambridge, Mass.: Harvard University Press, 1972], pp. 130, 137).

7. See Robert M. Jordan, "The Question of Unity and the *Parlement of Foules*," *English Studies in Canada* 3 (1977): 373–85.

8. For the poem as an interweaving of conflicting ideas, resolved not on earth but in heaven, see John P. McCall, "The Harmony of Chaucer's *Parliament*," *ChauR* (1970–71): 22–31. For antithesis as the source of aesthetic unity, see Michael R. Kelley, "Antithesis as the Principle of Design in the *Parlement of Foules*," *ChauR* 14 (1979): 61–73. See also Denis Walker, "*Contentio*: The Structural Paradigm of *The Parliament of Fowls*," in Paul Strohm and Thomas J. Heffernan, eds., *SAC, Proceedings*, no. 1 (Knoxville: University of Tennessee Press, 1984), pp. 173–80. On the multiplicity of authority, the disharmony, and "continuous self-reflexivity" undercutting any "pattern of orthodox theodicy," see David Aers, "*The Parliament of Fowls*: Authority, The Knower, and the Known," *ChauR* 16 (1981): 1–17. There exists no structural confusion but instead variable pluralisms with the poem being inconclusive and the narrator uninvolved in the action: see Larry M. Sklute, "The Inconclusive Form of the *Parliament of Fowls*," *ChauR* 16 (1981): 119–28. The fact of tension and conflict can perhaps be explained by its genre, the *demande d'amour*: see D. S. Brewer, "The Genre of the 'Parlement of Foules,'" *MLR* 53 (1958): 321–26. Such discord and discordant technique have led one critic to dismiss allegory in the poem altogether: Maureen Quilligan has argued for the deallegorization of the poem, in "Allegory, Allegoresis, and the Deallegorization of Language: The *Roman de la Rose*,

the *De planctu naturae*, and the *Parlement of Foules*," in *Allegory, Myth, and Symbol*, ed. Morton W. Bloomfield, *Harvard Studies in English*, vol. 9 (Cambridge, Mass.: Harvard University Press, 1981), pp. 163–83.

9. For the philosophic distinctions among its separate parts, see Laurence Eldredge, "Poetry and Philosophy in the *Parlement of Foules*," *Revue de l'Université d'Ottawa* 40 (1970): 441–59, who argues that Venus represents the nominalistic equivalent of individual desire and Nature, the realistic equivalent of concern for common good. However, other scholars arguing for unity and a single theme have presented alternatives to love: Victoria Rothschild sees the sections mirroring divisions of time so that the poem presents a natural rather than a social hierarchy in its epithalamion, in that the natural world is in time. See Victoria Rothschild, "The *Parliament of Fowls*: Chaucer's Mirror up to Nature?" *RES* 35 (1984): 164–84. Also arguing for unity through a single theme, the power of art as a means of providing closure where none exists, is James Dean, "Artistic Conclusiveness in Chaucer's *Parliament of Fowls*," *ChauR* 21 (1986): 16–25.

10. See the discussion in Christopher Baswell, "The Medieval Allegorization of the *Aeneid*: MS. Cambridge, Peterhouse 158," *Traditio* 41 (1985): 181–237.

11. Alan of Lille, *The Complaint of Nature*, trans. Douglas M. Moffat, Yale Studies in English, no. 36 (1908; repr., Hamden, Conn.: Shoestring Press, 1972), p. 56 (prose 5); see also *Liber de planctu Naturae*, in *PL* 210: 459–60. Subsequent references will be included by column or page numbers within the text. Alan's allegory of Venus-Hymen-Cupid and her adultery with Antigamus, producing Jocus, seems to be aptly summed up in the commentary of "Bernardus Silvestris" on Martianus. There, Venus and Bacchus, through the priest Hymen, produce five children, the three Graces, Jocus, and Cupid, who represent the five stages of love, " 'Visus et alloquium, contactus et oscula, factum.' " Most important are the latter, the desire, *voluptas*, of Jocus, that is, of the pleasure that exists in the kiss, of Cupid, or *coitus*, and of Hymen, or marriage: "Causa ergo est voluptas Ioci, id est delectationis que est in osculis, et Cupidinis, id est coitus, et Himenei, id est nuptiarum. Magne autem cure est Iocus voluptati nostre, maior coitus, maxime nuptie" ([Bern. Sil.] *Mart.*, pp. 75–76 [3.813–40]).

12. For a study of the role and sources of Alan's Genius, see Jane Chance Nitzsche, *The Genius Figure in Antiquity and the Middle Ages* (New York and London: Columbia University Press, 1975), chapter 5.

13. The three reproduce the race to forestall the Fates' violence: Venus, as the "subvicar" of Nature aided by husband Hymen and son Cupid, together work to form the living things of earth by applying hammers to anvils ("humani generis seriem indefessa continuatione contexeret, Parcarumque manibus intercisorum injurias repararet" [*PL* 210:454]). See also Moffatt, trans., *The Complaint of Nature*, pp. 44–45 (prose 4), and pp. 50–51 (prose 5 on sexual metaphors): in the text, *PL* 210:457, and Moffatt, p. 50.

14. See the analysis of the thematic link between love and creativity (or the lover and the poet) by Marion L. Polzella, " 'The Craft So Long to Lerne': Poet and Lover in Chaucer's *Envoy a Scogan* and *Parliament of Fowls*," *ChauR* 10 (1976): 279–86.

15. See the brief analysis of "voide cours" (113–14) in Oliver Farrar Emerson, "Some Notes on Chaucer and Some Conjectures," *PQ* 2 (1923): 81–96; repr. in *Chaucer Essays and Studies: A Selection from the Writings of Oliver Farrar Emerson* (Cleveland: Western Reserve University Press, 1929), pp. 378–404 (esp. pp. 380–82). See also Edgar S. Laird, "Chaucer's *Complaint of Mars*, Line 145: 'Venus valaunse,' " *PQ* 51 (1972): 486–89. And for astral evidence that Venus does become Mercury's mistress, see Edgar S. Laird, "Astrology and Irony in Chaucer's *Complaint of Mars*," *ChauR* 6 (1972): 229–31; see the astrological section in Chauncey Wood, *Chaucer and the Country of the Stars: Poetic Uses of Astrological Imagery* (Princeton: Princeton University Press, 1970), chapter 3, pp. 115–20.

16. For parallels between Venus, Mars, and Mercury and Elizabeth of Lancaster, John Hastings (the Earl of Pembroke), and Sir John Holland, see G. H. Cowling, "Chaucer's *Complaintes of Mars and of Venus*," *RES* 2 (1926): 405–10. For parallels to Isabel of York and Sir John Holland, see Haldeen Braddy, "Chaucer and Graunson: The Valentine Tradition," *PMLA* 54 (1939): 359–68. For parallels to Katharine Swynford (sister of Chaucer's wife) and John of Gaunt (as Mars), see George Williams, "What Is the Meaning of Chaucer's *Complaint of Mars*?" *JEGP* 57 (1958): 167–76; see the section on historical allegory in Wood, *Chaucer*, pp. 103–8.

17. See Gardiner Stillwell, "Convention and Individuality in Chaucer's *Compleint of Mars*," *PQ* 35 (1956): 69–89; Clemen, *Chaucer's Early Poetry*, pp. 188–97; and most fully, Neil C. Hultin, "Anti-Courtly Elements in Chaucer's *Complaint of Mars*," *AM* 9 (1968): 58–75. See also the full exposition on the Mars and Venus story, the astrological, mythographical, and iconographical background, and a comic reading of the tempering effect of the planet Venus on Mars in Wood, *Chaucer*, pp. 103–60.

18. See Melvin Storm, "The Mythological Tradition in Chaucer's *Complaint of Mars*," *PQ* 57 (1978): 323. For the frame story's origins in Ovid's *Metamorphoses*, see D. S. Brewer, "Chaucer's 'Complaint of Mars,'" *N & Q* 199 (1954): 462–63. For the source in the *Ars amatoria*, see Nancy Dean, "Chaucer's *Complaint*, a Genre Descended from the *Heroides*," *Comparative Literature* 19 (1967): 1–27. The story was retold in the *Ovide moralisé* 4.11.1268–1755 and in Gower's *Confessio* 5.635ff.: see Stillwell, "Convention and Individuality," pp. 69–89.

19. The astrological sources for the planets of Venus and Mars (but not Mercury) have been uncovered as Hyginus, *Poetica astronomica* 2.42, in *Mythographi latini*, ed. T. Mucherus (Amsterdam, 1681), according to Brewer ("Chaucer's 'Complaint of Mars,'" p. 462). See also Laird ("Astrology and Irony," pp. 229–31), who shows astrological correlations for the privy love between planet lovers, and Wood (*Chaucer*, pp. 115–20), who finds that the astrological background shows the adultery as unfortunate, the classical, as comic.

20. For the characterization of the lovers, see also the sympathetic account in *Ars amatoria* 1.9.29–30. For Venus's gentleness in restraining Mars from additional "carnage," and for Mars's suffering and bumbling as a lover, see Statius, *Thebaid* 3.269, discussed in Nancy Dean, "Chaucer's *Complaint*," pp. 1–27.

21. For the sources—in Plutarch, *Moralia* 1.101, Fulgentius, *Mitologiae*, Arnulf of Orleans, Walter Map, *De nugis curialem* 4.3, and Plutarch, *Isis and Osiris* 5.117—see Storm, "Mythological Tradition," p. 334 n. 3. Holkot also glosses the story in a similar way, drawing on the *Ars amatoria* and *Valerius ad Rufinum*, and influencing Walter Map's account (in *In librum Sapientiae*, p. 80, cited in Allen, "Mythology," pp. 391–92). Holkot attributes the adultery to "deliciae voluptatis"—and the weakness that follows the indulging of lust.

22. Chapter 7, par. William, *Macrob.*, pp. 71–72, taken in part from Fulg. *Mit.* 2.7, p. 47. See William, *Macrob.*, trans. p. 29.

23. Walter Clyde Curry, "O Mars, O Atazir," *JEGP* 22 (1923): 347–68.

24. On Henry Scogan, see George Lyman Kittredge, "Henry Scogan," *Harvard Studies and Notes in Philology and Literature* 1 (1892): 109–17. On the poem as a refusal to help Scogan with his love problem, see Walter H. French, "The Meaning of Chaucer's *Envoy to Scogan*," *PMLA* 48 (1933): 289–92. For a useful critical introduction, see volume 5 of the Variorum Chaucer, on *Chaucer's Minor Poems*, part 1, edited by George B. Pace and Alfred David (Norman: University of Oklahoma Press, 1980), pp. 149–51. The poem seems to bear affinities with French poems by Deschamps and Machaut and the *Parlement of Foules* in its discussion of courtly love. For the French sources, see R. T. Lenaghan, "Chaucer's *Envoy to Scogan*: The Uses of Literary Conventions," *ChauR*

10 (1975): 46–61. For the *Parlement,* see Polzella, "'The Craft So Long to Lerne,'" pp. 279–86.

25. For a view of the poem as having the same message as "Truth" but treated humorously, see Alfred David, "Chaucer's Good Counsel to Scogan," *ChauR* 3 (1969): 265–74.

26. See the edition of Martin of Laon (Dunchad) by Cora E. Lutz, in *Dunchad: Glossae in Martianum,* American Philological Monographs, no. 12 (Lancaster, Pa.: American Philological Association, 1944), p. 9 (74.13 of the commentary, on 2.192 of Martianus). Martin of Laon here copies from Macrobius, *Saturnalia* 1.21.3–6. See the very similar gloss in John Scot, pp. 23–24 (14.16).

27. On Saturn's ruin, or winter, in Martianus, William in the Florentine commentary presents a gloss, on 60v, on the Venus-Adonis myth (like 14.16 of Remigius, *Mart.* 1:94): Venus searches for Adonis in the woods, crying for him, "et ea Venus in silva querendo lacrimabatur." Equivocal names for Adonis, according to Remigius on Martianus, are Seraphis (191), Atthis (192), and Hammon and Adonis (192); the gloss on Atthis in 74.12, 1.200 parallels that of Adonis and Venus (14.16): Remigius says Atthis was a boy loved by Berecinthia, *terra,* whose name signifies *flos* and by whose figure the sun is adored because it is the principle and cause of all flowers.

28. In the manuscript next to "stremes hed" is written "Windesore" and next to line 45 is written "Grenewich," even though Chaucer was probably then living at North Petherton. See the note in the *Works,* ed. F. N. Robinson, 2d ed. (Boston: Houghton Mifflin, 1957; repr. 1961), p. 863.

29. On the relationship of the Tullius reference to the *Roman de la Rose,* see R. C. Goffin, "Lenvoy de Chaucer a Scogan," *MLR* 20 (1925): 318–21; on "Tullius" as Tullus Hostilius and not Cicero, see Thomas M. Phipps, "Chaucer's Tullius," *MLN* 58 (1943): 108–9.

30. See Samuel Moore, "The Date of Chaucer's Marriage Group," *MLN* 26 (1911): 172–74. Moore surmises that "Scogan" was written in autumn of 1393, so that the reference to Chaucer's Muse rusting in the sheath was true; the poem stimulated the writing of the Marriage Group.

31. William, *Macrob.,* p. 70, trans. p. 26, on Macrobius 1.2.10 (no. 6 of the commentary).

32. To represent his two forms as vines and wine, Bacchus, in William's glosses on Macrobius, is said to be twice-born, once from Semele, once from Jupiter's thigh: "for it impregnates the earth in winter, and thus Bacchus is born, for from this union comes the vines—but through Juno's mediation, for through the heavenly heat trees and fruit are generated. That Bacchus is said to be twice-born, first of Semele, then of Jupiter's thigh at the time of his nativity, contains so much of truth that the vines (which we understand by Bacchus, for he is their god), impregnated by the sun's heat, become green—this is what Bacchus's first birth refers to—and later they grow, until in summer they put forth grapes, and this is Bacchus' second birth" (p. 71, trans. p. 29 [7b]). In a later gloss (on 1.2.9), Bacchus transforms from "vines" to World Soul (William, *Macrob.,* p. 70); he represents a winnowing fan (*vannus*), or the World Soul, raised (or torn apart) by the giants, or human bodies, as if earth-begotten. They tear apart the World Soul, for "this is the purgation of the heavy and the light, likewise the disintegration of the heavy and the light— that is, of body and soul. But although the world-soul is divided throughout our bodies, it is nonetheless found whole and entire in each of the limbs—by virtue of its undividedness, that is, its indivisibility of nature, offering itself for division through its functions" (William, *Macrob.,* trans. p. 24). "Bernardus Silvestris" provides four significations in his commentary on Martianus Capella: as the natural earthly power for producing wine (that is, he is the product of the union of Semele and Jove); as the human soul (from the myth of *vannus* torn apart and raised to heavens by the giants), the three parts of the soul rep-

resenting imagination, reason, and memory; as temporal opulence (in the myth of Bris- eus, the giant, versus the gods); and as divine spirit—divine will (from the two sons, Apollo and Bacchus, divine wisdom and will) (pp. 55–56 [3.175–225]). For a discussion of the sources of Bacchus in the *Merchant's Tale*, see chapter 8, esp. notes 20 and 22.

33. "This is nothing but that the name Ceres is used to mean the earth, called Ceres on analogy with 'crees' (you may create), for all things are created from her" (William, *Macrob.*, p. 54). Compare William's etymology of Ceres in *Glossae in Iuvenalem*, ed. Bradford Wilson, Textes philosophiques du Moyen Age, 18 (Paris: J. Vrin, 1980), p. 197; see also Servius on the *Georgics* 1.39. Cf. this passage in [Bern. Sil.] *Aen.*, 6.59, trans. p. 161. Finally, the true role of Ceres involves "non ... aliud quam terre naturalis potencia crescendi" (William, *Macrob.*, p. 173), "earth's natural power of growing into crops and multiplying them," just as Bacchus is "earth's natural power of growing into vines" (William, *Macrob.* 1.2.17, p. 48 [13a]). The same passage appears in William's glosses on Plato 40d, in Édouard Jeauneau, ed., *Glosae super Platonem: Texte critique avec intro- duction, notes et tables*, Textes philosophiques du Moyen Age, no. 13 (Paris: Librairie Phi- losophique J. Vrin, 1965), p. 201. Finally, Ceres is the superior part of the earth in William's supposed commentary on Martianus Capella: the Florentine commentary can be found in the fifteenth-century MS. Conventi Soppr. J. 1.29 at the Biblioteca Nazionale Centrale in Florence, here, fol. 51v. The Bacchus-Ceres conjunction, coupled with a tropological gloss, reappears in the commentary of "Bernardus" on Martianus 3.123, p. 53.

34. See [Bern. Sil.] *Mart.*, p. 57 (3.245–47); the passage appears also in TVM 155.15–27 and [Bern. Sil.] *Aen.* 10.21.

35. Bernardus also explains the proverb in this same passage, by acknowledging the proximity of the sexual organs to those through which digested materials exit.

36. Chaucer's humorous depiction of sexual frustration uses as sources for Priapus Ovid's *Fasti* 1.437–48 and Boccaccio's *Teseida*, according to Emerson Brown, "Priapus and the *Parlement of Foulys*," *SP* 72 (1975): 258–74.

37. See the glosses of Adanan the Scot, who acknowledges his role as god of gardens because of the size of his virile member, in Hermann Hagen, *Scholia Bernensia ad Vergilii Bucolica atque Georgica*, Jahrbücher für classische Philologie. Suppl., vol. 4, part 5 (Leipzig: B. G. Teubner, 1867), 4.109–11. TVM also cites the gloss in the Berne scholia, on Priapus as god of gardens, *numen hortorum*, in 6.26, in Bode, p. 189. The size of his virile member may explain also why the TVM notes that wives extolled him as a god. Ar- nulf of Orleans echoes the Berne scholia and TVM in his explanation of the expulsion from the city, in Jean Holzworth, "An Unpublished Commentary on Ovid's *Fasti* by Ar- nulfus of Orleans" (Diss., Bryn Mawr, 1940), p. 93 n. 3. Walsingham also conveys this gloss (9.7.30–40): he is called Priapus from *priasse*, which is crowned, that is, the virile mem- ber, because it restores the damage to human generation (p. 140).

38. Remigius, *Mart.* 2:174 (par. 725, 363.17). See also [Bern. Sil.] *Mart.* 3.796–97, p. 75.

39. See Apuleius, *Metamorphoses* 7.22, which cites the transformation of Lucius into an ass; this reference is used as an example of the meaning of *nuptiae* as the monstrous change of form occurring in sexual intercourse, according to Charlton T. Lewis and Charles Short, *A Latin Dictionary founded on Andrews' Edition of Freund's Latin Dictionary* (Ox- ford: Clarendon Press, 1879; repr. 1969), p. 1229. On the various explanations for Priapus's departure from the scene during the Bacchic festivals, in Oxford, Bodleian, MS. Digby 221, interpolated within a Hercules series exists a gloss on Priapus and Lotus from the *Fasti* (and in echo of the *Georgics* glosses discussed earlier); because people were aroused by the voice of the ass of Silenus when Priapus was fleeing the arbor explains why the ass came to be sacrificed to Priapus. He is called Beelphegor, "deus tentiginis" (god of lust), or Beelzebuch, "deus muscarum" (god of the flies). Digby 221, a Bodleian MS, has been edited by Virginia Brown in "An Edition of an Anonymous Twelfth-Century *Liber de*

natura deorum," MS 34 (1972): 1–70, here, p. 53, and analyzed in full by Judson Boyce Allen, "An Anonymous Twelfth-Century 'De Natura Deorum' in the Bodleian Library," *Traditio* 26 (1970): 352–64. Arnulf of Orleans offers an alternate reason for sacrifice of the ass to Priapus, in a gloss on *Fasti* 1.400: perhaps the ass brayed in alarm when he saw the size of Priapus's member, so that Priapus was thereafter evicted. In a sense, the ass is sacrificed to Priapus because Priapus's lust for Lotus was sacrificed as a result of the ass (cited in Holzworth, "An Unpublished Commentary," p. 93).

40. See SVM, myth 38, in Bode: "Unde sacris ejus interesse dicitur; nam *sine Cerere et Libero friget Venus."* See also Servius on *Georgics* 4.111.

41. See Isidore, *Etymologiarum* 8.11.80, ed. W. M. Lindsay, 2 vols. (Oxford: Clarendon Press, 1911). Isidore was also responsible for much of the passage cited by Theodulf of Orleans, according to his editor Ernest Duemmler. See *Carmina* no. 45 in *Poetae latini Aevi Carolini,* ed. Ernest Duemmler, *Poetarum historica, latinorum Medii Aevi,* vol. 1, Monumenta Germaniae (Berlin: 1881), pp. 543–44.

42. See Kemp Malone, "Chaucer's Daughter of Cupid," *MLR* 45 (1950): 63.

43. Theodulf glosses his own lines by declaring that Cupid is *alatus,* or winged, because he is "fickle and naked because of his manifest crimes," and a boy (*puer*) because he lacks skill and reason (35–36), p. 171. It is possible that this Isidorean gloss on Cupid, taken up by Theodulf, was passed on by Remigius commenting on Martianus to "Bernardus Silvestris" in his twelfth-century commentary on Martianus 3.824–40, p. 76. See also the similar depiction of and glosses on Cupid in the fourteenth-century Holkot, *In librum duodecim,* fols. 6v-7r, cited in Allen, "Mythology," p. 254; Holkot attributes this picture to Remigius on Martianus.

44. The passage about the doors from *Aeneid* 6.893–96 in fact is based in part on myth 228, "Duae portae Elysiorum," which concerns the true gate of the eyes and the false gate of the mouth as glossed by the eighth- or ninth-century FVM in Bode.

Chapter 4. The Narrator as Mythographic Glossator: The Rape of Criseyde

Portions of this chapter were delivered as "Pandarus and Janus, 'God of Entree,' in *Troilus and Criseyde,* Book Two," at the Seventeenth Center for Early Medieval and Renaissance Studies Conference, "The Classics in the Middle Ages," at SUNY-Binghamton, October 17, 1986; and as "An Example of Feminist Mythography: Criseyde as Myrrha, Io, Athamas in *Troilus,* Book Four," Annual English Department Symposium at Rice University, February 13, 1988.

1. Other scholars have examined the use of classical mythology in the *Troilus,* but either without attention to the medieval mythographic tradition that informed so much of the poetic application of the individual myths (see A. J. Minnis's very literal and historical treatment in *Chaucer and Pagan Antiquity* [Bury St. Edmunds, Suffolk: D. S. Brewer; Totowa, N.J.: Rowman and Littlefield, 1982]), or without attention to the overall patterns of mythological and mythographic framing so important to Chaucer in the *Troilus* (see John P. McCall, "Classical Myth in Chaucer's *Troilus and Criseyde*: An Aspect of the Classical Tradition in the Middle Ages" [Diss., Princeton, 1955]). McCall's revision of his dissertation omitted much of the mythographic analysis: McCall, *Chaucer Among the Gods* (1979). See also Leah Zeva Freiwald, "Chaucer's Use of Classical Mythology: The Myths in the Context of the Medieval Audience" (Diss., University of California-Berkeley, 1983). The general approach has been dismissed because, in the words of Walter Clyde Curry, "the names of the pagan gods ... are employed merely as a literary device to symbolize the real destinal forces back of the drama" (*Chaucer and the Medi-*

aeval Sciences (1926; 2d ed. New York and London: Barnes and Noble, 1960); repr. in "Destiny in *Troilus and Criseyde,*" in Schoeck and Taylor, 2:66, 67.

2. The parallels between Troy/Troylus and Criseyde/Helen have been noted by John P. McCall, "The Trojan Scene in Chaucer's *Troilus,*" *ELH* 29 (1962): 263–75; Mary-Jo Arn, "Three Ovidian Women in Chaucer's *Troilus*: Medea, Helen, Oënone," *ChauR* 15 (1980): 1–10, esp. 4–6; and David Anderson, "Theban History in Chaucer's *Troilus,*" *SAC* 4 (1982): esp. 125–30.

3. E. Talbot Donaldson defended "The Ending of Chaucer's *Troilus,*" in *Early English and Norse Studies Presented to Hugh Smith in Honour of His Sixtieth Birthday,* ed. Arthur Brown and Peter Foote (London: Methuen, 1963), pp. 26–45; repr. as "The Ending of *Troilus,*" in E. Talbot Donaldson, *Speaking of Chaucer* (New York: Norton, 1970), pp. 84–101, and in Stephen A. Barney, ed., *Chaucer's "Troilus": Essays in Criticism* (Hamden, Conn.: Archon Books, 1980), pp. 115–30. Peter Dronke finds precedent for the conclusion in Dante, Boccaccio, and Boethius, in "The Conclusion of *Troilus and Criseyde,*" *MAE* 23 (1964): 47–52. Sister Frances Dolores Covella discovers that there are addresses to a courtly and general audience in the Epilogue that explain Chaucer's intentions, in "Audience as Determinant of Meaning in the *Troilus,*" *ChauR* 2 (1967–68): 235–45. The most complete study of antecedents for Troilus's ascent belongs to John M. Steadman, *Disembodied Laughter: Troilus and the Apotheosis Tradition. A Reexamination of Narrative and Thematic Contexts* (Berkeley, Los Angeles, and London: University of California Press, 1972). Finally, Winthrop Wetherbee argues that the narrator realizes his independence from his pagan material (especially given the Christianized Statius in Dante's *Purgatorio*) and discovers his role as a Christian poet, in " 'Per te poeta fui, per te cristiano': Dante, Statius, and the Narrator of Chaucer's *Troilus,*" in Lois Ebin, ed., *Vernacular Poetics in the Middle Ages,* Studies in Medieval Culture 16 (Kalamazoo, Mich.: Medieval Institute Publications, 1984), pp. 153–76.

4. Chauncey Wood, *The Elements of Chaucer's "Troilus"* (Durham, N.C.: Duke University Press, 1984).

5. Cindy Vitto, "The Figure of the Virtuous Pagan in Middle English Literature" (Diss., Rice University, 1985), in the last chapter finds Troilus to be an ironic type of the virtuous pagan—for example, Trajan. The dissertation minus this last chapter was published by the American Philosophical Society in 1989.

6. Some interpretations have invoked Chaucer's allusion to Dante's *Paradiso* 13 and 14, or 14 alone, to suggest that the ending is apt (Gerald Morgan, "The Ending of 'Troilus and Criseyde,' " *MLR* 77 [1982]: 257–71), or that it is not, with the moralizing left to the reader (Bonnie Wheeler, "Dante, Chaucer, and the Ending of *Troilus and Criseyde,*" *PQ* 61 [Spring 1982]: 105–23). Neither Morgan nor Wheeler mentions this reference, although it was discussed briefly by E. J. Dobson, "Some Notes on Middle English Texts," *English and Germanic Studies,* University of Birmingham, 1 (1947–48): 61–62, and included in Steadman's full discussion of possibilities (*Disembodied Laughter,* pp. 3–11), where he examines the *Paradiso* passage in more detail.

7. See Jane Chance Nitzsche, *The Genius Figure in Antiquity and the Middle Ages* (New York and London: Columbia University Press, 1975), pp. 68–75, on Bernardus Silvestris's use of the sphere of the fixed stars (Aplanon) in the *Cosmographia* and its astrological and literary analogues. The eighth sphere has been identified as the sphere of fixed stars and analyzed in detail, in Steadman, *Disembodied Laughter,* pp. 1–20, chapter 1: "The Eighth Sphere: Lunar Concave or Stellar Vault?"

8. See R. K. Root, ed., *The Book of Troilus and Criseyde by Geoffrey Chaucer* (1926; repr. Princeton: Princeton University Press, 1954), p. xlix, perhaps based on W. Farnham's view that Chaucer had altered *Il Filostrato* in line with *De casibus* tragedy, as expressed

in *The Medieval Heritage of Elizabethan Tragedy* (Berkeley: University of California Press, 1936), pp. 137ff. Subsequently, the poem was seen as falling into stages roughly corresponding to those in the *Consolatio*, in H. R. Patch, "Troilus on Determinism," *Speculum* 6 (1931): 242; repr. in Schoeck and Taylor, 2:71–85, esp. p. 83; the five-part structure has been analyzed as an inversion of the dramatic movement of the *Consolatio*, in John P. McCall, "Five-Book Structure in Chaucer's *Troilus*," *MLQ* 23 (1962): 297–308. See also Monica E. McAlpine, *The Genre of "Troilus and Criseyde"* (Ithaca, N.Y., and London: Cornell University Press, 1978).

9. Curry (*Chaucer and the Mediaeval Sciences*) denigrated this "sorry performance" because of the narrator's moralistic condemnation of earthly joy as false felicity and of the inefficacious paganism of Troilus in a poem whose time and setting by self-definition have been identified as pagan. Following from this lapse, Troilus's own apotheosis and judgment of this earthly world cause similar problems of credibility for the modern reader (Schoeck and Taylor, 2:66, 67). Alexander J. Denomy argues that the Epilogue was added out of fear of ecclesiastical censure, in "The Two Moralities of Chaucer's *Troilus and Criseyde*," in *Proceedings and Transactions of the Royal Society of Canada*, 44, ser. 3, sec. 2 (1950): 35–46; repr. in Schoeck and Taylor, 2:147–59.

10. See the vindication of the narrator by Minnis, *Chaucer*, pp. 66–73, here, p. 67. Another view, like Minnis's, ignores the role of the commentary tradition in its justification of the narrator: Winthrop Wetherbee traces Chaucer's development from a writer using courtly romance tradition to a writer in the classical (Virgil, Ovid, Statius, Dante) mode, in *Chaucer and the Poets: An Essay on Troilus and Criseyde* (Ithaca, N.Y., and London: Cornell University Press, 1984). For general critical discussion of the role of the narrator in the poem, mostly as it involves his view of Criseyde, for example, see Donaldson, "Criseide and her Narrator," *Speaking of Chaucer*, pp. 65–83; Carolyn Dinshaw, *Chaucer's Sexual Poetics* (Madison: University of Wisconsin Press, 1989), corrects Donaldson's biased reading (pp. 28–64).

11. D. W. Robertson, Jr., has compared the tragedy in the *Troilus* with the Fall of man, in "Chaucerian Tragedy," *ELH* 19 (1952): 1–37, repr. in Schoeck and Taylor, 2:86–121.

12. The late Bernard F. Huppé delivered a plenary address at the 1986 Center for Early Medieval and Renaissance Studies Conference, "The Classics in the Middle Ages," in which he commented on the influence of the Fulgentian journey in the Middle Ages and noted briefly Mercury's signal role at the end of this poem. Note also the discussion of Mercury's role in bedding Herse, with Aglauros as go-between, and the ironic aspects of Troilus's prayer to him in 3.729–30, in Michael Olmert, "Troilus and a Classical Pander: III, 729–30," *CN* 1:1 (1979): 18–19. Finally, recall that Mercury is Arcita's guide in Boccaccio's original; see Steadman's discussion of the parallels (*Disembodied Laughter*, pp. 38–41).

13. See Robertson, *Preface*, p. 471. Fulg. *Mit.*, trans., 1.7, also identifies Alecto, the first stage, as "unstoppable" and Megaera, the third, as "great contention"; Fulgentius concludes: "The first stage, therefore, is to create rage [*furiam concipere*] without pause; the second, to burst forth into words [*uoce erumpere*]; the third, to stir up a quarrel [*iurgium protelare*]" (see *Mit.*, pp. 20–21).

14. "Per Titium autem significantur luxuriosi, in iecori enim sedes est luxurie sicut in splene risus et in felle ira" (Remigius, *Boeth.*, p. 65).

15. On the four descents, see Nitzsche, *The Genius Figure*, pp. 43–62 (chapter 3).

16. On the underworld as earthly vice (the vicious descent), interpreted in a gloss on 3m12, see the excerpts from the Remigian commentaries on Boethius, p. 65.

17. In addition, Fulgentius says that Cerberus also represents roiling and contentious lawyers, in his exposition on the *Aeneid*, no. 22. In contrast, Bersuire interprets Cerberus as both death and avarice, in his gloss on 10.65 (*Ovidius*, trans. p. 350).

18. For Chaucer's use of the allegorization of the myth in structuring the *Troilus*, see also Patricia R. Orr, "Pallas Athena and the Threefold Choice in Chaucer's *Troilus and Criseyde*," in Chance, *Mythographic Art*, pp. 159–76. For the Judgment of Paris myth and the allegory of the three lives—voluptuous, active, and contemplative, each corresponding to one of the three goddesses, Venus, Juno, and Pallas Athena—see also Jane Chance, "The Medieval Sources of Cristoforo Landino's Allegorization of the Judgment of Paris," *SP* 81:2 (1984): 145–60. Margaret J. Ehrhart has also published a study of the myth of the Judgment of Paris, *The Judgment of the Trojan Prince Paris in Medieval Literature* (Philadelphia and London: University of Pennsylvania Press, 1987).

19. On the shepherd Phoebus's relationship with King Admetus's daughter, see Ovid's *Heroides* 5.151–2; for this passage as a possible medieval insertion from glosses into Ovid's text, see Sanford Brown Meech, "Chaucer and an Italian Translation of the *Heroides*," *PMLA* 45 (1930): 112–13. This myth does not appear in *Metamorphoses* or the three Vatican Mythographers.

20. Bersuire concludes that Niobe is too proud (*Ovidius*, trans., p. 256). He also concludes that Phoebus and Diana represent Christ and Mary, who attack with the arrows of tribulation and change us into stones, or what might be termed poor and fearful people. Finally, the seven sons and daughters represent the gifts of the Holy Spirit and the seven virtues. See the discussion of Niobe and her mythological significance in the last chapter of Freiwald, "Chaucer's Use of Classical Mythology."

21. On Apollo as tenth Muse: Fulg. *Mit.* 1.15, pp. 25–26; trans. p. 51. Brief Fulgentian interpretations of the nine Muses reappear in the TVM in Bode and in Robert Holkot, *In librum duodecim prophetas*, fols. 95v-96r, with Clio as *scientia* ("que fama interpretatur, et est cogitatio querende scientie"), in Holkot. However, in the catalog provided by Bernardus Silvestris commenting on Martianus, he lists as eighth this Muse, who represents glory, because in following wisdom she incites many: "Octava *Clio*, quasi 'cleo,' id est gloria, que ad sequendam sapientiam multum incitat" ([Bern. Sil.] *Mart.*, p. 234).

22. In the remainder of book 2, the various characters swear ironically by particular gods for help in making decisions or to attest to their credibility. Pandarus swears by Minerva (wisdom), Jupiter (benevolence), and Venus (love) in lines 232 and 233 in a bitterly ironic oath to Criseyde that he loves her best (232–38). He also protests his good intentions once again by swearing upon cruel Mars, the hellish Furies, and Neptune (435, 436, and 443). It is also ironic that Criseyde calls upon Pallas Athena, goddess of wisdom (425), upset over her uncle's betraying her by giving her such false counsel. Other comparisons, apostrophes, and petitions: Troilus on horse and armed is compared with Mars (630); Pandarus also asks Troilus to slow down for the love of Mars (988); Troilus summons Venus's grace (680, 972) and Minerva "the white" for help in devising a letter to win Criseyde (1062).

23. Two excellent studies of mythological references in Chaucer touch on this passage: McCall describes Janus as god of doors and gates, depicted with a key in his right hand and a staff in his left, and interprets Pandarus as a gate-opener, in his dissertation ("Classical Myth," pp. 245–46); Freiwald, in her dissertation ("Chaucer's Use of Classical Mythology," pp. 202–4), discusses the May 3 date, the allusion to Phoebus in the bull, Taurus, and Procne. She concludes that the astrological position, of Venus presiding with Apollo, is favorable to love—except that the white bull conjures up the image of Jove and Europa, the myth of abduction echoing the myth of rape conveyed by the image of Procne.

24. Cicero, *De natura deorum; Academica*, ed. and trans. H. Rackham (London: William Heinemann; New York: G. P. Putnam's Sons, 1933).

25. The Florentine is believed by Peter Dronke to be indebted to William of Conches's twelfth-century and lost commentary on Martianus. See the excerpts published in

William, *Macrob*. Janus is here associated with the month of January (or that month is sacred to him), whence he is said to be two-faced, in that he looks back to the past year and forward to the new, and is therefore also understood as *sapientia* ("qui bifrons est, propter duplicem cognitionem preteritorum et futurorum. Nam ex preteritis etiam futura debet conicere"). Janus in 53r is *sapiens* married to Argione (from 6.1).

26. For the twelfth-century TVM, see 1.2, Bode, p. 153, on Saturn, in which he repeats much of the historical account from Macrobius, and also 4.9, on Juno, pp. 169–70, in which ideas found in the Florentine commentary appear.

27. Janus in 6.1 of Remigius, *Mart.* 1:4, is god of the year, "deus anni," for an etymological reason, that is, because he opens the gate (*ianuam*) of the year. Thus the month of January is said to be two-faced because it is a month of ingress and egress for the year — but not four-faced because of the four seasons ("propter quattuor anni tempora") or the four regions of the sky ("propter quattuor caeli climata").

28. From Jean Holzworth, "Hugutio's *Derivationes* and Arnulfus' Commentary on Ovid's *Fasti*," *TAPA* 73 (1942): 259–76. Arnulf on the *Fasti* 1.103 (here, p. 263) identifies the god Janus as the world because he has two doors, one at Capricorn, through which one ascends, the other at Cancer, through which one descends. They called the heavens Janus, because it was the door for those ascending and descending. This identification resembles the gloss in Isidore, who mentions Janus's two faces, to represent east and west, in 8.11.37. Arnulf of Orleans used Isidore directly, as did Hugutio of Pisa, who actually mentions "orient" and "occident" in addition to Capricorn/Cancer (see Holzworth, "Hugutio's *Derivationes*," p. 263).

29. Ralph Miller has suggested that line 64 possibly alludes to the role of Procne in *Purgatorio*, canto 9: "Pandarus and Procne," *Studies in Medieval Culture*, ed. John R. Sommerfeldt (Kalamazoo: Western Michigan University Press, 1964), pp. 65–68. Miller remarks that the "dark uncertainties surrounding Pandarus's mission should be indicated by Procne, and that the probable joyful outcome of his good works is signified by the nightingale (though he [Chaucer] does not refer to it as Philomela [line 918])" (p. 65). But Miller also misreads canto 9: Dante makes a "casual reference to how the swallow cheeps sadly as if to keep fresh the memory of an old injustice" (p. 65).

30. The Feast of the Invention of the Cross is celebrated on May 3, Saint Helena's feast day. This link originated in France but passed to England before the end of the eighth century. See *Acta sanctorum, maius*, vol. 1, ed. Godefridus Henschenius and Daniel Papenrochius (Antwerp, 1680), pp. 450ff.; and *Inventio Sanctae Crucis*, ed. Alfred Holder (Leipzig, 1889). See also Kenneth Sisam, "Cynewulf and his Poetry" (Sir Israel Gollancz Memorial Lecture, Read March 8, 1933), *Proceedings of the British Academy*, 18 (1932): 303–31. For an analysis of the astrological significance of the dates May 3 and 4, to show their appropriateness for Pandarus's mission, see George Clark, "Chaucer's Third and Fourth of May," *Revue de l'Université d'Ottawa* 52 (1982): 257–65; see also Alfred L. Kellogg and Robert C. Cox, "Chaucer's May 3 and Its Contexts," in *Chaucer, Langland, Arthur: Essays in Middle English Literature*, ed. Alfred L. Kellogg (New Brunswick: Rutgers University Press, 1972), pp. 155–98, who find that its use is keyed to the particular poem involved (malevolent determinism in the *Troilus*, humanism in the *Knight's Tale*, and parody in the *Nun's Priest's Tale*). The date also has been linked with fertility rites and licentiousness, in relation to the Roman festival of the goddess Flora, and discussed in relation to the *Knight's Tale*, by Lorraine Kochanske Stock, "The Two Mayings in Chaucer's *Knight's Tale*: Convention and Invention," *JEGP* 85 (1986): 206–21, esp. 210–11. For another discussion of the use of the date in the *Knight's Tale*, see John P. McCall, "Chaucer's May 3," *MLN* 76 (1961): 201–5.

31. See Bersuire, *Ovidius*, trans., pp. 262–63. Bersuire glosses the myth as follows: the monster Tereus eats his own son, that is, delights in the flesh; Tereus cuts out Philome-

la's tongue to prevent scandal because he wishes to conceal the shamefulness of the deed and crime. But the web of Philomela's tapestry reveals the pregnancy following the crime. In Chaucer, the swallow's singing awakens Pandarus, who sets out on his mission; Procne's song of incestuous rape reminds the reader of Pandarus's incestuous voyeurism.

32. The reference to Oedipus is no doubt drawn from Statius's *Thebaid* to show a parallel with Troilus; see Julia Ebel, "Troilus and Oedipus: The Genealogy of an Image," *ES* 55 (1974): 15–21.

33. In FVM, myths 179 and 204; in SVM, myths 2 and 69, in Bode.

34. This Bodleian MS has been edited by Virginia Brown in "An Edition of an Anonymous Twelfth-Century *Liber de natura deorum*," *MS* 34 (1972): 1–70, here, p. 32.

35. Barry Windeatt, "Chaucer and the *Filostrato*," in *Chaucer and the Italian Trecento*, ed. Piero Boitani (Cambridge, England: Cambridge University Press, 1983), pp. 163–83, notes that Chaucer generally expands the Boccaccio concepts in the story through the characters' reflections on love and also references to death, time, fortune, and God. For Chaucer's changes in Boccaccio concerning Venus and the *prohemium* to book 3, making Venus's role much more important, see Wood, *The Elements of Chaucer's "Troilus"*, p. 99. In chapter 4, pp. 99–128, Wood does not find the view of Venus ambiguous in the *Troilus*, although in a few places she appears in multiple form: "for the most part Venus is a symbol used to show the extent to which Troilus has been mastered by the goad of the flesh" (p. 99). On Venus as planet, see Benson's note in the *Riverside Chaucer* on the astrological nature of the invocation; Earl G. Schreiber, "Venus in the Medieval Mythographic Tradition," *JEGP* 74 (1975): 519–35; and Robert Hollander, *Boccaccio's Two Venuses* (New York: Columbia University Press, 1977). For the poem in the tradition of the *concordia discors*, or the created world viewed as a contrarious harmony, see Donald W. Rowe, *O Love, O Charite! Contraries Harmonized in Chaucer's Troilus* (Carbondale and Edwardsville, Ill.: Southern Illinois University Press, 1976). On Troilus's hymn to love (from Boethius) as deriving from Neoplatonic cosmology and views of love, see Patricia Vicari, "Sparagmos: Orpheus among the Christians," in *Orpheus: The Metamorphoses of a Myth*, ed. John Warden (Toronto and Buffalo: University of Toronto Press, 1982), pp. 78–79 in particular.

36. See the discussion in McCall, *Chaucer Among the Gods*, pp. 16, 39, 168 n. 24.

37. In this role, she appears as a character at the opening of Fulgentius's *Mitologiae* to advise the African to receive the teachings of the Muses in his home, for she has heard that barbarians ban literature in their houses. To a certain extent, she may signify the personification of *mitologiae*, especially given the appearance of such myths in the classical epic. Note that she warns Fulgentius, "If such recondite and mystical matters [*secretis misticisque rebus*] are to be vigorously studied, the full approval of the authorities must be sought; for no trifling must be pursued, whereby we find ourselves patching up correct styles of verse with some frivolous lines" (Fulg. *Mit.*, Prol., p. 12, trans. p. 45). Satyra, the mistress she permits Fulgentius, seems to suggest that mixture of prose and verse, lying fiction and secret truth, classical and Christian, to which many medieval writers aspired. At any rate, Fulgentius's opening prologue provides a context and thesis for what will follow, through the linking of epic poetry with mythology, the firmly expressed purpose of stripping away alterations of the truth, or in other words the opposite of what happens in a fiction like *Troilus*. Unfortunately, if epic cloaks the truth with lying fictions, the product of such a "mother" surely is itself deluded, whether we are referring to untutored reading or to the son of Calliope, Orpheus as analogue to Troilus.

38. In a related but different allegorization, Calliope's role as the seventh Muse—just after Tersichore (Terpsichore), "artium delectatio," associated with Venus, or beauty, and just before Clio, "gloria, que ad sequendam sapientiam multum incitat"—in the process of knowledge, is identified with Mercury, "in eloquente," in Bernard Silvestris's com-

mentary on Martianus, [Bern. Sil.] *Mart.*, p. 234 (10.294–95), but most likely Chaucer is following the Fulgentian and not the Silvestran order, given Cleo's appearance in book 2. Through the incremental repetition of invocations to Muses, Chaucer provides an inverse mirror image of books 1, 4, and 5 (whose invocational Furies and Fates were linked with Pluto as ruler of the underworld, in the TVM, in Bode, and also in Bersuire, "De formis"). But in this book comes the formal rhetorical polishing of what has begun earlier. The reference may also be ironic: at the opening of his *Purgatorio* (1.7–9), Dante invokes Calliope as the Muse of epic poetry, that is, the best of human artistic endeavor necessary to describe—and complete—the epic and heroic process of penitence (see Benson's note in the *Riverside Chaucer*), because the Muses inhabited Helicon, a mountain like Parnassus (or Mount Purgatory in Dante). Penance is not a sacrament at work in the drama of book 3.

39. In "Blind Fortune, Blind Cupid, Blind Troilus" (pp. 153–63 of *The Elements of Chaucer's "Troilus"*), Wood analyzes Troilus as "Cupides sone" (5.1590) shown to be blind (he serves both blind Fortune and blind Cupid, who is not mentioned in the *Filostrato*). Blind Cupid was associated in the later Middle Ages with Fortune and Death, according to Erwin Panofsky, "Blind Cupid," in *Studies in Iconology: Humanistic Themes in the Art of the Renaissance* (New York: Harper and Row, 1939; repr. 1962), pp. 112–13. Wood also links blind Troilus with Oedipus (p. 161), a figure signifying *lasciuia* for Fulgentius in *Super Thebaid*, in *Opera*, p. 182, trans. p. 240.

40. Troilus is perhaps nineteen, Criseyde, several years older, according to Derek S. Brewer, "The Ages of Troilus, Criseyde and Pandarus," *Studies in English Literature* (Tokyo), English number (1972), 3–15, repr. in *Tradition and Innovation in Chaucer*, ed. Derek S. Brewer (London: Macmillan, 1982), pp. 80–88. Pandarus is probably only thirty, which deems his behavior less lecherous than we might otherwise imagine, according to Sally K. Slocum, "How Old is Chaucer's Pandarus?" *PQ* 58 (1979): 16–25.

41. On the question of incest between Pandarus and Criseyde, through puns on "deth" as intercourse, see Haldeen Braddy, "Chaucer's Playful Pandarus," *Southern Folklore Quarterly* 34 (1970): 71–81. But see also James F. Maybury, "Pandarus and Criseyde: The Motif of Incest in Chaucer's *Troilus*," in *XUS: Xavier Review* 2 (1982): 82–89.

42. On the significance of the smoky rain, changed from the smoky candle indicating generative love, in his source, Jean de Meun's *Roman*, and therefore of Pandarus as a type of Genius, generation god, see John V. Fleming, "Smoky Reyn: From Jean de Meun to Geoffrey Chaucer," in Leigh A. Arrathoon, ed., *Chaucer and the Craft of Fiction* (Rochester, Minn.: Solaris Press, 1986), pp. 1–21. The torrential rain, caused by the configuration of stars (Jupiter, Venus, and the moon) in late November 1984, which was identical to that of May 12, 1385, provides a *terminus a quo* for the third book in 1385, according to Kenneth Weitzenhoffer, "Chaucer, Two Planets, and the Moon," *Sky and Telescope* 69 (1985): 278–81.

43. See "Giovanni del Virgilio espositore delle Metamorfosi," ed. Fausto Ghisalberti, *Giornale Dantesco*, n.s., 4 (1933): 92. In Arnulf of Orleans, Adonis's preferred work is hunting and not lovemaking.

44. Fausto Ghisalberti, "Arnolfo d'Orléans, un cultore di Ovidio nel seculo XII," *Memorie del Reale Istituto Lombardo di Scienze e Lettere* 24 (1932): 223.

45. On the tree-vine topos, a literary convention describing a destructive or supportive relationship, here deliberately ambiguous to underscore the ambiguity of the secret marriage: see Patricia Bruckmann, "*Troilus and Criseyde*, III, 1226–32: A Clandestine Topos," *ELN* 18 (1981): 166–70.

46. See Robert A. Pratt, "Chaucer's 'natal Jove' and 'Seint Jerome … agayn Jovinian,'" *JEGP* 61 (1962): 244–48, who cites Saint Jerome's *Epistola adversus Iovinianum* 1.48 in support of this role of the god; "Jovius Gamelius" in this quotation means "ad nuptias

pertinens" and "Jovius Genethlicus" means "ad genus procreandum pertinens," so that "natal Jove" could be a translation of the second phrase. Significantly, the oath is sworn during the bedchamber scene at Deiphebus's house. Another interpretation identifies the phrase as the birthday festival of Jove, the pagan equivalent of Christ, in R. K. Root, ed., *The Book of Troilus and Criseyde by Geoffrey Chaucer* (Princeton: Princeton University Press, 1926; repr. 1954), p. 467; yet another suggests that the oath denotes "by the feast of Jupiter, who presides over nativities," according to W. W. Skeat, ed., *The Complete Works of Geoffrey Chaucer*, vol. 2, 2d ed. (Oxford: Clarendon Press, 1900), p. 476.

47. On Pandarus as a type of Tantalus who desires but cannot savor Criseyde, see Beryl Rowland, "Pandarus and the Fate of Tantalus," *Orbis Litterarum* 24 (1969): 3–15.

48. See Fulgentius, *Mit.* 2.15 and *Expos.*, p. 101, trans., no. 22; John of Garland also glosses him similarly: "Tantalides similis tibi Tantale vivit avarus / Qui sitit in pleno quem fugit id quod habet" ("a greedy man, a Tantalides who thirsts amid plenty, and whose possessions escape him" [p. 53; trans. p. 135; glossed with Tityus and Sisyphus, the first who signifies consuming care, the second, the man weighed down by burdens and cares]).

49. Remigius, *Boeth.*, p. 65: "Tunc abstinentibus cunctis Ceres brachium eius exedit quod ideo comesse dicitur quia ipsa est terra quae corpus resolvint."

50. For a discussion of the astrological nature of this prayer, see W. C. Curry, "Destiny in Chaucer's *Troilus*," *PMLA* 45 (1930): 142–45; see also Freiwald, "Chaucer's Use of Classical Mythology," pp. 183–84.

51. See Michael Olmert, "Troilus and a Classical Pander: *TC* III, 729–30," *CN* 1:1 (1979): 18–19.

52. The references begin with Jove and Europa (722) and Mars (724), move to Phoebus and Daphne (726), conclude with Mercury and Herse (729), with passing mentions of Diana, goddess of chastity (731), and the Parcae (733). See, for example, Bersuire's gloss on Diana as worldly glory, in *Ovidius*, p. 40, trans. p. 137; also the TVM, on Pluto (myth 6), including the Furies, and Proserpina (myth 7), including Diana-Proserpina-Luna, in Bode, pp. 174–97, and pp. 197–99. Michael E. Cotton, "The Artistic Integrity of Chaucer's *Troilus and Criseyde*," *ChauR* 7 (1972): 37–43, links Criseyde with the moon and Troilus with the sun; he also discusses infernal imagery conveying the idea of lost love, worldly pleasure.

53. Holkot also identifies Midas as "knowing nothing" to represent the prelate who may be learned but who, through evil habits, is changed into an ignorant ass: "Midas interpretatur nichil sciens, et signat prelatum qui et si primo sciat multa, tamen per malos mores suos vertitur in stulticiam asininam" (*In librum duodecim*, fol. 120r, cited in Allen, "Mythology," p. 360).

54. On the use of *adynata* ("listed impossibilities") in Criseyde's dawn songs, see Susan Schibanoff, "Criseyde's 'Impossible' *Aubes*," *JEGP* 76 (1977): 326–33.

55. In short, the saltiness of wisdom coupled with the fire of mind might have produced the renown of valor, TVM, myth 13, in Bode, p. 246.

56. See Thomas E. Maresca, *Three English Epics: Studies of Troilus and Criseyde, The Faerie Queene, and Paradise Lost* (Lincoln: University of Nebraska Press, 1979), who argues that the epic of *Troilus* uses the *descensus* both structurally and thematically, although it lacks a hero except in Everyman, who can choose *imitatio* of Christ (or, alternatively, of Troilus). More recently, Ann W. Astell, "Orpheus, Eurydice, and the 'Double Sorwe' of Chaucer's *Troilus*," *ChauR* 23 (1989): 283–99, traces the parallels between Troilus and Orpheus/Criseyde and Eurydice to show that both characters descend into hell, although Troilus, like Orpheus, descends at first only to ascend virtuously.

57. See Holkot, *In librum duodecim*, fol. 3r, cited in Allen, "Mythology," p. 274.

58. For an analysis of Chaucer's Digression on Predestination emphasizing Troilus's

wish to deny personal responsibility by denying freedom, see John Huber, "Troilus' Predestination Soliloquy: Chaucer's Changes from Boethius," *NM* 66 (1965): 120–25. For the argument that this is no digression, see Wood, *The Elements of Chaucer's "Troilus,"* pp. 57–62.

59. See Holkot, *In librum duodecim prophetas*, fols. 53v-5r, cited in Allen, pp. 380–82. But also, on Oedipus and Troilus in *Troilus*, book 4, connected through the image of blindness and observed as Statian (in that epic of the *Thebaid*, Oedipus is central to the narrative) rather than as medieval and Boccaccian, see Julia Ebel, "Troilus and Oedipus: The Genealogy of an Image," *ES* 55 (1974): 15–21.

60. See, for example, K. P. Wentersdorf, "Theme and Structure in *The Merchant's Tale*: The Function of the Pluto Episode," *PMLA* 80 (1965): 522–27, who acknowledges the Pluto legend as a type of pagan Fall (p. 527).

61. See Fulg. *Mit.* 1.8, p. 21: "Tria etiam ipso Plutoni destinant fata" ("They also assign to Pluto the three Fates"). Drawing on their etymologies and denotations (from *clitos*, for "summons," *lachesis*, meaning "destiny," and *atropos*, signifying "without order"), Fulgentius concludes that they represent the three phases of life—birth, living one's life, and death: "first, there is the summons of birth; second, one's lot in life, how one can live; and third, the state of death which comes without prescription" (trans. p. 52; also Bersuire, "De formis," p. 48).

62. See Jacqueline De Weever, "Chaucer's Moon: Cinthia, Diana, Latona, Lucina, Proserpina," *Names* 34 (1986): 154–74, who remarks that each name denotes a separate aspect of the goddess, invoked by different women in Chaucer in the *Troilus*, the *Franklin's Tale*, the *Knight's Tale*, and the *Merchant's Tale*.

63. [Bern. Sil.] *Aen.*, pp. 54–55 (6.119), trans. p. 54 (6.119–20). See also Bersuire, *Ovidius*, on *Metamorphoses* 10.3ff.; trans. p. 347: the serpent is the temptation of the devil, or the devil himself.

64. "Argyve," as the name of Criseyde's mother, is etymologized to show a contrast between the two, in Susan Schibanoff, "Argus and Argyve: Etymology and Characterization in Chaucer's *Troilus*," *Speculum* 51 (1976): 647–58.

65. See Holkot, *In librum Sapientiae*, p. 80 (22), cited in Allen, "Mythology," pp. 372–73. See also the brief reference in *Super librum Sapientiae* 195, p. 641, cited in Allen, "Mythology," p. 373.

66. On Calkas: Chaucer denigrates astrological prophecy and offers instead a Boethian view of destiny, according to Stanley B. Greenfield, "The Role of Calkas in *Troilus and Criseyde*," *MAE* 36 (1967): 141–51.

67. See Holkot, *In librum Sapientiae* 37, p. 130, cited in Allen, "Mythology," pp. 228–29.

68. Dante merely says he is on the beach; he does not say that Priam is dead or Hecuba enslaved (lines 17–18).

69. Book 5 also suffers from padding and jumbled sources, according to S. S. Hussey, "The Difficult Fifth Book of *Troilus and Criseyde*," *MLR* 67 (1972): 721–29, who argues that Chaucer did not revise this book as carefully as he did the other books of the *Troilus*.

70. On Chaucer's specific use of the *Thebaid*, especially in the fifth book, see Boyd Ashby Wise, *The Influence of Statius upon Chaucer* (New York: Phaeton Press, 1967), esp. pp. 20–36. On the source for Cassandra's dream in 5.1485–1510, a summary of *Thebaid* 2–12 in a series of eleven twelve-line Latin arguments, one each to the last eleven books (2–12) of the *Thebaid*, see F. P. Magoun, Jr., "Chaucer's Summary of Statius' *Thebaid* II-XII," *Traditio* 11 (1955): 409–20. For the contrast of Troy's fall with that of Thebes, which heightens the tragedy of Troilus, specifically through the use of Statius's Cassan-

dra in the *Thebaid* to develop the character of Troilus's sister in *Troilus* 5.1450ff., see Paul M. Clogan's "The Theban Scene in Chaucer's *Troilus*," *M & H* n.s. 12 (1984): 167–85. For disputes in families as responsible for Thebes's downfall, and therefore a warning for Troy, see David Anderson, "Cassandra's Analogy: *Troilus* V.1450–1521," *Hebrew University Studies in Literature* 13 (1985): 1–17 (see also, in the same issue, Paul M. Clogan's "Criseyde's Book of the Romance of Thebes," pp. 18ff.). For Theban parallels used as a "satirical counterpoint," especially in relation to the courtly concerns of Troilus and Pandarus instead of a concern with the ongoing war, see David Anderson, "Theban History in Chaucer's *Troilus*," *SAC* 4 (1982): 109–33.

71. "Sic autem erat: quod cum meleager natus esset tres sorores quae parcae dicuntur Illae scilicet deae infernales quae singulorum fata dictare dicuntur" (*Ovidius*, p. 130). Elsewhere in this passage, on *Metamorphoses* 8.271, Bersuire adds: "Say about the fate of the log that through the three goddesses who determine human life we are able to perceive, naturally speaking, the three powers of the sensitive soul [*tres potentias animae sensitiuae*]—that is the natural, the vital, and the animal [*naturalem vitalem & animalem*]—and through the log given by them the life fluid [*humidum radicale*]; for natural life [*vita naturalis*] is put out when the life fluid is totally consumed by the fire of accidental heat. Our life lasts as long as does the life fluid" (p. 131, trans. p. 314).

72. Fulg. *Mit.* 1.8, p. 21, trans. p. 52; see note 61 above.

73. "Haec est dea bellorum, quia bellis magis confert sapientia quam corporis fortitudo. Sap. 5 [6:1] Melior est sapientia quam vires, vir prudens magis quam fortis," from *In librum Sapientiae*, p. 380 (113), in Allen, "Mythology," p. 365.

74. See Chance, "Medieval Sources," pp. 145–60, and the discussion of Landino's treatment of the three lives in his interpretation of the *Aeneid.*

75. See Remigius of Auxerre on Boethius 3m12, p. 64; for William, *Boeth.*, pp. 50–51; for Nicholas Trevet, see Edmund Silk's transcription of Oxford University, Bodleian MS. Rawlinson G.187, p. 510.

76. Chaucer relies heavily on Trevet in the *Troilus*, according to Mark J. Gleason, "The Influence of Trevet on Boethian Language and Thought in Chaucer's *Troilus and Criseyde*," *DAI* 45 (1985): 2096A.

77. For William glossing 3m12.34, Juno represents the active life (so that the punishment on the Wheel of Fortune seems appropriate) and Ixion the desire for honors, but, in addition, this identification of Juno reminds him of the other two goddesses involved in the Judgment of Paris (William, *Boeth.*, pp. 50–51).

78. Holkot draws his gloss on Charybdis from the *Catholicon* of Hugutio of Pisa, in *Super librum Ecclesiastici*, fol. 52r (6.72), cited in Allen, "Mythology," pp. 250–51.

79. According to Pierre Bersuire, this tattletale noticed Proserpina eating three seeds of the pomegranate, an act that prevented her departure from the underworld to the real world because of Pluto's insistence that she eat nothing at all. As a punishment, she transformed Ascalaphus into an owl, a type of evil omen, witness of crime, informer, and envious detractor. "These things can be said against those who discover the deeds of others, those who practice detraction, and those who as soon as they see something having to do with the life of Proserpina—that is with some benefit for a miserable person—are accustomed to accuse this person and to reveal anything she has done harmful to herself" (*Ovidius*, pp. 95–96, trans. pp. 241–42).

80. See Arnulf's comments, p. 214 (on *Metamorphoses* 5.12). See also "Giovanni del Virgilio espositore delle Metamorfosi," ed. Fausto Ghisalberti, *Giornale Dantesco* n.s., 4 (1933): 65 (on *Metamorphoses* 5.17).

81. Fulg. *Mit.* 1.12 and 16, trans. pp. 23, 27–28, explains Phaethon etymologically and naturally: when the sun unites with water, creatures appear called apparitions (*fanon-*

tens, from *fanon*, in Greek, "is appearing"). They appear to bound up from earth; see also the discussion in Remigius, *Boeth.*, p. 46; Bersuire discusses him in 1.750ff. and 2.1ff., in *Ovidius*, p. 49, trans. pp. 152ff.

82. See the K-Reviser's interpolated gloss on 4m7 and the Labors of Hercules in Remigius, *Boeth.*, pp. 73–74. In general, the horses signify the perdition of ignorance and the sun, Christ, who dissipates the shadows of sin by means of the truth of the light and the four classical virtues given to the human race: temperance, prudence, fortitude, and justice. See also John of Garland, p. 44, trans. p. 129, on the *in bono* association of Phaethon and the wisdom of the philosopher.

83. Anderson, "Cassandra's Analogy," has investigated the significance of Troilus's dream, Cassandra's interpretation, and the relevance of the mythological (but not mythographic) background: the interpretation does not appear in the *Filostrato* and it appears to be a useless digression (p. 2). Anderson notes the following parallels between Troy's/Thebes's fortunes and Troilus's: just as the citizens of Troy do not believe Cassandra's prophecy that Troy will fall, Troilus does not believe Cassandra's prediction about Criseyde; Antenor's exchange for Criseyde will have disastrous results for both Troy and Troilus; the parallel between Cupid's cruelty to Troilus (596–602) resembles Juno's to the Trojans in her vendetta; the Calydonian boar parallels Diomede and Meleager parallels Troilus; the abduction of Helen by Paris resembles the seizure of Thebes by Eteocles, so that, to save Troy, the Trojans must give up Helen just as Cassandra warns Troilus he must give up Criseyde. In the figure of Cassandra, Chaucer emphasizes the destructivity of fortune, according to Peggy Ann Knapp, "Boccaccio and Chaucer on Cassandra," *PQ* 56 (1977): 413–17.

84. Anderson, "Cassandra's Analogy," is puzzled by the mention of Tydeus as descendant of Meleager, which differs from Boccaccio's *Genealogia* 11.21, wherein Tydeus is presented more conventionally as Meleager's half brother. He surmises that Chaucer may have been following Lactantius's commentary on *Thebaid* 1.463 (Meleager is the ancestor of Tydeus there), or *Filostrato* 7.27, in which Diomede's grandfather supposedly killed the boar (p. 2 n. 3).

85. The implications of this Theban genealogy for understanding book 5 have in part been examined earlier in this chapter (see notes 70–72), although without reference to the Ovidian version of the boar hunt and its signification in the commentaries. Diomede's boar-related genealogy, as presented by Cassandra, is also traced by Hyginus in his *Fabula* 69: after Polynices explains his lion garb by means of his lineage from Hercules, who defeated the Nimean lion, "Tydeus spoke too, saying that he was the son of Oeneus and traced his descent from Calydon, and so he wore a boar skin to recall the Calydonian Boar. Then the king, mindful of the oracular reply, gave Argia, the older daughter to Polynices, from whom Thersander was born; Deipyla, the younger, he gave to Tydeus, and she became mother of Diomede who fought at Troy" (Hyginus, p. 53 [69], trans. p. 69; see also pp. 51–52, trans. p. 68, Version A [no. 68]). Hyginus's first-century *Fabulae*, along with Firmicus Maternus's *Matheos* and Macrobius's *Somnium* and *Saturnalia*, became available at Chartres by the mid-twelfth century, according to A. Clerval, *Les Écoles de Chartres au Moyen-Âge (du Ve au XVIe siècle)* (Paris, 1895), pp. 223, 239.

86. The first reference, to Zephirus (10) at the opening, not only establishes the length of the relationship between Troilus and Criseyde but also emphasizes the cyclical nature of spring. The allusion to spring promises renewal and rebirth in the natural world, and therefore heightens the imminent irony of the turn of another cycle—the Wheel of Fortune. It has been three years since Hecuba's son fell in love with Criseyde, who is scheduled to leave the next morning. The same idea is restated through this

golden image: "The gold-tressed Phebus heighte on-lofte / Thries hadde alle with his be-mes cleene / The snowes molte, and Zepherus as ofte / Ibrought ayeyn the tendre leves grene" (8–11). The flossy rhetoric of the lines suggests that the pagan Troilus will not en-joy spiritual renewal in the spring, as Chaucer's Christian audience will during the sea-son of Lent and Easter, and, as we know, when he dies, his celestial journey through the heavens will end at the sphere of the fixed stars. Further, in the underworld of this earth, or of temporal good, only natural renewal appears possible. In addition, the reference here to Troilus as the son of Hecuba (12) reminds the reader, again, of the fourth book's use of *Inferno* figures Myrrha and Athamas, whose falsifying was linked in the same canto with the madness of Hecuba resulting after her loss of another son and a daughter at the end of the war—discord without renewal.

Chapter 5. Zephirus, Rape, and Saint Thomas à Becket: The Political Vernacular

Portions of this chapter were delivered as a paper, "Chaucer's Zephirus and the Idea of the *General Prologue*," in a session that I organized on the theme "Chaucer and Mythog-raphy" at the Twentieth International Conference on Medieval Studies, Western Michi-gan University, Kalamazoo, May 11, 1985.

1. J. Norton-Smith, "Chaucer's *Etas Prima*," *MAE* 32 (1963): 117–24.

2. Norton-Smith argues that this is not a Boethian meditation but a satiric exposé of contemporary society. However, he also notes that the appearance of the poem in two Cambridge University library manuscripts (MS. I.i.21 and MS. Hh 4.12) has Boethian connections: in the first, it appears with Chaucer's translation of Boethius in toto plus the gloss and commentary of Nicholas Trevet; also, the title in the manuscript is printed as "Chawcer vpon this fyfte metur of the Second book" (ibid., p. 117). Norton-Smith in-dicates that this Boethian connection does not appear in the second manuscript, and he also declares that "The last stanza shows Chaucer moving further away from Boethius in the introduction of his finest imagery: the double *exemplum*, one mythological, the other historical" (pp. 120–21).

3. See Notker's glosses on *Boethius De consolatione Philosophiae* in *Notkers des deutschen Werke*, ed. E. H. Sehrt and Taylor Starck, vol. 1, parts 1–3, Altdeutsche Text-bibliothek nos. 32–34 (Halle and Saale: Max Niemeyer, 1933–34), p. 216.

4. Note also the combats of Pseustis and Alithia; Bernard declares, "Boecius vero eos qui dum sunt impliciti terrenis, celestia discutere aut consequi nituntur," in Morton Yale Jacobs, "Bernard's '*Commentum in Theodulum: Editio Princeps*'" (Diss., University of North Carolina-Chapel Hill, 1963), p. 40 (14v). Note that the first appendix contains the whole of the *Ecloga* (pp. 218–29).

5. Ibid., fol. 15r, p. 41.

6. Ibid. The fifteenth-century Anonymous Teutonicus, commenting allegorically on the same passage of the *Ecloga Theoduli*, sees the giants as men who have accumulated riches upon riches to reach a state of honor. But Jupiter (God) takes his fabricator Mul-ciber (the Devil) and opposes the giants with flames (lightning) after death, that is, the promise of Judgment. The passage reads: "Item allegorice per istos gigantes intelligimus homines, qui per divicias temporales cumulantes MONTEM super MONTEM, i. denarium su-per denarium, volunt ascendere ad statum honoris, sed tandem Iupiter, i. Deus, mittit fabrum suum MULCIBERUM, i. dyabolum, cum FULMINE, i. cum flammis igneis, scilicet post mortem, et TRUDIT eos IN ANTRUM VULCANEI, scilicet in Infernum. Quare dicit Psalmista *Si divicie tibi affluant, noli cor apponere*" (*Anonymi Teutonici commentum in Theodoli*

eclogam e codice Utrecht, U.B. 292 editum [1]," ed. Arpád P. Orbán, in *Vivarium,* 11:1 [1973]: 37–38, on lines 85–88).

7. According to twelfth- and thirteenth-century dictionaries and encyclopedias by Papias and Giovanni Balbi, and commentaries like the fourteenth-century *Ovide moralisé,* the West Wind, Zephirus in Greek, also known as Favonius in Latin, makes the flowers and grasses bloom. See the facsimile of Papias, *Vocabulista* (Turin: Bottega d'Erasmo, 1966), s.v. (p. 380); and also the expanded but similar dictionary by Giovanni Balbi (Joannes Balbus), *Catholicon* (Mainz, 1460; repr. fac. Westmead, Farnsborough, Hants, England: Gregg International Publishers, 1971); see also under "Favonius." Of the commentaries, the *Ovide moralisé,* for example, mentions Zephirus in two places, once as one of the four winds, associated with the West and called Galerne (1.268, p. 66) and once as the force that vivifies the flowers: "Unz vens plesans et delitables, / Zephirus, fesoit les floretes / Nestre: vers, indes, vermeilletes, / Jaunes, blaunches et d'autre guise, / Sans semence qui i fust mise" (1.508–12, p. 72). In line with these definitions, most of the acknowledged sources for the Chaucerian passage about Zephirus echo his literal role as revivifying wind. Two important treatments come from Isidore, *De quadragesima,* 5, 59, cited by Bernard F. Huppé in *A Reading of the Canterbury Tales,* rev. ed. (Albany: State University of New York, 1967), p. 17, and from Pierre Bersuire in his *Ovidius moralizatus,* cited by Muriel Bowden in *A Commentary on the General Prologue to the Canterbury Tales,* 2d ed. (London: Macmillan; New York: Collier Macmillan, 1967), p. 20. Both passages mention zephyrs as synonyms for the balmy and fructifying westerly winds, as does Guido delle Colonne in his *Historia destructionis Troiae,* PL 83:97–105, cited by Huppé, p. 16. In addition, book 1, poem 5 of Boethius's *Consolatio Philosophiae* has been acknowledged as a source not only for the figure of Zephirus but also for the *reverdie* in Chaucer's *General Prologue,* according to Hubertis Cummings, "Chaucer's *Prologue,* 1–7," *MLN* 37 (1922): 86–90. Indeed, of all the possible sources for the *reverdie,* only the Boethius passage specifically mentions Zephirus. And in Boethius, as in other early passages, Zephirus, the wind of spring, the West Wind, functions exclusively as an agent for macrocosmic vitality and regeneration, in contrast to Boreas, the North Wind associated with winter: 1m5 of Chaucer's *Boece* addresses the "makere of the wheel that bereth the sterres" to note that "Thy myghte attempreth the variauntz sesouns of the yer, so that Zephirus, the debonere wynd, bryngeth ayen in the first somer sesoun the leeves that the wynd that hygte Boreas hath reft awey in autumpne." For a modern English translation of Boethius's *Consolation of Philosophy,* see Richard H. Green's translation (Indianapolis and New York: Bobbs-Merrill, 1962), p. 15.

8. "Hyemem autem resolvit et germina floresque producit, et dicitur Zephyrus a Zephs grece, quod latine vita sonat," in *Genealogia,* 4.61 (2:217).

9. *Aeneid* 4.705. Although this phrase in Latin is not uncommon and may only suggest the effects of moving air, it may also relate to the ancient Italian animistic—and later Stoic philosophical—belief in the soul as breath analogous to the fiery World Soul, *anima mundi.*

10. As if underscoring this analogy between life, wind, and breath, Fulgentius describes Psyche as "gently wafted by the breath of Zephyr" ("Zephyri ... anhelante vectura" [*Mit.,* p. 68, trans. p. 88]).

11. "Favonius autem eo quod faveat germinantia vel faveat germinibus; flat enim suaviter et placide a meridie usque in noctem, a principio veris usque ad estatis finem" (*Genealogia,* 4.61 [1:217]).

12. Rabanus Maurus, *De diis gentium,* in *De universo libri XXII,* 15.6, in *Opera omnia, PL* 111:282.

13. See Huppé, *A Reading of the Canterbury Tales*, pp. 14–15, and Jane Chance Nitzsche, "Creation in Genesis and Nature in Chaucer's *General Prologue*, 1–18," Papers on *Language and Literature* 14 (1978): 463.

14. For the Italian influence on Chaucer, specifically Boccaccio and Dante, see Howard H. Schless, "Chaucer and Dante," in *Critical Approaches to Medieval Literature: Selected Papers from the English Institute 1958–9* ed. Dorothy Bethurum (New York and London: Columbia University Press, 1960; repr. 1967); and Howard H. Schless, "Transformations: Chaucer's Use of Italian," in *Writers and their Background: Geoffrey Chaucer*, ed. Derek Brewer (Columbus: Ohio University Press, 1975). Schless notes that 1372 marks the first definite trip to Italy by Chaucer; there may also have been trips to Spain and Italy in 1366 and 1368. Italian (Dantesque) influence on Chaucer's earliest dream vision, the *Book of the Duchess*, has been noted by Robert Edwards in "The *Book of the Duchess* and the Beginnings of Chaucer's Narrative," *New Literary History* 13 (1982): 189–204, although there may have been stronger influences on his poetry both by Boccaccio and Dante after the second and much more important visit to Italy, in 1378, to interview Bernabò Visconti and Sir John Hawkwood in Milan (about the king's wars), when Chaucer examined the Visconti libraries: see especially Robert A. Pratt, "Chaucer and the Visconti Libraries," *ELH* 6 (1939): 191–99. See also Howard Schless's study, *Chaucer and Dante: A Revaluation* (Norman, Okla.: Pilgrim Books, 1984), as well as the studies of N. R. Havely, ed., *Chaucer's Boccaccio — Sources of "Troilus" and the Knight's and Franklin's Tales*, Chaucer Studies, vol. 3 (Cambridge, England: D. S. Brewer; Totowa, N.J.: Rowman and Littlefield, 1980); Piero Boitani, ed. *Chaucer and the Italian Trecento* (Cambridge, London, and New York: Cambridge University Press, 1983), esp. the essays by Boitani, "What Dante Meant to Chaucer," pp. 115–39, Wendy Childs, "Anglo-Italian Contacts in the Fourteenth Century," pp. 65–87, and J. A. W. Bennett, "Chaucer, Dante, and Boccaccio," pp. 89–113; R. A. Shoaf, *Dante, Chaucer and the Currency of the Word* (Norman, Okla.: Pilgrim Books, 1983); and Winthrop Wetherbee, *Chaucer and the Poets: An Essay on Troilus and Criseyde* (Ithaca, N.Y., and London: Cornell University Press, 1984), esp. chapter 5, "Dante and the *Troilus.*"

15. A date of 1377, however, was proposed by Edward I. Condren as the likely time of composition for the *Book of the Duchess*, in "The Historical Context of the *Book of the Duchess*: A New Hypothesis," *Papers on Language and Literature* 5 (1971): 195–212.

16. The Dante commentaries, which Chaucer may have seen, numbered at least twelve. Robert Hollander of Princeton has compiled a data base for many of these commentaries in what is known as "The Dartmouth Project." For additional information about the commentaries, see Bruno Sandkühler, *Die frühen Dantekommentare und ihr Verhältnis zur mittelalterlichen Kommentartradition*, Münchener romanistische Arbeiten, no. 19 (Munich: Max Hueber Verlag, 1967); and for the place of the commentaries within the whole of the mythographic tradition, see Jane Chance, *Medieval Mythography*, vol. 1: *From Roman North Africa to the School of Chartres, AD 433–1177* (Gainesville: University Press of Florida, 1994).

17. On *Paradiso* 12.46–52, see Charles Hall Grandgent, *Companion to the Divine Comedy*, ed. Charles S. Singleton (Cambridge, Mass.: Harvard University Press, 1975), p. 246. In support are cited these lines from Ovid's *Metamorphoses* 1.63–64: "Vesper et occiduo quae litora sole tepescunt, / proxima sunt Zephyro" ("The Western shores which glow with the setting sun are the place of Zephyrus"). According to Edmund Garratt Gardner, Petrus Ferrandi compares Saint Dominic to Hesperus, rising from the West: see *Dante and the Mystics: A Study of the Mystical Aspect of the Divina Commedia and its Relations with Some of its Mediaeval Sources* (New York: Dutton, 1913), p. 245.

18. See Grandgent, *Companion*, p. 246.

19. See Huppé, *A Reading of the Canterbury Tales,* p. 16, for the metaphor of impregnation and related rhetoric.

20. In *Genealogia deorum gentilium* 4.61 (1:217), Boccaccio cites Bede, Homer (*Iliad*), Lactantius in the *Divine Institutes,* Ovid, and Pliny to uncover interesting details about the West Wind favoring the growth of flowers through his anthropomorphized "breath." Boccaccio's simplest gloss, probably taken from Ovid's *Fasti* 5.183–371, notes that a nymph named Cloris was desired and later married by Zephirus; her marriage dowry gave her rule over flowers, and for this reason her name changed from Cloris to Flora. Boccaccio primarily draws upon Lactantius Firmianus's *Divinae institutiones* 1.20.6 and Arnulf of Orleans's commentary on the *Fasti* to clarify the relationship between Zephirus and Flora, goddess of flowers. Boccaccio cites a euhemeristic passage from Lactantius Firmianus on the lascivious nature of the activities of the Floralia, which originated in a prostitute's donations to the Roman populace of a large sum of money intended for games on her birthday and which were dignified by the Senate through an identification of the prostitute with the goddess of flowers (who must be placated in order to ensure ample fruit and vines). Finally, Boccaccio draws upon Pliny's *Natural History* 8.66.166 to indicate that near Lisbon, in Lusitania (Portugal), mares facing the west wind conceive the "breath of life" to produce a very fast colt; the mare from which this derives is known as "Thyella" and was mentioned by Homer. Transmission of these little-used antique and late classical sources to Boccaccio and also to Chaucer, if he did not know the *Genealogia,* may have been fostered by the twelfth-century Arnulf of Orleans's glosses on the *Fasti,* which unfortunately exist today only in the crabbed script of about six different manuscripts, the best of which is Vaticanus Reginensis 1548. Much of Arnulf's commentary reappeared in the more influential dictionary known as Huguccio of Pisa's *Magnae derivationes.* Portions of the Arnulf commentary are excerpted and discussed in Jean Holzworth, "An Unpublished Commentary on Ovid's *Fasti* by Arnulfus of Orleans" (Diss., Bryn Mawr, 1940). For a brief discussion of the Zephirus tradition as it appears in Ovid's *Fasti* and the relationship between Flora-Chloris, see Edgar Wind, *Pagan Mysteries in the Renaissance* (1958; rev. ed. London: Faber and Faber, 1968), p. 116.

21. In the FVM, Boreas is listed as "Aquilones" in Latin and Eurus, as "Africus"; the mythographer mistakenly lists "Auster" as the corresponding Latin name for Zephirus rather than as the South Wind. For no. 183.6, pp. 55–56, Bode notes that the sources of myth are the scholia on Statius's *Thebaid* 2.4 and Servius on *Aeneid* 1.132. A similar treatment of Zephirus and the other winds appears in Bede, *Didascalica genuina,* chapter 27, PL 90:248. The comments in myth 51 are similar to those of the FVM, myth 183, and according to Bode derive from Hesiod's *Theogony* 378 and Servius on *Aeneid* 1.587. Here the mythographer provides a gloss on a line from the *Aeneid* in reference to Aeolus as king of winds. Aeolus's anger and his order to curb that anger are explained naturally (Bode, p. 92). In addition, the two directions of each wind bear different names: Zephirus seeks Circius in the Northwest, but Favonius (a frequently cited alternate name of Zephirus) in the West; see John of Garland, *Integumenta,* lines 41–48. Favonius is regarded as especially fructifying in his effect on the double crops of India, as expressed in Martianus's *De nuptiis* (6, p. 345, or no. 694), where Zephirus's Latin name, Favonius, is used: "Stretching southward to the eastern Ocean, it [India] is a healthy land because of the invigorating breezes of Favonius; its soil is enlivened by a second summer each year, and it produces two crops" (trans. 2:259).

22. *Sir Gawain and the Green Knight,* ed. J. R. R. Tolkien and E. V. Gordon, 2d ed. rev. Norman Davis (Oxford: Clarendon Press, 1967).

23. Froissart's account is cited, in translation, in *The Peasants' Revolt of 1381,* ed. R.

B. Dobson, 2d ed. (Houndmills, Basingstoke, Hampshire and London: Macmillan, 1983; repr. 1991), pp. 139–40.

Chapter 6. Feminizing Theseus in the *Knight's Tale*: The Victory of Pallas Athena over Mars

1. Boyd Ashby Wise, *The Influence of Statius upon Chaucer* (Baltimore: J. H. Furst, 1911; repr. New York: Phaeton Press, 1967), pp. 46–48.

2. For Chaucer's direct and indirect use of Statius in the *Knight's Tale*, see ibid., pp. 46–54 and 78–126. Chaucer may have used the *Thebaid*, *Teseida*, and the anonymous *Roman de Thèbes*, for the features that do not appear in the *Teseida* include the Minotaur (980) and the mention of Fortune (p. 47). For Chaucer's use of Statius, "freely rearranged," in the *Anelida*, see p. 45; Wise notes that Chaucer follows Statius more closely here than in the *Knight's Tale* (p. 67).

3. For the impact of Boethius on the *Knight's Tale*, see Bernard L. Jefferson, *Chaucer and the "Consolation of Philosophy" of Boethius* (1917; repr. New York: Gordian Press, 1968), pp. 130–32, 142–44.

4. Robert W. Hanning, " 'The Struggle between Noble Designs and Chaos': The Literary Tradition of Chaucer's *Knight's Tale*," *Literary Review* 23 (1980): 519–41, compares the triumph of the courtly code in Boccaccio with Theseus, agent of order and civilization in Statius, battling chaos in Chaucer by means of the chivalric conflict.

5. See Henry Ward's notes to the Chaucer Society's *Six-Text Print of Chaucer's Canterbury Tales*, summarized in F. J. Furnivall, *A Temporary Preface to the Six-Text Edition of Chaucer's Canterbury Tales* (London, 1868), pp. 134–35. Of the 1,475 lines not taken from the *Teseida*, 260 are new, introduced into the Palamon-Arcite story. On comparison of the main source, *Teseida*, with the *Knight's Tale*, see Robert A. Pratt, "Chaucer's Use of the *Teseida*," *PMLA* 62 (1947): 598–621; Herbert G. Wright, *Boccaccio in England from Chaucer to Tennyson* (London: Athlone Press, 1957), pp. 45–58; and Piero Boitani, *Chaucer and Boccaccio*, Medium Aevum Monographs, n.s., 8 (Oxford and Cambridge: Society for the Study of Mediaeval Languages and Literature, 1977). Boitani includes a summary of the monograph in his essay "Style, Iconography, and Narrative: The Lesson of the *Teseide*," in his *Chaucer and the Italian Trecento* (Cambridge, England: Cambridge University Press, 1983), pp. 185–200. See also David Anderson, "The Legendary History of Thebes in Boccaccio's *Teseida* and Chaucer's *Knight's Tale*," *DAI* 40 (1980): 4585A, revised into a book entitled *Before the Knight's Tale: Imitation of Classical Epic in Boccaccio's Teseida* (Philadelphia: University of Pennsylvania Press, 1988), esp. chapter 4, on Chaucer's "translation" of the epic. For Chaucer's use of the *Teseida* in the depiction of Arcite, see Judith C. Perryman, "The 'False Arcite' of Chaucer's *Knight's Tale*," *Neophilologus* 68 (1984): 121–33. For a discussion of the *Teseida*'s influence on the two Mayings, see Lorraine Kochanske Stock, "The Two Mayings in Chaucer's *Knight's Tale*: Convention and Invention," *JEGP* 85 (1986): 206–21. Excerpts from the sources can be found in Robert A. Pratt, "The *Knight's Tale*," in Bryan and Dempster, pp. 82–105, in a section that includes even minor sources like Ovid and Vincent of Beauvais.

6. Of the few critical studies of the poem, only Michael D. Cherniss attempts to link it with the very similar *Knight's Tale*, in "Chaucer's *Anelida and Arcite*: Some Conjectures," *ChauR* 5 (1970): 9–21. He discusses the interrelationship of the *Teseida*, *Anelida*, and the *Knight's Tale*, to show that Arcite seems to be the common denominator in all three; he surmises that Chaucer probably intended to use the story of Palamon and Arcite in the *Anelida*, which would have consoled Anelida for the injustice of Arcite, but that Chaucer may have abandoned the *Anelida* because of the difficulty in integrating

the Anelida story with the Palamon and Arcite story (pp. 17ff.). He does conclude rather negatively that "In general, the story of Anelida and Arcite appears to have almost nothing to do with that of Palamon and Arcite" (p. 18). But note the echoes of the *Anelida* in the *Knight's Tale*, Prologue to the *Legend of Good Women*, *Squire's Tale*, *Merchant's Tale*, and *Parlement of Foules* in Alfred David, "Recycling Anelida and Arcite: Chaucer as Source for Chaucer," in Paul Strohm and Thomas J. Heffernan, eds., *SAC, Proceedings*, no. 1, 1984 (*SAC* 9 [1987], no. 93), pp. 105–15.

7. See F. N. Robinson's notes on the dating of the poem in *The Works of Geoffrey Chaucer*, 2d ed. (Boston: Houghton Mifflin, 1957; repr. 1961). Robinson remarks the *Anelida*'s metrical form and use of the *Teseida* mean it followed *Hous of Fame*, whereas its treatment of Arcite suggest a date earlier than the *Knight's Tale*. See also the range of dates provided by early scholars of Chaucer (Furnivall, Koch, ten Brink, Pollard, Mather, Bilderbeck, Tatlock), beginning in 1373 and ending in 1389, in J. S. P. Tatlock, *The Development and Chronology of Chaucer's Works*, Chaucer Society ser. 2, no. 37 (London: Paul, Trench, Trubner, 1907; repr. Gloucester, Mass.: P. Smith, 1963), pp. x-xi; it might have been written during the winter of 1373–74, before the *Knight's Tale*, and earlier than *Palamon and Arcite*, according to Viktor Langhans, "Chaucer's Anelida and Arcite," *Anglia* 44 (1920): 226–44. For a date not particularly early in Chaucer's career, linking it with the *Troilus* book 5 in the influence upon both of Italian humanistic verse, and making it a complete poem, see the essay by J. Norton-Smith, "Chaucer's *Anelida and Arcite*," in *Medieval Studies for J. A. W. Bennett, Aetatis Suae LXX*, ed. P. L. Heyworth (Oxford: Clarendon Press, 1981), pp. 81–99.

8. The *Anelida*'s flaws have been much discussed: it is fragmentary, lacks irony and ambiguity, and is conventionally courtly. See the discussion of Chaucer's dull, plain style in Stephen Knight, *Rymyng Craftily: Meaning in Chaucer's Poetry* (Sydney: Angus and Robertson, 1973), p. 11. But note its stylistic merits in Cherniss, "Chaucer's *Anelida and Arcite*," who acknowledges that "The Complaint of Anelida" has been praised for technical virtuosity and genuine human emotion (ideas seconded by William Paton Ker, *Essays on Medieval Literature* [London: Macmillan, 1905], pp. 76–100, here, pp. 82, 99; also Ker's *Medieval English Literature* [New York: H. Holt, 1912; repr. 1948], p. 175). See also Wolfgang Clemen, *Chaucer's Early Poetry*, trans. C. A. M. Sym (London: Methuen, 1963), pp. 198, 206–9; and Rossell Hope Robbins, "The Lyrics," *Companion to Chaucer Studies*, ed. Beryl Rowland (1968; rev. New York and London: Oxford University Press, 1979), pp. 322–23. For a study of the narrative section as "functionally complete," structured according to a principle of nonprogressive parallelism, see Adrienne Rosemary Lockhart, "The Draf of Storyes: Chaucer as Non-Narrative Poet" (Diss., Pennsylvania State University, 1972), *DAI* 33 (1973): 3592A. As testimony to its importance, see the annotated bibliography by Russell A. Peck, *Chaucer's Lyrics and Anelida and Arcite: An Annotated Bibliography 1900 to 1980*, The Chaucer Bibliographies (Toronto, Buffalo, and London: University of Toronto Press, 1983).

The *Anelida*, however, only *seems* to mix its major sources to no purpose. Statius's *Thebaid* (from which its setting and point of departure derive), is blended with Boccaccio's *Teseida* (for the story of Arcite) in this Italian-phase poem: note Robinson's comments on its misuse of Statius's *Thebaid* and Boccaccio's *Teseida* as sources (*The Works of Geoffrey Chaucer*, pp. 303–4). For other Italian sources, particularly important in placing of the *Anelida* in Chaucer's Italian period, see F. J. Snell, *The Age of Chaucer* (London: Bell, 1901; rev. 1906), pp. 121–236 on Chaucer, here, p. 163. For lines echoed from Dante, see John Livingston Lowes, "Chaucer and Dante," *MP* 14 (1917): 705–35. For a source in Boccaccio's *Fiametta*, see Tarquinis Vallese, *Goffredo Chaucer visto da un Italiano* (Milan: Società anonima editrice Dante Alighieri, 1930). This conflation of two sources explains the double genres of epic (Statius) in the narrative portion and lyric ("Corinne") in the courtly-love complaint portion. Note, for example, the Robinson introduction to the poem (pp. 303–4), in which it is criticized as a puzzling, unfinished cross between epic and lyric. Knight also notes that the poem wavers between three styles and two genres: "such a confusion must be a major flaw" (p. 20). For the epic sources and analogues — specifically its relationship with the *Knight's Tale* and Boccaccio's *Teseida* — see Langhans, "Chaucers Anelida and Arcite," pp. 226–44; Pratt, "Chaucer's Use of the *Teseida*," pp. 598–621; and Cherniss, pp. 9–21. For the poem as a lyrical complaint, derived from Ovid, see Edgar F. Shannon, "The Source of Chaucer's *Anelida and Arcite*," *PMLA* 27 (1912): 461–85. For related French (hence courtly) analogues and sources, especially by Machaut and also Froissart, see Madeleine Fabin, "On Chaucer's *Anelida and Arcite*," *MLN* 34 (1919): 266–72. This mixture of styles and genres could be explained by the term mock-heroic: see A. Wigfall Green, "Meter and Rhyme in Chaucer's 'Anelida and Arcite,'" *Studies in English (University of Mississippi)* 2 (1961): 55–63. Robert Pratt notes that its disunity and lack of plot have been influenced by "Boccaccio's incongruous juxtaposition of epic solemnity and medieval love complaint," which may also account for its chief character, Arcite, appearing unattractive and false in nature (p. 605). James I. Wimsatt, however, in analyzing its identity as pseudo-epic (that is, with passages borrowed from epic poems) colored by French love complaint, has witnessed some singleness of purpose in the major character of Arcite: although the poem's title refers to him, nevertheless he emblematizes falsity: see "*Anelida and Arcite*: A Narrative of Complaint and Comfort," *ChauR* 5 (1970): 1–8. For the creation of Arcite as a false lover, influenced by the *Roman de la Rose*, see Lisa Cipriani, "Studies in the Influence of the *Romance of the Rose* upon Chaucer," *PMLA* 22 (1907): 552–95, here, p. 554. On the image of the horse as a reflection on Arcite's failure to master either of his women, for he is restless in serving Anelida, tame with his new lady, see Doreen M. E. Gilliam, "Lovers and Riders in Chaucer's 'Anelida and Arcite,'" *ES* 63 (1982): 394–401.

    9. Wise, *The Influence of Statius upon Chaucer*, pp. 44–5, 66–77.

    10. For the former, see Vincent J. DiMarco in the note to the Benson *Riverside Chaucer* edition; for the latter, see p. 45; on Ovid (*Heroides*) as a source for "Corinne," see Douglas Bush, "Chaucer's 'Corinne,'" *Speculum* 4 (1929): 106–7.

    11. The three-stanza invocation in lines 1–21 is supposedly adapted or translated from Boccaccio's invocation in the *Teseida* (1.3,2,1) and without any narrative counterpart in the *Knight's Tale*; after the Statian homecoming passage in 22–42, Chaucer adapts Boccaccio's stanzas on the destruction of Thebes (*Teseida* 2, 10–12, which resemble the *Knight's Tale* 931–47). The poem breaks off at the description of the Temple of Mars.

    12. Whether Theseus is intended to be a positive or negative character has astrological as well as psychological and allegorical ramifications. A. J. Minnis, in *Chaucer and Pagan Antiquity* (Bury St. Edmunds, Suffolk: D. S. Brewer; Totowa, N.J.: Rowman and Littlefield, 1982), pp. 117–18, traces Theseus's qualities parallel to those of Jupiter — a good sense of humor, keen sense of justice, wisdom, pity, and so on — corroborated by John Ridevall's astrological mythography, and then, on p. 128, those more negative qualities, specifically the limitation of his justice, so uninformed by love; he provides an excellent critical summary of both views on p. 178 n. 40.

    13. The Knight's philosophical approach to life has been asserted by one camp (mostly predominant) in Chaucer criticism, as in the study of his pessimism and Stoicism by T. K. Meier, "Chaucer's Knight as 'Persona': Narration as Control," *English Miscellany* 20 (1969): 11–21, and of his Boethianism by Robert M. Lumiansky, "Chaucer's Philolosophical Knight," *Tulane Studies in English* 3 (1952): 47–68; repr. in revised form in *Of Sondry Folk: The Dramatic Principle in the "Canterbury Tales"* (Austin: Uni-

versity of Texas Press, 1955), pp. 29–48. For the controversial, and minority, argument that the Knight was a mercenary, see Terry Jones, *Chaucer's Knight: The Portrait of a Medieval Mercenary* (Baton Rouge: Louisiana State University Press, 1980); a more realistic modification of this argument appears in John H. Pratt, "Was Chaucer's Knight Really a Mercenary?" *ChauR* 22 (1987): 8–27.

14. For Theseus's change from the positive and heroic figure of the *Anelida*, derived from the *Thebaid*, to the more negative deserter of Ariadne in the *Legend of Good Women* and the *Hous of Fame*, and finally to the "morally ambivalent" figure of the *Knight's Tale*, see Walter Scheps, "Chaucer's Theseus and the *Knight's Tale*," *Leeds Studies in English* 9 (1976–77): 19–34. Note Melvin Storm's discussion of the two traditions, and the two faces, of Theseus, in "From Knossos to the Knight's Tale: The Changing Face of Theseus," in Chance, *Mythographic Art*, pp. 215–31. He concludes that the more favorable view of Theseus in the *Knight's Tale* reflects the character and values of Chaucer's mature and wise Knight.

15. Wise, *The Influence of Statius upon Chaucer*, p. 71. On his confusion of Bellona and Pallas, see, for a discussion of similar confusion in the *Thebaid* glosses, Paul M. Clogan, "Chaucer and the *Thebaid* Scholia," *SP* 61 (1964): 599–615. Clogan notes that "Statius tends to syncretize the different divinities and to consider them various manifestations of the same power. Although he keeps Bellona and Pallas distinct, I find the two being confused in several glosses on the *Thebaid*" (p. 606). See also Boyd Ashby Wise, "Chaucer's Use of the *Thebaid*," *English Miscellany* 18 (1967): 9–31, for Statian echoes in the "Complaint of Pity," *Book of the Duchess, Complaint of Mars, Hous of Fame, Anelida, Troilus*, and the *Knight's Tale*; he discusses the confusion of Bellona and Pallas, and the invocation to the Muses, in the *Anelida*, again, on p. 17.

16. Remigius of Auxerre glosses as minor deities gods of war like Abdella or Bellona, the arms of Mars, and Saturn (seen as a more advanced form of Discord) (*Mart.* 211.2). In the text, Silvanus, thinking that war approaches, begs for the bows of the Delians, the arms of Hercules, Portunus's trident, but does not dare "to ask for the spear of Gradivus Mars; being used to rustic warfare, he was considering the scythe of Saturn and, distrusting his own strength, was eying the missiles of the Thunderer" (trans., 2:156). Remigius glosses 211.6, as has John Scot earlier, although in 211.4 he misunderstands Bdella as Abdella (p. 64). The conventional interpretation of Mars here reappears: "he is god of power, *cratos divus*, or Gradivus, called so because he marches forth (in steps) to war, or from the lance that is called a *gradein* in Greek. He is like death, or the separation of body from soul. Death is the effect of war, and among the pagans no one thing was more laudable than death in defense of fatherland." Mars is linked with the number nine in book 7, the end of the first numerical series appropriately in Martianus par. 741, because it is he "by whom all things are brought to an end." Remigius explains (375.12, pp. 194–95) that Mars comes from "megalos Ares" (in Greek), or "magna virtus" (in Latin); so (implicitly) it is the end of all (numbers), or Mars is called so from mors, death, "FINIS EST OMNIUM"; or called so from *mactus virtute*, that is, full of virtue (*plenus virtutis*). Thus he is associated with nine, "quia mors finit omnia," because death ends everything.

17. Holkot, *In librum duodecim prophetas*, fols. 98r-98v, cited in Allen, "Mythology," p. 151; on p. 366, cited again, to which he added "Matt. 5 [5:9] Beati pacifici, quoniam filii dei vocabuntur."

18. Christine de Pizan, *The Epistle of Othea*, trans. Stephen Scrope, ed. Curt F. Bühler, EETS (London, New York, and Toronto: Oxford University Press, 1970), pp. 4–5.

19. Hoffman, *Ovid*, p. 39. Edgar Finley Shannon, *Chaucer and the Roman Poets*, Harvard Studies in Comparative Literature 7 (Cambridge, Mass.: Harvard University Press, 1929), declares that "though Chaucer was mainly following Boccaccio in the *Knight's Tale*, he has enriched his account from his extensive knowledge of Ovid" (p. 302). He

may have drawn even his knowledge of the Thebes story from moralized Ovid commentaries: Theban matter, taken from *Ovide moralisé* 9.1437–1838, Statius, the *Teseida*, and the *Roman de Thèbes*, is discussed by Bernard L. Witlieb, "Chaucer and a French Story of Thèbes," *ELN* 11 (1973): 5–9. On the possible influence of the *Ovide moralisé* on the Bellona-Pallas confusion at the opening, see 13.1–383 (esp. 284–87), in which Bellona is linked with "arms" and "temple," see Bernard L. Witlieb, "Chaucer and the *Ovide Moralisé*," *N & Q* 17 (1970): 204.

20. For the origin of Venus and her *citole* in the *Libellus* rather than Bersuire's moralization of Ovid, see Ernest H. Wilkins, "Descriptions of Pagan Divinities from Petrarch to Chaucer," *Speculum* 32 (1957): 511–22, esp. 520–22. Wilkins concludes (p. 522) that Mercury and Mars in the *Knight's Tale* (1387–88 and 2041–48) also came from the *Libellus* (what we call the TVM today), so that Petrarch's *Africa* led to the *Ovidius*, then the *Libellus de deorum imaginibus*, and then Chaucer. John M. Steadman, "Venus' Citole in Chaucer's *Knight's Tale* and Berchorius," *Speculum* 34 (1959): 620–24, argues that her *citole* links her depiction with Bersuire's *Ovidius moralizatus* rather than the *Libellus*, in that Bersuire saw her shell as symbolic of the musical aspect of the *vita voluptuosa*.

21. Walter Clyde Curry, *Chaucer and the Mediaeval Sciences* (1926; 2d ed. New York and London: Barnes and Noble, 1960), p. 126. On the gods, with the two knights representing the forces of Saturn and Mars, see Curry, pp. 119–65; also Curry, "Astrologizing the Gods," *Anglia* 47 (1923): 213–43. More particularly, the gods are actually the planets; the real conflict occurs between Saturn and Mars; Lycurgus and Emetrius are Saturnalian and Martian champions; Arcite dies because of an illness caused by his planetary adversary Saturn: "It is evident, therefore, that the final scene of conflict between the planets is in the body of Arcite" (p. 237). This conclusion fits in with the isolation of Arcite as the tale's hero: see A. V. C. Schmidt, "The Tragedy of Arcite: A Reconsideration of the *Knight's Tale*," *Essays in Criticism* 19 (1969): 107–17. Minnis adds: "Euhemerism has become a principle of characterization" since Bersuire, "by interpreting the gods as historical individuals and moral types" (*Chaucer*, p. 110). "So, in a different manner, did Chaucer, by modelling the characters of his pagans on the characters of the gods they worship" (p. 110). Chaucer's gods are astrologized deities, "and therefore another factor influencing characterization in *The Knight's Tale* would have been the notion that a man's character was affected (but not determined, of course) by the planet-god or planet-gods in the ascendant at his birth" (p. 110). V. A. Kolve, *Chaucer and the Imagery of Narrative: The First Five Canterbury Tales* (Stanford: Stanford University Press, 1984), thinks that the statues of the gods express primarily mythological roles and the wall paintings, planetary influence and hence astrological belief (see p. 115). He relates them to *Planetenkinder* of the gods—wall paintings. See Kolve's discussion of the iconography of the gods in pp. 114–27.

22. Note, for example, James S. Whitlark, "Chaucer and the Pagan Gods," *AM* 18 (1977): 65–75, who concludes that "As well as representing planetary influences, alchemical symbolism, psychological allegory of emotional states, and historical examples of virtues or vices, the pagan gods also served to dramatize the worldliness of Chaucer's characters and to relate it to the condition of pagans and apostates reviled in the Bible and denounced by the early Christians" (p. 75). Note the similar postmodern interpretation offered by H. Marshall Leicester, Jr., *The Disenchanted Self: Representing the Subject in the Canterbury Tales* (Berkeley, Los Angeles, and Oxford: University of California Press, 1990), in chapter 12, "The Unhousing of the Gods: Character, *Habitus*, and Necessity in Part III," in which the gods are deconstructed in prayers so that they can be replaced, in effect, by the characters (p. 299).

23. For astrological and mythological ramifications of Saturn, especially in the light of Bernardus Silvestris's link with determinism, Saturn's mythographic significance as

wisdom, and astrological malevolence in the zodiac, see Dorothy Bethurum Loomis, "Saturn in Chaucer's Knight's Tale," in *Chaucer und seine Zeit: Symposion für Walter F. Schirmer*, ed. Arno Esch, Buchreihe der Anglia: Zeitschrift für englische Philologie, no. 14 (Tübingen: Max Niemeyer, 1968), pp. 149–61, here, p. 160; for Saturn's source in Bernardus, Bethurum Loomis cites *Cosmographia* 1.3.33–56 (used by the Man of Law [194–212]) (pp. 156–57, 160). For an analysis of Saturn's roles and significations from varied traditions—astral, euhemeristic, moral, natural, Neoplatonic—see Theresa Tinkle, "Saturn of the Several Faces: A Survey of the Medieval Mythographic Traditions," *Viator* 18 (1987): 289–307. For Saturn as a summary of folly's effects, elaborating aspects of Mars and Venus, representing the old order overwhelmed by reason, moderation, and pity, see Alan T. Gaylord, "The Role of Saturn in the Knight's Tale," *ChauR* 8 (1974): 172–90.

24. See Wise, *The Influence of Statius upon Chaucer*, p. 50; Hoffman, *Ovid*, p. 50.

25. Richard H. Green has remarked on the mythographic conflict between rationality (Athens) and the land of appetite (Scythia), in "Classical Fable and English Poetry in the Fourteenth Century," in *Critical Approaches to Medieval Literature: Selected Papers from the English Institute 1958–59*, ed. Dorothy Bethurum (New York and London: Columbia University Press, 1960; repr. 1967), pp. 130–33. See also Robertson, *Preface*, pp. 260–66, on the issue of wisdom versus effeminacy in the conflict between Theseus and Hippolyta, and Hoffman, *Ovid*, pp. 45–47.

26. On the fraternal conflict of Palamon and Arcite and the divisiveness of their forebears Eteocles and Polynices, see David Anderson, "Theban Genealogy in the *Knight's Tale*," *ChauR* 21 (1987): 311–20.

27. See Holkot, *In librum Sapientiae*, p. 697 (212), cited in Allen, "Mythology," p. 367. But see also Bersuire's gloss, in *Ovidius*. For the interpretation of the conflict as the prudent man's victory over bestiality, see Boccaccio's *Genealogia deorum* 4.10, cited in the note in the Benson edition. For Ovid's Theseus slaying the Minotaur, see *Metamorphoses* 7.267–69; for Chaucer's use instead of the defeat of the Amazons in 865–66 to further the topos of Herculean wisdom and fortitude, see Hoffman, *Ovid*, pp. 41–47, esp. pp. 45–47.

28. For the seminal essay that first found central focus in the tale, see William Frost, "An Interpretation of Chaucer's *Knight's Tale*," *RES* 25 (1949): 289–304; repr. in Schoeck and Taylor, 1:98–116: the three focuses included lovers' rivalry, conflicts between love and friendship, and the "disintegrating human situation" stabilized by a "just providence." But, for the tale's opposition of order and chaos, with Palamon and Arcite as defining the struggle between such "noble designs" and chaos, and Theseus's faith in the "ultimate order," see Charles Muscatine, "Form, Texture, and Meaning in Chaucer's Knight's Tale," *PMLA* 65 (1950): 911–29; repr. in *Chaucer: Modern Essays in Criticism*, ed. Edward Wagenknecht (New York: Oxford University Press, 1959; repr. 1970), pp. 60–82. For chaos versus the ordered, noble life, see Charles Muscatine, *Chaucer and the French Tradition: A Study in Style and Meaning* (Berkeley and Los Angeles: University of California Press, 1957; repr. 1966), pp. 175–90. But see also Dale Underwood, who uncovers three realms of order (disorderly Fortune, disorderly human society, and God's true order), in "The First of *The Canterbury Tales*," *ELH* 26 (1959): 455–69; for the more medieval interpretation of the three orders, as nature, society, and the divine order of the cosmos, see John Halverson, "Aspects of Order in the *Knight's Tale*," *SP* 57 (1960): 606–21. For the idea that the *Knight's Tale* subverts the noble attempts to make order out of disorder, see Joseph Westlund, "The *Knight's Tale* as an Impetus for Pilgrimage," *Philological Quarterly* 43 (1964): 526–37. For the human will of Theseus as a means to order, reflecting the Knight's noble values, see Kathleen A. Blake, "Order and the Noble Life in Chaucer's Knight's Tale," *MLQ* 34 (1973): 3–19.

29. Hyginus, pp. 51–52, trans. p. 68 (no. 68).

30. "Oracular reply was given by Apollo to Adrastus, son of Talaus and Eurynome, that he would give his daughters in marriage to a boar and a lion. At the same time Polynices, *son of Oedipus, driven out by his brother Eteocles,* came to Adrastus, and *Tydeus, son of Oeneus and the captive Periboea, driven out by his father because he had killed his brother Menalippus at a hunt,* arrived at about the same time. When the servants had reported to Adrastus that two youths in unusual garb had come — one wearing a boar's skin, and the other a lion's skin, then Adrastus, mindful of the oracle given him, bade them be brought in, and inquired why they had come to his kingdom thus appareled. Polynices said that he had come from Thebes, and had put on a lion's skin because Hercules traced his descent from Thebes, and he was wearing the insignia of his race; Tydeus spoke too, saying that he was the son of Oeneus and traced his descent from Calydon, and so he wore a boar skin to recall the Calydonian Boar. Then the king, mindful of the oracular reply, gave Argia, the older daughter to Polynices, from whom Thersander was born; Deipyla, the younger, he gave to Tydeus, and she became mother of Diomede who fought at Troy. But Polynices begged an army from Adrastus for recovering his father's kingdom from his brother. Adrastus not only gave an army but set out himself with six other leaders, since Thebes was shut in by seven gates. For Amphion, who had surrounded Thebes with a wall, set in it seven gates named for his daughters. These were Thera, Cleodoxe, Astynome, Astycratia, Chias, Ogygia, Chloris" (from Hyginus, 69, p. 53, trans. pp. 68–69; my emphasis). For its currency among later poets, note that the FVM duplicates portions of the myth in myth 80, Bode, p. 28.

31. For Bersuire, see *Ovidius,* p. 127; see also Holkot on the devil and the labyrinth, in *In librum Sapientiae* 115, p. 387, cited in Allen, "Mythology," pp. 343–45. For prison (cycle, traps) imagery, showing sufferance in the face of divine influence, see Georgia R. Crampton, *The Condition of Creatures: Suffering and Action in Chaucer and Spenser* (New Haven: Yale University Press, 1974); and Kolve, who discusses the prison/garden (which share a common wall), related to iconographic depictions of the house of fortune and castles, and the circular theater, related to the Roman Colisseum, as a dominant image (*Chaucer and the Imagery of Narrative,* pp. 85–157): "The amphitheatre that Theseus builds for the tournament between Palamon and Arcite is to the theme of order in the poem what the prison/garden is to the theme of freedom" (p. 105). Echoing the mythographers, Kolve concludes, "For all the perfection of its form, his great amphitheatre can only encircle what is selfish, destructive, and violent in man's nature, released under the malign aspects of the planet-gods" (p. 130).

32. Fulgentius, *Thebaid,* trans. Leslie George Whitbread, in *Fulgentius the Mythographer* (Columbus: Ohio State University Press, 1971), p. 242.

33. Hoffman, *Ovid,* pp. 57, 60. Because of these adulteries, Thebes had a medieval reputation as a "fleshpot of pagan lust," and therefore Juno, as goddess of childbirth, presumably within marriage, appropriately opposed it. In the *Knight's Tale,* Theseus represents the ordered love of marriage in opposition to the city of fleshly lust, Thebes. For the Statian description of Junoesque enmity toward Thebes, see *Thebaid* 1.250ff.

34. Bode, p. 48. For Cadmus as founder of the Theban nation, see Wise, *The Influence of Statius upon Chaucer,* p. 89. Anderson, "Theban Genealogy," pp. 311–20, thoroughly discusses Chaucer's use of Theban genealogy in lines 1016–19 to show the parallels between Palamon and Arcite and Polynices and Eteocles; his study of Lactantius on the *Thebaid* indicates that the cousins in the *Knight's Tale* represent the equivalent of the sons of Oedipus's daughters Antigone and Ismene, thereby repeating the Theban themes of brotherhood versus the house divided.

35. Wise, *The Influence of Statius upon Chaucer,* pp. 88–89.

36. See *Lactantii Placidi qui dicitur commentarios in Statii Thebaida et commentarium in Achilleida*, ed. R. Jahnke (Leipzig, 1898), on 8.53. (Statius invokes *Aeneid* 6.617 later in this passage).

37. Hoffman, *Ovid*, pp. 52–54. See *Ovidius*, p. 127, for the Bersuire reference. For the friendship between Theseus and Pirithous and its sources in the Calydonian boar hunt described in *Metamorphoses* 8.303, the battle between the centaurs and the Lapiths in *Metamorphoses* 12.226–29, and their descent into the underworld to carry off Proserpina in *Metamorphoses* 8, probably all from the letters of exiled Ovid (*Tristia* 1.5.19–20, 1.9.31–32, and *Ex ponto* 2.3.43), or possibly the preserving *Roman* of Jean de Meun (8148–54), see Hoffman, "Ovid and Chaucer's Myth of Theseus and Prithoüs," *ELN* 2 (1965): 252–57.

38. Theseus is also the rational and virtuous man who descends virtuously into the underworld (in 6.122).

39. For the probable Ovidian source of Arcite's dreamed Mercury, see Richard L. Hoffman, "Mercury, Argus, and Chaucer's Arcite, *Canterbury Tales* I (A) 1384–90," *N & Q* 210 (1965): 128–29, and Hoffman, *Ovid*, p. 61.

40. Wilkins, "Descriptions of Pagan Divinities," p. 522, believes Chaucer used Bersuire and the TVM as sources for the messenger. Hoffman, *Ovid*, pp. 61–63, finds only verbal echoes from Bersuire; see "De formis," p. 44. But note the argument that Mercury here derives instead from the *Aeneid*: see Wolfgang H. Rudat, "Chaucer's Mercury and Arcite: The *Aeneid* and the World of the *Knight's Tale*," *Neophilologus* 64 (1980): 307–19.

41. On the significance of May 3 in Chaucer (used not only in the *Knight's Tale* but also in *Troilus and Criseyde* and in the *Nun's Priest's Tale*), see, for its association with the pagan goddess Flora, irrational love, and her celebration in Ovid, John McCall, "Chaucer's May 3," *MLN* 76 (1961): 201–5; for its varying relation to humanism and determinism, but in the *Knight's Tale* probably associated more with humanism, see Alfred L. Kellogg and Robert C. Cox, "Chaucer's May 3 and its Contexts," in *Chaucer, Langland, Arthur: Essays in Middle English Literature*, ed. Alfred L. Kellogg (New Brunswick, N.J.: Rutgers University Press, 1972), pp. 155–98; for its astrological meaning, see George Clark, "Chaucer's Third and Fourth of May," *Revue de l'Université d'Ottawa* 52 (1982): 257–65; and finally, for Emelye as a type of Flora combined with the goddess's antithesis, Diana, a comparison that hinges on this May 3 date, see Stock, "The Two Mayings," pp. 206–21. Chauncey Wood remarks that on this date Saint Helen threw down Venus's temple and raised instead the True Cross, in *The Elements of Chaucer's "Troilus"* (Durham, N.C.: Duke University Press, 1984), p. 101.

42. Bersuire, *Ovidius*, p. 62, trans. p. 180. Bersuire explains Cadmus's sister Europa as the human soul, whom Jupiter the devil has seized. Cadmus's search for her leads him to the place where he can construct the church. The serpent represents detractors devoted to Mars, the god of war. See also *Ovidius*, p. 63.

43. For the *Knight's Tale* as a vision of the Four Ages of Man, its human characters representative of the humors, see Douglas Brooks and Alistair Fowler, "The Meaning of Chaucer's *Knight's Tale*," *MAE* 39 (1970): 123–46. As a vision of the Three Ages of Man, see J. A. Burrow, "Chaucer's *Knight's Tale* and the Three Ages of Man," in Burrow, *Essays on Medieval Literature* (Oxford: Clarendon Press, 1984), pp. 27–48; and Piero Boitani and Anna Torti, eds., *Medieval and Pseudo-Medieval Literature: The J. A. W. Bennett Memorial Lectures, Perugia, 1982–3*, Tübinger Beiträge zur Anglistik, 6 (Tübingen: Gunter Narr; Cambridge, England: D. S. Brewer, 1984), pp. 91–108.

44. For the *Knight's Tale* in terms of humors psychology, Palamon and Arcite are melancholic and choleric; Emelye is phlegmatic, Theseus is jovial, like the Knight: see Brooks and Fowler, "The Meaning of Chaucer's *Knight's Tale*," pp. 123–46. As an allego-

rization of the faculties of the soul, see McCall, *Chaucer Among the Gods,* esp. pp. 64–86. He concludes that the tale allegorizes Aristotle's four moral virtues, concupiscence (Venus, part 1), irascibility (Mars, part 2) in the sensitive soul, will (Jupiter), and intelligence (Saturn, part 3) in the intellective soul; part 4 represents misfortune, suffering, death. Theseus sums up Mars and Venus within himself and allies with Jupiter as Egeus allies with Saturn.

45. According to Macrobius, *Somnium Scipionis* 1.19.2, the sun occupies the second sphere from the earth, and Mercury the third, although William Harris Stahl's note to this translated section (on p. 162 n. 1) reveals the Platonic order to be moon, sun, Venus, Mercury, whereas the later order, also mentioned in Cicero, *Somnium Scipionis* 4.2, placed Mercury and Venus beneath the sun (i.e., moon, Mercury, Venus, sun).

46. Susan Crane, "Medieval Romance and Feminine Difference in the *Knight's Tale,*" *SAC* 12 (1990): 47–63, notes that the feminine position represented by Emelye's plea for virginity to Diana is outside the "masculine designs of courtship and social order" and reflects aspects of the "romance sensibility" (p. 62).

47. See Joseph Harrison, " 'Tears for Passing Things': The Temple of Diana in the *Knight's Tale,*" *PQ* 63 (1984): 108–16.

48. See Hoffman, *Ovid,* pp. 71ff., who also notes the use of Jean de Meun's *Roman* 15663–70 for "Mount Cytheron." According to H. M. Cummings, *The Indebtedness of Chaucer's Works to the Italian Works of Boccaccio,* University of Cincinnati Studies, 10:2 (Menasha, Wis.: George Banta, 1916), p. 132, there are no lines translated from the *Teseida* in this temple description.

49. On patristic and literary variations of this garden, see D. W. Robertson, Jr., "The Doctrine of Charity in Mediaeval Literary Gardens: A Topical Approach through Symbolism and Allegory," *Speculum* 26 (1951): 24–49; repr. in *Essays in Medieval Culture* (Princeton: Princeton University Press, 1980), who discusses the cupidinous *hortus conclusus;* and Derek Pearsall, "Gardens as Symbol and Setting in Late Medieval Poetry," *Medieval Gardens* (Washington, D.C.: Dumbarton Oaks Research Library and Collection, 1986), pp. 237–51.

50. See Robertson, *Preface,* pp. 92–93 nn.

51. See Hoffman, *Ovid,* pp. 75ff., who outlines the mythographic commentary on the figure by Arnulf of Orleans, Benvenuto da Imola, and others (including John Gower) to show that Narcissus's beauty is a source of his pride.

52. In both Holkot and Bersuire, these iconographic details expose Venus's open carnality and concupiscence. In chapter 1 of Bersuire's *Ovidius moralizatus* ("De formis figurisque deorum," p. 66), he plunges immediately into a misogynistic Fulgentian gloss on these specific attributes, noting that, figuratively, this goddess signifies "the life of pleasure or a wanton person who is said to be a woman because of inconstancy and nude because of unconcealed indecency." The sea in which she swims signifies the pleasures (*deliciis*) with which she likes being surrounded, just as the seashell she uses for singing or for arranging her hair suggests the songs and joys with which she enjoys being surrounded. "Riotous living or the pleasure of riotous living is a woman because it does not last. It is nude because anyone who has it can scarcely keep it from appearing.... It is pretended that Venus was generated in the sea because riotous living is generated from opulence and transitory pleasures. Therefore, Scripture seems to speak to this harlot [*meretrici*] in Isaias 23:10: 'Pass your land as a river, O daughter of the sea' and also in Isaias 23:16: 'Take a harp; go about the city, you harlot who has been forgotten. Sing well, sing many a song'" ("De formis," p. 23, trans. pp. 66–67). See Holkot, *In librum duodecim prophetas,* fol. 85v, cited in Allen, "Mythology," p. 383, but the gloss continues through fol. 86v (in Allen, through p. 390). See note 20 for major sources of the description of

Venus; see also Meg Twycross, *The Medieval Anadyomene: A Study in Chaucer's Mythography*, Medium Aevum Monographs, n.s., 1 (Oxford: Medium Aevum Monographs, 1972), who concludes that Venus plays a *citole* because she represents the voluptuous life, therefore the musical "indicates the meritricious," or, as the planet Venus (often depicted with a stringed instrument), she may represent Venus *Urania* (p. 67). Also see chapter 4, "Venus in the *Knight's Tale*: Alle the Circumstaunces of Love," in Leah Zeva Freiwald, "Chaucer's Use of Classical Mythology: The Myths in the Context of the Medieval Audience" (Diss., University of California-Berkeley, 1983), pp. 116–72; on the basis of astrological and mythographic evidence, Freiwald concludes that "she is for the most part the astrological Venus, modified by her mythological roots and by her medieval associations in courtly poetry" (p. 118). Freiwald links the fighting of Palamon and Arcite with Mars, and Theseus with all three deities (since he has hunted/warred, loved, and remained chaste).

53. Hoffman, *Ovid*, p. 94, first noted the similarity between the wood of the suicides and Mars's temple description.

54. Wise, *The Influence of Statius upon Chaucer*, p. 99.

55. For discussions of the sources of the four and their appearance (or nonappearance) in the *Teseida*, see Hoffman, *Ovid*, pp. 82–89. For Callisto, Hoffman identifies as other possible sources *Fasti* 2.153–92 and Boccaccio 5.49. For Meleager, Hoffman differentiates between the two Atalantas in Ovid, one from 10.560–680 (of Boeotia) and one here (of Arcadia); he adds as a possible source *Heroides* 4. This "confusion" is straightened out in *Troilus* 5.1482–83.

56. Bersuire concludes that the Parcae represent the three parts of the soul.

57. Bersuire, "De formis," p. 28, trans. p. 75. The SVM relates Proserpina (Hecate) to the other goddesses by placing her in the lower world, just as Luna exists in the sky and Diana on earth: "Ipsa est enim Luna in caelo, Diana in terra, Proserpina in erebo" (in myth 15, in Bode, p. 79). The TVM notes that Diana the virgin is nevertheless invoked by women in childbirth, often by the names Juno or Proserpina: "Unde quum Diana sit virgo, tamen a parturientibus invocatur. Haec namque est secundum non paucos Diana Juno Proserpina" (in 8.3, in Bode, p. 201).

58. According to Wise, *The Influence of Statius upon Chaucer*, the three hearths (4.456) suggest the three abodes of Diana (pp. 98–99).

59. That Pluto rules the earth, as Proserpina rules the moon, has been noted by Remigius of Auxerre in his glosses on Boethius 3m12.40, p. 65, and by Bernardus Silvestris glossing Martianus 5.15, p. 94. Bernardus also remarks on the governance of the sublunary—as opposed to the superlunary—realm by Pluto and Proserpina, in glossing Martianus 5.660, p. 116. See also the discussion of Pluto and Proserpina in chapter 8, on the *Merchant's Tale*.

60. Hoffman, *Ovid*, p. 90. Other sources include *Roman de la Rose* 15675–750, as well as *Metamorphoses* 10.519–59 and 705–39, each representing the lover as a *miles amoris*.

61. Hoffman, *Ovid*, pp. 96–98. Other sources include the *Roman de la Rose* 13835–74, 14157–86, 18061–129, *Ars Amatoria* 2.561–92, and *Metamorphoses* 4.171–89.

62. Saturn *in bono* (mythographic Saturn) and *in malo* (astrological Saturn) has been widely examined, by medieval and modern commentators. For a full and comprehensive listing, see Bersuire, "De formis," in *Ovidius*, pp. 4–10, trans. pp. 36ff. See also Minnis, *Chaucer*, pp. 139ff., who cites Macrobius, Alexander Neckam, and John Ridevall, among others.

63. In Martianus, Mars and Saturn are linked through their weapons—for Saturn, the scythe. The last weapon Silvanus wants is the scythe of Saturn, glossed briefly by Remi-

gius in 211.7, p. 65: he is depicted with a scythe "quia dicitur amputasse virilia Caeli patris sui." See also William of Conches's twelfth-century gloss on Macrobius, *Somnium Scipionis* 1.2.10, no. 6, p. 70, trans. p. 26. In William's Juvenal glosses, Saturn, *sapientia,* old age, and Chronos are linked (p. 162). Note that in 1088, 1328, Arcite acknowledges that Fortune has given them such wicked aspects of Saturn, and that Palamon attributes being in prison to Saturn.

64. See Holkot, *In librum duodecim prophetas,* fols. 128v-129r, cited in Allen, "Mythology," p. 339; also Bersuire, "De formis," in *Ovidius,* p. 11, trans. p. 46.

65. Holkot even gives his gloss on Jupiter's gift of doctrine and knowledge to humankind a prelatical twist, in that the good shepherd, *bonus pastor,* should help guide men to heaven through a good life by means of these gifts, in *In librum duodecim prophetas,* fol. 60r, cited in Allen, "Mythology," pp. 341–42.

Chapter 7. *Maister* Alisoun's Feminist Self-Mythography

This chapter was delivered as a paper, "The Wife of Bath's Mythography of the Self," in a session on feminist mythography at the 22d International Congress on Medieval Studies, Western Michigan University, Kalamazoo, Mich., May 8, 1987 (and again, revised, at Notre Dame University on January 26, 1988).

1. On the English friars and their exegetical ability, see Beryl Smalley, *English Friars and Antiquity in the Early Fourteenth Century* (Oxford: Basil Blackwell, 1960; New York: Barnes and Noble, 1961); Judson Boyce Allen, *The Friar as Critic: Literary Attitudes in the Later Middle Ages* (Nashville, Tenn.: Vanderbilt University Press, 1971); and Alastair Minnis, *Medieval Theory of Authorship: Scholastic Literary Attitudes in the Later Middle Ages* (London: Scolar Press, 1984).

2. No other scholar, to my knowledge, has examined this mythographic question in regard to the Wife of Bath. Hoffman has probed Chaucer's use of Ovid and Ovid commentaries, primarily with an interest in sources; for his brief discussion of the Ovidian myths cited by the Wife of Bath, deriving from his earlier published notes, see *Ovid,* pp. 132–33, 141–42, and 145–49. An analysis of the patristic exegesis used in the *Wife of Bath's Prologue* can be found in Robertson, *Preface,* pp. 319–31, and her glossing as wordplay in Bernard F. Huppé, *A Reading of the Canterbury Tales,* rev. ed. (Binghamton: State University of New York Press, 1967), pp. 107–35: "As the word 'privetee' is of structural importance in the *Miller's Tale,* the word 'glose' has equal importance in the *Wife's Prologue.* The word is not insistently repeated as is 'privetee,' but Chaucer rings changes on its connotations; from biblical commentary to lying evasion, and finally to her own meaning of sexual play.... What the Wife does in fact is to *glose,* to play with words in order to make the worse seem the better reason. Her *glosing* is a key to her *Prologue,* so that the large number of word-plays in it will not seem surprising" (p. 109).

3. Carolyn Dinshaw (*Chaucer's Sexual Poetics* [Madison: University of Wisconsin Press, 1989], in "'Glose/bele chose': The Wife of Bath and her Glossators," chapter 4, pp. 113–31) sees Alisoun as opposed to the masculine glossation and preferring the tale of her "joly body." As the "excluded Other," she merely "*mimics* the operations of patriarchal discourse," however (p. 115). Her intention is to reform such discourse so as to accommodate the language of pleasure, female desire. Alisoun's view of glossing as carnal ("a masculine act performed on the feminine body," or text) leads to mutual gratification of both sexes. Cf. Peggy A. Knapp, "'Wandrynge by the Weye': On Alisoun and Augustine," in Laurie A. Finke and Martin B. Schichtman, eds., *Medieval Texts and Contemporary Readers* (Ithaca, N.Y.: Cornell University Press, 1987), pp. 142–57,

who also determines that Alisoun is a text to be glossed (a figure for the garrulous text) and an interpreter of texts, but analyzes Alisoun in the light of the theories of Derrida and Bahktin.

4. See Robert P. Miller, "Chaucer's Pardoner, the Scriptural Eunuch, and *The Pardoner's Tale," Speculum* 30 (1955): 180–99; repr. in Schoeck and Taylor, 1:221–44.

5. For an acute and extended analysis of Jankyn's book from the postmodernist perspective, see H. Marshall Leicester, Jr., *The Disenchanted Self: Representing the Subject in the Canterbury Tales* (Berkeley, Los Angeles, and Oxford: University of California Press, 1990), chapter 4, "Jankyn's Book: The Subject as Text."

6. A relatively recent treatment identifies Alisoun's four roles as entrepreneur, feminist, archetypal Eve figure, and sociopath: Peggy A. Knapp, "Alisoun Weaves a Text," *PQ* 65 (1986): 387–401. But see also Susan Crane, "Alisoun of Bath Accused of Murder: Case Dismissed," *ELN* 25:3 (1988): 10–15, who argues that Alisoun did not murder her fourth husband and that readers who believe so think that she "fulfils anti-feminist expectations." Finally, Dinshaw's binary dualism in *Chaucer's Sexual Poetics* in effect equates the female text with the body and thereby reproduces the misogynistic argument; but then Dinshaw interprets Alisoun as a male fantasy.

7. See Elizabeth Robertson, *Early English Devotional Prose and the Female Audience* (Knoxville: University of Tennessee Press, 1990), esp. chapter 3, "Medieval Views of Female Spirituality."

8. Note the analyses of the genre of the Wife's tale as bourgeois romance or "group fantasy" and as Old Wives' Tale in Louise O. Fradenburg, "The Wife of Bath's Passing Fancy," *SAC* 8 (1986): 31–58, and Sarah Disbrow, "The Wife of Bath's Old Wives' Tale," *SAC* 8 (1986), pp. 59–71. Note also Susan Crane, "Alisoun's Incapacity and Poetic Instability in the Wife of Bath's Tale," *PMLA* 102 (1987): 20–28, who finds that Alisoun is subversive in her response to conventions of genre, gender, and the estates; courtly romance is thus her choice for a good depiction of women.

9. See Barrie Ruth Straus, "The Subversive Discourse of the Wife of Bath: Phallocentric Discourse and the Imprisonment of Criticism," *ELH* 55 (1988): 527–54, who analyzes phallocentric discourse as a mode in which women are perceived as not telling the truth and in which male desire is secret. Alisoun subverts this mode by telling all their secrets (i.e., the truth). The association of female carnality with rhetoric, adornment, and subterfuge has been made by R. Howard Bloch, "Misogyny," *Representations* 20 (1987): 1–24.

10. Note the work of Kate Greenspan on "The Autohagiographical Tradition in Medieval Women's Devotional Writing," in *a/b:Auto/Biography* and, in longer form, in *Gender and Text in the Later Middle Ages,* ed. Jane Chance (Gainesville: University of Florida Press, 1995).

11. Theological and historical precedent for wives as preachers to their husbands existed in the late Middle Ages: see the texts cited and the principal argument in Sharon Farmer, "Persuasive Voices: Clerical Images of Medieval Wives," *Speculum* 61 (1986): 517–43. She concludes that, in the eleventh through the thirteenth centuries, "wives could, and should, employ their feminine characteristics in order to tame their husbands" (p. 543).

12. See Charlton T. Lewis and Charles Short, *Latin Dictionary* (Oxford: Clarendon Press, 1879; repr. 1969), p. 318; the proverb is found in Terence's *Eunuchus* 4, 5, 6 and Cicero's *De natura deorum* 2, 23, 60. In medieval mythographic texts, the proverb is cited in commentaries on the *Aeneid,* for example, in the twelfth-century commentary of Bernardus Silvestris on *Aeneid* 6.515–16, in which "horses" signify lechery, for "The Greeks made the horse, since the drunkenness and gluttony of lechery are in Troy, according to that saying: 'Venus grows cold without Ceres and Bacchus'" (trans. p. 96).

Note the repetition of the proverb on p. 91, in Bernardus's gloss on 6.450–76: "Dido sees *Sicheus* as a spiritual good — which we know as the vices of gluttony and intoxication — and the Epicureans claim the soul can have no greater good. He is Dido's husband, because lechery rejoices with gluttony: 'Venus grows cold without Ceres and Bacchus.' " The proverb reappears in Cristoforo Landino's commentary on the *Aeneid* included in the *Disputationes*: Lorenzo says that he disputes Venus interpreted as love, for "I see Venus interpreted in such a way that they mean by her nothing but the coming together of man and woman. Thus Terence: *sine Cerere et Baccho Venerem frigescere.*" He concludes that there are two Venuses, as does Pausanius in the *Symposium*. See Thomas H. Stahel, "Cristoforo Landino's Allegorization of the *Aeneid*: Books III and IV of the *Camaldolese Disputations*" (Diss., Johns Hopkins University, 1968), p. 57.

13. Robertson, *Preface,* pp. 319–31, notes that Alisoun's two arguments attack Saint Jerome's *Adversus Jovinianum*: first, because Christ attended only one wedding (Cana), therefore no one marries more than once; second, when Christ said that the Samaritan woman's current spouse is not her husband he implied that with more than one marriage, a true husband does not exist. In this exegesis, Robertson substantiates the Wife's literalism and oldness — and her concomitant desire for newness and spirituality — by referring to the turning of the five jars of water into wine at the Wedding at Cana. This transformation represents the turning away from the five senses, implying a numerical correspondence with the five husbands, and toward the wine of spiritual inebriation, what might be termed the sixth husband — to which Alisoun also looks forward, rather explicitly, at the beginning of her *Prologue,* when she cries, "Welcome the sixte, whan that evere he shal" (45). For a discussion of the Gospel story of the Wedding at Cana and its use in French sermons on marriage in the thirteenth century, see David d'Avray, "The Gospel of the Marriage Feast of Cana and Marriage Preaching in France," in *The Bible in the Medieval World: Essays in Memory of Beryl Smalley,* ed. Katherine Walsh and Diana Wood (Oxford: Basil Blackwell, 1985), pp. 207–24.

14. The tradition of two Venuses, one *scelestis* instead of *caelestis,* might explain the equation of Alisoun with the goddess as well as Martianus's Philology with Venus. For the two Venuses, see Earl G. Schreiber, "Venus in the Medieval Mythographic Tradition," *JEGP* 74 (1975): 519–35. Schreiber does not mention the influential Remigius of Auxerre, who also described two Venuses in his commentary on Martianus 1.3.14, 1:69.

15. Bacchus's first birth (as vines in winter), from Semele, resulted from the destructive sexual union of human Semele and Jupiter as lightning, or Jupiter as the ether, Juno the lower air, and Semele the earth, and his second birth (as grapes in summer), from Jupiter's thigh, or the impregnation of the vines by the sun, in 7b (William, *Macrob.,* p. 71, trans.). In a later gloss (on 1.2.9), Bacchus moves from his role as the "vines" to that of the World Soul (p. 70).

16. [Bern. Sil.] *Mart.* 13a, trans. p. 48. William discusses Ceres and Bacchus as bread and wine in his glosses on Juvenal's satires: see *Glosae in Iuvenalem,* ed. Bradford Wilson, Textes philosophiques du Moyen Âge 18 (Paris: J. Vrin, 1980), p. 91, in the Accessus, and on *Satire* 1.47–49. Also, in William's commentary on the second book of Plato's *Timaeus,* Earth, the most ancient and firstborn of the gods, made a guardian and artificer of night and day out of Ceres or Cibele, called a goddess because of "Cibeles," food or sustenance, in *Glosae super Platonem: Critique avec introduction, notes et tables,* ed. Édouard Jeauneau, Textes philosophiques du Moyen Âge 13 (Paris: Librairie Philosophique J. Vrin, 1965). See also Remigius on Martianus, 5.22 (2:3, 12–14), which is also found in SVM, myth 3; and 28.12 (1.118, 4–5) and 37.3 (1.136, 9); and Isidore's *Etymologiae* 8.40.59–61. For the four significations of Venus, see [Bern. Sil.] *Mart.,* pp. 56–57 (3.226–60).

17. She suffers from a split (astrological) self, partly Venerian and partly Martian (in

612–13 she has Mars in her heart, in her "sturdy hardyness," for her ascendant was Taurus, governed by Mars, and she has Mars's mark on her face [619]). See especially Chauncey Wood, *Chaucer and the Country of the Stars: Poetic Uses of Astrological Imagery* (Princeton: Princeton University Press, 1970), pp. 172–80. Walter Clyde Curry's excellent chapter on astrology in the Wife's *Prologue* can be found in *Chaucer and the Medieval Sciences*, 2d ed. (New York: Barnes and Noble, 1960). William of Conches, in his commentary on Macrobius, describes the adultery of Mars and Venus as the conjunction of the benevolent star Venus and the malevolent star Mars, which attempts to corrupt her through its "malice" (p. 72 [7c]); the gloss is taken from Fulg. *Mit.* 2.7.

18. See Remigius, *Mart.*, 1.22.16, 1:108. This passage reappears in the TVM, 9.2, Bode, p. 214.

19. Hoffman understands the reference to Argus—glossed by Alexander Neckam, Giovanni del Virgilio, John of Garland, and Benvenuto da Imola—to point to Alisoun's old husbands. See his *Ovid*, pp. 132–33, and p. 143 n. 6, and his note "Ovid's Argus and Chaucer," *N & Q* 210 (1965): 213–16.

20. "What would such a fantastic notion of the Greeks signify except that, with a sly blow of the scythe, the cunning of someone both thief and trader got the better of even a hundred guardians and the same number of artful ones, yet ones useless without barter, whence Argus is the Greek for idle" (Fulg. *Mit.*, pp. 30–31; trans. p. 60). The TVM also interprets Argus as *vacuus* and Mercury as wisdom.

21. Hoffman (*Ovid*, p. 143 n. 6) cites Holkot's statement in his commentary on the Book of Wisdom (*In librum Sapientiae*, p. 130 [37]) that a literate clerk morally is like Argus, a gloss we examined in chapter 5 on the *Knight's Tale*. But note also the explanation of the blinding of Argus by Mercury as one of the four kinds of dishonesty practiced by the merchant (of whom Mercury is god), in Holkot, *In librum duodecim*, fols. 17v-18r (cited in Allen, "Mythology," p. 353).

22. The full details of the myth can be found in the first two Vatican Mythographers: see the FVM, myths 58 and 171, and the SVM, myth 165, in Bode. Note also the summary contained in Hyginus in his *Fables* 33–36, to which the accounts in the first two Vatican Mythographers are indebted. Hyginus's version begins with Deianira's request that Nessus the centaur carry her across the river. In the process of doing so he tries to rape her and Hercules kills him. But before he dies, Nessus dips an arrow of Hercules in his own blood, then gives this to Deianira as a love philter that will ensure Hercules' continuing love. After she has sent the cape poisoned with Nessus's blood to Hercules, not knowing that it will burn him to death, she does try unsuccessfully to warn Hercules before he puts it on.

23. Douglas J. Wurtele, "Chaucer's Wife of Bath and the Problem of the Fifth Husband," *ChauR* 23 (1988): 117–28, notes that if Jankyn and Alisoun murdered husband number four, then Jankyn's books can be read as lessons to murderesses. If Alisoun, in her anger, threatened to reveal his role, the ending makes sense: Jankyn, frightened into reconciliation, leaves her free to tell tales of her own.

24. In the twelfth century, commentators on Boethius 4m7 gloss Agamemnon *in bono* as a priest who sacrifices his daughter like Calchas in the *Aeneid*; thereafter, beginning with the important glosses of William of Conches (which drove out the conventional commentary of Remigius of Auxerre on Boethius), Agamemnon is glossed *in malo* as pursuing *vanis gloria* (see British Library MS. Egerton 628, fol. 191v), a passage cited in Winthrop Wetherbee, *Platonism and Poetry in the Twelfth Century: The Literary Influence of the School of Chartres* (Princeton: Princeton University Press, 1972), p. 196 n. 6; see also Nicholas Trevet, in his gloss from *Exposicio* on Boethius. This derives from Edmund Silk's unpublished transcription of the commentary found in Oxford, Bodleian,

MS. Rawlinson G.187, p. 655. The whole myth (with Clytemnestra but without the moralization) is repeated in the SVM, myth 202, in Bode, pp. 141–42.

25. There has been much current debate on this subject: see the articles by Crane, "Alisoun of Bath Accused of Murder," and Wurtele, "Chaucer's Wife of Bath."

26. The contemporary antifeminist view has appeared in Judson Boyce Allen and Patrick Gallacher's examination of Alisoun's version of the Midas tale, based on Giovanni del Virgilio and Arnulf of Orleans, as a misuse of authority and a reflection of moral weakness, in "Alisoun through the Looking Glass; or Every Man his own Midas," *ChauR* 4 (1970): 99–105. Robertson also explores the implications of these changes, in "The Wife of Bath and Midas," *SAC* 6 (1984): 1–20, concluding that "the Wife is both Ovid's Midas and her own 'wife' of Midas, and she has been talking about herself without knowing it" (p. 11).

27. Her specific changes in the Midas story found in Ovid, *Metamorphoses* 11.172–93, center on the addition of Midas's wife and the omission of unflattering but related aspects of the myth of Midas. Alisoun's changes in Ovid, among others, have been glossed by Richard L. Hoffman, "Ovid and the Wife of Bath's Tale of Midas," *N & Q* 211 (1966): 48–50, which examines her references to the myth chiefly in lines 952 and 982. See also Hoffman's *Ovid*, pp. 145–49. Robertson, in "The Wife of Bath and Midas," includes a fine summary of the classical Midas story (pp. 6–8), with applications in Jean de Meun's *Roman* (pp. 9ff.).

28. "Midas interpretatur nichil sciens, et signat prelatum qui et si primo sciat multa, tamen per malos mores suos vertitur in stulticiam asininam" (Holkot, *In librum duodecim*, fol. 120r, cited in Allen, "Mythology," p. 360).

29. Hoffman, "Ovid and the Wife of Bath's Tale of Midas," p. 49–50, points to the music contest between Pan and Apollo, which resulted in Midas's ears being transformed, to prove that the Wife of Bath is a type of Midas. According to Arnulf of Orleans, says Hoffman, Midas figures forth stupidity and animalistic deference in that he has been deaf to the excellence of Apollo's music and has instead insisted on the excellence of Pan's. Therefore, like Midas, Alisoun signifies the old song of stupidity and asinine deference versus the new song of charity. The same idea can be found in Hoffman's *Ovid*, pp. 145–49. See also Robertson, "The Wife of Bath and Midas," p. 11.

30. The SVM conflated various myths associated with Midas, King of Lydia, and with Midas Rex; the TVM shaped this conflation. The Vatican Mythographers also gloss Midas's stupidity in the myths dealing with his avarice. The name "Midas" (say both the SVM and TVM, again drawing on Fulgentius) comes from the Greek for *medenidon*, or *nihil sciens*, "knowing nothing": a miser is so stupid that he does not even help himself, ("Avarus enim in tantum stultus est, ut etiam sibi prodesse nesciat" [myth 118, Bode, p. 115]). These two flaws dovetail in the instance of the music contest between Apollo and Pan judged by Midas, a contest anticipated by the music contest between Apollo and Marsyas (with similarly disastrous results for the human competitor or judge). In another myth, Midas's avarice is expressed literally, so that when he begs Bacchus for help in obtaining more wealth, everything he touches turns to gold, which means, unfortunately for him, that he must starve to death. The SVM (and the TVM) moralizes this myth by drawing on Fulgentius 2.10: "Veritas autem est, quia quisque avarus, quum omnia pretio destinat, fame moritur" ("The truth is, whoever is avaricious, fixing everything at a price, dies of hunger"). The SVM confuses Midas King of Lydia (from Fulg. *Mit.* 3.9) with the Midas Rex who petitions Apollo to divert the River Pactolus (from Fulg. 2.10). When Midas, whose touch turned all to gold, asked Bacchus for help, the god told him to stick his head in the river Pactolus three times, whence the river ran with gold. As a consequence, Midas irrigated and enriched the territory. The SVM derives myth 117 from the

FVM, in myth 88; the TVM repeats much of the SVM (in 10.8, Bode, p. 227). The SVM's version appears in Bode, p. 114.

31. In the TVM, the Marsyas and Apollo myth precedes the Midas myth; they form a related story because they all belong to the adventures of Minerva, wisdom, although Marsyas and Midas exhibit singular stupidity (Marsyas is *stultus* and Midas is *nihil sciens*). See TVM 10.7, in Bode, p. 226.

Chapter 8. The Merchant's *De Nuptiis Maii et Januarii*

1. For example, see Charles Muscatine, *Chaucer and the French Tradition: A Study in Style and Meaning* (Berkeley and Los Angeles: University of California Press, 1957; repr. 1966), pp. 231–32.

2. "Mercatorum kyrios, id est dominus, quia sermo maxime inter mercatores viget" (Remigius, *Mart.* 1, Pref., 1:66). See also Holkot, *In librum Sapientiae* 79, p. 277, in which he is called "deus mercatorum," and also *In librum duodecim prophetas*, fols. 17v-18r, in which four different versions of Mercury are tied to merchants' four different types of dishonesty (the passage is cited by Allen, "Mythology," p. 353), and including "mendacium sive periurium, mala sive iniusta mensura et ponderacio, carior vendicio casu non permisso," and "absconsio et unius pro alio ostensio." The four types are also cited in the TVM and probably drawn from Remigius, according to Allen, "Mythology," p. 354. The fourth version concerns the myth in which Mercury blinded and killed Argus; the deceit of "unius pro alio ostensio" is essentially that of Damyan stepping in for Januarie. Both the Merchant and Januarie are avaricious, either for money or May: see Paul A. Olson, "Chaucer's Merchant and January's 'Hevene in erthe heere,'" *ELH* 28 (1961): 203–14; see also the mythographic analysis of the Merchant and Mercury by Janet Levarie Smarr, "Mercury in the Garden: Mythographic Methods in the *Merchant's Tale* and *Decameron* 7.9," in Chance, *Mythographic Art*, pp. 199–214.

3. Martianus commentators typically gloss Mercury and Philology in the manner of Remigius, who before he begins his line-by-line commentary explains Mercury as eloquence, the go-between (etymologically, *medius currens*) who ferries speech between two people ("quia sermo inter duos seritur"), and Philology as the love or study of words, reason ("amor vel studium rationis"). For these reasons, Philology appears in the guise of wisdom and reason ("in persona sapientiae et rationis"), Mercury, in the likeness of eloquence and speech ("in similitudine facundiae et sermonis" [1:66]).

4. Although scholars have separately investigated many of the other major mythological references and characters in the *Merchant's Tale*—specifically Priapus, Pluto and Proserpina, and Pyramus and Thisbe—they have not discussed them as a related group, nor in the light of the Martianus Capella commentaries and associated mythographic (rather than merely mythological) texts. Further, scholars have made little attempt to justify the somewhat incongruous appearance of the infernal deities Pluto and Proserpina (glossed by Chaucer as "kyng of Fayerye," and his queen [2227]) in such a Christian tale—told by a pilgrim who could not possibly understand the intricacies of pagan mythology. The following explanations of the gods have been offered primarily to show the tale as unified, and comic: Pluto and Proserpina, as types of old Januarie and young May, are drawn from Claudian's *De raptu Proserpinae* in an adaptation of the pear-tree analogues in which husband and wife consult intervening deities Jupiter and Venus (or Mercury) for rationalizing explanations of infractions and are responsible for the Fall motif being introduced: M. J. Donovan, "The Image of Pluto and Proserpine in *The Merchant's Tale*," *PQ* 36 (1957): 49–60; K. P. Wentersdorf, "Theme and Structure in the Merchant's Tale: The Function of the Pluto Episode," *PMLA* 80 (1965): 522–27. Proserpina, in

addition, is a comically incongruous savior of adulterous May, akin to biblical saviors like Rebecca, Judith, Abigail, and Esther: Charlotte F. Otten, "Proserpine: *Liberatrix Suae Gentis,*" *ChauR* 5 (1971): 277–87. Priapus is a god of gardens whose frustrated fertility in Ovid's *Fasti* suggests that of Damyan (rather than of Januarie) in a comic story about infertility. Pyramus and Thisbe, a story of thwarted love, is meant to parallel the Damyan and May relationship: Emerson Brown, Jr., "*Hortus Inconclusus*: The Significance of Priapus and Pyramus and Thisbe in the *Merchant's Tale,*" *ChauR* 4 (1970): 31–40, and "Priapus in the *Parlement of Foulys,*" *SP* 72 (1975): 258–74. More recent critical analyses of individual gods will be mentioned at appropriate points within the text. Precedent for examining the mythographical associations of these characters has been established by Janet Levarie Smarr ("Mercury in the Garden"), for the god Mercury (although she does not examine his role in the Martianus epic and commentaries): she identifies as Mercurial the fact of the Sun in Gemini (in May: Mai); the emphasis on eloquence and deceit (Mai's) in Mercury's music, used to lull asleep and then blind Argus (as Januarie blinds himself); the telling of this tale by a Merchant, whose patron this god of trickery he was; and even the connection between the Merchant and Pluto (mythographically explained as the devotion to wealth).

5. See J. A. Burrow, "Irony in the *Merchant's Tale,*" *Anglia* 75 (1957): 199–208.

6. The topos of the three goods is founded on the text of the marriage in Cana. Hugh of St. Cher in the thirteenth century declared "there are three goods of marriage, namely: Faith, lest there be intercourse with another man or woman.... Children, that they may be brought up in a religious way.... The sacrament of matrimony, that they may not be separated" (in Bibliothèque Nationale, MS. lat. 15946 f.6vb-7ra, from the sermon on the text *Nuptiae factae sunt* [John 2:1], Schneyer, *Repertorium,* 2:759, no. 18, cited on p. 212 of David d'Avray, "The Gospel of the Marriage Feast of Cana and Marriage Preaching in France," in *The Bible in the Medieval World: Essays in Memory of Beryl Smalley,* ed. Katherine Walsh and Diana Wood [Oxford: Basil Blackwell, 1985]: "tria sunt bona matrimonii, scilicet: Fides, ne cum alio vel cum alia commisceatur.... Proles, ut religiose educetur.... Sacramentum coniugii, ut non separetur").

7. Note that Guibert of Tournai, in his sermon on the text *Vocatus est Jesus* (John 2:1), establishes marriage as the first sacrament, set up at the beginning of the world in paradise and confirmed by Christ's first miracle, that is, at the Wedding at Cana. See D'Avray, "The Gospel of the Marriage Feast," p. 211, from Schneyer, *Repertorium,* 2:283, no. 10.

8. On the "fall" of Januarie, see Lorraine K. Stock, "'Making it' in the *Merchant's Tale*: Chaucer's signs of January's fall," *Semiotica* 63 (1987): 171–83; see also the articles by Smarr ("Mercury in the Garden"), Donovan ("The Image of Pluto and Prosperpine"), and Wentersdorf ("Theme and Structure"), especially the latter, on the myth of Pluto and Proserpina as a classical version of the Fall (p. 527).

9. The Muses are celebrated in Martianus (par. 574) as "learned" and having one "Mind," glossed in Remigius, *Mart.,* in 286.17, 2:126, as daughters of Jove and Juno, because all music derives from air and ether, that is, out of that which is more crass and that which is more subtle and of purer spirit. See Remigius, *Mart.* 3.6, 1:67.

10. Medieval mythographers have normally glossed the poets, apart or together, as exemplars of reason or lawful order and harmony, the triumph of wisdom over passion, order over nature; together they appear in Martianus as Neoplatonic examples of the mastery of the underworld—*this world.* Martianus sees them as part of the harmony of a "chain of being" at the end of 908, "surpassing the great divinities whose praises you have sounded; you have been able with your song to subdue Erebus, the seas, the stones, the wild beasts, and to bring sensation to rocks" (trans. p. 352). Of the poets specifically,

Orpheus and Amphion are glossed in Remigius's tenth-century commentary but not in the twelfth-century commentaries (at least on this passage). The second part of the Orpheus myth—his taming of wild beasts—is more explicitly treated by Martianus and glossed by Remigius in 480.20–481.9, 2:310–11, but only in a prosaic, nonmoralistic way, as it is in [Bern. Sil.]'s commentary: see *Mart.* 5.124, 1:98. But Martianus is also interested in two other poets, Amphion and Arion (par. 908), both of whom epitomize harmony: Martianus says that when Amphion plays he brings life to bodies stiff with cold, animates mountains, and gives life to rocks (trans. p. 352); in addition, when he played at Thebes the city wall raised up and thereby protected the city.

11. Nicholas Trevet glosses Orpheus as *scientia*, in that passion is not greater than reason, in 3m12 of *Exposicio super librum Boecii Consolatione*, Oxford, Bodleian, MS. Rawlinson G.187, fols. 46rff. Chaucer relies heavily on Trevet in the *Troilus*, according to Mark J. Gleason, "The Influence of Trevet on Boethian Language and Thought in Chaucer's *Troilus and Criseyde*," *DAI* 45 (1985): 2096A.

12. This myth is glossed not only in Martianus commentaries but also in the equally influential Boethius commentaries, on 3m12, and in Bernardus Silvestris's commentary on the *Aeneid*. The poet-musician represents *sapientia et eloquentia* led astray by his wife Eurydice, *naturalis concupiscentia*: he follows her into the underworld after she has died from the bite of a serpent [*temporale bonum*] incurred as she fled from the shepherd Aristeus [*virtus divina*], and loses her again a second time when he looks back to see if she follows as he leads her out, thereby disobeying Pluto's injunction—that is, he prefers earthly to heavenly bliss. See Remigius, *Boeth.*, p. 63; see also Remigius, *Mart.* 480.15, 2:315, as well as 480.18 and 19. The fullest gloss on Orpheus and Eurydice appears in [Bern. Sil.] *Aen.*, p. 54 (6.119). The myths primarily glossed in the *Consolatio* concern, first, Orpheus's descent into the underworld and the underworld inhabitants in 3m12; second, Circe and Ulysses in 4m3, and Agamemnon's sacrifice of Iphigenia at the start of the Trojan War and Ulysses' conflict with Polyphemus in 4m7; and third, the Labors of Hercules, in 4m7.

13. Remigius on Martianus (in 480.15, 18–19) glosses Orpheus and Eurydice as an allegory of the arts: in Martianus 480.18, par. 907, he is called "Thracian bard," which Remigius explains was the region in which he flourished, "musica et poetria"; his wife Eurydice is defined in 480.19 as *profunda inventio* and Orpheus, as *pulchra vox*. John Block Friedman, in *Orpheus in the Middle Ages* (Cambridge, Mass.: Harvard University Press, 1970), pp. 101–2, explains that here Remigius varies the educational topos of *sapientia et eloquentia*: wisdom, profound thought (Eurydice), suspects eloquence, beautiful voice (Orpheus). I think Friedman misreads the mythographer: the point is that "profound imagination" must be coupled with a "beautiful voice" to be successful. The composer needs the musician.

14. Remigius, *Mart.*, glosses him and his story rather literally in 481.14, 2:311, as the best of poets and provides a long historical explanation of his relationship with Thebes.

15. The verse reads: "ma quelle donne aiutino il mio verso / ch'aiutaro Anfione a chiuder Tebe, / sì che dal fatto il dir non sia diverso" ("But may those ladies [Muses] aid my verse who aided Amphion to wall in Thebes, so that the telling may not be diverse from the fact") (canto 32, 10–12 [1:395]).

16. In Guido da Pisa's *Expositiones et glose super Comediam Dantis* or *Commentary on Dante's Inferno*, ed. Vincenzo Cioffari (Albany: State University of New York Press, 1974), pp. 671–72, *amor civium* is founded on the rocks used to build this city.

17. "There are however two Venuses, one voluptuous pleasure and mother of desire from whom Hermaphroditus is born, the other chaste who governs those honest and legitimate in love. There are accordingly two loves; one is indeed chaste love [*amor castus*], and one is unchaste [*incestus*]" (Remigius, *Mart.* 37.1, 1:135–36). Earlier scholarly exami-

nations of Venus posited two only: see Earl G. Schreiber, "Venus in the Medieval Mythographic Tradition," *JEGP* 74 (1975): 519–35 (he does not mention Remigius on Martianus, unfortunately). For Venus elsewhere in Chaucer, see: in the *Knight's Tale*, Betty N. Quinn, "Venus, Chaucer, and Pierre Bersuire," *Speculum* 38 (1963): 479–80; in the *Parlement of Foules*, Dorothy Bethurum Loomis, "The Venus of Alanus de Insulis and the Venus of Chaucer," in *Philological Essays: Studies in Old and Middle English Language and Literature in Honour of Herbert Dean Meritt*, ed. James L. Rosier (The Hague: Mouton, 1970), pp. 182–95; and in various places, McCall. See also the discussion in chapters 3 and 6 of this book.

18. In 8.8 of Remigius, *Mart.*, Aphrodite is glossed in the manner of John Scot, who more figuratively implies that desire ends when the "foam" subsides (1:79). Elsewhere, Remigius notes the connection between these desires and the five senses (8.7, 1:79).

19. Ibid.

20. Note [Bern. Sil.] *Mart.* 3.222–25, p. 56, on Bacchus, which is repeated in the Martianus commentary of Alexander Neckam and thereafter in the mythographic glosses of Holkot. Liber or Bacchus, said by Martianus (36.9) to be agreeable, drunk, and holding a sickle in his right hand and a "soporific bowl" (82), is also identified (in Remigius, *Mart.* 36.9, 1:134), as an honest and urbane companion because he stimulates the heart; the sickle cuts grapevines (36.10), and the bowl is full of wine. Unfortunately, the drunken man is also wanton: "Lascivia enim libido vel instabilitas ebriosorum est" (1:134). To this, Remigius appends the Terence quotation, "Sine Cerere et Libero friget Venus," "Without Ceres (bread) and Liber (wine) Venus grows cold" (*Eunuchus* 732). Finally, the whole process leads to the ultimate instability — insanity — with which drunkenness is linked: see [Bern. Sil.] *Mart.*, p. 56. See also *Alexander Nequam super Martianum de nupciis Mercurii et Philologie* (Oxford, Bodleian, MS. Digby 221), fols. 36v-37r, cited in Allen, "Mythology," pp. 239–40 n. 22, who indicates in his gloss on Bacchus that there are four types of inebriation: *vinolencia, rerum oblivio, libido, insania*. Holkot repeats Alexander's gloss and attributes it to him in *In librum duodecim prophetas*, fol. 25v: they are related to the four sisters Yno, Autonee, Agave, and Semele (mother of Bacchus), and the four types of inebriation are then explained by Fulgentius, with Yno representing *vinum*, Autonee, *non cognoscens*, Semele, *corpus solutum*, and Agave, *insanie*. See also Holkot's *In librum Sapientiae*, pp. 552–53 (167, on Sapientia 14:23), in which he links insanity with the sacrifices of night revelers and the festivities of Bacchus and Cybele (rather than Ceres).

21. On the connection between lascivious desire, liquor and folly, and death, see Remigius on Pluto, Bacchus, and Venus in the same section of book 1, *Mart.* 35.17–37.1, 1:134–36.

22. Bacchus is glossed by [Bern. Sil.] *Mart.* 3.107, as "opulentia vel gaudium" (p. 52). In 3.175–222, Bacchus has four significations (p. 56): the natural potency of earth in producing vines (wine); the human soul; temporal good; divine spirit ("ad naturalem potentiam terre producendi vinum; ad animam humanam; ad opulentiam temporalem; ad spiritum divinum" [3.176, p. 55]). These four are represented by the integuments of the myth of Semele and Jove, the latter as superior fire, Bacchus and the giants, Briseus, Apollo and Bacchus as sons of Jupiter. Bacchus is linked with Briseus, or *exprimentis* ("quia opulentia exprimit vinum ab uva, mel a favo, lac ab ubere" [3.220, p. 56]); and Apollo and Bacchus as sons of Jove represent divine wisdom and will ("divinam sapientiam et voluntatem" [3.222, p. 56]). See also the discussion in chapter 3.

23. Remigius, *Mart.* 22.16, 1:108.

24. See John Scot's very long (two-page) philosophical (Stoic) explanation of Hymen as the universal principle of harmony on 3.5, pp. 3–4, corresponding to the corporal membranes of the microcosm: "Universalis mundi huius visibilis structura quatuor contexi-

tur elementis," each of which has a certain quality, such as heat, humidity, cold, aridity; "Ex quibus IIII qualitatibus sex sizygias, id est coniugationes, naturali copula confici fysica perhibet ratio," and so on.

25. Remigius then explains that, just as there are two Venuses—*casta*, or chaste, and *turpis*, or filthy—so there are two Cupids: "Nam sicut sunt duae Veneres, casta et turpis, ita et duo Cupidines, cupiditas videlicet honesta et turpis" (3.14, 1:69).

26. "Paris quidem interpretatur sensus" ([Bern. Sil.] *Mart.* 6.688, p. 151). Helen is also glossed in the commentaries, but prosaically: Remigius, *Mart.* 488.1, 2:320, identifies the "Mother of the Spartan Beauty" as Leda, and the Spartan beauty as Helen (John: Lacena), so called because born and raised in Lacedemonia, and raped by the shepherd Paris, son of Priam. See the interesting analysis of Helen (associated with Venus and the Judgment of Paris) by Christopher C. Baswell and Paul Beekman Taylor, "The *Faire Queene Eleyne* in Chaucer's *Troilus*," *Speculum* 63 (1988): 293–31.

27. Hoffmann, *Ovid*, p. 156.

28. Brown, "*Hortus Inconclusus*," p. 33, examines Priapus in Ovid's *Fasti* (1.393–440 and 6.319–48), wherein his attempted seductions of Lotus and Vesta are interrupted by the braying of Silenus's ass. Whereas Brown interprets Januarie as a frustrated Priapus, I would argue that Damyan more closely resembles Priapus in Chaucer, with Januarie representing the old satyr Silenus—a darkly ironic parallel, for Januarie's oldness suggests infertility, not fertility (comic or otherwise). In addition, there exist other sources for Priapus in the Middle Ages aside from Ovid's *Fasti*, which was little read, and which was glossed in only one major commentary, by Arnulf of Orleans.

29. Hermann Hagen, ed., *Scholia Bernensia ad Vergilii Bucolica atque Georgica*, Jahrbücher für classische Philolologie Supplement, vol. 4, part 5 (Leipzig: B. G. Teubner, 1867), 4.109–11: "*Creditur* enim omnibus magicis artibus officere."

30. On Janus and Januarie, see Robertson, *Preface*, p. 256, who notes that "Januarie in the Merchant's Tale with his desire for both 'paradis' on earth and 'Paradis' above is obviously two-faced, like Janus who sits, as we are told in the Franklin's Tale, 'by the fyr with double berd.' The two faces of Janus could be interpreted to mean either prudence, which looks before and after, or gluttony and lechery, or other vices." See also the more recent Emerson Brown, Jr., "Chaucer and a Proper Name: January in *The Merchant's Tale*," *Names* 31 (1983): 79–87.

31. In 22.16 Remigius explains that Hermaphroditus's name comes from the Greek for Mercury (Ermes) and for Venus (Afrodite). Because Hermaphroditus thus signifies lascivious speech, Juno does not want Mercury to return to Venus to procreate a brother for Hermaphroditus, but to marry instead Philology (1:107–8). Note, however, the emphasis on doubleness in the Ovidian myth as interpreted by Bersuire, which allies better with other mythological "doubles" in this tale (including Januarie-Janus himself, and Tiresias): in his comment on Ovid's *Metamorphoses* 4.285ff., Bersuire declares of Hermaphroditus-Salmacis fused together (viewed as a two-natured Christ): "From them was formed one person who had both sexes and followed both the nature of man and the nature of woman. A double person is seen within one person. From then on, whoever washed in that spring was made effeminate and became, as it were, half a man. He lacked virility and was almost changed into a woman's nature. Thus it happened that Hermaphroditus was made double-natured. . . . This love is called feminine and half a man because he who was rigid and severed has become mild, capable of weeping, and benign. The Blessed Virgin made him a man because she changed his rigor into love" (*Ovidius*, p. 80, trans. pp. 213–14). In Chaucer, when Venus (Januarie) and Mercury (May) marry, they produce Hermaphroditus (Januarie's double, Damyan, fused to May in the tree, rather than Christ on the cross).

32. For the Anonymous Erfurt commentary on Boethius, see *Saeculi non auctoris in Boetii Consolationem Philosophiae commentarius,* ed. Edmund Taite Silk, Papers and Monographs of the American Academy in Rome, vol. 9 (Rome: American Academy, 1935), p. 290. The authorship of this commentary was resolved to be anonymous (rather than attributable to John Scot) by Edmund T. Silk, "Pseudo-Johannes Scottus, Adalbold of Utrecht, and the Early Commentaries on Boethius," *Medieval and Renaissance Studies* 3 (1954): 1–40, and the date resolved to be twelfth century by G. Mathon, "Le commentaire du Pseudo-Érigène sur la *Consolatio Philosophiae* de Boèce," *Recherches de théologie ancienne et médiévale* 22 (1955): 213–57.

33. The conclusion reads, "Nam, ut hoc certum sit, cecatur etiam a Iunone, illa uidelicet causa, quod hiemis tempus aeris nubilo caligante nigrescat, Iuppiter uero occultis uaporibus conceptionalem factum ei futuri germinis subministrat, id est quasi praescientiam; nam ob hac re etiam Ianuarius bifrons pingitur, quod et praeterita respiciat et futura."

34. Critics see the lovers Pyramus and Thisbe as foils for Damyan and May: Hoffman believes that the myth reveals how "amorous necessity was the mother of invention" (*Ovid,* p. 158). R. M. Lumiansky, *Of Sondry Folk: The Dramatic Principle in the Canterbury Tales* (Austin: University of Texas Press, 1955), finds that the May-Damyan relationship ironically contrasts with the affair of Pyramus and Thisbe (p. 167). Brown, "*Hortus Inconclusus,*" elaborates on Lumiansky's comparison (pp. 38–40).

35. In the pear-tree analogues for the *Merchant's Tale* in the *Novellino* tales and Aesopic fables, Saint Peter and God, Jupiter, Mercury, and Venus, not Pluto and Proserpina, provide the help for the husband and wife: see Germaine Dempster, "The Merchant's Tale," in Bryan and Dempster, pp. 341–56. Wentersdorf, "Theme and Structure," argues that Chaucer uses this change to reinforce "the truth of the arguments presented by Justinus against a marriage of old age with youth," and to show the likeness of January's marriage as a rape (p. 525); Donovan, "The Image of Pluto and Proserpine," argues that Januarie is modeled on Pluto as depicted by Claudian in his unfinished work, with Pluto's two brothers Neptune (and Amphitrite) and Jupiter (and Juno) replaced by Januarie's brothers Justinus and Placebo.

36. For Pluto as ruler of earth and Proserpina as ruler of moon, see Remigius, *Boeth.* 3m12.40, p. 65; see also [Bern. Sil.] *Mart.* 5.15, p. 94 (5.111). The division of the world into two parts, superlunary and sublunary, the latter designated as "inferior" and "infernal," is similarly related to the control of Pluto and Proserpina, who reign over the area from earth to the moon, into which all living things have fallen ([Bern. Sil.] *Mart.* 5.660ff., p. 116).

37. Hoffman thinks this definition of Pluto as god of sensuality explains his presence in the *Merchant's Tale,* with Proserpina the mistress of avarice and rapine: for these definitions he cites Coluccio Salutati (1.411), in book 3, and Bersuire, on p. 99. Note that Marcia A. Dalbey argues for their mythographic meaning as lust, derived from the *Ovide moralisé,* filtered through the Christian tradition of the gods as demons, in "The Devil in the Garden: Pluto and Proserpine in Chaucer's *Merchant's Tale,*" NM 75 (1974): 408–15.

38. See Remigius, *Mart.* 1.4 (5.18), 1:72. [Bern. Sil.] *Mart.* 5.660ff., p. 116, identifies Pluto, earth, with riches, in particular, precious metals, from "Dis," because, according to Boethius, men have always hidden in earth's "deepest caves" that which most excites the mind (3m10.13–14).

39. In Martianus, par. 81, Pluto brings a young girl, so overjoyed at the accessions that had come to them that she readily gave the fruits of the earth to those who asked her; thereafter humankind swore by a great deity to pay her back 1 percent (trans. p. 29). According to Remigius, *Mart.* (36.4), she is Proserpina (1:133). Called Proserpina from *proserpendo,* she renews the seeds of earth annually (1:133).

40. On Proserpina as Echate (Hecate) in Greek, goddess of trees and hunting whose name derives from the Greek word for one hundred, in that the earth duplicates one hundredfold what it receives as seed, see Remigius, *Mart.* 36.4, 1:133–34. Proserpina is called goddess of trees and hunting because she nourishes forest and pastures.

41. On Pluto and Proserpina and the analogy between generation/procreation in *Purgatorio* 27–28, see Pietro, p. 499.

42. On the discussion of the four descents into the underworld, which follows the gloss on Pluto and Proserpina, see [Bern. Sil.] *Mart.* 5.633–35, p. 115; Bernardus acknowledges that the first theologians referred to the human body as the underworld because there was nothing lower in the natural order.

Chapter 9. The Franklin's *Derke Fantasye*: Squire Aurelius as Ekko, Lady Dorigen as Narcissus's Image

Portions of this chapter were delivered as a paper in a session on the topic "Gender and Voice: Myth, Legend, Mythography" that I organized for the Twenty-third International Congress on Medieval Studies, Kalamazoo, Mich., as part of a Symposium on feminist studies and medieval literature sponsored by the *Medieval Feminist Newsletter*, on May 7, 1988.

1. See the excerpts from both of these texts in the handy anthology, *Chaucer: Sources and Backgrounds*, ed. Robert P. Miller (New York: Oxford University Press, 1977), p. 160 (trans. Diane Bornstein), p. 189 (trans. G. W. Coopland).

2. The Questione in Boccaccio reads, "Dubitasi ora quale di costoro fosse maggiore liberalità." The story from *Il filocolo* concerns a woman who rids herself of a lover (out of fear that her husband might hear him wooing her) by means of her request to him for fruit from a tree that blooms in January (4.4, trans. Donald Cheney, with the collaboration of Thomas G. Bergin [New York: Garland, 1985]; and in the *Decamerone*, 10.5). For Questione 4 of *Il filocolo*, which is closer to the *Franklin's Tale* than the story in the *Decamerone*, 10.5, see also Germaine Dempster and J. S. P. Tatlock, "The Franklin's Tale," in Bryan and Dempster, pp. 377ff. The question is cited on p. 383.

3. For the uncomplimentary view of the Franklin as a socially motivated landowner trying to better his status—and therefore a speaker without appropriately Christian motivations to speak on marriage—see Alfred David, "Sentimental Comedy in the 'Franklin's Tale,'" *AM* 6 (1965): 19–28. An analysis of his superficial literalism appears in R. A. Shoaf, "The *Franklin's Tale*: Chaucer and Medusa," *ChauR* 21 (1986): 274–90. An exoneration of the Franklin appears in the exhaustive study of his character and motives by Henrik Specht, *Chaucer's Franklin in the Canterbury Tales: The Social and Literary Background of a Chaucerian Character* (Copenhagen: Akademisk Forlag, 1981).

4. On "gentilesse" as a chivalric and Christian virtue unifying the *Tales*, see Gertrude White, "The 'Franklin's Tale': Chaucer or the Critics," *PMLA* 89 (1974): 454–62.

5. In Boccaccio, judge Fiammetta declares honor (the knight) to be greater than wealth (the clerk) or pleasure (the squire). According to Morton W. Bloomfield (*"The Franklin's Tale*: A Story of Unanswered Questions," in *Acts of Interpretation: The Text in Its Contexts 700–1600: Essays on Medieval and Renaissance Literature in Honor of E. Talbot Donaldson*, ed. Mary J. Carruthers and Elizabeth D. Kirk [Norman, Okla.: Pilgrim Books, 1982]), "a case can be made for each of the three noble characters" (p. 191), or none of them: "The Squire had no right to propose to a married woman anyway. Dorigen had no right to make a rash vow. The husband must support and back his wife regardless. Aurelius and Arveragus are then partly responsible for the dilemma. The clerk is not" (p.

192]. Dorigen, and even the teller of the tale, have been criticized as foolish and misdirected in their behavior, by Robert B. Burlin, "The Art of Chaucer's Franklin," *Neophilologus* 51 (1967): 72. All of the characters have been criticized by Chauncey Wood, *Chaucer and the Country of the Stars: Poetic Uses of Astrological Imagery* (Princeton: Princeton University Press, 1970), pp. 259–71, and by Russell A. Peck, "Sovereignty and the Two Worlds of the *Franklin's Tale*," *ChauR* 1 (1967): 253–71.

6. See the recent analysis of the problem in relation to troubadour poetry in Laurie A. Finke, *Feminist Theory, Women's Writing* (Ithaca, N.Y., and London: Cornell University Press, 1992), pp. 33–48.

7. The Narcissus myth appears in Ovid, *Metamorphoses* 3.338–507. Throughout its literary history, the myth is associated with distorted perception of reality and self-love, and usually with courtly love. See the excellent study by Frederick Goldin, *The Mirror of Narcissus in the Courtly Love Lyric* (Ithaca, N.Y.: Cornell University Press, 1967), although he discusses neither gender switching nor mythography. Narcissus is also linked with the crystals in the fountain that reflect the whole garden—one half at a time in Guillaume's *Roman* (1560ff.), glossed by Jean's Genius as the eyes that see the physical world as opposed to the sight possible in the heavenly carbuncle (20458ff.), and more recently glossed by John V. Fleming as autoeroticism expressive of the folly of self-love; see *Roman de la Rose: A Study in Allegory and Iconography* (Princeton: Princeton University Press, 1969), pp. 94ff. In his use of the Narcissus myth, Gower, providing perhaps a prototype for Chaucer's chivalric Arveragus, alters the courtly-love association by making hunting a masculine diversion from women and loving. In *Confessio Amantis*, Narcissus typifies pride (the sin governing the first book) but also, given Amans's character as a courtly lover, a type of *amor sui* that finds the pleasures of the opposite sex in oneself and therefore inappropriate for the lover. See 1.2285–2398, in which the hunter Amans, who spurns women, falls in love with an image that appears in the well as a nymph, in the G. C. Macauley edition of *The English Works of John Gower*, EETS, 2 vols. (London, New York, and Toronto: Oxford University Press, 1900; repr. 1957), 1:97–101. Genius glosses the tale as an exemplum of the vice that turns "wisdom to wenynge / And Sothfastnesse into lesynge / Thurgh fol ymaginacion."

8. Bersuire, *Ovidius*, on 3.359ff., pp. 195–96. Holkot links a scientific explanation of the "echo" with the Ovidian etiology from *Metamorphoses*, indicating her reduction to bone and then voice alone, in *In librum Sapientiae*, pp. 638–39 (194, in comment on Sapientia 17:18), which may have stimulated Chaucer's idea of character in the *Franklin's Tale*.

9. "Arveragus" also comes from the Briton Arviragus, who marries the daughter Genuissa of the Roman Claudius. Dempster and Tatlock ("The Franklin's Tale," pp. 383–84) conclude that Chaucer combined his main source of the story of Menedon (from Boccaccio's *Il filocolo*) with brief elements from Geoffrey of Monmouth's *Historia regum Britanniae* 4.15—and gave it a Breton ambience in imitation of the lays.

10. For courtly love and marriage in the *Franklin's Tale*, see C. Hugh Holman, "Courtly Love in the Merchant's and Franklin's Tales," *ELH* 18 (1951): 241–52; repr. in *Chaucer: Modern Essays in Criticism*, ed. Edward Wagenknecht (London, Oxford, New York: Oxford University Press, 1959; repr. 1970), esp. pp. 246–49; Paul Edward Gray, "Synthesis and the Double Standard in the *Franklin's Tale*," *Texas Studies in Literature and Language* 7 (1965–66): 213–24; Robert M. Lumiansky, *Of Sondry Folk: The Dramatic Principle in the "Canterbury Tales"* (Austin: University of Texas Press, 1955; repr. 1980), pp. 349–56.

11. That Chaucer is deliberately comparing this tale with the *Wife of Bath's Prologue and Tale* is clear from his use in both of Jerome's *Against Jovinian*, in the *Wife of Bath's*

Tale as one source of the examples from Jankyn's "Book of Wicked Wives," in the *Franklin's Tale* as source for Dorigen's long lament (1390ff.). But for the view that the *Franklin's Tale* does not end the Marriage Group, see, for example, Henry Barrett Hinckley, "The Debate on Marriage in the *Canterbury Tales*," *PMLA* 32 (1917): 292–305, who suggests that the *Second Nun's Tale* more aptly concludes the Group. Germaine Dempster, "A Period in the Development of the *Canterbury Tales* Marriage Group and of Blocks B^2 and C," *PMLA* 68 (1953): 1142–59, expands the Group to include the *Melibee* and the *Nun's Priest's Tale.* Donald R. Howard, "The Conclusion of the Marriage Group: Chaucer and the Human Condition," *MP* 57 (1959–60): 223–32, finds that the *Second Nun's Tale* and its description of virginal marriage is a more fitting conclusion. James L. Hodge, "The Marriage Group: Precarious Equilibrium," *ES* 46 (1965): 289–300, suggests that Chaucer did not wish to conclude the Marriage Group.

12. For Dorigen as a type of the Franklin in her dissatisfaction with reality, see Robert B. Burlin, "The Art of Chaucer's Franklin," *Neophilologus* 51 (1967): 55–73.

13. See William Langland, *The Vision of William Concerning Piers the Plowman in Three Parallel Texts Together with Richard the Redeless,* ed. Walter W. Skeat, 2 vols. (London, New York, Oxford: Clarendon Press, 1886; repr. 1968).

14. See John of Garland, p. 49 (3.164–64), trans. pp. 57–121, and trans. pp. 122–55; here, p. 132. Narcissus is also discussed (in a plain Ovidian/Hyginian way) by the SVM, myth 180, and by the FVM, myth 185, in nearly verbatim transcription, in Bode.

15. See Charles A. Owen, Jr., "The Crucial Passages in Five of the *Canterbury Tales*: A Study in Irony and Symbol," *JEGP* 52 (1953): 294–311; repr. in Wagenknecht, ed., *Chaucer,* on pp. 253–54. Bloomfield (*"The Franklin's Tale,"* pp. 189–98), continues the analysis of the rocks by discussing the series of questions (most unanswerable) initiated by Dorigen's questioning of God's benevolence in creating them. These questions proceed with Aurelius's to Apollo, to cover the rocks, and the Franklin's question of who is the most "free." For the Boethian signification of mutability and illusion in the symbol of the rocks, see W. Bryant Bachman, Jr., " 'To Maken Illusion': The Philosophy of Magic and the Magic of Philosophy in the 'Franklin's Tale,' " *ChauR* 12 (1977): 55–67. Shoaf (*"The Franklin's Tale,"* pp. 274–90) argues for the linking of Dorigen "astoned" at the rocks being away with the idea of being turned to stone, as if by Medusa, or the "monstre" of the letter.

16. Donald Baker divides into three the women in Dorigen's complaint (1355–1456)—women who kill themselves before and after ravishment, and women who remain faithful despite temptation or pressure; see "A Crux in Chaucer's *Franklin's Tale*: Dorigen's Complaint," *JEGP* 60 (1961): 56–64. Bloomfield believes the complaint makes clear her faithfulness to her husband (*"The Franklin's Tale,"* p. 193). See also Gerald Morgan, "A Defence of Dorigen's Complaint," *MAE* 46 (1977): 77–97, who analyzes Chaucer's adaptation of Jerome in *Adversus Jovinianum* 1.41–46, contained in Dempster and Tatlock, "The Franklin's Tale," pp. 395–96.

17. See Dempster and Tatlock, "The Franklin's Tale," p. 395.

18. "Alcestin fabulae ferunt pro Admeto sponte defunctam" (F 1442–43; ibid., p. 397); "Et Penelopes pudicitia Homeri carmen est" (F 1443–44; ibid.).

19. "Laodamia quoque poetarum ore cantatur, occiso apud Trojam Protesilao, noluisse supervivere" (F 1445; ibid.).

20. See Pietro's declaration, p. 563.

21. Ibid.

22. Ibid.

23. The Boethius commentaries frequently gloss 3 meter 12 (on Orpheus's descent into the underworld) and the line "arbiter umbrarum" as referring to Pluto, ruler of earth (underworld), one of three co-rulers of a tripartite world, including Jupiter (heaven) and

Neptune (water): see, for example, the twelfth-century Erfurt commentator (probably not the ninth-century John Scot), in Edmund T. Silk, ed., *Saeculi noni auctoris in Boetii Consolationem Philosophiae commentarius*, Papers and Monographs of the American Academy in Rome, vol. 9 (Rome: American Academy, 1935).

24. See Macrobius, *Saturnalia*, trans. Percival Vaughan Davies, Records of Civilization: Sources and Studies, no. 79 (New York and London: Columbia University Press, 1969), 1.7.9ff.

25. For medieval references to Janus, see 6.1 (1.4), of Remigius, *Mart.* 1:73; in the Florentine commentary on Martianus, with excerpts published, see William, *Macrob.* 6.1; TVM, in myth 1.2, Bode, p. 153, on Saturn, repeats much of the historical account from Macrobius, and in myth 4.9, on Juno, pp. 169–70, ideas from the Florentine commentary also appear. See also Jean Holzworth, "Hugutio's *Derivationes* and Arnulfus' Commentary on Ovid's *Fasti*," *TAPA* 73 (1942), for *Fasti* 1.103, here p. 263.

26. Dempster and Tatlock, "The Franklin's Tale," p. 378.

Chapter 10. Conclusion: The Artist Pygmalion, the Subject Chaucer, and Self-Seduction

A section of this chapter, on the Pardoner as Proteus, was delivered as a response to Britton Harwood's essay "Chaucer's Pardoner and the Dialectics of Inside and Outside" in a session on the topic "Contemporary Literary Theory and Medieval Studies" at the Midwest Modern Language Association Conference at Columbus, Ohio, on November 14, 1987.

1. See, for example, E. R. Amoils, "Fruitfulness and Sterility in the *Physician's* and *Pardoner's Tales*," *English Studies in Africa* 17 (1974): 17–37.

2. For excerpts from the *Roman*, see Edgar F. Shannon, "The *Physician's Tale*," in Bryan and Dempster, pp. 398–408; and also W. F. Dempster, "The Pardoner's Prologue," in Bryan and Dempster, pp. 409–14. For presentation of sources involving Pygmalion in the *Roman* and in Chaucer's *Physician's Tale*, see Hoffman, *Ovid*, pp. 179–81. For an analysis of Faus Semblant in the *Roman*, see Richard Kenneth Emmerson and Ronald B. Herzman, "The Apocalyptic Age of Hypocrisy: Faus Semblant and Amaunt in the *Roman de la Rose*," *Speculum* 62 (1987): 612–34. The relationship between the *Pardoner's Prologue and Tale* and the section on Faus Semblant in the *Roman* has been noted by Dean S. Fansler, *Chaucer and the Roman de la Rose*, Columbia University Studies in English and Comparative Literature 74 (New York: Columbia University Press, 1914), pp. 162–66; Felicity Currie, "Chaucer's Pardoner Again," *Leeds Studies in English* 4 (1971): 11–22; and Patricia M. Kean, *Chaucer and the Making of English Poetry*, 2 vols. (London: Routledge, 1972), 2:96–108. Stephen A. Khinoy has argued for the speeches of the *Roman*'s Reason as a source for the host's rebuttal to the Pardoner, in "Inside Chaucer's Pardoner?" *ChauR* 6 (1972): 255–67. See also parallels between the host and those who falsely reject repentance, as described by False Seeming, in David Lawton, "The Pardoner's Tale: Morality and Context," in *Studies in Chaucer*, ed. G. A. Wilkes and A. P. Reimer, Sydney Studies in English (Sydney: University of Sydney Press, 1981), pp. 38–63.

3. See Katherine B. Trower, "Spiritual Sickness in the Physician's and Pardoner's Tales: Thematic Unity in Fragment VI of the *Canterbury Tales*," *American Benedictine Review* 29 (1978):67–86; and Amoils, "Fruitfulness and Sterility," pp. 17–37.

4. For the Physician's misunderstandings, see Robert Longsworth, "The Doctor's Dilemma: A Comic View of the *Physician's Tale*," *Criticism* 13 (1971): 223–33. For his misunderstanding of morality, see Lee C. Ramsey, "'The Sentence of It Sooth is': Chaucer's *Physician's Tale*," *ChauR* 6 (1972): 185–97. For his misunderstanding of his own

tale, see Thomas B. Hanson, "Chaucer's Physician as Storyteller and Moralizer," *ChauR* 7 (1972–73): 132–39. According to D. W. Robertson, Jr., he also misinterprets the tale of Appius Claudius by chiding fathers not to be negligent toward their daughters, using an image of sheep and wolves that in the fourteenth century characterized false "maintainers" like himself; see "The Physician's Comic Tale," *ChauR* 23 (1988): 129–39. For the relationship of the tales, see Emerson Brown, "What Is Chaucer Doing with the Physician and His Tale?" *PQ* 60 (1981): 129–49; and Peter G. Beidler, "The Pairing of the *Franklin's Tale* and the *Physician's Tale*," *ChauR* 3 (1968–69): 275–79, who distinguishes the weak female hero, Dorigen, in one tale, from the strong hero, Virginia, in the other.

5. Trower, "Spiritual Sickness," p. 67.

6. These fables have appeared in the *Troilus*, discussed earlier, to document the incest motif between Criseyde and her father and her uncle and between Troilus and maternal Criseyde.

7. Arnulf of Orleans briefly glosses the importance of the statue and its sculptor's artistry in an influential passage that will be cited verbatim in the fifteenth-century *Archana Deorum* of Thomas Walsingham (10.9, p. 154). Identifying the catalyst of transformation as the illicit love of Pygmalion for the statue ("Motus ergo Pigmalion illicito amore sue statue obtinuit a Venere ut in veram feminam verteretur"), Arnulf nevertheless glosses the miraculous change in the statue as a result of Pygmalion, *mirabilis artifex*, whose abilities, somewhat narcissistically, are responsible for arousing this creator's desire ("eburneam fecit statuam cuius amorem concipiens ea cepit abuti ad modum vere mulieris" [p. 223]). Giovanni del Virgilio, in his Ovidian glosses, picks up Arnulf's first emphasis, on the statue, to elaborate rather literalistically on the *turpitudo* (deformity, turpitude) of the other women so repulsive to misogynistic Pygmalion and so different from the chaste statue: "They say [that Pygmalion's statue was transformed into a woman] because he despised all women on account of their turpitude," in "Espositore delle Metamorfosi," ed. Fausto Ghisalberti, *Giornale Dantesco*, n.s. 4 (1933): 3–110; here, p. 91 (10.100). Giovanni also specifies the sexual nature of the catalytic love of Pygmalion: after he had created the ivory statue, he began to sleep with it and inseminated it, so that it is said to have turned into a woman ("cum qua cepit dormire et ita spermatizabat cum ea tamquam cum femina unde dicitur conversa in feminam"). But only after he made it his wife did she engender Epaphos, for beforehand she was immovable without seductions or flatteries. Giovanni concludes that it was because of this *consuetudo* (habit of intercourse) that she responded. This misogyny will be picked up by Boccaccio in his fourteenth-century *Genealogia deorum gentilium* 1.2.49, in reference to the earlier viciousness of the women against which Pygmalion reacts with a life of celibacy.although Boccaccio acknowledges the virginity of the ivory statue, it is blamed for arousing the *concupiscentia* of the creator (p. 100). At the same time, Boccaccio also celebrates the *ingenium* (ingenuity, memory) of the creator Pygmalion in bringing to life the statue that so successfully arouses that desire (p. 100).

8. In another digression, forgers full of skill can duplicate human nature according to divine wisdom, if given an ivory form; God forms humans from matter, drawing from nature's beauty and bounty. See the *Ovide moralisé* 10.3617–28.

9. Hoffman, *Ovid*, understands this as moral metamorphosis, noting that there is a change not in the statue but in Pygmalion—that is, the foolish lover who translates a fantastic beauty into an image, a tangible image, which becomes the object of emotional passion. Therefore, in Chaucer, Virginia, to the lecherous Apius, becomes an "idol created by his own lust; and like Pygmalion himself, or the lover in the *Roman*, he burns with the deadly fire of concupiscence in the contemplation of possessing and enjoying

his idol" (pp. 180–81). While focusing on the lover-sculptor, Hoffman nevertheless leaves out the mythographic role of the female statue and the artistic, natural, and moral image of counterfeit so important to the *Physician's Tale.*

10. See especially Alfred L. Kellogg, "An Augustinian Interpretation of Chaucer's Pardoner," *Speculum* 26 (1951), 465–81; repr. in *Chaucer, Langland, Arthur: Essays in Middle English Literature,* ed. Alfred L. Kellogg (New Brunswick, N.J.: Rutgers University Press, 1972), pp. 245–68; Robert P. Miller, "Chaucer's Pardoner, the Scriptural Eunuch, and The Pardoner's Tale," *Speculum* 30 (1955): 180–99; repr. in Schoeck and Taylor, 1:221–44, and in *Twentieth-Century Interpretations of the "Pardoner's Tale": A Collection of Critical Essays,* ed. R. Faulkner (Englewood Cliffs, N.J.: Prentice-Hall, 1973), pp. 43–69; and Donald R. Howard, *The Idea of the "Canterbury Tales"* (Berkeley: University of California Press, 1976), pp. 339–70. For a review of "Augustinian criticism" of the Pardoner, see H. Marshall Leicester, Jr., "'Synne Horrible': The Pardoner's Exegesis of His Tale, and Chaucer's," in *Acts of Interpretation: The Text in Its Contexts, 700–1600. Essays on Medieval and Renaissance Literature in Honor of E. Talbot Donaldson,* ed. Mary J. Carruthers and Elizabeth D. Kirk (Norman, Okla.: Pilgrim Books, 1982), pp. 25–50; Leicester concludes that the Pardoner is "the first exegetical critic of his own tale." See also the chapters on the Pardoner in H. Marshall Leicester, Jr., *The Disenchanted Self: Representing the Subject in the Canterbury Tales* (Berkeley, Los Angeles, and Oxford: University of California Press, 1990).

11. See Britton Harwood, "Chaucer's Pardoner: The Dialectics of Inside and Outside," in "Medieval Literature and Contemporary Critical Theory," *PQ* 67 (1988): 409–22.

12. See Carolyn Dinshaw, *Chaucer's Sexual Poetics* (Madison: University of Wisconsin Press, 1989), chapter 6, "Eunuch Hermeneutics."

13. Figurative expressions should not be taken literally, for "'the letter killeth, but the spirit quickeneth.'" "That is, when that which is said figuratively is taken as though it were literal, it is understood carnally. Nor can anything more appropriately be called *the death of the soul than that condition in which the thing which distinguishes us from beasts, which is the understanding, is subjected to the flesh in pursuit of the letter. ...* There is a miserable servitude of the spirit in this habit of taking signs for things, so that one is not able to raise the eye of the mind above things that are corporal and created, to drink in eternal light." Various texts on medieval literary theory (including this passage) have been excerpted in Robert P. Miller, ed., *Chaucer: Sources and Backgrounds* (New York: Oxford University Press, 1977); here, p. 55; my emphasis.

14. For discussions of the quarrel between the Pardoner and the Host, see, on the Pauline text of 1 Tim. 6, which has the same homiletic theme of duplicity suggesting that false teaching leads to quarreling, Robert E. Jungman, "The Pardoner's Quarrel with the Host," *PQ* 55 (1976): 279–81. On the Pardoner's mocking of the host in his homily on tavern vices, see also Marc Glasser, "The Pardoner and the Host: Chaucer's Analysis of the Canterbury Game," *CEA Critic* 46:1–2 (1983–84): 37–45.

15. See Janet Adelman, "'That We May Leere Som Wit,'" in Faulkner, ed., *Twentieth-Century Interpretations,* pp. 96–106, who argues for parody in the prologue and tale, as literal versions of spiritual facts like the Trinity (= three rioters) and so on. See also the analysis of the Pardoner's literalism, which results from his avarice and incapacitates him as a preacher of God's word, in Warren Ginsberg, "Preaching and Avarice in the *Pardoner's Tale,*" *Mediaevalia* 2 (1976): 77–99.

16. On the parody of the Eucharist and the liturgy, see Clarence H. Miller and Roberta B. Bosse, "Chaucer's Pardoner and the Mass," *ChauR* 6 (1972): 171–84; and Rodney Delasanta, "Sacrament and Sacrifice in the *Pardoner's Tale,*" *AM* 14 (1973): 43–52.

17. For Servius's gloss, see *Servii Grammatici qui feruntur in Vergilii carmina com-*

mentarii, ed. Georg Thilo and Hermann Hagen, 3 vols. (1881–87; repr., Hildesheim: G. Olms, 1961).

18. TVM adds this Proteus section in 11.25, in Bode, pp. 242–43.

19. Ghisalberti, *Giornale*, p. 82.

20. The passage begins, "Protheus poterat se in diversas transmutare figuras."

21. Walsingham, *Archana deorum* 5.1.31–35, p. 82. Does this reference to lack of power from fear of virtue link up with the Pardoner's? The Host also refers to his "coillons" and his many holy relics. Note also Walsingham's earlier reference to "freeing from" (*carueret*) vices, in the manner of the spiritual eunuch presented in patristic commentary in Miller, repr. in Schoeck and Taylor, 1:221–44.

22. DeNeef has argued, in contrast, that the pilgrims appear to derive little benefit from the Pardoner's sermonizing: see A. Leigh DeNeef, "Chaucer's *Pardoner's Tale* and the Irony of Misrepresentation," *Journal of Narrative Technique* 3 (1973): 85–96.

23. See John Gower, *Confessio Amantis*, in *The English Works of John Gower*, ed. G. C. Macauley, EETS, 2 vols. (1900, 1901; repr. London, New York, Toronto: Oxford University Press, 1957), vol. 2: Amans wishes that he were as "wys" as Protheüs, "That couthen bothe of nigromaunce / In what liknesse, in what semblaunce, / Riht as hem liste, hemself transforme," but Amans would use his skill to flee into the chamber in the hopes that "I mihte under the palle / Som thing of love pyke and stele" (5.6670–81).

24. See David Marshall, "Unmasking the Last Pilgrim: How and Why Chaucer Used the Retraction to Close *The Tales of Canterbury*," *Christianity and Literature* 31 (1982): 55–74. See also Robert S. Knapp, "Penance, Irony, and Chaucer's Retraction," *Assays* 2 (1983): 45–67, who argues that irony and penance become interchangeable, with the Retraction an "authorial form of self-elimination."

Index

Jane Chance is a professor of English at Rice University. She is the author of numerous books on gender and mythography in medieval literature, including *The Genius Figure in Antiquity and the Middle Ages* (1975); *Tolkien's Art: A Mythography for England* (1980); *Woman as Hero in Old English Literature* (1986); and *Medieval Mythography*, vol. 1: *From Roman North Africa to the School of Chartres, AD 433–1177* (1994). She is also the editor of several critical volumes, the most important of which are *The Mythographic Art: Classical Fable and the Rise of the Vernacular in Early France and England* (1990) and the forthcoming *Gender and Text in the Later Middle Ages* (1995). She is series editor for the Focus Library of Medieval Women.